The publishers of Dr. Yusuf Al-Qardawi's important book, *Fiqh az-Zakat*, are deeply grateful to His Excellency, Mr. Easa Saleh Al-Gurg, CBE, for his generosity in making the publication of the book possible. In these days of the high cost of production of even the most valuable texts, such help as His Excellency has given is of great importance. It will enable the book to reach a wider readership than might otherwise have been the case.

بسم الله الرحمن الرحيم

In the name of God, most Gracious, most Merciful

From the Eternal Divine Charter:

"*Take* sadaqa *from their wealth to purify and cleanse them and pray for them. Your prayers bring relief to them. Allah is All-Hearing, All-Knowing.*"

Fiqh az-Zakat

A Comparative Study

The Rules, Regulations and Philosophy of Zakat in the Light of the Qur'an and Sunna

Dr. Yusuf al-Qardawi

DAR AL TAQWA LTD.
مكتبة دار التقوى

ISBN 1 870582 12 8

Translated by: Dr. Monzer Kahf
Editors: Abdalhaqq Bewley and Mohmed Isa Waly

Production: Bookwork, Norwich

Published by:
Dar Al Taqwa Ltd.
7A Melcombe Street
Baker Street
London NW1 6AE

www.daraltaqwa.com

Table of Contents

Foreword

I am delighted to have this opportunity both to be able to facilitate the publication of *Fiqh az-Zakat* and also to contribute this introduction to the book. I congratulate the publishers, Dar Al-Taqwa on their initiative in making so important a text available to non-Muslim and non-Arabic speaking readers.

Zakat is truly the financial and social cornerstone of the five pillars of Islam. An understanding of its role in Muslim society is crucial to understanding Muslim society as a whole.

Islam is a religion which cares deeply for the disadvantaged in society and which imposes a responsibility upon all Muslims to provide for their protection. *Zakat* is the means by which this responsibility is discharged and its discharge is one of the inalienable duties of all Muslim adults.

Zakat also demonstrates the integration of all aspects of Islam into the life of the community. All the great religions care for the poor and weak but it is particularly the concern of Islam to make this care an essential part of a Muslim's life.

Fiqh az-Zakat has been written by one of the foremost scholars of that great historic centre of Islamic learning, al-Azhar, Dr. Yusuf al-Qardawi. That his book should now be at the disposal of private individuals as much as public institutions and commercial organisations dealing with the Muslim world is a matter of great satisfaction to me, as it will be to all Muslims.

Easa Saleh Al-Gurg

Translator's Foreword

The writing of Yusuf al-Qardawi in Arabic is unique. Not only a scholar, he is also the Dean of the Shari'a College at the University of Qatar, in Doha, and also an enthusiastic preacher by nature. The present book, *Fiqh az-Zakat*, bears this out, being both scholarly and charged with the zeal of a religious writer.

The general approach taken in this translation has been to render the meaning of the Arabic sentence in English rather than attempt a verbatim translation, yet in so doing I have tried to keep his original ideas, words and syntax intact as much as possible. Details are omitted in some cases, e.g. the comparison of *nisab* in Egyptian gold currency of the beginning of the twentieth century, and a few paragraphs are abridged and summarised when the translator felt that they contained details irrelevant to the interest of the English reader. Sometimes a few words are added when the translation does not convey the intended meaning completely. Additions are usually put within square brackets [...]

Except when the meaning of the Arabic original did not have an exact equivalent, transliterated Arabic words have not been used. Thus the use of Arabic words in the English text is minimised. The letter (p) is used for "Peace and prayers be upon him" after the name of the Prophet.

Lastly, I should avail myself of this opportunity to express my gratitude to the author, Dr. Yusuf al-Qardawi, for granting his permission for this translation, the Centre for Research in Islamic Economics at the Faculty of Economics at King Abdulaziz University, Jeddah, for financial support, and to Abd al-Azim Islahi for his editorial work and valuable comments.

Monzer Kahf

Second Foreword

In the hierarchy of Islamic faith and religious duties, *zakat* is second only to the acclamation of Allah's unity and the prophethood of Muhammad (peace be upon him) and the five daily prayers. It is rather significant that a measure of far-reaching economic consequences should find such a high place in that hierarchy and be counted as one of the five pillars of Islam. *Zakat* is doubly important in the way of life that is Islam. On the one hand it is a means of spiritual purification and on the other a way to regain balance and equilibrium in social and economic life. One would expect religious scholars as well as economists not to miss these points and pay due attention to this unique institution. However, the subject of *zakat* has not attracted the attention of contemporary scholars to an extent commensurate with its importance. Despite the recent Islamic resurgence and the attempts by many a Muslim country to implement the economic teachings of Islam, *zakat* still awaits economists, legal experts and *Shari'a* scholars who would elaborate and analyse the laws of *zakat* in a contemporary manner.

Shaykh Yusuf al-Qardawi's book is one of the exceptions to the above which give one the necessary hope and reassurance to carry on. First published twenty years ago, *Fiqh az-Zakat* still remains unparalleled in its comprehensiveness, exposition and depth. It is, therefore, with great pleasure that we present it to the English reading public.

Zakat has always been a priority subject with us at the Centre for Research in Islamic Economics, King Abdulaziz University, Jeddah. Besides the papers on *zakat* included in the proceedings of the First International Conference on Islamic Economics (1980) and *al-Iqtisad al-Islami* (1980), the Centre has also published *Fatawa az-Zakat* (1985) by Shaykh Abdul A'la al-Mawdoodi and Prof. M. Raquibuzzaman's *Some Administrative Aspects of the Collection and Distribution*. (1987) Of special significance is our Arabic translation of the *Zakat Manual* prepared by the Central Zakat Administration in Pakistan. Translated by Rafiq al-Misri and comprising 526 pages,

Kitab az-Zakat (1984) is a compendium of operational details without parallel in modern times.

We hope these modest efforts for promoting *zakat* studies will help in attracting greater attention to the subject. The Centre will be glad to support further studies on the subject and welcomes any proposal for studying its legal, historical, and contemporary economic aspects.

Our author hardly needs an introduction. Dean of the Shari'a College at the University of Qatar, and member of several academies of Islamic Jurisprudence and Shari'a Advisory Bodies to Islamic financial institutions, Egyptian born Shaykh al-Qardawi is also a popular writer and frequent speaker on the subjects of Islam, contemporary Islamic movements and the economic system of Islam. We feel honoured in presenting his magnum opus on *zakat* to English readers. However, no scholarly work can be the last word on any subject. The same applies to this work, especially now that recent attempts to implement *zakat* in several countries – most were made **after** this book was written – have thrown up new problems. We hope that the publication of an English version of Qardawi's book will bring unattended issues into sharper focus while improving our understanding of the many issues already discussed.

We highly appreciate the support and co-operation of Dr. M. A. Yamani and Shaykh Saleh A. Kamel in the publication of the first edition of this book through Dar Al Taqwa.

We are very grateful to Shaykh al-Qardawi for his generous permission to translate and publish his book. Thanks are also due to Monzer Kahf in whom we found an excellent translator befitting the text. Abdul Azim Islahi's meticulous review of the translation has also helped in bringing out an error-free translation to the best of our capacity, for Allah alone is free of error, and to Him we turn for help and forgiveness.

Darwish Siddiq Jastaneiah, PhD
Director
Centre of Research in Islamic Economics
King Abdulaziz University, Jeddah

First Preface

Praise be to Allah and prayers and peace be upon the Messenger of Allah, his family, his Companions, and those who follow his guidance. Out of the five pillars of Islam, *zakat* is the socio-financial one. By performing *zakat*, along with *tawhid* (belief in the oneness of Allah) and establishing prayers, a person becomes Muslim. As a member of the Muslim community, he or she deserves the brotherhood and allegiance of Muslims, as indicated by the Qur'anic verse, *"But if they turn in repentance and establish the prayer and pay* zakat, *they are your brothers in the* deen." (9:11)

Even though *zakat* is usually mentioned with the acts of worship of Islam, such as prayer, it is in fact a part of the socio-financial system of Islam. For that reason it is always studied under the heading of "Financial and Political Issues of Islamic Society". It is no wonder, therefore, that Muslim scholars are eager to analyse the details of *zakat* from all angles.

Commentators on the Qur'an study and explain the verses about *zakat*, including verse 267 in *Surat al-Baqara*, verse 141 in *Surat al-An'am*, verses 34, 60 and 103 of *Surat at-Tawba*, and several other verses. Among commentators, those who specialise in *ahkam* (injunctions of the Qur'an), such as Abu Bakr ar-Razi, al-Jassas, Abu Bakr ibn al-'Arabi, and Abu 'Abdullah al-Qurtubi, have contributed detailed explanations of the verses of *zakat*.

Scholars of sayings study the traditions of the Prophet that deal with *zakat*, and there is a chapter on *zakat* in all books of *Sunna*, especially those arranged according to articles of *fiqh*, such as *al-Muwatta'* by Malik, *Sahih al-Bukhari*, *Sahih Muslim*, *Jami' at-Tirmidhi*, *Sunan an-Nasa'i*, *Sunan Abu Dawud*, and *Sunan Ibn Majah*. In *Sahih al-Bukhari* alone, the chapter of *zakat* contains 172 sayings attributed to the Prophet Muhammad (p). Muslim also agrees with him on all of the Prophet's sayings, and twenty sayings of the Companions and the Followers.[1]

---

1. See the last section of the book of *zakat* in *Fath al-Bari*, vol. 4, p. 120, al-Halabi ed., Egypt

Jurists study *zakat* in their books as the second major act of worship in Islam. It is usually listed directly after prayers, in line with the sequence found in the Qur'an and *Sunna*. Scholars specialising in the financial and administrative issues of Islam look at *zakat* as a component of its socio-financial system. So we find *zakat* in *Al-Kharaj* of Abu Yusuf, *Al-Kharaj* of Yahya ibn Adam, *Al-Amwal* of Abu 'Ubayd, *Al-Ahkam as-Sultaniyya* of al-Mawardi (Shafi'i), *Al-Ahkam as-Sultaniyya* of Abu Ya'la (Hanbali), and *As-Siyasa ash-Shar'iyya* of Ibn Taymiyya.

Since the subject of *zakat* has been extensively researched and its references are abundant, one may ask, why we need a new study of *zakat*? Does the contemporary Muslim library need a new work such as this (which includes a definition of *zakat*, its objectives, its effects on the life of the individual and the society, and its status among contemporary socio-financial systems)? The answer to this question is yes, for the following reasons:

1. This important tenet of Islam needs to be re-examined, combined in one volume and re-presented in a contemporary style. The authors of the past wrote for their own age in their own styles. Each era has its own style, as the Qur'an says, *"We have not sent any Messenger except with the language of his people so that he can make things clear to them."* (14:4)

There are two main areas in Islamic economics that deserve to be studied because of their relevance. The first is *zakat*, which is an essential obligation or a pillar of Islam. The other is *riba* (interest), which is prohibited as a major sin. There is no disagreement among Muslims about the obligatory nature of the first, nor the prohibition of the other, for denying these is tantamount to apostatising.

However, the issue of *riba* has captured the attention of scholars more than the issue of *zakat*. Great scholars such as Abu al-A'la al-Mawdudi[1], Muhammad 'Abdullah Draz[2], 'Isa 'Abdu[3], Muhammad

1. *Ar-Riba* published in Arabic.

2. His paper on *ar-Riba* read in the conference on Islamic jurisprudence, Paris, 1951.

3. His booklet, *Why did Allah prohibit riba?* (*Li-madha harrama Allah ar-riba*), published by Maktaba al-Manar al-Islamiyya, Kuwait, series title: "*Toward a Sound Islamic Economy*".

Abu Zahra[1], Muhammad 'Abdullah al-'Arabi[2], Mahmud Abu Sa'ud[3], Muhammad Baqir as-Sadr[4] , and Muhammad 'Uzair[5] have written books, papers and articles on the subject of *riba*, whether from a purely Islamic view or from a position influenced by Western capitalistic attitudes to money and life. Despite the fact that there can always be further rigorous and extensive research, one can note that a reasonable amount of research has emerged on this issue.

As for *zakat*, its research has largely been neglected by scholars. Such an important matter as *zakat* still needs study and research, especially since it is one of the fundamental obligations of Islam and a cornerstone of its financial, economic and social systems.

2. Muslim jurists differ on many details of *zakat*. Each has his own opinion and arguments and there are sometimes contradictions among their interpretations, which leaves the majority of people in confusion over which opinion to choose. There is a great need to review these interpretations, opinions, and arguments, to discuss them with a certain degree of neutrality, to examine them in the light of the criteria descending from Allah and to show which among them is the most worthy.

The late Shaykh Mahmud Shaltut referred to this need in his book, *Islam, Doctrine and Law*, writing in the chapter, "*Zakat*, a Principal Religious Pillar":

> "In spite of my belief that theoretical differences are indications of vitality of thought and the flexibility of the sys-

1. His booklet, *Prohibition of Riba as an Economic Institution.* (*Tahrim ar-Riba tanzim iqtisadi*), published in the above series.

2. His paper, *Private Ownership and its Limits in Islam* (*al-Milkiyya al-khassa wa hududuha fi'l-Islam*), read at the Congress on Islamic Research, Cairo and published in the first collection of the proceedings of the Congress.

3. His book *Outlines of Islamic Economics* (*Khutut ra'isiyya fi'l-iqtisad al-Islamic*) and his paper, *Is it possible to establish an Islamic Bank?* published by Maktaba al-Manar.

4. His book, *Our Economics* (*Iqtisaduna*), published by Dar al-Fikr, Lebanon; also his book, Interest Free Bank.

5 His paper, *Factors of Success in an Interest Free Bank* (*'Awamil an-naja fi'l-bank al-la-ribawi*), published by Maktaba al-Manar.

> tem that accommodates them, I feel uneasy when I see the range of difference among the schools of thought on the application of this obligation of *zakat*, as it is exposed in the books of jurisdiction and injunctions. This obligation of *zakat*, that is usually associated with prayer ought to be, like prayers, commonly understood. In prayers we see not much room for differences – just five prayers in the day and night. Unlike prayers, we observe that even the ratio, the exemptions, the kinds of wealth that are zakatable, are subject to differences among scholars. Such differences have serious implications for Muslims at large when it comes to their application of the Islamic obligation of *zakat*. For example, some scholars consider the wealth of children and insane individuals zakatable, others don't. Some scholars consider all agricultural products zakatable, others restrict *zakat* to specific kinds only. Some consider debts zakatable, others don't. Similar differences exist for business assets and women's jewellery. Some require certain minimum (*nisab*) for zakatability, some don't, etc. These kinds of differences also exist about the disbursement of *zakat*." (p. 109)

Shaykh Shaltut called for a revision of the differences among schools of thought which he feared would mar the essence of this obligation. Such a review should be based on the ultimate objectives of *zakat* as cited in the Qur'an, so that Muslims would be able to understand and apply it on the same level.

New financial institutions and practices have come into being which were not known to the earlier jurists. These new matters require new religious injunctions. Today Muslims ask many questions about *zakat* that must not remain unanswered. Questions such as how to consider new forms of wealth other than livestock, produce and fruits, for these new forms of wealth include huge buildings for rent or investment, enormous factories and plants, machines and equipment, and all kinds of fixed and circulating capital. There are things which generate a tremendous flow of income out of their production lines and rental proceeds such as ships, cars, planes and hotels. There are new trading and industrial corporations, new forms of income from professionals like physicians, engineers, and lawyers and huge numbers of employees receiving wages and salaries. Are all these subject to *zakat* or not, and if they are subject to *zakat*, what is the percentage of *zakat* on them? When is it due? And on what basis of *shari'a* is it founded.

Many measures and terms mentioned in the texts on *zakat,* such as the *wasq* in agricultural products, the *sa'* in the fast-breaking *zakat*, dirhams and dinars in the *zakat* on money, require new definitions and translation into the measures of today. Are these quantities given and fixed or can we change them in response to changes in economic and social circumstances, such as the changes in the purchasing value of money? There are new taxes with progressive or flat rates imposed by contemporary governments with certain social purposes attached to them. The relation between such taxes and *zakat* should be studied, and the areas of similarities and differences must be pointed out. The substitutability of these taxes for *zakat* must be investigated and their co-existence must also be examined.

Questions like these are waiting for answers and Muslim scholars are looked upon to provide such answers. To say that the door of *ijtihad* is closed would incorrectly leave these issues unsettled. No one can close the door of *ijtihad* since it was opened by the Messenger of Allah (p). Reliable scholars of *usul* (methodology of jurisprudence) have determined that *ijtihad* can be exerted on individual issues, since some people may specialise in certain areas of jurisprudence. In our days this specialised *ijtihad* has become the common rule rather than the exception. Hard work and extended preparation are required to understand the texts of the original sources of this religion from the linguistic and religious points of view, and those who have prepared themselves well for *ijtihad* can obviously exercise it in their particular fields of expertise.

While I believe that fulfilling answers to such questions requires a collective *ijtihad* exercised by a group of Muslim scholars, I maintain that individual effort and research undoubtedly pave the way for sound collective *ijtihad* until a time comes when Muslim states make it feasible for reliable scholars to work together as teams for collective *ijtihad.*

4. Unfortunately, there are a few misgivings among some Muslims about *zakat*. Some look at it as a very meagre amount given by the rich to the poor only to sustain the latter's life and keep him barely at the poverty line, i.e. in permanent need of the condescending charity of the rich. This picture has no place in the institution of *zakat* in Islam, though it is regrettably practised by many. We even find some reputable journalists in Egypt writing that *zakat* does not fit our society because contemporary social and economic systems must be based on work and production instead of charity, as if *zakat* was simply a charity for beggars or a support for the idle.[1] Another writer called Islamic justice "charity socialism".[2] All this reveals an ill intention to mislead readers or at least demonstrates an enormous ignorance about *zakat,* and emphasises the need for a new study which I believe is an obligation on Muslim scholars.

Researchers interested in financial and economic issues of Islam have expressed surprise that the contemporary Muslim literary corpus lacks a serious and comprehensive study on *zakat* in spite of its importance to Islam.[3] The Higher Council of Islamic Affairs in the Ministry of Awqaf in Egypt felt this need by announcing *zakat* some time ago as one of a few major research areas and allocating prizes to the best research papers written on it. This need was further stressed by the Congress on Islamic Research held in Cairo, March, 1963, and attended by Muslim scholars from more than forty countries. In their resolution, the conference declared, "The issues of *zakat*, financial resources in Islam, means of investment, their relation to individuals and society, and private and public rights are the major issues of contemporary concern because these subjects represent the point of convergence in the *Shari'a* of worship and social behaviour. For this very reason, the Congress considers these issues as a main theme for its coming session."[4]

---

1. The socialist writer, Ahmad Baha' al-Din in one of his weekly editorials in the newspaper, *Akhbar al-Yawm*, 1961, Egypt.

2. Khalid Muhammad Khalid, in his book *Min huna nubda'* (*From Here We Start.*)

3. Mahmud Abu Al Sa'ud in an article in the review *Al-Muslimun*.

4. Proceedings of the first session of the Congress of Islamic Research, p. 314.

The present book has been written in order to:

a. Collect the dispersed texts from their original sources in the Qur'an, *hadith*, and commentaries as well as from the books of jurisprudence of all the various schools, books on financial and religious policies and general books on Islamic culture, and rearrange them in one collection that will aid the understanding of *zakat* in Islam.

b. Investigate the differences among scholars in an attempt to find the most sound opinion that fulfils the criteria of the evidence in the *Shari'a*, Muslims' needs and their common contemporary interests.

c. Answer urgent questions on *zakat* arising from modern economic practices.

d. Reveal the facts about *zakat* as an Islamic obligation, comparing it with other modern taxes, and showing the similarities and differences between them.

e. Present the objectives of *zakat* and its effects on Muslim society in solving problems such as poverty, destitution and begging and in facing socio-economic miseries and showing the precedence of *zakat* with regard to social solidarity and social insurance.

f. Correct misgivings about *zakat*, which are caused by misunderstanding or erroneous application and objections raised by the enemies of Islam.

Method and Plan of Study

Depicting References and Collecting Material

The first thing I had to do was to collect relevant material from its sources, that is, texts, injunctions, opinions of scholars, new and ancient sources, religious texts and books. The Qur'an and *Sunna* are the main sources that I relied upon in understanding the reality of zakat, its injunctions, objectives, and position in Islam. I found abundant material in books of commentary from all ages, commentary by narration or commentary by means of explanation, especially the explanation of Qur'anic verses on *ahkam*.

Books of *hadith* gave me my second major source. I benefited from both texts and footnotes, especially in books dealing with *hadith* jurisprudence such as *Muntaqa al-Akhbar* and *Bulugh al-Maram* and their commentaries. I used books of jurisprudence representing various schools of thought as well as comparative studies, especially those that provide evidence from the *Shari'a* and debate the objections raised by others, as well as books of jurisprudence methodology and rules (*usul*) and books of financial and administrative jurisprudence such as *al-Amwal* by the great jurist Abu 'Ubayd al-Qasim ibn Sallam. Some material came from modern books and papers that deal with one or more aspects of the social, political and economic systems of Islam. I also used secondary sources such as books on language, history, bibliographies, encyclopaedias, indexes, etc.

Quotes from any of these books, ancient or contemporary, are attributed to their authors in the text or in footnotes, unless the reference is well-known or was mentioned earlier, in which case I only mention the name of the book. On rare occasions I quote certain statements that are very familiar to scholars without mentioning a specific source for them. In all this I follow our predecessor who said, "It is a blessing for any quote to be attributed to its author."

I would like to mention here that one of the blessings of the present study is that it allowed me to get involved in financial and economic readings from which I was formerly isolated as a result of my own speciality in *Shari'a*. Through this new window I came to understand many aspects of the financial and economic system in Islam, its principles and pillars and the kinds of transactions it deals with. Furthermore, while working on the present research I was able to publish my study entitled "The Problem of Poverty and its Islamic Solution."

The subdivision and sequence of chapters in this study

The nature of the subject, the interrelation of its parts, and the need to integrate its material required me to make an exhaustive study. Since every aspect is related, I have tried to make it a comprehensive scientific reference book on *zakat,* thus its considerable length. It is divided into nine parts and a conclusion. The sequence of these parts follows a logical pattern, starting with the obligation of *zakat*, the assets on which it is due, its ratios, those to whom it is distributed, cases where it must not be used, means of collection and distribution, objectives and effects of *zakat*, followed by the *zakat* paid at the end of the fast of Ramadan, and a discussion on whether there are other financial duties beyond *zakat* and the similarities and differences between zakat and contemporary taxes.

Part One deals with the obligation of *zakat*, in which I have showed that all religions share the concern for and care of the poor and weak members of society. Islam expressed concern in these matters as early as the Makkan period. This culminated in the imposition of *zakat* at the early Madinan period. The system of *zakat* preceded all similar legislation in the world.

Part Two deals with those people liable to pay *zakat*. In this part I have detailed the injunctions concerning *zakat* on children and the insane, and the issue of levying *zakat* on non-Muslims.

Part Three deals with funds and assets subject to *zakat* and with the ratios of *zakat* – what kinds of wealth are subject to *zakat* in respect of livestock, money and currency, business assets, agricultural products, minerals, marine assets, animal products, etc. In this part I explain the conditions of *zakat* on buildings for rent, plants and factories, on income of non-business capital, salaries and wages, and on the income of professionals.

In Part Four I discuss the eight areas of distribution of *zakat* mentioned in the Qur'an, how much should be appropriated to each category, whether or not all categories should be covered in each distribution of *zakat,* and disqualification for receipt of *zakat.*

Part Five deals with the means of *zakat* payment and collection, its relation to the state, and the prepayment of *zakat.* It deals also with the issues of transporting proceeds of *zakat* from one country to another and payment in value or in kind.

In Part Six I discuss the objectives and the effects of *zakat.* In this part I explain the objectives of *zakat* with reference to the *zakat* payer, the *zakat* recipient and the whole of society. Additionally, this part deals with the role of *zakat* in solving certain socio-economic problems such as unemployment, destitution and begging, natural catastrophes, community disputes and differences, in addition to the major problem of poverty.

Part Seven deals with the *zakat* paid at the end of the fast of Ramadan and its injunctions.

Part Eight studies the issue of other duties on wealth besides *zakat.* In this part I discuss the two opposing opinions on the matter, the arguments of each side and which one is sounder.

In Part Nine I compare *zakat* and taxes and depict the characteristics of *zakat* as a tax. The principles, objectives and guarantees of *zakat* are discussed in this part, as well as the fact that *zakat* supersedes contemporary thought on taxation with respect to its principles and regulations. This part also deals with the issue of whether other taxes are allowed in addition to *zakat* or whether *zakat* can be replaced by other taxes.

In the Conclusion I summarise the institution of *zakat* and provide testimony by writers, both Muslim and non-Muslim, on the virtues of *zakat* and its contribution to fulfilling justice, equality, and solidarity among the members of society.

Comparative Approach

Two kinds of comparisons are made in this study: comparison among schools of thought in order to select the opinion that is most supported by evidence of the *Shari'a*, and comparison between the *Shari'a* and other legal systems, divine or not, ancient or modern, in order to show the characteristics of this divine *Shari'a* as a final and perpetual law compared to prior divine laws that have been superseded or man-made systems that are inadequate.

While comparing the different views of the Islamic schools I did not limit myself to the four famous schools, for this might be unjust to other schools and opinions in Islamic jurisprudence. Since there are views expressed by scholars among the Companions, the Followers, and later generations, these views should not be neglected or disregarded. Regarding the Companions, there is no dispute as to their precedents and their knowledge. Beyond them there are views expressed by great Followers such as Ibn al-Musayyab, 'Umar ibn 'Abdu'l-'Aziz, az-Zuhri, an-Nakha'i, al-Hasan, 'Ata', ash-Sha'bi, Maymun ibn Mahran, and many others. Even in the generations after the Followers there are great names such as ath-Thawri, al-Awza'i, Abu 'Ubayd, at-Tabari, Dawud az-Zahiri, and many others. All these views in fact represent a very precious and valuable scientific heritage, the neglect of which would be a great mistake both from the scientific and religious points of view.

Furthermore, I did not limit my study to the Sunni schools, but expanded it to include the Zaydi and Imami schools of jurisprudence. Differences between them and Sunni schools in the matters of detailed injunctions are trivial and we have seen great scholars such as as-San'ani in his book *Subul as-Salam* and ash-Shawkani in his *Nayl al-Awtar* mention the views of the Zaydis and Imamis, including al-Hadi, al-Qa'im, al-Baqir, an-Nasir, and others. These works circulate among Sunni scholars without misgiving.

As for the comparison between Islamic thinking on *zakat* and other systems, it was necessary to compare the Islamic view of *zakat* with the stance taken by other religions regarding charity. It was also necessary to compare *zakat* with contemporary thoughts regarding taxation and social insurance.

Explanation and reasoning

Throughout the course of this research, I felt that it was not sufficient to give the *Shari'a* injunction on each matter, but that it was also necessary to explain the rationale and the virtues of the rulings and to show why those matters prohibited in Islam lead to detrimental results. This is in the spirit of the approach of the Qur'an itself in providing not just rulings but also their rationale, their objectives, and their benefits to mankind, individually and collectively. The Qur'an does not demand that believers merely submit to all rulings without knowing the reasoning behind them. If providing the reasoning for the rulings of the *Shari'a* is advisable in general, it is indispensable at this time, because there are malicious ideas circulating and misleading pressures from both the East and the West. It is no longer sufficient to simply state the injunctions of the *Shari'a* and expect believers to cry, "We hear and obey!"

Weighing different opinions

Any research that hopes to cover and collect all views and opinions from the different sources must also compare each with the other. But if the author himself is subject to one view or biased towards a certain school of thought, he will do his best to support the view he subscribes to. Therefore, I have freed myself from any such preconceptions or alliance to any specific school of thought. This non-partisan commitment is well appreciated in the tradition of this Muslim nation. Following one jurist in all his opinions, even those that are weakly supported by *Shari'a* texts, amounts to taking that jurist as a legislator or maker of *Shari'a* since imitation itself is a form of annulment of the mind and its virtue. "The mind is created to think and adore," said Ibn al-Jawzi. How could a person who has a lamp to shed light put it out and walk in the darkness? Others have said, "Those who imitate are insecure or stupid."

I read texts and views as an investigator, an examiner, and as a researcher seeking the truth regardless of where or from whom it comes. It may be found in opinionated schools of jurists or in schools of *hadith*, or in the school of the Zahiriyya. It could be found among the reputed schools or outside them. I do not ascribe to that fanaticism which places a taboo on all new opinions found after the first four Imams, believing that none are accepted after them, that *ijtihad* came to an end after the first three centuries of Islam and that truth lies only in the writings of those schools and those generations. On the other hand, I would not blindly follow those who claim to be making *ijtihad* without fulfilling all its requirements, those who call for a complete renovation, about whom the late ar-Rafi'i said mockingly, "They wanted to renovate religion, language, even the sun and the moon."

I am committed throughout my research to the principles of non-bias, non-partisanship, righteousness, open-mindedness to every useful innovation and keenness to retain every correct ancient view or opinion. The yellowed and wrinkled pages, bad printing and small script of the old texts did not prevent me from perusing them and extracting their treasures, whether in the original texts, commentaries, or footnotes. Consequently I benefited from old and new without being either cautionary or permissive. I analysed what I obtained and weighed the arguments of the different opinions and supported the strongest, that is, the one whose evidence is clearest, without adherence to any school. I may take the view of Abu Hanifa sometimes, Malik at other times, or ash-Shafi'i, Ahmad, Sufyan, al-Awza'i, Abu 'Ubayd, or any other thinker at certain other times. I may even leave aside all of them and take instead what is correctly reported from a Companion or Follower. This is not mingling ideas together, but rather it is a search for the truth and the best argument. Only one thing limits all scholars. That is the unmistakable words of the Book of Allah or the traditions of His Messenger. Ibn 'Abbas, Malik and 'Ata' said, "One may take or leave any opinion from anyone except the Messenger of Allah (p)."

This approach may allow me to take up an opinion that is otherwise neglected or not to accept an opinion of the majority, since truth does not always accompany great numbers. Even great Imams sometimes hold to an opinion that is in opposition to the majority. Ibn 'Abbas, arguing against following the majority, said, "A matter that came neither in the Book of Allah nor in the judgement of the Prophet (p), yet which all people accept, is the inheritance of a sister with a daughter of someone deceased." Malik gave his opinion on *shuf'a* (pre-emption) on fruits and said, "This is something I have not heard anyone else saying." Each one of the great Imams did not concern himself about whether or not he was alone on certain rulings and opinions. Issues on which Ahmad differed from the majority were even compiled in a special volume.

Criteria in weighing arguments and deductions

I have relied on a set of rules that represent the basis of the *Shari'a* in pointing out the opinion that overrules others and in deducing new opinions or quasi-new views. These rules can be summarised in the following way.

Texts are general, unless there is evidence that restricts them. Many texts in our religion are general in form so that they cover multiple cases as well as individual details and aspects. This in itself is one of the miracles of this religion which equips it to be the final religion and makes it suitable for all times and places.

Consequently Qur'anic verses and the Messenger's sayings should be received and taken as general, except when their scope is narrowed by another text that is correct, authentic and clear in its meaning. In this case, the restriction comes first. I am not among those who reject clear-cut (*muhkam*) and authentic (*sahih*) sayings because they oppose general texts in the Qur'an. On the other hand, I do not share the position of those who quickly accept a restriction coming in a *hadith* in spite of the fact that the *hadith* may not be exactly authentic or may not have a clear-cut indication. I do not, for example, subscribe to the position of Imam Abu Hanifa in rejecting the saying, "There is no *zakat* on dates below five *wasqs*" in order to preserve the generality of the text, *"and some of what the earth produces for you,"* (2:267) and the Prophetic text, "in what is watered by the sky there is one tenth," because the first saying is correct and agreed upon. The explanation given by Abu Hanifa that the saying deals with dates that are kept for trading is a very weak and clumsy explanation. For that reason I go along with the opinion of the two disciples of Abu Hanifa and the majority of scholars that there is a *nisab* on the produce of the earth, the same as on other sorts of wealth.

On the other hand, I fully agree with Abu Hanifa in holding to the generality of the text, *"and some of what the earth produces for you,"* and the *hadith*, "In what is watered by the sky there is one tenth," and I do not consider this generality modified by a *hadith* like, "There is no *zakat* on vegetables," because this is a weak *hadith*. Of course, one can find a reconciling explanation for this *hadith* by interpreting it to mean that vegetables cannot be collected in payment of *zakat* because they are perishable and cannot be stored for long. But if *zakat* is not collected in the form of vegetables, it is still required of their producer on the basis of the generality of these texts.

The generality of the texts of the Qur'an and the *Sunna* must be applied as is until they are modified by another correct and clear-cut text. Consequently, we must observe the general meaning of all verses and sayings that obligate *zakat* on all forms of wealth, such as the verses, *"Out of their wealth take* zakat", *"and in whose wealth, there is a well-defined right,"* and the saying of the Prophet (p), "Pay *zakat* on your wealth." These texts do not differentiate between one kind of wealth and another, so we need not make exceptions unless there are specific texts to support them.

Acceptance of true *ijma'*

The agreement of all scholars of this *umma*, especially in the early generations, on certain issues is an obvious indication that they have based their agreement on strong *shari'a* evidence, be it a text, general benefit, or a material fact. Consequently, we should respect such agreement so that we can preserve the value of *ijma'* in the *Shari'a*, that keeps balance in legislation and prevents chaos and legislative confusion. Examples of this *ijma'* is the agreement of the scholars that *zakat* is obligatory on gold assets at the same rate as it is on silver, i.e. one fourth of a tenth, and their agreement that a *mithqal* is one and three-sevenths of a dirham.

I say true *ijma'* because some jurists report *ijma'* on issues that are still controversial. This is because in early generations there were many scholars who were dispersed in several countries, so that it was very difficult to know their stance on certain issues. Imam Ahmad went so far as to state, "Whoever claims that *ijma'* on any matter ever existed is a liar, for how could he know? People may have differed without him knowing. Instead one may say, 'To my knowledge, there are no disagreements on such an issue' or 'No different opinions have been reported to me.'" There are examples of cases in which *ijma'* was claimed or no report of a disagreement was mentioned whereas there is concrete evidence that such cases were not agreed upon. Ash-Shafi'i, for example, said about *zakat* on cattle, "On each thirty, there is a one year old cow, and on each forty, there is a two year old cow, and I know of no difference among scholars on this." It is certain that a difference existed and was reported by Jabir ibn 'Abdullah, Sa'id ibn al-Musayyab, Qatada, and the collectors in Madina of Ibn az-Zubayr.[1]

Another example is that which is reported by Ibn al-Mundhir that there was *ijma'* that *zakat* may not be spent on non-Muslims while other scholars reported from az-Zuhri, Ibn Sirin and 'Ikrima that this is permissible, and it seems that this is the view of 'Umar, according to reports from him.[2] Also, Ibn Qudama said in *al-Mughni*, "We know of no disagreement on the view that the clan of Hashim are not allowed to receive *zakat*." This was commented on by Ibn Hajar in *al-Fath*: "But at-Tabari reported that Abu Hanifa said that they may receive *zakat* if they were not given the allowance of *dhawi'l-qurba* (the close relatives of the Prophet (p)." This is also stated by at-Tahawi. Similar views are attributed by some Malikis to al-Abhari, a Maliki, and it is an opinion expressed by some Shafi'is. Abu Yusuf said, "*Zakat* of the clan of Hashim is

1. Proceedings of the first session of the Congress of Islamic Research, p. 314.

2. See section on payment of *zakat* to non-Muslims in the part on disbursement of *zakat*.

lawful to members of the same clan." For this special case the Malikis have four different opinions.[1]

Such alleged *ijma'* is not binding because it is not in fact an *ijma'* and one may take a position that opposes it. As for true *ijma'*, i.e. *ijma'* that truly has no known opposition, it is an acceptable ruling in the *Shari'a* and I bind myself to following it in spite of objections raised about its binding nature.

Some *usul* scholars say that if Muslims of earlier generations differ on an issue and there are, for example, two opinions, a later generation may not formulate a third entirely new opinion. The argument given is that if there are only two opinions, an implicit *ijma'* to reject a third must exist. Al-Amidi said that if a third opinion contradicts both of the original two, then it is not acceptable, while if it coincides with one, or each, of them in certain aspects, then it can be accommodated. Let us take as an example what Abu Hanifa says, i.e. that the one-tenth imposed as *zakat* on land is obligated on the landlord. The majority say it is on the tenant. Apparently, all agree that the tenth is obligated, so one may say that this tenth is obligated on the tenant on his net agricultural products after deducting the rent which is paid to the owner, and that the landlord is required to pay *zakat* at the rate of 10% on the rent received. Obviously, this does not violate the implicit *ijma'* according to al-Amidi.

Others believe that the mere fact that scholars of a certain generation differ on an issue and express two opinions is in itself an indication that this issue is a controversial one in which all can exert effort and apply *ijtihad*. A third and later opinion is merely an outcome of such *ijtihad* and consequently should be accommodated. The Followers, for example, several times expressed views which had not been considered by the Companions, as is reported from Ibn Sirin, Masruq, and others.[2] This is the way I see it as long as such *ijtihad* issues are susceptible to new research and efforts.

1. *Fath al-Bari,* vol. 3, p. 227. See also section in Chapter 9 on *zakat* disbursement.

2. Al-Amidi, *al-Ahkam*, vol. 1, pp. 137-8.

The use of appropriate analogy

Analogy means applying to a case the same ruling given to a similar case because of common underlying cause (*'illa*). It is a matter of natural rationale implanted by Allah in human minds and, according to Ibn al-Qayyim, an ingredient of *al-Mizan* (right criteria) that descended from Allah with His Holy Book and made by Allah a support of the Book. Allah says, *"It is Allah who has sent down the Book with Truth and with the Just Balance,"* (42:17) and "*We sent Our Messengers with the Clear Signs and sent down the Book and the Balance with them so that mankind might establish justice."* (57:25) The "Balance" is meant here as justice, and the criteria and means by which we know what justice is. Appropriate analogy is the "Balance". It is better to give it the noble name that is given to it by Allah and to recognise that there is an obligation on every Muslim to apply it as much as possible. It is not so with the name 'analogy' because analogy may be right or wrong, praised or disclaimed, correct or incorrect. The right and correct analogy is the "Balance" that Allah sent along with his Book.[1]

Imam Ibn Taymiyya said, "Analogy is a global word. It includes correct analogy and incorrect analogy, but only correct analogy is accepted in the *Shari'a*. It implies treating similarly, cases that are similar and differentiating between cases that are distinct. The first application is called *qiyas at-tard* (positive analogy) and the second is called *qiyas al-'aks* (negative analogy). Analogy in this meaning is part of the justice and balance sent by Allah with His Messenger. Appropriate analogy is one in which the reason on which an injunction of the *Shari'a* is based exists in both cases without anything that opposes it or prevents the application of the same injunction. This kind of analogy is always consistent with the *Shari'a*. By the same token, analogy by disregarding irrelevant differences is also a correct analogy where an acclaimed difference between the two cases is shown as irrelevant. Again this kind of analogy is consistent with the *Shari'a*."[2]

1. *I'lam al-Muwaqqi'in*, vol. 1, p. 133.
2. Paper on analogy by Ibn Taymiyya, Salafiyyah Print, 1375 AH.

In brief, if the reason that is common between the two cases in analogy, is obvious and clear and if there is no relevant difference, apparent or otherwise, nor any factor preventing similarity, analogy should be applied and considered as evidence in the *Shari'a* which no one can disclaim. Some object to this on the basis that *zakat* is one of the acts of worship and in matters of worship there can be no analogy. It is agreed that matters of pure worship are not subject to analogy since the true reasons behind them may never be known by a human being, and in worship, obedience to Allah is the only rationale. Analogy is not applicable to acts of worship such as prayer, fasting and pilgrimage. This prevents human beings from inventing forms of worship out of their own imagination, without a clear order from Allah.

As for *zakat*, it is not purely worship, for, in addition to being an act of worship, it is a defined right of the poor, an established tax, and an ingredient of the social and economic system of the society. The reasons for enacting *zakat* are, in general, known and clear. Why should we not then use analogy in *zakat*?

The Prophet (p) collected the *zakat* paid at the end of the fast of Ramadan in the form of grains and fruits, such as barley, dates and raisins. By analogy, ash-Shafi'i, Ahmad and their disciples accept everything that is edible or the common food of the town of the one paying the *zakat*. They did not consider these special grains and fruits to be beyond analogy. On the other hand, the majority of scholars applied *zakat* on different kinds of grains and fruits by analogy with those grains and fruits mentioned by the Prophet (p), instead of restricting *zakat* to the items mentioned in the *hadiths*, such as wheat, barley, dates and raisins. It is reported that 'Umar used analogy with respect to *zakat* when he ordered *zakat* on horses after he realised that they had become high in value, saying, "Should we take one sheep out of every forty sheep and leave horses with nothing?" 'Umar was followed in that by Abu Hanifa.

Because of these precedents, I applied analogy to rented buildings because they are similar to agricultural land, and on wages because they are similar to the grants on which 'Abdullah ibn Mas'ud, Mu'awiya and 'Umar ibn 'Abdu'l-'Aziz used to collect *zakat*. These kinds of income and assets are included anyway under the general texts obliging *zakat*. By the same token we apply analogy to silk, milk and other animal products because they are similar to honey, which is mentioned in the traditions.

However, to emphasise the importance of analogy it may be sufficient to quote Imam ash-Shafi'i in *ar-Risala* about *zakat* on gold: "The Prophet of Allah ordered *zakat* on silver currency and Muslims after him collected *zakat* on gold. They were either depending on a saying of the Prophet that never reached our times or applying analogy because of the similarities between gold and silver as money, since both were used in several countries as measures and store of value." (pp. 193-4) Imposing *zakat* on gold, especially since gold has become an international reserve for currency in most countries, is not a trivial issue, yet Muslims after the death of the Prophet (p) applied analogy to it and made it subject to *zakat*. It is unlikely that there existed a saying about it that did not reach ash-Shafi'i, Malik, al-Bukhari, Muslim and others keen to collect all of the correct sayings of the Prophet (p). Malik considered the action of Muslims on this matter to be a *sunna* on which there is disagreement. Therefore, he said that *zakat* is obligated on gold (with a minimum of twenty dinars) the same way it is obligated on silver (with a minimum of two hundred dirhams).

Considering the objectives and common benefits

It is established among Muslim scholars that the injunctions of the *Shari'a* are ordained for the benefit of mankind in their earthly existence and in their resurrection after death. Ash-Shatibi argued that this can be verified by surveying the injunctions of the *Shari'a* and looking at the supportive evidence, whether of a universal or specific nature. This does not only apply to a unique case or one text – since the entire *Shari'a* has been established on this underlying fact.[1] Ash-Shatibi made this important point, stressing, "With regard to worship, the principle is that people accept and obey without seeking explanation or reasons. As for transactions and

1. *Al-Muwafaqat*, vol. 2, p. 51.

interrelations, the principle is to look for meanings and rationalisation."[1]

Ash-Shatibi provides strong arguments to support this view, but unfortunately, they fall beyond the scope of the present work. What should be emphasised here, however, is that *zakat*, despite the fact that it is associated with prayer under the heading of worship is, in reality, not solely an act of worship. It is closer in nature to a transaction, being as it is the major financial institution for Muslims. *Zakat* constitutes a three-way relationship between the state, the wealthy, and the poor. This is perhaps why all major works on financial and administrative issues in Islam include a chapter on *zakat* in the same way they include chapters on *kharaj*, state revenues, etc. *Zakat* is, as such, a part of the social system in Islam. If we were to reclassify issues of *fiqh* according to contemporary standards, we would classify *zakat* as part of the socio-financial system and not under the heading of pure worship. Similarly, when we talk about law, we talk about *zakat* as part of the financial law of the state.

This does not mean that all the rules of *zakat* are outside the boundaries of worship. Ash-Shatibi resolves this by saying that in transactions that have some characteristics of worship, we should limit ourselves to the texts. This applies not only to *zakat* but also to the requirements of *sadaq* (dowry) in marriage, the distribution shares in inheritance, the number of months women wait in *'idda* (the waiting period after divorce or being widowed), etc. I add to these the percentages of *zakat* and its *nisab* (minimum) because these are issues clearly defined by texts and on which Muslims never disagree. So it is essential to abide by these texts and this *ijma'*. For this reason I disagree with those who claim that the minimum exemption and rates of *zakat* are subject to change according to changing circumstances in time and place, on the grounds that such changes conform to the objectives and common benefits of *zakat*. I believe such changes alter the features of *zakat* and reduce it to a mere civil tax, like other taxes imposed by governments.

The objectives of the *Shari'a* are to achieve a common benefit for people and to avoid those things that would harm that benefit.

1. Ibid., p. 300.

Accordingly, Malik and his disciples went to the extent of considering common benefit a criterion of the *Shari'a* that should be applied like any other criteria in the *Shari'a*.[1] Curiously, many Hanbalis follow this trend, which is strongly supported by Imam Ibn Taymiyya and his disciple, Ibn al-Qayyim. In their writings, they show abundant evidence in support of this view.

Ibn al-Qayyim wrote a chapter illustrating the principle on which religious injunctions may be changed in accordance with changes in time, place, conditions, intentions and customs. At the outset of this chapter he writes:

> "This is a great very useful chapter; ignoring its ideas causes errors in understanding the *Shari'a* and imposes harassments and unnecessary obligations, which anyone of sense can conclude this great *Shari'a* would not accept or induce. Since the cornerstone of the *Shari'a* is to consider the benefit of people in both earthly life and afterlife, the *Shari'a* is most just and brings benefit and wisdom to people. In any case where one goes from justice to oppression, from mercy to cruelty, from benefit to harm, from wisdom to nonsense, one is deviating from the *Shari'a*. The *Shari'a* represents the justice of Allah among His servants, His mercy on His creatures, His shadow on this earth, His wisdom that leads to believing in Him and in the truthfulness of His Messenger (p). It is the light by which people of sight can see, the guide by which those that are guided can find the truth."[2]

These are words which we must preserve and make known to all people. Ibn al-Qayyim was quite correct in considering religious injunctions or opinions changeable in accordance with changes in time and conditions. It is not the ruling of the *Shari'a* that is

1. Al-Qarafi said, "Common benefit and interest (*al-masalih al-mursala*) is denied by some who at the same time as they deduce opinions, use benefit or interest in general without obligating themselves to providing proofs of present common benefit. They rather suffice themselves with the usefulness of their deductions. This is in the fact the given interest or benefit. See *Imam Malik* by Muhammad Abu Zahra.

2. *I'lam al-Muwaqqi'in*, vol. 3, p. 14.

changeable, but rather the application of the ruling in time and space and in the specific case under consideration. The *Shari'a* does not change, what changes is jurisprudence. The *Shari'a*, in the final analysis, is the Revelation of Allah, while jurisprudence, religious opinions, and judgements are man-made. For example, 'Umar refused to pay *zakat* to people to whom the Prophet (p) had given *zakat* to reconcile their hostility, saying, "Allah has given might and strength to Islam and we are not in need of them." He did not change a ruling of the *Shari'a*, nor did he reverse the application of the texts of the Qur'an as some people mistakenly think, but rather he changed the religious interpretation in response to the change in time and condition.

The specific individuals that used to receive *zakat*, including 'Uyayna and al-Aqra', were appeased during the early days of Islam in order to bring their hearts closer to the Message. The Prophet (p) did not write perpetual promises to those individuals. It is up to the contemporary ruler to determine who deserves it, and if no one fulfils those conditions, no one would be a recipient of that category of *zakat*. This is not a neglect of the texts of the Qur'an. Neither 'Umar nor any Muslim has a right to abandon the texts in the Book of Allah. But 'Umar found that the common interest of Muslims at his time could best be served by saving those grants. He never thought to abolish the ruling of the *Shari'a* on the share of *zakat* to be expended for the purpose of softening hearts. He simply refused to apply it to those ambitious individuals.

'Umar also changed the religious application in the case of horses. When some people from Syria asked him to take from them zakat on horses, he was hesitant because such a thing had not been done by the Messenger (p) nor by Abu Bakr. 'Umar was later reported to have imposed *zakat* on horses when he found out that horses had become very expensive – as much as one hundred camels for a horse – and he justified it by the above-mentioned analogy. This is in itself a form of considering the objectives of the *Shari'a* in observing justice and fulfilment of common benefit.

Another example of changing religious application to suit current conditions is that of Mu'adh ibn Jabal when he was sent by the Messenger of Allah (p) to Yemen. Mu'adh was ordered to collect *zakat* from the rich and render it to the poor. He was also told, "Take payment in grain out of grain holdings, sheep out of sheep holdings, and camels out of camel holdings." Mu'adh understood this to mean to make it easy for people: take *zakat* out of what is available. When he found out that people liked to pay the value of *zakat* because it was easier for them, he welcomed that. When Mu'adh governed in Yemen he said, "You may give me cloth and fabric instead of corn and barley as long as it is easier for you and beneficial for the migrants in Madina."

The consideration of common benefit and the fulfilment of the objectives of the *Shari'a* is what led Mu'adh – being one of the most knowledgeable Companions – to accept the value of *zakat* in terms of cloth instead of grain, despite what may be thought as a violation of the apparent words of the Prophet (p). Mu'adh clearly understood the objectives of the Prophet's command and applied it accordingly. This is why scholars of *usul* require a *mujtahid* to be knowledgeable on the ultimate goals and objectives of the rulings of the *Shari'a* as well as the common interest of the people in his time. Whoever obtains theoretical knowledge and the means of *ijtihad*, but lives isolated in an ivory tower, not knowing the concerns of society, the ideas and thoughts circulating among people and the desires and incentives of real life, cannot be among those who have the right to give religious opinions on the application of rulings of the *Shari'a*.

It is this consideration of common benefit and the general objectives of the *Shari'a* that led me to accept the religious application given by many Companions of the Messenger (p) regarding obligations on growing wealth. The amount of *zakat* collected would generally come out of the growth and the excess, leaving intact the original wealth. Since women's jewellery is lawful and does not grow, it should be considered as clothes or home furnishings, which are not taxable.

The consideration of justice on which all of the *Shari'a* is founded is what leads me to select and accept the view of the Follower, 'Ata' ibn Rabah, in deducting the expenses of agriculture out of the gross proceeds and considering only the net as subject to *zakat*. It is by the same principle that I consider the tenant of the land liable for *zakat* on his net income after deducting all expenses, including land rent, and that the landlord should pay *zakat* on the rent he receives.

Style of this book

Our aim in writing this book has been to use a style that combines easiness for the reader with accuracy of details, avoiding difficult wording and statements. Even when I quote, I have tried to select the clearest quotations with the simplest words, at times clarifying words in the quotation without altering its meaning. In my opinion the most successful style is that which has at once the accuracy of a scholar and the clarity of a preacher, and I hope I am successful in this.

I should mention that this study was prepared more than six years ago as my PhD dissertation but I was unable to present it then due to unavoidable circumstances. The papers remained in my hands and I began reviewing, correcting and editing them until Allah permitted this work to take this form. I hope it will be accepted among non-partisan researchers and that I may benefit from sincere criticism.

I hope Muslims will review the current practices of their religion and will return to it, having abandoned it long ago and make the obligation of *zakat* an important part of their socio-financial institutions, thus seeking the pleasure of Allah while solving many social problems, and protecting their youth from misleading and deviant ideas.

If I fulfil those objectives in this study, thanks and praise should go to Allah alone. I intended this effort for Him and He alone is asked to make it benefit people. If it does not reach that goal, it suffices that I tried to the best of my abilities and I hope Allah will give me the reward for the effort and good intention, since the reward of every person is in accordance with his intention.

Success can only come from Allah on Whom I depend and to Whom I return.

Yusuf al-Qardawi

Second Preface
The Words *Zakat* and *Sadaqa*

The meaning of the word *zakat*: linguistic definition and in terms of the *Shari'a*

The word *zakat* is the infinite of the verb *zaka*, meaning 'to grow and to increase'. When said about a person, it means 'to improve, to become better.' Consequently, *zakat* means 'blessing, growth, cleanliness or betterment.' In *Lisan al-'Arab*, it says, "The root of the word *zakat* in Arabic means cleanliness, growth, blessing and praise. All these meanings of the word are used in the Qur'an and *hadith*." It seems most obvious to al-Wahidi and others that the root '*zakat*' means increase and growth. With respect to plants, it means to grow, and with respect to things, it means to increase. But since plants grow only if they are clean of insects and other detrimental things, then the word '*zakat*' implies cleanliness and cleansing. If it is used with respect to persons, *zakat* then means betterment and righteousness. You may say of a man, "*zakat,*" that is, he had good character. or you may say that a judge "*zaka*" the witnesses, meaning he showed that they were of a higher level in their testimony.

In the *Shari'a* the word *zakat* refers to the determined share of wealth prescribed by Allah to be distributed among the categories of those entitled to receive it. It is also used to mean the action of payment of this share.[1] According to an-Nawawi's report from al-

1. Az-Zamakhshari said in *al-Fa'iq*, vol. 1m p. 536, "*Zakat* is like the word *sadaqa*. It is a common noun used to refer to a material thing which is the part of the fund paid out in the form of *zakat*. It also refers in an abstract sense to the action of sanctification. It was because of ignorance of this latter meaning of the word that some people did not understand the correct meaning of the verse, *"And those who are active in practising"*, thinking that it referred to money paid out while, in fact, it is a reference to the action of sanctification and purification.

Wahidi, this share of wealth is called *zakat* because it increases the funds from which it is taken and protects them from being lost or destroyed.[1] Ibn Taymiyya said that the inner soul of the *zakat* payer becomes better, and his wealth becomes cleansed.[2] Growth and cleanliness are not restricted to the assets from which *zakat* has been taken, but affects the person who pays *zakat*, in accordance with the verse, *"Take zakat from their wealth to purify and cleanse them."* (9:103) Al-Azhari says that it makes the poor grow too, meaning that *zakat* creates psychological and material growth for the rich in his soul and wealth.

An-Nawawi reports that the author of *al-Hawi* said, "It should be realised that *zakat* is an Arabic word known before Islam. It is well-known that it has been used in poetry." On the other hand, Dawud az-Zahiri said that this word had no source in the Arabic language before it was used in the Qur'an. The author of *al-Hawi* answered, "Although this is totally wrong, differences about the name do not affect the rulings on *zakat.*"

Knowing this, one can find no basis for the claims of the Jewish orientalist, Schacht, who wrote in the *Encyclopaedia of Islam* under the heading of *Zakat* that the Prophet (p) used the word *zakat* to mean more than what it meant for the Arabs and borrowed some of the meaning of the word from the Jews who used the Hebrew and Aramaic word *zakut*. Schacht said, "The Prophet, when he was in Makkah, used the word *zakat* and its derivatives to mean cleansing. This meaning has a close tie to the word *zaka* in Arabic and in the mind of the Arabs, but this word and its derivatives are not used except for that meaning in the Qur'an and this is not an original Arabic meaning: it is borrowed from Judaism where it means 'fear of Allah.' (vol. 10, pp. 355-6)

Orientalists such as Schacht have a fanatical desire to attribute as much as they can of Islamic concepts, words, rulings thoughts, and ethical values to Jewish or Christian origins or at least to any other origin, be it Eastern or Western, following only the whims of their own bias. It is sufficient, however, to disprove his claim by stating the following two points:

1. *Al-Majmu',* vol. 5m p. 324.
2. The collection of *Fatawa Shaykh al-Islam Ibn Taymiyya*, col. 25, p. 8.

• Firstly, the Qur'an uses the word *zakat* in the meaning known by the Muslims now as early as the beginning of the Makkah period. This is found in *suras*: 7:156, 19:31 and 55, 21:72, 23:4, 27:3, 30:39, 31:3, and 41:7. It is undoubtedly known that the Prophet (p) did not know Hebrew or any other language except Arabic, and that he had no contact with Jews before migrating to Madina. When and how could he have borrowed from Jews and Judaism?

• Secondly, it is more speculation that violates scientific methodology for anyone to claim that a language had borrowed a word from another language simply because he finds the word common to both languages. Such a common word does not necessarily mean that one language borrowed it from the other. It is even more speculative to point out one language as borrowing and the other as borrowed from without any proof.

The meaning of *sadaqa*

Zakat as known in the *Shari'a* is sometimes called '*sadaqa*' in the Qur'an and *Sunna*, to the extent that al-Mawardi said, "*Sadaqa* is *zakat*, and *zakat* is *sadaqa*. They are two names for the same thing."[1] Allah says, *"Take* sadaqa *from their wealth to purify and cleanse them."* (9:103), *"Among them there are some who find fault with you concerning the collected* sadaqa*"* (9:58) and *"Collected* sadaqa *is for the poor and the destitute..."* (9:60) A *hadith* says, "There is no *sadaqa* on what is less than five *wasqs*. There is no *sadaqa* on what is less than five camels and there is no *sadaqa* on what is less than five *uqiyyas*." (al-Bukhari, Muslim, and others). Addressing Mu'adh when he sent him to Yemen, the Prophet (p) said, "Inform them that Allah has prescribed *sadaqa* on their funds, to be taken from their rich."

All these texts are talking about *zakat* while using the word *sadaqa*, even the *zakat* collector and distributor is called *musaddiq*. But in the later history of Islam, *sadaqa* was traditionally used to

1. Al-Mawardi, *al-Ahkam as-Sultaniyya*, beginning of Chapter 11.

mean only voluntary charitable donations given to beggars and destitutes. But such a tradition must not be allowed to mislead us or divert us from the meaning of the word at the time when the Qur'an was being revealed. The root of the word *sadaqa* is the word *sidq*. Qadi Abu Bakr ibn al-'Arabi, commenting on interchanging the terms *zakat* and *sadaqa*, states that:

> "It is derived from *sidq*. *Sidq* is truthfulness in realising declared belief by action. The root *sidq* means realising and supporting something by something else. The word *sadaq* (a woman's dowry) means realising the lawfulness of intimacy by the contract and the dowry under specific conditions known in the *Shari'a*. The root *sidq* has several derivatives. The verb *saddaqa* with respect to statements means 'to accept and to realise'. The verb *tasaddaqa* with respect to funds means 'to give away, realising one's faith by action.' And the verb *asdaqa* means 'to give dowry in marriage to women'. The meaning of *sadaqa* is derived from the root *sidq* because *sadaqa* implies giving away goods and funds for the sake of Allah in expression of faithfulness and in realisation of the belief in resurrection and afterlife."[1]

It is for that reason that the Qur'an associated giving with the acceptance of faith and withholding with rejection of faith. Allah says, *"As for him who gives out and has taqwa and confirms the Good, We will pave his way to Ease. But as for him who is stingy and self-satisfied, and denies the Good, We will pave his way to Difficulty."* (92:5-10)

Sadaqa is thus an indication of truthfulness in faith and sincere belief in the Day of Judgement. Accordingly, the Messenger of Allah (p) said, "*Sadaqa* is a proof (or evidence)." (Muslim)

1. *Ahkam al-Qur'an*, pt. 2, p. 946, with commentary by al-Bijawi.

Zakat in the Holy Qur'an

The word *zakat* occurs thirty times in the Qur'an. In twenty-seven of them it is associated with prayer in the same sequence of verses, namely, *"Those who are humble in their prayer..."* and *"those who actively pay zakat."* (23:2, 4) Surveying these thirty places in the Qur'an shows that eight are Makkan verses and the others revealed in Madina. Some writers claim that *zakat* is associated with prayer in eighty-two places in the Qur'an,[1] but this is obviously an exaggeration. Even if we include the verses that have implicit reference to *zakat,* where words like spending, lending or feeding are mentioned, we would not reach that number. As for the word *sadaqa,* and its plural *sadaqat*, it is mentioned twelve times in the Qur'an, all of them in Madinan *suras*.

1. See *ad-Durr al-Mukhtar*, *al-Bahr*, *an-Nahr*, and other Hanafi books. Ibn 'Abidin quoted a correction in his commentary, *Radd al-Muhtar*. But the fact is that it came associated with the prayer in only 28 places.

Part One

The Obligatory Nature of *Zakat* and its Place in Islam

- The poor in ancient civilisations
- Religious concern for the poor
- The particular concern of Divinely revealed religions
- The special attention given by Islam to caring for the poor from its outset
- Encouragement of *zakat* in general from the Makkan period
- *Zakat* in the specific meaning becoming obligatory in the Madinan period
- The place of *zakat* in Islam and the ruling on those who deny it
- The difference between *zakat* in Islam and care of the poor in other religions
- Discussing the claims of Schacht regarding *zakat*

Introduction

Before illustrating the obligatory nature of *zakat* and its position in the religion of Islam, it would be useful to examine the position of the poor in the class structures of societies before Islam and to show the extent to which these societies responded to the needs of the poor and the kind of provision that was made for their relief in ancient laws and religions. By so doing, one can show the extent to which Islam superseded other religions in its care of the poor and how it established social justice, social insurance, and social solidarity on the firm basis stated in the Book of Allah and the *Sunna* of His Messenger (p).

The poor in ancient civilisations

Poverty and destitution are as old as history. It can be said that all human communities have had some individuals who have called for the care of the poor. Feelings for the sufferings of others has never ceased to be manifested throughout the history of humanity and attempts to provide relief and to solve problems have continued in all civilisations. Despite this, the condition of the poor has remained grave. It has always been a dark spot in human history. Injustice has continued to be a feature of societies that have failed to follow the humanitarian advice of their philosophers and prophets. One historian described relations between the rich and the deprived in ancient civilisations in this way:

> "In every nation that existed on earth one could easily recognise two classes of people, the rich and the poor. The rich class exercised power and always became richer while the deprived class was weak and downtrodden. With that contradiction the social structure of that civilisation would

> eventually fall apart, with the rich wondering why everything was deteriorating."[1]

Egypt, in its early history, was like a paradise on earth, producing all kinds of goods that were more than sufficient for its people, yet at the same time its poor did not even have the merest sustenance of food, because the rich left nothing of substance for them. When the great famine hit Egypt during the era of the Twelfth Dynasty, poor people sold themselves as slaves to the rich who made them suffer even more. In ancient Babylon the situation was the same. The poor had no rights to the produce of their land in spite of high production. The ancient Persian, Greek, and other kingdoms were also similar. The poor were driven by whips and sticks to the lowest jobs and were severely punished and sometimes savagely slaughtered for the slightest errors.

In Sparta the rich left for the poor rocky lands that were not fertile, so they lived in suffering. In Athens the rich used to sell the poor as slaves to pay for tolls imposed on them for debts. In Rome, the source of Western law, the rich ruled over the entire nation, distinct and high-ranked, reducing all others to the rank of untouchables in comparison to them. The poor were forced to obey them and this often drove them to flee Rome. Michelet said of the Roman Empire:

> "The poor were descending deeper and deeper into poverty while the rich were increasing their wealth. When the Roman empire was abolished and European kingdoms rose in its place, the plight of the poor became even worse. They used to be sold with the land like livestock under the feudal system of these kingdoms."[2]

---

1. The late scholar, Muhammad Farid Wajdi, author of *Da'irat Ma'arif al-Qarn al-'Ishrin* (Encyclopaedia of the Twentieth Century) and for many years editor of the *al-Azhar Review*. His book, *al-Islam Din 'Amm Khalid* (*Islam a Universal and Eternal Religion*) is quoted above, pp. 179-181.

2. Ibid.

Religious concern for the poor

Every religion, including those devised by man, has considered this to be a humanitarian social issue, without which brotherhood and a high standard of living cannot be realised. More than four thousand years ago in Babylon, Hammurabi, in introducing the first known recorded law on earth, stated, "God has sent me to prevent the strong from oppressing the weak and to guide people and secure prosperity for creatures." Thousands of years ago people in ancient Egypt expressed the sentiment that it was their religious duty to give bread to the hungry, clothes to the naked, and passage on their boats to the incapable, or to be father to the fatherless, husband to the widow and a protector to the outcast during cold winters."[1]

The concern of Divinely revealed religions

The voice of Divinely revealed religions in calling for the care of the poor and weak has been even louder than other religious systems, having a deeper effect than any human philosophy or man-made law. I cannot believe any Messenger of Allah has passed through the world without calling for the care of the poor, called *zakat* in the Qur'an.

In the Holy Qur'an, which is the most authentic Divine text existing on earth today, we find mention of the Messages of Ibrahim and Ya'qub. Allah says: *"We made them leaders, guiding by Our command and revealed to them the doing of good actions and the establishment of the prayer and the payment of* zakat, *and they worshipped Us."* (21:73) Isma'il's Message is described in the following: *"Mention Isma'il in the Book. He was true to his promise and was a Messenger and a Prophet. He used to command his people to pray and give* zakat *and he was pleasing to his Lord."* (19:54-55)

We also see the pledge of the tribe of Israel: *"Remember when We made a covenant with the tribe of Israel: 'Worship no one but Allah and be good to your parents and relatives and to orphans and the very poor.*

1. From a lecture by Dr. Karl Schobens in the Seminar on Social Studies, third session, p. 546.

And speak good words to people. And establish the prayer and pay zakat.*' But then you turned away – except a few of you. You turned aside."* (2:83) In another verse, this pledge is further elaborated: *"Allah made a covenant with the tribe of Israel and We raised up twelve leaders from among them. Allah said, 'I am with you. If you establish the prayer and pay the* zakat, *and believe in My Messengers and respect and support them, and lend a generous loan to Allah, I will erase your wrong actions from you and admit you into Gardens with rivers flowing under them. Any of you who reject after that have gone astray from the right way.'"* (5:12)

The Message of Jesus Christ is described by his own words as a baby in the cradle, *"He has directed me to pray and give* zakat *as long as I live."* (19:31) About the People of the Book in general, Allah says, *"They were only ordered to worship Allah, making their* deen *sincerely His as people of pure natural belief and to establish the prayer and pay* zakat *– that is the correct* deen*."* (98:5)

In the Old and New Testaments as they exist today, we find many recommendations and directives to have mercy on the poor and to care about widows, orphans, and the weak. From the Old Testament, we read in Proverbs 21:13-14: "Whoso stoppeth his ears at the cry of the poor, he also shall cry himself, but shall not be heard. A gift in secret pacifieth anger." In Proverbs 22:9, "He that hath a bountiful eye shall be blessed, for he giveth of his bread to the poor," and in Proverbs 28:27: "He that giveth unto the poor shall not lack; but he that hideth his eyes shall have many a curse."

And we read in Deuteronomy 15:7-11: "If there be among you a poor man of one of thy brethren ... thou shalt not harden thine heart, nor shut thine hand from thy poor brother, but thou shalt open thine hand wide unto him and shalt surely lend him sufficient for his need, in that which he wanteth. ... Thou shalt surely give him, and thine heart shall not be grieved when thou givest unto him, because that for this thing the Lord thy God shall bless thee in all thy works, and in all that thou puttest thine hand unto. For the poor shall never cease out of the land. Therefore I command you, saying: thou shalt open thine hand wide unto thy brother, to thy poor, and to thy needy, in thy land."

We read in 14:22-29 of the same chapter: "Thou shalt truly tithe all the increase of thy seed that the field bringeth forth year by year … At the end of three years thou shalt bring forth all the tithe of thine increase the same year, and shalt lay it up with thy gates, and the Levite (because he hath no part nor inheritance with thee), and the stranger, and the fatherless, and the widow, which are within thy gates, shall come and shall eat and be satisfied: that the Lord thy God may bless thee in all the work of thine hand which thou doest."

In the New Testament, Luke 12:33 reads: "Sell that ye have and give alms," and in Luke 3:11: "He that hath two coats, let him impart to him that hath none; and he that hath meat, let him do the same." And in Luke 11:41: "But rather give alms of such things as ye have; and behold, all things are clean unto you." And in Luke 14:12-14: "Then said he also to him that bade him, 'When thou makest a dinner or a supper, call not thy friends, nor thy brethren, neither thy kinsmen, nor thy rich neighbours, lest they also bid thee again, and a recompense be made thee. But when thou makest a feast, call the poor, the maimed, the lame, the blind: and thou shalt be blessed, for they cannot recompense thee, for thou shalt be recompensed at the resurrection of the just.'" In Luke 21:1-4 we find: "And he looked up, and saw the rich men casting their gifts into the treasury. And he saw also a certain poor widow casting in thither two mites. And he said, 'Of a truth I say unto you that this poor widow hath cast in more than they all. For all these have of their abundance cast in unto the offering of God, but she of her penury hath cast in all the living that she had."

Matthew 5:42 reads: "Give to him that asketh thee, and from him that would borrow of thee turn not thou away," and in Matthew 5:1-4: "Take heed that ye do not your alms before men, to be seen of them: otherwise ye have no reward of your Father which is in heaven. Therefore when thou doest thine alms, do not sound a trumpet before thee, as the hypocrites do in the synagogues and in the streets, that they may have glory of men. Verily I say unto you: they have their reward. But when thou doest alms, let not thy left hand know what thy right hand doeth. That thine alms may be in secret, and thy Father which seeth in secret himself shall reward thee openly." In Matthew 10:42: "And whosoever shall give to drink unto one of these little ones a cup of cold water only in the name of a disciple, verily I say unto you, he shall in no wise lose his reward."

Notes on the attitude of religions towards poverty

These are glorious examples of the care of previous religions toward the poor and the needy and this was the essence of the message of divine scriptures before the Qur'an. Some observations, however, must be noted.

- These texts do not go beyond recommendations and encouragement to be merciful toward the poor and to be wary of selfishness and miserliness. They are a call to voluntary and individual charity.
- These statements on charity do not make it compulsory so that those who abstain from charity do not feel that they have left an essential part of their religion and that they will be punished by Allah in this life and in the Afterlife.
- It is left to the human conscience to give charity: the state is not given any authority in its collection and distribution.
- The amount that should be given, the kinds of wealth that are subject to be taken from, and the circumstances and conditions of the fulfilment of this charity are not specified. This makes it impossible for the state to institutionalise care of the poor on any religious grounds.

In other words, in other dispensations, caring for the poor does not reach the extent of a rigorous attempt to deal with the problem of poverty as a whole, to eliminate it, to deny its sources, or to transform the poor into proprietors and landowners. These calls truly attenuate the misery and suffering of the poor.

Consequently, the poor and weak remain at the mercy of the rich and strong. If the latter are motivated by the love of God, the sense of an afterlife, or their own conscience, then the poor are helped and relieved. But if the faith of the wealthy is lacking, if they love accumulation and the exclusive pursuit of their own desires, the poor are left to their suffering without anyone to defend their rights against the rich.

The rigour of Islam in attacking poverty

Islam is unprecedented in the extent of its care for the poor and in its determination to solve the problem of poverty whether through directives and recommendations that exhort Muslims to show mercy to the poor, through legislation and laws, or through implementation and application.

The care provided in the Qur'an for the poor in the Makkan period

One of the clearest indications of Islam's care for the poor and its treatment of the problem of poverty is the fact that from the very outset in Makka, when the Muslims were still just a handful of men and women prevented from practising and calling for this new religion and not yet constituting a political entity, this humane and social aspect of Islam – caring for the poor and the destitute – was highly emphasised and constantly stressed by the Qur'an. This concept is expressed in the Qur'an as *'feeding the poor'*, *'spending of the sustenance that Allah has provided,'* *'a right to he who asks and to he who does not ask,'* or *'a right to the destitute and wayfarer'*, and sometimes the term *'establishing* zakat*'* is used.

Feeding the poor is a requirement of faith

In *Surat al-Muddaththir*, one of the earliest revelations of the Qur'an, we see a scene from the Day of Judgement. The righteous people in their heavenly Gardens ask the disbelievers and liars whom the fires of Hell encompass, what were the reasons for their punishment. Among those reasons are neglecting the rights of the poor, letting them be afflicted by hunger, nakedness and suffering, and turning their faces away from them. Allah says, *"Every self is held in pledge against what it earned except for the companions of the Right. In Gardens they will ask the evildoers: 'What caused you to enter Saqar?' They will say, 'We were not of those who prayed and we did not feed the poor. We plunged with those who plunged and denied the Day of Judgement until the Certain came to us.'"* (74:38-45)

Similar to feeding the poor is clothing, sheltering, and providing for their necessities. In *Surat al-Qalam*, Allah tells the story of some people who owned a garden and decided to collect its fruits at night in order to prevent the poor and needy that used to come on harvest day from taking some charity. Because of that, Allah sent a quick punishment to them. The verses read:

> *"So a visitation from your Lord visited it while they slept and in the morning it was like burnt land, stripped bare. In the morning they called out to one another, 'Leave early for your land if you want to pick the fruit.' So they set off, quietly saying to one another, 'Do not let any poor man into it today while you are there.' They left early, intent on carrying out their scheme. But when they saw it, they said, 'We must have lost our way. No, the truth is we are destitute!' The best of them said, 'Did I not say to you, "Why do you not glorify Allah?"' They said, 'Glory be to our Lord. Truly we have been wrongdoers.' They turned to face each other in mutual accusation. They said, 'Woe to us! We were indeed excessive. Maybe our Lord will give us something better than it in exchange. We make entreaty to our Lord.' Such is the punishment. And the punishment of the Next World is much greater if they only knew."* (68:19-33)

Encouragement to take care of the indigent

The Makkan verses did not stop at calling for mercy to the indigent, encouraging and providing for their needs, and making it dreadful to neglect or be harsh to them. The Makkan verses went further, in considering that each believer has a duty towards the indigent, i.e. believers should urge others to help the poor. The Qur'an considered abstention from encouraging others to aid the needy a feature related to disbelief in Allah, that implicates His anger and punishment in the Hereafter. Allah says in *Surat al-Haqqa*: *"But as for him who is given his Book in his left hand, he will say, 'If only I had not been given my Book and had not known about my Reckoning! If only death had really been the end! My wealth has been of no use to me. My power has vanished.'"* (69:25-29) And Allah, the Lord of the worlds, gives His just judgement in punishment on those who deserve it. *"Seize him and truss him up. Then roast him in the Blazing Fire. Then bind him in a chain which is seventy cubits long."* The cause of his punishment and humiliation in the sight of witnesses is: *"He used not to believe in Allah the Most Great, nor did he urge the feeding of the poor."*(69:30-34)

These verses, which promise so strongly the punishment of those who do not encourage the feeding of the indigent, motivated the companion Abu'd-Darda' to such an extent that he said to his wife, "O Umm ad-Darda', Allah has a chain that has boiled in the blazing Fire since Allah created Hell and it will remain there until it is thrown on the necks of people: Allah has saved us of half of its pain by bringing us into believing in Him, the Greatest, so encourage the feeding of the poor, Umm ad-Darda' (in order to fulfil the other condition mentioned in the verse above)."[1]

The world never witnessed before the Qur'an a text that considers abstention from encouragement to care for the indigent a sin that can send the perpetrator to Hell. In *Surat al-Fajr*, Allah calls the people of ignorance who claim to have a religion that brings them close to Allah and cling to the remnants of the religion of Ibrahim, *"No indeed! You do not honour orphans nor do you urge the feeding of the poor."* (89:17-18) Encouraging one another is a call to all humanity to co-operate and support one another in taking care of the poor. Shaykh Muhammad 'Abduh commented that "The Qur'an tells us to encourage one another to feed the poor, and not just to feed the poor, in order to indicate that members of the community should

1. *Al-Amwal*, p. 350.

have solidarity, mercy and grace towards one another, and should secure one another's needs.[1]

In *Surat al-Ma'un*, Allah made harshness to orphans and neglect of the poor signs of disbelief and of denial of the Day of Judgement: *"Have you seen him who denies the* deen*? He is the one who harshly rebuffs the orphan and does not urge the feeding of the poor."* (107:1-3) Shaykh 'Abduh said, "It is obvious that he who does not encourage others to feed the poor would not feed them on his own, so the sentence, 'does not urge the feeding of the poor' includes implicitly not giving anything of his own goods to the poor. It is mentioned in this form to show that even one who does not have enough to give the poor is required to call upon others to do so and to encourage all believers to relieve the poor, even if it were by collecting funds through, for example, charitable organisations."[2]

Surat al-Ma'un continues: *"So woe to those who pray, and are forgetful of their prayer. Those who show off and deny help to others."* (107:4-7) Ibn Kathir commented, "This means those who do not worship their Lord the right way and do not do good to His creatures even by lending them what they can benefit from without consuming the object lent. People like those gain no benefit from their prayers and are not categorised with the believers on the Day of Judgement." [3]

The right of one who asks, one who does not, the destitute and the traveller

In *Surat adh-Dhariyat*, Allah mentions sincere believers who deserve the Gardens of Heaven. One of their most obvious characteristics is *"And the beggars and destitute received a due share of their wealth."* (51:19-20) He who asks has a right, and he who is deprived, who has no wealth of his own, nor means of earning, nor a profession to live on, also has a right. Those sincere believers have

1. Commentary on part 30 of the Qur'an, p. 83.
2. Commentary on part 30 of the Qur'an, p. 162.
3. Commentary of Ibn Kathir, vol. 4, p. 555.

realised that their wealth is not only for their own use. They have realised that part of it belongs, in fact, to the needy, not as a charitable gift given with condescension but as a clear-cut right, without humbleness on the part of the receiver or pride on the part of the payer.

In *Surat al-Ma'arij*, this same characterisation is repeated with a slight difference in the scene pictured. It came with reference to the characters of the unbelievers who have overcome, by the strength of their conviction and sense of ethics, the weakness of the human being: *"Truly man was created headstrong. When something bad happens to him, desperate. When something good happens to him, begrudging, except for those who pray and who are constant in their prayer, those in whose wealth there is a known share for beggars and the destitute."* (70:19-25)

Here the right in their wealth is described as known and well-defined. This led some scholars to state that this *ayat* refers to *zakat* because it is the recognised, known right on the wealth of the rich. It is known, however, that this sura is Makkan while *zakat* as defined in the *Shari'a* was prescribed in Madina, as we shall see later. This recognised and well-defined right could not be anything except a part put aside by the believers out of their wealth to be given to he who begs and the destitute. The difference, therefore, between this right and *zakat* is that this is a portion determined by the believers themselves and put aside by their own action, while *zakat* is defined and determined by the *Shari'a*. In *Surat al-Isra'*, Allah says: *"Give relatives their due, and the very poor and travellers but do not squander what you have."* (17:26) And in *Surat ar-Rum*: *"Give relatives their due and the poor and travellers. That is best for those who are seeking the Face of Allah."* (30:38)

By these statements the Qur'an instilled in the being of Muslims as early as the Makkan period that kindred and those who are in need have well-defined rights on the believer's funds. It is not a mere voluntary charity which he can pay or refrain from paying according to whim.

The right due on crops at the time of harvest

In *Sura al-An'am* Allah says: *"It is He who produces gardens, both cultivated and wild, and palm-trees and crops of diverse kinds, and olives and pomegranates, both similar and dissimilar. Eat of their fruits when they bear fruit and pay their due on the day of their harvest, and do not be profligate. He does not love the profligate.* (6:141) Allah brings to the attention of His servants that there is a prescribed right on the fruits and crops of the earth. This right should be paid on the day of harvest.

Sa'id ibn Jubayr noted that, "Before *zakat* was revealed, a person was required to give out of the crops to orphans and indigents." This is a right that is not determined to be one-tenth or one half of a tenth. It is left to the sincerity of the farmer, and according to the need of the indigents. Later in Madina, the Messenger of Allah (ﷺ) determined the rate of this right by making it one-tenth or one half of a tenth on crops which are in excess of five *wasqs*. Some commentators found in this action of the Prophet an explanation of that due on crops and fruits as we shall discuss later.

Payment of *zakat* in Makka

There are many examples of the provision of the Makkan verses for the poor and destitute in assigning them a recognised right in others' wealth so that they would not be lost in the Muslim community. This was crowned by verses offering praise for those who pay it and humiliation for those who neglect it. In *Surat ar-Rum*, Allah holds a comparison between the effect of *riba*, which seems to increase wealth while it in fact shrinks it, and the effect of *zakat* which seems to reduce wealth while it in fact makes it grow. Allah says: *"Give relatives their due and the poor and travellers. That is best for those who are seeking the Face of Allah. They are the successful. What you give with usurious intent, aiming to get back a greater amount from people's wealth, does not become greater with Allah But anything you give as* zakat, *seeking the Face of Allah – all who do that will get back twice as much."* (20:38-39)

At the beginning of *Surat an-Naml*, Allah describes the believers for whom He made His book a guide and glad tiding as *"those who establish the prayer and pay* zakat *and are certain of the Next World."* (27:1-3) In connecting the giving of *zakat* to establishing prayers one finds a clear indication that what is meant here is the prescribed *zakat* on wealth. At the beginning of *Surat Luqman*, Allah says: *"Those are the Signs of the Wise Book – guidance and mercy for the good-doers: those who establish the prayer and pay* zakat *and are certain of the Next World."* (31:4) In *Surat al-Mu'minun*, He describes the faithful as *"those who actively pay* zakat." (23:4) In *Surat al-A'raf*, while telling the story of Musa and his tribe, Allah says: *"My mercy extends to all things but I will prescribe it for those who are godfearing and pay* zakat, *and those who believe in Our Signs: those who follow the Messenger, the Unlettered Prophet"* (7:156-7), and in describing the disbelievers Allah mentions, *"those who do not pay* zakat *and reject the Next World."* (41:6-7)

Some Qur'anic commentators infer that what is meant by *zakat* here is the sanctification and purification of the soul from evil and sin, following the idea in *Surat ash-Shams*: *"He who purifies* (zakka) *it has succeeded"* (91:9), and in *Surat al-A'la*: *"He who has purified* (tazakka) *himself will have success."* (87:14) The two verses use the verbs *'zakka'* and *'tazakka'* for 'purify'. To me, this is only an attempt to escape from the meaning that *zakat* in the above verses is the *zakat* on wealth that is prescribed later in Madina. At-Tabari holds that *zakat* in those verses means the same *zakat* on wealth that is known in the *Shari'a* and says that the word *zakat* was commonly used with regard to wealth.[1] This is supported by the verse itself, where the verb "give" is associated with the word *zakat*.

It should be observed that those Makkan verses on *zakat* were not giving commands, and did not clearly indicate the obligatory nature of *zakat* but rather they mentioned it in an informative manner as a practice essential to the character of sincere believers,[2]

1 *Tafsir at-Tabari*, vol. 24, p. 2.

2. Except what came in the last verse of *Surat al-Muzzammil*, *"So recite as much of it as is easy for you. And establish the prayer and pay* zakat," This is on the assumption that this *sura* is entirely Makkan which is the view of some scholars. Others

while not paying it is a characteristic of disbelievers. On the other hand, making *zakat* a criterion for distinguishing believers and unbelievers is itself an implicit reference that *zakat* is obligatory because it is always required to obtain the characteristics of believers and to avoid the characteristics of unbelievers.

Zakat in the Makkan period takes an undefined form

The *zakat* which is mentioned in Makkan verses was in the general form of voluntary payments. It did not take the specific definition as we know it now until it was prescribed in Madina when the rates, minimum exemption, and wealth subject to zakat were determined. That is when *zakat* collectors and distributors were sent to survey all Muslims and to collect *zakat* and distribute it, and when the state became responsible for *zakat* as an institution. In Makka, *zakat* was left to the faith and brotherly feelings of individuals, and the amount that was to be paid was not determined.

Some scholars infer from the Qur'anic terms of the Makkan verses like, "*right of the destitute*", "*right for him who asks and the destitute,*" "*a known right,*" that in Makka it was left to the Prophet (p) to determine the amounts of *zakat* on the funds of Muslims.[1] But such inference is not supported by any reports that the Prophet did so, while there are reports to the contrary.

It seems that in Makka there was no need for any specific determination because persecuted Muslims were then sacrificing all they had, including their own lives. However, the amounts may be determined by the payers of *zakat*, as stated by some commentators. Ibn Kathir says in his commentary on *Surat al-Mu'minun* about those who practise *zakat*, "The majority's opinion is that what is meant here is *zakat* on wealth, although the verse is Makkan while

say that the last verse is Madinan because it is different in style and content from the rest of the *sura*.

1. Muhammad 'Izzat Darwazah, *Biography of the Messenger as Derived from the Qur'an*, vol. 2, p. 341.

zakat was prescribed in Madina in the second year of the *Hijra*." Apparently, in the second year of the *Hijra*, *zakat* was prescribed in its specific form, with percentages and minimum exemption, while the principle of *zakat* was given in Makka as in the *ayat* in *Surat al-An'am*, "*and pay their due on the day of their harvest.*"[1] What is found by Ibn Kathir as the obvious meaning is supported by the many verses mentioned earlier.

Zakat in the Madinan period

In Madina, Muslims had their own society, political power and a state. This was not the case in Makka. Consequently, Islamic requirements took a new form that was suitable for this stage. These requirements now became specific and well-defined laws and regulations while in Makka they were general directions and advice. The authority of the state could now be counted on in the execution of these requirements in addition to the motivation of faith. The characteristics of this new Madinan era are clear in the treatment of *zakat*. The Lawgiver determines the exact kinds of wealth on which *zakat* is required, the conditions for its obligation, its percentages and ratios, and the areas of distribution of its receipts, as well as the institution that organises and administers it.

Madinan verses detailing the obligation of *zakat*

In Madinan *suras*, there is a very clear directive for the payment of zakat which is emphasised in different styles as in *Surat al-Baqara*, "*Establish the prayer and pay zakat.*" (2:110) Madinan verses on *zakat* are too numerous to list here, therefore I have selected *Surat at-Tawba* as an example, a *sura* which is among the last part of the Qur'an to be revealed.

1. Commentary of Ibn Kathir, vol. 3, pp. 238-239.

Surat at-Tawba as an example of the Madinan *suras* about *zakat*

At the beginning of this *sura*, the verses speak about fighting the unbelievers who broke their covenant with the Prophet, stating: *"If they turn in repentance and establish the prayer and pay* zakat, *let them go on their way. Allah is Ever-Forgiving, Most Merciful."* (9:5) Thus, three conditions are set to bring an end to fighting with pagans. Firstly, repentance from paganism. That is, bearing witness that there is no deity but Allah and Muhammad is the Messenger of Allah. Secondly, the establishment of prayer, which is the characteristic of faith and the greatest pillar of Islam, the criterion that distinguishes Muslims from non-Muslims, the spiritual bond among all Muslims. Thirdly, the practice of *zakat*, prescribed on the wealth of the rich for those who are in need, for the common benefit of the whole community. It is the political, social, and financial bond among all Muslims.

After another six verses, Allah speaks about another group of unbelievers: *"But if they turn in repentance and establish the prayer and pay* zakat, *they are your brothers in the* deen. *We mark out the Signs for people who know."* (9:11) Conversion from disbelief to become a member of the Muslim community cannot be done without repentance from associating partners with Allah, establishment of prayer, in which all Muslims share submission to Allah, and the practice of *zakat,* by which Muslims help one another and establish socio-economic solidarity.

Scholars as early as the era of the Companions point out an important issue in the Qur'anic style, namely the continuous association of *zakat* and prayer. One of them is seldom mentioned without the other. 'Abdullah ibn Mas'ud says, "You are ordained to establish prayer, to practise *zakat*, and the prayer of him who does not practise *zakat* is meaningless." Ibn Zayd says, "Prayer and *zakat* were prescribed together. One is not separated from the other." He read the verse, *"But if they turn in repentance and establish the prayer and pay* zakat, *they are your brothers in the* deen,*"* as an indication that Allah does not accept prayer without *zakat*. Ibn Zayd continued, "May the mercy of Allah be on Abu Bakr for his great understanding ,"[1] in reference to Abu Bakr's saying that we should not make a distinction between these two things Allah associated with each other.

In this *sura*, Allah refers to those who tend mosques as deserving acceptance by Him. He says: " *The mosques of Allah are only frequented by those who believe in Allah and the Last Day and establish the prayer and pay* zakat, *and fear no one but Allah. They are the people most likely to be guided."* (9:18) Establishing mosques and maintaining them is not sufficient for acceptance. There is a need to perform prayer and practise *zakat.*

There is a strong warning in *Surat at-Tawba* to those who hoard gold and silver without paying Allah's dues. Allah says: "*As for those who hoard up gold and silver and do not spend it in the Way of Allah give them the news of a painful punishment, on the Day it is heated up in the fire of Hell and their foreheads, sides and backs are branded with it: 'This is what you hoarded for yourselves! So taste what you were hoarding!'"* (9:34-35) Scholars comment that the warning against hoarding money is strong to counteract the instinct of loving money in most people.[2]

Areas of distribution are also given in the *sura*. With that, there should be no excuse for those who are eager to take for themselves the receipts of *zakat* without right. Allah says: "*Collected* sadaqa *is for: the poor, the destitute, those who collect it, reconciling people's hearts, freeing slaves, those in debt, spending in the Way of Allah, and travellers. An obligation imposed by Allah. Allah is All-Knowing, All-Wise."* (9:58-60) With this decisive verse, Allah left no room for favours in the distribution of the proceeds of *zakat*. He Himself took the issue of determining the eight deserving categories. Who could be more just than Allah in what He has ordained? *"Who could be better at giving judgement than Allah for people with certainty?"* (5:53) In these verses we find the assertion that there should be a group of workers to administer *zakat,* which indicates that *zakat* should be taken by the government and not merely paid by individuals on their own initiative.

---

1. Commentary of at-Tabari, vol. 14, p. 153.
2. *Ahkam al-Qur'an*, Abu Bakr ibn al-'Arabi.

In the *sura*, there are details about the characteristics of the believing society. Allah says: *"The men and women of the believers are friends of one another. They command the right and forbid the wrong, and establish the prayer and pay* zakat, *and obey Allah and His Messenger. They are the people Allah will have mercy on. Allah is Almighty, All-Wise."* (9:71) Thus, Allah made *zakat* one of the main features of communities of the faithful and distinguishes it from that of the hypocrites described in an earlier verse: *"The men and women of the hypocrites are as bad as one another. They command the wrong and forbid the right and keep their fists tightly closed. They have forgotten Allah so He has forgotten them. The hypocrites are degenerate people."* (9:67) The hypocrites close their hands because of their love of money and miserliness, so they deserve to be neglected by Allah, while the believers open their hands wide, giving out of faith, so they deserve the mercy of Allah.

In the *sura*, Allah instructs His Messenger (p) and every head of the Muslim state after him: *"Take* sadaqa *from their wealth to purify and cleanse them and pray for them. Your prayers bring relief to them. Allah is All-Hearing, All-Knowing."* (9:103) Commentators argue that by saying "from" before "their wealth", Allah meant to include some and not all of the wealth since *zakat* is not compulsory on all kinds of wealth. Further, the word "wealth" in the verse is in the plural form, and so it covers many kinds of wealth, and the pronoun "their" refers to all Muslims according to the majority of the commentators. This may be looked upon as proof that *zakat* is obligatory on all Muslims because they are equal in the application of religious ruling.[1] The verse also indicates that *zakat* should be collected by the head of state or his agents. This, in itself, is confirmed by the *Sunna* and the actual practice of the Rightly-Guided Caliphs (*al-Khulafa' ar-Rashidun*) as we shall discuss later.

At the time of Abu Bakr, some of the rebels who objected to the payment of *zakat* argued that this verse is addressed to the Prophet (p) alone, deducing that *zakat* must not be collected by others. However, it will be shown later in this study, that this interpretation is a false claim. Some scholars say that *sadaqa* in this verse does not necessarily mean *zakat*, since the verse, according to

1. See the commentary of at-Tubrusi, *Majma' al-Bayan*.

them, refers to those who stayed in the back of the lines and did not go to the Battle of Tabuk, those who mixed good deeds with bad. These scholars claim that *sadaqa* should only be taken from those who did not join the army as compensation for their sins. It is consequently a form of special voluntary contribution, restricted to those individuals as implicated by the context. These scholars go on to say that this verse, although general in its wording, is not general in its meaning, since *zakat*, which is a sign of submission to Allah and an obligation on all Muslims, cannot be part of the repentance of those individuals that stayed behind.[1] This is the opinion of at-Tabari, among others.[2]

Many commentators, however, insist that *sadaqa* in this verse means *zakat*. The majority of scholars in early and late generations used this verse to show the rulings of *zakat*, which means that they understood it as a clear reference to *zakat*, especially as there is no need grammatically or linguistically for this verse to be necessarily connected with the verses around it. This understanding is attributed to Ibn 'Abbas, among others. It is also the opinion of 'Ikrima, as reported by al-Qushayri.[3]

Ar-Razi offered an intelligent way of linking this verse to the verses before and after it, without sacrificing its general implication. He said that *zakat* was not accepted from the hypocrites and from those individuals who stayed behind and did not join the army. Upon repentance and acceptance by Allah, they were given the privilege of *zakat* being taken from them as it is taken from other Muslims. It should be remembered, however, that specific causes related to sending down a verse are not taken as restrictions on the general meaning of the words of the verse, as overwhelmingly accepted by scholars of *usul*.

Ironically, those who denied the payment of *zakat* during the time of Abu Bakr used the same verse in their argument that *zakat* should only be paid to the Messenger, without claiming at all that

1. *Ar-Rawd an-Nadir*, vol. 2,, p. 410.

2. Commentary of at-Tabari, vol. 14, pp. 454-456.

3. Commentary of al-Qurtubi, vol. 8, p. 244. See also Ibn Kathir, vol. 2, pp. 385-386, *Ahkam al-Qur'an* of Ibn al-'Arabi, pp. 997-998, and *at-Tafsir al-Kabir* of al-Fakhr ar-Razi, vol. 16, p. 177f. Also al-Qasimi, *Mahasin at-Ta'wil*, vol. 8, p. 3253.

the verse does not make *zakat* obligatory. None of the Companions or great scholars is reported to have interpreted this verse as referring to voluntary *sadaqa*. All arguments given by the Companions and scholars against those who denied the payment of *zakat* to Abu Bakr indicated that the verse is not limited to the Prophet (p), but generally to any head of state after him.

The interpretation of *sadaqa* in the verse as the obligatory *zakat* is further supported by the saying of the Prophet (p) to a young man of the Banu Hashim who asked him to be employed as a *zakat* collector. The Prophet answered, "It is not permissible for the family of Muhammad. It is the impurities filtered out of people's wealth." This implicitly refers to the verse "*to purify and cleanse them.*" This meaning of the verse is also supported by a report in *Sahih Muslim* from 'Abdullah ibn Abi Awfa, "Whenever somebody's *sadaqa* was brought to the Prophet (p), he used to pray for that person. My father brought his *sadaqa* to the Prophet, who then said, 'My Lord, grant mercy to the family of Abi Awfa.'" This action of the Messenger is in application of a word in the verse that says, 'and pray for them.' Scholars infer from this verse that the head of state or his agent who collects *zakat* should pray for its payer.

These are the most important points about *zakat* in *Surat at-Tawba*. They represent the general trend of the Madinan *suras* in asserting the obligation of *zakat* and giving its main regulations. According to the Qur'an, a person cannot attain to righteousness or truthfulness, nor can he or she truly fear Allah and believe in Him, unless he or she practises *zakat* among other things. Without the payment of *zakat* there is nothing to distinguish a person from the hypocrites or the unbelievers: *"My mercy extends to all things but I will prescribe it for those who are godfearing and pay* zakat, *and those who believe in Our Signs."* (7:156)

Without *zakat* a person does not deserve Allah's mercy or the support and commitment of Allah, His Messenger (p), and the believers: *"Your friend is only Allah and His Messenger and those who believe, those who establish the prayer and pay* zakat, *and bow. And those who make Allah their friend, and His Messenger and those who believe: it is the party of Allah who are the victorious!"* (5:58-59) Without *zakat*, a person does not deserve the victory promised by Allah: *"Allah will certainly help those who help Him. Allah is All-Strong, Almighty. Those who, if We establish them firmly on the earth, will establish the prayer and pay* zakat, *and command the right and forbid the wrong. The end result of all affairs is with Allah."* (22:40-41)

The *Sunna* provides details on the general directives of the Qur'an

The Qur'an, as the main charter of Islam, and its basic reference, gives usually only the main principles without minute details except in a few areas where there is fear of misconception. The *Sunna* is the practical manifestation of the Qur'an. It explains, gives details, provides the scope and the specifications of the general verses of the Qur'an, in accordance with the understanding given by Allah to His Messenger (p). Allah says: *"And We have sent down the Reminder to you so that you can make clear to mankind what has been sent down to them."* (16:44)

As far as *zakat* is concerned, the *Sunna* undeniably asserted its obligation as early as the Makkan period. Ja'far ibn Abi Talib, informing the King of Abyssinia about the Prophet (p) on behalf of the Muslim migrants, said, "And he ordains us to pray, pay *zakat*, and fast." (Ibn Khuzayma) This is a reference to the general concept and not to the specific obligations of *zakat*. In Madina, the opportunity was open for the *Sunna* to give the details of *zakat*, its minimum exemption, its ratios, its conditions, and its role and importance in the life of the Muslims, as well as practical examples of the execution of this major tenet of Islam.

The *Sunna* determines the specific details of *zakat*

The *Sunna* gave us the detailed specifications of the kinds of wealth subject to *zakat*, the minimum amount exempt of each of them, and the applicable rates. The *Sunna* also gave us the details of the categories who receive *zakat*. This section is devoted to finding out the history of the obligation of *zakat* as a defined amount due on particular varieties of wealth.

We know that the general principle of *zakat* was prescribed in Makka without any determination of its details. This is what I believe most reasonable and acceptable, in accordance with many scholars, since it is indicated by many verses of the Qur'an and many sayings of the Messenger (p). Moreover, it was shown earlier that Madinan *suras* emphasised this obligation and gave some of the definitions and details of *zakat*. The *Sunna* took the task of delineating the minute specification determining the kinds of wealth on which *zakat* is levied, the percentages of wealth owed in *zakat*, and the methods of its collection. The question of determining the exact year in which *zakat* in this specific sense was prescribed finds an answer during the Madinan period.

It is overwhelmingly recognised that *zakat* was made compulsory in the second year after the *Hijra*. It is said that *zakat* was prescribed before the fasting of Ramadan was prescribed. An-Nawawi pointed out this opinion in the part of *ar-Rawda* which was devoted to *as-siyar* (biography). On the other hand, it is authentically reported by Ahmad, Ibn Khuzayma, an-Nasa'i, Ibn Majah, and al-Hakim that Qays ibn Sa'd ibn 'Ubada said, "The Messenger of Allah commanded us to pay *sadaqa* of *al-Fitr* before *zakat* was revealed. Later on, the obligation of *zakat* was revealed." Al-Hafiz noted that. This would mean that *zakat* was made an obligation after the fast of Ramadan.[1] It is not disputed, however, that the fast of Ramadan was obligated after the *Hijra* since the verse that talks about it is indisputably Madinan.

In his *History*, Ibn al-Athir stated that *zakat* was made obligatory in 9 AH. This is supported, according to some, by the story of Tha'laba ibn Hatib which states, "When the verse of *sadaqa* was revealed, the Prophet (p) sent a collector to collect *zakat* from Tha'laba, who riposted, 'This resembles nothing but a *jizya* or the sister of *jizya*.'" *Jizya* was obligated in 9 AH, so the concept of *zakat* must have been around then. The author of *Fath al-Bari* said, "This saying is weak and does not stand in argument."[2]

1. Fath al-Bari, vol. 3, p. 171.
2. In *Takhrij al-Kashshaf*, p. 77, the author said that is very weak.

Ibn Hajar argued, however, that *zakat* was made obligatory before 9 AH, citing the saying of Anas concerning the story of Dammam ibn Tha'laba (reported in the two *Sahih* collections) who asked the Prophet (p) in the name of Allah to give him the right answer on a few matters. Dammam said, "By Allah, did Allah order you to take this *sadaqa* from the rich among us and distribute it to the poor among us?" The Prophet (p) answered, "Yes." Dammam came to the Prophet (p) in 5 AH. But in 9 AH, the Prophet (p) sent *zakat* collectors for the first time to collect *zakat*. This implies that *zakat* was made obligatory well before that.[1]

Additionally, the verse that starts, "Sadaqa *is for ...*" which closed the door in the face of the hypocrites and their ambitions, indicates implicitly that *zakat* was definitely in practice and that the Prophet (p) was having *zakat* collected and distributed by his appointees at the time of its revelation.

Zakat after Ramadan (*Zakat al-Fitr*)

It seems to be evident from all the sayings together and from the historical development of the imposition of Islamic obligations that the five prayers were the first to be made obligatory. That happened in Makka on the Night Journey. Fasting was obligated in 2 AH, and then *Zakat al-Fitr* was also obligated as a purification for fasters and to bring happiness to the poor on the Day of the Feast. *Zakat* on wealth was made compulsory later on. But it is very difficult to find decisive evidence that tells the exact year when it was imposed as an obligation, although the saying of Dammam ibn Tha'laba indicates that *zakat* had already been made obligatory by 5 AH according to Ibn Hajar.

In *al-Furu'*, Ibn Muflih mentioned the report of al-Walibi from Ibn 'Abbas: "Allah has sent His Prophet (p) with the testimony that there is no god but Allah. When they accepted that, they were increased by the prayer. When they accepted that, fasting was added. After they accepted that, *zakat* was added. When they

1. *Fath al-Bari*, vol. 3, p. 171.

accepted that, *hajj* was added. After they accepted that, *jihad* was added, and thus the religion was perfected and completed." And he quoted, "*Today I have perfected your* deen *for you and completed My blessing upon you and am pleased with Islam as a* deen *for you.*" (5:3) This is consistent with what Ibn 'Aqil said in *al-Wadih*, i.e. *zakat* was prescribed after fasting.[1]

Zakat, the third pillar of Islam

The Prophet (p) affirmed the obligation of *zakat* in Madina. He pronounced its importance and rank in this religion as one of its principal pillars. He encouraged its performance and strongly warned against rejecting its payment. All this came in many sayings. We see it in the well-known *hadith* when Jibril came to teach Muslims their religion by politely questioning the Prophet (p). He asked the Prophet (p), "What is Islam?" The Prophet (p) answered, "Islam is to testify that there is no god but Allah and Muhammad is the Messenger of Allah, to establish prayer, pay *zakat*, fast Ramadan, and to make pilgrimage to the House if you are able to do so." (Agreed upon) In the famous saying narrated by Ibn 'Umar, "Islam is founded on five: testifying that there is no god but Allah and Muhammad is the Messenger of Allah, establishing prayer, paying *zakat*, fasting Ramadan, and pilgrimage to the House for whoever can do so." (Agreed upon). In these two sayings and in many others, the Messenger (p) declared that the pillars of Islam are five, among them *zakat* is the third. *Zakat* is declared as the third pillar in the *Sunna* as well as in the Qur'an, without which the structure of Islam does not stand.

In some sayings the Prophet (p) only mentioned some of those pillars, but he always mentioned prayer and *zakat* in the forefront of what he called for and took covenant on. An example is the saying narrated by Ibn 'Abbas in the *Sahih* collections. When the Prophet (p) sent Mu'adh to Yemen,[2] he told him, "You are going

1. *Al-Furu'*, in *Hanbalite Fiqh*, vol. 2, p. 217 and p. 318.

2. Ash-Shawkani said, "He was sent in 10 AH just before the Prophet (p) went on pilgrimage as reported by al-Bukhari at the end of the chapter, "Travels

to some of the People of the Book. Call upon them to testify that there is no god but Allah and I am the Messenger of Allah. If they obey you in that, inform them that Allah has prescribed for them five prayers every day and night. If they obey you in that, inform them that Allah has made it obligatory that *sadaqa* be collected from their rich and rendered to their poor. If they obey you in that, then carefully avoid their other wealth and valuables. Be very fearful of the prayer of an oppressed person since there is no veil between such a prayer and Allah."

The saying only mentions prayer and *zakat* in order to show how much importance Allah has given them, especially when the matter is the call to Islam. These two tenets, along with the declaration of faith, should be sufficient indication of Islam as it is in the *ayat*: *"But if they turn in repentance and establish the prayer and pay* zakat, *they are your brothers in the* deen." (9:11) This saying indicates that the job of collecting and distributing *zakat* was a specifically assigned task and that payment and distribution of *zakat* was not left to the individual's initiative.

Al-Bukhari reports from Jabir ibn 'Abdullah, "I gave a pledge to the Prophet (p) to establish prayer, pay *zakat*, and give sincere advice to each Muslim." Ibn 'Umar narrates in the two *Sahih* collections that the Messenger of Allah (p) said, "I am commanded to fight disbelievers until they testify that there is no god but Allah and Muhammad is the Messenger of Allah, and establish prayer and pay *zakat*." This saying refers, in principle, to the Arab pagans. Allah wanted Arab land to be sanctified for Islam and cleansed from all remnants of paganism, blind ignorance and oppression.

There is a *hadith* reported by al-Bazzar from Anas that the Messenger of Allah (p) said, "He who dies having sincere faith in Allah, worshipping Him without partners, establishing prayer, and paying *zakat*, ends up with the pleasure of Allah." Anas said, "This is the religion of Allah for which Messengers are sent. They reveal

and Battles of the Prophet." Some said he was sent in 9 AH upon returning from the Battle of Tabuk. Others said that he was sent the same year as the Conquest of Makka in 8 AH. It is agreed, however, that he stayed in Yemen until after the death of the Prophet and his succession by Abu Bakr. There are also differences on whether he was sent as a governor or only a judge. Ibn 'Abdu'l-Barr believes the latter while an-Nasa'i confirms the former. See *Nayl al-Awtar*, vol. 4, p. 115.

it to people from the Lord. It was there long before vain talk and differences of whims." There he quoted the *ayat*: *"If they turn in repentance and establish the prayer and pay* zakat, *let them go on their way."* (9:5) He said, "Repentance is by their dissociation from idols, by the worship of Allah alone, by the practice of the prayer and by paying *zakat*." Anas then quoted another verse: *"But if they turn in repentance and establish the prayer and pay* zakat, *they are your brothers in the* deen.*"*[1] (9:11)

Strong warning against to pay *zakat*

Several *hadiths* mention the warning the Messenger (p) gave to those who reject the payment of *zakat*. Warning of severe punishment in the Hereafter is aimed at awakening dormant hearts and shaking miserly souls to give by both positive encouragement and fear of punishment. If they do not perform this duty with an awakened conscience, the power and authority of the state is used to collect *zakat*.

Punishment in the Hereafter

Al-Bukhari reported from Abu Hurayra, "The Messenger of Allah (p) said, 'If someone is given wealth by Allah but does not pay its *zakat*, that wealth will appear to him on the Day of Judgement in the form of a huge bald serpent with two horns, encircling him and squeezing him all day, then holding him by the lips and telling him, 'I am your wealth, your treasure which you hoarded.' Then the Prophet quoted the verse, *'Those who are stingy with the bounty Allah has given them should not suppose that that is better for them. No indeed, it is worse for them! What they were stingy with will be hung around their necks on the Day of Rising.'* (3:180)"

In another *hadith*, Muslim reports that the Prophet (p) said, "If someone owns gold and silver and does not pay what is due on

1. Commentary of Ibn Kathir, vol., 2, pp, 235-238.

them, on the Day of Rising they will be made like sheets heated by the fire of Hell. His front, back and sides will be ironed with these sheets on a day which is as long as fifty thousand years, until judgement is given to all human beings, and he will be shown his way to the Garden or the Fire. He who owns cattle or sheep and does not pay what is due on them, they will be brought on the Day of Resurrection to stamp on him with their hoofs and stab him with their horns. When the last one finishes with him, the first will be brought again to continue that stamping and stabbing until Allah gives judgement to all His servants, on a day that is as long as fifty thousand years of yours. Then he will be shown his way to the Garden or to the Fire."

Punishment in this life of those who refuse to pay *zakat*

The *Sunna* did not merely threaten punishment in the Hereafter for those who do not pay *zakat*, but went on to warn them of a punishment in this life: punishment from Allah and a penalty from the state. A *hadith* states: "There is no people who do not pay *zakat* who are left without being made to suffer by Allah through disasters, famine or drought."[1] Another says, "Any people who do not pay zakat on their wealth would be denied rain from the sky were it not for animals and livestock."[2] Yet another says, "*Zakat* is never intermingled with any amount of wealth without destroying and rotting it."[3] This *hadith* has two meanings according to al-

1. Reported by at-Tabarani in *al-Awsat*, with a trustworthy chain of narrators, and by al-Hakim and al-Bayhaqi, but the latter's words were: "Whenever any people refuse to pay zakat, Allah will withhold rain from them." Al-Hakim said that it is *sahih* according to the criteria of Muslim. See *at-Targhib wa't-Tarhib*, vol. 1, p. 270 and *Majma' az-Zawa'id*, vol. 3, p. 96.

2. Reported by Ibn Majah, al-Bazzar and al-Bayhaqi from Ibn 'Umar. It is also reported by al-Hakim who said it is *sahih*. He was followed by adh-Dhahabi. This saying also has other narrations that support it. See the series of *sahih hadiths* of al-Albani, 105.

3. Reported by al-Bazzar and al-Bayhaqi as in *at-Targhib*. In *al-Muntaqa* it is reported by ash-Shafi'i and al-Bukhari in his *History*, and al-Humaydi, who added that if *zakat* has become due but is not paid out, the whole asset is ruined. See *Nawl al-Awtar*, vol. 4, p. 126.

Mundhiri. Firstly, that whenever *zakat* is not paid, it will be a cause of ruining that wealth. This meaning is upheld by another *hadith* which says, "Whenever any amount of wealth is destroyed in the land or in the sea it could be because its *zakat* was not paid.[1] Secondly, if someone receives *zakat* without being entitled to it and mixes it with his wealth, that will be a reason for rotting all his wealth, according to Imam Ahmad.[2]

Legal penalty for someone who does not pay *zakat*

The legal penalty for someone who does not pay *zakat* is mentioned by the Prophet (p): "He who pays it seeking the reward from Allah will be rewarded and he who refuses to pay it, we shall take it from him along with half his wealth, and by the authority given to us by our Lord. The clan of Muhammad are not allowed to take anything of its proceeds."[3] This saying includes a few important principles:

- *Zakat* is, in principal, paid out of sincerity by the believer for the sake of pleasing Allah and seeking reward from Him, since a Muslim is ordained to worship Allah by paying *zakat*.
- Anyone who is overcome by his miserliness and refuses to pay *zakat* is not left without payment being extracted from him anyway. *Zakat* is a legal institution that is supported by the executive power of the state. The state must use its authority to collect *zakat* in addition to the penalty (equal to half the wealth

1. *Majma' az-Zawa'id*, vol. 3, p. 93. Reported by at-Tabarani in *al-Awsat*. 'Umar ibn Harun is in the chain and he is weak.

2. *At-Targhib wa't-Tarhib*, op. cit.

3. Reported by Ahmad, an-Nasa'i and Abu Dawud from Bahz ibn Hakim from his father from his grandfather. It is also reported by al-Bayhaqi in his *Sunan*, vol. 4, p. 105. Al-Bayhaqi continued, "This is a *hadith* reported by Abu Dawud, it was not reported by al-Bukhari and Muslim because they have the condition that the Companion or the Follower should have more than one narrator of the next generation in order to put the saying in their *Sahih* collections. The grandfather, in this saying, is only narrated from by his son. Ibn at-Turkumani followed in his *al-Jawhar an-Naqi* that this was not a universal condition of al-Bukhari and Muslim. See the note on this saying in *Nayl al-Awtar*, vol. 4, p. 132.

of the hoarder), imposed by Allah and His Messenger (p). Some say that this penalty was levied only at the beginning of Islam but was annulled later.[1] There is no evidence whatsoever of this annulment, and the state can impose this penalty in order to prevent people from abusing this tenet of Islam.

• The strong penalty imposed on those who refuse to pay *zakat* shows the extent to which Islam cares about the rights of the poor and the other deserving categories. As the Prophet (p), all members of his family and his descendants are not allowed to receive any of the proceeds of *zakat*. It is made unlawful to them under any circumstances, in contrast with charity in Judaism, where one-tenth of it is assigned to the Levites, the descendants of Harun, and part of it was formerly used for other religious leaders.[2]

Fighting those who refuse to pay *zakat*

Those who refuse to pay *zakat* on their wealth are fined as above. But if it so happens that a group of people refuse to pay *zakat* collectively, that group should be fought by the Islamic government because that represents a rebellion against the state and Islam. Although fighting leads to bloodshed and the destruction of property which Islam aims to avoid, it becomes legitimate and permissible when it is done for the establishment of justice on earth. As for those who reject *zakat*, they have lost the respect and protection of their lives and property by declaring their rebellion against Allah and His Messenger (p) by rejecting this basic pillar of Islam.

This command to fight rebels who reject *zakat* is affirmed by *sahih hadiths* and the unanimous stand of the Companions. Al-Bukhari and Muslim reported from 'Abdullah ibn 'Umar that the Messenger of Allah (p) said, "I am commanded to fight unbelievers until they testify that there is no god but Allah and Muhammad is

1. This is stated by ash-Shirazi in *al-Muhadhdhab*. See *al-Majmu'*, vol. 5, p. 332, 334.

2. Abu'l-Hasan an-Nadwi, *al-Arkan al-Arba'a*, p. 129.

the Messenger of Allah, establish prayer and practise *zakat*. If they do all that, their blood is protected except by the due course of Islamic law and to Allah is left their reckoning." They also reported from Abu Hurayra, "The Messenger of Allah (p) said, 'I am commanded to fight unbelievers until they testify that there is no god but Allah and believe in me and in what I brought. If they do so, then they have protected their blood and property except by due course of law, their reckoning is left to Allah." A similar *hadith* is reported by Muslim and an-Nasa'i from Jabir ibn 'Abdullah.[1]

These *hadiths* clearly indicate that those who refuse to pay *zakat* must be fought until they pay. It may be that these sayings were not known to Abu Bakr and 'Umar when they argued whether they should fight those who refuse to pay *zakat* without denying the other pillars of Islam, such as prayer and fasting.[2]

After the death of the Messenger of Allah (p), several Arab tribes rebelled and refused to pay *zakat* though they continued their regular prayer and they declared faith in Allah. There were also totally rebellious tribes who turned back from Islam and claimed false prophets such as Musaylima the Liar, Saja, Tulayha al-Asadi and their clans. Abu Bakr then took a historic stand. He refused to acknowledge any differentiation between bodily worship (prayer) and financial worship (*zakat*). He rejected the reduction of what used to be paid to the Messenger of Allah (p), no matter how small that reduction might be (a baby goat or a camel's tether). He was not weakened by the apostates' preparation to invade Madina, and the hesitation of some Companions to fight the rebels.

Abu Hurayra describes this historic stand when the Messenger of Allah (p) died and Abu Bakr came to power and many Arabs turned back as apostates. 'Umar said, "By what virtue should we fight those people, knowing that the Messenger of Allah (p) said, 'I am commanded to fight pagans until they testify that there is no god but Allah. Once they say that, they have protected their blood

1. *Nayl al-Awtar*, vol. 4, p. 121.

2. This is not surprising. It may happen that some Companions did not hear from the Prophet what some others heard. An example is the statement of 'Umar about the *hadith* narrated by Abu Musa on seeking permission, "I missed it by getting busy with my trade in the markets." It is possible that Abu Bakr knew that *hadith* since he used its meaning in his argument with 'Umar.

and their property, except by due course of justice, and their reckoning is left to Allah Almighty.'" Abu Bakr answered, "By Allah, I shall fight those who differentiate between prayer and *zakat. Zakat* is the right due on wealth. By Allah, if they refuse to give me one baby goat they used to give to the Messenger of Allah as *zakat*, I shall fight them for it." 'Umar said, "And by Allah, it was not until I realised that Allah had opened the heart of Abu Bakr to fighting that I knew it was the truth." Reported by all except Ibn Majah. (In another version Abu Bakr said, "A tether of a camel" instead of a "baby goat".)[1] 'Umar took the words of the saying of the Prophet (p) literally to mean the declaration of faith alone is sufficient to protect the pagans, without attention to the essential implications of that declaration, without which the declaration itself is merely vain talk.

On the other hand, Abu Bakr brought out some basic points. Firstly, the text of the saying itself suspended protection by the condition of "due course of Law." *Zakat* is what is due on wealth in Islamic Law. 'Umar did not disagree on this point. Secondly, there is an analogy between *zakat* and prayer, as two sisters always associated together in the Book of Allah and the *hadiths* of His Messenger (p). The conclusion of the argument of Abu Bakr and 'Umar was that the Companions were unanimously agreed that those who refuse to pay must be fought, including those who were hesitant at first. 'Umar realised that Abu Bakr was correct and accepted his argument and his evidence.[2]

This is what was done by the first Caliph Abu Bakr the Truthful with regard to those Arab clans who insisted on refusing to pay *zakat* after the death of the Messenger of Allah (p). Consequently, fighting those who refused to pay *zakat* has become a matter of *ijma'* that cannot be altered. An-Nawawi said, "If a person or a group of people refuse to pay *zakat* and resist the law enforcement of the state, then the state must fight them, because it is authentically reported in the two *Sahih* Collections from Abu Hurayra that the Companions, after an initial debate, realised the value of the opinion given by Abu Bakr and the strength of its supportive evi-

1. *Nayl al-Awtar*, vol. 4, p. 119.
2. Ibid., p. 120. See also *Ma'alim as-Sunan*, vol. 2, p. 165.

dence and agreed with him in making the ruling on fighting those of reject *zakat* unanimous among the Muslims."[1]

It should be pointed out that for the first time in the history of humanity, a state, that is, the Islamic state of Abu Bakr, fought for the purpose of protecting the rights of the poor and the weak sectors of society. Most states stand in support of the rich and strong. Abu Bakr and the Companions rejected the idea that *zakat* should only be paid to the Prophet (p) and after his death no one would have the right to collect *zakat*, claiming that verse 103 of *Surat at-Tawba* gave the right to collect *zakat* to the Prophet (p) alone. The judge, Abu Bakr ibn al-'Arabi, said about this claim, "These are the words of a person who is totally ignorant of the Qur'an, who does not know how the rulings of the *Shari'a* are derived, who wants to tamper with religion and whose viewpoint is falling apart on its own. The verse is addressed to every head of state after the Prophet (p), though it speaks to him at that particular time. It is not addressed to the personal affairs of the Prophet (p), like the verses that speak about his family life or his personal prayers."[2]

Al-Khattabi said, "The address of speech in the Book of Allah is of three kinds. One is general address, such as the verse, '*O you who believe, when you stand for the prayer, wash your faces...*' (5:6) The second is that which is addressed specifically to the Prophet (p) alone. This is clearly indicated in the verse itself such as, '*And stay awake for prayer during part of the night as a supererogatory action for yourself*' (17:79) and '*exclusively for you as opposed to the rest of the believers.*' (33:50) The third is that which is addressed to the Prophet (p) but includes the entire Community in meaning and action as, '*Establish the prayer from the time the sun declines...*' (17:78), '*Whenever you recite the Qur'an, seek refuge with Allah from the cursed Shaytan*' (17:98) and '*Take* sadaqa *from their wealth.*' Such verses are not restricted to the Prophet alone. They are in fact addressed to him and to the entire Muslim Community." It should be mentioned that the speech is addressed to the Messenger of Allah (p), because he is required to preach and explain Allah's commandments, and he is an example for all Muslims to follow.

1. *Al-Majmu'*, vol. 5, p. 995.
2. *Ahkam al-Qur'an*, vol. 2, p. 995.

Verse 103 of *Surat at-Tawba* mentions that the Prophet (p) should pray for those who give *zakat*. However, no one can make the claim that only the Prophet (p) should pray for those who pay *zakat*. All *zakat* collectors are also addressed by this verse. The payment of *zakat* itself is related in the verse to sanctification and purification of those who pay it. Muslim scholars comment that purification, sanctification, and prayer for those who pay *zakat* are consequences of their obedience to Allah and His Messenger (p) in paying *zakat*, and every reward for good deeds that is mentioned with respect to the time of the Prophet (p), remains in effect after his time for all doers of such good deeds without interruption until the Day of Judgement.[1]

Zakat is part of what is necessarily known of the religion

It is important lastly to point out that *zakat* as a pillar of Islam is among those principles that are necessarily known of religion. It was instituted by clear verses in the Qur'an, by abundant sayings of the Prophet (p) and has been affirmed by the *ijma'* (consensus) of Muslims, generation after generation.[2]

Denying *zakat* is equivalent to denying faith

We have shown how important *zakat* is in Islam and how high it is ranked among Islam's obligations. We should here point out

1. See al-Khattabi, *Ma'alim as-Sunan*, vol. 2, p. 165, *Ahkam al-Qur'an*, part 2, pp. 884-996, and *Nayl al-Awtar*, vol. 4, pp. 102-104.

2. Some scholars said that its obligation is also deduced by the rational thinking of the Muslims. The author of *al-Bada'i'*, vol. 3, p. 3, said the following reasons are used to rationalise the obligation of *zakat*: 1. The payment is a help and relief to the poor, the incapable and the needy, it helps them to support their own lives and to perform prayers and other forms of worship. 2. *Zakat* purifies the soul of the *zakat* payer from sins, trains him to become generous and helps him avoid misery. This training is very useful to each soul. 3. The payment of *zakat* is an expression of thankfulness to Allah by the rich who are granted their wealth as a bounty from Allah.

that scholars have established that the denial of its obligation is equal to disbelief and apostatising from Islam. An-Nawawi said, "Anyone who does not pay *zakat* on the basis of denying its obligation is considered a disbeliever except if that person is new in Islam or has lived all his or her life far from sources of information (in an isolated desert, for example.) Then he or she should first be made aware of the importance of the obligation of *zakat*. If he or she insists on denying it, then that is disbelief, because the obligation of *zakat* is basic to this religion, without which Islam becomes annulled. One who denies this obligation denies the words of Allah and His Messenger (p), and therefore is a disbeliever."[1] This ruling is also established by Ibn Qudama and other scholars.[2] With this unanimous ruling we should realise the low rank that those who deny or ridicule *zakat*, assume in the eyes of Allah.

The main differences between *zakat* in Islam and alms in other religions

Zakat in Islam is not a mere charity left to the righteousness of individuals as part of their good deeds. It is rather an essential pillar of this religion, one of its major rituals, and the second of its four main forms of worship. Not paying it is like going astray. He who denies its obligation is considered a disbeliever. It is an obligation supported by the ethical values of Islam as well as by the power of law in the Islamic state.

Zakat is the right of the poor in the wealth of the rich, a right decided by the true Owner of wealth - Allah, and imposed on those who have been given control of that wealth by Him. *Zakat* thus does not humble or humiliate the receiver nor does it elevate the rich to a higher rank, ethically or socially. *Zakat* is a recognised and defined due, determined by the *Shari'a* so that Muslims may know with clarity the ratios, the conditions and exemptions of this due.

1. *Al-Majmu'*, vol 5, p. 334.
2. *Al-Mughni,* vol., 2, p. 573.

The Islamic state is charged with the responsibility of collecting *zakat* and distributing it. *Zakat* is in this respect like a tax that must be collected and not like a contribution that is proffered. The Qur'an says, *"Take* sadaqa *from their wealth"* and the *Sunna* says, "...to be taken from the rich." The state has the right to penalise anyone who refuses to pay *zakat.* This penalty may include a fine of as much as half the assets as mentioned in the *hadith*, "We shall take it along with half the wealth of the rejecter." Any group of people who think of using force in resisting the payment of *zakat* should be fought by the Islamic government. War is declared on them until they accept to pay the due on their wealth, imposed by Allah, to the poor.

The individual Muslim is called upon to establish this essential obligation of Islam even if the state does not collect it, since the payment of *zakat* is in itself a form of worship that a Muslim offers to his Lord. If the government does not require its collection, it is required by the faith and by the Qur'an. Each Muslim should know of all the rulings of *zakat* so that he or she may pay it according to the conditions stipulated by the *Shari'a.*

The proceeds of zakat are not left to government or to religious leaders or priests to determine their distribution. The distribution of *zakat* and the deserving categories are determined in this religion in the verse *"Collected sadaqa is for: the poor, the destitute..."* (9:60) The *Sunna* brought the details of distribution. It is known from human experience that merely collecting funds is not supremely important but that what is more important is the disbursement of funds collected. So the Messenger of Allah (p) announced that neither he nor any member of his family or descendants would be allowed to take any part of the proceeds of *zakat. Zakat* is taken from the rich in every area and rendered to the poor in that same area.

Zakat is not merely temporary relief of the immediate needs of the poor and for the attenuation of their misery, leaving them in the long run to their poverty. *Zakat* aims at eliminating poverty and making the poor at least self-sufficient, helping them with sufficient financial means to enable them to work and produce for their own sustenance. *Zakat* is a periodical due repeated each year, aimed at raising the level of living of the poor.

Zakat in its distribution aims at achieving several spiritual, moral, social and political purposes. For that reason, it may be spent for the reconciliation of hearts, for the liberation of slaves, for those who are in debt, and for the sake of Allah in the widest meaning of the word.

With these characteristics of *zakat* that are so distinct from alms in other religions, we realise that *zakat* is an institution unique in its characteristics and features. It is different from taxes and other dues as much as it is different from alms known in other religions.

Disproving the claims of Schacht about the nature of *zakat*

It may be useful to go through the biased claims of some who assume the position of knowledge in the West without exhibiting the necessary honesty that is required for any scientific research. Schacht said under the title "Zakah" in the *Encyclopaedia of Islam*, "The tradition of the Prophet (p) includes some cases where *zakat* is obligated which are not consistent with the institution of *zakat* as it came to be known later. In all cases, the nature of *zakat* at the time of the Prophet (p) was still ambiguous and it was not one of the taxes required by religion. That is why many Arab tribes refused to pay it after the death of the Prophet (p). They considered that their covenant to pay to the Prophet (p) came to an end at this death. Some believers, including 'Umar ibn al-Khattab, were inclined to accept that view." (p. 358)

Schacht did not mention which sayings of the Prophet (p) he was referring to so that we could discuss his unfounded claims. Furthermore, his words, "...the institution of *zakat* as it came to be known later" imply that this system of *zakat* was fabricated by the Muslims after the time of the Prophet (p), that is, it is not a system revealed by Allah, but it was created by the conditions and human experience that Muslims gained from the Persians and the Romans. This, in itself, is an old falsehood for which Schacht and other orientalists have been branded. The truth, confirmed by verses of the Holy Qur'an, *sahih* and *hasan hadiths* of the Messenger (p), and the heritage of the Companions and the Wise Successors (*al-Khulafa' ar-Rashidun*), is that *zakat* is a pure Islamic system. It is a unique and unprecedented institution which any person not ridden by prejudice would agree is a tenet from Allah.

The claim that there is ambiguity in the concept of *zakat* at the time of the Prophet (p) is even more ridiculous. I wonder how a person who claims to be a researcher with insight into Islamic jurisprudence and the *Shari'a* could prove his statement that *zakat* at the time of the Prophet (p) was ambiguous and was not a religious requirement, especially since we have shown the sayings of the Prophet (p) that determine the kinds of assets that are subject to *zakat*, which includes all kinds of wealth known to the Arabs in the Prophet's time, such as livestock, agricultural products, and gold and silver.

The percentages and ratios of *zakat* are also determined clearly in the *hadiths*, ranging from ten percent to two and a half percent on different kinds of wealth. The *Sunna* of the Prophet (p) also defined the time of payment and the pattern of periodicity of *zakat*. The disbursement of *zakat* is also well-defined in the Qur'an and, in more detail, in the *Sunna*. The *Sunna* also determined methods of collection and administration of *zakat,* called in the Qur'an, '*zakat*-collectors'. Accordingly, the Prophet (p) sent his agents and collectors to different regions and tribes and ordered them to collect and distribute *zakat*. Can anyone, after all these details, claim that there is any ambiguity concerning the nature of *zakat* during the Prophet's time?

Even more surprising is Schacht's claim that *zakat* was not a due required by religion, when on the contrary, we find the Prophet (p) always listing *zakat* as one of the pillars and essential obligations of Islam, to the extent that some *hadiths* mention prayer and *zakat* immediately after the declaration of faith and leave out fasting and pilgrimage. We have quoted above the saying that requires Muslims to fight those who refuse to pay *zakat*, such as the sayings narrated by Ibn 'Umar, Abu Hurayra and Jabir. We have noted that the Prophet (p) put a clause on prayer and *zakat* in every treaty he concluded with any tribes that were entering in the religion of Islam. We have seen *zakat* mentioned in every letter he sent with his agents and deputies in the different regions or with the delegations that would come to visit him.

It is obvious that the importance of prayer and its ranking in this religion of Islam is not denied by Schacht and his colleagues. How could he then throw any doubt on *zakat*? The Prophet's messages record in detail the ordinances regarding *zakat* and its ratios, leaving no room for any ambiguity or doubt. For those who would like more references, I may mention the collection of political documents of the time of the Prophet (p) and the *Khulafa' ar-Rashidun* by Dr. Muhammad Hamidullah.

Schacht used the fact of the refusal to pay *zakat* by some Arab tribes to imply that *zakat* was ambiguous. Those tribes who refused to pay *zakat* fell into several categories. Some completely denied Islam and followed individuals who falsely claimed prophethood, such as Musaylima, Saja, al-Aswad and Tulayha. Others denied the whole of the Islamic *Shari'a*, including prayers and *zakat*, but Schacht did not use this to claim that the prayer was also ambiguous. Some other tribes accepted prayer and the rest of the Islamic *Shari'a* but raised objections to *zakat* as we noted earlier. Most of these were either very new in Islam and unversed in it, or did not deny the payment of *zakat* but rather, like Banu Yarbu', were prevented by their leaders from paying *zakat* to Abu Bakr.[1]

Muslim scholars such as Imam Abu Sulayman al-Khattabi did not consider this category to be apostates. He only considered them rebellious because their refusal to pay *zakat* was caused mainly by their lack of comprehension and understanding of the religion and its obligations. Regarding this last category, 'Umar debated with Abu Bakr; but it is obvious from studying the story that 'Umar was convinced by the evidence provided by Abu Bakr and it became unanimous among all the Companions that even this category of Arab tribes were to be fought.

Schacht claimed that the stand of Abu Bakr toward those who refused to pay *zakat* was responsible for giving *zakat* its obligatory nature. However, he forgot that Abu Bakr gave his proofs and evi-

1. *Nawl al-Awtar*, col. 4, p 102.

dence from the verses of the Qur'an and the sayings of the Prophet (p), and was not bringing any new argument from his own mind, but rather following the Messenger of Allah (p). In his statement, "By Allah, I shall fight them if they refuse to pay me any portion of *zakat*, be it as little as a baby goat, that they used to pay to the Messenger of Allah (p)." Abu Bakr was only following the tradition of the Messenger (p). 'Umar, on the other hand, thought that they should accept the establishment of the prayer now from those tribes and wait on the matter of *zakat* until the Muslim government in Madina was strongly established because of the dangers he anticipated from the apostates.[1] Abu Bakr was more convincing even to 'Umar himself because he had undeniable evidence from the Qur'an and *Sunna*: *"But if they turn in repentance and establish the prayer and pay* zakat, *they are your brothers in the* deen."

1. *Ahkam al-Qur'an*, part. 2, p. 995.

Part Two

Those on whom *Zakat* is Obligatory

Chapter One

Zakat is not required from non-Muslims

There is agreement among Muslim jurists that *zakat* is obligatory for any Muslim who has reached puberty, who is sane, who is free, and who owns the minimum (*nisab*) according to the conditions of the *Shari'a*.[1] We have previously discussed the clear texts of the Qur'an and authentic sayings of the Prophet that indicate this obligation. All these texts necessarily imply that *zakat* is an obligation. This has been inherited by Muslims generation after generation, and is overwhelmingly reported in both theory and application as a well-known tenet of Islam. He who denies this obligation, without an excuse of being new in Islam and not having had a chance to study it, is a disbeliever, since such a denial amounts to apostatising from Islam.

Muslims have also agreed that *zakat*, as an obligation of Islam, is not required from non-Muslims because it is a part of the religion and could not be expected from those not believing in Islam. By the same token, *zakat* will not be considered due for the past period of disbelief of a person who converts to Islam. Muslim jurists point to the *hadith* narrated by Ibn 'Abbas in the two *Sahih* collections of al-Bukhari and Muslim: "When the Prophet (p) sent Mu'adh to Yemen he said, 'You are going to a people who have a Book. When you come to them, call on them to testify that there is no god but Allah and that Muhammad is the Messenger of Allah. If they obey you in respect of that, then tell them that Allah has made the five prayers obligatory for them every night and day. If they obey you in respect of that, inform them that Allah has made it obligatory for *zakat* to be taken from the wealthy among them

1. Jurists cite several studies concerning the obligation of *zakat* on slaves. I do not discuss this issue because of its irrelevance to our time. Those who wish to study it may refer to *al-Majmu'*, vol. 5, pp. 326-7, *al-Mughni* with *Sharh al-Kabir*, p. 494, *Radd al-Muhtar*, vol. 1, p. 209. This last work provides a good summary of the opinions of different schools of jurisprudence long with their supporting arguments.

and given to the poor.'"[1] This saying indicates, according to an-Nawawi and others, that all obligations in Islam come only after the declaration of faith. That much is universally agreed upon.[2]

"And because *zakat* is one of the pillars of Islam," said the jurists, "it is not required from a disbeliever." In that sense, it is similar to prayer and fasting. There is another reason for the exemption of disbelievers from payment of *zakat* mentioned by ash-Shirazi and approved of by an-Nawawi among the Shafi'is. They both contend that *zakat* is an obligation that is not binding on disbelievers because they did not accept it to start with,[3] be they the 'People of War' or the 'People of Pledge'. Consequently, a disbeliever is not obliged to pay it as long as he remains a disbeliever and if he converts to Islam he should not be asked for any past dues of *zakat* for the period of disbelief.[4]

Not only is *zakat* not required from non-Muslims, it is also not acceptable from them as a form of worship since the pre-requisite for its acceptance is the declaration of faith in Islam. Allah says, *"We will advance on the actions they have done and make them scattered specks of dust."* (25:23) But it should be added that good deeds reduce the severity of punishment in the Hereafter, since punishment has degrees just as enjoyment has degrees.

All this applies to the born disbeliever. In the case of someone who turns back from Islam to disbelief, *zakat* shall not be waived if it had already become due while he was Muslim. *Zakat* is a direct responsibility on a Muslim and tampering with one's faith by apostatising does not waive this responsibility, just as financial responsibilities and due fines may not be waived. This is the Shafi'i opinion, which contradicts that of Abu Hanifa.[5]

1. See *Fath al-Bari*, vol. 3, p. 229.

2. There is a question of principle here: Are disbelievers addressed with the detailed requirements of the *Shari'a,* so their punishment will increase in the Hereafter because of lack of performance? The majority view is that they are addressed, as opposed to the Hanafi view.

3. This justification brings a new issue, i.e. if the People of Pledge agree to pay *zakat,* as Muslims in the same way they nowadays accept military service, would it be possible to extend the rules of *zakat* to cover them, since military service for the Muslims is *jihad*, which is, like *zakat*, a form of worship.

4. *Al-Majmu'*, vol. 5, pp. 327-8.

5. *Al-Majmu'*, vol. 5, pp. 327-8.

As for *zakat* due during the period of apostasy, Shafi'i jurists differ between themselves. Some say *zakat* is due for that period. I agree with them, since it is a right of the poor and other deserving people and should not be waived by apostasy. It is similar to due fines and financial responsibilities.

Why Islam exempts non-Muslims from paying *zakat*

A question may occur to us when we consider that Islam has made bountiful provisions for the People of the Book and other non-Muslims, providing them with the pledge of Allah and the pledge of His Messenger (p) that their lives, properties and liberties be protected under the Islamic state and that they have the same rights and obligations as Muslims. So why then did Islam make the difference with respect to *zakat* between Muslims and non-Muslim minorities that live under the Islamic state, despite the fact that *zakat* is a social obligation and a financial due, whose proceeds help the economically weak and needy citizens of the state?

To answer this question, we should consider two points. The first consideration is that *zakat* is a social duty, a defined right of the needy and destitute, a financial tax obligated by Allah to be taken from the wealthy in the nation and rendered to its poor in fulfilment of the right of brotherhood, the right of society, and the right of Allah.

The second consideration is that *zakat* is a form of worship in Islam and one of the five pillars on which Islam is established. In this way, *zakat* is similar to the declaration of faith, establishment of prayer, fasting during the month of Ramadan, and pilgrimage to Makka.

We have shown in previous pages that *zakat* is associated with prayer in tens of verses of the Qur'an and that the establishment of prayer is the symbol of becoming Muslim and something by which one gains the brotherhood of other Muslims. In other words, it is related to repentance from believing in that Allah has partners.

Additionally, some of the proceeds of *zakat* are to be spent for the support of Islam, for raising high its banner, and for the general interests of its message and state. This is the part known as "for the sake of Allah". Another portion is spent on reconciling hearts with Islam and establishing them on its path. The justice of Islam, its sensitivity in dealing with non-Muslims and its respect for their beliefs precludes obligating them to pay a due that has clear religious character to the extent that it is one of the major symbols of Islam, one of its four principal forms of worship and one of its five basic tenets.

Can an equivalent of *zakat* be taken from non-Muslims as a tax?

After settling that *zakat* is not required religiously from non-Muslims because it is a form of worship, the question arises: Is it permissible to take an amount equal to *zakat* in the form of a regular tax from wealthy non-Muslims to be rendered to the poor? Hence for Muslims what is paid as an obligation and a form of worship would be a simple tax for non-Muslims. By so doing we avoid differentiating between citizens of the same state by imposing a financial burden on Muslims that has no equivalent on non-Muslims and creating technical and administrative difficulties inherent in applying different rules to Muslims and non-Muslims.

This is a new matter which needs collective *ijtihad* by capable Muslim jurists. But until this happens, I find no reason why I should not put forward my opinion based on my research and my understanding of the subject, believing that such individual exertion of effort could open the way for a sound collective *ijtihad*. If this opinion is correct, Allah alone deserves praise, and if it is wrong it is I who should be blamed. What appears to me after research is that there is no reason why an equivalent to *zakat* should not be taken from the 'People of the Pledge' in the form of a tax if it is decided by the proper authorities. The following points elaborate this assertion.

- When Muslim jurists state that *zakat* is not required from non-Muslims, they are speaking of the religious kind of requirement which is related to reward and punishment in the Hereafter. There is nothing, however, that prevents its establishment as a political requirement by the proper authorities, based on public need as perceived by legislators.

- The reason jurists give for not obliging non-Muslims to pay *zakat* is that it is a duty to which non-Muslims did not commit themselves.[1] This means that if non-Muslims accept such a duty there is no reason why it may not become mandatory.

- The 'People of the Pledge' in Muslim lands formerly paid a financial due to the Islamic state called by the Qur'an '*jizya*' as a contribution towards the public expenditure of the state that covers disability, old age and poverty insurance, like Muslims. This is clear in the action of 'Umar, who made these provisions when he saw an elderly Jew begging at doors. The reality in Muslim countries today is that the People of the Book do not pay *jizya* and reject the word itself. Is it thus possible that they should pay a substitute tax calculated like *zakat* but without the label of *jizya*?

Historians, compilers of *hadith*, and jurists specialising in Islamic finance report that 'Umar ibn al-Khattab provided us with a precedent in this matter in his stand with the Christians of Banu Taghlib. Abu 'Ubayd reports that an-Nu'man ibn Zur'a asked 'Umar ibn al-Khattab about the question of the Banu Taghlib. 'Umar was about to collect *jizya* from them, which would drive them to disperse in the land. An-Nu'man ibn Zur'a told 'Umar, "O Commander of the Believers, the Banu Taghlib are Arabs. They are dismayed at the word '*jizya*'. They do not own gold and silver. They are people of agriculture and livestock and they can be instigated by our enemy. Please do not help your enemy by driving them away." Then 'Umar reconciled with them on the condition that they pay double the amount of *zakat*.

Al-Bayhaqi reported from 'Ubada ibn an-Nu'man in a long account that the tribe argued, "We are Arabs. We don't pay what

1. *Al-Majmu'*, vol. 5, p. 327.

the non-Arabs pay. Take from us as your people take from each other," meaning *zakat*. 'Umar said, "No, this is an obligation on Muslims." They replied, "Impose whatever you want, but under that name, not under the name of *jizya*." He agreed and then they settled on doubling the amount due from them. In some versions of this report, 'Umar said, "Call it whatever you like."[1]

Abu 'Ubayd comments on the action of the Commander of the Believers, 'Umar, with Banu Taghlib by saying, "In my opinion 'Umar used the word *zakat* and left the word *jizya* because he noticed their abhorrence and rejection of the word *jizya*. He feared that they would join and help the Romans against the Muslims, and realised that no harm would be done to the Muslims by leaving aside that word as long as what needed to be collected was collected. So he agreed to collect the dues under the name of *zakat,* thus reconciling them with the state while still collecting their dues. He was correct in so doing, especially since it is reported in a *hadith* of the Prophet (p) that Allah has put truth in the mouth and heart of 'Umar. 'Abdullah ibn Mas'ud said, "I have not seen 'Umar except as if an angel were on his forehead between his eyes holding him straight." 'Ali is reported as having said, "It was not unrealistic to say that wisdom always came from 'Umar's mouth," and 'A'isha said, "He was of a unique nature, as if he had prepared, for all difficulties, solutions that are exactly what is needed."

Abu 'Ubayd said, "What he did with the Banu Taghlib was one of those exact solutions and one of the uncountable good deeds of 'Umar."[2] So, 'Umar did not see any wrong in collecting a due from Christians under the name of *zakat,* because of their dislike of the title *jizya*, and doubled the amount of *zakat* owed by them through mutual agreement. For that reason az-Zuhri said, "There are no financial dues on the livestock of the People of the Book

1. *Al-Amwal*, p. 541 and its footnote, p. 28-9. Ibn Hazm considered the story of the Banu Taghlib to be weak (see *al-Muhalla*, vol. 6, p. 111), but it is well-known, and has been reported by Ibn Abi Shayba and Abu Yusuf in *al-Kharaj*, p. 143, Yahya ibn Adam in *al-Kharaj*, pp. 66-7, and al-Baladhari in *Futuh al-Buldan*, p. 189. Ahmad Shakir comments on the story of the Banu Taghlib, "It is narrated by many chains of narrators so one feels satisfied with its authenticity."

2. *Al-Amwal*, p. 541.

except the Christians of Banu Taghlib, or Christian Arabs for whom livestock is the major part of their wealth."[1]

What 'Umar did was approved by other Companions. So why can we not make a tax on the People of the Pledge in Muslim countries today in place of the *jizya* levied on them by the Islamic system. This tax would be in substitution for two mandates on the Muslims: that of *jihad*, in which they sacrifice their own blood, and that of *zakat*, in which they sacrifice part of their wealth. Why could we not legislate such a tax after consultation with prominent figures, Muslims and non-Muslims? This tax need not even be called *zakat*. I believe that the act of 'Umar is an enlightening precedent for those who would like to take such an approach in contemporary circumstances with relation to problems of our age.

The Shafi'is and Hanbalis have said, "If a group of non-Muslims was potentially powerful and refused to pay *jizya* except with an agreement similar to that of the Banu Taghlib, and there was danger in not accepting its demand, and the Imam agreed to accept it to prevent such danger, it is permissible to do so if the amount collected from them is equal to or greater than *jizya*."[2] Undoubtedly, this is a sound opinion that has strong support in the action of 'Umar regarding the Banu Taghlib.

There is no doubt that *zakat* on all growing forms of wealth is much more than *jizya*. *Jizya* is a small due exacted from men who are capable of carrying weapons, while *zakat* is imposed on all individuals according to the view of the majority of jurists. However, doubling the amount of *zakat* on the 'People of Pledge' is not necessary. 'Umar did not do that to the Banu Taghlib only because it was a condition of an agreement they signed and accepted. Such a matter depends on the religiously conducted political decisions and on the public interest as well as that of the state and religion.

Ibn Rushd correctly raised this question in his work, "*Zakat* on the People of the Pledge", saying, "As for the People of the Pledge, the majority view is that they are not compelled to pay *zakat*. The only exception is the view of some scholars concerning the dou-

1. *Al-Kharaj* by Yahya ibn Adam, p. 65.

2. *Ahkam Ahl adh-Dhimma wa'l-Musta'minin* (Rules of the People of Pledge and Non-Citizen Residents) by Dr. 'Abd al-Karim Zaydan, p. 149, as quoted from *al-Mughni*, vol. 8, p. 526, and *Matn al-Minhaj*, vol. 4, p. 261.

bling of *zakat* on the Christians of Banu Taghlib. Ash-Shafi'i, Abu Hanifa, Ahmad and ath-Thawri offered such opinions too. However, it is not reported whether Malik expressed such a view. The former take the action of 'Umar ibn al-Khattab as applicable only to that specific case since it does not seem to fit with the basic rules of the *Shari'a*."[1]

I may add that we have previously quoted Abu 'Ubayd's explanation of 'Umar's move. It was not in violation of the basic rules of the *Shari'a*. Rather, it was a realisation of the interests of Muslims and the removal of a potential threat to them. This means that there is no reason why it should be applicable only to that specific incident, especially in the light of the Prophet Muhammad's command to follow the tradition of his Wise Successors (*al-Khulafa' ar-Rashidun*).

Our position is supported by a precedent mentioned by Muhammad ibn al-Hasan ash-Shaybani, a disciple of Abu Hanifa, who said, "If a Muslim sells his land on which *zakat* can be levied (*'ushri*), that is not subject to *kharaj* for a 'Person of the Pledge', that person becomes liable to the *zakat* on that land (*'ushr*). Being subject is a description of land that does not change because of a change of ownership. It is not permissible to let one of the 'People of the Pledge' use the land without paying any dues.[2]

The People of the Book are ordained in their own religions to give alms and to care for the poor. We have quoted earlier the verses of the Qur'an which point to this ordinance, such as the verse: *"They were only ordered to worship Allah, making their* deen *sincerely His as people of pure natural belief, and to establish the prayer and pay* zakat *– that is the correct* deen." (98:5) We have also quoted from their books as they exist today. Both Old and New Testaments have many statements that call for and encourage caring for the poor. So if the People of the Book are called to implement

1. *Bidayat al-Mujtahid*, vol. 1, p. 209.

2. *Bada'i' as-Sana'i'*, vol. 2, p. 10, *al-Hidaya* and its commentary, *Fath al-Qadir*, vol. 2, p. 10. Muhammad ibn al-Hasan stands in opposition to the opinion of Abu Hanifa and Abu Yusuf on this matter. Abu Hanifa says the buyer is obligated by *kharaj* and the land becomes subject to *kharaj*. Abu Yusuf says that the land remains *'ushri* land, but *'ushr* should be doubled as was the case with the Banu Taghlib.

zakat, they are asked for something which has its seed in their own religion. The only new issue being the estimation of the amount due and its compulsory character.

It is narrated from 'Umar ibn al-Khattab and some Followers that spending the proceeds of *zakat* on the 'People of the Pledge' is permissible. This will be discussed in detail in the section on the disbursement of *zakat*. If it is permissible to spend zakat on them which is collected from Muslims, why should it not be permissible to take *zakat* from their wealthy members and render it to their poor? This fulfils the social solidarity that must exist among all Muslims and non-Muslims who live under the Islamic state. In such a case, this duty may be called a "social insurance tax" or "care tax" or any similar name that distinguishes it from Islamic *zakat*, so that their consciences are not disconcerted or those of Muslims. The disbursement of the proceeds of each of these taxes should be distinctly separate. they are similar in ratio, rate, conditions and the assets taxed, but they are different in name and disbursement since they have two different natures and are mandated by different authorities.

Chapter Two

Zakat on Children and the Insane

Jurists who agree that *zakat* is compulsory on the assets of sane Muslims after puberty disagree about whether it is compulsory on the assets of children and the insane. There are two contrasting points of view. The first is that *zakat* is either not obligatory at all or only mandatory on specific kinds of wealth belonging to children and the insane, and the second asserts that *zakat* is obligatory on all of their assets.

Those who do not consider *zakat* required

A. Abu 'Ubayd reports from Abu Ja'far al-Baqir and ash-Sha'bi that there is no *zakat* on the assets of orphans.[1] Ibn Hazm mentions a similar view from an-Nakha'i and Shurayh.[2]

B. It is reported from al-Hasan that there is no *zakat* on the wealth of orphans except on agricultural produce and livestock.[3] Ibn Hazm reports in *al-Muhalla* that Ibn Shibruma had a similar view.[4]

C. In *al-Amwal* Mujahid is reported as saying that any form of wealth owned by orphans that has growth potential such as livestock, agricultural produce, and business funds, should be subject to *zakat*, but any kind of wealth that is stagnant is not subject to *zakat* until the orphan reaches puberty, when it should be given to him.[5] Al-Lakhmi, a Maliki jurist, stated that foregoing *zakat* on a child whose wealth does not grow is like the case in which an owner cannot make his wealth grow, e.g. when it is buried treasure whose

1. *Al-Amwal*, p. 453.
2. *Al-Muhalla*, vol. 5, p. 205.
3. *Al-Amwal*, p. 453.
4. *Al-Muhalla*, vol. 5, p. 205.
5. *Al-Amwal*, p. 453.

whereabouts is unknown, or an inheritance not known to the heir. Ibn Bashir explained that incapacity in the case of a child is related to the nature of his ownership. There is no disagreement that for the person who must pay *zakat*, inability to invest his wealth is not sufficient reason to make him exempt from *zakat* except in the case where the property is of a stagnant nature. Ibn al-Hajib contends that the argument of al-Lakhmi is weak.[1]

D. Abu Hanifa and his disciples argued that *zakat* is only obligatory on agricultural produce and all other assets are exempt.[2] Ibn Hazm commented that he knew of no one before Abu Hanifa who made such a distinction. But the author of *al-Bahr az-Zakhkhar* of the Zaydi school reported it from Zayd ibn 'Ali and Ja'far as-Sadiq, contemporaries of Abu Hanifa.[3] However, it seems incredible that this view of Zayd, as-Sadiq and an-Nasir, who are of *Ahl al-Bayt*, contradicts what is correctly reported from 'Ali. 'Ali used to pay *zakat* on the assets of Abu Rafi's children, who were orphans. When Zayd was asked about this he replied, "We of the *Ahl al-Bayt* deny this report."[4]

Evidence supporting this group of scholars

This group of scholars looked mainly at the second consideration mentioned earlier, i.e. that *zakat* is a pure form of worship which requires intention. Children and the insane cannot fulfil this requirement. They are not, therefore, addressed with command of worship. Prayer is not required from them, and for the same reason, *zakat* should not be.[5]

This opinion is supported by the *Sunna*. The Prophet Muhammad (p) said, "The Pen is suspended from three: children until puberty, sleepers until they wake, and the insane until they

1. *Sharh ar-Risala* by Ibn Naji, vol. 1, p. 328.
2. *Bada'i' as-Sana'i'*, vol. 2, p. 4.
3. Zayd was killed in 122 AH and Ja'far died in 148 AH. About the latter Abu Hanifa said, "I have not seen a person who has better understanding." Abu Hanifa died in 158 AH.
4. *Ar-Rawd an-Nadir*, commentary on *Majmu' al-Fiqh al-Kabir*, vol. 2, p. 416.
5. *Radd al-Muhtar*, vol. 2, p. 4.

recover."[1] Suspension of the Pen refers to the recording of sins and release from obligations, since obligation applies only to those who understand the instruction of Allah. Childhood, insanity and sleep prevent that understanding.

Their stance is also supported by the verse, *"Take* sadaqa *from their wealth to purify and cleanse them."* (9:103) Purification is needed from sins and evil. Children and the insane have none of these and need no purification or cleansing, so they should not be among those from whom *zakat* must be taken.

It is ironic to note that these three arguments do not stand in support of the Hanafi stance that *zakat* is obligatory on some kinds of a child's wealth and not others. On the other hand, these arguments may bolster the view of as-Saqir, ash-Sha'bi, an-Nakha'i, and Shurayh since they perceive *zakat* as not being required of any kind of wealth belonging to a child or someone insane.

The well-being of children and the insane demands that their wealth stay intact and not be used up by *zakat* payments. Growth is not realised in the assets of children and the insane because of their weakness and inability to sustain their affairs. There is always the fear that the repetitive collection of *zakat* over years may consume all their wealth and leave them poor and in need.

This may be the rationale behind the opinion of Mujahid that *zakat* is mandatory on children and the insane in respect of those kinds of wealth that grow on their own, such as agricultural produce and livestock, and wealth that grows by action such as money used in business. It could also be the reason for the report that al-Hasan al-Basri and Ibn Shibruma only excluded the gold and silver of a child from *zakat*. As for fruits, produce and livestock, they considered them to be subject to *zakat* since growth is realised in them, whereas money, gold and silver, do not grow except through business ventures. Children and the insane cannot engage in such ventures, so they are exempt from *zakat* on this kind of wealth.

1. An-Nawawi said this is a *sahih hadith*. It is reported by Abu Dawud and an-Nasa'i in *Kitab al-Hudud* in their respective books, as narrated from 'Ali ibn Abi Talib with a sound chain. It is also reported by Abu Dawud in *al-Hudud*, an-Nasa'i and Ibn Majah in *Kitab at-Talaq* as from 'A'isha with a good chain. See *al-Majmu'*, vol. 6, p. 253.

Those who consider *zakat* on the wealth of children and the insane to be obligatory

This opinion is expressed by 'Ata', Jabir ibn Zayd, Tawus, Mujahid, and az-Zuhri, all of whom were Followers. Of the second generation, Rabi'a, Malik, ash-Shafi'i, Ahmad, Ishaq, al-Hasan ibn Salih, Ibn Abi Layla, Ibn 'Uyayna, Abu 'Ubayd, and Abu Thawr agreed. This view is expressed by al-Hadi and al-Mu'ayyad-billah among the Shi'ites. It is also the view of the Companions, 'Umar, his son, 'Ali, 'A'isha, and Jabir. They did not make any exceptions like those made by Mujahid, al-Hasan, Ibn Shibruma, and Abu Hanifa.

The arguments of this group

They argue that the verses and authentic texts concerning the mandate of *zakat* on the assets of the wealthy are general. They do not exclude children or the insane. Take for example the *ayat*, *"Take* sadaqa *from their wealth to purify and cleanse them."* Ibn Hazm explains, "And see how general it is. It includes children, adults, the sane and the insane. All these are in need of purification and cleansing by Allah. They are all believers." Similarly, the Prophet (p) told Mu'adh before he left for the Yemen, "Inform them that Allah has made it obligatory for *zakat* to be taken from the wealthy among them and given to the poor." Children and the insane receive *zakat* if they are poor, so they must pay it if they are rich. Ibn Hazm continues, "This general text is addressed to all wealthy Muslims, including children and the insane."[1]

Ash-Shafi'i reported from Yusuf ibn Mahak that the Messenger of Allah (p) said, "Invest the funds of orphans so that they may not be depleted by *zakat*." The chain of narrators of this *hadith* is sound, as confirmed by al-Bayhaqi and an-Nawawi. But Yusuf is a follower who never met the Messenger of Allah (p), so his *hadith* is *mursal*. However, ash-Shafi'i says that this *mursal hadith* is supported by the general implication of other texts and by what is authenti-

1. *Al-Muhalla*, vol. 5, pp. 201-2.

cally reported from the Companions that *zakat* is compulsory on the assets of orphans.[1]

At-Tabarani reported in *al-Mu'jam al-Awsat* from Anas ibn Malik that the Messenger of Allah (p) said, "Invest the funds of orphans so that they may not be depleted by *zakat*." Referring to Zayn al-'Iraqi, al-Haytami said in *Majma' az-Zawa'id*, "I was told by my shaykh and teacher that the chain of his *hadith* is correct."[2] At-Tirmidhi reported from 'Amr ibn Shu'ayb from his father from his grandfather that the Prophet (p) said, "He who is a guardian of an orphan should trade for the orphan and not let his assets be depleted by *zakat*." The chain of this *hadith* is controversial, but its meaning is reported authentically as being said by 'Umar ibn al-Khattab. Al-Bayhaqi reported through Sa'id ibn al-Musayyab that 'Umar ibn al-Khattab said, "Trade with the funds of orphans so that they are not consumed by *zakat*." Al-Bayhaqi found the chain to be correct and supported by other reports.[3]

Accordingly, these ordinances of the Prophet (p) indicate that *zakat* is compulsory on the wealth of orphans since guardians are not permitted to make voluntary contributions out of such wealth because these contributions would unnecessarily make the orphan poorer.[4] Allah ordained in the Qur'an that a guardian must not use the funds of an orphan, except in the latter's best interest, until the orphan reaches the age of puberty (see 6:152, 17:34).

The views that are authentically reported from the Companions also support this group. Abu 'Ubayd, al-Bayhaqi and Ibn Hazm report that 'Umar, 'Ali, 'Abdullah ibn 'Umar, 'A'isha and Jabir ibn 'Abdullah said that *zakat* is obligatory on the assets of children.[5]

1. *Al-Majmu'*, vol 5, p. 329, *as-Sunan al-Kubra*, vol. 4, p. 107 and *ar-Rawd an-Nadir*, vol. 2, p. 417.

2. Vol. 3, p. 67. As-Suyuti in *al-Jami' as-Saghir* referred to it as "*sahih*". But it seems that this was not the original designation of the author. The commentator al-Manawi said that as-Suyuti marked it as "*sahih*" in his book, *Jami' al-Jawami'*, while here he only marked it as *'hasan'*, However, Ibn Hajar supports the fact that it is *hasan*. *Fayd al-Qadir*, vol. 1, p. 108.

3. *As-Sunan al-Kubra*, vol. 4, p. 107. See also *al-Majmu'*, vol. 5, p. 329.

4. *Muqaranat al-Madhahib fi'l-Fiqh*, Mahmud Shaltut and Muhammad as-Sayes, p. 48 (1953); also *al-Mughni*, vol. 2, p. 493.

5. See *al-Amwal*, p. 448, as-Sunan al-Kubra, p. 107, *al-Muhalla*, vol. 5, p. 208, *Musannaf Ibn Abi Shayba*, vol. 4, pp. 24-5 and *at-Talkhis* by Ibn Hajar, p. 176. An-

There is no report that any Companion opposed this view, except for a report from Ibn 'Abbas, which is too weak to be used in argument.[1]

It is argued that the purpose of *zakat* itself supports this view. The aim of *zakat* is to satisfy the needs of the poor from the assets of the affluent, as a sign of thankfulness to Allah, and to purify these assets. The funds of children and the insane can accommodate *zakat*, just as they accommodate other financial responsibilities or fines.[2] It is argued that guardians are responsible for paying *zakat* from the funds of the two categories the same way that sane adults pay it. Guardians act on behalf of children or the insane. This is required of them, and must be fulfilled. The intention of the guardian can substitute for the intention of the funds' owner.[3]

Some Malikis say that the guardian must only pay *zakat* for a child if he is assured that what he is doing would later be approved by the child, but if not, he is not obliged to pay. When the guardian pays *zakat*, his action should be approved by the child, but if not, he is not obliged to pay. When the guardian pays *zakat*, his action should be witnessed, but Ibn Habib says that if he is trustworthy, his word alone is accepted.[4] On the other hand, according to some Malikis, if the guardian fears that a child, after puberty, or an insane person after regaining his senses, would not approve that payment and ask him for compensation, the guardian should seek a ruling from a judge who believes *zakat* is mandatory from children and the insane in order to protect himself against any future liability.[5]

Nawawi added al-Hasan ibn 'Ali in *al-Majmu'*, vol. 5, p. 329. He did not add Ibn Mas'ud because the report from him is weak as stated in *Sunan al-Bayhaqi*, *al-Majmu'* and *at-Talkhis*. An-Nawawi's opinion is that the guardian should keep a record of all *zakat* due on the assets of his orphan ward. When the latter reaches puberty he should be informed and it is up to him to pay *zakat*.

1. *Al-Muhalla*, vol. 5, p. 209, and *al-Mughni*, vol. 5, p. 329. The reason it is weak is that the chain contains Ibn Lahi'a, who is weak.

2. *Al-Majmu'*, vol. 5, p. 330.

3. *Al-Mughni*, vol. 2, p. 494.

4. *Sharh ar-Risala*, vol. 1, p. 329.

5. *Hashiya as-Sawi 'ala ad-Dardir*, p. 205.

Weighing the two arguments

The arguments provided by those who regard *zakat* as mandatory on the assets of children and the insane seem to outweigh that of those who do not. It is the stance of the majority of scholars among the Companions, the Followers and later generations.

The universality of the texts and their covering of children and adults, sane and insane, is a sound argument that should not be underestimated. Allah made *zakat* a right of the poor, the needy, and other deserving categories, from the assets of the affluent. These texts did not make special provisions regarding the age or sanity of the rich, in spite of the special attention the *Shari'a* gives to preserving the assets of orphans. Those who want to exclude children and the insane from *zakat* are called upon to furnish evidence from Qur'anic texts or from the *Sunna*.

The *hadith* reported by Yusuf ibn Mahak that calls for investing the funds of orphans in order to prevent payment of *zakat* eating them away is authentic and clear in its indication. Although it is *mursal*, it is strengthened by corroborating reports and by the generality of the texts. Additionally, it is supported by sayings of the Companions, as well as the *hadith* of Anas reported by at-Tabarani and confirmed by al-Haytami and al-'Iraqi.

There is no doubt that the agreement of many Companions such as 'Umar, 'Ali, 'A'isha, Ibn 'Umar, and Jabir has great importance in an issue of such public concern and that occurred so frequently, especially in a society in which martyrs and orphans were numerous. No scholar could dare to neglect this agreement in understanding, especially since these Companions lived at the same time as the Messenger (p), and were fully aware of the warnings to those who squandered the assets of orphans. It is significant that there is not a single report from any Companion to the effect that *zakat* is not mandatory on the assets of orphans. What is narrated by Ibn Mas'ud and Ibn 'Abbas is weak to the extent that it could not stand up to critical analysis.[1]

If we look carefully at the objectives of *zakat* we can conclude that the assets of a wealthy child or insane person should be cov-

1. See *Mir'at al-Mafatih* by al-Mubarakuri, vol. 3, p. 25.

ered by *zakat*, like other financial responsibilities on their assets. There is no doubt that *zakat* is a right of other people. It is covered by the verses, *"And the beggars and destitute receive a due share of their wealth."* (6:141) and *"Collected* sadaqa *is for the poor, the destitute..."* (9:60) This was the perception of the first Caliph as seen in his saying to 'Umar, "By Allah, I shall fight him who differentiates between prayer and *zakat*, since *zakat* is the right on wealth." This is reported in the two *Sahih* collections. There is universal agreement among scholars that the assets of children and the insane are subject to the right of other people. Childhood and insanity do not preclude financial liability to others, including fines, due expenses, and other contractual responsibilities.[1]

Consequently, we come to the conclusion that *zakat* is binding on the wealth of children and the insane under the same conditions applied to the wealth of other people. We see that the view of the other three major schools of jurisprudence outweigh the view of the Hanafi school. The Hanafi school made *zakat al-fitr* and *'ushr* (*zakat* on crops) obligatory for children or the insane, so why exclude them from other forms of *zakat*? If *'ushr* is obligatory, *zakat* should be as well. There should be no distinction between *'ushr* that is made necessary by the verse, *"pay their due on the day of their harvest"* (6:141), and *zakat* that is made necessary by the *ayat*, *"And the beggars and destitute received a due share of their wealth."* (9:60) Additionally, there is *'ushr* in what is "watered by the sky" and his saying, "There is one fourth of ten percent on silver."

Therefore, the Hanafi distinction between fruits and produce on the one hand and other kinds of wealth on the other, based on the claim that the former are provision for sustenance unlike the other, is neither justified rationally nor by reference to texts. Hence, Ibn Hazm came down hard against this distinction, saying, "I wonder about such acclaimed difference between *zakat* on produce and fruits and *zakat* on livestock, gold, and silver! If someone reversed it, i.e. obliging *zakat* on the latter and exempting the former, would it not be as arbitrary?" Ibn Rushd said, "I am aware of no

1. *Bada'i' as-Sana'i'*, vol. 2, pp. 4-5, and *Radd al-Muhtar*, vol. 2, p. 4.

rationale for those who differentiate between produce of the land and other funds or between apparent and non-apparent assets."[1]

Refuting the arguments of those who believe *zakat* is not obligatory on children

Those who do not oblige *zakat* on children and the insane claim that they are not covered by the verse, *"Take* sadaqa *from their wealth to purify and cleanse them"* (9:103) because purification means cleansing from sins and children and the insane are not sinful. However, the fact that purification is not merely removal of sins should be emphasised. Purification includes moral uplifting, psychological growth and training to be helpful and merciful. It also means purification of the assets themselves. Even if we accept purification to be only for sins, the meaning of the verse need not be limited, according to an-Nawawi.[2] *Zakat* is not only purification. It is undisputed that there is another reason for *zakat*, i.e. fulfilment of the needs of Muslims. Children and the insane can share in such a fulfilment.

As for the *hadith*, "The Pen is suspended from three...," according to an-Nawawi it means that those three may not be held sinful. No one claims that they are sinful. No one says *zakat* must be paid by them personally. My opinion is that *zakat* is obligatory on their assets. Their guardians are required to pay it just as they are asked to dispose of other financial responsibilities.[3] The suspension of the Pen from them does not imply waiving their financial responsibilities towards others, such as wives and other relatives. Why then should the responsibilities toward the needy and the wayfarer be abandoned?

There is the argument that *zakat* is a form of worship, just like prayer, and requires intention. Since children and the insane are

1. *Bidayat al-Mujahid*, col. 1, p. 209.

2. He said in *al-Majmu‘* that most likely it is a purification, but this is not a condition since we agree that *zakat al-fitr* and *‘ushr* are obligatory on their assets, even though originally all these are purifications. Vol. 5, p. 330.

3. *Al-Majmu‘*, vol. 5, p. 330, *al-Mughni*, vol. 2, pp. 493-4, and *Muqaranat al-Madhahib*, p. 49.

not able to express valid intentions, they should not be required to pay *zakat*. The reply to this is that we all agree that *zakat* is an act of worship, the twin of prayer, and one of the pillars of Islam, but it should be added that *zakat* is distinct because of its financial and social character. It is a financial act of worship that can be done by proxy. Rules applicable to rights of others (*huquq al-'ibad*) apply to it. According to the Hanafis, a Person of the Pledge can be assigned to pay it on behalf of the *zakat* payer. Ibn Hazm added, it is true that *zakat* requires intention, but Muslims and Muslim governments are ordered to collect *zakat* by the verse, *"Take* sadaqa *from their wealth ."* Therefore, if the *zakat* collector has that intention, he can take it from the funds of the absentee, the person who is in a coma, the insane, and children, without any need for an intention on their part.[1]

In summary, *zakat* is a form of financial worship that can be done by proxy, and the guardian, as an operator on behalf of children or the insane, can fulfil it. It is unlike bodily worship such as prayer and fasting that needs to be done by the person himself. Exempting children and the insane from prayer does not mean waiving *zakat*, because each is an obligation independent from the other. Allah did not ordain all obligations as a 'package deal', so that if one becomes compulsory the other does, and vice versa.[2] If prayer is missed for certain reasons, *zakat* need not be abandoned. An obligation ordained by Allah or His Messenger (p) can be waived only in accordance with a text from Allah or His Messenger (p). It may not be neglected without a text from the Qur'an or *Sunna* because another obligation is relaxed.[3]

The statement of Abu 'Ubayd in this respect is most brilliant: "The obligations of Islam must not be taken merely by analogy with one another since each of them is basic, independent and essential, each of them is performed in accordance with the way it is ordained in the Qur'an and *Sunna*.[4] Prayer is a right of Allah on

1. *Al-Muhalla*, vol. 5, p. 206.
2. *Al-Umm*, ash-Shafi'i, vol. 2, p. 24.
3. *Al-Muhalla*, vol. 5, p. 206.
4. *Al-Amwal*, p. 454. Abu 'Ubayd made a full account of the differences between the two obligations.

all His servants. *Zakat* is a right given by Allah to the poor from the assets of the wealthy."[1]

The special interests of children and the insane are to be balanced against the special interests of the poor and needy as well as those of the state and religion, and by imposing *zakat* on children and the insane their interests are not sacrificed. *Zakat* is taken from assets that grow actually or potentially. It is only obliged on properties that are in excess of essential needs. Some Hanafi jurists went as far as considering *zakat* not obligatory on money saved for necessary expenditure even if it is above the minimum amount, i.e. *nisab*. This will be discussed in Part Three, and it is what I see as applicable on children or the insane that only applies to owned liquid assets saved for necessary expenditure, until puberty, or the expected life-span in the case of the insane.

Three points of importance should be mentioned before concluding:

Firstly, it should be remembered that children who are responsible for paying *zakat* are not necessarily orphans. They may have inherited their wealth from their mother's side or from someone other than their parents. "*Zakat* on the Assets of Children" would be a more appropriate way of entitling this section, and not "*Zakat* on the Assets of Orphans". This way, we can eliminate the sentimental aspect of the issue. Let us not forget that a child's wealth may come to hundreds of thousands of dinars.

Secondly, there are reports that instruct guardians to invest orphans' assets so that such assets will not be depleted by *zakat*. An example is the saying of 'Amr ibn Shu'ayb from his father from his grandfather: "The Messenger of Allah (p) gave a talk to some people saying, 'For those who care for orphans, they should invest their assets on their behalf and not leave them idle to be consumed by *zakat*,'" (at-Tirmidhi and ad-Daraqutni), and the saying of Yusuf ibn Mahak that the Messenger of Allah (p) said, "Invest the assets of orphans so that they will not be depleted by *zakat*." Guardians of orphans are obliged to invest these assets the same way they are required to pay *zakat* from them. It is true that there

1. *Al-Amwal*, p. 455.

is weakness in the chain of these two *hadiths*, however they are strengthened by the following facts:

- The meaning is reported through other chains that support each other.[1]
- Similar statements are correctly attributed to some Companions.
- The order to invest orphans' assets is in line with the verse, *"provide for them and clothe them out of it,"* (4:5), because the verse does not say, "from their assets," but "out of it", which implies the idea of using their assets for growth and investment and feeding them from the proceeds.
- This kind of investment is well suited within the general approach of Islam in economic matters, i.e. the preference for investment and the prohibition of hoarding.

The ordinance (in the above *hadiths*) is addressed to the guardians of orphans specifically and to the Muslim community and authorities in Muslim countries in general. It is therefore mandatory for Muslim society and its government to preserve the assets of orphans, to see that they are invested and to provide necessary guarantees and detailed legislation to serve this purpose.

Thirdly, Islamic society provides guarantees for orphans and the economically weak, so there should be no fear that orphans would be lost if their assets were subject to *zakat*. Wealthy relatives are required, legally, to guarantee the sustenance of their orphaned relatives. Orphans are also insured by the state. Allah says: *"They will ask you what they should give away. Say, 'Any wealth you give away should go to your parents and relatives and orphans and the very poor and travellers.' Whatever good you do, Allah knows it."* (2:215) *"It is not devoutness to turn your faces to the East or to the West. Rather, those with true devotion are those who believe in Allah and the Last Day, the Angels, the Book and the Prophets, and who, despite their love for it, give away their wealth to their relatives and to orphans and the very poor, and to travellers and beggars and to set slaves free."* (2:177) *"Know that when*

1. Al-'Iraqi considered some versions of its chain sound.

you take any booty a fifth of it belongs to Allah, and to the Messenger, and to close relatives, orphans, the very poor and travellers." (8:41) *"Whatever booty Allah gives to His Messenger from city dwellers belongs to Allah and to the Messenger and to near relatives and orphans and the very poor and travellers so that it does not become something which merely goes by turn to the rich among you."* (59:7)

Consequently, in the assets of all individuals, there exists a share for orphans: it may be under the name of *zakat* or not. A part of the revenue of the state is assigned to orphans as ordained by Allah. The Prophet (p) said, "I am more entitled to every believer than his own self. Whoever leaves property, it is for his family. Whoever leaves a debt or family, it is for me and on me." (Agreed upon) Therefore, if the well-being of orphans is guaranteed by Muslim society, there is no need to fear that they may be neglected or lost if they are not wealthy.

Conclusion

Zakat is obligatory on the property of children and the insane because it is a right on the property and is not waived through youth or insanity. It makes no difference whether those assets are in the form of livestock, agricultural produce, fruits, business assets or money, except for liquid cash earmarked for future necessary expenditure, whereby it is not considered in excess of essential needs. The guardians of children or the insane are required to pay *zakat* on their behalf. It is preferred, according to some Malikis, that a court order be sought so the guardian can protect himself against future claims based on the opposing viewpoint.

Part Three

Kinds of Wealth on which *Zakat* Must be paid and their Ratios

Chapter One

Assets Subject to *Zakat*

The Qur'an does not give the definition of the kinds of wealth on which *zakat* should be paid nor does it provide the required percentages of *zakat*. It is left to the *Sunna* to give, by example or by directives, details of the general Qur'anic command and to convert the theoretical axioms of the Qur'an into a living reality in human life. The Prophet (p) was assigned this responsibility and he is the one who knows most about what Allah ordains in His Holy Book. Allah says: *"And We have sent down the Reminder to you so that you can make clear to mankind what has been sent down to them so that perhaps they may reflect."* (16:44) It must be realised, however, that the Qur'an does mentions a few kinds of zakatable assets, such as:

- Gold and silver in the verse: *"As for those who hoard up gold and silver and do not spend it in the way of Allah, give them the news of a painful punishment."* (9:34)
- Crops and fruits that are referred to in: *"Eat of their fruits when they bear fruit and pay their due on the day of their harvest."* (6:141)
- Earnings from trade and other business ventures, referred to in the verse: *"O you who believe! Give away some of the good things you have earned."* (2:267)
- What is brought out from beneath the earth: *"and some of what the earth produces for you."* (6:141)

Except for these items, the Qur'an mentions *zakat* in general and the word *amwal* (assets or wealth) in its plural form, such as in the verse, *"Take* sadaqa *from their wealth to purify and cleanse them,"* (9:103) and *"And the beggars and destitute received a due share of their wealth."* (51:19)

The meaning of *amwal* in Arabic and the *Shari'a*

The word *amwal*, meaning wealth, property, goods, possessions, mentioned in the Qur'an is the plural of *mal*. *Mal* meant in the minds of the Arabs at the time of the Qur'anic revelation all things that people like to acquire and own, including, for example, camels, cattle, sheep, land, palm orchards, gold and silver. Arabic dictionaries such as *al-Qamus* and *Lisan al-'Arab* define the word *mal* as "all things one owns," knowing that Bedouins use the word in reference to their livestock and urban dwellers use it in reference to gold and silver, despite the fact that all are *mal*. Ibn al-Athir says that the original meaning of the word *mal* referred to owned gold and silver but then it became generalised to include all material things that are obtained and owned.

Jurists express several opinions on the meaning of the word *mal* in the *Shari'a*. Hanafi jurists say *mal* is everything that a person acquires and usually uses, so there are two conditions for anything to be considered to be *mal*: the possibility of acquiring it, and the possibility of using it in general. Consequently *mal* includes all that is owned: land, animals, furniture, equipment, and money. As for things that are not actually acquired or usually used, if there exists a possibility of obtaining and using them, then they are considered to be *mal*, such as lawful things like fish in the sea, birds flying in the sky or animals in the wild.

Things that cannot be acquired are not considered *mal* even though they may be useful, such as sunlight and heat. By the same token, things that are usually not usable but can be obtained, such as a handful of soil, a drop of water, a bee, or one grain of rice are not *mal*. This definition implies that *mal* must be a material thing, because non-material things cannot be obtained. Consequently, services are not *mal*, such as inhabiting a house, travelling by car, or wearing a garment, because these are not acquirable. Similarly, rights such as custodianship and guardianship, are also not *mal*.

Shafi'i, Maliki, and Hanbali jurists, on the other hand, consider services as *mal*. According to them, possibility of acquisition is not a condition, rather the condition is the possibility of obtaining the source of *mal*. Since a car can be physically acquired, use of it is considered a *mal*. Scholars of man-made laws consider both usage and rights such as authorship rights and patents as *amwal*. This means that *mal* as defined in man-made legal systems includes more than it includes for the jurists.[1] My opinion is that the definition of the Hanafis seems to be closer to the linguistic meaning given in dictionaries, and more sensible with regard to the application of the texts on *zakat*, since it is material assets and not services that *zakat* must be paid on.

In *al-Bahr* Ibn Nujaym states that *mal* is what can be obtained and saved to be used at the time of need, and this can only be applied to material things. The author of *Kashf al-Kabir* says *zakat* can only be fulfilled by giving the recipient something of material value, so if a poor person was allowed to inhabit free of charge the house of a *zakat* payer, this would not fulfil the responsibility of the payment of *zakat*, since this utility is not a material thing that can be acquired. Ibn Nujaym continues, "This is one opinion. The other is, however, that the utility is also a *mal*. But when the word *mal* is used, without any specification, it applies to material acquisitions only."[2] For the purposes of this book, *mal* means material things, and that is where *zakat* applies.

Conditions for collecting *zakat* from a *mal*

If we agree that all obtainable and owned materials are *mal*, is *zakat* required on all kinds of *mal*, no matter how little it may be or how much the owner is in need of it? A house inhabited by the owner is *mal*, as are clothes worn and books used and the tools of tradesmen who work with their hands. Is *zakat* required on all these? Is a bedouin who owns two she-camels or a few sheep from which he derives his essential food, liable for *zakat*? How about a peasant whose crop is only a small quantity that can barely satisfy the food needs of his household, or a business man who has inventory and cash funds, but at the same time is overridden by debts that are in excess of his business assets? Is *zakat* due on all these?

1. See Shaykh 'Ali al-Khafif, *Ahkam al-Mu'amalat ash-Shar'iyya*, pp. 3-4.
2. *Al-Bahr ar-Ra'iq*, vol. 2, p. 217.

Justice in Islam and ease in the *Shari'a* would not allow such people to be burdened by what would bring great difficulty and anxiety into their lives. Consequently, it is important to define the conditions of assets subject to *zakat*.

Undivided and absolute right of ownership

One condition is undivided and absolute right of ownership. All *amwal* in the ultimate analysis belongs to Allah. He is the Creator of them. He is the One who gives them for human sustenance. The Qur'an repeatedly refers to this final reality by attributing the *mal* to Allah, such as in the verses, "And *give them some of the wealth Allah has given you*" (24:33) and *"O you who believe! Give away some of what We have provided for you"* (2:254). It also refers to, *"Those who are stingy with the bounty Allah has given them"* (3:180), or to humans as only vicegerents or agents with regard to the wealth they own, such as in the verse, *"Give from that to which He has made you the successors"* (57:7).

Allah, although He is the True Owner, honours His servants with the privilege of authority over the gifts He bestows on them and holds them responsible and accountable for what they control. It is similar to when a father gives his child some of his property in order to make the child experience his or her independence and tests him or her with that. It is no surprise, therefore, that the Qur'an in other places mentions wealth (*amwal*) as attributed to people: *"O you who believe! Do not let your wealth or children divert you."* (63:9) *"Your wealth and children are a trial."* (64:15) *"He thinks his wealth will make him live forever."* (104:3) *"His wealth has not helped him nor anything he has earned."* (111:2) *"And the beggars and destitute received a due share of their wealth."* (51:19) *"Take* sadaqa *from their wealth."* (9:103) *"Do not let their wealth and children impress you." (9:55) "Hand over their property to them."* (4:6) *"Do not consume one another's property by false means."* (4:29)

Allah highly honours humans by using the concept of "borrowing from people" with reference to Himself in respect of those assets, although they are, in fact, bestowed by Allah on his servants.

Allah says, *"Is there anyone who will make Allah a generous loan so that He can multiply it for him many times over?"* (2:245) *"Who will make a good loan to Allah so that He may multiply it for him? He will have a generous reward."* (57:11) *"And lend a good loan to Allah."* (73:20) *"Allah has bought from the believers their selves and their wealth in return for them having the Garden."* (9:111) Al-Hasan comments here that He "buys" persons that He created and wealth that He bestowed.

Ahmad ibn 'Abdu'r-Rahim ad-Dihlawi, the philosopher of Islam in India, comments on the verses that attribute ownership to human beings, "When Allah made it permissible for people to use what He created for them in and on the earth, people became greedy about things, so there was a need to establish a rule based on the priorities of acquiring things. All land is for all human beings, but those who come first are served first. Consequently, the human ownership of these created things depends on the priority of extracting utilities and usefulness from them."[1]

However, it should be pointed out that titling this section "Undivided and Absolute Right of Ownership", I do not mean the ultimate ownership which belongs to Allah alone. What is meant here is the right of control over assets and material things as attributed to humans in the above-mentioned verses.

What exactly is meant by "undivided and absolute ownership"? This is a jurist's term that is composed of two factors, *milk* (ownership) and absoluteness of ownership. *Milk* (ownership) is the noun from the root *malaka* (to own) which means to obtain and have control and authority of disposition of, as stated in *al-Qamus*. In *al-Muj'am al-Wasit*, the verb *'malaka'* means to obtain and have exclusive right of disposition over. This linguistic meaning in the *Shari'a* is defined by jurists. In *al-Fath*, al-Kamal ibn al-Humam defines ownership as the power of disposition which is original or derived from another person. In *al-Furuq*, al-Qarafi defines ownership as "a conjunction of the *Shari'a* on material things or on their utilities which allows the person to whom those things belong to utilise them and/or their services, or to exchange them for a substitute, except when a lawful obstacle [that prevents the exercise of such authority] exists."

1. *Hujjat Allah al-Baligha*, vol. 2, pp. 640-641.

Sadr ash-Shari'a, in his commentary on *al-Wiqaya*, defines the right of ownership as a legal relation between a person and a material whereby the person is absolutely authorised to use the material, an authorisation that prevents others from having any power over that thing. All these definitions include the idea of exclusiveness referred to in Arabic dictionaries. Experts in law have similar definitions. For them, ownership is "an authority that enables the owner to use the owned thing and get the benefit of all its utilities in a perpetual and exclusive manner."[2]

The meaning of absoluteness and undividedness of the ownership is that the owned material is exclusive to the owner.[3] No one else has any share in it, nor does the owner's right to use it depend on authorisation from others.[4] For that reason, it is said that whenever the right of ownership is not absolute, such as merchandise purchased but not yet received, *zakat* is not obligated. Nor is *zakat* obligated in the case in which the asset is used as a lien holder or the asset is stolen and actually in the possession of the thief."[5]

Jurists express the condition of absoluteness of ownership by the ability to dispose of the asset, as is known among the Zaydis. The Zaydis deem that for a thing to be subject to *zakat* that the owner must have authority of disposition over the *nisab* throughout the whole year, or at least sufficient reason to hope that if he so wishes he can have total authority of disposal, such as if he has funds deposited with others. Zaydis say if the owner does not have that power of disposal or sufficient expectation of having it at his wish, then *zakat* is not required on that *mal* until the owner gets it back. In such a case, the year for this *mal* starts when he gets it back.

The rationale of this condition

Private ownership is a great boon from Allah. It is one of the fruits of freedom and of humanity itself. Animals cannot own;

1. Shaykh 'Ali al-Khafif, "*Al-Milkiya al-Fardiya wa Tahdiduha fi'l-Islam*" in the proceedings of the first conference of the Islamic Reference Congress, p. 99.
2. Ibid.
3. *Al-Bahr ar-Ra'iq*, vol. 2, p. 213.
4. *Matalib uli Nuha, Sharh Ghayat al-Muntaha*, vol. 2, p. 16.
5. *Al-Bahr ar-Ra'iq*, op cit.

humans can. Ownership gives the feeling of authority and power and satisfies the acquisitive desire. Complete ownership enables people to extract the benefits of owned materials, as well as putting assets to grow. The grace of Allah should be recognised by people. The payment of *zakat* is an expression of thankfulness to Allah and recognition of His bounty.

The proof of this condition

This condition is justified by two major points. Firstly, the fact that assets and wealth are attributed to people in the Qur'an and *Sunna* implies that individuals liable for *zakat* must have ownership of these assets. This general form of ownership requires owning in an exclusive manner. Secondly, the fulfilment of *zakat* requires that the recipients, such as the poor and destitute, should become owners of what is given to them as *zakat*. They would not become owners if the *zakat* payers did not have the absolute right of ownership over what they pay.

Implications of this condition

The case of assets which do not have a specific owner

This condition implies that assets which do not have a specific person as owner are free of *zakat*, such as the state's revenue collected from taxes, *zakat*, and other sources. These are not subject to *zakat* because they are not owned by an individual and the right to them belongs to the entire society, including the poor and needy. Additionally, the government is the agency that collects *zakat* and there is no reason why it should collect from itself. Scholars have said, "There should be no *zakat* on state resources like *fay'* (wealth taken from enemies without fighting) or on the government's share of *ghanima* (wealth gained as a result of lawful war with enemies) because these revenues belong to all Muslims and are spent for their benefit."[1] In general, all publicly owned property is not subject to *zakat*.

Property in public trust

Property put in public trust for, say, the poor, mosques, orphans, schools, fighters for the sake of Allah, etc., is not subject to *zakat*. On the other hand, the property of private trusts that are held for the benefit of an individual or a group of beneficiaries, such as children's trusts, is subject to *zakat*, since the right of private ownership is transferred on these properties to the benefit of the children, although they cannot, for some time, dispose of the property themselves.[2] This is more akin to privately owned things than to public trusts, since the most important element of private ownership is the exclusivity of benefit of the property and this feature exists in private trusts. Some jurists, however, consider *zakat* to be obligated on all trusts, public and private. Ibn Rushd says, "It seems that imposing *zakat* on public trusts designated for the benefit of the indigent is meaningless for two reasons. Firstly, their ownership is incomplete, and two, they are not subject to *zakat*, but on the contrary recipients of *zakat*.[3]

Unlawful wealth

This condition excludes from *zakat* any wealth acquired by unlawful means, such as theft, counterfeiting, bribery, interest, monopoly, or cheating. This may include the most part of the wealth of autocratic rulers, interest financiers, thieves, etc. Such individuals do not indeed own the stolen property in their hands, although they might have mixed them with property obtained by lawful means. Scholars declare that evil wealth is not subject to *zakat* because all such wealth must be returned to its true owners if known, or to their heirs, and if not, then to the poor and needy. It is not sufficient for only a small part of such ill gotten gains to be given out in the form of *zakat*.[4] The authentic *hadith* speaks for itself: "Allah does not accept *sadaqa* from stolen property." (Muslim)

---

1. *Matalib uli'n-Nuha*, vol. 2, p. 16.
2. An-Nawawi, *al-Majmu'*, vol. 5, pp. 339-340.
3. Ibn Rushd, *Bidayat al-Mujtahid*, vol. 1, p. 239.
4. *Al-Bahr ar-Ra'iq*, by Ibn Nujaym, and its commentary by Ibn 'Abidin, vol.

Jurists justify the non-zakatability of such wealth by the fact that it is not actually owned by those who have control over it. Therefore, they have no authority to pay *zakat* or to make any other disposal except returning it to its lawful owner.[1] Thus a person whose methods of gain are unlawful is not considered rich in the *Shari'a*, even though he might control huge wealth. Some Hanafi jurists, including as-Sarakhsi, go to the extent of permitting the giving of charity to dictators on the grounds that they are in fact poor, although they unlawfully dispose of the riches of the whole country.[2] Such bold opinions mean to us that unlawfully acquired wealth cannot be owned or transferred to an heir or any other recipient.[3] On the other hand, giving charity, per se, to such oppressors is not acceptable because, although they are legally poor, they use their holdings to oppress people and for other evil purposes. The rule is that even a poor person should not be given *zakat* if it is known that he will use such income in disobedience to Allah.[4]

2, p. 221. It should be noted that Abu Hanifa thinks that a person who takes by use of unlawful force money from another and mixes it with his own, is considered to be changing its nature. He becomes a guarantor of the stolen money to its owner, and the total that the thief possesses becomes his property. On the other hand, Abu Yusuf and Muhammad ash-Shaybani do not agree on the guarantee or on attributing ownership of stolen property to the thief.

1. *Fath al-Bari*, vol. 3, p. 180.

2. Mentioned by Ibn al-Humam in *Fath al-Qadir* from *al-Mabsut*. He also reports from Qadi Khan that he said in *al-Jami' as-Saghir*, "If he made a last will of one-third of his wealth to the poor, and that third was given to an oppressing ruler, the will is satisfied." See *Fath al-Qadir*, vol. 1, pp. 513-514. These kinds of religious opinions are in fact written protests against oppressive rulers.

3. Ibid. See also *al-Bahr*, vol. 2, p. 240.

4. *Al-Muhalla*, vol. 2, p. 101. It is narrated from Ibn al-Qasim, a disciple of Malik, that usurped property is in the custody of the usurper from the time of its usurpation; consequently, the latter must pay *zakat* on it. Some Malikis apply that only to the case in which the thief has other property that can be used to satisfy the guarantee. If not, they say there is no *zakat* on stolen wealth. In the commentary of ad-Dusuqi, it is mentioned that *zakat* must be taken on materials stolen by force by the thief every year as long as they remain in his possession. This is done without affecting the obligation of the owner in paying *zakat* the moment he gets his stolen property back. This means *zakat* may be paid twice on such stolen property, once every year by the thief, and when it is returned, by the owner. The thief has no right to claim any liability on the part of the owner for the amount of

Zakat on debts

Another implication of this condition relates to *zakat* on debts. Who should pay such *zakat*? The creditor, the debtor or both? None of the jurists say both. 'Ikrima and 'Ata' are reported to be of the opinion that neither are subject to *zakat* on the basis that the debtor does not own the asset and the creditor does not have control of it.[1] Ibn Hazm reports from 'A'isha, *Umm al-Mu'minin*, "There should be no *zakat* on debts." This means that neither party – debtors and creditors – are subject to *zakat*. Ibn Hazm and his Zahiri colleagues support this opinion on the grounds that the right of ownership of both the debtor and the creditor is incomplete. The debtor does not own borrowed property although he makes use of it, while the creditor does not have control over the debt and does not extract benefit from it. The author of *al-Amwal* attributes to an-Nakha'i that "unreasonably delayed debts are subject to the payment of *zakat* by the debtors."[2] This opinion is a violation of the condition of completeness of ownership which is unanimous among all jurists.

The majority of jurists since the era of the Companions distinguish between two kinds of debts. The first are debts which creditors expect to be repaid, meaning debts made to parties who are capable of payment. *Zakat* is obliged on this category of debts yearly, as if they were property under control. Abu 'Ubayd reports this opinion from the Companions, 'Umar, 'Uthman, Ibn 'Umar and Jabir, and from the Followers, Jabir ibn Zayd, Mujahid, Ibrahim and Maymun ibn Mihran. The second are doubtful or dead debts, which are debts on individuals who are incapable of repayment or are denied by debtors.

There are three views about *zakat* on these debts. The first is that the creditor must pay *zakat* for all past years upon repayment of the debt. This is the opinion of the Companions 'Ali and Ibn

zakat paid by him. See *ash-Sharh al-Kabir* and its commentary by ad-Dusuqi, vol. 1, pp. 456-457.

1. *Al-Muhalla*, vol. 2, p. 101, and al-Bayhaqi says in his *Sunan*, vol. 4, p. 150, "It is mentioned by Ibn al-Mundhir from Ibn 'Umar and 'A'isha.

2. *Al-Amwal*, p. 432. A similar report is narrated from 'Ata'. However, the contrary is also reported from them.

'Abbas. The second is that the creditor should pay *zakat* for the last year only upon repayment of the debt. This is the view of al-Hasan and 'Umar ibn 'Abdu'l-'Aziz. It is also the view of Malik on all debts.[1] The third is that the creditor does not owe any *zakat* whatsoever and the debt when paid back starts a new year of *zakat*, which is the view of Abu Hanifa and his two disciples.[2] Abu 'Ubayd is of the opinion that if the creditor hopes to get back the debt, *zakat* should be imposed as if the debt were part of his current assets, in accordance with 'Umar, 'Uthman, Jabir, and Ibn 'Umar. Abu 'Ubayd, however, cautiously allows deferring the payment of *zakat* until the receipt of the amount of the debt, provided that *zakat* is then strictly paid for all the preceding years.

As for doubtful and bad debts, Abu 'Ubayd is of the opinion of 'Ali and Ibn 'Abbas, that payment of *zakat* should be made by the creditor for all past years if the debt is ever repaid. He argues that since the right of ownership on the debt is not annulled by the doubtfulness, then the right of Allah should also remain.[3] I agree with Abu 'Ubayd in the first case, but differ with him in the case of doubtful and dead debts, because the right of ownership on such debts is not complete, since the creditor has no hope of extracting benefit and so disposing of the debt.[4] This is also the argument of Abu Hanifa and his two disciples. That is, all assets whose owner is not capable of extracting benefit from them should be excluded from paying *zakat*, since such an owner is not rich and *zakat* is only imposed on the rich.[5]

1. According to Malik, *zakat* is due for one year only from the time the debt is paid back, even if the debt is for many years. Once the creditor receives the debt back, he should pay its *zakat* for one year, provided it is equal to the *nisab*. This is subject to the condition that the delay in getting the debt back was not merely to avoid payment of *zakat*. If it was for that reason only, *zakat* is due on it for every year. On the other hand, if the debt results from a gift or charity, i.e. a gift is pledged but not surrendered to the receiver by the donor, *zakat* is not obliged until a year has passed from the time of acquiring it physically. Debts that are expected to be paid back and those that are not, are the same in this regard, except for business credit on which *zakat* is due. Business credit is a loan which results from sales. See *ash-Sharh al-Kabir* and *Hashiyat ad-Dusuqi*, vol. 1, p. 466.

2. *Al-Amwal*, pp. 434–435.

3. Ibid.

4. *Matalib Uli'n-Nuha*, vol. 2, p. 14.

5. *Bada'i' as-Sana'i'*, vol. 1. p.9.

I agree with Abu Hanifa that all doubtful and dead debts are like assets from which their owner is incapable of deriving benefit and, therefore, not subject to *zakat* for all past years. But if the debt is repaid, it should be treated as a newly-earned asset, and the creditor, upon receipt of the debt, should pay *zakat* for one year only, as on any other newly-earned asset.

Pension contributions and savings of employees

A question which commonly arises these days concerns retirement savings and pension contributions that are retained by governments, employers or other independent agencies to which the contributor has no direct access, except upon retirement or termination of employment. The *zakat* on such funds is determined by whether they can be defined as being completely owned by the contributor. Can he dispose of them at will or not? Are these funds the right of the contributor or mere contributions whose value will be determined at the time of retirement? If they are purely contributions or gifts, they accrue only to the contributor at the time of receipt. But if they are part of what the contributor has access to and may dispose of at will, then they should be treated like debts owed to people who are capable and ready to pay, i.e. they are subject to *zakat* every year, once they reach the *nisab* for *zakat* to be taken as will be discussed later.[1]

Growth

The second condition for *zakat* is that the wealth concerned must either be actually growing or have the potential for growth. Growth means something that provides the owner with profit and benefit. Or the asset itself should be the result of growth, being surplus or a newly acquired item. This has been established by Muslim jurists in a clear and specific manner. Linguistically, "growth" is any surplus. In the *Shari'a*, growth has two meanings, actual and potential growth. Actual growth is increase by genetic or business means.

1. As we have mentioned above Malik's view on debts is that *zakat* is not taken on them until they are received, and then *zakat* is due on them for one year only.

Potential growth is when the asset can increase if it is used properly for that purpose. This implies the availability of the asset for potential use.[1]

The rationale for this condition

Ibn al-Humam writes, "*Zakat* is legislated to help and relieve the poor without impoverishing the rich, by having the rich pay from their surplus, taking a little from the plenty. Imposing *zakat* on wealth that does not, by definition, grow, reverses this purpose, since *zakat* is paid year after year, in addition to living expenses."[2] This condition of growth applies to the *hadith* of the Messenger of Allah (p), "Wealth never decreases as a result of *sadaqa*," (at-Tirmidhi) since the payment of a small fraction as *zakat* out of growing wealth does not make the wealth diminish.

What is actually considered, however, is the growth potential of the assets and not actual growth, because as mentioned by the author of *al-Mughni* actual growth can hardly be measured and is subject to difference in measurement.

It is mentioned in *al-Bada'i'* that "The very naming of *zakat* – which in itself means growth or increase – is not realised except in growing assets. It is not necessary, however, for wealth to actually grow but the ability to grow through business, animal breeding, or seed planting, is sufficient, since growth by reproduction, profit, and multiplicity is realised by those means. The possibility of using the means is alone sufficient. This is similar to travelling, which allows the traveller to reduce the prayer even if he can pray without hardship."[3] On the other hand, the asset itself may be a result of growth, as in crops and fruits. In this case, *zakat* is only obliged after growth has occurred.

The proof for this condition

This condition is derived from the spoken and practised tradition of the Prophet (p), which was sustained in application by his

1. *Hashiyat Ibn 'Abidin*, vol. 2, p. 7, as quoted from *al-Bahr*.
2. *Fath al-Qadir*, vol. 2, p. 482.
3. *Bada'i' as-Sana'i'*, vol. 2, p. 11.

successors and Companions. The Prophet (p) did not oblige *zakat* on assets which are obtained for personal use, as indicated by the sound *hadith*, "A Muslim is not accountable for *zakat* for his mare or slaves." (Muslim) An-Nawawi says, "This *hadith* plants the seed of the principle that assets obtained for personal use are not subject to *zakat*." the Prophet (p) did not impose *zakat* except on growing and producing assets, of which Arabs in his time had several kinds:

- Livestock such as camels, cows and sheep.
- Money, gold or silver in the form of cash, business assets and as savings.
- Crops and fruits, especially basic foods, such as wheat, barley, dates, and raisins. Honey is included in this category according to some jurists.
- Treasures hidden underground by people in the past and minerals stored by Allah inside and on the surface of the earth.

About the disbursement of the proceeds of dues on this last category, there are two opinions. One states that it should be treated like *zakat*, and the other is that it should be treated like *fay'*.

Jurists who believe that rulings of the *Shari'a* are always justifiable – and they are the majority – have agreed that the justification for payment of *zakat* on the above-mentioned assets is actual or potential growth. Livestock physically grows by weight increase, reproduction and milk production. Business assets also grow. They are there to make profit and bring return. This growth is not simply natural like that of animal and agricultural wealth, but is caused by the action of people. Since it is considered lawful in Islam as well as in all heavenly and earthly religions and laws, business growth is put in the same category as natural growth. Money also grows, because it is the means of exchange and the measure of value as a substitute for goods.

When money is used in industry and trade, it brings income, which is what is meant by growth in this section. If money is hoarded and prevented from fulfilling its role in circulation and production, the hoarder is held responsible for leaving it idle. He is not by that action exempt from *zakat*, but rather *zakat* gives him the impetus to utilise his money in growth and useful business, otherwise it will perish. Crops and fruits are themselves the result of growth, being produced by the process of agricultural reproduction. Honey, discovered treasures and minerals are similar.

This condition is founded by jurists on the basis of the guidance of the Messenger of Allah (p) and the practice of the Rightly-guided Khalifs. It is also consistent with the meaning of *zakat* itself, since one of the most clear meanings of the word '*zakat*' is growth. What is being paid as *zakat* is given this name because it brings blessing and growth, in accordance with the promise of Allah: *"Anything you expend will be replaced by Him,"* (34:39) and *"But anything you give as* zakat, *seeking the Face of Allah – all who do that will get back twice as much."* (30:39) Giving the name *zakat* for what is paid in fulfilment of the requirement of *zakat* may have yet another meaning, according to some scholars. That is, the amount paid is called *zakat* because it comes out of the surplus or excess that is the result of the process of growth. Consequently, *zakat* is obliged on growing assets but not on assets held for personal and family use.[1] In application of this condition, Muslims since the early times exempted animals used for personal transportation, homes inhabited by the owner, tools of craftsmen and household furniture from *zakat*. Also exempted are assets that cannot be made to grow, such as assets unlawfully controlled by others.[2]

On the other hand, it is because of this condition that scholars declare that *zakat* on harvested crops and fruits does not recur every year. Once the ten percent *zakat* has been paid on them, no more *zakat* is imposed even though these crops and fruits may remain owned in storage by the same owner for several years, because crops and fruits after being harvested do not grow anymore, and *zakat* is repeated yearly only on growing assets. In contrast, livestock is subject to *zakat* annually because of its continuous growth.[3]

It should be pointed out that the school of Malik extends the application of this condition more than other schools. One of these

1. *Al-Muntaqa*, a commentary on *al-Muwatta'* by Abu'l-Walid al-Baji, vol. 2, p. 90.

2. *Al-Bahr ar-Ra'iq*, vol. 2, p. 222.

3. An-Nawawi, *al-Majmu'*, vol. 5, p. 569.

applications is related to debts. Since all kinds of debts do not grow, they are, according to the Malikis, not subject to *zakat*, but once they are paid back, the creditor must pay *zakat* on them for the final year only. Similarly, *zakat* on lost property is only due once the property is found, and for one year only. According to Malik, this applies to all debts, except for debts owed to non-monopolistic businesses, which are subject to *zakat* as part of the net worth of businessmen.[1]

According to the Malikis, the exemption of all debts from *zakat* is simply an application of this condition for growth. Additionally, Malik goes as far as exempting from *zakat* traders who keep an investment for years, on the basis that the investment does not actually give increase to the owner during this period. This assumes that investment shows an increase only at the time of selling. Malik says at that time the money from the investment is liable for *zakat* for one year only.[2]

Assets with owners who are unable to invest them

Since growth, actual or potential, is a requirement for *zakat* to be imposed, what should be the status of wealth whose owner is unable to make it grow? A distinction must be drawn between two cases of inability to cause growth in an asset: incapacity implied by the nature of the asset such as unpaid debts and property which has been stolen, and incapacity on the part of the owner. In the former case, the asset is not subject to *zakat*, but once the owner becomes able again to make it grow, such as when lost property is recovered, then the *zakat* is due on the asset only from that year on. On the other hand, if the incapacity is on the part of the owner, i.e. if the owner withholds his wealth from investment, then he is not excused from the yearly payment of *zakat*. It is assumed that Muslims will do their best to invest their assets.

Incapacity to make one's assets grow is not an excuse for exemption from *zakat*.[3] Inability to invest is rather blameable

1. *Ash-Sharh al-Kabir*, with commentary by ad-Dusuqi, vol. 1, p. 457.
2. Ibid., p. 473.
3. Some jurists expand the use of incapacity as an excuse to the extent that

because it indicates lack of will or means on the part of the owner. Against this kind of incapacity, the Prophet (p) strongly warned and he reprimanded those who demonstrate it. He used to pray, "My Lord, I seek your protection from incapacity and laziness." (al-Bukhari) Abu Hurayra narrates from the Prophet: "Be keen to hold to what benefits you, seek the help of Allah, and do not stay in a state of incapacity or stand still," (Muslim) and the Prophet (p) once told a man, 'Verily Allah reprimands for incapacity." (Abu Dawud)

All growing assets are subject to *zakat*

The condition of growth for *zakat* to be due can be used as a criterion for determining the kinds of wealth that are subject to *zakat*, even if they were not specifically mentioned by the Prophet (p), as long as they are covered by the general texts of the Qur'an and *Sunna*. This is not accepted by some jurists who restrict *zakat* to those items mentioned by the Prophet (p). Ibn Hazm, for example, restricts *zakat* in *al-Muhalla* to eight kinds of wealth: camels, cows, sheep, wheat, barley, dates, gold and silver.[1] For him, even raisins are not subject to *zakat*, nor is livestock other than camels, cows, and sheep. The same applies to agricultural crops except wheat, barley and dates, and to minerals and money except gold and silver. Moreover, according to him, there should be no *zakat* on business assets.

Jurists differ on the extent to which *zakat* is obliged as far as the different kinds of wealth are concerned. While some are very restrictive, others are liberal. Abu Hanifa is one of those who extend *zakat* to most categories. For example, he considers everything produced by the land, without any minimum, subject to *zakat*. He includes horses among the livestock from which *zakat* should be taken. He also obliges *zakat* on jewellery. On the other hand, in his view *zakat* is not required from minors or the insane,

they exempt a lender from *zakat* on debts, even if payment is expected, because it is not growing and its ownership is not complete. They also exempt from *zakat* the assets of children and the insane, because they are incapable of making assets grow.

1. *Al-Muhalla*, vol. 5, p. 209.

nor does he require the tenth on the output of *kharaj* land owed by Muslims.

The theory of Ibn Hazm, and those who restrict *zakat* along with him, such as ash-Shawkani and Siddiq Hasan Khan, is based on two principles: that a Muslim's wealth is protected by clear texts and must not be taken, so nothing must be imposed on it without virtue of a text, and that *zakat* is a religious obligation. Thus, in order to prevent anyone from incorporating in religion anything that Allah does not ordain, it is necessary that people must not be placed under obligation without a text. Analogy should especially not be used in the area of *zakat*.

My theory is exactly the opposite. It is based on other equally important principles in the *Shari'a*.

- The general texts of Qur'an and *Sunna* confirm that there is a right, a *sadaqa* or *zakat*, on all wealth. The *ayats*, *"And the beggars and destitute received a due share of their wealth..."* and *"Take sadaqa from their wealth...* " and the *hadith* of the Prophet (p), "Inform them that Allah has obliged *sadaqa* to be collected from their rich and rendered to their poor," and "Pay the *zakat* on your wealth," are sufficient evidence. We know that the word *amwal* in the *Sunna* means growing assets and not those things designated for personal use. It is not allowed to exclude some kinds of wealth from this *zakat* or *sadaqa* without clear evidence. There is no such evidence.

- Each rich person is in need of purification and cleansing – cleansing through giving for the sake of Allah and purification from miserliness, selfishness, and the overwhelming desire for money. Allah says, *"Take* sadaqa *from their wealth to purify and cleanse them."* (9:103) It is unreasonable to think that peasants who own wheat and barley should be purified and cleansed while owners of large orchards or landlords of luxurious high-rise buildings or owners of factories are not in need of that purification and cleansing. The return of the latter's property is far greater than that in wheat and barley.

- Wealth of any kind is in need of purification, since it may have been mixed with some sort of unlawfulness in the process of its generation and earning. Purification of wealth can only be achieved by the payment of *zakat*, and it is authentically reported from Ibn 'Umar, "Allah has imposed *zakat* as a purification of wealth." It is also reported in some *hadiths*, "If you pay *zakat* on your wealth, you will have removed its evil."(Ibn Khuzayma and al-Hakim) It does not seem rational to restrict such purification to the eight items mentioned by Ibn Hazm and to exclude the bulk of the other kinds of wealth which are nowadays the backbone of private and public wealth, since all kinds of wealth are in need of purification.

- *Zakat* is ordained in order to satisfy the needs of the poor, the destitute, and travellers, and to pay for the fulfilment of some public affairs of the Muslim community, such as *jihad* for the sake of Allah, reconciling people's hearts to Islam, and helping those who carry disproportionately large burdens of financial responsibility in the public interests of Muslims. The satisfaction of these needs and the achievement of those interests is a duty of all rich individuals. It is unthinkable that the *Shari'a* meant to throw this burden on those who own five camels or forty sheep or five *wasqs* of barley and to exempt businessmen who own factories, buildings and other big businesses, or professionals, such as physicians, lawyers, executives, etc., who earn in one day much more than five camels or forty sheep. According to the religion of Islam, riches are in reality the property of Allah, human beings only vicegerents or agents. The right of poor brethren who are in need is established on these riches because they are dependent on Allah. By the same token, the public interests of the nation also have rights on these riches. Every rich person must share this responsibility, whether he or she invests in agriculture, industry, business or professional services.

- Analogy, as was shown earlier, is one of the essential axioms of the *Shari'a*, according to the majority of scholars, despite the disagreement of Ibn Hazm and other Zahiris. Consequently, I say that every growing wealth is subject to *zakat* by analogy with those items mentioned by the Messenger (p). We are certain that the *Shari'a* does not treat differently cases which are similar, nor does it treat similarly cases which are different, thus we can use analogy in the matter of *zakat*. This cannot be treated as being an addition to religion, which is not allowed by Allah, especially since *zakat* is not pure worship, but an essential component of the socio-economic system in Islam as well.

• No one would disagree with the postulate that "The wealth of a Muslim is protected, and that he or she has a right to private ownership." But it can be shown that the right of Allah, the right of the community and the right of those who are in need of *zakat* are also well-established by the texts themselves. Ibn Hazm agrees with this principle because he believes that on assets of individuals there are rights besides *zakat*. He further gives authority to the government to force the rich to pay for the support of the poor, and even says that the poor have the right to revolt until their needs are satisfied. Ibn Hazm would have been more sensible had he imposed *zakat* on all items of wealth before talking about additional dues to satisfy the needs of the poor. After the complete practice of *zakat* on all items of wealth, if there is still need for more funds, additional dues can be imposed.

• Finally, concerning the allegation that *zakat* should not be extended to items from which the Prophet did not take *zakat*, two points should be raised. Firstly, the growth of such items was very negligible in his time, so he did not consider them. Secondly, he left *zakat* on such items to individual practice and the conscience of the owner. If the Messenger of Allah (p) did not collect *zakat* from certain items, this does not necessarily mean that they are not subject to *zakat* on the initiative of individuals, especially if the latter are informed as to the requirement of *zakat* and the need of all items to be purified.

Reaching the minimum for *zakat*

Islam does not impose *zakat* on all amounts of growing wealth. There is a minimum required for *zakat* to be taken, which jurists called the *nisab*. Sayings of the Prophet (p) exempt anything that is less than five camels, forty sheep, two hundred silver dirhams or five wasqs of grain, fruits or agricultural crops. Shaykh al-Islam ad-Dihlawi[1] says about the rationale behind these quantities:

> "Five *wasqs* of grain or dates is considered the minimum because that much would be the minimum required for sustaining a household for a year, a household composed of three people. On the average, people ate one *ratl* or *mudd* of grain per person per day. Five *wasqs* would therefore be sufficient for three people for a whole year, and a small extra quantity should be left as provision for emergencies. For silver, the minimum required for *zakat* to be taken is two hundred dirhams, because this would be sufficient for the same household for one full year, at prices similar to those prevailing at the time of the Prophet (p). Five camels are the minimum for *zakat* and the *zakat* on them is one sheep. In principle, *zakat* is collected from the same kind of wealth as the asset on which *zakat* is due, but camels were exchanged for sheep at the time of the Prophet (p) at the rate of eight to one, ten to one, or twelve to one, as reported in many *hadiths*. One camel out of five would be too much, so one sheep is considered the amount of *zakat* due on five camels, since five camels would be equal to at least forty sheep, on which the *zakat* due is one sheep." (*Hujjat Allah al-Baligha*, vol. 2, p. 506)

1. He is the great scholar and renovator of the practice of Islam in India, Ahmad ibn 'Abdu'r-Rahim, known as Shah Waliyullah, b. 1114 AH, died 1176 AH, author of *Hujjat Allah al-Baligha* and several other valuable books. See his biography in detail in *Nuzha al-Khawatir* by as-Sayyid 'Abdu'l-Hayy al-Hasani, vol. 6, pp. 398-415, *Tarikh ad-Da'wa al-Islamiyya fi'l-Hind* by Mas'ud an-Nadwi, p. 129f, *Mujaz Tarikh Tajdid ad-Din wa ihya'ah* by Abu'l-A'la al-Mawdudi, pp. 101-121, and in *al-A'lam* by az-Zirkili, vol. 1, pp. 144-145.

The condition of *nisab* for *zakat* is agreed upon among all scholars, except in the case of crops, fruits and minerals. Abu Hanifa considers anything that comes out of the earth to be subject to *zakat*, no matter how little it may be. The *zakat* on it is ten percent. Also a report from Ibn 'Abbas, 'Umar ibn 'Abdu'l-'Aziz and others says, "There is on each ten bundles of parsley one bundle as obligated *sadaqa*." The majority of scholars see *nisab* as a necessary condition for *zakat* on all kinds of wealth, whether it comes from the ground or not. They argue that there is the *hadith*, "There is no *sadaqa* on what is less than five *wasqs*." This argument is supported by analogy, since other kinds of wealth have *nisabs* of their own.

The rationale behind this condition is very obvious. *Zakat* is a due on the rich to relieve the poor and to share in the expenses of common interest to Islam and the Muslims. It can only be taken from those who can afford it. It is meaningless to take *zakat* from those who are themselves in need of help, knowing that the Prophet (p) said, "There is no *sadaqa* except from wealth." (al-Bukhari) It is on the same grounds that contemporary taxation systems tend to exempt those with limited resources from taxes, in consideration of their inability to pay. It is worth registering that the *Shari'a* of Allah precedes those systems by fourteen hundred years.

Excess above essential needs

Some jurists add another condition to the condition of growth. That is that the *nisab* must be in excess of the basic needs of the owner. In most of their literature, the Hanafis try to establish this principle on the basis that wealth itself is not realised without this condition, since if the person who owns the assets needs them for essential necessities, they are not considered rich, nor would such a person be happy to sacrifice anything of what they own for the payment of *zakat*. The Prophet (p) said, "Pay *zakat* on your wealth with your hearts willing and pleased."[1] Some other jurists feel that

1. *Bada'i' as-Sana'i'*, vol. 2, p. 11. The *hadith* is reported by at-Tabarani from Abu'd-Darda'. It is weak.

the condition of growth is alone sufficient since things needed to satisfy basic needs are not usually growing or designated for growth, as in the case of homes inhabited by owners, personal animals for transportation, personal clothing, personal weapons, books for personal study and handicraft tools. All these satisfy basic needs and at the same time are not growth assets. These jurists argue that true personal need is something very subjective and usually cannot be recognised positively by others. Consequently, what is in excess of those needs cannot be known, so instead of the condition of excess above personal needs, we can use a recognisable condition, like designation of the assets for business and growth purposes.[1]

In fact, the condition of growth does not cover all the cases of the condition of excess above essential needs. Money, for example is considered a growth asset, because it is created for circulation and investment, even if the owner does not actually use it for growth. Without the condition of being in excess of needs, an amount of money that is equal to *nisab* is subject to *zakat*, even if it were designated for providing food, clothing, shelter, or medical care for the owner and his household. It is known among the deeply involved scholars that assets designated to satisfy basic needs are treated as non-existent from the point of view of *zakat.*[2]

We should, however, note that this condition refers to essential or basic needs. People have an infinite amount of needs, especially in this time of ours, when many goods that used to be considered luxuries have become necessities. Not anything that is desired can be considered a basic need, since if the son of Adam had two valleys full of gold, he would want to obtain a third one. Basic needs are those human beings cannot survive without, such as food, shelter, clothing, and items needed for a job, such as books for study and tools for work.

Some Hanafi scholars define essential needs in an accurate and scientific manner, as "those things that are used to avoid the realised or potential destruction of human beings; realised ones, such as expenses for living, clothing, personal weapons; and potential ones, such as the need to pay one's debts, tools for handicraft,

1. Ibid.

2. Ibn 'Abidin, commentary on *ad-Durr al-Mukhtar*, vol. 2, p. 6.

home furniture, animals for personal transportation, and books for study, because ignorance is like destruction. If a person has money designated for such needs, it is considered non-existent with regard to *zakat*. This is similar to the case of someone who has no water except that designated for drinking. This water is considered non-existent with regard to performing *wudu'*, and one is allowed to do *tayammum* instead."[1]

It should be gratefully and proudly recorded that our scholars consider knowledge like life and ignorance like destruction, and consider what prevents ignorance an essential need just like food that prevents hunger or clothes that prevent nakedness, and consider freedom like life and imprisonment like destruction. It should be noted however, that the essential needs of human beings evolve and change with time and circumstances, so determining them should be left to people of intelligence and understanding and to the exertion of best effort (*ijtihad*) of the proper authorities in the Islamic state. Basic needs include the needs of the *zakat* payer, his household, and all family members whom he is required by the *Shari'a* to support.

This condition in Islamic jurisprudence precedes the latest theories in taxation that call for exempting a certain minimum amount from taxes and puts an end to the materialist theory that taxes all assets, regardless of the circumstances of the owner, his or her business, and family needs. Modern theorists take consideration of the personal circumstances of the taxpayer as a sign of advancement in taxation theory and legislation. Unfortunately, much of the legislation does not actually apply this principle in levying taxes. For example, sometimes tax laws exempt a minimum of living expenses for the taxpayer alone, regardless of the number of mouths he or she has to feed.

Evidence from the Qur'an and *Sunna* supporting this condition

In the *Musnad* Ahmad reports from Abu Hurayra that the Prophet (p) said, "*Sadaqa* is only taken out of wealth," and in

1. *Ibid*, and *al-Bahr ar-Ra'iq*, vol. 2, p. 222, as quoted by Ibn al-Malik in *Sharh al-Majma'*.

another version, "There should be no *sadaqa* taken except out of wealth."[1] Al-Bukhari mentioned this *hadith* as suspended (without complete chain) in the chapter of advice and wills in his *Sahih* collection. He makes it the title of a section in the chapter on *zakat*, "Section: *Sadaqa* is only taken from wealth; he who would give *sadaqa* while he or his family are in need or while he is under the burden of debts, should first pay his debts out of what he would give as *sadaqa*." Ibn Hajar comments on the title, "It seems that al-Bukhari wants to explain the above-mentioned *hadith* by stating that it is a required condition for *sadaqa* that the payer or his family must not be in need."[2] There is no doubt that *zakat* is *sadaqa*, as expressed in the Qur'an and *Sunna*.

In the Qur'an, Allah says: *"They will ask you what they should give away. Say, 'What is surplus to your needs.'"* (2:219) Ibn 'Abbas is reported to have said, "This means what is in excess of you and your family's needs." Ibn Kathir says, "This is also reported from Ibn 'Umar, Mujahid, 'Ata', 'Ikrima, Sa'id ibn Jubayr, Muhammad ibn Ka'b, al-Hasan, Qatada, al-Qasim, Salim, 'Ata' al-Khurasani, ar-Rabi' ibn Anas, and several others. They say, *'What is surplus to your needs'* is what is in excess."[3] This means that Allah – may His wisdom be glorified – makes subject to spending only what is in excess of basic needs, i.e. the needs of the person, his family and all those he is required to support. The needs of the person and his family have priority for him, over the needs of other people. So the *Shari'a* does not ask him to sacrifice his own needs to which his heart is attached in order to satisfy other people's needs. Al-Hasan is reported to have commented on the preceding verse, *"That is so as not to extinguish your wealth so you have to go begging from people."*[4]

Ibn Kathir says that this condition is also supported by what is reported by Ibn Jarir, narrated through his chain to Abu Hurayra: "A man said, 'O Messenger of Allah, I have a dinar.' He said, 'Spend it as *sadaqa* on yourself.' He said, 'I have another.' He said, 'Spend it on your wife.' He said, 'I have another.' He said, 'Give it

1. *Hadith* 7155 in the *Musnad*. Ahmad Shakir comments, "Its chain is correct." See commentary in vol. 12, *al-Musnad*, See also *Fath al-Bari*, vol. 3, p. 189.
2. *Fath al-Bari*, vol. 14, p. 189.
3. *Tafsir Ibn Kathir*, vol. 1, p. 256.
4. Ibid.

as *sadaqa* to your child.' The man said, 'I have a fourth,' and the Messenger answered, 'You best know your needs.'" This *hadith* is also reported by Muslim in his *Sahih* collection. It indicates that the needs of the person, his wife and children have priority over the needs of others. Muslim reports also from Jabir, "The Messenger of Allah said to a man, 'Start with yourself and spend *sadaqa* on yourself. If anything is left, give it to your family. If anything is left after your family, then give to your relatives, and if anything is left after your relatives, then give this way and that way.'" Some of those traditions are about voluntary charity and not the obligatory one, but in all cases they indicate the intention of the *Shari'a* in spending, which is that all spending, voluntary and obligatory, should come out of surplus. The surplus, as understood by the majority of scholars, and as defined by Ibn Kathir, is the excess after satisfying needs.

Freedom from debt

That the *nisab* should be free of debt is, in fact, an implication of the first condition, i.e. completeness of ownership, and of excess above essential needs. If the owner is burdened by debts that exceed the *nisab* or reduce the assets' worth to below the *nisab*, *zakat* is not obliged.

Jurists have varying opinions on debts, especially those debts that are related to apparent assets [assets that can be detected by *zakat* collectors]. The reason for this variety of opinion is that they do not agree on the classification of *zakat* – as mentioned by Ibn Rushd – as worship or a financial right due to the poor. Those who see *zakat* as a right to the poor, consider that the person who is burdened by debts in a manner that reduces his current assets to below the *nisab* is not liable for *zakat* since the right of the creditors comes first before the right of the poor, because the creditors are the true owners of that asset.

Those who see *zakat* as a form of worship say that *zakat* is due from such a person because the condition for *zakat* is the presence of assets above the *nisab*; no mention of debts is made. They add that there is in this case a conflict between two rights, the right of Allah and the right of a person, and the right of Allah has priority[1] Ibn Rushd remarks, "What seems to be more consistent with the *Shari'a* is waiving *zakat* on the debtor."[2] It should be added, however, that what is selected by Ibn Rushd is what can be derived from texts of the *Shari'a*, its spirit, and its major principles concerning all kinds of assets. This can be shown in the following:

- The ownership of the debtor is in fact weak and incomplete, because of the authority the creditor has over his due debts in asking for payment, to the extent that the creditor may take back the lent asset if it is still in the debtor's hands, even without the consent of the debtor, according to the Hanafi school and others.[3] The first condition for *zakat* is that the right of ownership should be complete.
- The creditor is required to pay *zakat* for the loan, being the real owner, according to the majority of scholars. If the debtor was also asked to pay *zakat* on that same debt, then there would be a double *zakat* on the same asset. This double jeopardy is prohibited by *Shari'a*.[4]
- A person who is overwhelmed by debts that exceed what he owns, or at least reduce it to below the *nisab*, can be a recipient of *zakat* on the grounds of being poor or of being overwhelmed by debts. How could he be a *zakat* payer and a *zakat* recipient at the same time?
- *Zakat* is only legitimately taken from wealth, as mentioned in the *hadiths*. The debtor who needs to pay back his debts is not rich. Moreover, he is under stress caused by the debt.
- *Zakat* is legislated to relieve those who are in need. An overwhelmed debtor is in need of paying his debts. He is like the poor. It is not rational to leave the needs of the debtor unsatis-

1. *Bidayat al-Mujahid*, p. 238
2. *Al-Majmu'*, vol. 5, p. 46, and *al-Bahr*, vol. 2, p. 219.
3. Ibid.
4. Ibid.

fied in order to provide for the needs of others,[1] knowing that the Messenger (p) said, "Start with yourself, then with those for whom you are responsible."

- Abu 'Ubayd reports from as-Sa'ib ibn Yazid, "I heard 'Uthman ibn 'Affan saying, 'This is the month of your *zakat*. Those of you who have debts should pay back your debts so you can start paying *zakat* on your assets.'"[2] In another version reported by Malik, "He who is in debt should pay back his debt and then pay *zakat* on the rest of his assets."[3] A version is reported by al-Bayhaqi from as-Sa'ib who heard 'Uthman ibn 'Affan giving this speech from above the minbar of the Messenger of Allah (p). 'Uthman said, "This is the month of your *zakat* ..." This last version means that 'Uthman's speech took place in the presence of many Companions, and none of them disagreed, meaning they all knew and accepted that opinion.[4]

It is for those reasons that the majority of jurists hold the view that debts prevent *zakat*, or at least reduce *zakat* on the assets by the amount of the outstanding debts, in non-apparent assets, money and business assets. This is the opinion of 'Ata', Sulayman ibn Yasir, al-Hasan, an-Nakha'i, al-Layth, Malik, ath-Thawri, al-Awza'i, Ahmad, Ishaq, Abu Thawr, Abu Hanifa and his disciples. Only Rabi'a, Hammad ibn Salman and ash-Shafi'i in his new opinion, disagree.

As for the apparent assets – livestock and crops – some jurists say that debt does not prevent *zakat*, differentiating between these assets and the former ones because *zakat* is clearly mentioned on these items by the texts, and also because these items are seen more by the poor and they feel envy in their hearts about them. This may be confirmed by the fact that the *Shari'a* instituted sending collectors to collect *zakat* on those assets from the time of the Prophet (p) and the first khalifs. Abu Bakr fought those who

1. *Al-Mughni*, vol. 3, p. 41.

2 *Al-Amwal*, p. 437. The month is said to be Ramadan or Muharram.

3. In *at-Talkhis*, p. 178, Ibn Hajar says it is reported by Malik in *al-Muwatta'* and ash-Shafi'i from Malik from Ibn Shihab from Sa'ib from 'Uthman.

4 *Al-Mughni*, op cit.

refused to pay *zakat* on these assets, while it is not reported that *zakat* payers were forced to pay *zakat* on non-apparent assets, especially since collectors used to take *zakat* on any apparent assets they found without asking about possible existing debts of owners.[1] This is the view of Malik, al-Awza'i, ash-Shafi'i and a version from Ahmad.[2] On the other hand. Abu Hanifa believes that debts are a reason to waive *zakat* on all assets except crops and fruits.[3]

Ibn 'Umar and Ibn 'Abbas have two different views with respect to debts on a person who owns crops. Ibn 'Abbas says the debtor should take out an amount equal to the debt used for farming expenses, and then pay *zakat* on the residue. Ibn 'Umar says that the debtor should deduct an amount equal to the debt that is spent on farming expenses or on himself and his family and then pay *zakat* on the rest.

It seems to me, however, that the distinction between apparent and non-apparent items of wealth is unclear, since those are relative matters that change from time to time. For example, in our time, business assets are apparent and very visible to the poor, much more than livestock and crops. I do not see in the above-mentioned reasoning anything that stands against the opinion given earlier which indicates that the presence of debts waives *zakat* on all assets.

We should also remember that the *Shari'a* also tends to make things easier on debtors in order to help them by all means to be rid of the burden of debt. This approach obviously contradicts forcing the debtor to pay *zakat*. This is the view of 'Ata', al-Hasan, Sulayman, Maymun ibn Mihran, an-Nakha'i, ath-Thawri, al-Layth, Ishaq, and a version from Ahmad.[4] Abu 'Ubayd reports it from Makhul and continues, "It is also reported from Tawus."[5]

1. *Al-Mughni*, vol 3, pp. 42-43.

2. This is similar in modern taxation in real estate taxes levied on properties, which is usually taken from the income of the property, regardless of the tax payer and his or her circumstances. The same thing applies to stocks and interest income in many countries. See *at-Tashri' ad-Daribi* by Dr. Muhammad Hilmi Murad, vol. 1, p. 78.

3. *Al-Mughni*, vol. 3, pp. 42.

4. Ibid.

5. *Al-Amwal*, p. 510.

Abu 'Ubayd, however, chooses the following stand: "If the debt is certain (not merely a claim), it waives *zakat* in the case of agricultural produce and livestock, following the Prophet's tradition, which ordered *zakat* to be collected from the rich and rendered to the poor. How can *zakat* be collected from the debtor, since he or she is a recipient on *zakat* on two grounds, being in debt and being poor?[1] This is if the debt is certain and known."

In the case when the debt is not known and not certain, *zakat* collectors are not supposed to accept the claim of the debtor, and should collect *zakat* on all present crops and livestock because *zakat* on those items is a very obvious obligation, binding the owner, while the claimed debt is unknown. This is similar to a case where a person has definite obligations that are known and claims to have paid them without having sufficient evidence. His or her word is not sufficient as proof.[2] Apparently, Abu 'Ubayd is making the certainty of the debt a condition in order to take it into consideration in waiving *zakat* or deducting the amount of the debt from assets subject to *zakat*. This is a sound position which protects the right of Allah and the poor.

Conditions of deductible debts

For debts to cause *zakat* to be completely waived, the amount of the debt should be large enough to cover all present assets, or at least bring them down below the *nisab*. For example, if the amount of debt is ten dinars and the taxable person has thirty dinars, then what is left after the debt is deducted is still *nisab*, which is subject to *zakat*. But if the amount of debt is more than ten dinars, then this person is not liable for *zakat*.[3]

As for deferred or immediate debts – debts that are due in either a long or short period – it seems that it makes no difference from the point of view of *zakat* whether debts are deferred or immediate. The selected view is that all debts, immediate and deferred are deductible from assets subject to *zakat*. Some scholars, however,

1. Ibid., p. 511.
2. Ibid.
3. *Al-Mughni*, vol. 3, p. 43.

hold to the view that deferred debts are not deductible.[1] One of the common deferred debts could be part of the wife's dowry that is deferred until death or divorce. Some scholars argue that this deferred *mahr* is not deductible, while others consider it deductible like other debts.[2] Alimony due to a wife and held as debt on the husband by court order, or relatives whose support is an obligation, are deductible debts.[3]

There is a discussion also about debts that belong to Allah and debts that belong to human beings. An-Nawawi, a Shafi'i, says if debts are deductible, then this applies to all debts, whether they are Allah's or a person's.[4] Hanafis say only debts to people are deductible because people seek payment and are protected by the judicial system. Debts to Allah, such as pledges and *kaffarat* [recompense for a violation of some religious obligation such as fasting] are not deductible. It should be noted, however, that past due *zakat* is considered like debts to other people. It is deductible because the state is authorised to collect it on behalf of the recipients.[5]

I agree with the view of the Hanafis on this issue; if the Islamic state takes the responsibility of collecting *zakat*, this rule shuts the door on false claims of pledges to Allah and *kaffarat* made in order to reduce the amount of *zakat* since there are no accessible means of verifying those pledges and *kaffarat*. if the state does not collect *zakat* and individual Muslims pay *zakat* on their own and make their own calculations, these debts to Allah can be deducted and paid before *zakat*. because the texts are general, such as the *hadith*, "The debt to Allah has priority in payment." (al-Bukhari)

The passage of a year

Twelve full lunar months should pass from the beginning of ownership, or past the due date of *zakat* for *zakat* to accrue again

1. Ibid.
2. *Al-Bahr ar-Ra'iq*, vol. 2, p. 219.
3. Ibid.
4. *Al-Majmu'*, vol. 5, p. 345.
5. *Al-Mughni*, vol. 3, p. 45. See also *al-Hidaya* and its commentaries, vol. 1, pp. 436-437.

on assets. This condition is restricted to livestock, money and business assets. It does not apply to crops, fruits, honey, extracted mineral, treasure, etc., where there is no condition of one year on the grounds that *zakat* on those items is a sort of *zakat* on income.

The value of this condition for certain assets

Ibn Qudama expresses his opinion on the essence of the distinction between zakatable items as far as the passage of a year is concerned. "Items where the passage of a year is considered are those designated for growth, such as business assets, or as storage of value, such of money, because it is of the nature of being used for growth, so that *zakat* would be paid at the end of each year out of their profits and income. As for crops and fruits, they themselves are the income, and *zakat* is taken out of them. Once they are produced they obviously do not grow. Extracted minerals are considered similar to plants and fruits."[1]

Reasons for this condition

Ibn Rushd states,[2] "The majority of jurists believe that this condition is required for *zakat* on gold, silver, and livestock. It is confirmed that the four khalifs applied this condition, and it is commonly known among the Companions, which means that all these people would not agree on such a matter without knowing that the Prophet (p) had said something about it. It is reported from Ibn 'Umar that the Prophet (p) said, 'There is no *zakat* on an asset until a year has passed.'"[3] This is agreed upon among jurists in all coun-

1 *Al-Mughni*, vol. 1, p. 625.

2. *Bidayat al-Mujtahid*, vol. 2, pp. 261-262.

3. Ibn Hajar in *at-Talkhis,* p. 175, "This saying is reported by ad-Daraqutni and al-Bayhaqi from Ibn 'Umar. Its chain contains Isma'il ibn 'Ayyash, whose narration from other than people of Syria is weak. Some narrators report the same as a statement made by Ibn 'Umar, and not linked to the Prophet. Ad-Daraqutni in *al-'Ilal* views the non-linked version as correct. The saying, however, is unanimously graded as weak. Variation on this issue is known since the time of the Companions and Followers. This is stated by Ibn Rushd from Ibn 'Abbas and Mu'awiya in correct reports. The report from Ibn Mas'ud is also correct.

tries, and there is no dispute about it in the Companions' generation except for a report from Ibn 'Abbas and Mu'awiya. It seems that the reason for that exception is the lack of an authentic *hadith*.[1]

Variations among the Companions and Followers on this condition

Ibn Mas'ud, Ibn 'Abbas and Mu'awiya are reported to hold the view that *zakat* is due on assets when acquired, without requiring the passage of a year. These Companions, along with a few Followers, departed from others on the issue of acquired *mal*, and believed that it was subject to *zakat* when acquired if it reaches the *nisab* on its own, or after being added to what was in the owner's possession before it was acquired.[2] Ibn Rushd explains this difference on the grounds that no *hadith* is authentically reported on this issue. This seems to be a correct judgement as will be seen later.

What is agreed upon about the passage of a year

There is no disagreement among scholars, both the *Salaf* and later scholars, that *zakat* on capital assets such as livestock, money, and business inventory, is required only once a year. Ibn Abi Shayba reports from az-Zuhri, "Nothing has reached us from any scholar or commissioner of this community who was in Madina – Abu Bakr, 'Umar and 'Uthman – to the effect that they collected *zakat* twice. They sent collectors every year, fertile or barren. Collecting it this way is the tradition of the Messenger of Allah."[3]

This shows the justice of the Islamic *Shari'a*. The periodicity of *zakat* is not left to rulers and governments to impose at will, or to the desire and miserliness of individuals. The year is considered the pattern of repetition because it is the cycle of all seasons, and it is long enough for growth and profitability to accrue.[4] Ibn al-Qayyim

1. *Bidayat al-Mujtahid*, op. cit.

2. *Al-Muhalla*, vol. 6, pp. 82-83; *Nayl al-Awtar*, vol. 4, p. 143, *ar-Rawd an-Nadir*, vol. 2, pp. 411-412, and *Subul as-Salam*, vol. 2, p. 129.

3. *Kanz al-'Umma*, vol. 6, p. 296, which also reports similar statements from ash-Shafi'i and al-Bayhaqi in *as-Sunan* as a narration from az-Zuhri.

4. *Bidayat al-Mujahid*, vol. 1, pp. 261-262.

says about the guidance received from the Messenger (p) on *zakat*, "He [the Prophet] obliged it once every year. He made the time of accrual of *zakat* on crops and fruits the time of ripening and harvest. *Zakat* is an expression of the utmost justice, because had it been obliged every month or every week, it would have heavily burdened the rich, but if it were made once in a lifetime, it would not have satisfied the needs of the indigent. The best way was to make it once every year."[1]

Variation on the issue of accrued assets

Accrued assets or goods include regular income, periodical salaries and wages, grants, windfall profits, gifts, etc. Some of those accrued goods, such as crops, fruits, honey, treasure trove, and extracted minerals, are subject to *zakat* once acquired if they meet the amount of *nisab*. That much is not disputed. There is, however, a difference of opinion on the *zakat* of capital assets, like money, business inventory, and livestock that are acquired during the year. Is *zakat* due on them at the time they come into one's possession? On this we should present some details mentioned by Ibn Qudama in *al-Mughni* which distinguishes between three cases:

- If acquired assets are the result of already owned capital, such as profit on business assets and the offspring of already owned livestock, *zakat* is due on them. This income should be added to the original assets in calculating *zakat*. Ibn Qudama says, "I am aware of no dispute on this. It goes by the year of its principal and it is like continuous growth, such as the increase in the value of inventory."[2]
- The second case is when the accrued asset is not of the same kind of capital a person already owns such as a person who owns the *nisab* of camels and is given a gift of cows. According to the majority of scholars, this acquired asset is not added to the capital he or she owns, but rather starts a new year and a new *nisab* of its own. If it is below the *nisab*, the new asset is

1. *Zad al-Ma'ad*, vol. 1, p. 307.
2. *Al-Mughni*, vol. 2, p. 625.

not subject to *zakat*. There is, however, a report from Ibn Mas'ud, Ibn 'Abbas and Mu'awiya that *zakat* is due on it once it is acquired. Ahmad says that *zakat* should be taken upon receipt. Ahmad reports via his own chain from Ibn Mas'ud, "'Abdullah used to deduct *zakat* when he gave us the grants." Al-Awza'i is reported as saying about the case of a person who sells his home or slave, "He should pay *zakat* on the price once he receives the money, unless he has already established an accounting month for payment of *zakat*, in which case he may delay payment until the last month of his accounting year.[1] Supporting evidence for this opinion shall be presented later in the section on *zakat* on salaries.

• The third case is if the acquired asset is the same kind as already owned assets that have reached the *nisab*, and have started the *zakat* year, but acquiring the new assets is independent of the already-owned assets. For example, someone owns forty sheep and during the year he purchases or is given as a present another twenty. *Zakat* is not due on those sheep in that year according to Ahmad and ash-Shafi'i. Abu Hanifa says that it should be added to what he already owns and *zakat* is due on the total at the end of the *zakat* year, except in the case when this new asset is obtained merely in exchange for an older one that *zakat* has already been paid on. He adds that letting the acquired *mal* have a separate time for *zakat* would cause accounting and collection difficulties, all of which should be avoided in accordance with the *ayat*, *"... He has not placed any constraint on you in the* deen*."* (22:78)

The *Shari'a* always considers the removal of difficulties, such as in the case of taking one sheep on each five camels because a camel is indivisible. Adding profits to original capital in *zakat* is of the same case. Malik agrees with Abu Hanifa in the case of pastured livestock, while in money he tends to agree with Ahmad and ash-Shafi'i because according to him, the above-mentioned difficulty does not arise.[2] The author of *al-Mughni*

1. Ibid.
2. *Al-Mughni*, vol. 2, p. 617.

argues against the Hanafi point of view, but it seems that the latter is definitely simpler in application and much less complicated, and for that reason I tend to agree with it.

Chapter Two

Zakat on Livestock

The animal kingdom has many species. Mankind has made use of only a few of them. These are what are known by the Arabs as *al-an'am*. Camels, cows, buffalo, sheep, goats, are all part of what Allah bestowed on His servants. Their benefits are mentioned in several places in His Holy Book. In *Surat an-Nahl* (sometimes called *Surat an-Na'am* (livestock), Allah says: *"And He created livestock. There is warmth for you in them, and various uses, and some you eat. And there is beauty in them for you in the evening when you bring them home and in the morning when you drive them out to graze. They carry your loads to lands you would never reach except with great difficulty. Your Lord is All-Gentle, Most Merciful."* (16:5-7) Also: *"There is instruction for you in cattle. From the contents of their bellies, from between the dung and blood, We give you pure milk to drink, easy for drinkers to swallow."* (16:66) And: *"Allah has made your houses resting places for you and made houses for you out of cattle hides which are light for you to carry, both when you are travelling and when you are staying in one place. And from their wool and fur and hair you obtain clothing and carpets and household utensils for a time."* (16:80)

And we read in *Surat Yasin*: *"Have they not seen how We created for them, by Our own handiwork, livestock which are under their control? We have made them tame for them and some they ride and some they eat. And they have other uses in them and milk to drink. So will they not show thanks?"* (36:71-73) Allah fashioned this livestock for mankind, and He subjects them to humans to ride and to make use of their skin and hair. It is not surprising that Allah asks people to be thankful.

The most obvious and practical means of expressing the gratitude urged by the Qur'an and the *Sunna* of the Prophet (p) is the obligation of *zakat*. Its *nisab* and rates are determined, collectors are sent every year to livestock owners, and warning is given to those who refuse to pay it. Livestock, especially camels, were the most useful asset for the Arabs at the time of the Prophet (p). Consequently, the *Sunna* determined their *nisab* and rates very clearly. In many countries today, especially Muslim countries, livestock still represents one of the most important national assets and sources of income. The following sections attempt to provide a full account of *zakat* on livestock.

Section One: General conditions for *zakat* on livestock

Zakat is not imposed on livestock of all quantities and kinds. There are certain conditions that should be fulfilled for the *zakat* of livestock which are enumerated here:

The minimum for *zakat* (*nisab*)

The first condition is the *nisab*, since *zakat* is only for the rich and not every owner of livestock is rich. There must always be a limit above which people are considered rich. This limit is the *nisab*. By the unanimous agreement of the Muslims for centuries it is five camels. *Zakat* is not obliged on anything less than five camels. The unanimous *nisab* for sheep is forty sheep. The *nisab* is determined by the *hadiths* of the Prophet (p), his actual practice, and the application of his successors. The *nisab* for cows varies from five, to thirty, to fifty, depending on the school of jurisprudence one adopts.

The passage of a year

It is reported authentically from the Prophet (p) and his successors that they used to send *zakat* collectors once a year to take account of livestock. It was shown in the previous chapter that the condition of the passage of one full lunar year for non-earned assets is accepted unanimously. One can add here that the majority who posit this condition on earned income do not require it on the offspring of livestock that result from reproduction during the year, and accept the *zakat* for offspring to be that of their mothers.

Natural pasturage

Pastured livestock are those that are grazed on natural and cost-free pasture land during the major part of the year for the purpose of breeding, milking and putting on weight.[1] The opposite of natural grazing is buying feed.

This condition is satisfied if livestock is pastured naturally most of the year. The pasturing should be for the purpose of growth, reproduction and milking: thus if it is for the purpose of personal riding or eating, the animals concerned are not subject to *zakat*, since such allocation removes animals from being growth assets and puts them in the category of personal use which is not liable to *zakat* as shall he shown in the next sub-section.

The reason for this condition is that *zakat* is obliged on the surplus, on what is easy for people to pay, in accordance with the verse, *"Take what is extra"* (7:199), and the verse, *"They will ask you what they should give away. Say, 'Whatever is surplus to your needs'"* (2:219), that is, on what does not cost much and grows rapidly. This can only be fulfilled if the animals are pastured cost-free, since artificially fed animals have a high cost, which makes it hard for people to give them away as *zakat*.

This condition is derived from what is reported by Ahmad, an-Nasa'i, and Abu Dawud from Bahz ibn Hakim from his father from his grandfather, who said, "I heard the Messenger of Allah (p) saying about naturally (cost-free) pastured camels, for each forty, there is one as *zakat* ..." This saying is judged to be sound by a group of leading scholars. The adjective "naturally pastured" here implies that artificially-fed camels are not subject to *zakat*. Otherwise adding such an adjective becomes meaningless, and the Prophet (p) does not speak in vain. It is obvious from this *hadith* that camels characterised as naturally pastured are not the same as those that are

1. *Ad-Durr al-Mukhtar* and its commentary, *Radd al-Muhtar*, vol. 1, pp. 20-21.

not. Al-Khattabi comments, "When something may have either of two characteristics, and a ruling of the *Shari'a* is applied to one of them, then the opposite ruling applies to the other characteristic implicitly.[1] It is also accepted by scholars of the methodology of jurisprudence that giving a specific characteristic in a ruling implies that when the characteristic is absent the ruling does not apply,[2] i.e. camels fed by purchased feed are treated differently.

This saying is further supported by a report in the *sahih* collection of al-Bukhari and others from Anas that "If sheep are naturally pastured and reach 40 in number, there is one sheep as *zakat*." If the condition of natural free pasture is required on sheep, it should also be, by analogy, required on camels and cows, since there should be no distinction between them. *Hadiths* without such restriction should be taken with reference to those that came with the restriction of natural free grazing.

This is the opinion of the majority of scholars. Rabi'a, Malik and al-Layth differ on this point. They maintain that *zakat* is obligatory on manually-fed livestock the same way as it is on naturally pastured livestock, as implied by the *hadiths* that do not have the restriction. Their explanation of the restricting *hadiths* is that the words "natural or cost-free pasture" is a general description because this was a common adjective of livestock at the time of the Prophet (p).[3]

Livestock on which *zakat* is due does not include working animals

This is the fourth and last condition for *zakat* on livestock. It means that they should not be used for cultivation, carrying water or loads, or riding, etc. This condition only applies to cattle and camels. Abu 'Ubayd reports from 'Ali that "There is no *sadaqa* on working cattle." There is also a report that Jabir ibn 'Abdullah said, "Animals working in cultivation are not subject to *zakat*.[4] In his

1. *Ar-Rawd an-Nadir*, vol. 2, p. 399.
2. Ibid., p. 400.
3. Ibid. p. 399.
4. *Al-Amwal*, p. 380.

Sunan, Abu Dawud reports from Zuhayr, "We are told by Abu Ishaq from 'Asim ibn Damura and al-Harith from 'Ali (Zuhayr said, "I think it is from the Prophet") that he said, "Bring me one-fourth of a tenth," i.e. on each of forty dirhams one dirham..." and he continued, "...and there is nothing due on working animals." This is reported also by Ibn Abi Shayba linked to the Prophet (p), and by 'Abdu'r-Razzaq in his *Musannaf*, via ath-Thawri and Ma'mar, ending at 'Ali only.[1] Similar reports exist as coming from Ibrahim, Mujahid, az-Zuhri, 'Umar ibn 'Abdu'l-'Aziz and some other Followers.[2] It is also the view of Abu Hanifa, ath-Thawri, ash-Shafi'i and the Zaydis. It is the opinion of al-Layth as far as cows are concerned.

Two things support these narrations and this point of view. The first is the principle that *zakat* is not paid on assets designated for personal use and service, and by the same token livestock designated for cultivation or personal transportation should not be subject to *zakat*. It is apparent that such animals are not part of the assets invested for growth.[3] Secondly, the report of Abu 'Ubayd from az-Zuhri that *zakat* is not paid on cattle and camels used for carrying riders nor for cattle used for cultivation.[4] All these are like tools for agriculture. Sa'id ibn 'Abdu'l-'Aziz at-Tanukhi says, "Cattle used in cultivation are not subject to *zakat* because the *zakat* is taken from the grain produced, and it involves the work of cattle."[5] If animals used in the process of farming were to have *zakat* levied on them, *zakat* would then be double on agriculture; taken once on the means of production and again on the produce, as rightly stated by Abu 'Ubayd.

Malik disagrees with the majority on this ruling, and according to him *zakat* is obliged on cattle and camels, working or not, naturally pastured or not. When the view of Malik was mentioned to ath-Thawri, he replied, "I did not think that anyone would say that."[6] In fairness, one should add that some Maliki jurists lean

1. *Nasb ar-Rayah*, vol. 1, p. 360.
2. *Al-Amwal*, pp. 380-382, and *ar-Rawd an-Nadir*, vol. 2, p. 408.
3. *Ar-Rawd an-Nadir*, op cit.
4. *Al-Amwal*, p. 381.
5. Ibid., p. 382.
6. Ibid., p. 281.

toward the majority. Ibn Naji quotes Ibn 'Abdu's-Salam as saying, "In this regard, the view of the majority is the one that one feels more comfortable with." Abu 'Umar ibn 'Abdu'l-Barr shows that the Maliki view on working animals is in conflict with their position on jewellery designated for personal use; the latter is not subject to *zakat*, according to them.[1]

Section Two: *Zakat* on camels

The unanimous agreement of Muslims, as well as several correct traditions from the Messenger of Allah (p) and reports from his Companions indicate the *nisab* of camels and the rate of *zakat* on them are as follows:

Number of Camels	Amount Due as *Zakat*
5 - 9	1 sheep
10 - 14	2 sheep
15 -19	3 sheep
20 - 24	4 sheep
25 - 35	*bint makhlad* (female camel between 1 and 2 years old)
36 - 45	*bint labun* (female camel between 2 and 3 years old)
46 - 60	*hiqqa* (female camel between 3 and 4 years old)
61 - 75	*jadh'a* (female camel between 4 and 5 years old)
76- 90	2 *bint labun*
91 - 120	2 *hiqqa*

There is consensus on this schedule[2] except for a report from 'Ali that there are five sheep on 25 camels and one *bint makhlad* on

1. Ibn Naji, *Sharh ar-Risala*, vol. 1, p. 339.

2. This *ijma'* is quoted by Ibn al-Mundhir and an-Nawawi in *al-Majmu'*, vol. 5, p. 400, and also by Abu 'Ubayd in *al-Amwal*, 364-5, Ibn Qudama in *al-Mughni*,

26 camels.[1] Ibn al-Mundhir says, "The unanimity is not broken, because what is reported from 'Ali is not authentic. The *hadith* from Anas on those quantities and amounts is *sahih* and there is unanimous agreement on its content.[2] For more than 120 camels the majority view is that for each additional 50 camels, the *zakat* is a *hiqqa*, while for each additional 40 camels, the *zakat* is a *bint labun*.[3] This is shown in the following table:

Number of Camels	Amount Due as *Zakat*
121 - 129	3 *bint labun*
130 - 139	1 *hiqqa* and 1 *bint labun*
140 - 149	2 *hiqqa* and 1 *bint labun*
150 -159	3 *hiqqa*
160 - 169	4 *bint labun*
170 - 179	1 *hiqqa* and 3 *bint labun*
180 - 189	2 *hiqqa* and 2 *bint labun*
190 - 199	3 *hiqqa* and 1 *bint labun*
200 - 209	4 *hiqqa* or 5 *bint labun*

It is seen from the table that for the higher numbers, an increase of less than ten camels does not affect the amount of *zakat*. Once it is increased by ten, then you go one step higher in the amount of *zakat* due according to the same rule mentioned above. It is obvious from these two tables that if the number of camels owned is less than five then there is no *zakat*. Once they reach five the amount due is one sheep. The author of *al-Mabsut* quotes a scholar as saying, "This means that the value of the livestock is considered. Camels between one and two years old used to be priced at forty dirhams and a sheep at five dirhams, so five camels equalling 200 dirhams also equal 40 sheep. This implies that the minimum for

as-Sarakhsi in *al-Mabsut*, and by al-'Ayni. See *al-Mir'a*, vol. 3, p. 49.

1. *Al-Majmu'*, vol. 5, p. 400. An-Nawawi comments, "It is supported by a *hadith* from 'Asim ibn Damura from 'Ali, linked up to the Prophet (p), but its weakness is agreed upon."

2. Ibid.

3. The Hanafis, an-Nakha'i and ath-Thawri are exceptions, as will be shown.

zakat in camels, sheep, and silver is the same."[1] Ibn al-Humam in *al-Fath* and Ibn Nujaym in *al-Bahr* reply that there is a *hadith*, "Whoever is obliged to give as *zakat* a camel of a certain age group, but does not own any of that age, can pay in substitution on the average of ten dirhams for a sheep, if he does not have any. This is an explicit text that contradicts the explanation of as-Sarakhsi."[2] The *hadith* referred to is reported by Anas.

The *Shari'a* obliges sheep in place of camels when the number of camels liable for *zakat* is less than 25, although *zakat* is usually paid out of the same kind of assets as those on which the *zakat* is being levied . The obvious reason for this is that while the amount due is less than one camel, at the same time the *Shari'a* considers five camels a sufficient amount to consider one as rich. This represents a careful consideration of the interests of the poor by obliging *zakat* to be paid. The tables above are derived from the practice of the Messenger of Allah (p). An-Nawawi in *al-Majmu'* says that the quantities and amounts of *zakat* on livestock come from the *hadiths* narrated by Anas and Ibn 'Umar.[3]

Anas narrated that Abu Bakr wrote this message when he was sent to Bahrayn:

> "In the name of Allah, the Merciful, the Compassionate. This concerns the obligation of *zakat* which the Messenger of Allah (p) made obligatory for the Muslims and to which Allah commanded His Messenger. Any Muslim who is asked to pay the correct amount should pay it and anyone who is asked for more than that should not pay it. For twenty-four camels or less it is paid in sheep, one sheep for every five camels. From twenty-five to thirty-five, it is a one-year-old she-camel. From thirty-six to forty-five, it is a two-year-old she-camel. From forty-six to sixty, it is a three-year-old female fit for breeding. From sixty-one to seventy-five, it is a four-year-old she-camel. From seventy-six to ninety, it is two two-year-old she-camels. From ninety-one to one hundred and twenty, it is two three-

1. As-Sarakhsi in *al-Mabsut*, vol. 2, p. 150.
2 *Al-Bahr ar-Ra'iq*, vol. 2, p. 230 and *Fath al-Qadir*, vol. 1, p. 496.
3. *Al-Majmu'*, vol. 5, p. 382.

year-old she-camels fit for breeding. If there are more than one hundred and twenty, it is a two-year-old female for every forty and a three-year-old for every fifty. If someone has only four camels, he does not have to pay any *zakat* unless he wishes to. When the camels reach five in number a sheep is owed for them.

As for the *zakat* of grazing sheep, from forty to one hundred it is one sheep. If there are between one hundred and twenty and two hundred, it is two sheep. If there are between two hundred and three hundred it is three. If there are more than three hundred, it is one sheep for every hundred. If the man's flock is less than forty sheep, there is no *zakat* on them unless their owner wishes. For silver it is one-fortieth. If the amount is only one hundred and ninety dirhams, nothing is owed unless its owner wishes. If someone's *sadaqa* payment should be a one-year-old she-camel, which he does not have, while he does have a two-year-old she-camel, it should be accepted from him and the *zakat*-collector should give him twenty dirhams or two sheep in compensation. If he has no one-year-old she-camel but does have a two-year-old male camel, it should be accepted from him and he does not receive anything in compensation.

Anyone whose *zakat* is a four-year-old she-camel and who does not have one but does have a three-year-old she-camel, the three-year-old is accepted from him and he adds two sheep to it, if they are easily available to him, or alternatively twenty dirhams. Anyone whose *zakat* is a three-year-old she-camel and who does not have one, but does have a four-year-old she-camel, the four-year-old is accepted from him and the *zakat*-collector gives him twenty dirhams or two sheep. Anyone whose *zakat* is a three-year-old she-camel and who only has a two-year-old she-camel, the two-year-old is accepted from him and he adds two sheep or twenty dirhams. Anyone whose *zakat* is a two-year-old she-camel who has a three-year-old she-camel, it is accepted from him and the *zakat*-collector gives

> him twenty dirhams or two sheep. Anyone whose zakat is a two-year-old she-camel and who does not have one, but who does have a one-year-old she-camel, the one-year-old is accepted from him and he adds twenty dirhams or two sheep.[1] Neither an old animal, one with a defect nor a ram should be taken as *zakat* unless the *zaka*t-collector wishes to do so. The wealth of individuals should not be combined, nor shared wealth split up, merely because of the fear of having to pay (more) *zakat*.[2] If there are two equal partners, they pay in equal parts between them."

An-Nawawi says, "This letter is reported by al-Bukhari in his *Sahih* collection, scattered throughout the chapter on *zakat*. I put it back together."[3] It is also reported by Ahmad, Abu Dawud, an-

1. An-Nawawi says in al-*Majmu'*, vol. 5, p. 409, quoting al-Khattabi, "It seems that the Prophet (p) made two sheep or 20 dirhams equal the difference in one year of age for camels, because of the difficulty of going to court or for appraisers to determine the exact worth of different age camels in the remote places where *zakat* was collected on camels. The Prophet (p) did not want to leave this value for the *zakat* collector to decide. Al-Khattabi thinks that this estimation of two sheep or 20 dirhams is binding, like a religious rule. This is the opinion of ash-Shafi'i, Ahmad and the school of *hadith*. The author of *al-Fath* writes that it is reported from ath-Thawri that the difference is ten dirhams; a version is also reported from Ishaq. Ash-Shawkani quotes Zayd ibn 'Ali as saying, "The difference of one year of age equals the sheep or ten dirhams." According to Malik, the owner of camels is required to buy a camel of the necessary age to fulfil *zakat*, while according to Abu Hanifa, they should resort to evaluation. See *al-Fath*, vol. 4, p. 62, and *Nayl al-Awtar*, vol. 4, p. 109.

2. Ibn Hajar quotes Malik in *al-Muwatta'* as saying, "The meaning of this *hadith* is that if you have three people, each owning forty sheep, they are charged *zakat* to the amount of one sheep each, but if they add their herds together, there will be only the sheep due on the 120. Also, when two individuals together own 202 sheep, they are charged the amount of three sheep, but if they divide the herd into two halves, each of them is obliged to pay *zakat* to the amount of one sheep." According to this interpretation, this saying is addressed to the payer of *zakat*. Ash-Shafi'i, on the other hand, considers this saying addressed to both payers and collectors; each of them is ordered to neither combine or separate assets in order to influence the amount of *sadaqa*, the payer would be interested in reducing it, while the collectors would like to increase it. It seems more logical that the words of the sayings are addressed to the payer, but Allah knows best. See *al-Fath*, vol. 4, p. 26.

3. *Al-Majmu'*, vol. 5, p. 383.

Nasa'i, and ad-Daraqutni. The latter adds, "The chain is sound and the narrators are all trustworthy," as in *al-Muntaqa*.[1] Ash-Shawkani says, "It is also reported by ash-Shafi'i, al-Bayhaqi and al-Hakim. Ibn Hazm says this message is completely reliable. It is also graded *sahih* by Ibn Hibban and others.[2]

There is also a saying from Ibn 'Umar narrated by Sufyan ibn Husayn from az-Zuhri from Salim from his father, 'Abdullah ibn 'Umar: "The Messenger of Allah (p) wrote the message on *sadaqa*, but did not send it to his governors before he died. He tied it to his sword, and after he died, Abu Bakr applied it until he in turn died, and then 'Umar until he died. The letter contains, "For five camels there is one sheep due, for ten, two sheep ...", continuing with the same rates listed in the *hadith* from Anas. An-Nawawi said it is reported by Abu Dawud and at-Tirmidhi who grades it a *hasan hadith*.[3] Ash-Shawkani adds, "This *hadith* is reported also by ad-Daraqutni, al-Hakim and al-Bayhaqi."[4]

Ibn Hazm says in his commentary on the saying from Anas, "This *hadith* is completely sound."[5] Abu Bakr applied it in the pres-

1. *Nayl al-Awtar*, vol. 4, p. 107.
2. Ibid.
3. *Al-Majmu'*, vol. 5, p. 383-384.
4. *Nayl al-Awtar*, vol. 4, p. 112.
5. Ibn Hazm upholds that all narrators of this *hadith* are trustworthy and criticises the view of Yahya ibn Ma'in as weak, commenting, "The words of Yahya ibn Ma'in or others may be accepted when they tell about narrators who are not commonly reputed for their trustworthiness. But his claim that a *hadith* whose narrators are trustworthy is weak, unbacked by proof, is rejected for lack of evidence. Allah says, *'Say: Bring your proof if you are truthful.'*" See *al-Muhalla*, vol. 6, pp. 20-21. The affirmation of Ibn Hazm is accepted under two conditions. Firstly, that all narrators are well-reputed for their honesty and precision, and secondly that the *hadith* must not have a strong reason for being rejected. In the above-mentioned *hadith*, 'Abdullah ibn al-Muthanna is included in the chain, and he is disputed by critics. He is described once by Yahya ibn Ma'in as righteous, and once as "nothing". Abu Zur'a, Abu Hatim and al-'Ijli consider him a strong link, while an-Nasa'i says that he is not very reliable. Al-'Ijli comments, "Most of what he narrates has no witnessing chain (other chains supporting his narration)." Ibn Hajar says, "He is followed in this by Hammad ibn Salama, who narrates from Thumama that the latter gave the former a letter, claiming that Abu Bakr wrote it for Anas and it has the seal of the Messenger on it. This is the report by Ahmad in his *Musnad*, "I am informed by Abu Kamil, who was informed by Hammad, who said, 'I took this letter from Thumama ibn 'Abdullah ibn Anas, from Anas, that

ence of all the Companions, and none of them is known to have disagreed, although *ijma'* is usually claimed in cases of much less unanimity than this. The great majority of scholars of this nation have received these two messages with acceptance, and apply them practically, although some of the leading scholars of *hadith*, such as Yahya ibn Ma'in, hesitate to consider them *sahih*, in consistency with their special approach in scrutinising narrators and the links among them.

It seems that the orientalist Schacht abuses the stand of Ibn Ma'in in order to cast doubt on all the *hadiths* on *zakat* and the whole institution itself. He claims that the jurists' opinions on the issue have put their stamp on the *hadith* itself, and adds, "We note, in this respect, that the detailed system of *zakat* commonly attributed to Abu Bakr is sometimes attributed to the Prophet (p), to 'Umar ibn al-Khattab, or to 'Ali ibn Abi Talib. Schacht is known for his hostility towards the *hadiths* of the Prophet (p). Very often he fabricates reasons to shed doubt on them and to disorient the reader regarding them. In his books he collects all the misinterpretations and misleading statements and the fabrications and misrepresentations against the *Sunna*.

Praise be to Allah, my dear and respected colleague, Dr. Muhammad Mustafa al-'Azami, refuted these falsehoods in his extensive study on *hadith* in English which was submitted to Cambridge University as his PhD dissertation. To be fair and reasonable, the orientalists should have realised that it is extremely unlikely that the Prophet (p) would leave such an important issue as *zakat* on camels, sheep, etc. without determining its minimums and its rates, since this was where the majority of the wealth of the

Abu Bakr ...'" and he narrated the tradition. Ishaq writes in his *Musnad*, "An-Nadr ibn Shumayl told me that Hammad ibn Salama told him, 'I took this letter from Thumama, narrating it from Anas from the Prophet (p),' and he repeated the whole *hadith*." Ibn Hajar says, "It is obvious that Hammad heard it from Thumama and read the letter, so the claim that it was only transmitted in writing and the claim that 'Abdullah ibn al-Muthanna was not supported by other chains are both refuted." (See *Fath al-Bari*, Chapter on *Zakat*, section on *zakat* on sheep, vol. 4, p. 59.) This saying is also supported by the fact that it quotes a famous letter preserved by the descendants of Anas ibn Malik, sealed with the seal of the Messenger of Allah (p), and reported by al-Bukhari in his *Sahih* collection through a chain of the descendants of Anas.

Arabs at his time lay. *Zakat* collectors and governors were sent by him to oases and desert areas to collect and distribute *zakat* every year from the scattered tribes. There are many reports on the sending of those collectors and on the way they were instructed to treat individuals who owed *zakat*, on what to take, what not to take, what the response of cattle owners should be, and how they should treat the collectors. No impartial researcher could claim that all these *hadiths* are fabrications.

It is no surprise that the Prophet sent instructions determining *nisabs* and rates of *zakat* on cattle and other growing items of wealth that were most prevalent at his time and within his environment. This is attested to by the letters of Abu Bakr as well as those of 'Umar, and both of them are linked to the Prophet (p). It was shown in the previously quoted message of Abu Bakr that "This concerns the obligation of *zakat* which the Messenger of Allah (p) made obligatory for the Muslims ..." The letter written by 'Umar, as narrated by his son, 'Abdullah, reads, "Indeed the Messenger of Allah wrote the letter of instruction on *sadaqa*..." As for the letter of instruction of 'Ali ibn Abi Talib, there is no agreement among scholars about whether or not it can be conclusively linked to the Prophet (p). This letter in any event is not as well-known as the letters of Abu Bakr or 'Umar, nor is its chain of transmission as solid. It should be noted that these were not the only letters with instructions that provide details of *zakat* on livestock. There are several other letters, such as that of 'Amr ibn Hazm which was addressed to the people of Najran regarding the details of obligatory *zakat*, and amounts of compensation for accidental death or loss of limbs. We also have the message of Mu'adh that delineates *sadaqa* on cattle, and several other letters.

It is noteworthy that these instructions unanimously agree on certain major points:

- There is no *zakat* obliged on anything less than five camels.
- There is no *zakat* on any number of sheep less than forty.
- There is no *zakat* on less than 200 dirhams of silver.
- The amount of *zakat* obliged on less than 25 camels is calculated in sheep.

- *Zakat* on up to 25 camels is one sheep for every five camels.
- They agree on the ages and number of camels due as *zakat* on wealth of 25 to 120 camels.
- They also agree on the rate of *zakat* on sheep from 40 to 300, and that the rate afterwards is one for each 100.
- The rate on silver and silver money is one-forth of one-tenth.
- Neither damaged animals nor top quality animals are taken as *zakat*. What is required are animals of average quality.

Those instructions do not agree, however, on certain minute and secondary details such as the rate on camels after 120. The instructions of Abu Bakr put the rate at one she-camel two to three years old for each 40, and one she-camel three to four years old for each 50, while the instructions in the letters of ʻAli and ʻAmr ibn Hazm start again with the same rate as that between 5 and 125. Also, these instructions do not mention some other items of wealth, such as gold and cattle. It seems to me that this in itself provides some additional proof that these texts are rightly attributed to the Prophet (p) and that they were not influenced by the jurists' opinions as Schacht claims, because the Prophet (p) was writing practical instructions to different people according to their needs and circumstances. He did not mention gold because the Arabs of his time did not frequently use it and he did not mention cattle because they were not common in Madina. Only in his instructions to Muʻadh, who was being sent to Yemen, did the Prophet (p) mention cattle because they were common in Yemen.

Variations on the rates after 120 camels

It was mentioned earlier that there are varying views among jurists on *zakat* on more than 120 camels. Malik, ash-Shafiʻi, Ahmad and the majority consider the rate to be one three to four-year-old she-camel for each additional 50 and one two to three-year-old she-camel for each additional 40,[1] as mentioned in the

1. There is a slight difference on the quantity between 121 and 129. According to Malik, the collector has a choice between taking two three-year-old

letters of Abu Bakr and 'Umar narrated by Anas and Ibn 'Umar. The same also appears in the letters of Ibn Hazm and Ziyad ibn Labid to the people of Hadramawt,[1] in the words of the Prophet: "If they exceed 120, then for each 40 is one two to three-year-old she-camel, and for each 50 one three to four-year-old she-camel." Some versions of the last *hadith* are summarised by that narrator as "In each 50 one she-camel..." without mentioning the rate for each additional 40, but the different versions complete each other.

Abu Hanifa's view

An-Nakha'i, ath-Thawri and Abu Hanifa[2] say that "for what is above 120, we start the rates from the beginning, i.e. for an additional 5 to 24 camels, the rate is one sheep for each 5 camels, and for an additional 25 camels *zakat* due is one one to two year old she-camel, etc." The following table shows the amount due according to this opinion:

Number of Camels	**The Rate**			
	Hiqqa		**Sheep**	**Others**
125	2	+	1	
130	2	+	2	
135	2	+	3	

camels, or three two-year-old camels, while according to ash-Shafi'i it must be only three two-year-old camels. A third view given by Ibn al-Majishun, a disciple of Malik, is that the collector must only take two camels that are three or four years old. Once the camels reach 130, all agree on the rest of the table. See *Bidayat al-Mujtahid*, vol. 1, p. 221 and *Bulghat as-Salik* with commentary, vol. 1, p. 208, and *al-Mir'a,* vol. 3, pp. 49-50.

1. Az-Zayla'i, in *Nasb ar-Rayah*, gives a full account of these letters, vol. 2, pp. 335-45. The first three are reported by ad-Daraqutni, pp. 208-210, al-Hakim in *al-Mustadrak*, vol. 1, pp. 390-397, and al-Bayhaqi in his *Sunan*, vol. 4, pp. 85-92. See *al-Mir'a*, commentary on *al-Mishkat, vol.* 3, p. 50.

2. It is also narrated by al-Mahdi in al-Bahr from 'Ali, Ibn Mas'ud, Hammad, al-Hadi, Abu Talib, al-Mu'ayyad bi'llah, and Abu'l-'Abbas. See *Nayl al-Awtar*, vol. 4, p. 109, *al-Majmu'*, vol. 5, p. 400, *al-Hidaya*, with commentary, vol. 1, p. 495 and afterword, and *ad-Durr al-Mukhtar* with its commentary, *Radd al-Muhtar*, vol. 2, pp. 22-23.

Number of Camels	**The Rate**			
	Hiqqa		**Sheep**	**Others**
140	2	+	4	
145	2	+	0	1 *bint makhlad*
150	3	+	0	
155	3	+	1	
160	3	+	2	
165	3	+	3	
170	3	+	4	
175	3	+	0	1 *bint makhlad*
186	3	+	0	1 *bint labun*
196	4			
200	5			or 5 *bint labun*

After 200 the rate repeats again, one sheep for each additional 5 camels, and each time the additional zakatable camels reach 50, the amount of *zakat* due is one three to four-year-old she-camel.

The Hanafis argue that Abu Dawud reports as *mursal*, Ishaq in his *Musnad* and at-Tahawi in his *Mushkil* from Hammad ibn Salama who said, "I told Qays ibn Sa'd to get me the message of Muhammad ibn Hazm, so he gave me a letter which he said that the Prophet (p) wrote to my grandfather. I read it and found it contained the rates of *zakat* on camels..." and he narrated the saying until "Once they exceed 120, make due on each 50 one *hiqqa*. For the increments, restart the rates from the beginning, and for what is less than 25 camel increments, the amount of *zakat* is due in sheep, one sheep for each five." This is reported in *Nasb ar-Rayah* by az-Zayla'i.[1] A similar version is narrated by 'Asim ibn Damura from 'Ali, linked to the Prophet (p) as well as ending at 'Ali,[2] and Ibn Mas'ud is reported to have said similar things. The Hanafis are said by Ibn Rushd to have argued that such a thing

1. *Al-Mir'a*, vol. 3, p. 51, *as-Sunan al-Kubra*, vol. 4, p. 94, and its commentary by Ibn at-Turkumani, and *al-Muhalla*, vol. 6, pp. 33-34, with commentary of Ahmad Shakir, pp. 34 & 36.

2. See *as-Sunan al-Kubra*, vol. 4, pp. 93-94, *al-Muhalla*, vol. 6, pp. 38-39, and *al-Mir'a*, vol. 3, p. 52.

cannot be decided but by instructions from the Prophet (p), because it is not a thing that can be deduced by analogy.[1]

The majority of scholars disapprove of the arguments of the Hanafis and see weakness in their findings. Al-Bayhaqi shows that whatever is reported from Ibn Mas'ud in this matter is not correct.[2] The version of the *hadith* of 'Ali which is linked to the Prophet (p) is also incorrect, and there are also differing opinions on the version that is attributed to 'Ali. In one version, it is reported in a consistent manner with the letters of Abu Bakr and 'Umar, while in another version it is reported differently. The usual rule applicable in such a case is that we give more weight to the version that is consistent with other correct *hadiths* which are not disputed. This was noted by al-Hazimi.[3] Moreover, the same version of the *hadith* from 'Asim contains a number of points that scholars agree to disregard because of their unreliability. For example, one statement that reads that for each 25 camels the *zakat* due is five sheep instead of a *bint makhlad*. At the same time, it is possible to interpret differing versions in a way that makes them consistent with other correct *hadiths*.

As for the saying of Ibn Hazm, some scholars interpret the starting over of the rates as a reference to the calculation of the rates on 40 or 50 camels as mentioned in the two *hadiths* of Abu Bakr and 'Umar.[4] However, the majority of scholars are of the opinion that this version is weak for the following reasons:

- It contradicts what came correctly in an exact *hadith* from Anas.
- It is in opposition to other versions of the same *hadith*, and those other versions are consistent with the two letters of Abu Bakr and 'Umar. Those other versions are sustained by al-Bayhaqi and others.[5]
- This differing version is not consistent with the general rule in *zakat* collection, that *zakat* is due in the same kind of assets as

1. *Bidayat al-Mujtahid*, vol. 1, p. 222.
2. *Al-Mir'a,* vol. 3, p. 52 and *al-Muhalla*, vol. 6, pp. 42.
3. *Ibid.*
4. *Nayl al-Awtar*, vol. 4, p. 109 and *al-Muhalla*, vol. 6, pp. 37-38.
5. *As-Sunan al-Kubra*, vol. 4. pp. 89-90.

> those on which the *zakat* is being levied except when nothing else is possible. The case of camels below 25 is an obvious necessity, but it is not necessary to take sheep when the number of zakatable camels is above 120. Another inconsistency in this version is that the increase of five camels (from 145 to 150) requires an increase in *zakat* from a *bint makhlad* to a *hiqqa*, which is a large increase.

Other scholars consider the report of Ibn Hazm to be superseded by those of Abu Bakr and 'Umar. Ibn Taymiyya supports this last view on the basis that Ibn Hazm was given these instructions when he was appointed governor of Najran, some time before the death of the Prophet (p), while the message of Abu Bakr was written by the Prophet (p), just before he died, and since he did not have a chance to send it to his governors it was sent by Abu Bakr after he succeeded him.[1] Thus it seems that Ibn Taymiyya goes along with those who consider the instructions of Ibn Hazm annulled by the later instructions of Abu Bakr and 'Umar, since it is known that Ibn Hazm's instructions preceded the latter.

The majority view, including Ahmad, ash-Shafi'i, and al-Awza'i, is much stronger and better supported by proofs than that of the Hanafis. Some fair-minded Hanafis even give more weight to the majority view, such as the later 'Abdu'l-'Ali, known as the "Ocean of Knowledge", al-Luknawi, from India. In his *Rasa'il al-Arkan al-Arba'a*, pp. 170-171, he says, "What seems to be stronger is the view of ash-Shafi'i and Ahmad."[2]

The view of at-Tabari

Abu Ja'far at-Tabari expresses a third, reconciling view, stating that both opinions are acceptable, and it is up to those responsible for *zakat* collection to select which view to apply.[3] In my opinion, this is a better approach, since one should not consider the content of any *hadith* superseded and annulled if there is the slightest chance of a reconciliation between the reports from the Prophet (p). The

1. *Al-Qawa'id an-Nuraniyya*, p. 87.
2. *Al-Mir'a*, vol. 3, p. 51.
3. *Al-Majmu'*, vol. 5, pp. 400-401.

reconciliation proposed by at-Tabari is undoubtedly acceptable if we keep in mind that the determination of ages and quantity of camels due as *zakat* is meant to facilitate *zakat* calculation, payment, and collection, and to reduce the procedures so that the untangled freedom of the *zakat* agency enhances its activities.

The slight difference in the letters on *zakat*

Looking at the different versions of letters on *zakat* reported from the Messenger of Allah (p) and his Rightly-guided Khalifs, one finds some minor differences. An example is whether the difference in value between different aged camels is ten dirhams (or two sheep) or twenty dirhams (or two sheep).[1] How can the difference between the letter of 'Ali and those of Abu Bakr and 'Umar be explained? It is known that the report of 'Ali is incorrectly linked to the Prophet (p). It is known to be a saying of 'Ali himself. How could 'Ali differ from the letter of the Prophet (p)? How could he, who lived in the era of Abu Bakr and 'Umar, not be aware of their letters and application? Did he believe that he had information which superseded that contained in the other letters? If so, why did he not mention it in their time?

In my opinion all these questions are answered negatively and it seems to be that another interpretation of these minor differences must be offered. I believe that some of these equalities, like the value of sheep in silver, are given by the Prophet (p) in his capacity as head of state. Their prices at his time were such that a sheep was worth approximately ten dirhams. It is known that prices vary from time to time, and when the Prophet (p) gave a ratio as twenty dirhams for two sheep, he was quoting his period's current prices. At the time of 'Ali's caliphate, prices of sheep were different, and his quotation of those prices were ten dirhams for two sheep.

This is not a violation of the Prophet's *hadiths*, but rather an application of the rule used by the Prophet (p) as to the suitability of the time. This interpretation is, in my opinion, better than any attempt to disregard the differing texts, as Yahya ibn Ma'in did in claiming that nothing was correctly reported on the determination

1. *Al-Muhalla*, vol. 6, p. 39.

of rates and quantities of *zakat*,[1] Ibn Hazm rejected such a claim and questioned how a person like Ibn Ma'in could state such a thing without even the slightest supporting evidence.[2] An orientalist like Schacht abuses to the utmost that claim in his attempt to reject all the correct *hadiths* about *zakat*.

Section Three: *Zakat* on cattle

Cattle, used by mankind for land cultivation, meat and milk, are another gift from Allah to His servants. The usefulness of this animal was so great at times that some people, such as the ancient Egyptians and modern Hindus, have worshipped it. The buffalo is considered as a cow by all Muslim jurists, as stated by Ibn al-Mundhir.[3]

Zakat on cattle is made obligatory by *Sunna* and *ijma'*. Al-Bukhari, in his *Sahih* collection, reports from Abu Dharr, "I came to the Prophet (p)[4] and he said, 'I swear by He who holds my soul in His hand,' or 'I swear by the One beside whom there is no God, every man who has camels, cattle or sheep whose due is not paid will be presented with them on the Day of Rising larger and fatter than they were and they will trample him with their hooves and gore him with their horns. Every time the last one leaves him the first comes back again, until all the judgements between people are decided.'"

Imam al-Bukhari said, "It is narrated by Bakir from Abu Salih from Abu Hurayra from the Prophet (p). The "due" mentioned in the *hadith* means *zakat* before any other thing. *Zakat* is the right due on wealth as defined by Abu Bakr at the time of fighting those

1. Ibn Hajar, *at-Takhlis*, p. 143.
2. *Al-Muhalla*, vol. 6, p. 21.
3. *Al-Mughni*, vol. 2, p. 594.
4. This is the way it is recorded in al-Bukhari with the commentary by al-Qastallani, whereas in the version which has the commentary of Ibn Hajar, it reads as follows: He said, "I came to him, i.e. al-Ma'rur talked about Abu Dharr, which implies the *hadith* ends at Abu Dharr [and it is not linked to the Prophet (p). However, it is confirmed by Muslim and al-Bukhari himself that the *hadith* is linked to the Prophet (p). See *al-Fath*, vol. 4, pp. 66-67.

who rejected *zakat* and this definition was approved by 'Umar and all other Companions (reported by al-Bukhari and Muslim). In the version reported by Muslim the word "*zakat*" is used in place of the word "due". Moreover, Muslims through all generations have unanimously confirmed that *zakat* is obliged on cattle. Not a single scholar disagrees.[1] There are, however, differences in determining *nisab* and *zakat* rates on cattle.

Nisab and rates of *zakat* for cattle

There is no *sahih hadith* that provides us with the *nisab* and rates of *zakat* for cattle as we have seen for camels. This may be because cattle were rare in the Hijaz. It may also be because cattle are close in size and value to camels, so the Prophet (p) did not determine their rates on the assumption of their obvious similarity. But the fact that there is no *sahih hadith* on the issue left the jurists with varying views on the determination of *nisab* and rates.

The popular opinion: the *nisab* is 30 cows

The reputed position upheld by the four schools of jurisprudence is that the *nisab* is 30 cows, and there is no *zakat* obliged on less than 30 cows. For 30 cows, a one-year-old cow is due, and for 40-59 cows there is one two year-old-cow. For 60 cows, two one-year-old cows are due; for 70 cows, a one-year-old and a two-year-old; for 80 cows, two two-year-olds; for 90 cows, three one-year-olds; for 100 cows, one two-year-old and two one-year-olds; for 110, two two-year-olds and one one-year-old, and for 120 cows, three two-year-olds or four one-year-olds.

This opinion relies on the *hadith* reported by Ahmad and the four books of Sunan (at-Tirmidhi, an-Nasa'i, Abu Dawud and Ibn Majah) from Masruq from Mu'adh ibn Jabal who said, "The Messenger of Allah (p) sent me to Yemen. He instructed me to collect a one-year-old cow on each 30 cows and one two-year-old on each 40 cows."[2] This tradition is rated *hasan* by at-Tirmidhi and

1. *Al-Mughni*, vol. 2, p. 591, and *al-Amwal*, p. 379.
2. *Al-Mughni*, with commentary, vol. 2, p. 462.

sahih by Ibn Hibban and al-Hakim. Ibn 'Abdu'l-Barr comments, "Its chain is correct, continuous and authentic," and a similar statement is made by Ibn Battal. Ibn Hajar said in *al-Fath*, "We need to scrutinise any ruling about the correctness of this saying, because Masruq did not meet Mu'adh." At-Tirmidhi considers it *hasan* because there are other *hadiths* that testify with it, such as the one in *al-Muwatta'* from Tawus from Mu'adh, but Tawus did not meet Mu'adh either.[1] Abu Dawud has a similar saying from 'Ali.[2]

Ibn al-Qattan comments on the narration of Masruq from Mu'adh, "It is probable; it should be considered connected in accordance with the majority view."[3] Ibn Hazm first considered this *hadith* weak on the ground that Masruq did not meet Mu'adh, but he later corrected himself and said, "I found that Masruq merely mentioned the practice of Mu'adh in Yemen regarding *zakat* on cows; there is no doubt that he lived in Mu'adh's era, witnessed his governorship, and recognised his well-known practices. Consequently his quotation of Mu'adh is accepted, because he is quoting many people that witnessed the same practice, a practice that reflected the instructions of the Messenger of Allah (p), so we must accept that report.[4]

1. Ash-Shafi'i says, "Tawus was well aware of Mu'adh's action, even though he did not meet him, because he met many people who knew Mu'adh." This is not, to the best of my knowledge, disputed by anyone. Al-Bayhaqi says, "Tawus did not meet Mu'adh, but as a Yemeni he was very familiar with details about the biography of Mu'adh, which is commonly known in Yemen. (See *al-Mir'a*, vol. 3, p. 71.

2. *Al-Fath*, vol. 4, pp. 65-66, *Nayl al-Awtar*, vol. 4, p. 132, *Nasb ar-Rayah*, vol. 2, p. 346, and afterward. This saying has support from other than 'Ali. Among them are reports from Ibn Mas'ud, Ibn 'Abbas, and Anas, and also the long report from 'Amr ibn Hazm. See *Sunan al-Bayhaqi*, vol. 4, pp. 98-99, and *al-Mir'a*, vol. 3, p. 71.

3. Because according to the majority of critics, it is not necessary that a report must exist to the effect that a narrator met the person from whom he narrates. Information about them being contemporaries and having the possibility of having met together is sufficient. See *Nayl al-Awtar*, ibid., and *al-Mir'a*, ibid. On the other hand, al-Bukhari, along with his teacher, Ibn al-Madini, require the knowledge that narrators met at least once. This is the reason why al-Bukhari does not report in his *Sahih* collection anything about the *nisab* of cattle. This is quoted by Ibn Hajar from Zayn ibn al-Munir. See *al-Fath*, vol. 4, p. 65.

4. *Al-Muhalla*, vol. 6, p. 16.

In *at-Talkhis*, Ibn Hajar quotes Ibn 'Abdu'l-Barr from the latter's *al-Istidhkar*, "There is dispute among scholars that the tradition concerning *zakat* on cattle is what exists in the report from Mu'adh. That is the agreed upon *nisab*."[1] The report of Mu'adh is supported by the letter of the Prophet (p) to 'Amr ibn Hazm, which says, "On each 30 cows and one two-year-old on each 40 cows." Several scholars of *hadith* consider this last one good. (*Sunan al-Bayhaqi*)

It should be noted, however, that neither of these sayings explicitly set the minimum for *zakat* at 30, and that their wording does not preclude the possibility of imposing *zakat* on less than 30 cattle. Thus any claim of *ijma'* like that of Ibn 'Abdu'l-Barr is rejected, because it is known that Ibn al-Musayyab, az-Zuhri, Abu Qilaba, at-Tabari and others disagree, as will be shown later. Ibn Hajar quotes 'Abdu'l-Haqq as saying, "There is no saying about *nisab* of cattle on whose correctness there is agreement."[2]

The saying of Mu'adh also indicates that there is no additional *zakat* on between 40 and 59 cattle, and this is also supported by the report that Mu'adh was brought additional *zakat* on cattle and refused to take it on this number, as mentioned in *al-Muwatta'* and other works. This is the opinion of the three schools of jurisprudence, Abu Yusuf, Muhammad ash-Shaybani, and the majority of scholars. Abu Hanifa disagrees and expresses the view that what is above 40 cattle is liable for *zakat* at the rate of two and a half percent of the price of a two-year-old cow for each additional cow above 40. Al-Hasan has another report from Abu Hanifa that additional amounts of *zakat* are due only when the number reaches 50, whereby one two-year-old cow and one quarter of that becomes the due *zakat*. There is yet a third report from Abu Hanifa that goes along with the majority view.[3]

The view of at-Tabari that the *nisab* is 50

At-Tabari argues that *nisab* must be 50 cows, that it is undoubtedly unanimous that for each 50 cows there is an obligatory *zakat*

1. *Nayl al-Awtar*, op. cit.
2. *Nayl al-Awtar*, op. cit., and *at-Talkhis*, p. 174.
3. *al-Mir'a*, vol. 3, p. 70.

of one cow. Anything below 50 is controversial and not supported by any clear text.[1] Ibn Hazm in *al-Muhalla* supports this opinion on the same grounds as at-Tabari. He comments, "Anything that is controversial and on which there is no text making it obligatory must not be imposed on people, because it means confiscating a part of a Muslim's wealth without being certain of its requirement by virtue of a correct text from Allah or His Messenger.[2] He went on to quote, through his own chain, from 'Amr ibn Dinar, "The governors of Ibn az-Zubayr as well as ibn 'Awf[3] used to collect one cow from each 50 cattle, two cows from every 100, and for more than that, the rate was one cow out of each 50.[4] These governors were performing their duties in the presence of many, many Companions and this performance was not objected to." But one may disprove this opinion on two grounds:

- From the point of view of the text. The long *hadith* of 'Amr ibn Hazm on *zakat* says, "take one one-year-old cow from each 30 cows and one cow from each 40." This is graded as *hasan* by a handful of leading scholars and it was used by at-Tabari against the view of Ibn Daqiq al-'Id in his book, *al-Imam*.[5] Additionally, the saying of Mu'adh according to which *zakat* should be collected on 30 and 40 cattle is graded *sahih* by a group of leading scholars. It is by virtue of this saying that Ibn Hazm corrected himself and reverted to the view of the majority.[6]
- From the point of view of the rationale. It is very unlikely that the *Shari'a*, which is most just and wise, would oblige *zakat* on only five camels or 40 sheep and leave the minimum for *zakat* on cattle to be 50. Cattle may not be as large as camels, but they are certainly larger, more useful and more valuable than sheep.

1. Mentioned by Ibn Hajar in *at-Takhlis*, p. 174.
2. *Al-Muhalla*, vol. 6, p. 16.
3. He is Talha ibn 'Abdullah ibn 'Awf, cousin of 'Abdu'r-Rahman ibn 'Awf, and was one of the leading Followers in Madina according to Ibn Hazm, *al-Muhalla*.
4. *Al-Muhalla*, vol. 6, p. 7-8 .
5. As in *at-Talkhis*, op. cit., and *Nayl al-Awtar*, vol. 4.
6. At the end of his section on *zakat* on cattle. See *al-Muhalla*, vol. 6, p. 16.

The opinion of Ibn al-Musayyab and az-Zuhri

Two leading scholars, Sa'id ibn al-Musayyab and Muhammad ibn Shihab az-Zuhri, along with Abu Qilaba and others think that the *nisab* on cattle is the same as the *nisab* on camels, and that the *zakat* rate of camels is the same for cattle with only a minor change, that is, disregarding the ages of camels. A similar opinion is reported as a version of the letter of 'Umar ibn al-Khattab on *zakat*, from Jabir ibn 'Abdullah and others who paid *zakat* at the time of the Prophet (p). Abu 'Ubayd reported from Muhammad ibn 'Abdu'r-Rahman that the instructions which 'Umar ibn al-Khattab wrote on *zakat* included: "from cattle one should take the same as from camels." Abu 'Ubayd continues, "Others were asked about *zakat* on cattle and the answer was, "it is the same as on camels."

Ibn Hazm reports with his own chain from az-Zuhri and Qatada, both from Jabir ibn 'Abdullah: "For every five cows there is one sheep due, and two sheep for ten, three sheep for 15, and four sheep for 20." Az-Zuhri says, "*Zakat* on cattle is like *zakat* on camels except in respect of ages. That is, if the number of cattle were between 25 and 75, the amount of *zakat* due is one cow, and two cows between 76 and 120. Above 120, for an additional 40 cows there is one additional cow. We were told that in the statement, "There is a one-year-old cow due for every 30 and one cow for every 40" was only a simplification and reduction in the rates for the people of Yemen which was disregarded later.[1]

It is also reported that 'Ikrima ibn Walid said, "I was commissioned to collect *zakat* from 'Akk and I met some old people who had paid *zakat* at the time of the Messenger of Allah (p). They disagreed: some of them said that the *zakat* on cattle should be made like the *zakat* on camels, and others said that you should take a one-year-old cow from every 30 cows, while others said that you should take one two-year-old cow from every 40 cows."[2] Ibn Hazm reports through his own chain from Ibn al-Musayyab, Abu Qilaba and another scholar a view similar to that of az-Zuhri. He also reported from 'Umar ibn 'Abdu'r-Rahman ibn Khulda al-

1. *Al-Amwal*, p. 379, and *al-Muhalla*, vol. 6, p.2.
2. *Al-Muhalla*, vol. 6, p. 3.

Ansari, "*Zakat* on cattle is the same as *zakat* on camels except for the ages."[1]

Evidence supporting this view

This opinion is supported by a report of Abu 'Ubayd with his own chain from Muhammad ibn 'Abdu'r-Rahman, "It is in the Prophet's letter on *zakat* and in the letter of 'Umar ibn al-Khattab that one should take from cattle the same as from camels."[2] Also this view is supported by what is reported by 'Abdu'r-Razzaq from Ma'mar, who said, "Sammak ibn al-Fadl gave me a letter from the Prophet (p) to Malik ibn Kuflanis in which I read, "...and on cattle is due the same as on camels."[3]

This is confirmed by what is mentioned by az-Zuhri that it was the last report from the Messenger of Allah (p), and that taking a one-year-old cow from each 30 cows was, at the beginning, a matter of favour for the people of Yemen. This report is *mursal*, but it is supported by the previous saying and by statements from some Companions. Ibn Hazm comments, "If a *mursal hadith* would be accepted from anyone, it deserves to be accepted from az-Zuhri because he was well-versed in the *Sunna* and met a number of Companions."[4]

This view is also supported by the general rule implied in the saying mentioned at the beginning of Section Three, "And anyone who owns cattle and does not pay their due, will be laid out for the cattle to trample on the Day of Rising." It is argued that this is a general text that includes cattle of any number except for restrictions brought in by a text or any *ijma'*. It is further argued that the report that there is one one-year-old cow due on each 30 and a two-year-old due on each 40 also supports this opinion because it does not waive *zakat* on cows below 30. It is only a statement of the rate of *zakat*.

It is further argued by analogy that cattle are similar to camels. In the *'Id* sacrifice, for example, a cow is sufficient for seven indi-

1. Ibid.
2. *Al-Amwal*, p. 379, and *al-Muhalla*, vol. 6, p.4.
3. *Al-Muhalla*, ibid.
4. *Al-Muhalla*, vol. 6, p. 9.

viduals, just as a camel is. Also in the sacrifices made after the *Hajj* the rate of camels and cows is the same, so *zakat* on cattle should be like that on camels.[1]

However, Ibn Hazm disproves these arguments on the basis that the *hadiths* attributed to the Prophet (p) are not completely linked to him and one can only give as evidence a *hadith* whose chain is complete to the Prophet (p). He notes that the argument that the *hadith* about *zakat* on cattle being general for any number of cattle is binding only on the Hanafis and Malikis who oblige *zakat* on business assets by the generality of texts alone, but not those who require a specific text for obliging any rulings in the *Shari'a*. As for the argument that *zakat* on cows should be similar to that on camels by analogy, I say that if analogy is accepted as a tool in deducing rulings in the *Shari'a*, then this application of it is a correct one, since I am aware of no agreed upon difference between camels and cows. Thus, this conclusion must be binding on those who accept analogy – the Hanafis, Malikis, and Shafi'is – but I do not accept it.[2]

On the other hand, scholars of the known schools of jurisprudence argue that the *nisab* should not be deduced by analogy; the *nisab* should only come from a text, and it is evident that there is no text on the *nisab* of cattle. Ibn Qudama adds that such an analogy is incorrect, since in sacrifice and the *Hajj*, 35 sheep equal five camels, but 35 sheep are not the *nisab* in *zakat*.[3]

A fourth opinion

Ibn Rushd gives yet another opinion without providing the name of its author nor its argument. On each ten cows there is one sheep until they reach 30 cattle, on which a one-year-old cow is due.[4] I find that Ibn Abi Shayba attributes this view to Shahr ibn Hawshab in his *al-Musannaf*. The latter says, "*Zakat* should be one sheep on each ten cows, two sheep on each twenty cows, and one

1. *Al-Muhalla*, vol. 6, p. 4.
2 Ibid., pp. 8–11
3. *Al-Mughni*, vol. 2, p. 463.
4. *Bidayat al-Mujtahid*, vol. 1, p. 225.

one-year-old cow on 30 cows."[1] This means that the *nisab* of cattle is ten as compared to five in the previous opinion. No evidence of support is given by Ibn Abi Shayba. It may come to mind that this argument can be supported by the *hadith* that estimates the compensation for loss of life to be 100 camels or 200 cattle. This is reported to have been stated by 'Umar, as well as linked to the Prophet (p).[2] This implies that one camel is equal to two cows. If the *nisab* for camels is five, then that of cows must be ten, and if for each five camels the amount of *zakat* due is one sheep, there should be one sheep due for each ten cows.

Analysis and evaluation

After listing all these opinions,[3] it seems to me that the view of the majority about the rate on each 30 and 40 cows is the one that carries more weight, on the basis of the *hadiths* of Mu'adh and 'Amr ibn Hazm. However, it is notable that these two sayings do not give information regarding what is below 30 cows, whether negative or positive, but only determine the rate of *zakat* rather than its *nisab* except by contrast. Interestingly enough, the saying of Ibn Hazm goes on to state, "And on each 40 dinars, there is one dinar due." The majority of jurists agree that the *nisab* on gold is 20 dinars and not 40, which indicates that this saying was given to determine the rate of *zakat* and not necessarily its *nisab*, since the rate on gold is two and a half percent or one fortieth.

1. *Al-Musannaf*, vol. 3, p. 221.

2. Reported by Abu Dawud in his *Sunan* in the chapter on ransom, section on the amount of ransom. From 'Amr ibn Shu'ayb from his father from his grandfather who said, "The ransom at the time of the Messenger of Allah (p) was 600 dinars or 600 dirhams ... this remained in effect until 'Umar became Caliph and he announced, 'Camels have become expensive.' Then he ordered the ransoms to be 1000 dinars of gold or 1200 silver dirhams or 200 cows or 2000 sheep or 200 garments ..." Abu Dawud reports from 'Ata' ibn Abi Rabah, "The Messenger of Allah (p) gave his judgement on ransom. For those who own camels it is 100 camels, for those who own cattle, it is 200 cows..." This is *mursal*. In another version 'Ata' narrates from Jabir ibn 'Abdullah, "The Messenger of Allah (p) imposed..."

3. Schacht mentions in the *Encyclopaedia of Islam* that the *nisab* is 20 cows. I am aware of no place where he might have got this figure.

It is impossible to combine this opinion with that of Ibn al-Musayyab, az-Zuhri and their group of followers in putting *nisab* on cattle at five, especially since it is put at five in a version of 'Umar's letter on *zakat*, as a report from Jabir ibn 'Abdullah, a Companion, and is sometimes attributed to the letter of the Prophet (p). Abu 'Ubayd comments that this opinion was not known by people,[1] but it was shown earlier that it was in fact known to a number of Companions and Followers. Additionally, one can argue that the analogy of cattle and camels is a strong one and the objection of Ibn Hazm can be disregarded as based on his personal view that all analogy is invalid. The majority of scholars are in accord on the principle that the correct analogy is a source of deduction in the *Shari'a*.

Allah knows best, but it seems to me that the Messenger of Allah (p) intentionally left certain issues in *zakat* undefined and undetermined in order to make its application flexible with changing circumstances. It is left to the Islamic state and its *zakat* institution to draw up those details from time to time. Cattle may become more expensive and useful than camels. In this case *nisab* may be set at five, and the rate of one sheep for each five cows could be applied, and when they number in the 30's and 40's, such a course is practical and clear when cattle rearing becomes a big and profitable business. In some countries or times, cattle may carry a lower value than camels, to the extent that five of them would not be such substantial wealth as to stand as a minimum liable for *zakat*, in which case the *nisab* could be put at 30.

This flexibility has its root in the comment of az-Zuhri that 30 cows as a *nisab* was only given to make things easier for the people of Yemen. Given what az-Zuhri said, the sequence in time between the letters setting the *nisab* at 30 and at five does not necessarily imply that the latter annuls the former, but can be interpreted as different applications in two different circumstances by the Prophet (p) in his capacity as head of state and not just as a Messenger. Consequently, for different circumstances he may have given another opinion.

1. *Al-Amwal*, p. 379.

Section Four: *Zakat* on sheep

Zakat on sheep is obligatory by virtue of the *Sunna* and *ijma'*. In the *Sunna*, Anas narrates in the letter of instruction of Abu Bakr mentioned earlier that:

> "As for the *zakat* of grazing sheep, from forty to one hundred it is one sheep. If there are between one hundred and twenty and two hundred, it is two sheep. If there are between two hundred and three hundred it is three. If there are more than three hundred,[1] it is one sheep for every hundred. If the man's flock is less than forty sheep, there is no *zakat* on them unless their owner wishes. Neither an old animal, nor one with a defect, nor a ram is taken as *zakat* unless the *zakat*-collector wishes to do so."

Similar statements appear in the report from Ibn 'Umar and in several others.

Jurists unanimously agree that *zakat* is obligatory on sheep. There is also a unanimous opinion that the word "*ghanam*" (sheep) includes sheep and goats, in such a way that they are combined together as one item.[2]

According to this, the following table can be drawn up:

1. The author of *Sharh as-Sunna* writes, "This means an increase of another 100 until the number of sheep reaches 400. Then four sheep are required." This is the opinion of the majority of jurists. Al-Hasan ibn Salih indicates that if the quantity becomes 301, then four sheep are required. This is also the view of an-Nakha'i. (See *al-Mir'a*, vol. 4, pp. 144-145.)

2. See the chapter on *zakat* on sheep in *al-Majmu'*, vol. 5, p. 417, and afterword, *al-Mughni*, vol. 2, p. 472, and afterword; *Bidayat al-Mujtahid*, vol. 1, p. 224, and *Sunan al-Bayhaqi*, vol. 4, p. 99, and afterword.

Number of sheep From	To	Amount of *zakat* (in sheep)
1	39	None
40	120	one
121	200	two
201	300	three
301	400	four
401	500	five
		and so on.

We will discuss in Section 6 the description of what animal should be taken as *zakat* as to its size, age, and sex.

Discussion of the rate on sheep

It is notable that the *Shari'a* reduces the rate on sheep as their number increases. From the previous schedule it is observed that as the number grows above 120 the rate stabilises at one per cent in contrast with the usual two and a half per cent on business assets, money and other assets. What is the rationale for this reduction? Some contemporary researchers[1] attempt to explain this reduction with the argument that the *Shari'a* intends to encourage animal breeding by this reduction, since the rate on 40 sheep is two and a half per cent and it regresses at 200, going down to one per cent. But one wonders if this explanation is correct and why the same is not applied to the *zakat* of other kinds of livestock. The rate on both camel and cattle stabilises at around two and a half per cent on large numbers, which is consistent with the general rule of *zakat*. If the above interpretation is correct, it should apply to other animals as well.

The way I see it – and Allah knows best – is that once the number of sheep grows, the herd will contain many baby lambs because

1. He is Shawqi Isma'il, in an article entitled "The Accounting System of *Zakat*" in *al-Iqtisad as-Siyasa fi daw' al-Islam*, a review published by the Faculty of Commerce at the University of Cairo more than fifteen years ago.

most sheep give birth more than once a year. These lambs are counted in the number of sheep but not accepted as payment of *zakat*, as shall be shown in the following two sections. It seems to me that justice requires a certain reduction in the rate for this reason. If the rate is kept at one out of forty while the herd contains many lambs, the actual rate becomes much higher. As for the first forty, the rate is two and a half per cent because it is expected that lambs would not be counted in the first forty, as will be explained in Section Five.

This shows that the rate of *zakat* is in fact consistent, not progressive or regressive, which will be discussed at length in the last part of this book. In his commentary on the *Risala*, the Maliki, Shaykh Zarruq, writes on the declining rate of *zakat* on sheep between 40 and 200: "As the number of sheep grows, their cost increases, and the desire for accumulation increases also. Therefore the rate on some assets is as low as one fourth of one tenth per cent, while it goes up to ten per cent on other assets."[1] I could not understand the reason given by Shaykh Zarruq. The known fact is that when wealth increases, its costs decline. This is perhaps why cattle owners like to pasture together on a large scale, to spread the cost of shelter and herding. This is known now as the economy of scale. If the explanation given by Zarruq is correct, it should have applied to all livestock, but we see the rate is not reduced for large quantities of camels and cattle.

Section Five: Is *zakat* due on baby animals?

Ahmad, Abu Dawud, and an-Nasa'i report from Suwayd ibn Ghafala that "...the *zakat* collector of the Messenger of Allah (p) came to us. We sat close to him and I heard him saying, 'In my instructions it says that I should not take from nursing animals.'"[2]

1. *Sharh ar-Risala*, vol. 1, p. 337.

2. Mentioned in *al-Muntaqa*, Ash-Shawkani comments, "Reported by ad-Daraqutni and al-Bayhaqi. Hilal ibn Khabbab is one of the links in the chain, and he is graded trustworthy by more than one scholar, while some speak critically of him. See *Nayl al-Awtar*.

This indicates that baby livestock are not liable for *zakat*, and this is the opinion of a group of leading scholars. But the chain of this tradition is contested. On the other hand, in *al-Muwatta'*, Malik reports that 'Umar told his collector, Sufyan ibn 'Abdullah ath-Thaqafi, "Count the lambs among them, even those carried by the shepherd in his arms, but do not accept them in payment."[1] This is also reported by ash-Shafi'i and Abu 'Ubayd.[2] This report of 'Umar contradicts the previous report and indicates that baby animals are counted in the *nisab* and consequently *zakat* is due on them. This is what a group of jurists adopt, to the extent that if all the animals subject to *zakat* were lambs, one of them would be acceptable as payment,[3] though others say the owner should be asked to buy an older animal from outside to fulfil the payment of *zakat*.[4]

Some scholars attempt to reconcile the report of 'Umar with the saying of Suwayd by not obliging *zakat* on baby animals if they comprise the entire zakatable amount, saying that is where the saying of Suwayd applies, while counting baby animals if they are with their mothers. However, some jurists consider that baby animals are counted in the total number of the zakatable herd only if older animals make up the *nisab* required for *zakat* to be levied. This is the view of Abu Hanifa, ash-Shafi'i, Ibn Hazm, and others.[5]

It is, in my opinion, the closest to Islamic justice to exempt from *zakat* a person who owns, for example, four old camels and collect it from a person who owns five baby camels or four baby lambs, since the latter is less rich than the former. Once the *nisab* is fulfilled by counting adult animals alone, then baby animals can be counted in determining the total number subject to *zakat*. For larger quantities, the rate structure itself is flexible because it takes stratas of quantities and applies the same rate on the lower and higher ends of each layer. Thus five camels are liable to *zakat* at the rate of one sheep, the same as nine camels. It seems to me that this

1. *Al-Muwatta'*, vol. 1, p. 265.

2. *Nayl al-Awtar*, vol. 4, p. 134.

3. Ash-Shawkani comments, "This is done on the basis that restricting the meaning of a text is validated by the opinion of a Companion, but this is an incorrect basis." Ibid.

4. *Bidayat al-Mujtahid*, vol. 1, pp. 252-254.

5. *Al-Muhalla*, vol. 5, p. 274 and afterword.

was intentionally set up by the Prophet (p) in order to give leeway for the presence of baby animals. It seems that this becomes more apparent in sheep, and more especially goats, which give birth more than once a year. This is perhaps why the rate of sheep is lower at larger quantities, and becomes one per cent after the sheep reach 200 in number.

Section Six: Conditions for animals given as *zakat*

A few conditions are required for the animals that can be paid as *zakat*.

Free of defects and damage

The animals paid as *zakat* should be free of illness, bone fracture, old age, or accidental defects or damage. The Qur'an says: *"Do not have recourse to bad things when you give,"* (2:267) and the Prophet (p) stated, "Neither an old animal, one with a defect nor a ram should be taken as *zakat* unless the *zakat*-collector wishes to do so." This is part of the *hadith* from Anas. Accepting animals with defects as *zakat* payment is not fair to the poor and other deserving recipients; it is a bias in favour of the owner, which is improper.

As for the definition of defect or damage, the majority are of the view that it is the same definition as used in sales contracts, though some say that anything not accepted for sacrifice is not accepted as *zakat*.[1] One should mention the unique case where a defective or damaged animal is accepted as *zakat*, which is if all the animals being offered as *zakat* have the same defect or damage, such as a common disease. This is because the ordinance of *zakat* asks payment from what the person paying *zakat* owns without forcing him or her to purchase from outside a good animal only for the payment of *zakat*.[2]

1. *Fath al-Bari*, vol. 4, p. 63.
2. *Al-Mughni*, vol. 2, p. 473.

Specification of the animal's sex

The animal given as *zakat* must be a female of the species. This applies only to camels, except in the cases mentioned in the *hadith* of Anas, whereby a male of a higher age group is accepted instead of the due female. The Hanafis accept the payment of male animals on the basis of estimating their value,[1] because according to them, the value of the due item can be paid instead of it.

As for cattle, the text requires a male or female one-year-old out of every 30, which is not disputed. However, there is a variation on whether to accept a two-year-old bullock out of every forty. The majority do not approve of that, while the Hanafis accept it on the grounds that male and female cattle are similar. There is the tradition reported by at-Tabarani from Ibn 'Abbas, "For each 30 cows one one-year-old cow is due, and for each 40 one older, male or female."[2]

With regard to sheep, the Hanafis do not distinguish between male and female because the text mentions a sheep due without distinguishing the sex.[3] Malikis go along with the Hanafis in respect of *zakat* on sheep,[4] while the Hanbalis do not approve of taking a male sheep as *zakat* as long as there are females in the herd. This is taken by analogy with camels.[5] Furthermore, Malik and ash-Shafi'i leave it to *zakat* collectors to select the male or the female, depending on which is better for *zakat* recipients.[6] An-Nawawi writes, "If the male sheep is given as *zakat*, it is permissible, according to the majority of Shafi'is." It is also the opinion of ash-Shafi'i himself. Some Shafi'is do not approve of this view because of 'Umar's report mentioned earlier, which states, "And take a female sheep more than one year old."[7] After reviewing the different opinions, I

1. *Al-Bada'i'*, vol. 2, p. 33.

2. The author of *Majma' az-Zawa'id*, vol. 3, p. 75, writes "Layth ibn Abi Salim is in the chain, and he is trustworthy but *mudallis* (he may intentionally delete names in the chain.)

3. *Al-Bada'i'*, op cit.

4. *Bulgha as-Salik*, vol. 1, p. 209.

5. *Al-Mughni*, vol. 2, pp. 473-474.

6. Ibid.

7. *Al-Majmu'*, vol. 3, p. 397. The statement of 'Umar is reported by Malik with a correct chain as quoted by an-Nawawi. We will discuss it in detail later in

am inclined to go along with the Hanafi view regarding cattle and sheep because I think it carries more weight and has more convincing evidence than the others.

Age requirement

Traditions give specific ages for *zakat* regarding camels and cattle which must be complied with, on the ground that taking less or more is unfair towards either payers or recipients of *zakat*. This is agreed upon. As for sheep, there is a variation of opinion. According to Malik, sheep accepted as *zakat* should be at least one year old, to comply with the *hadith*, "Our right is at the least, a one-year-old sheep or goat." Ash-Shafi'i and Ahmad believe that what is paid as *zakat* should be at least one year old for goats and six months old for sheep.[1] This is also reported by Abu Dawud and Muhammad ash-Shaybani, while Abu Hanifa agrees with Malik, although he allows giving a six-month-old sheep on the basis of value.[2] I take that view shared by Ahmad, ash-Shafi'i, Abu Yusuf and Muhammad ash-Shaybani, because it has strong proofs.

If the age necessary for payment is not available and other ages are available, how should *zakat* be paid? Ibn Rushd summarises the diverse opinions, "According to Malik, the *zakat* payer is required to buy the necessary animal. Others say that the payer should give a lower age animal plus compensation at the rate of 20 dirhams or two sheep for each year difference in the age of camels, as was mentioned in the letter of Abu Bakr on *zakat*, and there should be no differences about it. This is also the view of ash-Shafi'i and Abu Thawr. Some jurists say that payment must be made of the available age and a compensation for the difference should be paid.[3] According to Abu Hanifa, the value of the necessary animal is due. It seems to me, however, that Abu Hanifa's view is also consistent with the *hadith* because the Prophet (p) estimated the difference in age in his capacity as head of state rather than as a religious ordi-

this section.

1. *Al-Mughni*, vol. 2, p. 479.
2. *Ad-Durr al-Mukhtar* with its commentary, *Radd al-Muhtar*, vol. 2, p. 25.
3. *Bidayat al-Mujtahid*, vol. 1, pp. 222-223.

nance, and such estimation varies with time. 'Ali quoted different prices from the estimation of the Prophet (p).[1]

The average

The *zakat* collector should not take the best or the worst in quality, but the average of the animals owed. Ibn 'Abbas narrates that the Prophet (p) said to Mu'adh, "Avoid the best of people's wealth, and be fearful of the prayer of the oppressed, for there is no veil between it and Allah." Ibn Abi Shayba reports that the Prophet (p) noticed an excellent she-camel among the camels collected as *sadaqa*. He was furious at the collector and asked, "What is this?" The collector answered, "I exchanged it for two lesser quality animals." The Prophet (p) said, "Then it is all right."[2]

This is essentially because *zakat* is based on fairness to the two parties, payers and recipients, and taking the best or the worst means favouring one of them. However, it is obvious that the worst or the best can be taken on the basis of value at the option of the livestock owner. Abu Dawud reports through his chain from the Prophet (p), "There are three things and if anyone fulfils them, he will taste the sweetness of faith: to worship Allah alone, realising that there is no god but Allah, to pay *zakat* on your wealth with your soul pleased at paying it year after year ... and to give not the old or the ill or the young or the defective animal that gives little milk, but to give from the average of your wealth. Allah does not ask you for the best of it, nor does He order you to give the worst of it."[3]

As in payment of *zakat*, the collector must not take an animal that is nursing or pregnant, nor should he take the ram out of sheep, or an animal that is intended to provide meat for the household of the *zakat* payer.[4] Malik reports in *al-Muwatta'* from 'A'isha

1. This is the opinion of ath-Thawri. It is also attributed to Ishaq, as in *al-Fath*, vol. 4, p. 62.

2. *Nasb ar-Rayah*, vol. 2, p. 361.

3. The same is reported by at-Tabarani who rates its chain as *hasan*. See *Nayl al-Awtar*, vol. 4, p. 114.

4. *Al-Bada'i'*, op. cit., *al-Mughni*, vol. 2, p. 476, and *al-Muhadhdhab* and its commentary, *al-Majmu'*, vol. 5, pp. 426-427.

that 'Umar ibn al-Khattab passed by the sheep taken as *sadaqa* and saw one with large udders and asked, "What is this sheep?" He was answered, "One taken as *sadaqa*?" He replied, "Its owners did not give it with pleasure, so do not subject people to trials, and do not take the best of the wealth of the Muslims."[1]

As an application of this condition, baby animals, while counted for *zakat*, are not accepted in payment of *zakat*. When Umar ibn al-Khattab sent Sufyan ibn 'Abdullah ath-Thaqafi to collect *zakat*, he started counting the baby lambs and was asked, "Are you counting these lambs while you do not accept them in payment?" When he returned to 'Umar and told him that, 'Umar said, "Yes, count baby lambs, even those which are so young that they must be carried by the shepherd, but do not accept them in payment, nor should you take that which is meant for meat for the household, nursing ewes, pregnant sheep or the ram. Take only sheep and goats which are one year old."

Ahmad, Abu Dawud, and an-Nasa'i report from a person named Si'r from the two men commissioned by the Messenger of Allah (p) to collect *zakat*. They said, "The Messenger of Allah (p) prevented us from taking pregnant animals." And Suwayd ibn Ghafala said, "A *zakat* collector sent by the Messenger of Allah came to us and I heard him saying, 'In my instructions it was written that I should not take from nursing animals...' and when a man wanted to give him a pregnant she-camel, he refused to accept it."[2]

Section Seven: The effect of mixing and partnership on *zakat* on livestock

It is common for livestock owners to put their cattle together in order to save on overheads. Should all gathered livestock be treated as one unit in determining the *nisab* and rate of *zakat* or should they be considered for each owner alone?

1. *Al-Muwatta'*, vol. 1, p. 267, chapter on *zakat*, section on preventing embarrassing people in *sadaqa*.

2. *Nayl al-Awtar*, vol. 4, p. 133.

To deal with this question, one should note that there are two leading forms of collective breeding. One involves keeping the ownership separate and sharing in certain expenses and the other is when the cattle is owned commonly among the partners. In the latter form, the share of each owner is not determined in number but only as a proportion of the total, whereas in the former each person's own animals are distinguished.[1] These two forms of investing together need not have the same effect on *zakat* rulings.

In *Bidayat al-Mujtahid*, Ibn Rushd summarises the views of jurists in the following way:

> Most jurists view mixing animals as affecting the conditions of *zakat* except for Abu Hanifa and his disciples, who believe that mixing animals together does not have any effect on the nisab or on the applicable rate. Malik, ash-Shafi'i and most jurists agree that a group of breeders who mix their camels together are treated as if they were one owner. Those jurists, however, differ, in two areas: the determination of *nisab* and the definition of effective mixing together.
>
> It should be noted that the reason for these different opinions is different interpretation of the *hadiths* of the Prophet (p). In the letter on sadaqa, the Prophet (p) said, "What is separate should not be counted together, and what is together should not be counted separately in order to avoid *sadaqa*, and as for what belongs to two persons, they must settle their account in proportion to their ownership."
>
> Those who say that mixing together does not affect the *zakat* interpret this to mean that the *zakat* collector should not divide herds owned by one person in such a way that would increase *zakat*. For instance, 120 sheep owned by one person should not be divided into three groups of 40 to make the *zakat* three sheep instead of one. They also say that what is owned by one person should not be added to what is owned by another in order to make the *nisab*.

1. *Ar-Rawda* by an-Nawawi, vol. 2, p. 170.

> Ash-Shafi'i and his disciples interpret this saying to mean that cattle put together are treated as if they were owned by one person, both in the application of the *nisab* and in the determination of the *zakat* rate. On the other hand, Malik and his students interpret it to mean that if each owner alone has the minimum *nisab*, then the applicable rate is that of the total and not that which applies on what belongs to each owner alone.[1]
>
> As for the variation on the definition of mixing together, ash-Shafi'i is of the opinion that mixing animals together means in pasturing, milking, sheltering and watering, to the extent that putting animals together is like partnership. Accordingly, *nisab* is applied on the total and not on each owner alone. Malik sees effective mixing together as where watering, pasturing and sheltering and rams are common.[2]

In *al-Muhalla* Ibn Hazm strongly criticises the opinion that mixing animals together affects *zakat*, on the grounds that this ends up in fact violating the essential texts of *zakat*. For example, a person who owns less than the *nisab* is exempt from paying *zakat*, so how could such a person pay *zakat* if he puts his cattle with others? This, according to Ibn Hazm, contradicts the principle of individual responsibility and private ownership, making one person's property affect the duties and obligations of others. This is a violation of the Qur'an and *Sunna*.[3] It should be noted finally that the view of the Shafi'is has the widest concept of the effect on *zakat* of mixing the wealth of several owners. It goes as far as affecting the *zakat* not only on livestock, but also of crops, fruits, and gold and silver that are mixed.[4] This view may serve as a basis for the treatment of contemporary corporations as the *zakat* agency may find best, because it provides for simplicity in procedures and thrift in collection expenses.

---

1. *Bulghat as-Salik*, vol. 1, pp. 210-212.
2. *Bidayat al-Mujtahid*, pp. 254-255.
3. *Al-Muhalla*, vol. 6, pp. 31-39.
4. *Ar-Rawda*, vol. 2, pp. 172-173.

Section Eight: *Zakat* on horses

Horses used for personal transportation and fighting are exempt from *zakat*. It is agreed upon among Muslims that horses owned for the purpose of personal riding, carrying personal loads and fighting for the sake of Allah are exempt whether they are naturally pastured or fed in ranches, because they are for personal and household use and are not growing assets in excess of personal needs. On the other hand, all Muslims except the Zahiris have agreed that horses used as a business investment owned by horse merchants should have *zakat* paid on them, whether they are naturally pastured or hand-fed on the grounds that such horses are a commodity, like other business assets. It is also agreed upon that horses that are fed by owners most of the year, which are not owned for any of the previously mentioned purposes, are exempt from *zakat*, because natural free pasturing is a condition for the payment of *zakat* on animals according to the majority of scholars.[1]

Zakat on naturally pastured horses designated for breeding

There are two opinions on the *zakat* of naturally pastured horses that are designated for breeding and growth. Abu Hanifa believes that *zakat* should be paid on them provided that not all horses owned are males, since in this case they could not breed.[2] The majority of jurists consider these horses exempt from *zakat*, and this is narrated by Ibn al-Mundhir from 'Ali, Ibn 'Amr, ash-Sha'bi, 'Ata', al-Husayn al-'Abdi, 'Umar ibn 'Abdu'l-'Aziz, ath-Thawri, Abu Yusuf, Muhammad ash-Shaybani, Abu Thawr, Abu Khaythama, and Abu Bakr ibn Shayba. Others attribute this opinion to 'Umar, Malik, al-Awza'i, al-Layth and Dawud.[3]

1. *Al-Bada'i'*, vol. 2, p. 34.
2. *Radd al-Mukhtar*, vol. 2, pp. 25-26.
3. *Al-Majmu'*, vol 3, p. 339.

Evidence of the majority for not paying *zakat* on horses

It is reported in the two *Sahih* Collections and elsewhere from Abu Hurayra that the Prophet (p) said, "A Muslim does not have to pay *zakat* on his horse or slave."[1] This exemption includes all horses, naturally pastured or not, female or male because it is general.

The report of Ahmad, Abu Dawud, and at-Tirmidhi from 'Ali from the Prophet (p), "I have waived for you *sadaqa* on horses and slaves. Pay *sadaqa* on silver, one dirham for every forty."[2]

The actions of the Prophet (p) did not include collecting *zakat* on horses, even though it was collected on camels, cattle and sheep. The Messenger is the one who gives the details of the obligation outlined in the Qur'an, and his word and deed indicate that *zakat* is not paid on horses.

They also argue that livestock which is subject to *zakat* is obviously very different from horses and that horses cannot be made objects for *zakat* by analogy because of the basic differences in use and in the purpose of owning these different kinds of animals. Horses are acquired for use in fighting, in establishing Islam and in defence against enemies, so people should be encouraged to obtain them and keep them for such purposes. Allah says: *"Arm yourselves against them with all the firepower and cavalry you can muster."* (6:60) War horses are fighting equipment, like weapons and like other fighting equipment are not subject to *zakat* as long as they are not used as a commodity for trade.[3]

Abu Hanifa's opinion and its supporting evidence

Abu Hanifa, who believes that *zakat* should be paid on naturally pastured horses provides the following arguments.

1. The author of *al-Muntaqa* is quoted by ash-Shawkani, "This is reported by all the group." See *Nayl al-Awtar*, vol. 4, p. 136.

2. Ibid., p. 137. At-Tirmidhi mentioned that al-Bukhari rates this *hadith* as *sahih*, Ibn Hajar rates it *hasan* and ad-Daraqutni says, "What is correct is that it ends at 'Ali."

3. *Ar-Rawd an-Nadir*, commentary on *Majmu' al-Fiqh al-Kabir* on comparative Zaydi jurisprudence, vol. 2, pp. 408-109.

Al-Bukhari reports in his *Sahih* collection from Abu Hurayra that the Prophet (p) said, "Horses are for three purposes. They are a reward for one man, and a shelter for another man and a burden for another man. As for the one who has a reward, that is the man who ties them in the way of Allah and gives them a long tether in pasture or meadow. He will have good deeds for whatever it gets from the pasture or the meadow for the extent of its tether. If it breaks its tether and crosses a hill or two, then he has good deeds for its tracks and dung. If it crosses a river and drinks from it, that will be good deeds for him even if he did not intend to give it water. There is a man who ties them up out of boasting and showing-off and enmity towards the people of Islam. It is a burden for that man."[1] This *hadith* indicates that Allah has a right on horses, *zakat* and giving lifts on their backs.[2] Other jurists argue that what is meant by the right on horses is the use of horses in fighting.[3]

It is reported from Jabir that the Prophet (p) said, "On every naturally pastured mare there is due one dinar or ten dirhams." This *hadith* is reported by ad-Daraqutni and al-Bayhaqi, who graded it weak. For this reason, the majority of jurists argue that it cannot stand against the *sahih hadith* of waiving *zakat* on horses: "A Muslim does not have to pay *zakat* on his horse or slave."

By analogy to camels, both are growing and useful animals, and in both, the condition for *zakat* – natural pasturage – is fulfilled. The claimed differences between horses and other livestock are no more than those among the other kinds of livestock, since each animal has its unique characteristics. There are many differences between camels and sheep, yet *zakat* is paid on both. Abu Hanifa holds to this argument on the basis that the reason for the obligation of *zakat* is a matter that can be rationalised and not a matter of worship only. This reason is growth or growth potential and once growth exists in another asset, the ruling of *zakat* must be extended to it.

1. These are the words of al-Bukhari in the chapter of sharing water, section on people and livestock drinking from rivers. The hadith is also reported by Ahmad and Muslim. See *Nayl al-Awtar*, vol. 4, p. 117.

2. *Al-Mirqa*, vol. 4, p. 122.

3. *Al-Muhalla*, vol. 5, p. 228 and *Nayl al-Awtar*, vol. 4, p. 118.

At-Tahawi and ad-Daraqutni report, with a correct chain, from as-Sa'ib ibn Yazid, "I witnessed my father evaluating his horses and paying their *sadaqa* to 'Umar ibn al-Khattab."[1] 'Abdu'r-Razzaq and al-Bayhaqi report from Ya'la ibn Umayya that 'Abdu'r-Rahman, the brother of Ya'la, bought a mare from a man in Yemen for the price of 100 camels. The seller felt sorry and went to 'Umar complaining, 'Ya'la and his brother forced me to sell my mare.' 'Umar asked Ya'la to come and meet with him and he gave 'Umar the true story. 'Umar wondered, 'Would a steed reach that high a price in your area? I never realised that a mare would reach that value. Would it be just to take one sheep out of each forty and not take anything from horses? Collect one dinar per horse.' He then imposed *zakat* on horses at the rate of one dinar each."[2]

Ibn Hazm reports, with his own chain from Ibn Shihab az-Zuhri, that as-Sa'ib ibn Yazid told him that he used to bring 'Umar ibn al-Khattab *zakat* on horses. Ibn Shihab adds, "'Uthman used to collect *zakat* on horses."[3] Anas ibn Malik narrates that 'Umar used to collect ten dirhams on each mare and five on each male horse.[4] Zayd ibn Thabit had similar views to that of 'Umar. In the reign of Marwan ibn al-Hakam, jurists disputed the *zakat* on naturally pastured horses, and when Marwan consulted the Companion, Abu Hurayra, he narrated the *hadith*, "A Muslim does not have to pay *zakat* on his horse or slave." Marwan turned to Zayd ibn Thabit and asked, "What do you say, O Abu Sa'id?" Abu Hurayra said, "I wonder at Marwan. I tell him the *hadith* of the Messenger of Allah (p) and he asks, 'What do you say, Abu Sa'id?'" Zayd answered, "The Messenger of Allah (p) spoke the truth, but he meant the horse of a fighter for the sake of Allah. For a merchant who keeps horses for breeding, *zakat* is due." Marwan asked, "How much?" He replied, "One dinar or ten dirhams on each horse."[5]

In *Kitab al-Amwal*, Ibn Zanjawayh reports with his chain from Tawus, "I asked Ibn 'Abbas whether *zakat* was due on horses and he answered, 'There is no *sadaqa* on the horse of the fighter for the

1. *Nasb ar-Rayah*, vol. 2, p. 359.
2. Ibid.
3. *Al-Muhalla*, vol. 5, p. 227.
4. Ibid., p. 226.
5. *Nasb ar-Rayah*, op. cit.

sake of Allah.'"[1] This implies that *zakat* is due on other horses. Ibrahim an-Nakha'i, a Follower, had the same view as 'Umar and Zayd. He said, "Naturally pastured horses raised for breeding are subject to *zakat* at one dinar or ten dirhams on each horse, or else evaluate them and pay ten dirhams for each 200 dirhams of their value." (Mentioned by Muhammad in *al-Athar*.) Abu Yusuf reports a similar statement[2] also from Hammad ibn Abi Sulayman that he said, "...and *zakat* is due on horses."[3]

Nisab and rates of *zakat* on horses

Abu Hanifa does not determine a *nisab* for horses. The author of *ad-Durr al-Mukhtar* writes, "It is best known that Abu Hanifa does not estimate a *nisab* for horses; we have no report from him."[4] Ibn 'Abidin in his commentary quotes al-Quhustani as saying, "Some indicate *nisab* at three and others indicate it at five."[5] It seems that the estimation of five is more correct because of its similarity to camels. The number five is often used in *nisab*. *Nisab* is five camels, five *uqiyyas* of silver (equals 200 dirhams) and 5 *wasqs* of grain.

The rate is explained by Ibn 'Abidin from Abu Hanifa: Owners of Arabian horses are given the choice of paying one dinar on each or evaluating their horses and paying five dirhams for each 200 dirhams of value – the rate is just two and a half percent. For non-Arabian horses, only the value is considered.[6]

Analysis

After discussing the two arguments, it seems to me that the Messenger (p) did not negate *zakat* on horses in a clear way but neither did he oblige it clearly. The *hadith* from Abu Hurayra, "A Muslim does not have to pay *zakat* on his horse or slave", does not

1. Ibid., p. 357. The commentator notes, "Ibn Hajar in *ad-Diraya* says that its chain is correct.

2. Ibid., p. 359.

3. *Nayl al-Awtar*, vol. 4, p. 136.

4. *Radd al-Muhtar*, commentary on *ad-Durr al-Mukhtar*, vol. 2, p. 26.

5. Ibid., p. 25.

6. Ibid.

touch on anything other than the horse used for personal transportation and as a mount for war. This explanation is supported by the interpretation from Zayd ibn Thabit and Ibn 'Abbas, correctly reported to him. The very words, "his horse or slave" in the *hadith* seem to indicate this meaning. It is also unanimous by *ijma'* among the jurists – except the Zahiris – that *zakat* is obligatory on horses and slaves when they are business assets. Abu Hurayra was known for holding to the letter of texts, and was also known among the Companions for his precise memory, and did not have a reputation for analysing and elaborating like Zayd and Ibn 'Abbas.

The *hadith* from 'Ali, "I have waived for you *sadaqa* on horses and slaves," is noted by ad-Daraqutni as correct when it ends at 'Ali and is not linked to the Prophet (p). It is well known that ad-Daraqutni is the expert on such matters. However, the words, "waived for you," imply that these assets should be in principle liable for *zakat,* but the Prophet (p) waived *zakat* on them for certain reasons.[1] This could be the pressing need for war steeds or the fact that horses were not a substantial item of wealth in Arabia.

The lack of a text clearly obliging *zakat* on horses does not necessarily mean that they are not subject to *zakat.* The Prophet (p) is not reported to have said anything about obliging *zakat* on gold. It is apparent that most coins used at his time were silver and the ruling on gold is derived by analogy because of the similarity in the use of the two metals. The story of 'Umar with Ya'la ibn Umayya has, in my opinion, an extremely important significance. The action taken by 'Umar indicates that analogy and *ijtihad* have an important position in *zakat.* The fact that the Prophet (p) took *zakat* from certain kinds of asset does not mean that Muslims after him may not take it from other kinds that are similar. In fact, *zakat* must be payable on every substantial growing asset. The rates, wherever there is no text, are subject to *ijtihad.*

The majority of jurists consider the action of 'Umar as his own *ijtihad*, which is not binding. They also argue that 'Umar obliged *zakat* on horses after it was requested from him by a group repre-

1. At-Tibi explains that 'waived' means "I removed or overlooked in respect of *zakat*", referring to the fact that it should originally have been zakatable. Al-Qari comments, "It implicitly means that the matter was left to the Prophet (p) (see *al-Mirqa*, vol. 4, p. 149.

senting the people of Syria who said to him, "We have acquired certain wealth, including horses and slaves, and we would like it to be purified and sanctified." 'Umar replied. "How could I do a thing which was not done by my two predecessors before me!" He consulted the Companions of Muhammad (p). 'Ali suggested, "It is a good idea as long as it does not become a regular due enforced by rulers after you."[1]

It seems to me that this incident precedes the above-mentioned story about the people of Yemen. The story of the Yemenis explains the reasoning of 'Umar, which was spurred on by the high prices horses had assumed in Yemen. His words were, "Should we take one sheep out of each forty and take nothing on horses?" What seems reasonable is that the story with the Yemenis took place after that with the Syrians, since with the latter he was hesitant and consulted the Companions, while with the Yemen he was determined because he had already made up his mind after consultation.

On the other hand, the rate imposed by 'Umar (one dinar per horse) does not seem to be binding on us because of changes in the purchasing power of the dinar as well as in the prices of horses in both time and place. I prefer at our time to revert to the opinion of an-Nakha'i and Abu Hanifa, who suggest the evaluation of horses and the application of the rate of two and a half per cent. Obviously, this is the required rate on livestock. It seems most likely that the Prophet (p) intentionally left certain undetermined areas in *zakat* to make things more flexible for Muslims after him, and in order to leave freedom of decision to the proper *zakat* authority.

The different possibilities regarding Prophetic instructions

The above discussion leads us to devote a few paragraphs to the distinction between the orders of the Prophet (p) as a Messenger of Allah and his orders as head of state. One should always look at the

1. Reported by Ahmad and at-Tabarani in *al-Muj'am al-Kabir.* The author of *Majma' az-Zawa'id*, vol., 3, p. 69, says, "The men in its chain are trustworthy." See *Nayl al-Awtar*, vol. 4, p. 136

circumstances that surround a statement made by the Prophet (p) and the subject matter of the *hadith* to see whether it relates to temporal, political, economic, military or administrative affairs (or to the principles of the Islamic way of life). There may sometimes exist another text that indicates the enduring principle of a special temporal application or similar events that may have been treated differently, which indicates that this treatment may be temporal rather than religious.

An example is given by al-Qarafi in *al-Ihkam* regarding the *hadith*, "Anyone who kills an enemy soldier may have his personal property." Malik says this is a decision by the Prophet (p) as head of state and not a general rule. If the leaders of the Islamic state declare such a regulation at the beginning of a war, then it should apply, but otherwise the general principle that war booty is distributed according to the text of the eighth chapter of the Qur'an remains applicable. Malik gives the following arguments to support this view:

- The verse about the distribution of war booty in *Surat* 8 contradicts this.
- Such a regulation may interfere with, and divert the intentions of the fighters from being for the sake of Allah to being the desire for the enemy's property.
- The reason why this statement was made by the Prophet (p) was to encourage the fighters in a particular battle.[1]

The late Shaykh ad-Dihlawi mentions in *Hujjat Allah al-Baligha*[2] that what is reported from the Prophet (p) is of two categories. The first is what he said as Messenger to explain the Message of Allah, according to the verse, *"Whatever the Messenger gives you you should accept and whatever He forbids you you should forgo."* (59:7) This category includes all sayings about the Unseen. The second category includes what he said in his capacity as a human being and head of state, as he himself stated, "I am only a man. If I ordain something

1. *Al-Ihkam*, al-Qarafi, pp. 106-108.

2. *Hujjat Allah al-Baligha*, vol. 1, pp. 271-272. See also Shaykh Mahmud Shaltut, *al-Islam 'aqida wa Shari'a*, Part Three, section entitled "*Sunna*, a Legislation and not a Legislation."

as your religion, you should take it. If I give you something as my personal opinion, then I am merely a man." (Muslim)

Included in this category are his sayings on medicine because they are based on experiments and customs of his time and are not a form of obedience to Allah or worship. Also in this category is what he did by chance and accident and not by intention and determination. Ad-Dihlawi continues that this category also contains those sayings that reflect temporal concerns which do not relate to all generations of this nation, such as the commands he gave in preparing armies and selecting emblems. Many *hadiths* that contain regulations of this kind are considered in this category, such as his *hadith*, "Anyone who kills an enemy soldier may have his personal property,"[1] and "Anyone who revives a wasteland owns it." (Abu Dawud and at-Tirmidhi) According to the Malikis, a soldier who kills an enemy is not entitled to his property unless the commander stipulates that before or during the battle, and according to the Hanafis, the rejuvenation of wasteland requires prior permission from the Islamic government.

It seems to me that the waiver the Prophet (p) gave concerning *zakat* on horses – if correctly reported – is also part of this category because it is related to temporal benefit, i.e. the encouragement of owning steeds for fighting for the sake of Allah. The very words of that waiver also indicates that it may only be temporary, because they imply that *zakat* should have been there but "was waived for you". This means that the Islamic state has the choice of imposing *zakat* on horses or not according to considerations of public interest. If horses represent substantial wealth, *zakat* may be levied on them in order to apply *zakat* to all those who are wealthy, while if they are not an important item of wealth they may be exempted. This interpretation reconciles the action of 'Umar with the *hadith* of the Prophet (p) and Allah knows best in all cases.

1. Reported by al-Bukhari, Muslim, and others from Abu Qatada al-Ansari. The Prophet (p) said this in the Battle of Hunayn.

Section Nine: Other naturally-pastured domestic animals

This part deals with the general case of naturally-pastured domestic animals obtained for profit. Can we generalise the case of *zakat* on such animals or not? In other words, should *zakat* be restricted to the four previously mentioned species or should it include all domestic animals? Some of today's leading professors of Islamic studies, including Muhammad Abu Zahra, 'Abdu'l-Wahhab Khallaf, and 'Abdu'r-Rahman Hasan, deduce from the practice of 'Umar that one can apply analogy on *zakat*.

'Umar ibn al-Khattab obliged *zakat* on horses by analogy, on the grounds that horses were becoming valuable assets. This is upheld by Abu Hanifa, the master in the application of analogy. Those who do not oblige *zakat* on horses do not do so in denial of analogy, but because they consider the edible character of livestock an important reason for their liability to *zakat*. Since horses are not edible, they refuse to extend *zakat* to include horses. The author of *al-Mughni* writes, "The analogy of horses and livestock is incorrect, because the latter are growing wealth that is used for milking and meat and can be used for sacrifice." The majority of scholars do not consider growth to be a sufficient reason to impose *zakat*.

These three professors add: If the caliph 'Umar considered growth the essential requirement for *zakat* and was followed by Abu Hanifa, then we can extend their application to other animals and declare that all animals that are growing and naturally-pastured should have *zakat* paid on them if they reach the minimum for *zakat* (*nisab*), which equals twenty dinars, at the rate of two and a half per cent. *Nisab* is estimated in relation to gold, because 'Umar accepted the principle of evaluating horses in determining the *zakat* owed on them and value is currently estimated in gold.

This is supported by the fact that when the Messenger (p) was asked about *zakat* on donkeys, he did not negate the obligation of *zakat* in a clear statement, but said, "Allah did not reveal to me anything on this matter except the comprehensive succinct verse: *'Whoever does an atom's weight of good will see it. Whoever does an atom's weight of evil will see it.'*" (Ahmad and Muslim) The ratio of two and a half per cent is supported by the *hadith* from Bahz ibn Hakim from his father from his grandfather that the Prophet (p) said, "Out of all naturally pastured camels, one two to three-year-old she-camel is due on every forty." This is a general rate for camels exceeding forty. Applying this rate on all other animals acquired for breeding for profit is undoubtedly a correct *ijtihad*, based on analogy between similar growing assets. Consequently, mules, reindeer, and other animals would be included in this concept.

I disagree with these professors on the estimation of *nisab* on these animals at 20 dinars, on the basis that to equate the *nisab* on animals and the *nisab* on money is not, in my opinion, valid. I have quoted earlier from *al-Mabsut* that five camels or 40 sheep equal 200 dirhams, and noted that Ibn al-Humam objected to this equation because there are *sahih hadiths* indicating that two sheep equal 20 dirhams, which means that 40 sheep equals 400 dirhams, i.e. the *nisab* on livestock is twice as much as the *nisab* on money. Thus, if we take the *nisab* on money as a reference, the *nisab* on animals should be estimated at twice as much as that on money since those who possess money have more freedom of choice than animal owners.

I prefer to determine *nisab* on animals as growing assets on two grounds. Firstly, this number should not be less than five, because the *Shari'a* does not oblige *zakat* on any amount less than five camels, five *wasqs* of grain or five *uqiyyas* of silver. This indicates that five should be the lowest quantity considered for *zakat* to be imposed. Secondly, that the value of the *nisab* should equal that of five camels or forty sheep in an area where prices are close to average. Estimating value on the basis of the value of camels or sheep is better than estimating on the basis of money, because (a) the purchasing power of money is usually unstable, and (b) it is much more correct to draw an analogy between two animals than between animals and money; likewise it is better to estimate *nisab* on new animals in reference to old animals than in reference to money.

Section Ten: General principles derived from the previous sections

The above discussion concerning *zakat* on livestock has been necessary because the *Shari'a* itself dictates many principles and rulings about *zakat* on livestock that may not be as detailed in other areas of *zakat*, and because an analysis of this issue uncovers important principles that will be of great benefit in understanding the essence of *zakat* in general. Among these principles are the following:

- *Zakat,* although an act of worship, is also a public institution supervised by the Islamic state. Appointing and sending *zakat* collectors is the duty of the Islamic state.
- *Zakat* regulations balance the concerns of the poor on one hand and the interests of the rich on the other hand, so that small quantities of wealth are exempted from *zakat* and average quality assets only are accepted in payment of *zakat*.
- The expensive upkeep of an asset reduces *zakat* or waives it on that asset. For that reason, the majority of leading jurists consider hand-fed animals exempt from *zakat* on the grounds that they cost as much as they profit the owner.
- A transformation of a growing asset from its use for profit to personal use exempts it from *zakat,* according to the majority of scholars with regard to cattle and camels used for watering, cultivation, and carrying personal loads.
- The *Shari'a* treats the common property of partnerships as one unit, which may constitute a basis for handling contemporary corporations.
- The *Shari'a* refuses to accept any wilful avoidance in matters of *zakat* and does not allow the combination or separation of assets for the purpose of decreasing *zakat*.
- Analogy can be used in *zakat* because its rulings have rational causes behind them. If these reasons exist in another asset, *zakat* can be extended to them. That is why 'Umar obliged

zakat on horses. I advocate obliging *zakat* on all naturally cost-free pastured animals, even though they may not have been known at the time of the Prophet (p) or his Successors.

- Some rulings given by the Prophet (p) can be categorised as regulations coming from the head of the Islamic state and not religious principles deriving from his capacity as a Prophet. These two types of rulings must be clearly known and distinguished. This, for example, explains the slight differences among the letters of instruction given by the Prophet (p) and his Successors.
- The *nisab* for animals is twice as much as the *nisab* for money. In *sahih hadiths*, two sheep are estimated at 20 dirhams, so 40 sheep equal 400 dirhams. It is unanimously known that the *nisab* for money is 200 dirhams.
- *Zakat* – even on livestock – is a proportional due. It is not regressive as misunderstood by some contemporary writers. The reduction of the rate for larger quantities of sheep is made for the specific reason explained earlier.
- The rate of *zakat* on animals is approximately one-fourth of one-tenth (2.5%) as is obvious in the case of camels and cows, and taking into consideration the explanation given earlier in the case of sheep. The rate of *zakat* on animals is similar to that on money and business assets.

These principles are noteworthy for they will help, Allah willing, in the understanding of the following chapters.

Chapter Three

Zakat on Gold and Silver

Gold and silver are useful precious metals. Many nations have used gold as money and as a measurement of value. The *Shari'a* considers gold and silver growing wealth by definition and *zakat* should be paid on them whether they are used in the form of coins or bullion or even as ornaments and decorative materials. However, they carry a different ruling when they are used as a woman's ornaments and jewellery. This chapter will have two sections, one devoted to *zakat* on money and another to *zakat* on jewellery and ornaments.

Section One: *Zakat* on money

The role and development of money

Barter was the method of exchange for primitive tribes. Once society and trade grew, the barter system could not satisfy all transactions because of the difficulty of finding two parties whose bartering requirements coincided. Allah guided humanity to use money as a medium of exchange and as a measurement of value in order to facilitate exchanges and transactions.[1] Man used different items as money until the rise of precious metals. Gold and silver dominated international and national trade for centuries because of the natural physical characteristics Allah implanted in them.[2]

1. 'Ali 'Abdu'l-Wahid Wafi, *al-Iqtisad as-Siyasi*, pp. 140-144, and 'Abdu'l-'Aziz Mar'i, *an-Nudhum al-Naqdiyya*, pp. 11-15.

2. This includes the stability of the metal, its characteristic of not rusting and non-deterioration, the stability of its relative value, its divisibility, the divisibility of its value, the difficulty of cheating, and the ease of inspecting its purity, the low but stable production of the metal throughout centuries, etc.

Money used at the time of the Prophet Muhammad

During the time the Messenger (p) was receiving the Revelation, the Arabs used these two metals as money. Gold was used in the form of the dinar and silver in the form of the dirham. Dinars and dirhams came to Arabia from the Arabs' neighbouring kingdoms, gold mainly from the Byzantines and silver mainly from the Persians. Dirhams came in both heavy and light weights and so pre-Islamic Makkans used silver dirhams by weight and not by number, as if they were not minted. They had their weight measurement system which was composed of: *ratl* (equalling twelve *uqiyyas*), *uqiyya* (equalling 40 dirhams), *nash* (equalling 20 dirhams or one-half *uqiyya*), and *nawa* (equalling five dirhams).[1]

The Prophet (p) said, "Our system of weight measurement is that of the Makkans."[2] He obliged *zakat* on dirhams and dinars, as we will see. This gave gold and silver recognised status as currency in Muslim lands. They have come to be the subject of many rulings of the *Shari'a* in transactions related to civil and commercial matters in addition to *zakat*, and they are used as measures in determining many values, such as dowries, ransoms, and *nisab* in *zakat*.

Evidence for the obligation of *zakat* on money

The obligation of *zakat* on money is confirmed by the Qur'an, *Sunna* and *ijma'*. Allah says, *"As for those who hoard up gold and silver and do not spend it in the Way of Allah, give them the news of a painful punishment, on the Day it is heated up in the fire of Hell and their foreheads, sides and backs are branded with it: 'This is what you hoarded for yourselves! So taste what you were hoarding!'"* (9:34-35) These two verses indicate with a strong warning that there is a right for Allah

1. See the booklet on currencies by al-Maqrizi, printed as part of *an-Nuqud al-'Arabiyya* ("Arabian Currencies"), p. 25f.

2. Ibid., p. 30, with regard to the saying, Ibn Hajar says in *at-Talkhis* (p. 183), "Reported by al-Bazzar, who grades it *gharib*, and by Abu Dawud and an-Nasa'i from Tawus from Ibn 'Umar, graded *sahih* by Ibn Hibban, ad-Daraqutni, an-Nawawi, and al-Qushayri." Al-Albani adds, "and Ibn Daqiq al-'Id and al-'Ala'i as in *Silsilat al-Ahadith as-Sahiha*, part 2, *hadith* no, 164." The rest of the *hadith* says, "and our volume measurements are those of the Madinans."

on gold and silver. The words, "spend it" refer to the monetary character of gold and silver, since money can be spent. The verse says "spend it" instead of "them" because "it" refers to money while the pronoun "them" could have been used to refer to gold and silver. These verses indicate also that there is a grievous penalty promised for two evil actions, hoarding and abstention from spending for the sake of Allah. No doubt non-payment of *zakat* is the most obvious sort of abstention from spending for the sake of Allah.

The *Sunna* gives some details of these verses. Muslim reports from Abu Hurayra that the Messenger (p) said, "If someone owns gold and silver and does not pay the dues on them, on the Day of Rising they will be made like sheets, heated by the fire of Hell. His front, back and sides will be ironed with these sheets on a day which is as long as fifty thousand years, until judgement is given to all human beings, and he will be shown his way to the Garden or the Fire." (Muslim) All this warning is for non-payment of dues on gold and silver. Another version of this *hadith* shows the meaning of this due to be *zakat*: "If someone has a treasure and does not pay its *zakat*, it will be heated in the fire of Hell..."[1] In the *hadith* from Anas that gives the instructions on *zakat* that were ordained by Allah to His Messenger, as written to Anas by Abu Bakr when he was sent to Bahrayn,[2] "And on silver, for each two hundred dirhams, the due is 2.5%. If there are only one hundred and ninety, *zakat* is not due on them unless the owner volunteers to pay."

As for *ijma'*, the Muslims have unanimously agreed throughout all generations that *zakat* is obligatory on these two currencies.

1. Ibn Hajar quotes ash-Shafi'i as saying, "The Messenger of Allah (p) imposed *zakat* on silver. The Muslims after him collected *zakat* also from gold, either on the basis of a *hadith* that did not reach us, or analogy." Ibn 'Abdu'l-Barr adds, "Nothing is authentically reported from the Prophet concerning gold." See *Subul as-Salam*, pt. 2, p. 129. In my opinion, the verse about hoarding is sufficient evidence for *zakat* on gold. It is supported and explained by the *sahih hadith* mentioned above. The statements of ash-Shafi'i and Ibn 'Abdu'l-Barr refer to the *nisab* and rate, since there is no *hadith* correctly reported about the *nisab* and rates of *zakat* on gold. However, these are unanimously agreed upon, as will be shown.

2. Bahrayn, as in *al-Fath*, vol. 4, pp. 59-60, was the name of a well-known land to the east of the Arabian peninsula. Its centre is the town of Hajar (today Hasa').

The reason for payment of *zakat* on money

Money should always be circulating. Hoarding money nullifies its usefulness and leads to stagnation in business, the spread of unemployment and regression in economic activity in general. Hoarding can become epidemic sometimes, and it is feared by economists to the degree that some have proposed the issuance of currency with a determined expiration date to prevent any possibility of hoarding. They call this kind of currency "melting money". Some Western economists have experimented with another idea to discourage hoarding, which entails cutting off monthly vouchers from paper currency in order to reduce its value and prevent its hoarding.[1] These various means aim at enhancing circulation and penalising hoarding, but they are surrounded by complexities and practical difficulties; however, they all reaffirm the Islamic point of view against hoarding.

By imposing a due of two and a half per cent every year, Islam encourages people to invest money which would otherwise become depleted by annual *zakat* payments. Thus the Prophet (p) urged the guardians of orphans to invest the wealth of their charges so that they would not be consumed by *zakat*. This urging for investment of the wealth of orphans comes since it is assumed that adults would not neglect to invest their own wealth, because of the inner impulse to become richer, while orphans do not have control over their own wealth.

The rate of *zakat* on money

There is unanimous agreement among Muslims that the rate of *zakat* on money is two and a half per cent. The author of *al-Mughni* says, "I am aware of no dispute among scholars that *zakat* on gold and silver is 2.5%." This is authentically reported from the Prophet (p), "On silver 2.5% is due."[2] It is apparent that the *Shari'a*

1. Mahmud Abu as-Sa'ud, *Outlines of Islamic Economics*, p. 40f. There you will find the details of this experiment which was carried out in Vorgel, Austria. It had succeeded in reducing unemployment, interest rates and hoarding, and was repeated in some countries, where it was strongly opposed by central banks.

2. *Al-Mughni*, vol. 3, p. 7.

makes the rate of *zakat* on money low, because it is calculated on both principal and accumulated profit. This rate is much lower than the one-tenth or one-twentieth imposed on crops and fruit, but crops and fruit to land are like profit to capital. *Zakat* on fruit and crops is calculated only on the profit, while *zakat* on money is taken from the capital itself, whether it actually grows or not and whether it has made a profit during the year or not.

Is it possible to increase this rate today?

Some non-specialised writers argue that the proceeds of *zakat* as regulated in the *Shari'a* may not be sufficient to satisfy all the complex needs of today's life, especially with changing economic circumstances, so there is a need to revise the regulations of *zakat* and possibly raise the rate of *zakat* on money.[1]

I reject this proposal on the following grounds:

- It contradicts clear and authentic texts from the *Sunna* of the Messenger of Allah (p) and the Rightly-guided Khalifs. We are commanded to hold strongly to this *Sunna* and are warned by Allah about the consequences of deviating from it. Allah says: *"Those who oppose his command should beware of a testing trial coming to them or a painful punishment striking them."* (24:63)
- It is in opposition to the consensus of all Muslims throughout fourteen centuries, during which many social and economic changes have taken place and many internal and external political situations changed. Needs arose for additional funds and the state treasury emptied many times, but in spite of all that, not a single Muslim scholar suggested a change in the rate of *zakat*.

1. Such as Dr. Fadl ar-Rahman, who assumed the chairmanship of the Committee on Islamic Research in Pakistan at the time of Ayyub Khan. He called for an increase in the rate of *zakat* at this time and for determining *nisab* at 2939 Pakistani rupees because people were exempt from income taxes below that level. This opinion raised a wave of rejection and hostile responses from Pakistani scholars. See the magazine, *al-Bata's al-Islam*, vol. 12, no. 2, the article by Shaykh al-Binnari. It is reported that Fadl ar-Rahman was dismissed from the committee after he made a few statements that were considered ill-intended and unIslamic.

- This *ijma'* is supported by the existence of controversy among Muslim scholars on the question of additional dues besides *zakat*. If the rate of *zakat* could be increased, there would be no reason for this controversy.

- Jurists accustomed to applying analogy, such as the Hanafis, argue that the rates of *zakat* cannot be derived by analogy, because their determination comes only from the Legislator and have been given once and for all. If these rates cannot be derived by analogy, how could a rate fixed by tests and *ijma'* be changed?

- *Zakat* is, before anything else, a religious obligation, fixed and eternal, one of the pillars of Islam, and one of its great institutions. Allowing its rates to change according to changing circumstances is *sine qua non* to removing this sacred character of *zakat* and putting it in the hands of governments and rulers to tamper with. This pillar of Islam symbolises the unity of all Muslims by the fact that Muslims in all places under all governments are required to apply the same rates.

- Moreover, if the rates of *zakat* are allowed to increase, they should also be allowed to decline or to be eliminated. If a time of prosperity comes to a Muslim land with huge resources (such as oil), those who call for its increase today may then call for its reduction or complete elimination. *Zakat* loses its validity as a given act of worship and becomes a tool in the hands of the state.

- The allowance of any change in the rates of *zakat* would pave the way for changes in other areas of the *Shari'a*. If today's society needs more resources, we can impose other taxes in addition to *zakat* to the degree that is needed. We need not change *zakat*.

Nisab of money

The agreed upon *hadith* states, "There is no *sadaqa* on anything less than five *uqiyyas* of silver." (Ahmad and Muslim) An *uqiyya* equals 40 dirhams, according to many texts and *ijma'*, as quoted by an-Nawawi.[1] Thus five *uqiyya* equals 200 dirhams. It seems, however, that silver currency was predominantly used by the Arabs at the time of the Prophet,[2] so the *hadiths* determine *nisab* and rates on silver currency. These are not disputed by Muslim scholars.[3]

As for gold currency (dinar), we have no *hadiths* determining its *nisab*, or at least not as strong and commonly known *hadiths* as those about silver. Hence the *nisab* of gold is not agreed upon unanimously, but the great majority of scholars are of the opinion that the *nisab* on gold is 20 dinars. It is reported from al-Hasan al-Basri once that it is 40 dinars, and once that it is 20 dinars. The *nisab* on gold is independent from that on silver, except according to Tawus, who evaluates gold by silver. Hence, according to him, an amount of gold whose value is 200 dirhams has reached the *nisab*.[4] A similar view is reported from 'Ata', az-Zuhri, Sulayman ibn Harb and Ayyub as-Sakhtiyani.[5]

The opinion of the majority is supported by the following evidence. There are a few *hadiths*, none of them free from criticism, but which, when taken together strengthen one another. They include:

- Ibn Majah and ad-Daraqutni (p. 199) reporting from Ibn 'Umar and 'A'isha that the Prophet (p) used to collect half a dinar on each 20 dinars.[6]

---

1. Commentary on Muslim, vol. 7, p. 48, at the beginning of the chapter on *zakat*, and *al-Majmu'*, vol. 6, p. 5.

2. That is why 'Ata' said they had silver and not gold currency. See *Musannaf Ibn Abi Shayba*, vol. 3, p. 222.

3. *Al-Mughni*, vol. 3, p. 1.

4. *Nayl al-Awtar*, vol. 4, p. 139.

5. *Al-Mughni*, vol. 3, p. 4.

6. Ibrahim ibn Isma'il ibn Majma' is in its chain, who is described by Ibn Ma'in as 'nothing'. Abu Hatim noted that his *hadiths* cannot be relied on since he has illusions. In al-*Muhalla*, vol. 6, p. 69, Ibn Hazm mentions the *hadith* and rates it weak on p. 72 because of 'Abdullah ibn Waqid, whom he calls unknown. The late Ahmad Shakir asks, "How could he be unknown, when he is 'Abdullah ibn Waqid ibn 'Abdullah ibn 'Umar?" He is trustworthy; he narrates from his grandfather and died in 119 AH. Ibn Hazm was wrong in making his narration from Ibn 'Umar and 'A'isha, since it is reported by Ibn Majah and ad-Daraqutni from both Ibn 'Umar and 'A'isha."

- Ad-Daraqutni (p. 199) reporting from 'Amr ibn Shu'ayb from his father from his grandfather from the Prophet (p), " There is no *sadaqa* obliged on any amount less than 20 *mithqals* [dinars] of gold or 200 dirhams."[1]
- Abu 'Ubayd, with his own chain, reports from Muhammad ibn 'Abdu'r-Rahman al-Ansari, a Follower, that in the letter of the Messenger of Allah and in the letter of 'Umar, it is written, "From gold, nothing must be taken until it reaches 20 dinars. Once it is 20 dinars then on it there is one half dinar due."[2]
- Abu Dawud reports from 'Ali from the Prophet (p), "If you have 200 dirhams, and a year passes on them, there must be five dirhams [taken as *nisab*]. You are not obliged to pay anything [on gold] until you have 20 dinars. If you have 20 dinars and a year passes on them, there is a half dinar due on it." Some critics of the *hadith* grade this *hasan*. Ad-Daraqutni considers it correct when it ends at 'Ali.[3]

Those jurists who view the quantities as given by the *Shari'a* and not deduced through reasoning, like the Hanafis,[4] say, "If it is

1. Also mentioned by Abu Ubayd in *al-Amwal*, p. 409, and Ibn Hazm in *al-Muhalla*, vol. 6, p. 69. The latter grades it weak on p. 71 because it is *mursal* and it has Ibn Abi Layla, who is weak in memory in its chain. Ibn Hajar in *at-Talkhis*, p. 132, writes, "Its chain is weak." It is also reported by Ibn Zanjawayh in *al-Amwal* from al-'Arzami, whose narration is disregarded. See *Nasb ar-Rayah*, vol. 2, p. 369; *ad-Diraya*, p, 161, and *al-Mir'a* on *al-Mishkat*, vol. 3, p. 43.

2. Mentioned by Ibn Hazm in *al-Muhalla*, vol. 6, p. 69. On p. 72, he says, "It is *mursal* and has an unknown link in its chain." On p. 31 he says, "Muhammad ibn 'Abdu'r-Rahman is unknown." Ahmad Shakir disagrees with this, claiming that he is known, saying that he is Muhammad ibn 'Abdu'r-Rahman al-Ansari, a trustworthy Follower.

3. The *hadith* is graded weak by Ibn Hazm in *al-Muhalla*, vol. 6, under the title "*Zakat* on Gold". Later on, he revised his view and graded it as *sahih*. It is graded as *hasan* by Ibn Hajar in *Bulugh al-Maram*, but he held it defective in *at-Talkhis*, p. 182. Ad-Daraqutni says, "It is correct as a statement of 'Ali." This seems to be correct. See *Nayl al-Awtar*, vol. 4, pp. 137-138.

4. In his *Usul*, as-Sarakhsi says, "There is no disagreement among our scholars, whether ancient or modern, that what a Companion says is accepted as evidence in respect of the questions that cannot be derived by analogy. The quantities are of that nature." He mentions several examples that are accepted by Hanafis, p. 110.

authentically reported from 'Ali that the *nisab* of gold is 20 dinars, then this has the same authority as if it were linked up to the Prophet (p)," because 'Ali would not state it from his own opinion.

It is known historically that, at the time of the Prophet (p), one dinar equalled ten dirhams.[1]

Muslims since the time of the Companions have paid *zakat* on gold on the basis of this *nisab*, on which an *ijma'* has been established after the era of al-Hasan (who had a different view according to a version of one report from him). From the time of the Companions we have a report from Anas ibn Malik stating, "I was commissioned by 'Umar to collect *sadaqat*. He instructed me to take from each 20 dinars one-half of a dinar, and from more than 20 at the rate of one dirham from each four dinars." 'Ali says, "There is nothing due on less than 20 dinars. On 20 dinars there is one-half a dinar due."[2] This is part of the *hadith* that is linked to the Prophet (p) by some narrators. Ibrahim an-Nakha'i says, "The wife of Ibn Mas'ud had a necklace that contained 20 *mithqals*. Her husband instructed her to give five dirhams as its *zakat*."[3]

That on each 20 dinars one-half of a dinar is due is also reported from prominent Followers such as ash-Sha'bi, Ibn Sirin, Ibrahim, al-Hasan, al-Hakam ibn 'Utba, and 'Umar ibn 'Abdu'l-'Aziz.[4] Abu 'Ubayd and Ibn Hazm report from Zurayq ibn Hibban, "'Umar ibn 'Abdu'l-'Aziz wrote me a letter saying: 'Look out for Muslims who pass by you and take out of their apparent wealth and their profits from trade, one dinar out of each 40 dinars, and apply the same proportion to what is less than that until you reach the amount of 20 dinars. Once it is less than 20 dinars, even by one-third of a dinar, leave it intact.'"[5]

On this estimation of *nisab*, *zakat* stabilised and has continued since the time of 'Umar ibn 'Abdu'l-'Aziz. No variation or dispute

1. *Al-Amwal*, p. 419; see also *Sunan* Abu Dawud, chapter on the amount of ransoms. There is a *hadith* there from 'Amr ibn Shu'ayb from his father from his grandfather that, "Ransom at the time of the Messenger of Allah (p) was 800 dinars or 8000 dirhams.

2. *Al-Muhalla*, vol. 6, p. 69.

3. Ibid.

4. Ibid., p. 69-70.

5. Ibid., p. 66.

is mentioned, and some leading jurists consider there to be virtual unanimity. Malik relies on such an established practice, especially among Madinans. In affirming this ruling in *al-Muwatta'*, Malik writes, "The undisputed *Sunna*, in my opinion, is that *zakat* is obligatory on 20 dinars of gold as it is on 200 dirhams."[1] Ash-Shafi'i says in *al-Umm*, "I know of no controversy that there is no *sadaqa* on gold until it reaches 20 dinars, and once it does, then *zakat* is paid on it."[2] Abu 'Ubayd comments in *al-Amwal* on the *hadith* of 'Amr ibn Shu'ayb that the *nisab* on gold is 20 *mithqals*, "There is no controversy about this among all Muslims. If, at the beginning of the year, a person owns an amount on which *zakat* should be paid (i.e. 200 dirhams, 20 dinars, five camels, 30 cows, or 40 sheep) and continues to own it until the end of the year, *zakat* is obliged on him indisputably among all people."[3] 'Iyad says, "*Ijma'* is relied upon in determining the *nisab* of gold, although a disregarded deviant view is reported."[4]

Many leading scholars have established that if all Muslims embrace a *hadith*, even if it is criticised from the point of view of the chain, this embracing raises it to the degree of acceptance, as in the case of the *hadith*, "There must be no final bequest to an heir." This principle is supported by ash-Shafi'i, Ibn 'Abdu'l-Barr, Ibn al-Humam, Ibn Hajar, Ibn al-Qayyim, and others. On this ground we notice that at-Tirmidhi may sometimes report a *hadith* about which he expresses doubt or which he considers weak with the qualifier being that it is accepted among scholars. Also Ibn 'Abdu'l-Barr says that a *hadith* is sometimes *sahih* because scholars espouse it, or that the *ijma'* of the people on the meaning of a *hadith* renders any criticism of its chain invalid.[5]

However, this principle must not be applied indiscriminately. I think it is only applicable if the *hadith* is not extremely weak, if the

1. *Al-Muwatta'*, chapter on *zakat*, section on *zakat* on gold and silver, vol. 1, p. 246.

2. *Al-Umm*, vol. 2, p. 34.

3. *Al-Amwal*, p. 409.

4. *Al-Mir'a*, vol. 3, p. 43.

5. See *al-Ajwiba al-Fasila*, by the late scholar al-Luknawi, pp. 51-52, and the works of Shaykh Husayn al-Ansari on the acceptance of weak *hadiths* when received with approval by people, p. 228, and the commentaries of my colleague, Shaykh 'Abdu'l-Fattah Abu Ghidda.

acceptance is expressed by the generations of the Companions and Followers and not only by later generations, and lastly, if the *hadith* does not stand in opposition to a well-established principle or ruling in the *Shari'a*. These three conditions are satisfied in the case regarding the *nisab* of gold. The chains of narrators in the above-mentioned saying are close to being accepted. The Companions and Followers paid *zakat* on gold in accordance with the meaning of these *hadiths*, and there is no ruling in the *Shari'a* that opposes them. In fact there is a ruling which supports their meaning since 20 dinars equals 200 dirhams.

Disproving an objection

Some argue that al-Hasan's opinion – according to one version of the report from him – that the *nisab* is 40 dinars, may be supported by the *hadith* from 'Amr ibn Hazm that the Prophet (p) wrote for him. That letter continues, after the mention of the *nisab* of silver, "and on each 40 dinars there is one dinar."[1] One can easily disprove this argument by the very text cited, which obviously refers to the rate of *zakat* and not to the *nisab*.

Dirhams and dinars in the *Shari'a*

We know that the *nisab* for *zakat* is 200 silver dirhams or 20 gold dinars, but we still must ascertain the actual amount of metal contained in the dirham and dinar so that we can discover their equivalent in modern terms. Many scholars, both modern and early, have attempted to find out the exact quantity of the dirham

1. The *hadith* is reported by Ibn Hibban in his *Sahih* collection and al-Hakim in *al-Mustadrak*, vol. 1, p. 395. The latter rates it *sahih* and this is approved by adh-Dhahabi. It is also reported by al-Bayhaqi, vol. 4, pp. 89-90. He quotes a group of critics who grade this *hadith* as *hasan* as raised to the Prophet (p). Al-Haytami mentioned it in *Majma' az-Zawa'id,* vol. 3, p. 72, and says it is reported by at-Tabarani in *al-Kabir* with Sulayman ibn Da'ud in its chain, who is considered trustworthy by Ahmad, but is criticised by Ibn Ma'in. Ahmad says that the saying is correct. Al-Haytami says, "The roots of the chain's links are trustworthy." The late Ahmad Shakir supports it as correct in his commentary on *al-Muhalla* as mentioned in vol. 6, p. 13, and p. 34.

and dinar. They include Abu 'Ubayd in *al-Amwal*, al-Baladhuri at the end of *Futuh al-Buldan*, al-Khattabi in *Ma'alim as-Sunan*, al-Mawardi in *al-Ahkam as-Sultaniyya*, an-Nawawi in *al-Majmu'*, al-Maqrizi in *an-Nuqud al-Qadima al-Islamiyya*, Ibn Khaldun in *al-Muqaddima*, and several others. Ibn Khaldun summarises: "One must realise that it is unanimously agreed upon since the early ages of Islam, the era of the Companions and Followers, that the dirham in the *Shari'a* is a coin, ten of which are equal in weight to seven *mithqals* of gold. An *uqiyya* is 40 dirhams. Consequently the weight of a silver dirham is equal to seven-tenths the weight of a gold dinar. One dinar of pure gold is equal to 72 grains of barley of average weight; thus, one dirham weighs fifty and two-fifths grains. All these measures are affirmed by unanimous agreement."

The dinar [which is the same as a *mithqal*] did not change from the pre-Islamic era. Muslim currencies, however, at the above-mentioned weights, were used over a wide area from the time of the Umayyad caliph 'Abdu'l-Malik ibn Marwan. During his reign, there were different dirhams with different weights, which he unified in accordance with the above ratios. But changes were incorporated in later mintings of dirhams and dinars after 'Abdu'l-Malik in several countries, so the above-cited definition by Ibn Khaldun became only theoretical, and people had to find out the proportion between their local currencies and those definitions, when determining the *nisab* and other *Shari'a* quantities. The same problem is posed again in regard to contemporary currencies in Muslim countries today.

The Prophet (p) guides us to a very useful practice in unifying measures and quantities all over the country. He said, "Our weight measurements are those used by Makkans, and our volume measurements are those used by Madinans." The Makkans were people of trade, accustomed to circulating dinars and dirhams by weight and they were more precise in their weight measurements. Madinans were cultivators of crops and fruits and they were more accurate in using volume measures, such as the *wasq*, *sa'*, and *mudd*. It was hoped that all Muslim countries would unify and standardise their measures of weight and volume in accordance with those of the Makkans and Madinans, in order to make the application of quantities mentioned in the *Shari'a* easier.

Unfortunately, the Muslims have not given sufficient attention to that useful directive of the Prophet (p). They have differences in their measures of weight and volume from one country to another and we have come to see the *ratl* defined differently in Baghdad, Madina, Egypt and Syria. In the same way the dirham and dinar were given different weights in different countries. All this makes our task of finding the exact equivalent of the dirham and the dinar today even more difficult. Those grains that were used in defining the dirham and the dinar are not themselves precise which adds yet another difficulty to the problem in hand. Yet we must determine the exact weight of the dirham and the dinar in order to define the *nisab* of gold and silver in our time.

In his book, *Coin Weights in the Early Ages of Islam*, 'Abdu'r-Rahman Fahmy of Cairo's Museum of Islamic Art, after a careful examination of a number of historical weights, estimated that one dirham was the equivalent of 3.104 grams of silver. Ibn 'Abidin, after narrating several Hanafi views, came to the conclusion that it was very difficult to agree on the exact weight of dirhams and dinars.[1] A more recent researcher, basing himself on the writings of al-Maqrizi and comparing Greek and Islamic weights for the dirham and dinar, concluded that the dirham should be 3.12 grams of silver, which is very close to Fahmy's figure. But it seems that the latter study does not distinguish between the dirham that used to be a unit of weight and the dirham that was used as a unit of silver currency. Al-Maqrizi himself quotes from al-Khattabi that there used to be several dirhams, one a weight unit and another a currency unit.[2]

Other studies were based on actually weighing coins that were saved from early Islamic periods and preserved in museums throughout the world. It seems, however, that the *mithqal*, which is

1. *Radd al-Muhtar*, vol. 2, p. 40.

2. See *al-Khutat at-Tawfiqiyya*, vol. 2, p. 33 and the *Encyclopaedia of Islam*. Zembaur says, "Dirham is also the name of a weight measure." A dirham equals 3.184 grams. It is completely different from the coin that carries the same name. This weight measure remained in use until our days, and it is used by chemists and goldsmiths.

the same as the dinar, is a more constant and stable measure than the dirham. If we can determine the weight of a *mithqal*, then the weight of a dirham can easily be derived. Fortunately, several dinars that were minted at the time of 'Abdu'l-Malik have been preserved.

Some European scholars and the Egyptian, 'Ali Basha Mubarak, in separate studies, took the weight of several Islamic dinars that exist in London, Paris, Madrid, and Berlin. They came to the conclusion that the dinar of 'Abdu'l-Malik weighed 4.25 grams. The *Encyclopaedia of Islam* cites this as the same weight as the Byzantine dinar. Thus the dirham would be 4.25 x 7/10 = 2.975 grams.[1]

This is supported by many contemporary archaeological researchers, Arab and European, including the orientalist Zembaur, who writes in the *Encyclopaedia of Islam* under the title "Dirham and Dinar": "Historians differ greatly on the exact weight of the dirham and dinar. But they agree that ten dirhams equal seven dinars, which is the same as seven *mithqals*. The *mithqal* of the Makkans equals 4.25 grams. This means that a dirham is 2.97 grams, which coincides with the weight of coins minted at the time of al-Muqtadir (295/908 - 320/932), discovered by Rogers in al-Fayyum, Egypt. It seems that 'Umar was the first to stabilise the legal weight of the dirham, and later 'Abdu'l-Malik unified all coins on that legal weight – 2. 97 grams."

Zembaur continues, "Historians are unanimously of the opinion that 'Abdu'l-Malik in his currency reform did not alter the weights of gold coins. The weight of the gold coins can easily be determined by weighing the existing dinars in museums. The exact weight of the dinar is 4.25 grams. This is also equal to the actual weight of the Byzantine dinar."

It seems that the survey of preserved coins is the most accurate means of determining the exact weight of the dinar and the dirham. The *nisab* of silver must then be 200 x 2975 = 595 grams,

1. It is noted that this result is very close to the conclusions of the later Maliki scholar ad-Dardir in *as-Sharh as-Saghir*, that the *nisab* of silver dirhams is 185 and five-eighths, which equals 579.15 grams. Thus a dirham is equal to 2.896 grams, although we do not know the basis for his conclusion. See *as-Sharh as-Saghir*, commentary on *Bulgha as-Salik*, vol. 1, p. 217.

and the weight of the *nisab* of gold should be 20 x 4.25 = 85 grams of gold.

The *nisab* of non-metal money

Paper currency is now predominantly used in transactions throughout the world, and gold and silver have disappeared from circulation as currencies. What then is the *nisab* of paper money? Is it that of silver and gold? It is apparent that 20 dinars of gold (85 grams) and 200 dirhams of silver (595 grams) are no longer equal in value to each other as they were at the time of the Prophet (p).

It is expected that, since this is a matter of human reasoning, some scholars will be inclined to consider the *nisab* of silver most appropriate for non-metal money because it is determined explicitly by *Sunna* and *ijma'*, and it is the smaller amount of the two in today's value, so using it as *nisab* would be of more benefit to the poor. This is perhaps why it is commonly used in countries like Egypt, Saudi Arabia, the Gulf states, India and Pakistan.[1]

Other scholars tend to consider the nisab of gold more appropriate because the value of gold has not changed through the centuries as much as the value of silver has.[2] Scholars favouring the gold *nisab* include the late Abu Zahra, Khallaf and Hasan.[3] This view can be supported by comparing the *nisab* on gold with the *nisab* on camels, sheep, and crops, because one finds that with today's price, the *nisab* of gold is more comparable to the *nisab* on other items of wealth than the *nisab* of silver. Five camels or forty sheep equal a value that is very close to 85 grams of gold, while the 595 grams of silver may not equal the price of one camel.

1. Estimated by al-Ghazipuri at 60 rupees and by al-Luknawi at 55 rupees.

2. This is indicated by historians' reports that the dinar was equal to ten dirhams during the first era of Islam. In the Umayyad era it became equal to 12 dirhams, and during the Abbasid period it became equal to 15 dirhams or more. See *al-Kharaj in the Islamic State*, p. 347. 'Ali Mubarak quotes al-Maqrizi, "At the time of al-Halim, the Fatimid, the number of dirhams increased to the extent that a dinar was exchanged for 35 dirhams. See *al-Khutat at-Tawfiqiyya*, vol. 2, p. 43. 'Abdu'r-Rahman Fahmy discusses the same thing in his book using a table that shows the rates of exchange between dinar and dirham in the different Islamic eras.

3. *Halqat ad-Dirasat al-Ijtima'iyya*, p. 238.

In *Hujjat Allah al-Baligha*, Shah Waliyullah ad-Dihlawi says, "The *nisab* on silver was estimated at five *uqiyyas* because that was sufficient for the smallest household to live on for one year under reasonable prices and with average dietary habits." (p. 505) Can we find any country today in which the value of 595 grams of silver would be sufficient for one year's expenses for a small household? In fact, that much silver would hardly be sufficient for one month or even one week. It is much better to determine the *nisab* on money today at the equivalent of that on gold, i.e. the value of 85 grams of gold, because doing it otherwise would inflict great injustice on *zakat* payers.

Can we find a stable, permanent *nisab* for money?

The value of money is not fixed; it fluctuates from time to time in accordance with many variables. The real value of money is its purchasing power,[1] and the only reason paper currency has any validity is because it has purchasing power. We noted that silver money decreased in value to the extent that made the silver *nisab* extremely low compared to the *nisab* on other items of wealth. What would happen if the value of gold declined drastically? Can we discover a standard and stable measurement that could be used as a *nisab* for money? Some may look to the *nisab* applicable on other items, such as animals, crops, or fruits, whose value may be more stable than that of money.

Can the *nisab* of crops and fruits be used?

The immediate observation on the *nisab* of crops (five *wasqs*) is that its current value is very low in relation to the *nisab* on livestock. This may be explained by the following points. Firstly, the bounty of Allah is more apparent in agriculture, where the role played by the human hand is relatively less than when generating

1. This may be supported by a report from Abu Dawud, "Ransom used to be 800 dinars or 8000 dirhams, at the time of the Prophet (p)." During his caliphate 'Umar declared that camels had become expensive and determined rates of ransom at 1000 gold dinars or 12,000 silver dirhams.

other forms of wealth. Allah says, *"So they may eat its fruits and their hands did not make it. So why do they not show thanks?"* (36:35) Secondly, humanity cannot survive without that which comes out of the soil as crops and fruits the way they can do without animals for food. The *nisab* on crops is made low in order to provide large proceeds of *zakat* to benefit the needy. Thirdly, crops and fruits are to land as profit is to capital. While *zakat* on cows, camels and sheep is obliged on the capital and profit together, *zakat* on crops and fruits is only taken from the profit. To compensate for this difference, the *nisab* is made low and the *zakat* rate is made high.

Can the *nisab* of livestock be used?

If the *nisab* on crops is not suitable, can the *nisab* on livestock be an alternative? To start with, the *nisab* on cattle must be disregarded because it is not obliged by a clear-cut text. The *nisab* on camels and sheep is defined in non-controversial texts and confirmed by *ijma'*. Can we take the value of five camels or forty sheep as the *nisab* for money?

To answer this question, we must first consider whether the *nisab* of camels and sheep equalled the *nisab* of silver money at the time of the Prophet (p). In *al-Mabsut*, as-Sarakhsi argues in favour of the possibility. A one-year-old she-camel used to be valued at about 40 dirhams, and sheep at five dirhams. Thus, five camels would equal 200 dirhams of silver.[1] But we mentioned earlier that Ibn al-Humam in *al-Fath* and Ibn Nujaym in *al-Bahr* both critically investigated the argument of the author of *al-Mabsut*, contrasting it with a *hadith* reported in the *Sahih* of al-Bukhari, which indicates that the difference in the value of different age camels was estimated by the Messenger (p) at two sheep or 20 dirhams per year of difference. This is an explicit text that contradicts the calculation of as-Sarakhsi.[2] According to this authentic *hadith*, at the time of the Prophet (p) 40 sheep were equal to 400 dirhams, that is, twice as much as the *nisab* of silver money.

1. *Al-Mabsut*, vol. 2, p. 150.
2. *Fath al-Qadir*, vol. 1, p. 494, and *al-Bahr*, vol. 2, p. 230.

It seems, however, that the *nisab* of silver was intentionally made lower than the *nisab* of livestock for a special reason in the *Shari'a*. Money can be used in many ways, giving a greater choice than the owning of camels or sheep presents. Money is a liquid asset while camels and sheep are not. Saving money for an entire year, despite all temptations to spend it, is more of an indication of wealth than retaining livestock for a year. There is an implication, especially according to the Hanafis who make it an explicit condition, that this money is above and beyond the basic needs of the owner. These reasons may have been considered by the Legislator in determining the *nisab* of money as below that of livestock.

Thus, if we decide to determine a *nisab* for paper money that can be stabilised and used as a standard when the purchasing power of money varies drastically, this *nisab* should be equal to one-half the value of five camels or forty sheep in an average country. I suggest an average country in order to avoid the two extremes, lands where these two animals are scarce and very expensive, and lands where they are plentiful and very cheap.

Types of paper money

Paper money is printed by the government, or a government-authorised body, and circulated among people for use in their transactions. This kind of money is commonly used all over the world for many national and international transactions. Paper money is used as a means of exchange, a store of value, a measurement of future values and as a means of evaluating financial transactions.

Paper money evolved through time from obligatory convertibility to non-convertibility. In its early stages, paper money took the form of simple IOU's issued by banks, that guaranteed their substitution for fixed amounts of gold or silver. Banks were obliged to convert these IOU's into gold or silver on demand. As time went on, the banking machinery was able to influence the government and gain permission to hold only partial reserves of gold and silver against issued IOU's. Governments themselves went into the business of producing paper money because it seemed lucrative.

At first, governments issued paper money on partial reserves of gold or silver, but with time, changing needs, and the general acceptance of paper money, governments shifted from the system of partial precious metal reserves to the system of government authorisations given to central banks to issue a certain quantity of paper money. Thus we entered the phase of non-convertibility, where national currencies became compulsory and non-convertible to gold or silver within the borders of each country.

Zakat on paper currency

Obviously, we do not expect to find an opinion on the *zakat* of paper money in the early generations of Islam because paper money is an invention of the last few centuries. Contemporary scholars looking at various aspects of money have expressed different opinions concerning the application of the rules of *zakat* on it. Shaykh 'Ulaysh, a Maliki in Egypt, gave the opinion that paper, stamped by the government and used like dinars and dirhams is not subject to *zakat*.[1] Some Shafi'is add a condition for the *zakat* on paper money being the actual substitution of money into gold and silver.[2] The group of scholars who compiled the book, *al-Fiqh 'ala al-Madhahib al-Arba'a* write that:

> The Shafi'ites consider paper money to be drafts representing debts of the issuing banks. Since the bank is fully capable of payment, the rules of *zakat* on debts apply. *Zakat* is due on this draft.
>
> The Hanafis consider paper money to be claims on the bank that can quickly be exchanged into silver. They are subject to *zakat*.
>
> The Malikis find in these bank notes a means of exchange, representing gold and silver, convertible into these metals on demand. They are amenable to *zakat*.

1. The booklet *at-Tibyan fi Zakat al-Athman*, by Shaykh Muhammad Hasanayn Makhluf al-'Adawi, p. 33.
2. *Al-Fiqh 'ala al-Madhahib al-Arba'a*, p. 486.

> The Hanbalis consider paper currency not liable to *zakat* until it is converted into gold or silver, and then the conditions of *zakat* on gold and silver apply.

It is apparent that all these views are based on the principle of obligatory convertibility, whereas the latest developments in paper currency make it completely non-convertible, which means that these views, even those that count paper currency as being subject to *zakat*, should be revised according to this reality.

We should realise the fact that paper currency is now the main tender for transactions. Gold and silver are only used in exceptional circumstances. Paper currency, issued and guaranteed by the state, is the measure of current and future values. Laws provide for its acceptability and enforce its non-convertibility. Paper money is used to perform all the activities and functions of monetary gold and silver. It is true, however, that precious metals have values of their own which may at times be different from their monetary value, a value that is determined by the supply and demand for these two metals, merely on the grounds of their industrial and commercial value. *Zakat* is imposed on gold and silver in consideration of their characteristics as growing assets used as a measure of value. That is perhaps why gold and silver are usually called in juridical terms "the values" or "the two currencies".

It is not fair or acceptable for anyone to claim that some schools of thought do not consider paper money amenable to *zakat* or to attribute such a view to the schools of Ahmad, Malik or ash-Shafi'i. In fact, paper money is a new invention and was not in existence at the time of these leading scholars.

One should note what is written by the later scholar, Muhammad Hasanayn Makhluf al-'Adawi, in his booklet, *at-Tibyan fi Zakat al-Athman*. He comments on those who consider paper currency as representing bank debts:

> It is obvious that there are essential differences between paper currency and real debts. Real debts are not growing assets. Paper currency is a growing asset, used for obtaining goods and services. *Zakat* on debts is based on the ability of debtors to repay, knowing that debts do not grow, while *zakat* on money is based on its use as a means of exchange.

The fact that paper currency is not any kind of debt known to jurists means it must be liable to *zakat* because it is useful and growing like any other present wealth while debts do not grow nor provide benefit to creditors as long as they are not paid back to him. Paper currency cannot be described as similar to debt documents since such documents are usually made as evidence of indebtedness, not for growth or to be used in transactions. Nor can it be argued that paper currency only becomes zakatable after being exchanged for gold or silver since the exemption of debts from *zakat* is because they do not grow nor are they left in the debtor's vault.

Paper money is subject to *zakat* for four reasons:

• It represents funds deposited in the bank, which is similar to present disposable assets.

• It represents the stock of gold or silver in the vaults of the bank.

• It is a debt on the bank, which is fully capable of payment.

• It is a measure of value acceptable in transactions, so it is also amenable to *zakat* like coins and other things used as currency.

The first three reasons mentioned here are actually untrue and only the last consideration of Shaykh Makhluf is, in my opinion, relevant, because of the prevalence of non-convertible paper currency. In the early use of paper currency, because of its vagueness and unknown future, people's opinions differed, but now that the use of paper money is well-established, we must be certain about its treatment in terms of *zakat*. Besides, money can be anything used as a measure of value, a means of exchange, and store of value, regardless of the actual material used.[1] This form of money is used for all the monetary functions of gold and silver as known in the *Shari'a* and must therefore be subject to *zakat*.

1. *An-Nudhum*, op. cit., p. 29.]

Conditions for the *zakat* of money

Four conditions are required for the *zakat* of money.

The *nisab*

The first condition is that the amount of money should be at least equal to the *nisab*. Anything that is below the *nisab* is exempted from *zakat* since the possessor is not considered rich. We have learned from the preceding pages, the various statements regarding the *nisab* of money. My preference is to consider it the value of 85 grams of gold which is equal to 20 dinars.

Is sole ownership necessary?

What happens in the case of a partnership or a corporation, in which the owners are several individuals and the company has cash assets of more than the *nisab*, but the share of each partner in the cash is less than the *nisab*? According to Abu Hanifa and Malik, partners pay *zakat* only if the share of each one individually reaches the *nisab* or more.

Ash-Shafi'i treats this common property as one unit and considers it subject to *zakat* if the total is at least the *nisab*. The reason for this difference in opinion is, according to Ibn Rushd, the general terminology of the saying of the Prophet (p), "On that which is less than five *uqiyyas* there is no *sadaqa* due." It is undetermined in this text whether these five *uqiyyas* (200 dirhams) belong to one owner or more, but I may add that the very reason for which *nisab* is a condition of *zakat* should perhaps be applied to one owner, as it otherwise loses its virtue. Ash-Shafi'i looks at the similarity between common property in a partnership and mixing cattle together in grazing, but here again the same difference in views appears with respect to the effect of mixing cattle in grazing.[1]

The majority view is based on the assumption that since *zakat* is an obligation on the rich only, a partnership may contain some poor partners, and why should these poor people pay *zakat* simply

1. *Bidayat al-Mujtahid*, Ibn Rushd, vol. 1, p. 250.

because of their association with others who are rich? On the other hand, ash-Shafi'i's view appears to be simpler in application in a time when corporations have become of major importance in the business world. However, it could be suggested that part of the proceeds of *zakat* taken from corporations be distributed among the poor shareholders or partners of that corporation.

The passage of a year

The second condition is that a full lunar year must have passed on the ownership of the *nisab*. *Zakat* on money is a yearly obligation and cannot be imposed at shorter intervals. Hanafis require that the *nisab* at least exists at the beginning and end of the year. Thus a decline from the level of the *nisab* during the year has no effect. But if the wealth vanishes completely, the year is disrupted and a new year should be counted for any newly earned wealth.[1]

The other three schools of jurisprudence require the *nisab* to remain in ownership during the whole year. They argue that the Prophet's saying, "There is no *zakat* on an asset until a year passes on it," implies that the year should pass on it all, since what is considered at the two ends of a year must also be considered at its middle, such as ownership or faith.[2]

All this applies to money as a saved asset. Earned money, such as salaries, wages, awards, professional income and the rental proceeds of leased buildings or cars, are all disputed. The majority of jurists stipulate that a year must pass on any amount of money, stock or flow for *zakat* to become obligatory. Abu Hanifa suggests adding the flow to the stock and making *zakat* due on the total at the end of the year (that started for the stock). An exception is made in the case where the flow of cash is a substitution for an asset whose *zakat* was already paid.[3] It is authentically reported from some Companions that such a flow of money is liable for *zakat* at the time of its receipt. We shall study this issue in detail in the proper chapter.

1. *Ad-Durr al-Mukhtar* and its commentary, *Radd al-Muhtar*, vol. 2, p.45.
2. *Al-Mughni*, vol. 2, p. 499.
3. Ibid., p. 497.

Freedom from debt

The third condition is that the person possessing the *nisab* must be free of any debt whose payment would reduce the amount of money below the *nisab*. Debts that prevent the payment of *zakat* are those that are due to other human beings, including personal debts and past due *zakat*,[1] while debts that belong to Allah are not deductible, such as the cost of making pilgrimage. The Hanafis have different opinions regarding deferred debts and whether they prevent the liability of present sums of money or not.[2] An-Nawawi summarises the Shafi'i view, "If debts prevent the conditions of *zakat*, then debts due to Allah and debts due to others should be treated the same."[3]

Excess above basic needs

Some leading Hanafi jurists require that the *nisab* be counted only above the satisfaction of the basic needs of the owners. According to Ibn Malik, basic needs are those that prevent the destruction of a person and his dependants, such as food, shelter, arms for defence, clothes that protect from the elements, money to pay back debts, furniture, household utensils, basic transportation, and books of knowledge. According to the Hanafis, ignorance is like personal destruction.[4] If a person owns an amount of money

1. Ibn 'Abidin, a Hanafi, quotes from *al-Bada'i'*, "The person who claims it here is the governor, because he is the one who has the responsibility of collecting *zakat* on livestock. When wealth increased tremendously at the time of 'Uthman he realised that investigating all the wealth would create great inconvenience for the owners, and preferred to leave the calculating of *zakat* to the owners themselves. This was unanimously approved by the Companions. Owners of wealth became like agents of the government in calculating their own *zakat*, without affecting the right of the government to collect it if it so decided. It is for this reason that jurists of our school say that if it were known that owners of wealth in certain towns did not pay *zakat* on non-apparent wealth then the governor must collect it." *Radd al-Muhtar*, vol. 2, p. 6.

2. Ibid.

3. *Ar-Rawda*, vol. 2, p. 199.

4. Some Hanafis argue with Ibn Malik on the basis that *zakat* is obligatory on money even if it is designated for these expenses. But it seems that Ibn Malik's opinion is more consistent with the clear words of the texts in the Hanafi school.

that is above the *nisab*, but needs it for any of the above expenses, he or she is not considered liable for *zakat*,[1] on the grounds that this person is not rich and *zakat* is only collected from the rich. The Prophet (p) proclaims: "There is no *sadaqa* except out of wealth," and "Start with those you support."

Section Two: *Zakat* on gold and silver jewellery, ornaments and antiques

In order to complete our study of *zakat* on gold and silver, we must consider the basis on which *zakat* is paid on utensils, ornaments, decorative objects, statuary, and jewellery made of gold and silver.

Gold and silver utensils and ornaments are amenable to *zakat*

It is not disputed among Muslim scholars that whenever gold and silver are used in a forbidden manner they are subject to *zakat*. Authentic and reliable *hadiths* are reported which forbid the use of gold and silver as kitchen and dining utensils because doing so indicates a lavish and ostentatious way of life and constitutes a form of hoarding.[2] The author of *al-Mughni* explains that whatever is prohibited for use is also prohibited for decoration, regardless of whether such utensils and decorative objects are owned by men or women. Women's jewellery is allowed on the grounds that women wear it for their husbands. This need cannot be extended to utensils and other ornaments.

That is why some Hanafi scholars opt for it. It is described as the correct view in *Radd al-Muhtar*, vol. 2, p. 8. It is also the strongest in my opinion, because of its consistency with the principle of "being surplus above basic needs."

1. What is meant by clothing is what satisfies essential needs, and not luxurious clothes, described by Ibn Malik as clothes needed to protect the body against heat and cold.

2. About the prohibition of silver and gold utensils, see my book, *al-Halal wa'l-Haram fi'l-Islam*.

Additionally, statues are prohibited regardless of the metal or stone they are made from. If they are made of gold or silver, the grounds for their prohibition is doubled. Ibn Qudama adds, "Once this is realised, ornaments and utensils are indisputably subject to *zakat*, if they reach the *nisab* either alone or when added to other owned gold and silver."[1] The author of *al-Mughni* attributes an opinion to some Hanbalis that the market value of such items should be considered and not only their weight, because of the high value of the artistic work incorporated in them.

Men's jewellery

Men are forbidden to wear jewellery made of gold, silver or any other substance, except for a plain silver ring which is permissible. Men's jewellery is thus subject to *zakat* if it reaches the *nisab*, like that of women.[2] *Zakat* is obliged on men's jewellery as a reminder of the error of having jewellery and of the need to put its value back into productive use. As for the use of gold by men, it is completely prohibited, except for such necessities as caps for teeth, tooth fillings or as a substitute for a broken nose or severed ear.

Abu Dawud reports from 'Abdu'r-Rahman ibn Tarafa that, "The nose of his grandfather, 'Araja ibn Sa'd, was severed in the Battle of al-Kilab. He got an artificial nose made of silver, but it became rotten and bad-smelling. The Prophet (p) ordered him to get a gold nose." Ahmad says, "It is permissible in cases of necessity to tie the teeth with gold thread, if it is feared that the teeth may fall out." Any other use of gold by men is forbidden and is subject to *zakat*. We should recognise, however, that it is preferred to consider value and not only weight in the case of men's jewellery, because of the value added by artistic labour. Once the value of this jewellery reaches the equivalent of 85 grams of gold, *zakat* is paid on it.

1. *Al-Mughni*, vol. 3, pp. 15-16.

2. Ibn Qudama said, "For men, a silver ring is allowed because the Prophet (p) wore a silver ring," and this is agreed upon. Also lawful is the decoration of a sword by making its handle out of silver or decorating it with silver. Anas reports that the handle of the sword of the Messenger of Allah (p) was made of silver, and Hisham ibn 'Urwa says that az-Zubayr's sword was decorated with silver. Both are reported by al-Athram with his own chain. See *al-Mughni*, vol. 1, pp. 14-15.

Pearls, precious stones, and women's jewellery are not subject to *zakat*

Women's jewellery made of materials other than gold and silver, such as pearls, diamonds, and other precious stones and metals, are not subject to *zakat* because they are designated for personal and lawful use by women, as determined by Allah, *"and bring out from it ornaments to wear,"* (16:14) and are not considered growing assets. Some leading Shi'ite scholars disagree and consider any women's jewellery that reaches the *nisab* in value subject to *zakat,* on the grounds that jewels are valuable items of wealth and Allah says, "*Take* sadaqa *from their wealth.*" They maintain that the words "their wealth" in this verse refers to all Muslims, the general implication of the verse being that wealth should be taken from each of them. Women's jewels, precious stones, and metals are items of wealth included in this general meaning.[1]

The majority of scholars argue that even if the generality of the verse is accepted, we must recognise that the *Sunna* restricts the meaning of the verse to only growing wealth or wealth with growth potential. Thus, actual or potential growth is the reason for *zakat* being levied on it and not the precious nature of the item.[2] These jewels are usually obtained for personal ornamentation and not for growth or investment, as long as they are not kept for the purpose of hoarding wealth and do not exceed a reasonable amount.

The difference between women's gold and silver ornaments

In the letters on *sadaqat* sent by the Prophet (p), there is no reference to women's gold and silver jewellery, nor do we have any authentic, explicit texts which oblige *zakat* or exempt it on this jewellery. All we have are a few sayings whose authenticity and indications are controversial. The reason for the differences in opinion is that some scholars take into consideration the metal of

1. *Ar-Rawd an-Nadir*, vol. 1, pp. 409-410.
2. Ibid.

which jewellery is made. Gold and silver are both amenable to *zakat* as forms of money, so these scholars consider gold and silver jewellery also subject to *zakat*.

Other scholars consider the labour involved and the industrial process required to make jewellery and transform the metal from its basic substance as a monetary form into a commodity for personal use that satisfies a natural need of women. Thus jewellery is treated similarly to clothes, furniture and other personal objects that scholars unanimously exempt from *zakat*. According to these scholars, *zakat* is not paid on women's jewellery. This controversy only concerns lawful jewellery. Forbidden jewellery is unanimously accepted as something on which *zakat* must be paid. Accordingly, there are two groups of scholars: those who consider jewellery items subject to *zakat* exactly like money, and those who consider them beyond or within the realm of *zakat* barring certain restrictions.

Scholars who consider jewellery subject to *zakat*

Al-Bayhaqi and others report from 'Alqama that the wife of Ibn Mas'ud asked him about her jewels. He replied, "If they reach 200 dirhams, *zakat* is paid on them. She said, "May I spend their *zakat* on my orphaned nephews whose guardian I am?" "Yes," he answered. Al-Bayhaqi comments, "This is also narrated and linked to the Prophet but is unsupported." He also reports from Shu'ayb ibn Yasar that 'Umar wrote to Abu Musa, "Instruct Muslim women in your area to pay *zakat* on their ornaments." But this is not authentically reported from 'Umar.[1] Ibn Abi Shayba quotes al-Hasan as saying, "I know that none of the first four Khalifs said that ornaments are subject to *zakat*.[2] Al-Bayhaqi reports from 'A'isha, "It is permissible to wear jewellery if its *zakat* is paid." But we have another correct report from 'A'isha contradicting this, as will be seen later. It is reported that 'Abdullah ibn 'Amr used to write instructions to his treasurer Salim to pay *zakat* on the ornaments of his daughters every year. (al-Bayhaqi) Abu 'Ubayd reports from

1. He says it is *mursal* because Shu'ayb did not see 'Umar.
2. *Al-Musannaf*, vol. 4, p. 28.

him that he gave his three daughters ornaments worth six thousand dinars. He used to send his slave Jalid every year to pay their *zakat*.[1]

The chains of transmission of all the above reports are controversial. Abu 'Ubayd comments, "We have nothing authentic concerning ornaments from any of the Companions except from Ibn Mas'ud.[2] Ibn Hazm says, "The report of Ibn Mas'ud is foremost in its authenticity."[3] Among those who believe that ornaments are liable for *zakat* are Sa'id ibn al-Musayyab, Sa'id ibn Jubayr, 'Ata', Mujahid, 'Abdullah ibn Shaddad, Jabir ibn Zayd, Ibn Shibruma, Maymun ibn Mahran, az-Zuhri, ath-Thawri, Abu Hanifa and his disciples, al-Awza'i and al-Hasan ibn Hayy.[4]

Evidence supporting this opinion

One factor is the general implication of the verse, *"As for those who hoard up gold and silver and do not spend it in the way of Allah, give them the news of a painful punishment"*. (9:34) The gold and silver mentioned in this verse includes what is used for making women's ornaments as much as it indicates money and bullion. Consequently, unless *zakat* is paid, the owner will be branded with its heat on the Day of Resurrection.

The general meaning of the *hadiths* of the Prophet (p), "On silver, 2.5% is obliged. No *sadaqa* is required on what is less than five *uqiyyas*." This implies that *zakat* is paid on silver once it reaches five *uqiyyas*, as do the general texts of *zakat* on gold, such as, "There is no owner of gold that does not pay its *zakat*..."

There are a few *hadiths* about *zakat* on ornaments in particular that are considered correct by some leading scholars. Among these *hadiths* are the following:

---

1. *Al-Amwal*, p. 440.
2. Ibid., p. 446.
3. *Al-Muhalla*, vol. 6, p. 75.
4. *Musannaf Ibn Abi Shayba*, vol. 4, p. 27, *al-Amwal*, pp. 441-442, *al-Muhalla*, vol. 6, p. 76, and *al-Mughni*, vol. 3, p. 100. It should be noted that it is reported from Ibn al-Musayyab that "*Zakat* on jewellery is lending it."

• Abu Dawud reports from 'Amr ibn Shu'ayb from his father from his grandfather that a woman[1] with her daughter came to the Prophet (p). On her daughter's wrists were two thick gold bracelets. The Prophet (p) asked, "Do you give *zakat* on this?" "No," she replied. "Would you prefer Allah to make you wear two bracelets of fire in place of these two on the Day of Resurrection?" he warned. The narrator says, "She took them off and tossed them to the Prophet (p), saying, 'They belong to Allah and His Messenger.'"[2]

• Abu Dawud, ad-Daraqutni, al-Hakim and al-Bayhaqi report that 'A'isha said, "The Messenger of Allah (p) entered my room and found in my hands a few rings of silver. He said, "A'isha, what is this?' I said, 'I made them in order to use them as ornaments to please you, Messenger of Allah.' He said, 'Do you pay their *zakat*?' I answered, 'No.' He said, 'That would be enough for you of the Fire.'"[3]

• Abu Dawud and others report from Umm Salama, "I used to wear some ornaments of gold and I asked, 'Messenger of Allah, is this hoarding?' He said, 'That which reaches the *nisab*, if *zakat* is paid on it, is not hoarding.'" Al-Mundhiri comments, "In its chain there is 'Atab ibn Bashir (Abu'l-Hasan al-Harrani). Al-Bukhari reports from him, but others criticise him."[4]

---

1. In Ibn Abi Shayba and Abu 'Ubayd, it says it was a woman from Yemen.

2. Abu Dawud does not comment on this, saying, "Al-Mundhiri in his *Mukhtasar as-Sunan* says that at-Tirmidhi reports it similarly and comments, 'Nothing is authentic on this question from the Prophet (p).'" An-Nasa'i also reports it connected and *mursal*, indicating that the *mursal* version is more correct. See *Mukhtasar as-Sunan* of al-Mundhiri, vol. 2, p. 175. Al-Mundhiri also mentions this *hadith* in the chapter on *zakat* in *at-Targhib*. He marks it weak and does not make any further comment. In *at-Talkhis*, p. 183, Ibn Hajar says, "Reported by Abu Dawud from Husayn al-Mu'allim, who is trustworthy, from 'Amr." This disproves the claim of ar-Tirmidhi, who affirms that it is only reported from Ibn Lahi'a and al-Muthanna ibn as-Saban from 'Amr.

3. Ibn Hajar in *at-Talkhis*, p. 184, says, "Its chain satisfies the conditions for the sahih. But this *hadith* contradicts what is authentically reported from 'A'isha that she did not pay *zakat* on her nieces' jewellery, although it is authentically reported that she paid *zakat* on their other wealth.

4. *Mukhtasar as-Sunan, vol.* 2 p. 175.

Those who exempt ornaments from *zakat*[1]

In *al-Muhalla*, Ibn Hazm writes, "Jabir ibn 'Abdullah and Ibn 'Umar said, 'There is no *zakat* on ornaments.'" This is also the view of Asma' bint Abu Bakr, and a similar view is correctly reported from 'A'isha. This is also the opinion of ash-Sha'bi, 'Amra bint 'Abdu'r-Rahman, and Abu Ja'far Muhammad ibn 'Ali. It is reported from Tawus, al-Hasan, and Sa'id ibn al-Musayyab. There are two differing reports from Sufyan ath-Thawri, one that *zakat* is paid on women's jewellery and one that it is not.[2] Al-Qasim ibn Muhammad ('A'isha's nephew), Malik ibn Anas, Ahmad ibn Hanbal, and Ishaq ibn Rahawayh say that women's jewellery is not subject to *zakat*. This is the most famous opinion of ash-Shafi'i, according to al-Khattabi,[3] and it is the opinion of Abu 'Ubayd as well.

Evidence supporting this view

In principle, people are not obliged to pay *zakat* without a text from the *Shari'a*, and there is neither an authentic text about *zakat* on women's jewellery nor a correct analogy with a ruling based on an authentic text. Moreover, *zakat* is obliged on actually or potentially growing wealth, and jewellery is neither. Jewellery is for wearing and not for investment. The analogy to animals for personal use is obvious. *Zakat* is not paid on animals because they are not used for growth.

There are also authentic reports from some Companions to the effect that *zakat* is not obliged on ornaments. In *al-Muwatta'* Malik reports from al-Qasim ibn Muhammad[4] that 'A'isha, the wife of

1. Under this title one can also include those who say that jewellery is subject to *zakat* only once in a lifetime, as reported from Anas and those who say that *zakat* on jewellery is satisfied by lending it free of charge, as reports from some Companions and Followers indicate.

2. *Al-Muhalla*, vol. 6, p. 176.

3. *Ma'alim as-Sunan*, vol. 3, p. 176. This is now the accepted view of Shafi'ites, as reported in *al-Majmu'*, vol. 6, p. 136.

4. He is al-Qasim ibn Muhammad ibn Abi Bakr, nephew of 'A'isha and one of the famous seven jurists of Madina.

the Prophet (p), was the guardian of her orphaned nieces. They used to wear ornaments, and she did not pay *zakat* on their ornaments. He also reports from Nafi' that 'Abdullah ibn 'Umar's daughters and female slaves wore gold ornaments and he did not pay *zakat* on their ornaments.[1] Ibn Abi Shayba reports from al-Qasim, "Our assets were kept with 'A'isha. She used to pay *zakat* on them, except for the ornaments," and from 'Amra, "We were orphans under the guardianship of 'A'isha. We had ornaments and she did not pay *zakat* on them."

Ibn Abi Shayba and Abu 'Ubayd and others report similar things from Jabir ibn 'Abdullah and Asma' bint Abi Bakr in addition to 'A'isha and Ibn 'Umar.[2] Ibn az-Zubayr narrates from Jabir, "There is no *zakat* on ornaments. I said, 'It may be as much as a thousand dinars.' He answered, 'It is for wearing or lending.'" In another version he says, "Verily it is too much." It is reported from Asma' that she did not pay *zakat* on ornaments, and ash-Shafi'i adds, "It is also reported from Ibn 'Abbas and Anas ibn Malik, but I do not know whether it is authentic from them. The meaning of these reports is that there is no *zakat* on ornaments."[3]

Qadi Abu'l-Walid al-Baji, in his commentary on *al-Muwatta'*, writes, "This is a known opinion among the Companions. 'A'isha is perhaps the most knowledgeable, since she is the wife of the Prophet (p) and not a person who may have missed his ordinances on such a matter. Also 'Abdullah ibn 'Umar is the brother of Hafsa, the wife of the Prophet (p), and she would have been aware of any requirement on them."[4] One can use as supporting evidence what Yahya ibn Sa'id said, "I asked 'Amra about *zakat* on ornaments. She said, 'I have never seen a person who pays *zakat* on them.'" Al-Hasan is reported to have said, "I know of none of the Rightly-guided Caliphs who said there is *zakat* on ornaments."(al-Bukhari)[5]

1. *Al-Muwatta'*, vol. 1, p. 250.

2. Ibn Abi Shayba, vol. 4, p. 28, and *al-Amwal*, p. 443.

3. *Al-Umm*, vol. 2, p. 41. Non-payment of *zakat* on it is reported from Anas by Abu 'Ubayd, p. 442, and al-Bayhaqi, vol. 4, p. 138.

4. *Al-Muntaqa*, commentary on *al-Muwatta'* by Abu'l-Walid al-Baji, vol. 2, p. 107.

5. Ibn Abi Shayba, vol. 4, p. 28, and *al-Amwal*, p. 442.

Ibn al-Jawzi in *at-Tahqiq* reports, with his own chain, from 'Afiyya ibn Ayyub from al-Layth ibn Sa'd from Abu Zubayr from Jabir from the Prophet (p), "There is no *zakat* on ornaments."[1] Al-Bayhaqi notes that 'Afiyya is unknown. "We know of no criticism of him," Ibn al-Jawzi counters. Ibn Daqiq al-'Id adds, "I have read it hand-written by our teacher, al-Mundhiri, that "...nothing reached me that makes 'Afiyya ibn Ayyub weak."[2] The Prophet (p) said, "O womenfolk, give for charity even out of your ornaments." This is reported by al-Bukhari, at-Tirmidhi, and others.

Ibn al-'Arabi comments, "The obvious literal implication of this saying is that there is no *zakat* obliged on ornaments. His telling women to '...give charity, even out of your ornaments', means that *zakat* is not obliged on them, and they are urged to give voluntary contributions."[3] It is not linguistically correct or usual to ask someone to give voluntarily something he or she is obliged to give anyway as *zakat*. It makes more sense to encourage someone to give voluntarily what is spared from *zakat*.

Analysis of different views

After presenting the differing views of jurists, I may add that what seems to carry most weight is that *zakat* is not obligatory on jewellery, within certain limits. This opinion is consistent with the general conditions of *zakat*. That is, *zakat* is compulsory on actually or potentially growing assets, such as money and business investments. Women's jewellery is worn not for growth but for personal use and lawful ornamentation. It satisfies personal needs of women, natural desires which are taken into consideration in Islam. Gold and silver jewellery is lawful for women, while it is not for men. Hence jewellery for women is something like expensive clothes, furniture, and other sorts of personal ornaments that are lawful for

1. Reported by al-Bayhaqi in *al-Ma'rifa* from 'Afiyya ibn Ayyub from al-Layth from Abu'z-Zubayr from Jabir. He notes, "It is sourceless." It is reported as a statement of Jabir himself. 'Afiyya is described as weak. Ibn al-Jawzi says, "I know of no criticism of him." Al-Bayhaqi says he is unknown, and Ibn Abi Hatim quotes a citation of his as trustworthy from Abu Zar'a. See *at-Talkhis*, p. 183.

2. *Nasb ar-Rayah*, vol. 2, pp. 374-375, and *al-Mir'a*, vol. 3, p. 82.

3. Commentary on at-Tirmidhi, vol. 3, pp. 130-131.

her. It carries great similarities to jewellery made of pearls, diamonds and other precious stones, which are made lawful for women by the texts of the Qur'an. These pearls, precious stones and valuable clothes are exempt from *zakat* by the unanimous opinion of leading scholars, in spite of their high value.

We realise from the Prophet's *Sunna* that *zakat* is not required on all kinds of wealth, but only on growing items. This is in order to preserve the principal and take *zakat* from out of its increase. This also explains the conditions of free grazing in livestock and of growth and excess over basic needs. Thus homes inhabited by their owners, means of personal transportation and tools, are indisputably exempt from *zakat*. Even the Hanafi jurists, who consider *zakat* obligatory on jewellery, have decided that the reason for *zakat* being paid on it is its position as an asset in excess of personal needs that is designated for profit.[1] Does this reason apply in the case of lawful jewellery for women, which is neither designated for growth nor in excess of personal needs?

Hanafis also exempt from *zakat* working animals used in watering and cultivating, in spite of the fact that *zakat* would be paid on the same animals were they naturally pastured and not in work. Being working animals makes them similar to tools and things designated for personal use. How can the same Hanafis oblige *zakat* on jewellery, which is also for personal use?

I firmly believe that the *Shari'a* treats similarly things that are similar, and whenever similar things are not treated thus, it is an error of judgement on the part of the jurists. This is perhaps the reason for which Abu 'Ubayd criticises those who oblige *zakat* on jewellery while exempting working animals. It is extremely unlikely that the *Shari'a* would exempt jewellery made of pearls, diamonds and other precious stones, which are very often more expensive than gold and silver, and oblige *zakat* on jewellery made only of gold and silver. The first kind of jewellery is usually used by rich women, while the second is used by middle class and sometimes poor women. Does it make sense for the *Shari'a* to make middle class and poor women pay *zakat* on their jewellery and exempt the higher class women from similar payment? Exempting

1. *Al-Bahr ar-Ra'iq*, vol. 2, p. 218.

them all from *zakat* is just and reasonable according to the whole spirit of *zakat* rulings.

The leading Zaydi scholar al-Hadi is consistent when he declares that *zakat* is required from all jewellery, whether made of gold and silver or of pearls and precious stones. On the other hand, exempting one and obligating the other does not seem rational to those who look for the reason behind the rulings of the *Shari'a*, and who constitute the majority of Muslim scholars. The opinion I select is supported by the rule of *zakat* collection which states that *zakat* should be paid out of the same asset which is liable for *zakat* and its increment. This rule is not broken except in necessity, as in the case of owning less than 25 camels, where *zakat* is paid in sheep and not camels, for reasons described earlier in this book.

How can a woman pay *zakat* out of her jewellery, except by being unnecessarily forced to sell some or all of it? In all other applications of *zakat* there is no such requirement. Why should an exception be made here? The theory of "growing assets" assumes that *zakat* is collected out of the increments of the asset without reducing the asset itself, in order to preserve it as a source of income for the owner. The result of obliging *zakat* on jewellery, which does not grow, is to consume the asset itself as the years go by. Maymun ibn Mahran points out, "We have a necklace whose *zakat* I paid throughout the years reached about its value.."[1] I think that the spirit of the *Shari'a* in regard to *zakat* does not approve of this.

In *Ahkam al-Qur'an* Ibn al-'Arabi argues: "The intent of growth would oblige *zakat* on things that since they do not grow on their own are not otherwise subject to *zakat*, such as all assets that consist of business investments. By the same token, the intent of abstention from growth in gold and silver by making them into jewellery for personal use waives *zakat*. If a condition's existence makes *zakat* required on an asset on which *zakat* is not otherwise paid, its absence must exempt from *zakat* an asset that would otherwise make the payment of *zakat* on it obligatory."[2]

1. *Al-Amwal*, p. 442.

2. *Ahkam al-Qur'an*, vol. 2, p. 919, and *Sharh at-Tirmidhi*, vol. 3, p. 131. Both by Ibn al-'Arabi.

Additionally, the texts that talk about the conditions for *zakat* on gold and silver consider their use as a measure of value, that is, as money. Even the verse, *"As for those who hoard up gold and silver and do not spend it in the way of Allah..."* (9:35) indicates by using the words "hoard" and "spend" that gold and silver are meant here as money, because money is what is usually hoarded and not spent, while common jewellery is not considered a treasure and is not for spending.

The view that I select here is the same as that expressed by the great scholar Abu 'Ubayd, who says in *al-Amwal*:

> "The Prophet (p) said, 'If silver money reaches five *uqiyyas*, there is one-fourth of a tenth due on it.' Here the Messenger of Allah (p) restricts *zakat* to silver money. He does not include all forms of silver, but minted silver only, by using a word that is only used for silver coins that have been minted and are used as money. By the same token, the word *uqiyya* only refers to dirhams. Each *uqiyya* is worth forty dirhams, and *zakat* is obliged on dirhams. Muslims unanimously consider dinars as monetary units on which *zakat* is paid and dinars are also mentioned in some *hadiths* linked to the Prophet (p). Muslims have no differences of opinion in regard to the dirham and the dinar but they do differ on jewellery because the latter is for personal use, while the only use for gold and silver money is in circulation. The rulings on *zakat* on money must then be different from that of jewellery, which more resembles furniture and clothes, and this is the reason many scholars consider jewellery outside *zakat*.
>
> "On similar grounds, the Hanafis, who oblige *zakat* on jewellery, say that *zakat* is not paid on working camels and cows because of their similarity to things designated for personal use. Jurists of the Hijaz oblige *zakat* on working camels and cows but exempt jewellery. Neither of these schools are consistent. Since these items are similar with regard to being commodities designated for personal use, they should either all be exempt from *zakat* or not.

"In my view, neither are liable for *zakat* on the grounds mentioned above. As for the saying in which the Prophet (p) asked the Yemeni woman who had two gold bracelets, 'Do you pay their *zakat*?' it is only known through one chain, which is criticised by many scholars in the past and present.[1] If this *hadith* is correct, the Prophet (p) may have meant by '*zakat*', lending those bracelets to others free of charge, as explained by some scholars, including Sa'id ibn al-Musayyab, ash-Sha'bi, al-Hasan and Qatada, who say, 'Its *zakat* is lending it to other women free of charge.'[2]

"If *zakat* on jewellery were obliged in the same way it is obliged on silver money, the Prophet (p) would not have

1. This *hadith* is from 'Amr ibn Shu'ayb from his father from his grandfather. His grandfather was Muhammad ibn 'Abdullah ibn 'Amr ibn al-'As. 'Amr ibn Shu'ayb was a scholar of his time, and died in 118 AH. He was controversial as far as his trustworthiness as a reporter of *hadith*. Ibn Ma'in, Ibn Rahawayh, al-Awza'i and Salih Jazra grade him trustworthy. Al-Bukhari in his *Tarikh* mentions his trustworthiness, although he does not report from him in his collection of *sahih hadiths*. Ahmad ibn Hanbal says, "'Amr ibn Shu'ayb has *hadiths* which are rejected. I write his reports just for consideration, but he is not acceptable." Ibn Hanbal further says, "I may sometimes accept his reports, but I have some doubts about him." Abu Zar'a says, "He is criticised because of the numerous *hadiths* which he reports from his father from his grandfather. It is said that he only heard a few *hadiths* and that he inherited a written pamphlet which he quoted. He is also criticised for telling everything he heard." Ibn al-Madini answered when asked about him, "All that is reported from him by Ayyub and Ibn Jurayj is correct, but what he reports from his father from his grandfather is weak." Yahya ibn Ma'in has a similar opinion about him. Ibn Hibban says that when he reports from trustworthy narrators other than his father, it is acceptable, but in what he reports from his father from his grandfather there are many rejected *hadiths*. Consequently, he must not be accepted. In *al-Mizan*, adh-Dhahabi concludes that his narrations are good. (vol. 3, pp. 263-268). In *al-Fath*, Ibn Hajar says, "the biography of 'Amr seems to be strong, but only when his narrations are not opposed by others." With respect to the question on hand, his narration is opposed by correct reports from 'A'isha, Ibn 'Umar, Jabir and other Companions that they used to pay *zakat* on jewellery. 'Abdullah ibn 'Amr was a contemporary of those Companions and does not oblige them with the *hadith* he heard from the Messenger of Allah (p) about the Yemeni woman and her daughter. Had he done so they would have accepted it and it would have been frequently reported to us.

2. Ancient Arabs used to lend jewellery and wedding clothes to the bride for her wedding celebration. Prominent families do that today for expensive fees. This may be a form of *zakat* on jewellery and wedding clothes.

limited himself to giving that advice to a particular woman when he saw her bracelets. That issue would have been treated like *zakat* on other items that are repeatedly mentioned in many of his letters, instructions, and traditions. It would have been practised by the Rightly-guided Khalifs after him. In none of their instructions do we find anything about *zakat* on women's jewellery. As for the saying from 'A'isha, 'It is permissible to wear jewellery if you pay its *zakat*,' I find that its *zakat* is lending it freely to others, especially since her nephew al-Qasim ibn Muhammad denied that she instructed any women in her family, including her nieces, to pay *zakat* on their jewellery.

"Nothing is authentic about the *zakat* on jewellery from a Companion except from Ibn Mas'ud. The statement of 'Abdullah ibn 'Amr that he used to pay *zakat* on the jewellery of his daughters has problems in its chain similar to those in the *hadith* linked to the Prophet (p) mentioned above. The other opinion [that jewellery is not subject to *zakat*] is reported from 'A'isha, Ibn 'Umar, Jabir ibn 'Abdullah, and Anas ibn Malik [Companions] and many Followers after them. This is also supported by our explanation of the tradition of the Prophet (p)."[1]

After this lengthy but brilliant quotation from Abu 'Ubayd, I would like to mention the following remarks on the arguments presented by those who oblige *zakat* on jewellery.

Disproving the arguments for obliging *zakat* on jewellery

The use of the verse *"As for those who hoard up gold and silver and do not spend it in the way of Allah..."* , along with the interpretation of hoarding to include women's jewellery is not acceptable.[2] The verse refers to gold and silver that can be spent and circulated and not to gold and silver that are designated as jewellery for the per-

1. *Al-Amwal*, p. 446.
2. As stated by ad-Dihlawi in his *Hujjat Allah al-Baligha*, vol. 2, p. 509.

sonal use and enjoyment of women. No one requires jewellery to be circulated and spent in the way of Allah, except in emergencies.

The *hadiths* used by those who oblige *zakat* on jewellery are also disputed by others from the point of view of their authenticity as well as from the point of view of their indications. The first saying, "And there is one-fourth of a tenth due on silver, is agreed upon as *sahih*, but the Arabic word used for silver in this *hadith* is *"ar-riqqa"* which literally means silver that has been minted in the form of coins. The word is not used in Arabic for manufactured jewellery.

Some of the other *hadiths* are not proven to be authentic, to the extent that at-Tirmidhi could say, "No saying is correct on this question."[1] Ibn Hazm, who obliges *zakat* on jewellery, does not depend on these *hadiths*. He, in fact, disagrees with the very use of those *hadiths* as arguments for obliging *zakat* on jewellery. He argues that "Those who see that *zakat* is required on jewellery use fumbling sayings and reports which we need not be occupied with."[2] In his argument, Ibn Hazm depends only on the comprehensive implications of the basic texts on *zakat* on gold and silver. However, let us take the time to review the chains of those *hadiths* anyway.

The *hadith* from 'Amr ibn Shu'ayb is reported by an-Nasa'i as both *musnad* and *mursal*, and he evaluated it as *mursal*. Al-Mundhiri marks it in *at-Targhib wa't-Tarhib* as weak. We have discussed it earlier and quoted the opinion of Abu 'Ubayd on it. The *hadith* reported from 'A'isha about the bracelets has Yahya ibn Ayyub al-Ghafiqi in its chain. Yahya is acceptable to al-Bukhari and Muslim. He was trusted, but adh-Dhahabi quotes differing opinions about him from several critics. He quotes Ibn Ma'in as saying, "His reports are fair," and Ahmad as saying, "He had a bad memory." Ibn al-Qattan and Abu Hatim are quoted as saying, "His reports must not be accepted," an-Nasa'i as saying he was not a strong link, and ad-Daraqutni as saying, "Some of his reported narrations have discrepancies."[3] The latter mentions several discrepancies of Yahya, which are rejected. The report of a person who is extremely con-

1. *Commentary* by Ibn al-'Arabi on at-Tirmidhi, vol. 3, p. 131.
2. *Al-Muhalla*, vol. 6, p. 78.
3. *Al-Mizan*, vol. 3, p. 282.

troversial should not be used on issues that are not agreed upon, especially when we have available correct reports that 'A'isha's practice contradicted his saying.

The tradition from Umm Salama is commented on by al-Mundhiri, who says, "'Attab ibn Bashir is in its chain. Al-Bukhari uses his reports, but more than one scholar criticises him." In *al-Mizan*, adh-Dhahabi says about 'Attab, "Ahmad said, 'I hope he is all right. He reports from Khasif some unacceptable reports which I think are the mistake of Khasif.'" An-Nasa'i says, "He is not that [good] in [reporting] sayings." Ibn al-Madini notes, "Our colleagues consider him weak." Ibn Ma'in once remarked, "He is trustworthy," and another time, "He is weak." "We leave his reports aside," 'Ali indicates. Lastly, Ibn 'Adi says, "I hope he is all right."[1] All this means that none of the leading critics are firm regarding Yahya ibn Ayyub's trustworthiness and some of them even grade him weak. The fact that al-Bukhari reports from him should not be overestimated. Ibn Hajar notes that, "Al-Bukhari reports only two *hadiths* from him." In one of them, there is another chain supporting it, while in the other his name is associated with other names."[2]

In *Nasb ar-Raya*, az-Zayla'i says, "The authors of the two *Sahih* collections [al-Bukhari and Muslim] may report from a person who is controversial, but when they do so, they select from his sayings that are either supported by other chains or that are obviously witnessed and known from other sources. They do not report from the controversial sayings in whose chain he is singled out, especially in cases where trustworthy reporters contradict his reports."[3] Moreover, in the chain of this *hadith*, Thabit ibn 'Ajlan is the only one who reports from 'Attab ibn Bashir, as stated by al-Bayhaqi.

Thabit, whose report is used by al-Bukhari, is also controversial. Ibn Ma'in views him as trustworthy. Ahmad says, "I abstain from giving an opinion on him. Abu Hatim says, "He is fair," and Ibn 'Adi give three strange examples reported by him. Al-'Uqayli comments on him in his book, *ad-Du'afa'*, "He is not usually followed

1. Ibid., p. 27.
2. *Hadi as-Sari*, the introduction of *al-Fath*, vol. 2, pp. 189-190.
3. *Nasb ar-Raya*, vol. 1, p. 342.

by others in reports." Al-Bayhaqi adds, "And among his reports that are negated is the *hadith* reported from 'Attab ibn Bashir from 'Ata' from Umm Salama," and he cites the *hadith* we have. 'Abdu'l-Haqq says, "It is authentic but must not be used in argument." This is rejected by Abu'l-Hasan ibn al-Qattan, who continues, "Al-'Uqayli is biased against him. Those who are not known at all as trustworthy may be described as such, but if a person who is known as trustworthy is singled out in the chain, this does not bring harm to the chain, unless singling out occurs very often."

Adh-Dhahabi argues with Ibn al-Qattan, "This is true if the person is known as trustworthy, but a person about whom a leading critic like Ahmad abstains from giving an opinion, while some others consider him trustworthy and Abu Hatim calls him 'fair',[1] must not easily be upgraded to the degree of trustworthiness. If such a person is singled out in the chain, then it must be negated. Thus adh-Dhahabi gives weight to the opinion expressed by al-'Uqayli and 'Abdu'l-Haqq.[2]

Moreover, al-Bukhari only reports one saying from Thabit in the chapter on slaughtering. This saying is supported by other sayings in the chapter on cleansing, according to al-Hafiz.[3] As we know from the methods of al-Bukhari and Muslim, the inclusion of this saying must not be taken as grading Thabit as absolutely trustworthy. Neither Muslim nor al-Bukhari mention the *hadith* under discussion, or any other on the subject of *zakat* on jewellery. The *hadith* reported from Umm Salama through Thabit and 'Attab, in view of this controversy about them, must not be accepted as proof in such a controversial question.

Ibn Hajar, in the introduction to *Tahdhib at-Tahdhib*, says: "The benefit of bringing out all that is said about a reporter, whether good or bad, becomes obvious in controversial matters." (vol. 1, p. 5)

---

1. The description "has a good narration" is one of the low grades of acceptability, the fourth of sixth, according to different classifications. See as-Sakhawi in the commentary on *al-Alfiya*, and *as-Sundus*, commentary on *an-Nukhba*. See also *ar-Raf' wa at-Takmil*, pp. 109, 116, 124.

2. *Al-Mizan*, vol. 1, pp. 364-365.

3. *Hadi as-Sari*, the introduction of *al-Fath*, vol. 2, pp. 189-190.

Furthermore, I should mention that I see these reported *hadiths* as even more dubious because they were not commonly known to the Companions, in spite of the fact that the Companions had different opinions on the *zakat* of jewellery. If such *hadiths* were known to the Companions, they would not have been so varied in their opinions and practices. This may mean that those reported hadiths are either overridden by later *hadiths* or are not authentic, since it is extremely unlikely that the Companions would differ on an issue and not use what they heard from the Messenger of Allah (p) to support their views. We know, however, that 'A'isha's practice which is opposite to these *hadiths* is authentically reported.[1]

Lastly, al-Bayhaqi, supported on this point by an-Nawawi and al-Mundhiri,[2] says, "The report of al-Qasim and Ibn Abi Mulayka from 'A'isha that she was not paying *zakat* on the jewels of her nieces, in spite of the fact that she is correctly reported to have believed in paying *zakat* on an orphan's wealth, brings some doubt to the report raised to the Prophet (p) [that there is *zakat* on jewellery] for how could she not practise something that she herself reports from the Prophet (p), unless she knew it was annulled?"[3]

Some scholars attempt to find a consistent interpretation of these *hadiths*, assuming they are acceptable, in that *zakat* on jew-

1. In *at-Talkhis*, Ibn Hajar says, "One may reconcile her action and her narration if we assume that she used to believe in the obligation of *zakat* on jewellery and not on orphan's assets." But it seems that this reconciliation is difficult to accept and is not obvious from the wording of the saying itself.

2. *Al-Majmu'*, vol 6, p. 35, and *Mukhtasar as-Sunan*, vol. 2, p. 176.

3. Al-Kamal ibn al-Humam in *Fath al-Qadir*, vol. 1, p. 526, comments on this saying, "This is opposed by a report in *al-Muwatta'* from 'Abdu'r-Rahman ibn al-Qasim from his father that 'A'isha was the guardian of her orphaned nieces, and did not pay *zakat* on their jewellery." 'A'isha is the Companion who narrates the *hadith* about the large rings. The action of a narrator in contradiction to his or her reports means to us that the report is annulled. This annulment is disputed on the basis of a report that 'Umar wrote to al-Ash'ari about *zakat* on jewellery, which implies that this is accepted as a ruling. If the annulment is disputed and the rule is verified, a ruling of the annulment cannot be accepted."

It is known, however, that the report about 'Umar writing to al-Ash'ari is not *sahih*, and al-Hasan denies that any of the four *Khulafa'* ordered *zakat* on jewellery. Abu 'Ubayd says that *zakat* on jewellery is not authentically reported from any Companion except Ibn Mas'ud. The doubt thrown by al-Bayhaqi and others on the report about the large rings is well-supported.

ellery was obligatory in the early stage in Madina, when the use of gold as jewellery by women was itself forbidden, but the moment that gold jewellery became permissible for women, *zakat* on that jewellery was waived in the same way that *zakat* was waived on working livestock. Al-Bayhaqi says, "This is the view of many of our colleagues." He gives a report of sayings which indicate the prohibition of gold jewellery and an account of sayings that allow it for women. He comments that these sayings indicate that the use of gold jewellery by women is permissible. This is unanimously agreed upon, which means that these reports on its prohibition are superseded by the newer sayings that allow it.[1] But this interpretation has no bearing on the report from 'A'isha that *zakat* be paid on silver bracelets since not a single scholar claims that silver jewellery was also prohibited for women.[2]

- The difference of opinion among leading jurists on the *zakat* of women's jewellery implies that they agree on the lawfulness of jewellery for women, since if jewellery were prohibited for women, it would be paid without dispute.
- The lawfulness of women's jewellery has been well-established throughout all Muslim lands since the era of the Companions. No Muslim scholar objected to it and the whole Muslim community cannot agree to a thing that is prohibited and preserve that agreement in theory and practice for centuries. This means that the sayings that imply the lawfulness of gold and silk to women are the latest. They supersede any other reports, because it is inconceivable that the sayings prohibiting gold for women came later and yet all the Companions agreed otherwise. I fully agree with al-Albani's view that anything that reaches the level of extravagance is prohibited, such as large and expensive rings. One may argue that those sayings mentioning prohibition refer only to extravagance and excess.

1. This unanimity is quoted by al-Bayhaqi in his *as-Sunan*, vol. 4, p. 142, and by Ibn Hajar in *al-Fath*, vol. 10, p. 260. It has been an established practice throughout the centuries in all Muslim countries, which opposes the claim of al-Albani in his booklet on wedding manners, that wearing gold is prohibited for women the same way it is for men, except when it is cut into pieces, like gold buttons, for instance. This unanimity is supported by two things.

2. *As-Sunan al-Kubra*, vol. 4, pp. 140-142.

Another interpretation may be viewed with regard to the two sayings from 'A'isha and from Umm Salama, assuming they were authentic. The Prophet (p) may have had a special and stricter approach in dealing with his own family, taking them further away from the desire for luxury and ornaments, since they are supposed to set an example for all other women, as indicated by the verse: "*O wives of the Prophet! You are not like other women...*" (33:32) and *"O wives of the Prophet! If any of you commits a clear act of indecency she will receive double the punishment."* (33:30) So it may be a special ruling restricted to the wives of the Prophet (p), not given as a religious opinion applicable to other Muslim women. On these groups, 'A'isha's not paying *zakat* on the jewellery of her nieces who were in her custody may be understood.

Some other scholars have yet a third interpretation of these *hadiths*, again assuming they are authentic. That is that the Prophet (p) noticed extravagance and excess above that which is customary[1] in those specific cases mentioned in the sayings, so he obliged *zakat* on those grounds. This interpretation is supported by the words in one of the *hadiths*, describing the bracelets are large or huge or describing the rings as large. Those *hadiths* may be used to support the view that prohibited or disapproved jewellery is subject to *zakat*.

Some other Companions and Followers have another interpretation of *zakat* on jewellery. It is that *zakat* is fulfilled by lending jewellery free of charge to other women to use on festive occasions. This is reported by al-Bayhaqi in his *Sunan* from Ibn 'Umar and Ibn al-Musayyab, and it is also reported by Abu 'Ubayd and Ibn Abi Shayba from Ibn al-Musayyab, al-Hasan al-Basri, Qatada, and ash-Sha'bi.[2]

All these different interpretations make it impossible to use these sayings as evidence supporting the payment of *zakat* on jewellery, in accordance with the well-known rule of jurisprudence: "If the evidence has different possible interpretations, it cannot be used to support one of them against the others." This is assuming that the

1. *Nihayat al-Muhtaj*, vol. 2, p. 88.
2. *Al-Amwal*, p. 443 and *al-Musannaf*, vol. 4, p. 28.

hadiths are acceptable from the point of view of their authenticity, though in fact, each of them is also disputable on that ground.

Surprisingly enough, the jurists who belong to the school of rationalisation use sayings and reports as evidence in this debate, while jurists belonging to the school of *hadith* use rationalisation as their evidence.[1] As for the reports from some Companions like Ibn Mas'ud (authentically reported) and Ibn 'Amr (disputed in authenticity), it should be noted that they do not give their opinions as applicable to all people. All that is indicated by these reports is that these Companions paid *zakat* on the jewellery of their own wives and daughters, which may be an indication of their piety and preference for removing all doubt on their part in a manner on which they do not have a ruling from the Messenger (p). The only report that falls beyond this interpretation is the one attributed to 'Umar when he wrote to Abu Musa to order Muslim women to pay *zakat* on their jewellery. This report is not proven correct, and al-Hasan denies that any of the first Khulafa' obliged *zakat* on jewellery.

Jewellery used as hoarded treasure is amenable to *zakat*

The opinion preferred by us that jewellery is not zakatable applies only to jewellery that is used by women as ornaments. As for jewellery that is used as a storage of value for the purpose of hoarding, and is looked upon as an accumulation of wealth, this is subject to *zakat*, just like money. It is reported from Sa'id ibn al-Musayyab that if jewellery is worn and used, it is not subject to *zakat*, but if it is not worn or used, *zakat* is paid.[2] Malik says, "Those who own gold and jewellery made of gold or silver which is not used for ornamental wearing must pay *zakat* on it every year. Jewellery should be weighed and *zakat* paid at the rate of one-fourth of one-tenth, unless the total weight is less than the equiva-

1. This may indicate that the classification of the leading scholars into the people of opinion (*ra'y*) and the people of *hadith* is unrealistically exaggerated, since the people of opinion do not reject *hadiths* and the people of *hadith* do not refuse to apply human reasoning. Shaykh Muhammad Abu Zahra shows in his book on Malik that he was one of the People of Opinion as much as he was one of the people of *hadith*.

2. *Al-Amwal*, p. 443.

lent of 20 dinars or 200 dirhams. Then they are not liable for *zakat*. As for jewellery that is broken and in need of repair in order to be worn, it is still considered jewellery in use and *zakat* is not paid on it."[1]

An-Nawawi says, "Our colleagues say that if jewellery is not held for the purposes of customary use (lawful, desired or prohibited) but rather for the purpose of hoarding and accumulation, then *zakat* is paid on it, as correctly confirmed by the majority."[2] Similarly, al-Layth ibn Sa'd says, "Jewellery used for wearing and lending to others is not liable to *zakat*, but that used as hoarded treasure has *zakat* paid on it."[3]

This means that when jewellery is not intended for customary use, it is treated as an attempt to escape *zakat*. Ibn Hazm argues with al-Layth, "If this is so, then a person who buys a house or orchard in order to avoid *zakat* should also be made to pay *zakat*."[4] I believe that the spirit of the *Shari'a* which annuls all mischief and treats cheats in such a way that gives them the opposite of their intent confirms this. The Hanbalis have also established the opinion that any person who holds jewellery as a means of avoiding *zakat* is subject to *zakat*. We discuss further tactics trying to evade *zakat* in our chapter dealing with *zakat* payment. Jewellery owned by men and used as ornamentation by their female family members or other females is treated like jewellery owned and used by women, i.e. *zakat* is not paid on it, since it is designated for lawful customary use and not for growth.[5]

***Zakat* is paid on jewellery above a customary limit**

If the quantity of jewellery exceeds the customary amount and reaches extravagance, the extra is subject to *zakat*. This is on the

1. *Al-Muwatta'* with its commentary, *al-Muntaqa*, vol. 2, p. 107. This is indicated by Malik's statement that if jewellery is broken and becomes irreparable, or if the owner does not want to repair it, then *zakat* is paid on it. See *Bulghat as-Salik*, vol. 1,. p. 19, and *ar-Rau-da* by an-Nawawi, vol. 2, p. 261.

2. *Al-Majmu'*, vol. 6, p. 36, and *ar-Rawda*, vol. 2, p. 260.

3. *Al-Muhalla*, vol. 6, p. 76

4. Ibid.

5. *Al-Mughni*, vol. 3, p. 11.

grounds that *zakat* is waived on jewellery because it is used by women just like clothes and household goods. What is above the customary and moderate use is either prohibited or at least discouraged. It is in all cases not approved by the *Shari'a*. An-Nawawi says, "Our Shafi'i colleagues argue that jewellery is made lawful for women only within the limits of non-apparent extravagance, but once it reaches the extravagant limit, then it becomes prohibited according to most jurists from Iraq.[1] Ibn Hamid, a Hanbali, says, "If jewellery is below one thousand *mithqals*, it is lawful. Once it reaches that amount, it becomes unlawful and consequently *zakat* is paid on it, in accordance with what is reported by Abu 'Ubayd and al-Athram from 'Amr ibn Dinar: "Jabir was asked if *zakat* was taken on jewellery and he answered that it was not. He was then asked, 'Even if it amounts to one thousands dinars?' He answered, 'That is indeed too much.'[2] Jewellery exceeding customary limits is surely extravagance and no longer needed as normal ornamentation."[3]

This is a strong argument, but the author of *al-Mughni* argues that the *Shari'a* makes the use of jewellery lawful without limit, thus it is not acceptable to limit that use by personal opinions.[4] It seems that he forgets that the use of lawful things in the *Shari'a* is restricted by two principles: avoidance of extravagance and avoidance of ostentation. The Prophet (p) is reported to have said, "Eat and drink and dress without extravagance or pride."[5]

The *hadith* about the Yemeni woman who entered the presence of the Messenger (p) with her daughter, who had two huge golden bracelets on the daughter's arm and was told by the Prophet that *zakat* should be paid on them may be considered a case for this argument. That is, the Prophet (p) found that the amount of jewellery was far beyond the limit of customary use and was extravagant for that young woman. Some scholars take this saying to mean

1. *Al-Majmu'*, vol. 6, p. 40.

2. *Al-Mughni*, vol. 3, p. 11. See narration no. 1675 in *al-Amwal*, p. 442. It is also reported by ash-Shafi'i and al-Bayhaqi. See as-*Sunan al-Kubra*, vol. 4, p. 138.

3. *Al-Mughni*, vol. 3, p. 11.

4. Ibid.

5 Reported by al-Bukhari as suspended. See Ibn Kathir, vol. 2, p. 182. Also reported by an-Nasa'i in his *Sunan*, chapter on *zakat*, "*Zakat* Evasion", vol. 5, p. 79.

exactly that. That is, *zakat* is obliged on what exceeds the customary amounts.[1] This may be the reason why 'Abdullah ibn 'Amr used to pay *zakat* on his daughters' jewellery. He was reported to have bought his three daughters jewellery worth 6000 dinars. This is definitely more than the customary limit.[2]

Does *zakat* then become obligatory on all the jewellery owned by the person or on that part which is above the customary limit? It seems from the above-mentioned sayings that all the jewellery becomes amenable to *zakat* as a means of cleansing the whole amount, because of its exaggeration in exceeding the lawful limit. The opinion that claims that all jewellery of any amount is not subject to *zakat* ends up putting a large portion of the wealth of the Muslim Community in the idleness of extravagant amounts of jewellery and ornaments that are only rarely used by women and that are usually stored in private boxes in banks.

What is the limit of extravagance? It seems difficult to put an objective definition of extravagance, since its boundaries differ from one community to another and from one neighbourhood to another. An amount that is extravagant in a poor country for a poor family may be very customary or less than normal for a rich family in a rich country. The real determinant of the limit of extravagance is the customs of the area.[3]

I should mention that pearls, diamonds, and other precious stones must be treated the same way as gold and silver jewellery. If they are within the limit of customary use *zakat* is not paid on them, but if they exceed that limit and become a means of prohibited extravagance, they must not be exempt from *zakat*. If they are held as a store of treasure and an accumulation of wealth or in order to escape *zakat* payment, *zakat* must be paid.

---

1. *Nasb ar-Raya*, vol. 2, p. 375, and *al-Mir'a*, vol. 4.

2. *Al-Amwal*, p. 440.

3. Ar-Ramli in *Nihayat al-Muhtaj* says about men's rings and their weights, "What is acceptable is to leave this matter to the usual customary practices of the time. What is above this custom may be considered extravagant."

Summary

The preceding rules and opinions can be summarised in the following points:

- Jewellery made of gold and silver that is held as a treasure and an accumulation of wealth is subject to *zakat*, the same as if it were being held as bullion or coins.
- If the jewellery is obtained for personal use as ornaments, then we should distinguish between lawful and unlawful use. Jewellery and ornaments designated for house decoration, utensils, or use by men are prohibited. *Zakat* is paid on this jewellery and ornamentation.
- Jewellery that is extravagant even though it is used by women is subject to *zakat*. Extravagance is the excess above the customary use by women within their community.
- Jewellery held for lawful use as women's ornamentation without extravagance or for lawful use by men, such as silver rings, is not subject to *zakat*, because it is not designated for profit and is in fact part of the materials used personally, like clothes and furniture, designated for lawful use.
- There is no difference regarding these rulings whether the legal ownership of the jewellery is in the hands of men or women.
- Once *zakat* becomes obligatory, then the rate is that of money, two and a half per cent every year.
- Definitely, the minimum amount, the *nisab*, should be observed at 85 grams of gold. It should be noted, however, that the value of the jewellery and ornaments is the criterion and not their weight only, because craftsmanship contributes to the value of the jewellery.

Chapter Four

Zakat on Business Goods

Allah makes it lawful for Muslims to engage in business and to make profit, provided that they do not indulge in trading in commodities that are prohibited in Islam and that they observe ethical values in their transactions, such as honesty, truthfulness, and kindness. Also, business engagements must not be a hindrance to the remembrance of Allah, or to the fulfilment of the spiritual and material obligations prescribed by Him.[1]

Since practising trade is lawful, several sayings order the guardians of orphans to invest orphans' wealth in trade so that it is not exhausted by the repetitive payment of *zakat*. It is normal that a part of the wealth of any nation is used in trade and business exchange, and it is no wonder that Islam prescribes *zakat* on assets invested in business and commerce as well as on the income derived therefrom. Like *zakat* on money, *zakat* on business is an expression of thankfulness to Allah for His bounties by caring about those of His servants who are in need.

Islamic jurisprudence addresses itself to the details of this kind of *zakat*. Business goods are called by jurists *'urud at-tijara*,[2] which means anything obtained for the purpose of trade for profit, except liquid monetary assets. This definition includes machinery, furniture, clothing, foodstuffs, ornaments, jewellery, livestock, agricultural produce, land, buildings, etc. Some jurists define *'urud at-tijara* as anything that one buys in order to sell for profit.[3] A Muslim who owns business goods equal to the *nisab* of money or more at

---

1. See al-Qardawi, *al-Halal wa'l-Haram*.

2. Jurists use for "trade wealth" the Arabic "*'urud at-tijara*". "*Tijara*" means "trade" and "*'urud*" is the plural of "'ard", which means commodities and wares other than gold and silver, according to the dictionary *at-Taj*. An-Nawawi says that the *mal* of trade is anything that, when obtained, is intended for trade.

3. *Matalib Uli an-Nuha*, vol. 2, p. 96.

the end of a *zakat* year must pay its due *zakat* at the rate of two and a half per cent. This *zakat* is levied on the principal and increments accruing above the principal.

This chapter has four sections. The first deals with the obligation of *zakat* on business goods, the second disproves the arguments of those who do not oblige *zakat* on business, the third section describes the conditions for this kind of *zakat* and section four deals with the methods of paying *zakat* on business goods.

Section One: The obligation of *zakat* on trade

Evidence of this obligation is taken from the four sources of the *Shari'a* in Islam: Qur'an, *Sunna*, *ijma'* and analogy.

The Qur'an

Allah says:

> *"O you who believe! Give away some of the good things you have earned and some of what the earth produces for you."*
>
> (2:267)

Imam al-Bukhari indicates in his chapter on *zakat* in his *Sahih* collection under the section on *sadaqa* on crafts and business that this *sadaqa* is taken in accordance with the verse, *"Give away some of the good things you have earned."* Imam at-Tabari comments, "Pay *zakat* out of the good things you earn in your economic activity, such as business, industry, or gold and silver." He also reports through several chains, from Mujahid that the words, "good things you have earned", means by making trade.[1] In *Ahkam al-Qur'an*, Imam al-Jassas says: "It is reported that a group of our predecessors explain Allah's words, *'good things you have earned',* as meaning through trade. These include al-Hasan and Mujahid. However, the general implication of the words also covers all assets earned by other economic activities."[2] Imam Abu Bakr ibn al-'Arabi says, "Our schol-

1. Commentary of at-Tabari, vol. 5, pp. 555-556.
2. Al-Jassas, *Ahkam al-Qur'an*, vol. 1, p. 543.

ars interpret the words of Allah, *'that you have earned'*, as things earned by means of trade, and the words, *'what the earth produces for you'*, as things earned by means of agriculture."

It should be noted that earning may come either from the earth or from human effort in trade, industry, hunting and booty obtained in war. As Allah commands the rich to give to the poor out of all the earnings He gives them, trade is no exception as was made clear by the Prophet (p). Imam ar-Razi points out that the obvious meaning of the verse is that *zakat* is obliged on every asset human beings earn, including trade assets, gold and silver, and livestock, since all these are earned.[1] This is supported by the verse that read, *"His wealth has not helped him nor anything he has earned."* (111:2) *"He has earned"* refers to his accumulations from trade.

In addition to that, we must remember that other verses about *zakat* are general and therefore include business assets, such as the verse, *"And the beggars and destitute received a due share of their wealth"* (51:19), and *"Those in whose wealth there is a known share for beggars and the destitute"* (70:24-25), and *"Take* sadaqa *from their wealth to purify and cleanse them."* (9:103) There is not a single statement in the Qur'an or *Sunna* that exempts the assets of Muslim merchants from this recognised right by which Muslims are purified and cleansed.

Ibn al-'Arabi indicates that the verse *"Take* sadaqa *from their wealth"* is general and covers all assets, no matter how they are classified or named, and no matter what purpose they are assigned to. Thus anyone who desires to restrict the meaning of this verse is asked to produce supporting evidence.[2]

Remarkably enough, some Arabic tribes meant by *"mal"* (the word used in the verse to mean "wealth"] only clothes, furniture, and trade assets, and did not include gold and silver in their meaning of the word. It is reported from Abu Hurayra, "We went with the Messenger of Allah (p) to the Battle of Khaybar, where we did not acquire gold or silver, but only *mal*," i.e. clothes and other assets.[3]

1. Ar-Razi, *at-Tafsir al-Kabir*, vol. 2, p. 65.
2. *Sharh at-Tirmidhi*, vol. 3, p. 104.
3. *Commentary of al-Qurtubi*, vol. 8, p. 245.

The *Sunna*

Abu Dawud reports from Samura ibn Jundub, "The Prophet (p) used to order us to pay *sadaqa* from what we have for sale."[1] To "order" implies "to oblige" and it is clear that the word *sadaqa* means *zakat*, especially when it is preceded by the definite article "*al*". This implies that Ibn Hazm's claim that if the saying is sound, then *sadaqa* is not the same as *zakat*, is very far from the text.[2] Ad-Daraqutni reports from Abu Dharr, "I heard the Messenger of Allah (p) say, 'Camels are subject to *zakat*; lambs are subject to *zakat*; and *zakat* is paid on clothes and housewares." There is no disagreement that clothes and other housewares for personal or household use are exempt, which means that the housewares and clothes mentioned in this *hadith* refer to business goods for resale. This is in addition to the general *hadiths* that oblige *zakat* on all kinds of wealth without discrimination, such as "Pay *zakat* on your wealth."[3] It is noted that trade goods are the first kind of wealth that come under the term "*mal*" used in the texts, because trade goods are general and may include anything purchased for sale.[4]

The *ijma'* of the Companions, Followers and Salaf

Abu 'Ubayd reports from 'Abdu'l-Qari, "I was appointed treasurer at the time of 'Umar ibn al-Khattab. When he paid stipends,

1. Reported by ad-Daraqutni, p. 214, and Abu Dawud via Ja'far ibn Sa'd from Khubayb ibn Sulayman ibn Samura from his father Sulayman, Abu Dawud made no comment nor did al-Mundhiri. See *Mukhtasar as-Sunan*, vol. 2, p. 175. Ibn al-Humam says this means they approve the saying, as in *al-Mirqa*, vol. 4, p. 158. Ibn 'Abdu'l-Barr grades it as good. See *Nasb ar-Raya*, vol. 2, p. 376. Al-Hafiz says in *Bulugh al-Maram*, p. 124, "Its chain is soft." Ibn Hazm claims that Ja'far, Khubayb and Sulayman are unknown. Ahmad Shakir writes in his footnote on p, 234, vol. 5 of *al-Muhalla* that "they are known; they are mentioned by Ibn Hibban as among the trustworthy." Adh-Dhahabi quotes from Ibn al-Qattan, "The trustworthiness of either of them is not determined, in spite of the effort made by critics of *hadith*. There are several other *hadiths* reported through that chain. 'Abdu'l-Haqq al-Azdi says Khubayb is weak and Ja'far is not dependable. Anyhow this chain is dubious and does not stand. See *al-Mizan*, vol. 1, p. 150.

2. *Al-Muhalla*, vol. 5, pp. 234-235.

3. At-Tirmidhi reports it and comments, "*hasan sahih*", vol. 3, p. 91.

4. *Matalib Uli'n-Nuha*, vol. 2, p. 96.

he used to calculate the assets of merchants, both present and absent assets, and then collect *zakat* on them all out of the assets that were present.[1] Reported also by Ibn Hazm in *al-Muhalla* where he adds that its chain is sound. There is a report from Abu 'Amr ibn Hammas[2] from his father who said, "'Umar passed by me and said, 'O Hammas, pay the *zakat* due on your wealth.' I answered, 'I have no wealth except hides and bags.' 'Umar replied, 'Evaluate them and pay the *zakat* due on them.'"[3] The author of *al-Mughni* comments, "The likes of such stories are common, and none of the Companions neglect this ruling which implies a sort of *ijma'* on this matter."[4]

Abu 'Ubayd reports from Ibn 'Umar, "Slaves and clothes intended for trade are subject to *zakat.*"[5] Al-Bayhaqi and Ibn Hazm report from Ibn 'Umar, "There is no *zakat* on housewares and clothes, except when they are used for trade." Ibn Hazm adds that this is a sound narration.[6] Moreover, Abu 'Ubayd also reports the obligation of *zakat* on trade from Ibn 'Abbas.[7]

There is no report whatsoever that any Companion disagreed with the opinion of 'Umar, his son, and Ibn 'Abbas. The collection of *zakat* on trade assets continued during the time of the Companions and the era of the Followers. In the preceding chapter, I mentioned that 'Umar ibn 'Abdu'l-'Aziz is correctly reported

1. The story is reported by Ibn Abi Shayba too. See *al-Muhalla*, vol. 6, p. 34, where Ibn Hazm comments that its chain is *sahih.* But he claims that the word "assets of merchants" means gold and silver and not merchandise. This interpretation seems to be far from the obvious words of the text.

2. The author of *Usd al-Ghaba* says Hammas al-Laythi is mentioned by al-Waqidi among those born at the time of the Prophet and usually reports from 'Umar.

3. In *at-Talkhis*, p. 185, al-Hafiz says this is reported by ash-Shafi'i, Ahmad, Ibn Abi Shayba, 'Abdu'r-Razzaq, Sa'id ibn Mansur, and ad-Daraqutni. See also *al-Umm* of ash-Shafi'i, vol. 2,. p. 38; *Sunan al-Bayhaqi*, vol. 4, p. 147. Ibn Hazm grades the story weak, claiming that Hammas and his son are unknown, while Ahmad Shakir writes in his footnote in *al-Muhalla*, vol. 5, p. 235, that they are known and trustworthy.

4. *Al-Mughni*, vol. 3, p. 35.

5. *Al-Amwal*, p. 425.

6. *Al-Muhalla*, vol. 5, p. 234, and as-*Sunan al-Kubra*, vol. 4, p. 147.

7. *Al-Amwal*, p. 426. Ibn Hazm grades the story good, but makes a twisted interpretation. See *Al-Muhalla*, vol. 5, pp. 234-235.

to have written to one of his deputies to "...look for Muslims who pass by your area and take *zakat* out of their merchandise at the rate of one dinar for every 40 dinars, and apply the same percentage on what is less than that up to a minimum of 20 dinars."

Jurists of the Followers' era and the generations after them agreed that *zakat* is obligatory on trade goods. This *ijma'* is reported by Ibn al-Mundhir and Abu 'Ubayd. Ibn al-Mundhir writes, "People of knowledge unanimously agreed that *zakat* is paid on items intended for trade once a full fiscal year passes. This is reported from 'Umar, his son, Ibn 'Abbas, the seven renowned jurists, al-Hasan, Jabir ibn Zayd, Maymun ibn Mihran, Tawus, an-Nakha'i, ath-Thawri, al-Awza'i, ash-Shafi'i, Abu 'Ubayd, Ishaq, Abu Hanifa and his disciples.[1] It is also the stand of Ahmad and the Maliki school. Abu 'Ubayd says, "All Muslims unanimously agree that trade goods are subject to *zakat*, and no other opinion is attributed to any of the people of knowledge." [2]

The judge Ibn al-'Arabi says that *zakat* is obligatory on trade goods for four reasons. One, Allah says, *"take* sadaqa *from their wealth,"* which means all sorts of wealth; two, 'Umar ibn 'Abdu'l-'Aziz ordered *zakat* to be taken from trade goods on the advice of many scholars in the era of the Followers and no one raised objections to his action; three, 'Umar ibn al-Khattab collected *zakat* on trade goods long before 'Umar ibn 'Abdu'l-'Aziz, as correctly reported from Anas; and four, the report of Abu Dawud from Samura ibn Jundub that "The Prophet (p) used to order us to pay *zakat* on what we had for sale." There is no authentic report to the contrary from any of our predecessors.[3] Al-Khattabi writes that some later people among the Zahirites claimed that there was no *zakat* on trade goods, but they are preceded by the *ijma'*.[4]

Analogy and Reasoning

Ibn Rushd mentions that trade goods are wealth intended for growth, like the other three forms of wealth that are unanimously

1. *Al-Mughni*, vol. 3, p.30.
2. *Al-Amwal*, p. 429.
3. *Sharh at-Tirmidhi*, vol. 3, p. 104.
4. *Ma'alim al-Mujtahid*, vol. 1, p. 217.

considered amenable for *zakat* – agricultural products, livestock, and gold and silver. Thus the analogy is clear and fitting.[1] As for the reasoning that supports this premise, trade goods are like monetary assets. They are exchangeable, valued and prepared for investment and growth. If *zakat* were not to be imposed on trade goods, rich people would always keep their wealth in the form of merchandise and goods and avoid keeping cash, to escape the payment of *zakat.*[2] It is natural that businessmen – although not with the intention of evading *zakat* – keep little cash, since most business transactions take place through credit or through bank transfers, cheques and drafts.

According to the late Rashid Rida, the rationale for this matter is that Allah imposed *zakat* on the wealth of the rich in order to relieve the poor and needy and to pay for some of the public interests of Muslims and Islam. *Zakat* also aims at reducing capital concentration in the hands of a few individuals, in accordance with the principle laid down by the verse, "*so that it does not become something which merely goes round and round among the rich among you.*" (59:7) Moreover, it gives the rich the benefit of purification and cleansing and trains them to be helpful and merciful. With all that in mind, is it reasonable that merchants and business, who may own the bulk of the wealth of a nation, be exempt?[3]

One could also say that merchants need purification more than anyone else, because the ways they earn their wealth may not always be completely clean. The Prophet (p) indicated, "Merchants are resurrected wicked on the Day of Judgement, except for those who fear Allah, speak the truth and are righteous."[4] He once said, "Merchants are the wicked," and he was asked, "O Messenger of Allah, did not Allah make business lawful?" He answered, "Yes indeed, but merchants often swear, commit sins, and lie in their speech."[5] Abu Dawud reports from Qays ibn Abi Gharaza, "The

1. *Bidayat al-Mujtahid*, vol. 1, p. 217.

2. Commentary *al-Manar*, vol. 10,p. 591.

3. Ibid.

4. Reported by at-Tirmidhi, who calls it *hasan sahih*, Ibn Majah, Ibn Hibban (in his *Sahih* Collection), and al-Hakim. The latter grades it *sahih*.

5. Reported by Ahmad (via a good chain) and al-Hakim. The latter indicates that the chain is *sahih*. See *at-Targhib*.

Messenger of Allah (p) passed by us and said, 'O merchants, sales are associated with vain talk and swearing, so let it be mixed with *sadaqa*.'"

This *sadaqa* is not a reference to *zakat*, but the *hadiths* stress the point that traders need purification because of errors and impurities that intermingle with their transactions. If merchants need to pay voluntary charity for their own purification – as also held by Ibn Hazm – they certainly are in need of paying *zakat*, the prescription for purification and cleansing for all Muslims.

Section Two: Arguments of the opponents of *zakat* on trade goods

The Zahiri School

According to al-Khattabi, Sunnis are generally of the opinion that *zakat* is obligatory on trade goods,[1] except for a few late jurists of the Zahiri school. Ibn Hazm in his book, *al-Muhalla*, adopts this view.[2] Some scholars known for their inclination to restrict *zakat*, such as ash-Shawkani and Siddiq Hasan Khan, also support this view. Their arguments can be summarised in the following points.

Firstly, they draw on the *hadiths*, "No *zakat* is obliged on Muslims on their slaves and horses," and "I have exempted you from *sadaqa* on horses and slaves." The literal meaning of these *hadiths* is that *zakat* is waived on these two items, whether or not they are trade goods. The reply of scholars in the majority camp is that studying these two sayings indicates that they waive *zakat* on slaves in household service and horses used for personal transportation. Both serve needs that are unanimously exempt from *zakat*.

Secondly, they argue that in principle it is forbidden to take any part of a Muslim's wealth without clear evidence from Allah through Qur'an or *Sunna*. Trade was practised in the time of the

1. An old opinion that no *zakat* is obliged on trade is attributed to ash-Shafi'i, but many of his disciples challenge that. See *ar-Rawda* of an-Nawawi, vol. 2, p. 16.

2. *Al-Muhalla*, vol. 6, pp. 233-240.

Prophet (p) and there is no *sahih* report obliging *zakat* on trade. As for the reports from Samura and Abu Dharr, the argument is that they are weak and do not stand as evidence for obligation, especially on matters experienced by people.[1]

The answer to this claim is that there are several verses and *hadiths* that oblige, by virtue of their generality, *zakat* on all wealth. Furthermore, we have specific evidence to the effect that *zakat* is obliged on trade assets from the Qur'an, *Sunna*, Companions' sayings, and the *ijma'* of recognised people of knowledge. The *hadith* of Samura is not criticised by Abu Dawud and al-Mundhiri which means they consider it *hasan*. It is graded *hasan* by Ibn 'Abdu'l-Barr, and the later Ahmad Shakir says of it, "Its narrators are known and classified as trustworthy by Ibn Hibban." The *hadith* of Abu Dharr is marked as *sahih* by al-Hakim. Al-Hafiz mentions several weak chains for it and marks one of them as permitted. These *hadiths* are supported by the generalities of the main texts, the actions of the Companions and the *ijma'*, in addition to analogy and reasoning.

Thirdly, Abu 'Ubayd mentions that some jurists claim that *zakat* must always be paid out of the asset itself, and in the case of trade goods, all scholars accept payment on the basis of value. Abu 'Ubayd continues, "This is an error in judgement, because we know in the tradition of the Messenger of Allah (p) that *zakat* obliged on one kind of asset may be paid in the form of another kind. For example, in the Prophet's letter to Mu'adh about *jizya* is written, "On each person who is past puberty, there is a due of one dinar, or its value in clothes."[2]

Also, part of the Prophet's treaty with the people of Najran reads, "They are obliged to give two thousand articles of clothes every year, or their equivalent in silver." 'Umar accepted camels as *jizya* payment, while its levy was in gold and silver, and 'Ali accepted ropes and needles in payment of *zakat*. He said, It is also reported from Mu'adh that he took merchandise in place of *zakat*. He said, "Bring me clothes and menswear. I accept it in payment

1. *Ar-Rawda an-Nadiyya*, vol. 1, pp. 192-193.

2. Reported by Ahmad, Abu Dawud, an-Nasa'i, at-Tirmidhi, ad-Daraqutni, Ibn Hibban, al-Hakim, and al-Bayhaqi from Masruq from Mu'adh. At-Tirmidhi grades it *hasan*.

of *sadaqa* since it might be easier for you and more beneficial to the migrants in Madina." It is reported that Ibn Mas'ud's wife said to him, "I have a necklace that weighs twenty *mithqals*." He replied, "Pay five dirhams on it." (Ten dirhams was equal to one *mithqal*.)

Abu 'Ubayd notes that in all these examples, dues are levied on certain items and collected in the form of another. This negates the statement that *zakat* must be waived if it cannot be paid in the form of the same item on which *zakat* has been paid. As for trade goods, *zakat* may be collected in kind unless such collection harms the asset by forcing the division of the indivisible, in which case the value should be designated and *zakat* is then paid in terms of value. Muslims agree on the taking of *zakat* on trade goods, and its opponents are not known as people of knowledge. *Zakat*, however, is not obliged on these items when they cease to be trade goods or are assigned for personal or household use, similar to the waiver of *zakat* on cattle and camels used for family transportation. Trade goods, like livestock, are designated for growth, exchange, and profit, and as such *zakat* is paid on them. The ratio of *zakat* on livestock is given, while *zakat* on trade is estimated in terms of value.[1]

The Imami school

Imami jurists are of the opinion that *zakat* is recommended rather than obliged on trade goods.[2] They have, however, another prescription for trade earnings (excluding capital), saying one-fifth is due on those profits. They argue that the verse, *"Know that when you take any booty a fifth of it belongs to Allah, and to the Messenger, and to close relatives, orphans, the very poor and travellers"* (8:41), covers all earnings from business, buried treasures, and other gains. This obligation of one-fifth on business profits comes after deducting the personal and household expenses of the trader. The author of *Jawahir al-Kalam* writes, "One-fifth is levied on the residual of profits from trade, industry, and agriculture after the living expenses for the entire year has been deducted." He adds, "This is not

1. *Al-Amwal*, p. 427.
2. *Al-Mukhtasar an-Nafi' fi Fiqh al-Imamiyya*, p. 54.

disputed."[1] Using contemporary terms, this means a levy of twenty percent on net income.

Sunnis argue that this verse refers only to booty acquired in war, as explained by the Messenger of Allah (p). This interpretation is supported by the context of the verse in *Surat al-Anfal* itself. If the term acquired booty (*ghanima*) is used in a general sense and not restricted to the case of war, then a percentage on bequests would be due. This obviously contradicts the *ijma'*, and what necessitates the wrong is itself wrong.[2]

Section Three: Conditions of *zakat* on business goods

Trade is exchange with the intention of making a profit.[3] Trade goods are commodities obtained for the purpose of selling at a profit.[4] Thus two elements are involved in trade – the action of buying or selling and the intention of making profit.[5] Buying for the intention of using the asset is not trade. Items bought for personal and household use are not trade goods. These two elements must always co-exist in trade.[6] Changing the intention from selling for profit to personal use of an item must remove its liability for *zakat*."[7]

These are the two main conditions for the definition of trade goods. A few scholars add another condition,[8] that there should be no duplication in *zakat* on any item in one single *zakat* year,[9] since

1. *Jawahir al-Kalam*, vol. 2, p. 126.

2. *Ar-Rawda an-Nadiyya*, vol. 1, p. 219.

3. *Radd al-Muhtar*, vol. 2, p. 18.

4. *Matalib Uli'n-Nuha*, vol. 2.

5. *Radd al-Muhtar*, vol. 2, p. 18-19. See also its commentary and *Bulghat as-Salik*, vol. 1, p. 224, and its commentary.

6. This is the majority view. Among the Hanbalis, Ibn 'Aqil and Abu Bakr consider the change of intention from personal use to trade for any item is sufficient to include that item in those which are subject to *zakat*.

7. *Radd al-Muhtar*, vol. 2, p. 19.

8. Ibid., p. 18.

9. *Al-Mughni*, vol. 2, p. 529.

the Prophet (p) said, "There should be no duplication in *sadaqa*."[1] Duplication may take place in the case when a commodity, e.g. agricultural land, is purchased for resale with profit, but it is cultivated and harvested while in the possession of the merchant. Many scholars suggest that *zakat* on agriculture (ten per cent) is applicable on the produce, while others consider *zakat* on trade assets alone is applicable. Although a few suggest that the two *zakats* must apply in this case,[2] the majority are of the opinion that the two forms of *zakat* must not apply together, because that would be duplication in *zakat*.

The above are the conditions of *zakat* with respect to trade goods. We should, however, remember that there are also the general conditions of *zakat* which are the same as those of *zakat* of money, i.e. the *nisab*, the passage of one full lunar year, the absence of debts and similar liabilities, and being in excess of essential needs.

The *nisab* is the equivalent of the value of 85 grams of gold. As for the time of the *zakat* year at which the *nisab* condition should be fulfilled, there are three opinions among jurists. The first is that it is sufficient that the *nisab* exists at the end of the *zakat* year. This is reported from Malik and the text of ash-Shafi'i in *al-Umm*.[3] Secondly, there is the opinion that the *nisab* must be fulfilled throughout the whole *zakat* year and any moment this condition becomes unsatisfied interrupts the conditions of *zakat*, and a new *zakat* year begins until the *nisab* remains held for a full *zakat* year. This is the opinion of ath-Thawri, Ahmad, Ishaq, Abu 'Ubayd, Abu Thawr and Ibn Mundhir.[4] Thirdly, there is the opinion of Abu Hanifa and his followers. It aims at removing the apparent inconvenience of requiring continuous evaluation of trade assets in order to verify the fulfilment of the *nisab* throughout the year.

In my opinion, there is no correct text to support requiring *nisab* at the beginning of the year or during it. At the end of the the year, if the condition of *nisab* is fulfilled, we have on hand a zakatable asset. Consequently, I prefer the opinion of Malik which is

1 *Al-Amwal*, p. 375.

2. *Radd al-Muhtar*, vol. 2, p. 19, and *al-Mughni*, vol. 2, p. 630.

3. *Al-Majmu'*, vol. 1, p. 55.

4. *Al-Mughni*, vol. 3, p. 32.

also the most acceptable one to the Shafi'is.[1] The state can determine the date when a *zakat* year ends (i.e. when *zakat* is due). Any merchant who owns the *nisab* on that date is liable for *zakat*. This approach was practised at the time of the Prophet (p) and his Khulafa' with respect to *zakat* on livestock. The collectors were sent on a certain date to collect *zakat* on all livestock that was at the *nisab* and above, without asking the owners whether the *nisab* was fulfilled throughout the whole year.

Section Four: How *zakat* on trades is paid

Trade assets may take one of the following three forms:

- Merchandise and goods for sale.
- Cash in hand or in the bank.
- Debts and credit extended to agents and others.

Also, traders may have liabilities in the form of debts due to other people.

Abu 'Ubayd reports the ways of calculating *zakat* as perceived by some of the great Followers.[2] He quotes Maymun ibn Mihran as saying, "When *zakat* is due, calculate the amount of money, add to it the value of the goods and the amount of debts on customers that you expect to be paid, make a sum of the total, deduct whatever debts you owe to others, and pay *zakat* on the net amount." Al-Hasan al-Basri states, "When *zakat* is due, one must add the amount of money in hand, plus the amount owed by others as outstanding debts, except the amount of hopeless debts, and pay *zakat* on the total." Ibrahim an-Nakha'i indicates that one must evaluate one's trade goods and pay their *zakat* along with the *zakat* due on one's other holdings.[3]

1. *Ar-Rawda*, vol. 2, 267.
2. *Al-Amwal*, p. 426.
3. Ibid.

It is clear from these quotations that a Muslim merchant, in calculating the *zakat* on his assets, must add together what he owns, be that capital, profit, savings, and debts which are likely to be paid. He or she is required to take stock and evaluate it in addition to money and debts and then pay 2.5% of the total. As for hopeless debts, I already mentioned my preferred opinion that they are not subject to *zakat* unless they happen to be paid back. Then *zakat* must be taken once only,[1] on the basis of similarity with earned wealth on which *zakat* is paid at the time it is acquired. It is obvious that liabilities are deducted from assets and only the net is subject to *zakat*.

Malik distinguishes between monopolistic and non-monopolistic traders

According to Malik, a monopolistic trader is one who buys commodities and waits until prices go up to sell while a non-monopolistic trader is one who buys to sell on a regular basis without giving much attention to storage or to waiting for price changes.[2] Ibn Rushd writes, "Malik says a monopolistic trader must pay *zakat* on his goods when he sells them, once only, even if his stock was kept for several years, while the other trader is required to pay *zakat* on his stock every year.

The majority, including ash-Shafi'i, Abu Hanifa, Ahmad, ath-Thawri, al-Awza'i, and others do not make any distinction between these two kinds of traders.[3] Ibn Rushd comments on Malik's view, "This seems to be an intrusion into *Shari'a*, rather than a deduction from its principles. Things like this are usually called loose analogy (*al-qiyas al-mursal*), which do not rely on a principle mentioned in the *Shari'a*, but only on pure rationalisation of the *Shari'a's* interests. Malik accepts such an approach."

1. This is the view of Malik regarding all debts.

2. *Bulghat as-Salik*, vol. 1, p. 224. As-Sawi in his commentary quotes Ibn 'Ashir: "It seems that craftsmen are among the non-monopolistic merchants and those who transport merchandise from one location to another are also non-monopolistic.

3. *Bidayat al-Mujtahid*, vol. 1, pp. 260-261.

Furthermore, Malikis have different opinions about the case in which the merchandise of a non-monopolistic trader remains in stock for several years. Is he required to pay *zakat* every year, or should he be treated like the monopolistic trader who at the time of purchase anticipates a long waiting period? Sahnun says that the stagnant stock may be treated like the goods of a monopolistic trader, while Ibn al-Qasim does not agree. But what defines stagnation? There are two opinions reported from Sahnun and 'Abdu'l-Malik: two years or according to custom.[1]

It is obvious that the majority view is stronger than that of Malik, because *zakat* is levied on the grounds that trade assets are potentially growing assets, like money, and there is nothing to substantiate Malik's distinction. It should be mentioned, however, that at times of general economic recession, the opinion of Malik may have a certain applicability in order to reduce the burden of merchants by collecting *zakat* on actual sales instead of on stock.

Fixed assets are not subject to *zakat*

Business assets referred to with respect to *zakat* are only those assets that are liquid or circulating, or what is usually called turnover capital. Buildings, furniture and fixtures of stores that are not acquired for sale are not included in the zakatable assets. Jurists define trade goods which are subject to *zakat* as those items which are purchased for resale with profit.[2] The *hadith* narrated by Samura states: "The Prophet (p) used to order us to pay the *sadaqa* on what we designate for sale." Consequently, it is said that containers, cages, scales, machinery, and tools are not included in *zakat*.[3] Some jurists go on to distinguish between containers and packages sold with the merchandise and those that are not sold, the former being subject to *zakat* while the latter are not.[4]

1. *Sharh ar-Risala* by Zarruq, vol. 1,p. 325.

2. *Matalib Uli'n-Nuha*, vol. 2, p. 96.

3. Ibid., *Fath al-Qadir*, vol. 1, p. 427, *Bulghat as-Salik*, vol. 1, p. 235, and *Sharh al-Azhar*, vol. 1, pp. 479-480.

4. *Matalib Uli'n-Nuha*, vol. 2, p. 96.

Pricing of stock for *zakat* purposes

The majority view is to use current prices on the due date of *zakat*. This is also reported from the Follower, Jabir ibn Zayd. Evaluation is done according to the price on the day *zakat* becomes due. Ibn 'Abbas is reported to have said, "It is permissible to wait until the merchandise is sold and then the due *zakat* is paid (according to the actual proceeds)."[1] Yet a third view is reported by Ibn Rushd without attribution to any particular jurists, which is to appraise the stock at its purchase price.[2] Since prices may go up or down, it is not fair for the payer or the recipient of *zakat* to consider anything but prices that are current on the day of payment, especially since *zakat* is, in fact, due on principal and accrued profit. The majority view is obviously the most reasonable here. But it should be noted that wholesale prices, and not retail prices must be used, if any liquidation of stock is to be done, it will be at current wholesale prices.

Payment of *zakat* in kind or in value

Naturally, there are several opinions. Abu Hanifa and a report from ash-Shafi'i leave it to the merchant to make the choice, especially when the stock takes the form of consumer goods.[3] Another report from ash-Shafi'i makes it obligatory to give payment in kind and says it is not permissible in terms of value.[4] Al-Muzani says, "*Zakat* on merchandise is paid in kind and not in value."[5] Yet another view is that of Ahmad and a third report from ash-Shafi'i that *zakat* must only be paid in value because the *nisab* in trade assets is only a matter of valuation.[6] The author of *al-Mughni* writes, "We do not think that *zakat* is levied on the kind of the asset but only on its value."[7]

1. *Al-Amwal*, p. 426.
2. *Bidayat al-Mujtahid*, vol. 1, p. 260.
3. *Al-Mughni*, vol. 3, p. 31.
4. *Ar-Rawda*, vol. 2, . p. 273.
5. *Bidayat al-Mujtahid*, vol. 1, p. 260.
6. *Al-Mughni*, vol. 3, p. 31, and *ar-Rawda*, vol. 2, . p. 273
7. *Al-Mughni*, ibid.

This last opinion seems to me the most rational, because it is most beneficial to the poor, leaving them with the choice of commodities they need most. This method is also easier for the state to collect. Paying *zakat* in kind may also be practised when the payer knows that the poor need that commodity and the merchant pays it directly to them. Ibn Taymiyya was asked whether a merchant could pay *zakat* in value or not, and he answered, "That depends. Some people say it is permissible always, others say it is never allowed, while a third opinion says it is sometimes permissible depending on needs, so that if someone has a need for clothing and is given clothes, purchased for him by the payer, that is well and good. But if the payer gives clothes that he owns, their fair evaluation may be a matter of controversy. Moreover, clothes in kind may be given to poor people who may not need them. Then they stand to lose when selling them [in order to be able to buy what they need].[1]

1. *Fatawa Ibn Taymiyya*, vol. 1, p. 299.

Chapter Five

Zakat on Agriculture

Land is one of the greatest bounties of Allah. He subjects this earth to mankind and makes it cultivable, to produce plants and fruits. He created the laws of nature and made them benefit human beings in their living and subsistence. The importance of land as an origin of agricultural and other resources has always been recognised, to the extent the physiocrats in Western economics called for one single tax on land. Allah says:

> *"We have established you firmly on the earth and granted you your livelihood in it. What little thanks you show!"* (7:10)

Who created land and submitted it to our authority? Who made land arable or non-arable? Who created the seeds that, put inside the soil, grow into bushes and trees? Who nourishes seeds and waters them from clouds or springs? Who makes plants breathe the carbon gas that human being discharge, and discharge the oxygen that human beings need in a fantastic exchange of benefit? Who created the sun that provides plants and trees with light and heat indispensable for their growth?

All these are only a few of the bounties Allah created for us, human beings. Should we not indeed be thankful? Allah says: *"Have you thought about what you cultivate? Is it you who make it germinate or are We the Germinator? If We willed We could have made it broken stubble. You would then be left devoid of fruit, distraught: 'We are ruined, in fact we are destitute!'"* (56:63-67)

"As for the earth, We stretched it out and cast firmly embedded mountains in it and made everything grow in it in due proportion. And We put a livelihood in it for you and for those for whom you do not provide. There is nothing that does not have its store with Us and We only send it down in a known measure. We send forth the pollinating winds and send down

water from the sky and give it to you to drink. And it is not you who keep its store." (15:19-22)

"Man has only to look at his food. We pour down plentiful water. Then split the earth into furrows. Then We make grain grow in it; and grapes and herbs; and olives and dates; and luxuriant gardens; and orchards and meadows; for you and your livestock to enjoy." (80:24-32)

"A Sign for them is the dead land which We bring to life and from which We bring forth grain of which they eat. We place in it gardens of dates and grapes, and cause springs to gush out in it. So they may eat its fruits and from their own labour. So why do they not show thanks?" (36:33-35)

Indeed, all that the ground produces is but a part of the bounties of Allah. It is therefore natural that we are required to give thanks to Allah for these bounties that we use. The first expression of thankfulness is to give due *zakat* on it, showing gratitude to Allah and helping His needy servants. This *zakat* on grain, lands and fruits is known in the Shari'a as "*'ushr*" (10%).[1] Unlike other forms of *zakat*, *zakat* on agriculture does not require the passage of one full year. It is payable at the time of harvest because at the moment they are harvested, produce and crops represent the realised growth from land, and we have seen in Chapter One of this part that growth is the reason for *zakat*.

Section One: Obligation of *zakat* on agriculture

In the Qur'an

Allah says:

1. This is famous among Hanafis. Strangely enough, some Hanafis claim that calling it *zakat* is only allegorical, or in accordance with the view of the two disciples, Abu Yusuf and Muhammad ash-Shaybani, who require for the *'ushr* the preconditions of *nisab* and storability that apply to *zakat*. This is in opposition to Abu Hanifa. Ibn al-Humam says, "That does not matter. There is no doubt that *'ushr* is *zakat*, since it is spent in the same way. The matter is that certain kinds of *zakat* require certain conditions, which are not necessary for other kinds." See *Fath al-Qadir*, vol. 2, p. 2.

> *"O you who believe! Give away some of the good things you have earned and some of what the earth produces for you. Do not have recourse to bad things when you give, things you would only take with your eyes tight shut!"* (2:267)

The obligation of *zakat* is inherent in this command to spend. Very often the Qur'an uses the word 'spending' for *zakat*. Al-Jassas comments on this verse, "What is meant is *zakat*, especially since the following sentence forbids selecting bad goods as payment. Earlier and later generations agree that *zakat* is what is meant in this verse."[1]

Allah says: *"It is He who produces gardens, both cultivated and wild, and palm-trees and crops of diverse kinds, and olives and pomegranates, both similar and dissimilar. Eat of their fruits when they bear fruit and pay their due on the day of their harvest."* (6:141)

Many of the predecessors interpret the word 'due' in this verse to be *zakat*. At-Tabari reports that Anas interprets this verse to mean the obligatory *zakat*. He also reports from Ibn 'Abbas through several chains, "It refers to the one-tenth and the half-tenth dues." Another version from Ibn 'Abbas says, "Due means the prescribed *zakat* on the day when the quantity of the harvest is measured and known." It is reported that Jabir ibn Zayd, al-Hasan, Sa'id, Muhammad ibn al-Hanafiyya, Tawus, Qatada, and ad-Dahhak interpret the verse as the obligatory *zakat*, i.e. the one-tenth or half-tenth dues.[2] Al-Qurtubi says that Ibn Wahb and Ibn al-Qasim report the same from Malik. It is also the opinion of some of the disciples of ash-Shafi'i,[3] and of Abu Hanifa and his disciples as well.[4]

Others claim that this order came before the specific *zakat* was prescribed. It was replaced by it when the one-tenth and half-tenth dues were prescribed. At-Tabari reports from Ibn 'Abbas and Ibrahim an-Nakha'i, "The sixth *sura*, *al-An'am*, is Makkan, and the command was later replaced by the one-tenth and half-tenth dues. There is also a narration from Muhammad ibn al-Hanafiyya to the

1. *Ahkam al-Qur'an* by al-Jassas, vol. 1, p. 543.
2. *Commentary of at-Tabari*, vol. 12, pp. 158-161.
3. *Commentary of al-Qurtubi*, vol. 7, p. 99.
4. *Bada'i' as-Sana'i'*, vol. 2, p. 53.

same effect. Sa'id ibn Jubayr and al-Hasan are also reported to share this view. As-Suddi says, "They were taught to give to whoever comes to them on the day of the harvest, then *zakat* was ordained to replace that, and Allah prescribed on what comes forth from the earth dues of one-tenth and one half-tenth." A similar report is also narrated from 'Atiyya al-'Awfi.[1]

At-Tabari, after giving all these reports, concluded that the verse was superseded later by *zakat*. He adds that *zakat* cannot be paid on the day of harvest because drying or cleaning the grain or fruit is necessary.[2] This is surprising from at-Tabari since he is usually very cautious about the superseding of one verse by another. Throughout his commentary he denies many claimed supersedings and annulments. As a matter of principle, annulment of one text by another can only be resorted to when there is complete contradiction between their rulings, to the extent that both texts cannot be worked out together. The relation between the verse "*pay their due on the day of their harvest*" and the sound *hadith* that imposes one-tenth and half-tenth dues is not that of total contradiction, but rather the relation of the general to the specific.

It seems that the confusion is a matter of terminology, because the word 'annulment' [in Arabic *'naskh'*] is commonly used by predecessors, including many Companions, in a general text as defined by the scholars of jurisprudence, but also for any restriction of a general text, or the limitation of an absolute, or the details of a universal rule. In *al-Muwafaqat*, ash-Shatibi writes, "It seems that earlier scholars of *usul* used the word *naskh* when limiting an absolute text or removing some of the implications of an earlier one by a later one. All this used to be called annulment or *naskh*, since they all have some common element in their meaning."[3] Ibn al-Qayyim adds, "Early scholars use the term *naskh* sometimes in the meaning of eliminating a previous ruling completely – which is the only use of the term by later generations of scholars – but also used the term to mean the restricting or limiting of a general or absolute text."[4]

1. At-Tabari, vol. 12, pp. 168-170.
2. Ibid., pp. 170-173.
3. *Al-Muwafaqat*, vol. 3, p. 75.
4. *I'lam al-Muwaqqi'in*, vol. 3, p. 75.

In commenting on the reports of substitution of the 'due' mentioned in the above verse by the later prescription of *zakat*, Ibn Kathir says, "Calling this supercession or annulment is not correct, because we have something that was first made obligatory, then its details were provided, and the ratios and quantities were given later on. It is said that details were given in the second year of Hijra."[1]

One can conclude that the 'due' in the verse is something whose details and description were given later as one-tenth and half-tenth. As for the objection that the right due could not possibly be paid on the day of harvest because of the necessary operations of cleaning or drying, the reply is that it might be true about some crops, but the four kinds of produce mentioned in the verse – grapes, dates, olives and pomegranates – do not require drying and can be dispensed on the day of harvest. Additionally, a few scholars interpret the words, "pay their due" as "be ready to pay it."[2]

In the *Sunna*

Ibn 'Umar narrates that the Prophet (p) said, "On that which is watered by the sky or by springs or water running from mountains, one-tenth is obligatory, and on that which is watered by carried water, a half-tenth is obligatory."[3]

Jabir narrates from the Prophet (p), "One tenth is obligatory on that which is watered by rivers or clouds, and a half-tenth is obligatory on that which is watered by means of transported water." (Ahmad, Muslim, an-Nasa'i and Abu Dawud)

There are also several *hadiths* that determine the *nisab* of grains and fruits and others that talk about sending out collectors of *zakat* on agriculture.

1. *Commentary of Ibn Kathir*, vol. 2, p. 182.
2. Commentary of *al-Futuhat al-Ilahiyya*, with *Hashiyat al-Jamal*, vol. 2, p. 99.
3. The author of *al-Muntaqa* says it is reported by the group except for Muslim. See *Nayl al-Awtar*, vol. 4, pp. 139-140.

In *Ijma'*

Muslim scholars have unanimously agreed on the obligation of the one-tenth or the half-tenth dues, although they may have differences about details.[1]

Section Two: Agricultural products on which *zakat* is paid

In this section I will review the different scholarly opinions and then conclude with a comparison and reflection to select the best among them.

The view that *zakat* is obliged only on four food items

'Abdullah ibn 'Umar and a few Followers consider *zakat* obligatory only on wheat, barley, dates, and raisins. This is also reported from Musa ibn Talha, al-Hasan, Ibn Sirin, ash-Sha'bi, al-Hasan ibn Salih, Ibn Abi Layla, Ibn al-Mubarak, Abu 'Ubayd, and a report from Ahmad.[2] They put forward the following evidence in support of their view:

- Ibn Majah and ad-Daraqutni report from 'Amr ibn Shu'ayb from his father from his grandfather, "The Messenger of Allah (p) only collected *zakat* on wheat, barley, dates and raisins." Ibn Majah's version adds "corn".[3]
- A report narrated by Abu Burda from Abu Musa and Mu'adh that the Messenger of Allah (p) sent them to Yemen to teach people and ordered them not to take *sadaqa* except from the four foods – wheat, barley, dates and raisins.[4]

1. *Bada'i' as-Sana'i'*, vol. 2, p. 54.

2. *Al-Muhalla*, vol. 5, pp. 209f.

3. Ash-Shawkani says Muhammad ibn 'Ubaydullah al-'Arzami is in its chain, and he is disregarded. See *Nayl al-Awtar*, vol. 4, p. 143.

4. Al-Hafiz says it is reported by at-Tabarani and al-Hakim (see *Bulugh al-Maram*, p. 122. He says in *at-Talkhis* that al-Bayhaqi says, "Its narrators are trustworthy, and the *hadith* is connected to the Prophet (p)." The author of *ad-Diraya* writes on page 174, "Yahya ibn Talha is in the chain and people disagree about

• There is no text or known *ijma'* that imposes *zakat* on other than these four products. Other crops are not as common as these four and must not be considered similar to them.

The view that imposes *zakat* on all edible preservable items

Malik and ash-Shafi'i consider edibility and preservability as the necessary conditions for *zakat* on agricultural products. Consequently, *zakat* can be taken on wheat, barley, millet, grain, and rice. By 'edibility' they mean that the item should be a major foodstuff and not a secondary one, an item that people normally eat for subsistence. Consequently, almonds, walnuts and pistachios are not subject to *zakat*, although they can be stored. *Zakat* is not taken on apples, pomegranates, pears, peaches, and plums because they cannot be dried and stored. Malikis differ on whether figs are subject to *zakat*. Malik himself is reported to have excluded figs, plums, pomegranates and all fruits from *zakat*,[1] while some of his followers consider figs under the fruits from which *zakat* can be taken because the two conditions of edibility and preservability are fulfilled. Al-Kharashi counts twenty food items from which *zakat* may be taken which include chick peas, lentils, wheat, barley, rice, dates, olives, raisins, sesame and others.[2]

Al-Qurtubi says that ash-Shafi'i believes in no obligatory *zakat* on fruits except dates and grapes, because the Prophet (p) took *zakat* on these two products, as primary preservable foods in Hijaz. On the other hand, *zakat* is not taken on walnuts and almonds although they are non-perishable, because they were not primary foodstuffs in Hijaz, but were used only as fruits. Ash-Shafi'i continues, "*Zakat* is not taken on olives because they are associated with pomegranates in a verse, "*...and olives and pomegranates.*" (6:141)

him. This *hadith*, however, is the best that we have on the subject." The author of *al-Mir'a*, vol. 3, p. 39, adds, "It is not agreed upon whether the *hadith* is connected to the Messenger or not." See also *al-Kharaj* by Yahya ibn Adam, p. 153, *as-Sunan al-Kubra*, vol. 4, p. 125, *Nasb ar-Raya*, vol. 2, p. 319, and *al-Muhalla*, vol. 5, p. 221.

1. *Al-Muwatta'*, vol. 1, p. 276.
2. *Sharh al-Kharashi* on Khalil with *Hashiyat al-'Adawi*, vol. 2, p. 163.

There is, however, another report from ash-Shafi'i that *zakat* is taken on olives.[1] This is also the opinion of Malik.[2] Al-Qurtubi continues, "They both agree that pomegranates are not liable for *zakat*, while according to the verse quoted at the beginning of this chapter, pomegranates should be liable for *zakat*."[3]

The argument of ash-Shafi'i is based on two points. The first is a *hadith* narrated by Mu'adh which reads: "Cucumbers, watermelons, pomegranates, sugar cane and vegetables are exempt: the Messenger of Allah (p) exempted them," reported by al-Bayhaqi in *as-Sunan al-Kubra*. He also reports a few other *hadiths* and comments, "All these *hadiths* are *mursal*, but there are several narrations of them which must strengthen them." This is further supported by the statements made by some Companions such as 'Ali, 'Umar, and 'A'isha. And the second is that foodstuffs are highly useful, like livestock, so they must likewise be liable for *zakat*.[4]

Neither of these two points stand up in the face of the generalisation of the texts in the Qur'an and *Sunna* which indicate that the obligation of *zakat* is on all that comes from the earth or is watered by the sky.[5]

The view that all non-perishable crops that can be dried and measured are amenable to *zakat*

Ahmad is reported in *al-Mughni* to have said that these three conditions must be met for *zakat*, whether the crop is a food item or otherwise.[6] Thus grain, cotton, sesame, some vegetables and many fruits are included. However, *zakat* is not taken on some fruits, like apples, pears, peaches, and apricots, and some vegetables like cucumbers, eggplants, and carrots.

This view is based on the generality of the *hadith*, "There is one tenth obliged on that which is watered by the sky," the Prophet's

1. Al-Qurtubi, op cit.
2. *Al-Muwatta'*, vol. 1, p. 272. Malik says that the one-tenth is taken from olives after they are pressed, provided that the crop reaches five *wasqs*.
3. Al-Qurtubi, op cit.
4. *Al-Muhadhdhab* with *al-Majmu'*, vol. 5, p. 493.
5. *Sharh ar-Risala*, Zarruq, vol. 1, p. 329.
6. *Al-Mughni*, vol. 2, pp. 690-692.

order to Mu'adh, "Take grain out of grain,"[1] and the *hadith*, "There is no *zakat* on grain or dates that are less than five *wasqs*"[2] reported by Muslim and an-Nasa'i. This last *hadith* means that for *zakat*, measurability is a required precondition.[3]

The view that anything that stems from the soil is liable to *zakat*

According to Abu Hanifa anything that is planted and harvested with the intention of making a profit, is liable for *zakat.* Natural forests, bushes and plants that grow on their own are not subject to *zakat* except when the owners intend to use the land for lumber or fodder production. In this case those products become liable for *zakat.*[4] Abu Hanifa does not consider any of the conditions of edibility, driability, non-perishability, or measurability. Abu Dawud and his Zahiri followers oblige *zakat* on every land product and do not exempt anything. This is also reported to be the view of 'Umar ibn 'Abdu'l-'Aziz, Mujahid, Hammad, and a report from an-Nakha'i.[5] Abu Yusuf and ash-Shaybani do not agree with their teacher Abu Hanifa on the *zakat* of vegetables.

According to Abu Hanifa and his two disciples, sugar cane, saffron, cotton, and other fibres are subject to *zakat.* So also vegetables are subject to *zakat* in his view only. Abu Hanifa uses the following in support of his opinion. Firstly, he says the general terms of the verse in *Surat al-Baqara*, *"...some of what the earth produces for*

---

1. This is part of the *hadith* reported by Abu Dawud and Ibn Majah as stated in *al-Muntaqa.* Ash-Shawkani says al-Hakim grades it *sahih* according to the criteria of al-Bukhari and Muslim, but in its chain 'Ata' narrates from Mu'adh. In fact, he did not listen to Mu'adh.

2. *Nasb ar-Rayah*, vol. 2, p. 384.

3. *Al-Mughni*, vol. 2, pp. 692.

4. *Al-Hidaya*, with *al-Fath*, vol. 2, pp. 2-5. The author of *al-Fath*, p. 2, says there is no *zakat* on medicines or tree sap. But his must be applied only to the case where medicinal plants and products from tree trunks are not produced on a commercial basis. In such cases they would be liable to *zakat.*

5. *Al-Muhalla*, vol. 5, pp. 212-215.

you".[1] Secondly, the verse, *"pay their due on the day of their harvest"* comes after the mention of several kinds of trees and fruits.

If *zakat* should cover fruits, it must also cover vegetables because the latter are easier to produce and to transfer to the poor and needy, even more so than grains.[2] Finally the *hadith*, "One-tenth is obligatory on that which is watered by the sky and a half-tenth is required on that which is watered by carried water" does not distinguish between edible or non-edible, perishable or non-perishable, measurable or non-measurable crops.

Discussion and analysis

The view of Abu Hanifa seems to be the strongest. It suits the general objectives of *zakat* and the justice of its implementation as expressed in the texts of the Qur'an and *Sunna*. It does not seem reasonable to impose *zakat* on grain farmers while oranges, mangoes and apples are exempt. We must also remember that this is also the opinion of several great scholars, such as 'Umar ibn 'Abdu'l-'Aziz, Mujahid, Hammad, Da'ud and an-Nakha'i.[3] The few *hadiths* that talk about four food items are either *munqati'* (interrupted) or weak.[4] Even if one were to accept the *hadiths*, the restriction to the four items can be interpreted as a mere reference to items present at the time of the Prophet.[5] It is remarkable that

1. Ar-Razi says in his commentary, vol. 7, p. 65, "Apparently the verse indicates the obligation of *zakat* on all that is produced by the earth, in accordance with the view of Abu Hanifa. His use of this verse makes his argument very strong. His opponents, however, restrict the general implication of this verse by the *hadith* of the Prophet, 'No *zakat* is obliged on vegetables.' But I think this *hadith* is not strong enough to restrict the general implication of a verse. This leaves Abu Hanifa's argument very difficult to challenge."

2. *Bada'i' as-Sana'i'*, vol. 2, p. 59.

3. I find no substantial difference between the opinion of Abu Hanifa and that of the mentioned scholars, because the exception Abu Hanifa makes for firewood, cane and grass does not really make a restrictor of the general concept of *zakat* on what is produced by the earth through agriculture, since it is a very minor exception.

4. *Al-Mir'a*, vol. 3, p. 39.

5. *Al-Mirqat*, vol. 4, p. 153.

none of the four schools of thought took such limitation for granted.

Amazingly enough, the late Rashid Rida supports this narrow view, after he adds corn to the other four crops, saying, "If anything must be added by analogy it is rice especially in areas where rice is the main subsistence."[1] This is amazing because Rida himself uses the argument of generality with respect to trade assets. The generality argument is in fact far more applicable to the produce of the earth that is referred to in the verses than to anything else, especially since the grace of Allah is more evident in the produce of the earth than in any other form of wealth. This is perhaps why the farmer's *zakat* is made due on the harvest.

As well as this, a Maliki like Ibn al-'Arabi supports the position of Abu Hanifa in *Ahkam al-Qur'an*.[2] The commentary on at-Tirmidhi states: "The strongest view is that of Abu Hanifa, because it is more advantageous to the needy, most supported by the general terms of the texts and more appropriate as an expression of gratitude for Allah's grace."[3]

In his explanation of the verse, *"and pay their due..."* Ibn al-'Arabi says, "Abu Hanifa hits the truth in obliging *zakat* on foodstuffs and other crops, as implied by the general terms of the Prophet's *hadith*, 'And one-tenth is obliged on what the sky waters.' Ahmad's opinion depends on a weak argument in mistakenly interpreting the *hadith*, 'There is no *zakat* on what is less than five *wasqs*' to mean there is a condition of measurability, instead of a minimum for *zakat* that applies to all crops, measurable or not. The edibility condition of the Shafi'is is baseless. Allah reminds us of His grace in providing food and fruits and obliges dues on both, in spite of differences in kinds of crops or in the way a given group is used, such as using oil extracted from a crop for light to enjoy the grace of vision and the removal of darkness.

"How could anyone claim that *zakat* is not obligatory on vegetables because they are usually distributed fresh and not dried knowing that fresh dates and fresh grapes are both subject to *zakat*

---

1. *Al-Mughni* with *ash-Sharh al-Kabir*, vol. 2, p. 551.
2. *Ahkam al-Qur'an*, pt. 2, pp. 749-752.
3. *Sharh at-Tirmidhi*, vol. 3, p. 135.

without any need for drying. Fresh fruits are an essential part of the bounties Allah bestows on us. He even mentions them as some of the enjoyments offered in Heaven as in the verse, *'In them are fruits and date-palms and pomegranates,'* (66:68)" Ibn al-'Arabi continues, "One may argue that we have no report that the Prophet (p) collected *zakat* from the vegetables in Madina and Khaybar. My answer to this is that lack of evidence that he collected *zakat* is not evidence that *zakat* is not required, especially since we have sufficient proof in the Qur'an itself."

The *hadith* that reads, "No *zakat* is obliged on vegetables," has a weak chain and does not help as evidence.[1] At-Tirmidhi indicates that the chain of this *hadith* is incorrect: nothing authentic is reported from the Prophet (p) on this issue.[2] Some Hanafi jurists tend to understand this *hadith* as a reference to the perishability of vegetables and advice to a *zakat* collector not to collect vegetables because they cannot be preserved.[3] Those jurists require that producers of vegetables distribute their *zakat* directly although some suggest that *zakat* be assessed and collected in value instead of in kind. It is reported by Yahya ibn Adam from az-Zuhri, "Anything other than wheat, barley, dates, grapes and olives should have their *zakat* taken in value."[4]

'Ata' al-Khurasani says, "Vegetables, walnuts, almonds and fruits are not subject to one-tenth. But whatever is sold of them is subject to *zakat* if the value is two hundred dirhams or more." A similar opinion is reported from ash-Sha'bi. Abu 'Ubayd attributes similar views to Maymun ibn Mihran, az-Zuhri and perhaps al-Awza'i. Az-Zuhri and Maymun apply here the *nisab* and rate applicable to silver.[5] Abu 'Ubayd further reports that Malik applies the same to

1. See the comment of al-Hafiz in *at-Talkhis*, p. 179, also *Fath al-Qadir*, vol. 2, p. 3. Al-Haythami mentions this *hadith* in *Majma' az-Zawa'id* as connected to the Prophet from Talha and says, 'At-Tabarani adds it in *al-Awsat* and *al-Batra'*. The chain has al-Harith ibn Nabhan, who is disregarded." Ibn 'Adi abstains from giving an opinion about him, vol. 2, pp. 668-69.

2. Chapter "*Zakat*," section "Texts on the subject of *zakat* on vegetables". See the *sahih* collection of at-Tirmidhi with the commentary of Ibn al-'Arabi, pp. 132-233.

3. *Bada'i' as-Sana'i'*, vol. 2, p. 59.

4. *Al-Kharaj*, Yahya ibn Adam, p. 145.

5. *Al-Amwal*, p. 594.

fresh dates, grapes and olives. The latter adds, however, another condition, that the crop must be five *wasqs* or more.[1]

The idea of calculating *zakat* of perishable vegetables and fruits on the basis of value is very practical, but I tend to differ with the above scholars on the *nisab* and ratio, since changing the mode of payment from kind to value does not necessitate a change in the rate and *nisab* of *zakat*. I believe that the rates and *nisab* of agriculture must still be applicable. We have on hand a report from ash-Sha'bi that *zakat* is taken on the value of grapes at the rate of one-tenth or one half-tenth.[2] In *ar-Risala*, Ibn Abi Zayd mentions, "Olives are subject to *zakat* if the crop is five *wasqs* or more and *zakat* can be paid out of the olive oil or the proceeds of sale." And in his commentary on *ar-Risala*, Ibn Naji says, "This is also reported from Malik. The generally accepted opinion in the Maliki school is that *zakat* on olive oil is paid in oil, while *zakat* on olives sold unpressed is paid in value."[3]

Section Three: The *nisab* of agriculture

The majority of Muslim scholars since the era of the Companions and Followers believe that crops must be at least five *wasqs* for *zakat* to be taken,[4] based on the Prophet's *hadith*, "No *sadaqa* is obligatory on anything less than five *wasqs*," which is *sahih* and agreed upon.[5]

Abu Hanifa says that *zakat* is obligatory on agriculture regardless of the amount of the crop, since the *hadith* of the Prophet, "A tenth is obliged on that which the sky waters," is general. This is also *sahih* and reported by al-Bukhari and others.[6] According to Abu Hanifa the condition of *nisab* is not applicable because the condition of the passage of one year is not required. Yahya ibn

1. Ibid., p. 496.
2. *Al-Kharaj*, op. cit. p. 152.
3. *Sharh ar-Risala*, Ibn Naji, vol. 1, pp. 320-321.
4. *Al-Mughni*, vol. 2, p. 695.
5. The author of *al-Muntaqa* says it is reported by the group, from Abu Sa'id.
6. *Al-Mughni*, vol. 2, p. 695.

Adam reports a similar opinion from Ibrahim an-Nakha'i.[1] 'Ata' is said to be of the same view.[2] Abu Raja' al-'Utaridi says that Ibn 'Abbas used to collect *zakat* in Basra even from bunches of fresh onions.[3]

Furthermore, Ibn Hazm indicates that Mujahid, Hammad, 'Umar ibn 'Abdu'l-'Aziz, and an-Nakha'i all oblige *zakat* on all that the land produces, whether big or small in quantity. Reports from the last three are extremely correct.[4] 'Umar ibn 'Abdu'l-'Aziz says that of each ten bunches of spinach and the like, one bunch must be paid as *zakat*.[5] Da'ud az-Zahiri holds that for items that are measurable, the condition of five *wasqs* is necessary, while this condition does not apply to crops that are not measurable.[6] This seemed to be a reconciliation of the above two *hadiths*.[7] The author of *al-Bahr* reports yet another opinion from al-Baqir and an-Nadir, that the *nisab* is a necessary condition on dates, raisins, wheat and barley, since these were the most common foodstuffs at the time of the Prophet (p).[8] Ash-Shawkani comments, "This looks like restricting a general text without any supportive evidence."[9]

Discussion and analysis

I incline to prefer Abu Hanifa's view of imposing *zakat* on all produce but his opinion in obliging *zakat* on any quantity, with no consideration of *nisab*, contradicts the *sahih hadith* that does not oblige *zakat* on what is less than five *wasqs*. It also appears to be in direct conflict with the general principle that *zakat* should be levied on the rich alone, and the *nisab* is the criterion for richness. The seeming opposition of this *hadith* by the *hadith*, "A tenth is obliged on that which the sky waters," is not an argument, because both of them can be interpreted in a way that removes contradiction.

1. *Al-Kharaj*, p. 152.
2. Ibid.
3. Ibid., p. 145; the *hadith* is weak.
4. *Al-Muhalla*, vol 5, p. 112.
5. Ibid., p. 113, and *Fath al-Qadir*, vol. 2, p. 3.
6. *Al-Muhalla*, vol 5, p. 212.
7. *Nayl al-Awtar*, vol. 4, p. 151.
8. *Al-Bahr az-Zakhkhar*, vol. 2, p. 169.
9. *Nayl al-Awtar*, op. cit.

According to Ibn al-Qayyim, "The *hadith*, 'a tenth is obliged on that which the sky waters,' is said in the context of distinguishing between cases that require a rate of one-tenth and cases where a rate of only a half-tenth is required. This *hadith* does not touch the matter of *nisab*. On the other hand, the *hadith* of the five *wasqs* is a clear text on the issue of *nisab*. This cannot be challenged by the general text of the former *hadith*."[1]

Ibn Qudama says, "Since the *hadith*, 'There is no *sadaqa* obliged on that which is less than five *wasqs*;' is specific, it has priority in determining the *nisab* and restricts the general *hadith*. This is like the case of other zakatable items, such as camels and silver. In both cases there are general *hadiths* whose purpose is to indicate whether the item is subject to *zakat*, while there are texts whose purpose is to set the *nisab*, like 'There is no *sadaqa* obliged on less than five camels,' and 'There is no *sadaqa* obliged on less than five *uqiyyas*.'"

Ibn Qudama goes on, "The passage of a year is disregarded in agriculture because the time of harvesting represents the complete cycle of growth for the land. So there should be no association between the *nisab* and the passage of a year. Finally, the *nisab* is the determinant of wealth in matters of *zakat*, and *zakat* is only obliged on the rich."[2]

The required *nisab* on grain and fruits

Sahih hadiths determine the *nisab* at five *wasqs*. A *wasq* unanimously equals sixty *sa's*. This is even mentioned in a *hadith*, although it is a weak one.[3] A *nisab* is thus three hundred *sa's*. Unanimity on this estimation is mentioned by Ibn al-Mundhir and others.[4]

1. *I'lam al-Muwaqqi'in*, vol. 3, pp. 229-230.

2. *Al-Mughni*, vol. 2, pp. 695-696.

3. Reported by Ibn Majah from Jabir. Its chain is weak. Also reported by Abu Dawud, an-Nasa'i and Ibn Majah through Abu'l-Bakhtari from Abu Sa'id, connected to the Prophet (p). This is interrupted because Abu'l-Bakhtari did not hear from Abu Sa'id, as stated by al-Bukhari. He was not even a contemporary of Abu Sa'id, according to Abu Hatim. Ad-Daraqutni reports the *hadith* from 'A'isha, but it is also weak. Ibn Hajar shows the weakness of all chains of this *hadith* in *at-Talkhis*, p. 180.

4. *Al-Majmu'*, vol. 5, p. 447.

The *sa'*

According to *Lisan al-'Arab*, the *sa'* is a measure of volume or capacity used in Madina. It is equal to four *mudds*. The *sa'* is mentioned in several *hadiths* with regard to the *zakat* for breaking the fast of Ramadan.[1] It is said that the Prophet (p) used one *sa'* of water for his *ghusl* and one *mudd* for *wudu'*,[2] so that *sa'* of the Prophet (p) is four *mudds*. One *mudd* is equivalent to what fills the two hands put together with the fingers extended. The Prophet guided Muslims about measures of capacity, stating, as narrated by Ibn 'Umar, "The (standard) measures are the measures of Madina, and the (standard) weights are the weights of Makka."[3] The people of Madina were farmers and their measures of capacity were more widely known and more accurate, while the people of Makka were men of trade, and their weights were more common and accurate.

Differences on the weight equivalent of the *sa'* among jurists of the Hijaz and Iraq

Abu Hanifa and his Iraqi disciples estimate the weight of one *sa'* at eight Baghdadi *ratls*, while Malik, ash-Shafi'i, Ahmad and other Hijazis estimate it at five and one-third Baghdadi *ratls*.

Iraqi jurists argue that the *sa'* at 'Umar's time weighed eight *ratls*.[4] They also depend on the claim that the Prophet (p) used eight *ratls* for his *ghusl*, two *ratls* for *wudu'*, or one *sa'* for his *ghusl* and one *mudd* for his *wudu'*.[5] They conclude that one *sa'* must equal eight *ratls*, while one *mudd* equals two *ratls*.

1. The *sa'* is also needed to determine *kaffara* for a broken oath, and the recompense in pilgrimage.

2. Reported by Ahmad, Muslim, at-Tirmidhi and Ibn Majah from Safina from the Prophet. At-Tirmidhi adds, "There are also reports on the same from 'A'isha, Jabir and Anas." See *Sunan at-Tirmidhi*, edited by Ahmad Shakir, vol. 1, p. 84.

3. Ibn Hajar says on page 183 of at-Talkhis that it is reported by al-Bazzar, who grades it *gharib*. Also reported by Abu Dawud and an-Nasa'i from Tawus from Ibn 'Umar. This *hadith* is graded *sahih* by Ibn Hibban, ad-Daraqutni, an-Nawawi and Abu'l-Fath al-Qushayri.

4. *Bada'i' as-Sana'i'*, vol. 2, p. 75.

5. These *hadiths* are mentioned in *al-Amwal*, pp. 514-516. Abu 'Ubayd explains that the Prophet (p) used to bathe sometimes with one *sa'* of water and

As for the Hijazis, their evidence is the predominant practice of the residents of Madina, generation after generation, from the time of the Prophet (p). Ibn Hazm says, "This is overwhelmingly known in Madina, and it is obvious to everyone, young or old, righteous or wicked, knowledgeable or ignorant. Rejecting such a fact is like rejecting the site indicated by Makkans as the Mosque in Makka or rejecting the known site in Madina of the dome of the Prophet's Mosque – it is absurdly unreasonable." He continues, "Even Abu Yusuf, upon visiting Madina and coming across their *mudds*, changed his view to that of the Hijazi jurists."[1]

He is referring to the story reported by al-Bayhaqi from al-Husayn ibn al-Walid: "We went to visit Abu Yusuf upon his return from the pilgrimage. He told us, 'I want to inform you of a matter that worried me for some time until I went to Madina. There I asked about the *sa'* and they answered that the *sa'* they have today is the same *sa'* used by the Messenger of Allah (p). I asked if they could provide proof for this statement. They said that they would bring me their proof the following day. The next day, about fifty elderly sons of the Ansar and Muhajirun appeared before me, each of them carrying a measure of one *sa'*. Each narrated from his father and his ancestors that this was the measure used at the time of the Prophet (p). I looked at those measures and found them all equal. I compared the weight of the *sa'* contents and found it a little less than five and a third *ratls*. This was overwhelming evidence and I change my view from that of Abu Hanifa to that of the residents of Madina."[2] Al-Husayn continues, "I went on pilgrimage the following year and met Malik and asked him about the *sa'*. He said, 'The *sa'* we have today is the same *sa'* of the time of the Prophet (p).' I asked him how much it weighed and he replied, 'This is a measure of capacity. It cannot be converted into weight.'"[3]

sometimes with eight *ratls*. He also used to perform *wudu'* sometimes with one *mudd* and other times with two *ratls*. These *hadiths* thus talk about different occasions.

1. *Al-Muhalla*, vol. 5, p. 246.

2. *As-Sunan al-Kubra*, al-Bayhaqi, vol. 4, p. 171.

3. Ibid. It seems that a story similar to that of Abu Yusuf was repeated with some other Madinans. Ad-Daraqutni reports from Ishaq ar-Razi, "I asked Malik

In the third century of Hijra, Ahmad said, "I weighed the contents of one *sa'* of wheat and found it five *ratls* and one-third." Hanbal quotes his father, Ahmad, "I took that *sa'* from Abu'n-Nadr, who told me he took it from Abu Dhu'ayb, who told me that this is the *sa'* which was known in Madina at the time of the Prophet (p)." Ahmad says, "I weighed the contents of a *sa'* of lentils and found it equal to five and one-third *ratls*. This is the best I know and what becomes clear to me about the *sa'* of the Prophet (p)."[1]

Reconciliation of these two estimates

Three propositions are suggested to reconcile the two views on the weight of the contents of the *sa'*.

- Some Hanafis suggest that the *ratl* of Baghdad is two-thirds of the *ratl* of Madina. Ibn al-Humam supports this proposition. It means that the *sa'* as a capacity measure is the same both in Madina and Baghdad, but the weight of the *ratl* is different.[2]
- Ibn Taymiyya suggests that there used to be two measures of capacity and the Hijazi *sa'* is used only for grain and foodstuffs. A *sa'* of grain equals five and one-third *ratls* in weight. Another measure was used only for liquid, also called a *sa'*, and is equal to eight *ratls* in weight.[3] According to this reconciliation, the

ibn Anas about the size of the *sa'* of the Prophet. I said, 'It is five and one-third Baghdadi *ratls*. I personally verified it.' I mentioned to him that he differs with Abu Hanifa, who says it is eight *ratls*. Malik was very angry and told the people sitting around, 'Bring the *sa'* of your grandfather, and you bring the *sa'* of your uncle, and you bring the *sa'* of your grandmother,' etc.'" Ishaq says, "Several *sa's* were brought by the people. Then Malik asked them, 'What do you remember about these?' One said, 'My father told me that his father used this *sa'* in measuring for the Prophet (p).' Another said, 'My father told me that his mother did the same.' etc. Malik said, 'I verified these measures and found them equal to five and a third *ratls*.' Ad-Daraqutni and al-Bayhaqi report this story via a good chain, according to ash-Shawkani's *Nayl al-Awtar*, vol. 4, p. 196.

1. *Al-Mughni*, vol. 3, p. 59.
2. *Sharh Fath al-Qadir*, vol. 2, p. 42.
3. *Al-Qawa'id an-Nuraniyya*, Ibn Taymiyya, p. 89.

ratl is the same in Iraq and the Hijaz, while there are two different volume measures, depending on the materials measured.

- For our modern age, 'Ali Mubarak suggests a third means of reconciliation. He claims that there is no real difference in the volume of the *sa'* in Iraq and the Hijaz, nor is there any difference between their ratls as a measure of weight. If you weigh one *sa'* full of grain it is five and one-third *ratls*, and if you weigh one *sa'* full of water, it is eight *ratls*. It should be noted that the eight *ratls* is only an approximation, because the exact weight of the water is a little bit less than eight *ratls*. Thus, according to Mubarak, the Iraqis considered the weight of water, while the Hijazis considered the weight of grain.[1]

With all this, it becomes apparent that the weight of one *sa'* of grain is five and one-third *ratls*. The late ar-Rayis says, "There should be absolutely no doubt about this. It is supported by the strong experience of the residents of Madina. Malik himself studied the measure of the *sa'* and the weight of one *sa'* full of grain in the presence of the Abbasid caliph, Harun ar-Rashid, and convinced Abu Yusuf of it." Ar-Rayis continues, "Who knows the traditions of Madina better than Malik? And whose testimony is more valuable than that of Abu Yusuf? This determination of the weight of one *sa'* best suits the proportion of the *nisab* on grain as compared with other *nisabs*. It is known that one *sa'* is four *mudds* and one *mudd* is a double handful. Who can imagine that the double handful of an average-sized man can be more than one and one-third *ratls*?"[2]

Determination of this *nisab* in contemporary measures

After we have determined the *nisab* as five *wasqs*, each *wasq* being sixty *sa's,* we can easily transfer these to contemporary capacity measures. In order to give the amount of the *nisab* in weight we

1. *Al-Kharaj fi'd-dawla al-Islamiyya*, Diya' ad-Din ar-Rayis, p. 301, as quoted from the article of 'Ali Mubarak entitled, "*Al-Mizan fi'l-Aqyisa wa'l-Awzan*," pp. 86-88.

2. Ibid., pp. 302-303.

must remember the experiment of Ahmad. He weighed a *sa'* full of wheat and the weight was five and one-third *ratls*. It is known that some crops are lighter than wheat, such as barley or corn. There is no disagreement among the *Ahl al-Hadith* that the weight of a *sa'* is five and one-third *ratls* of average wheat. We must not forget that the quantity of the *nisab* is determined by capacity measures and not in weight. If the volume of the *nisab* of another crop happens to weigh less than the same volume of wheat, that volume of the other grain is subject to *zakat* in spite of its lighter weight.[1]

'Ali Mubarak studied the Baghdadi *ratl* and concluded that one *ratl* equals four hundred and eight grams.[2] He also estimated that one *sa'* of water is 2.75 litres. Consequently, the weight of one *sa'* of grain is 2.176 kg. By simple arithmetic we find that one *wasq* is 130.56 kg of wheat, or 165 litres. This means that the *nisab* is 825 litres or 652.8 kg.[3]

Nisab for crops that are not measured by volume

A few crops cannot be measured by volume measures because they are usually administered without being condensed or pressurised, such as saffron and cotton. Abu Yusuf suggests that the value of such products should be the criteria for *zakat* purposes. He proposes to consider the value of a *nisab* of the cheapest grain, barley, for example, and apply that value on those crops.[4]

Muhammad suggests using the largest unit used actually in trade, such as a ton, for example, saying that the *wasq* was the highest unit of volume measure at the time of the Prophet (p). Thus, for those new crops, we should take five of their highest units of measurement as a *nisab*. This definitely means the *nisab* will differ from one country to another.

Some jurists suggest that in all crops which are not measured by volume, the *nisab* must be determined as the quantity whose value is two hundred dirhams, applying the *nisab* of money the same way

1. *Al-Mughni*, vol. 2, p. 701.
2. *Al-Kharaj*, pp. 304-305.
3. *Hashiyat al-'udul 'ala Sharh al-Kharashi*, vol. 2, p. 168.
4. *Bada'i' as-Sana'i*, vol. 2, p. 61

it is applied to trade goods.[1] Da'ud suggests that crops not usually sold by measures of volume all come under *zakat* without any consideration of *nisab*. Lastly, Ahmad suggests that we should use the weight equivalent of the *nisab* of grain.[2] This means that for crops that are not usually measured by volume measures, the weight of 653 kg must be applied in our times.

Ibn Qudama accuses all these views of being void of any support from a text, a valid analogy, or a sound rationale. He argues that *zakat* cannot be due on all assets regardless of any minimum, nor can the estimation of *nisab* on certain crops be done on the basis of another crop, nor can the value be considered, because in agriculture it is essential that *zakat* be paid in kind.[3]

In my opinion, other crops that are not measurable by volume must have a *nisab*. Their *nisab* should be estimated on the basis of the value as Abu Yusuf says, but I think that the estimation at the cheapest measurable crop is unfair from the point of view of *zakat* payers, although it benefits the poor. An estimation of the *nisab* must be fair with both parties, so I suggest taking a crop that is average in value among all land produce. Since this may differ from time to time and place to place, I suggest that the *nisab* in each case be determined according to the socio-economic variables on the basis of the value of five *wasqs* of an average crop as declared by people of wisdom and knowledge in each country.

Time and method of determination of the *nisab*

The estimation of nisab should be made on the dry product after it takes its final form for sale (after threshing, cleaning, filtering, skinning, etc.) Al-Ghazali in *al-Wajiz* writes that the five *wasqs* must be measured in the dried form of raisins, and in grain after cleaning and removal of its bran, except for crops that are sold fresh or with their bran. In this case the *nisab* is estimated on them as they are.[4]

1. *Al-Bahr az-Zakhkhar*, vol. 2, p. 170.
2. *Al-Mughni*, vol. 2, p. 697.
3. Ibid., pp. 697-698.
4. *Al-Wajiz* and its commentary, printed with *al-Majmu'*, vol. 5, p. 568.

Section Four: Ratios of *zakat*

The one-tenth and half-tenth rates

Al-Bukhari reports from Ibn 'Umar that the Prophet (p) said, "One-tenth is obliged on that which is watered by the sky or springs or that which is not watered at all, and a half-tenth is obliged on that which is watered by carried water."[1] Muslim reports from Jabir that the Prophet (p) said, "On that which rivers or clouds water, there is one-tenth due, and on that which is watered by water carried by camels, there is half a tenth."[2] Yahya ibn Adam reports from Anas, "The Messenger of Allah (p) imposed a one-tenth on that which the sky waters and half a tenth on that which is watered by animals or men carrying water in containers."[3] Ibn Majah reports from Mu'adh, "The Messenger of Allah (p) sent me to Yemen and commanded me to collect one-tenth from that which the sky waters or is not watered, and half a tenth from that which is watered by pails."[4]

Consequently Abu 'Ubayd concludes that anything watered without the use of machinery and the payment of labour, whether by rain from the sky or by rivers or springs or without water at all, the charge on it is one-tenth.[5] The author of *al-Mughni* writes, "In all, whenever cost and effort from people or their animals or water-wheels are involved, the ratio is half a tenth. On the other hand, what is watered without such cost and effort is charged at one-tenth. Since cost may eliminate the obligation of *zakat*, it can evidently reduce its rate. Moreover, *zakat* is only obliged on growing assets, and cost reduces growth, thus it must also reduce the rate.[6]

1. Ibn Hajar writes on p. 180 of *at-Talkhis* that this is reported by al-Bukhari, Ibn Hibban, Abu Dawud, an-Nasa'i, and Ibn al-Jarud. Muslim reports the same from Jabir; and at-Tirmidhi and Ibn Majah from Abu Hurayra, and an-Nasa'i and Ibn Majah from Mu'adh.

2. Also reported by Ahmad, Abu Dawud and an-Nasa'i. See *Nayl al-Awtar*, vol. 4, p. 139.

3. *At-Talkhis*, p. 181.

4. Reported by Ibn Majah, chapter on *sadaqa* on grain and fruit, from Mu'adh; see *Nasb ar-Rayah*, vol. 2, p. 244.

5. An-Nawawi, *ar-Rawda*, vol. 2, p. 244.

6. *Al-Mughni*, vol 2, pp. 698-699.

When water is purchased and paid for, the rate is also reduced, according to an-Nawawi and others.[1]

Crops watered sometimes at cost and sometimes without cost

If plants are watered by carried water half of the year and left to rain the other half, the percentage of *zakat* becomes seven and a half per cent. Ibn Qudama says, "This is not disputed, to my knowledge, since if watering takes place fully with cost or completely without it for the whole year, the ratio is five or ten per cent respectively, so for half a year the rate will be half of it."[2]

If plants are watered most of the year, the ratio becomes five per cent and the small portion of the total season is disregarded. By the same token, the ratio must be ten per cent if they are not watered most of the season. This is according to 'Ata', ath-Thawri, Abu Hanifa, one of two reports from ash-Shafi'i and the official position of the Hanbalis.[3]

If the ratio of watering to the total season is not known, the percentage applicable must be one-tenth since the tenth is obliged in general and only reduced by cost. If cost is not ascertained, the original due must remain. Additionally, the general case is watering without cost and the existence of cost must be proved without leaving any room for doubt.[4]

Consideration of effort and costs other than watering

The question arises of whether costs spent on other than watering are considered in the reduction of the *zakat* percentage. This might include digging trenches and canals for irrigation, establishing a sprinkling system, and the like. Ibn Qudama suggests that the cost of canals and trenches should have no effect on *zakat* because

1. *Ar-Rawda*, vol. 2, p. 245.

2. *Al-Mughni*, op. cit.

3. The other view is to make it proportionate to the number of waterings. But the opinion mentioned in the text is more acceptable because of the difficulty involved in keeping records of watering, See *al-Mughni*, vol. 2, p. 700.

4. *Al-Mughni*, op. cit.

such cost is implied in the reclamation of land and its preparation for agricultural use.[1] Ar-Rafi'i expresses a similar view,[2] while al-Khattabi distinguishes between the initial cost of irrigation canals and the cost of maintaining them, and concludes that if a substantial amount is assumed yearly for the operation and maintenance of such canals and wells, the rate must be reduced to five per cent.[3] Ar-Rafi'i reports that some Shafi'is share the same view as al-Khattabi.[4]

Section Five: Pre-harvest estimation of *zakat*

The Messenger of Allah (p) started a tradition of estimating the amount of dates and grapes before the harvest, while the fruits are still on the trees, with no need for actual measuring or weighing. The purpose of this pre-harvest estimation, made by experts, is to determine the amount of *zakat* due, thus benefiting both parties: farmers and the poor. The farmers are given the freedom of disposing of the crop any time, without having to wait for the *zakat* collector, and the *zakat* collectors, who represent the poor, know the amount due in advance.[5] Al-Khattabi says, "While securing the rights of the poor from being tampered with by farmers attempting to dispose of some of their produce before collectors arrive after the harvest, pre-harvest estimation allows farmers to take the best opportunities for collecting their fruits and selling them without having to wait for the *zakat* officers, provided that, when pre-estimation is done and the due amount of *zakat* is determined, the farmer guarantees the delivery of *zakat* due to its collector. Fruits are estimated when they start to ripen but before they become edible."[6]

1. Ibid.
2. *Ash-Sharh al-Kabir* with *al-Majmu'*, vol. 5, p. 578.
3. *Ma'alim as-Sunan*, vol. 2, p. 207.
4. Ibid., and *ar-Rawda*, vol. 2, p. 244.
5. *Al-Muhadhdhab* with *al-Majmu'*, vol. 5, p.477.
6. *Ma'alim,* vol. 2, p. 210.

'Umar ibn al-Khattab, Sahl ibn Abi Hathama, Marwan, al-Qasim ibn Muhammad, al-Hasan, 'Ata', az-Zuhri, 'Amr ibn Dinar, Malik, ash-Shafi'i, Ahmad, Abu 'Ubayd, Abu Thawr, and the majority of scholars approve of the pre-harvest estimation. On the other hand, Abu Hanifa does not accept it on the grounds that it is mere speculation.[1]

The majority provide the following supporting evidence.

- Sa'id ibn al-Musayyab reports from 'Attab ibn Usayd, "The Prophet (p) used to send officers to estimate – before the harvest – grapes and fruits."[2]

- Sa'id ibn al-Musayyab also said, "The Messenger of Allah (p) commanded that grapes be estimated before the harvest as dates are estimated and their *zakat* be collected in the form of raisins, in the same way that the *zakat* on dates is collected (after drying)."[3]

- The Prophet (p) practised pre-harvest estimation. He estimated the crop of an orchard that belonged to a woman in Wadi al-Qura at ten *wasqs* and told the woman to measure the actual crop. She did, and it came to exactly what the Prophet (p) estimated.[4]

- Abu Dawud reports from 'A'isha about Khaybar: "The Prophet (p) used to send 'Abdullah ibn Rawaha to the Jews to estimate the date crop before it was ripe and edible."[5]

- From Sahl ibn Abi Hathama, "The Messenger of Allah said, 'When you estimate before the harvest, do not count one-third of the fruits, or at least one-fourth (to be fairer in estimation.'"[6]

1. *Al-Amwal*, pp. 492-493.

2. Reported by Abu Dawud, at-Tirmidhi, and Ibn Majah. It is interrupted since Sa'id ibn al-Musayyab did not listen to 'Attab. But it is strengthened by other sayings and by the practice of the Companions and the majority of scholars, according to an-Nawawi. See *at-Talkhis*, p. 181.

3. Reported by Abu Dawud, an-Nasa'i, at-Tirmidhi, Ibn Hibban and ad-Daraqutni. It is also interrupted. See ibid.

4. Agreed upon as narrated by Abu Humayd as-Sa'idi. Ibid.

5. In its chain is an unknown man. See al-Mundhiri, *Mukhtasar as-Sunan*, vol. 2, p. 213.

6. Reported by the five, not including Ibn Majah. Also reported by Ibn

In *Ma'alim as-Sunan*, al-Khattabi says, "This *hadith* confirms the practice of pre-harvest estimation which is the view of the majority, except for a report from ash-Sha'bi that estimation is a fabrication. Scholars who prefer opinion deny estimation, claiming that estimation was used only to put pressure on farmers not to cheat rather than to determine the actual amount of *zakat*, and estimation is only speculation, i.e. a sort of gambling that may have been permissible only before gambling was prohibited."

Al-Khattabi continues, "...but pre-harvest estimation was practised a long time after the prohibition of gambling during the era of the Messenger (p), Abu Bakr and 'Umar. The bulk of Companions permitted it, since none of them is reported to have opposed such a practice. Moreover, claiming that estimation is merely speculation is not valid because estimation is the result of the exertion of their best efforts by experienced experts. It is therefore like *ijtihad*, and although *ijtihad* is subject to error, it is always practised when a fixed rule is not available. This is similar to estimating the value of destroyed property (in order to impose the compensation on the person who destroyed it. Judging things on this basis, *de jure*, is a principle with a wide ranging application. No scholar denies this."[1]

Time and procedure of pre-harvest estimation

Pre-harvest estimation must be done when fruits start to ripen and before the time of the harvest, because the need for this estimation becomes important at that time. The time is in accordance with the *hadith* from 'A'isha mentioned above.[2] If the estimation is found to be far from the actual reality of the crop, the due amount of *zakat* remains as estimated and needs not be adjusted. Al-Qasim ibn Muhammad answered such a question saying, "You must pay

Hibban, al-Hakim in his al-Mustadrak, vol. 1, p. 402, Abu 'Ubayd in *al-Amwal*, p. 485, al-Bayhaqi in *as-Sunan*, vol. 4, p. 123, and Ibn Hazm in *al-Muhalla*, vol. 5, p. 355. Abu Dawud and al-Mundhiri are silent about its grade, while Ibn Hibban and al-Hakim grade it *sahih*. This is agreed with by adh-Dhahabi. At-Tirmidhi adds, "most scholars agree with its content." See *Mukhtasar as-Sunan*, vol. 2, p. 213.

1. *Ma'alim as-Sunan*, vol. 2, p. 213.
2. *Al-Mughni*, vol. 2, p. 707.

according to the estimation. It is the error of the person who made it." This is also the opinion of Malik, provided that the estimator is honest and experienced because according to him the estimation is final as far as the due amount of *zakat* is concerned. Abu 'Ubayd comments, "This is agreeable if the variance is within reasonable limits which are usually forgiven in normal transaction, but if the difference is large, a correction becomes necessary as in other transactions.[1]

Ibn Hazm argues that the mistake of the estimator must be corrected because Allah says, *"Be establishers of justice and balance."* (4:135) Whether the estimation is more or less than the actuality, it is unjust to either the payer or the recipient of *zakat*. A claim that the estimator made an error or was dishonest must be proven by factual evidence.[2] I, however, believe that the opinion of Abu 'Ubayd is more reasonable and practical.

Estimation of other crops

The majority of scholars believe that only dates and grapes can be estimated before the harvest and this estimation must not be applied to other fruits like olives which are, unlike dates and grapes, difficult to estimate and not usually needed for the owner's food. This is also the view of Malik and Ahmad.[3] Az-Zuhri, al-Awza'i and al-Layth extend pre-harvest estimation to other fruits, such as olives, because the need for such an estimation exists with respect to other fruits the same way it exists for dates and grapes.[4]

I conclude that pre-harvest estimation must be practised only according to need, whatever the fruit. This is a matter that depends on the practical experience of people and the opinions of experts as well as on the technology of the times. If pre-harvest estimation is needed for any fruit for the benefit of *zakat* administrators or farmers, it can be applied in analogy to estimation of dates and grapes.

1. *Al-Amwal*, pp. 494-495.
2 *Al-Muhalla*, vol. 5, p. 256.
3. *Al-Mughni*, vol. 2, pp. 710-711.
4. *Al-Bahr az-Zakhkhar*, vol. 2, p. 172.

Section Six: Facility in estimation

There are several indications that the estimation of the amount of *zakat* on crops should be easy on the payer. These include the following:

- Sahl ibn Abi Hathama narrates that the Prophet (p) said, "When you estimate, leave one-third, and if not, leave one-fourth (uncounted)."

- Ibn 'Abdu'l-Barr reports from Jabir that the Prophet (p) said, "Take it easy in estimation...."[1]

- Abu 'Ubayd reports from Makhul, "When the Messenger of Allah (p) sends estimators he tells them, 'Make it easy, because orchards usually include trees left for charity and trees left for passers-by to eat from.'"[2]

- Al-Awza'i is reported to have said, "It reached us that 'Umar ibn al-Khattab said to make it easy for people when you estimate, since trees usually include those designated for charity, passers-by, and the family to eat from."[3]

- From Bashir ibn Yasar, "'Umar ibn al-Khattab sent Abu Hathama from the Ansar to make the estimation of fruits of Muslims and told him, 'If you find them eating among their trees, do not count the trees they are eating from.'"[4]

- Sahl ibn Abi Hathma reports that Marwan appointed him an estimator of dates. He estimated the palm grove of Sa'd ibn Abi Sa'd at seven hundred *wasqs* and said, "If it were not for the forty cabins and booths with people living in them which I found in it, I would have estimated it at nine hundred *wasqs*, but I left for them what they were eating."[5]

---

1. Mentioned in *Nayl al-Awtar*, vol. 2, p. 144. Ibn Lahi'a is in its chain.

2. *Al-Amwal*, p. 487. Also reported by at-Tahawi, p. 315, with a good chain as "Go easy when charging *sadaqa*, since there are trees left for charity and for passers-by." See *Fayd al-Bari*, vol. 3, p. 47.

3. *Al-Amwal*, p. 487.

4. Reported by al-Hakim in brief, vol. 1, pp. 402-403, and Ibn Hazm, *al-Muhalla*, vol. 5, p. 259.

5. Reported by al-Hakim in brief, vol. 1, pp. 402-403, and Ibn Hazm, *al-Muhalla*, vol. 5, p. 259.

The first of these *hadiths* is graded *sahih* by a group of leading scholars, and is supported by the saying from Jabir and that of Makhul, as well as by the practices of the Companions. Ibn Hazm says, "Here we have the practice of the Companions, 'Umar, Abu Hathama and Sahl, in the presence of all other Companions, without any report to the contrary from any of them."[1] Several traditions and stories from the Companions imply the urging of easiness and kindness in estimation.

Ibn Qudama says, "The estimator must not count one-third or one-fourth of the total fruits as a gesture of kindness to the payer, because they usually need that much for their own food, for charity, passers-by and guests. If one counts everything, it becomes harsh on them. Ishaq, al-Layth, and Abu 'Ubayd are reported to be of the same view. How much is left is a matter that is decided by the estimator on the basis of his observation and the location of the orchard. But if the estimator does not leave anything uncounted, the owner may eat as much as one-fourth and deduct that from the estimated total of *zakat*. If the government does not send an estimator, the owner may get a non-partisan estimator and may deduct between one-third and one-fourth for the above-mentioned purposes.[2]

If the fruit or crop is not estimated prior to the harvest day, owners may still eat or give gifts up to a reasonable amount without being charged *zakat* on it. Ahmad was asked about wheat eaten before being dried and answered, "It is permitted, because it is customary for growers to eat from this crop in the same way as fruit growers."[3] Abu Yusuf and ash-Shaybani say that what is eaten by growers, their guests, and families, is always deductible, even if it equals all the crop.

On the other hand, Malik and Abu Hanifa believe that nothing should be left uncounted. Even fruits eaten by growers must be estimated and included in the total count of the *zakat* of crops.[4] Ibn al-'Arabi says that ath-Thawri also shares this view.[5] Ibn Hazm

1. *Al-Muhalla*, vol. 4, p. 260.
2. *Al-Mughni*, vol. 2, pp. 709-710.
3. Ibid.
4. *Bidayat al-Mujtahid*, vol. 1, and *Bada'i' as-Sana'i'*, vol. 2, p. 64.
5. *Sharh at-Tirmidhi*, vol. 3, p. 143.

claims it is not permissible to charge *zakat* on what is eaten by growers and their families or given in charity, on the grounds that *zakat* is due after the harvest, so things eaten or given away before the harvest are not included in principle. This is also the view of ash-Shafi'i and al-Layth. He adds that otherwise we would be imposing hardship on the payers, because what is eaten in that period is difficult to estimate, and Allah says, *"Allah does not charge any self beyond what it can bear."* (2:286) Ibn Hazm depends on the *hadith* from Sahl and similar stories in his presentation.[1]

Those who disagree on leaving anything uncounted have their own answers to the *hadith* from Sahl. Some of them claim it was only meant for a specific case, that of Khaybar. Some others, including ash-Shafi'i, explain "leaving some to them" as not to collect all the *zakat* due from them, although they are charged the whole amount due according to accurate and comprehensive estimation, but to leave one-third or one-fourth of the *zakat* for growers to distribute privately to their poor neighbours or kin.[2] Others provide yet a different explanation, saying that what is left uncounted is merely for the expense of the growers in cultivating and planting the land.

In my opinion, the *hadith* of Sahl must be applied, especially since it is supported by the practice of 'Umar and by Ahmad, Ishaq, al-Layth, ash-Shafi'i – his former view – and Ibn Hazm. This *hadith*, in fact, provides us with an important rule, the consideration of the reasonable convenience of the *zakat* payer and his family and of circumstances surrounding the case that might require certain reductions in the estimation of required fruit. This complies with the general condition in *zakat* assets, which is that they must be in excess of the essential needs of the owner. This approach of considering special circumstances has only recently been discovered by man-made taxation systems.

1. *Al-Muhalla*, vol. 5, p. 259.

2. In *ar-Rawda*, vol. 2, p. 250, an-Nawawi says, "This is the old opinion," mentioned also in al-Buwayli as quoted by al-Bayhaqi.

Section Seven: Deduction of debts and expenses

Are debts and expenses deductible?

Two kinds of debts may be owed by owners of crops, namely personal debts and debts for other purposes. Abu 'Ubayd reports from Jabir ibn Zayd about debts for farming and debts for family use that Ibn 'Abbas said, "Debts spent on the land must be paid back first," and Ibn 'Umar said, "Both debts on farming and family debts must be deducted."[1] Yahya ibn Adam quotes Ibn 'Umar, "The farmer should start by paying back his debts, then must pay *zakat* on what is left, while Ibn 'Abbas says, "Debts spent on farming must be paid back and what is left is liable for *zakat*."[2] Obviously, Ibn 'Abbas and Ibn 'Umar agree that debts on farming are deductible, but they do not agree on deducting debts for family and personal use.

Abu 'Ubayd reports from Makhul, "*Zakat* is only due on what is left after debts are deducted, if it satisfies the conditions for *zakat*. Similar views are reported from 'Ata' and Tawus,[3] as well as a group of Iraqi jurists, including Sufyan ath-Thawri.[4]

There are two reports from Ahmad, one in agreement with the view of Ibn 'Abbas and the other in agreement with the view of Ibn 'Umar. Ibn Qudama comments, according to one report, "All debts are deductible; one-tenth is obliged on what remains if it reaches the *nisab* or more, because we are dealing with *zakat*, and the principle is that debts are deductible."[5] Abu 'Ubayd supports the view of Ibn 'Umar, and adds the condition that the debts must be valid. "Valid debts that are due on the farmer are deductible for crops liable to *zakat*, as stated by Ibn 'Umar, Tawus, 'Ata', and Makhul. It is in accordance with the *Sunna*, since the Prophet (p) imposed *zakat* on the rich to be given to the poor. Those who are

1. *Al-Amwal*, p. 509.
2. *Al-Kharaj*, p. 162. In the commentary, Shaykh Ahmad Shakir states that its chain is sound.
3. *Al-Amwal*, p. 509.
4. *Al-Kharaj*, p. 163.
5. *Al-Mughni*, vol. 2, p. 727.

in debt are not rich; they may even deserve *zakat* as recipients," Abu 'Ubayd remarks.[1]

Concerning the deductibility of *kharaj*, a real estate tax on land, Yahya ibn Adam reports from Sufyan ath-Thawri that debts and *kharaj* are deductible, and if the remainder reaches five *wasqs*, it is zakatable.[2] Abu 'Ubayd reports from Ibrahim ibn Abi 'Abla that 'Umar ibn 'Abdu'l-'Aziz wrote to his officer in Palestine, 'Abdullah ibn 'Awf, that *kharaj* should first be collected from the *kharaj* land in the hands of the Muslims, and then *zakat* should be levied on the remainder.[3] This is also the view of Ahmad, on the basis that *kharaj* is a cost of the land which is deductible from *zakat*, as in *al-Mughni*. This is consistent with Ibn 'Abbas and Ibn 'Umar's view that costs of farming are deductible.[4]

The rent of land rented for farming must be treated like *kharaj*, by analogy since the majority of jurists consider *kharaj* a form of land rent. Yahya ibn Adam asked Sharik about a person who rents a lot to a farmer for a given amount of grain. He was answered, "He should deduct the amount of rent from the output of the land and pay *zakat* (ten or five percent) on the remainder, the same way debts are deductible.[5]

Now we come to considering expenditure on farming even when it does not take the form of debts. This may include the cost of seed, fertiliser, pesticide, labour involved in cultivating, irrigation, harvesting, weeding, drying, etc. Are these costs deductible like *kharaj*, debts and rent? Ibn Hazm argues that these expenses are not deductible, whether their total is high or low. He reports from Jabir ibn Zayd that Ibn 'Abbas and Ibn 'Umar disagree on this issue. The first says expenses are deductible, while the other says they are not. 'Ata' is reported to reduce the amount of the crop by the amount of the expenses. Ibn Hazm continues, "It is not permissible to make any reduction of a due imposed by Allah without valid textual support from the Qur'an or *Sunna*." He further states

1. *Al-Amwal*, p. 510.
2. *Al-Kharaj*, op. cit.
3. *Al-Amwal*, p. 88.
4. *Al-Mughni*, ibid.
5. *Al-Kharaj*, p. 161.

that Malik, ash-Shafi'i, Abu Hanifa, and the Zahiris are of the same view."[1]

It should be noted that the report he cites about Ibn 'Abbas and Ibn 'Umar agreeing on deducting expenses was mentioned earlier in this section, where the word used was debt caused by farming expenses. We learned that both Ibn 'Abbas and Ibn 'Umar agree on deducting the amount of a debt that was used toward farming expenses, although Ibn 'Umar allows deducting other debts too. But Ibn Hazm attributes to them approval of the deduction of expenses in the case where there is no borrowing.

The most remarkable and direct statement about expenses comes from 'Ata' and is referred to by Ibn Hazm. Yahya ibn Adam reports from Isma'il ibn 'Abdu'l-Malik that he asked 'Ata' about farming a lot of land and 'Ata' answered, "Deduct your expenditure and pay *zakat* on what is left."[2] "There seems to be no agreement among our scholars on deducting the costs of farming," Ibn al-'Arabi says, "and my opinion is that the costs of farming must be deducted and *zakat* charged on the remainder only. The statement in the saying, 'Leave aside one-third or one-fourth' is a reference to the cost of farming." He continues, "I even ran a few experiments and found the cost is about that much."[3]

This view of Ibn al-'Arabi implies that the deduction of costs and expenses and the exclusion of one-third or one-fourth in the estimation must not be implemented together, though the deduction of expenditure seems to be accepted by Ibn al-'Arabi even if it were more than one-third, and on all kinds of crops and fruits, whether they are estimated or not.

Ibn al-Humam rejects the view that the Prophet (p) judged that what is due varied according to expenses. Even if the expenses are high, what is due is the same: it is always a tenth on the remainder, because it is only reduced to half of that by expenses. The obligation is that after removing the amount of expenses, there is no expense in what remains, and so the obligation is always a tenth. However, the amount due varies in the *Shari'a*: sometimes it is a tenth and sometimes half of that because of expenses. So we know

1. *Al-Muhalla*, vol. 5, p. 258.
2. *Al-Kharaj*, p. 161, and also reported by Ibn Abi Shayba, vol. 4, p. 23.
3. *Sharh at-Tirmidhi*, vol. 3, p. 143.

that in the *Shari'a* one does not consider that there is no tenth on the expenses at all."[1]

It seems to us that the Prophet decided that what is due varies according to the difference in effort expended in irrigating the land. That is the most notable expense in agricultural lands. There is no text indicating whether one takes other expenses into consideration or not. The most likely position which is in keeping with the spirit of the *Shari'a* is that there is no *zakat* on the amount spent on expenses. Two points support this view:

- The first point is that effort and expense was taken into consideration by the Prophet (p). It lessens the amount due, as is the case when the land is irrigated by artificial means. What is due on such land is only half of one-tenth. In some cases, it prevents anything being due at all, as is the case with livestock fed by fodder for most of the year. Therefore it is not odd that there should be no *zakat* on what is spent on agricultural expenses.

- The second point is that the reality of growth is increase. Wealth is not said to increase and be earned when a similar amount is spent in the effort to acquire it. This is why some *fuqaha'* said that the amount of the expenses is in the same position as advance payment. It is like purchasing it. This is a sound view.

So according to the *Shari'a* the cost of irrigating the land reduces what is due from a tenth to half of a tenth. If someone has land which produces ten *qintars* of wheat worth a hundred pounds, and the costs – excluding irrigation but including land taxes – is sixty pounds (or the equivalent of three *qintars*), then *zakat* is paid only on seven *qintars*. If it is naturally watered, there is a tenth due on that and if it is artificially irrigated, there is a half of a tenth due. Allah knows best

1. *Fath al-Qadir*, pt. 2, pp. 8-9.

Section Eight: *Zakat* on rented farmland

Zakat is obliged on the owner when he farms the land

When agricultural land is farmed by the owner, its *zakat* is due from the owner himself, but when the owner lends his land, free of charge, for someone else to farm, *zakat* is then paid by the farmer.[1]

The owner as a partner in farming

When farming is done in certain forms of partnership, such as sharecropping, within the conditions required in the *Shari'a*, and each partner's share reaches the *nisab*, either alone or when combined with output accruing to the partner from other sources, *zakat* is due. If the share of one partner does not fulfil the condition of *nisab*, he is not charged *zakat*, although the other partner or partners may have *zakat* taken from them. Ash-Shafi'i differs on this issue, suggesting that if the total output of the partnership reaches the *nisab*, it fulfils the condition for the *zakat*, and the partners are obliged to pay *zakat*, each in proportion to his or her share in the output.[2] This is also one of the opinions of Imam Ahmad.

Rented land

When land is rented to a farmer for a given amount of money or any commodity, *zakat* (the ten or five per cent) becomes due on the owner, according to Abu Hanifa. He argues that *zakat*, though usually collected from the output, is, in fact, a levy on the land. In renting, the land remains owned by the owner and not by the user, and since *zakat* is a charge on the land, similar to *kharaj*, it is his responsibility to pay it.[3] Renting is like farming, a sort of growth of the land, and out of this increase *zakat* is paid.[4] A similar view is reported by an-Nakha'i.[5]

1. *Al-Mughni*, vol. 2, p. 728.
2. Ibid.
3. Ibid.
4. *Fath al-Qadir*, vol. 2, p.8.
5. *Al-Kharaj*, Yahya ibn Adam, p. 172. The latter reports it from al-Hasan ibn

On the other hand, the majority are of the opinion that *zakat* is charged to the renter, on the grounds that *zakat* is a levy on the output and not on the land. Consequently, the owner of the output is responsible for *zakat*. It becomes obvious to us, along with Ibn Rushd, that there is a difference in the philosophy of *zakat*. Is it on the land or on the output, or maybe on both together? There seems to be no one who mentions that *zakat* could be on both land and output together, although this looks to be the truth of the matter. When the owner is the same as the farmer, the problem does not exist, but when the owner and the farmer are different persons, the majority argues that since *zakat* is paid out of the output, it is the responsibility of the person who owns the output, while Abu Hanifa refers to the basis of *zakat*, which is the growth of the land itself.[1]

Analysis and discussion

Ibn Qudama prefers the majority view. He challenges the position of Abu Hanifa, saying that if *zakat* is a charge on the land, it should be calculated on acreage instead of amount of produce and levied even when the land is not farmed, and it should be due on *dhimmis* as well, especially since *kharaj* is imposed regardless of farming and output. Furthermore, if *zakat* is on the land, its disbursement should be like that of *fay'*.[2]

Ar-Rafi'i says that the renter is required to pay *zakat* regardless of the rent, like a businessman who is required to pay *zakat* in addition to the rent he might be paying for his store.[3] But one may differ with ar-Rafi'i on this analogy, because the merchants pay *zakat* at the end of the year after rent and other costs have already been paid during the year. *Zakat* on agriculture has no yearly condition. It is due on the harvest, and if rent is not deducted from the harvest, where would it otherwise be deducted from? It seems unfair that the renter should be asked to pay both *zakat* and rent, while the owner is charged nothing. Justice requires that both par-

'Amara, who is disregarded.

1. *Bidayat al-*Mujtahid, vol. 1, p. 239.
2. *Al-Mughni*, vol. 2, p. 728.
3. *Sharh ar-Rafi'i al-Kabir* with *al-Majmu'*, vol. 5, p. 566.

ties share in the payment of *zakat*. Neither should be allowed to escape it while the whole burden is unjustly thrown on the other. Ibn Rushd was intelligent enough to realise that *zakat* is in fact in the land and its output together.

In my opinion, the farmer who pays rent should be allowed to deduct the rent along with other expenses and debt from the output and pay *zakat* on the remainder, if it reaches the *nisab*, while the owner must be required to *pay* zakat on his share of the growth of the land, which in this case is the total rent he or she receives, if it reaches the *nisab*. Payment is calculated according to the rate that applies on the output itself, i.e. ten per cent or five per cent. The owner is certainly allowed to deduct from the rent costs that might be involved, such as real estate taxes, along with expenditures and debts.

This approach of sharing in the payment of *zakat* prevents duplication in *zakat*, because the rent that is deducted from the output of *zakat*, as far as the farmer is concerned, is included in the output of *zakat* of the land-owner. Each is charged with what belongs to him or her from the profit on the land, and on the basis of the income that accrues to him or her from it. I suggested this reconciliation in 1963, and it was rejected then by many of the scholars of al-Azhar, but recently I read in *Tanzim al-Islam li'l-Mujtama'* by the late Shaykh Abu Zahra, on page 159: "Some contemporary scholars suggest in a proposal for a *zakat* act that *zakat* be shared by the owner and renter, where each of them is charged according to the profit he or she gets after payment of taxes, as far as the owner is concerned." This is, praise be to Allah, the opinion I feel most comfortable with and I share and support.

Section Nine: The case of *'ushr* and *kharaj*

The Hanafis have a condition for *zakat*, which is that the land from which it is taken must not be *kharaj* land. If the owner pays *kharaj* on his land, then *zakat* is waived. On the other hand, the majority of scholars believe that Muslims must pay *zakat* on their agriculture, regardless of whether *kharaj* is obliged on the land or not.

'Ushri land

Lands may be classified as either *'ushri*, i.e. lands on whose output *'ushr* (the *zakat* of ten or five per cent) is due, or *kharaji* land, on which *kharaj* is due.

Abu 'Ubayd lists the following as *'ushri* lands: Firstly, all lands whose owners accepted Islam, as in Madina, Yemen and Bahrain. To this Makka is added, because although there was brief fighting, the Prophet (p) protected the persons and properties of the Makkans. Secondly, lands acquired by fighting and distributed among the Muslim conquerors, after one-fifth had been set aside as prescribed by the Qur'an. The distributed four-fifths is considered *'ushri* because ownership has been transferred to Muslims. Thirdly, land not owned by anyone and given by the state to individuals to farm, and fourthly, land not in use that is reclaimed by Muslims. These sorts of lands are all mentioned in *hadiths*, and are all subject to *zakat*, according to the texts of *zakat* in the Qur'an and *Sunna*.[1]

Kharaji lands and the origin of their definition

Abu 'Ubayd defines *kharaji* lands as, "lands that are either conquered in war, but left in the hands of local farmers instead of being confiscated and distributed among the Muslim conquerors (like the lands of Iraq, Persia, Syria, Egypt, and North Africa), or land whose owners entered under the authority of the Islamic state as a result of the treaties that included a clause to this effect (such as some areas in the southern tip of the Arabian Peninsula, some areas in Persia, and certain Armenian areas). Whatever taxes are imposed on these lands is called *kharaj*, and goes to the state budget, to be spent for the general interests of the Muslims."[2]

By "lands conquered in war," Abu 'Ubayd means those lands whose people were defeated in war with Muslims. Such lands are

1. *Al-Amwal*, pp. 512-513.
2. *Al-Amwal*, pp. 513-514 and *al-Kharaj* by Abu Yusuf, p. 69.

treated in accordance with the Qur'an[1] and *Sunna*,[2] which require that ownership be transferred to the whole Muslim society, present and future generations, as represented by the Islamic state. This policy was applied *en masse* at the time of 'Umar, making his era rich in the minute details that arise out of application. Jurists use the term "*waqf* for all the Muslims" to express the principle that the land becomes a trust for the benefit of all Muslim generations, whereby a tax is levied on it on a yearly basis. This tax, called *kharaj*, is like rent for the land paid to the treasury of the state, and is not waived even if the ownership of the land is transferred to Muslims or if the users themselves convert to Islam, because of its nature as a rent payment.[3]

This policy was applied by 'Umar on the conquered lands in Iraq and Syria, instead of dividing these lands and distributing them among the soldiers as he was asked to do by Bilal and a few other Companions. 'Umar provided verses from *Surat al-Hashr* to support his decision:

> *"Whatever booty Allah gives to His Messenger from city dwellers belongs to Allah and to the Messenger and to near relatives and orphans and the very poor and travellers, so that it does not become something which merely goes by turn to the rich among you. Whatever the Messenger gives you you should accept and whatever He forbids you you should forgo. Show fear of Allah – Allah is Severe in Retribution. It is for the poor of the Muhajirun who were driven from their homes and wealth desiring the favour and the pleasure of Allah and supporting Allah and His Messenger. Such people are the truly sincere."* (59:7-9)

'Umar argued that according to these verses, Allah includes all future generations of Muslims in land distribution and if land is distributed to the present soldiers, nothing will be left for future generations, while if it is kept in trust with the state and a charge

1. *Surat al-Hashr* (59:7-11) speaks about the distribution of *fay'*. 'Umar uses these verses as evidence for requiring holding the land as trust for future Muslim generations.

2. The Prophet (p) distributed half the land of Khaybar among the soldiers and retained the other half as a trust for the public interest of the Muslims.

3. *Al-Mughni*, vol. 2, p. 716.

imposed on it to benefit the treasury, then even a shepherd in Yemen would receive his share from the state treasury without his dignity suffering.[1]

The purpose of this policy is so that wealth "*does not become something which merely goes by turn to the rich among you.*" The distribution of the return, called *fay'*, according to these verses, included that generation of soldiers, i.e. the *Muhajirun* and *Ansar*, as well as all future generations. By this form of distribution, Islam avoids the common capitalist mistake of preferring the interests of the present generation over those of future generations, as well as the mistake of Communism of imposing heavy sacrifices on the present generation for the benefit of development.

It is perhaps for that reason Mu'adh, the great Companion scholar, told 'Umar, "If you distribute the land now, something very undesirable might happen. You will create a class of very rich individuals whose wealth will be inherited by their sons and daughters, and nothing will be left for the future generations who will carry out the responsibility of defending Islam and its society. Please do something that helps future as well as present needs."[2] 'Umar's basic argument, derived from these verses, was that "...he must not leave future generations with nothing."[3] Ibn Qudama says, "Khaybar is, to the best of my knowledge, the only conquered land which was distributed among Muslim soldiers. The Messenger of Allah (p) divided half of its land among the Muslims. All that was conquered during the time of 'Umar and his successors, including Syria, Iraq, and Egypt, was not distributed."[4]

Sale of *kharaji* land

The majority of scholars, including Malik, ash-Shafi'i and Ahmad, believe *kharaj* lands cannot be sold because they are *waqf*. 'Umar questioned 'Utba ibn Farqad because he bought a lot of *kharaj* land, "From whom did you buy it?" "From its owners,"

1. *Al-Kharaj*, Abu Yusuf, pp. 23-24.
2. *Al-Amwal*, p. 59.
3. Ibid., p. 58.
4. *Al-Mughni*, vol. 2, p. 716.

'Utba answered. When the people in Madina gathered, including *Muhajirun* and *Ansar*, 'Umar told 'Utba, "These are the owners. Did you buy it from them?" "No," he said. Then 'Umar said, "Return it to whomever you bought it from and take back your money."[1]

Some scholars approve of the inheritance of *kharaj* land. Some others allow purchasing this kind of land only from the original non-Muslim holders. It is reported that Ibn Mas'ud bought a piece of land from a Persian and pledged to pay its *kharaj*.[2]

Ibn Qudama points out, "Even if purchasing this kind of land is permitted, buyers have to continue the payment of *kharaj* that was imposed on the sellers. This purchase then is actually a transfer of holding the land, without a real transfer of ownership. When Ibn Mas'ud set the condition that the buyer continue paying *kharaj*, he made this contract a form of rent and not a sale."[3]

Kharaj is perpetual

It is obvious then that *kharaj* lands belong to the whole Muslim nation. A transfer of holding of such land from one person to another cannot be considered a transfer of ownership. *Kharaj* imposed on the land is like a rent paid to the owner, as represented by the Islamic state, which uses this rent to serve public interests, including improving the productivity of *kharaj* lands. If the holders of *kharaj* land become Muslim, or if the holdings are transferred to Muslims, *kharaj* remains undisturbed. On this Muslim jurists have no differences, because no one has the authority to waive such a rent that belongs to all Muslim generations.

A question arises about *kharaj* lands which – for any reason – are held by Muslims who are subject to *zakat*. Are these Muslims required to pay *kharaj* and *zakat* simultaneously, or must one be waived in order to avoid paying two taxes on the same land? Abu Hanifa and his disciples decided that the output of *kharaj* land is exempt from *zakat*. They set out for the *zakat* of agriculture the

1. Ibid., p. 821.
2. Ibid., p. 720.
3. Ibid., p. 722

condition that the land must not be *kharaji*. Abu 'Ubayd reports from al-Layth and Ibn Abi Shayba from ash-Sha'bi and 'Ikrima that *kharaj* and *'ushr* must not be combined on the same land.[1]

- Ibn Mas'ud reports from the Prophet (p), "*'Ushr* and *kharaj* are not due together on a Muslim's land."[2]

- Abu Hurayra narrates from the Messenger of Allah (p), "Iraq will refuse to pay its dues on its dirhams and *qafiz* [volume measure of food], Syria will refuse the payment of dues on its *madi* [volume measure] and dinars. And you will return to where you started." Abu Hurayra adds, "The Prophet (p) said that three times: my flesh and blood give witness." Reported by Muslim and Abu Dawud. This *hadith* in which the Prophet (p) predicts that in later days people will not pay their dues, indicates that these dues refer to *kharaj* and not to *'ushr*, because *'ushr* is only on the output, while *kharaj* can be either money or a given amount of measured food.

- Abu 'Ubayd reports from Tariq ibn Shihab that 'Umar ibn al-Khattab wrote regarding a woman who became Muslim in the region of Nahr al-Malik,[3] "Give her her land, and she should continue the payment *kharaj* on it,"[4] indicating that 'Umar ordered the collection of *kharaj* and not *'ushr* from her.

- No political ruler, oppressive or just, is reported to have collected *'ushr* from *kharaj* lands that are in the hands of Muslims, since 'Umar imposed *kharaj* although many *kharaj* lands were owned by Muslims. This position may be interpreted as a practical *ijma'*.

- *Kharaj* is imposed on the same principle as *'ushr*, i.e. on arable farmland. If the land is not arable, no *kharaj* or *'ushr* is imposed. Consequently, they may not be imposed concurrently on the same land. This is like owning cattle for the purpose of trading.

1. *Al-Amwal*, p. 91, and *al-Musannaf*, vol. 3, p. 201.

2. The author of *Fath al-Qadir*, vol. 2, p. 14, says, "It is reported by Abu Hanifa from Hammad from Ibrahim from 'Alqama from Ibn Mas'ud, connected to the Prophet (p)."

3. Nahr al-Malik is a large orchard near Baghdad.

4. *Al-Amwal*, p. 87.

Even after the passage of a year, *zakat* on livestock and *zakat* in trade assets are not both imposed. This is a unanimous position of Muslims, taken in order to avoid duplication, which is forbidden by the *hadith*, "No duplication in *zakat*."

- *Kharaj* was originally imposed on conquered land that was left in the hands of pre-Islamic owners, as a form of penalty to the conquered, while *'ushr* is imposed on Muslims as a form of worship and an expression of gratitude to Allah Who purifies the person and the property. The two dues are obliged for different reasons, and therefore must not be combined.[1]

However, the majority of scholars believe that *'ushr* as a required obligation must not be waived on *kharaj* lands. This opinion is founded on the following evidence:

- The texts that make *zakat* obligatory on agriculture are general, clear-cut, and lack any distinction between the two kinds of land. Examples are the verses, *"O you who believe! Give away some of the good things you have earned and some of what the earth produces for you,"* and "*pay their due on the day of their harvest,"* and the agreed-upon *hadith*, "There is one-tenth obliged on that which the sky waters." *Kharaj* is imposed on the land itself, whether cultivated or not, whether it happens to be in the hands of a Muslim or an unbeliever, while *'ushr* is imposed on the output if it belongs to Muslims.
- *'Ushr* and *kharaj* are two separate dues imposed for different reasons. Nothing precludes their co-existence. The reason for *kharaj* is controlling the land in such a way that offers the ability to make use of it, while the reason for *'ushr* is the presence of output. *'Ushr* relates directly to the output of the land, while *kharaj* relates to the liability of the holder. Just like those of *zakat*, the proceeds of *'ushr* are distributed to the eight categories mentioned in the verse, *"Sadaqa is for the poor…"* while the proceeds of *kharaj* are used for salaries of soldiers and civilians and for public expenditure. With all these differences, there should be no reason why *'ushr* and *kharaj* cannot be

1. *Ahkam al-Qur'an*, al-Jassus, vol. 3, pp. 17-19.

levied together on the same land. It is just like paying a rent for a store and *zakat* on stock. This is similar to the case of a person who, while in the state of *ihram* for pilgrimage, kills an animal that is owned by someone else. This person is required to compensate the owner, in addition to the *kaffarat* required from him because he or she was in a state of *ihram*.

- *'Ushr* is obliged by clear texts from the Qur'an and *Sunna*. It must not be waived because of *kharaj* that came about through *ijtihad*.[1]

Weighing these opinions

The documents given by the majority of jurists are clear-cut and strong, both in their authenticity and their indications. The Hanafis cannot challenge them and the waiving of *zakat* they suggest is not accepted. Ibn al-Mubarak, after looking at this evidence, comments, "Should we leave what Allah says for what Abu Hanifa says?"[2]

The majority of scholars disprove the Hanafi argument as follows:

- The *hadith*, "*'Ushr* and *kharaj* must not be combined" is, according to an-Nawawi, false and unanimously graded weak. In its chain, Yahya ibn 'Anbasa singly narrates from Abu Hanifa from Hammad from Ibrahim from 'Alqama from Ibn Mas'ud from the Prophet (p). Yahya is openly known as weak, because he attributes to trustworthy individuals false *hadiths*.[3] As-Suyuti in *al-La'ali* quotes Ibn Hibban and Ibn 'Adi, "This *hadith* is false, narrated by Yahya, who is a liar."[4]

- An-Nawawi says about the *hadith* from Abu Hurayra which begins, "Iraq will refuse…", "There are two well-known interpretations of this *hadith*, namely that they will become Muslims and therefore *jizya* will be eliminated or that there will be so

1. *Al-Majmu'*, vol. 2, pp. 549–550.
2. *Al-Mughni*, vol. 2, p. 726.
3. *Al-Majmu'*, vol. 5, pp. 550–553.
4. *Al-La'ali al-Masnu'a*, vol. 2, p. 70.

many disasters and so much misery that people will refuse to pay the dues obliged on them. This *hadith* does not mean that *'ushr* will not be obliged, because it speaks about the *zakat* due on gold and silver. If it implies the elimination of *'ushr*, it must also mean the elimination of all *zakat*.[1]

- As for the story of the Persian woman who converted to Islam, *kharaj* was mentioned by 'Umar to make it clear that *kharaj* remains obliged, and is not like *jizya*, which is cancelled by conversion to Islam. The story does not say anything about *'ushr*. Some scholars also mention that this might be an instruction from 'Umar to the *kharaj* collector, who is usually a different officer than the *'ushr* collector.[2]

- The claim that rulers since 'Umar have agreed not to collect *kharaj* and *'ushr* from the same land is defeated by the authentic report that 'Umar ibn 'Abdu'l-'Aziz collected *'ushr* and *kharaj* together. Yahya ibn Adam reports that 'Umar ibn Maymun ibn Mihran said, "I asked 'Umar ibn 'Abdu'l-'Aziz about a Muslim who holds *kharaj* land. 'Umar replied, 'Take *kharaj* from here,' as he pointed to the land with his hand, 'and take *zakat* from here,' as he pointed to the crop with his hand. Sharik thought that 'Umar may not have said exactly that, so he researched until he was informed, and then he followed suit."[3] The claim that 'Umar and the Companions did not collect *'ushr* and *kharaj* simultaneously is refuted, because during that time the holders of land in conquered areas were still unbelievers. No one can make the assertion that they did not collect *'ushr* from those who became Muslim.[4]

- The claim that *kharaj* and *'ushr* are imposed for the same reason is disproved by the fact that *'ushr* is imposed on crops while *kharaj* is imposed on the land, whether it is cultivated or not. In other words, *kharaj* is imposed for having the ability to use the land, while *'ushr* is imposed for having an output.[5]

1. *Al-Majmu'*, vol. 5, pp. 554-558, and also *al-Amwal*, pp. 87-88.
2. *Al-Majmu'*, ibid.
3. *Al-Kharaj*, Ibn Adam, p. 165.
4. *Al-Muhalla*, vol. 2, p. 247.
5. *Al-Majmu'*, vol. 5, pp. 558-559.

- The claim that *kharaj* is a punishment for the owner's disbelief is disproved by the similarity between rent and *kharaj*. *Kharaj* is a rent taken for permitting the holder to use the land. It is like real estate taxes imposed by many countries today not on any punitive grounds.[1] *Kharaj* is paid for obtaining the land in order to cultivate it, while *'ushr* is a religious duty on the products, and they do not contradict each other.

As for the calculation of the payment due as *'ushr*, my position is to treat *kharaj* as a debt on the farmer that must be deducted from the output before the calculations of 'ushr.

What has happened to *kharaj* land today

Let us look at a map of the Muslim world today to see what has happened to *kharaj* lands in Egypt, Syria, Iraq, etc. Are they still subject to *kharaj*?

Many late Hanafi jurists declare that the lands of Syria and Egypt are no longer *kharaji*, because upon the deaths of their owners, those lands were returned to the treasury, and any selling that took place by the state treasury is complete and final, without *kharaj*.[2] Accordingly, if *kharaj* is eliminated, *'ushr* is obliged as the *zakat* on Muslim agriculture. Real estate taxes on agricultural land is the common practice of all modern states, regardless of whether the land is *'ushri* or *kharaji*. Consequently, the only suitable solution is to impose *'ushr* on all land owned by Muslims if the output reaches the *nisab*, in addition to the real estate tax levied on all lands.

Contemporary comments on combining *'ushr* and *kharaj*

Dr Ahmad Thabit 'Awaida says, "We are supposed to refer to the distinction Muslims made between agricultural income and real estate income when they separated *kharaj* from *zakat*. This distinction constitutes the basis for the contemporary distinction of the source of income in taxation. Many countries today have taxes on real estate income different from the taxes on agricultural income.

1. *Al-Mughni*, vol. 2, p. 115.
2. *Al-Bahr ar-Ra'iq*, vol. 5, p. 115.

The majority of jurists consider *kharaj* a tax on real estate income, while *zakat* on crops is like a tax on agricultural income. A Muslim who farms land owned by a non-Muslim must pay *zakat* on his output, in addition to *kharaj* paid by the owner. By the same token, a Muslim who owns and farms *kharaj* land must pay *'ushr* as well as *kharaj*."[1]

After disproving the evidence of the Hanafis and supporting the majority view, the late Shaykh Mahmud Shaltut and Muhammad as-Sayis write, "Once we note that *'ushr* is a religious obligation on Muslims and *kharaj* is an obligation by *ijtihad* created to finance the needs of the Muslim community, we can understand the state's right to impose taxes on Muslims and non-Muslims in order to satisfy public needs, in addition to what Allah imposes on Muslims. The levying of *kharaj* does not mean an exemption from *zakat*, which is obliged by the Qur'an and *Sunna*.[2]

1. From a lecture, "Islam Laid Down the Foundations of Modern Taxation," from Dr. Ahmad Thabit 'Awaida in *al-Mawsim ath-Thaqafi al-Amwal li-Muhadarat al-Azhar*, 1959, p. 302.

2. *Muqaranat al-Madhahib*, Muhammad as-Sayis and Mahmud Shaltut, p. 54.

Chapter Six

Zakat on Honey and Animal Products

Section One: *Zakat* on honey according to those who oblige it and those who do not

Honey is one of the goods bestowed by Allah on humanity as a food, medicine, and sweet. Allah mentioned it as a sign of His grace to human beings in a *sura* which is named after bees, *Surat an-Nahl.* Allah says:

> *"Your Lord revealed to the bees: 'Build dwellings in the mountains and the trees, and also in the structures which men erect. Then eat from every kind of fruit and travel the paths of your Lord, made easy for you to follow.' From their bellies comes a drink of varying colours, containing healing for mankind. There is certainly a Sign in that for people who reflect."* (16:68-69)

Those who believe *zakat* is due on honey

Abu Hanifa and his disciples say that *zakat* is obliged on honey, provided that the beehives are not located in *kharaj* land. This is an extension of their principle that *kharaj* and *'ushr* are not combined. *Zakat* is also obliged on honey produced on non-arable land, which is by implication not subject to *zakat.*[1] This is also Ahmad's opinion. Al-Athram says that Ahmad was asked whether he believed that *zakat* was due on honey and answered, "Yes indeed, 'Umar collected *zakat* on honey." Al-Athram then asked whether honey growers should contribute their *zakat* voluntarily. Ahmad answered, "No, it was imposed on them."[2]

1. *Al-Hidaya* with *Fath al-Qadir*, vol. 2, pp. 5-7, and *ad-Durr al-Mukhtar* with commentary, vol. 2, pp. 604-605.

2. *Al-Mughni*, vol. 2, p. 713.

This view is shared by Makhul, az-Zuhri, Sulayman ibn Musa, al-Awza'i and Ishaq.[1] The author of *al-Bahr* also attributes it to 'Umar, Ibn 'Abbas, 'Umar ibn 'Abdu'l-'Aziz, al-Hadi, al-Mu'ayyad bi'llah, and one narration from ash-Shafi'i. At-Tirmidhi mentions that most scholars accept this view. This is challenged by ibn 'Abdu'l-Barr, who asserts that the opposite is true.[2]

Evidence for this view

This opinion is supported by two groups of evidence: reports from the Prophet (p) and the Companions, and rationale and analogy. Firstly, the texts:

- 'Amr ibn Shu'ayb, from his father from his grandfather, narrates that the Prophet (p) "...collected the one-tenth due from honey." Reported by Ibn Majah. Ad-Daraqutni says, "This is narrated from 'Abdu'r-Rahman ibn al-Harith and Ibn Lahi'a from 'Amr as linked to the Prophet (p), and from Yahya ibn Sa'id al-Ansari from 'Amr as *mursal*." Al-Hafiz notes that this is the problem with this *hadith*, especially since 'Abdullah and Ibn Lahi'a are not known as accurate. It is noted that 'Amr ibn al-Harith, who is trustworthy, and Usama ibn Zayd also narrate the same from 'Amr ibn Shu'ayb, as reported by Ibn Majah, and others.[3]
- Abu Dawud and an-Nasa'i report that Hilal, of Banu Mat'an, used to pay the Prophet (p) the one-tenth due on the beehives he had, and had the Prophet (p) protect a valley known as Salaba for him. When 'Umar became head of state, Sufyan ibn Wahb wrote to him about this. 'Umar replied, "As long as Hilal gives you that which he was giving the Messenger of Allah (p), the one-tenth due on his honey, then keep protecting Salaba for him. If he does not, then what is in that valley is

1. Ibid., and *Ma'alim as-Sunan*, vol. 2, p. 209.

2. *Nayl al-Awtar*, vol. 4, p. 146. There different reports from 'Umar ibn 'Abdu'l-'Aziz. Al-Bukhari, Ibn Abi Shayba and 'Abdu'r-Razzaq also report that he believes *zakat* is obliged, but via a weak chain, as stated by Ibn Hajar in *al-Fath*.

3. *Mukhtasar as-Sunan*, vol. 2, pp. 209-210.

for everybody." In *al-Fath*, Ibn Hajar says the chain of this *hadith* is sound up to 'Amr ibn Shu'ayb. 'Amr's record is strong, at least when he is not opposed by stronger narrators.[1]

• It is reported from Sulayman ibn Musa that Abu Sawara al-Muta'i told the Messenger of Allah (p), "I have bees." The Prophet (p) said, "Pay the one-tenth due." He said, "Messenger of Allah, preserve its mountain for me." The Prophet (p) then protected that mountain for him. Reported by Ahmad and Ibn Majah.[2]

• Al-Bayhaqi reported from Sa'id ibn Abi Dhubab, "The Prophet (p) employed him (for collecting *zakat*) from his clan. He ordered people to pay the one-tenth due on honey, then brought it to 'Umar, who sold the honey and added its value to the *zakat* funds of Muslims." Munir ibn 'Abdullah is in the chain of this *hadith*, and he is graded weak by al-Bukhari and others.[3] In another version, Sa'd tells his clan, "There is no good in wealth from which *zakat* is not taken." He continues, "I took out of each ten containers one container and brought it to 'Umar, who put it with the *zakat* funds of the Muslims." This version is reported by Sa'id in his *Sunan*.[4] Al-Athram reports from him that 'Umar commanded him to collect ten per cent from honey.[5]

• At-Tirmidhi reports from Ibn 'Umar that the Messenger of Allah (p) said, "On honey, one out of every ten jars is due." However, Sadaqa as-Samin is in its chain. He had a weak memory and is disagreed with.

---

1. *Fath al-Bari*, vol. 3, p. 223. Ibn Hajar mentions a report by 'Abdu'r-Razzaq from 'Umar ibn 'Abdu'l-'Aziz indicating that Hilal gave that *zakat* voluntarily. Ibn Hajar adds that the chain of the first *hadith* is stronger, but it is argued that Hilal's payment was in exchange for protecting property, as indicated by 'Umar's letter.

2. Mentioned in *al-Muntaqa* from them both. Ash-Shawkani says, "This is also reported by Abu Dawud and al-Bayhaqi, but is interrupted because Sulayman did not meet any of the Companions, as stated by al-Bukhari. *Nayl al-Awtar*, vol. 4, p. 146, and *at-Talkhis*, p. 180.

3. *At-Talkhis*, p. 180.

4. *Al-Mughni*, vol. 2, p. 715.

5. Ibid., p, 71.

Although all these *hadiths* and stories are not free from criticism, they support one another, indicating that there is substance in the ruling on honey. Ibn al-Qayyim comments, "Ahmad and his group believe that *zakat* is due on the basis that these *hadiths* strengthen one another because they have different sources and chains. Abu Hatim ar-Razi was asked about the narration of 'Abdullah, Munir's father, from Sa'd ibn Abi Dhubab, and answered that it was sound."[1]

Secondly, the payment of *zakat* on honey is further supported by reasoning and analogy. Since honey is derived from flowers, is not perishable, can be measured, and its cost is very low, it must be liable for *zakat*, like grains and dates.[3] Abu Hanifa believes that honey is subject to the *'ushr* in *'ushr* land, but when it is in *kharaj* land, there is no *zakat* on it based on the principle that *'ushr* and *kharaj* are not combined because the owner of the *kharaj* land must pay the *kharaj* in return for cultivating it. Therefore, a second due is not imposed on it because of that. Imam Ahmad said that both types of land are the same in that respect and he obliged it on the honey someone takes from his own property or from the wild, and whether the land is *'ushri* or *kharaji*.[2]

The position of those who believe there is no *zakat* on honey

Malik, ash-Shafi'i, Ibn Abi Layla, al-Hasan ibn Abi Salih, and Ibn al-Mundhir say that there is no *zakat* on honey. They produce two things to support their position:

- Ibn al-Mundhir said that there is no established report or consensus that *zakat* is obliged on honey. Therefore there is no *zakat* due on it.
- It is a liquid which comes from an animal and so it resembles milk, and there is no *zakat* on milk by consensus.[4]

1. *Zad al-Ma'ad*, vol. 1, p. 314. the *hadith* is from Munir ibn 'Abdullah from his father from Sa'd ibn Abi Dhubab.
2. Ibid., p. 314.
3. Ibid.
4. *Al-Mughni*, vol. 2, p. 713.

The view of Abu 'Ubayd

Abu 'Ubayd took a middle position between those who oblige *zakat* on honey and those who do not since it seems to him that there is conflict between the traditions reported about it, even though he inclines to take the view that *zakat* is due on it.

After recounting both positions regarding *zakat* on honey and the various reasons for their positions, I incline to the view that the owners are commanded to pay *zakat* on it and are encouraged to pay it. It is disliked for them to refuse to pay it and it may well be a sin for them to conceal it, even if it is not, technically speaking, obligatory for them in the manner that *zakat* is due on land and livestock.

People are not fought when they refuse to pay its *zakat*, as they would be if they refused to pay *zakat* on land and livestock. That is because there is no authentic *Sunna* from the Messenger of Allah (p) about it as there is about the other two forms of wealth and it is not found in the books of *zakat*. If it had been of the same status as the *zakat* due on those two categories, it would have times and definitions about its quantities, like the five *wasqs* in grain and forty sheep. There is nothing firm from any of the Imams. Nonetheless, when the owner of honey brings the ruler his *sadaqa*, he should accept it, as 'Umar did with Abu Dhubab. This is its limit on the matter. If someone does not pay it, no judgement can be taken against him.[1]

It is more likely that *zakat* is due on honey

My preference in this matter is that honey is a form of wealth from which there is earning and thus it is a property on which *zakat* is obliged. Our evidence for that is the following:

- The texts about *zakat* are general and do not distinguish between one form of wealth and another, as when Allah says: *"Take* sadaqa *from their wealth," "Give away some of the good things you have earned and some of what the earth produces for you"* and *"Give away some of what We have provided for you,"* etc.

1. *Al-Amwal*, pp. 506-50.

- There is an analogy between honey and grains and fruits on which *zakat* is due. The output of farming is like the output of beehives, and must be treated the same.
- The relevant particular traditions and *hadiths* which, although they are criticised, support each other, as stated by Ibn al-Qayyim. That is perhaps why at-Tirmidhi does not negate their authenticity but rather says, "Nothing of importance is authentically reported from the Prophet (p) on this issue."[1] This statement implies that small things may have been reported. At-Tirmidhi continues, "But this is the view of most scholars."[2]

In *ad-Durar al-Bahiya*, ash-Shawkani selects the view that honey is subject to *zakat*, saying, "One-tenth is obliged on honey." In his commentary on that, Siddiq Hasan Khan supports this view, noting, "The sayings, taken together, do not fall short of substantiating the conditions of *zakat*."[3] The argument that honey, being a liquid produced by animals, is not amenable for *zakat* by analogy to milk, is refuted on the basis that milk is in principle subject to *zakat* through *zakat* paid on livestock, while bees are not charged anything, so the similarity requires that *zakat* be paid on honey.[4]

Section Two: The ratio of *zakat* on honey

All those who oblige *zakat* on honey agree that the ratio is ten percent, based on the texts reported on the issue and in analogy to fruits and grains.[5] As for consideration of production costs, Abu 'Ubayd reports that 'Umar said that honey produced in valleys and plains is due a rate of *zakat* based on ten percent, while honey produced in mountains is charged *zakat* at five percent.[6] This is apparently in consideration of production costs.

1. *Sharh Sahih at-Tirmidhi*, Ibn al-'Arabi, vol. 2, p. 123.
2. Ibid.
3. *Ar-Rawda an-Nadiya*, vol. 1, p. 200.
4. *Al-Mughni*, vol. 2, p. 714.
5. Ibid., p. 713.
6. *Al-Amwal*, p. 498.

An-Nasir from Ahl al-Bayt disagrees, arguing that the rate must be one-fifth, as in the case of *fay'*, because honey is not measurable, nor does it come from the earth.[1] The reply to him is that honey is similar to fruits, because like fruits, it comes from trees' flowers (the nectar). Moreover, one-tenth is indicated by the texts.[2] I think ten per cent should be the rate, but it must apply to the net income from honey after deduction of production costs, as with grains and fruits.

Section three: The *nisab* of honey

We have no reports about the *nisab* of honey, so people differ on it. Abu Hanifa argues that there is no *nisab*. Abu Hanifa argues that there is no *nisab*, as with grains and fruits. Abu Yusuf considers the *nisab* to be the value of five *wasqs* of the cheapest grain, such as barley, in accordance with his view of considering the value of the lowest measurable *nisab* applicable to products that are not measurable. There is also a report from him that the *nisab* is ten *ratls*. There are several narrations from Muhammad which set the *nisab* at five *faraqs*, five *manns*, or five *qirbas*, following his rule of using five units usually used for items not mentioned in sayings. One *faraq* is thirty-six *ratls*, one *mann* is two *ratls* and one *qirba* is one hundred *ratls*. There is also a report from Ahmad that the *nisab* is ten *faraqs*, attributed to 'Umar. It is reported from Ahmad that one *faraq* is sixteen *ratls*.[3]

My personal opinion is to estimate the value of five *wasqs* of an average grain, such as wheat, since it is an average universal food. The Prophet (p) made five *wasqs* in grain and fruits, and honey must be treated the same by analogy. It is by analogy that the rate is determined at one-tenth, so why not determine the *nisab* on the same basis of value, especially since considering the value of the lowest grain is not fair to *zakat* payers?

1. *Al-Bahr az-Zakhkhar*, vol. 1, p. 174.
2. Ibid.
3. *Bada'i' as-Sana'i'*, vol. 1, p. 61.

Section Four: Animal products such as silk and milk

Today many industries revolve around animal products like milk, silk, eggs, and meat. Most of these were not large-scale businesses in the time of the Prophet (p), the Companions and the great scholars. The result is that we have no reports about these products. One can derive an answer to the question regarding the *zakat* on these products from the reasons cited by jurists to establish *zakat* on honey and to exempt the milk of pastured animals from *zakat*. The main reason cited is that the source of milk – livestock – is charged with *zakat*, while the source of honey is not. This implies that *zakat* is due on all products whose sources are not subject to *zakat*. Therefore, milk and other products of non-zakatable fed livestock are charged *zakat*, like honey. Each of these is an animal product where *zakat* is not due on the animal itself.

I believe that *zakat* must be taken from animal products at ten per cent of the net output unless the animals themselves are considered trade assets. The rule is that anything whose source is not liable for *zakat* must be charged with *zakat* as an output, like crops with respect to land, honey with respect to bees, dairy products with respect to livestock, eggs with respect to poultry, and silk with respect to the silkworm. This is the opinion of Yahya, a Shi'ite, who obliges *zakat* on silk.[1]

Some jurists treat non-pastured animals used for their products and reproduction like trade assets and oblige one-fourth of one-tenth on both the principal and growth. This is reported from some Zaydi jurists, such as al-Hadi, al-Mu'ayyad, and others. A person who buys a horse for breeding or a cow for its products is treated as a merchant and charged the *zakat* on trade assets. This is not restricted to producing animals, but to any asset that is used for business, such as houses and buildings owned for the purpose of renting. This issue will be discussed in detail in Chapter Eight.

1. *Al-Bahr az-Zakhkhar*, vol. 1, p. 173.

Chapter Seven

Zakat on Minerals and Sea Products

Minerals, Buried Treasure, and *Rikaz*

Ibn al-Athir writes in *an-Nihaya*, "Minerals are the valuables extracted from the earth, like gold, silver, copper, and other things."[1] Ibn al-Humam says, "The root of the word '*ma'dan*' (mineral) means to stay or reside. '*Ma'adin*' (minerals) receive their name because they stand still in the earth. Buried treasure (*kanz*) refers to the wealth put in the earth by human beings. *Rikaz* means both mineral and buried treasure. The root of the word '*rikaz*' also means 'to stay still.'"[2]

Ibn Qudama defined minerals as anything put by Allah in the earth of a nature different from the earth itself and extracted therefrom which has value. This definition excludes things extracted from the sea, things put in the earth by human action, things that are of the nature of the earth such as soil and things that carry no value. Examples of minerals are gold, silver, lead, iron, diamonds, oil, sulphur, etc.[3]

Section One: Buried Treasure

Buried treasures include all things of value left in the earth by people in the past, such as gold, silver, used metals and the like. Jurists oblige a charge of one-fifth on the person who finds such wealth, in accordance with the narration of Abu Hurayra that the Prophet (p) said, "One-fifth is obliged on *rikaz*." It is defined by

1. *An-Nihaya*, Ibn al-Athir, vol. 3, p. 82.
2. *Fath al-Qadir*, vol. 1, p. 537.
3. *Al-Mughni*, vol 3, p. 23.

the group.[1] Things buried in the earth are defined unanimously as *rikaz*. An-Nasa'i reports from 'Amr ibn Shu'ayb from his father from his grandfather, "The Messenger of Allah (p) was asked about lost and found things, and said, 'When you find things on the roads used by people or in inhabited areas, you must announce it for one year. If the owner appears, give him what belongs to him, and if not, it is yours. But things found in deserted roads or villages are charged, as in the case of *rikaz*, one-fifth.'" (an-Nasa'i)

These two *hadiths* indicate the following:

- One-fifth is due on things found where no owner exists, regardless of whether they are on the surface of the earth or inside it. Things found in private lands must be given to the landowners.
- The majority of scholars believe that *rikaz* includes anything that exists on the surface of the earth or under it. Ash-Shafi'i is an exception, because he restricts the meaning of *rikaz* to gold and silver only.[2] The view of the majority is consistent with the general texts.
- The two *hadiths* apparently indicate that the fifth is obliged on the finder, Muslim or not, minor or adult. This is the view of the majority. Ash-Shafi'i says non-Muslims are not obliged to pay a fifth, because this payment is a form of *zakat*. It is claimed that he says children and women are not allowed to own found *rikaz*. Ibn Qudama contends, "We rely on the generality of the *hadith*, 'One-fifth is obliged on *rikaz*,' to ascertain that one-fifth is obliged on all *rikaz*, and the remainder belongs to the finder."[3] Ibn Daqiq al-'Id notes that the closest view to the text of the *hadiths* is that one-fifth is obliged on all or, at least, most forms of *rikaz*.[4]
- Apparently, the *hadith* does not refer to any *nisab*. The fifth is obliged on any quantity of found treasure, according to Malik, Abu Hanifa and his disciples, Ahmad, Ishaq and ash-Shafi'i in

1. Mentioned in *al-Muntaqa*. See *Nayl al-Awtar*, vol. 4, p. 147.
2. *Nayl al-Awtar*, vol. 4, p. 143.
3. *Al-Mughni*, vol. 3, pp. 22-23.
4. *Nayl al-Awtar*, vol. 4, p. 140, and *Fath al-Bari*, vol. 3, p. 235.

the old school. This wealth, on which one-fifth is flatly obliged as on *ghanima*, needs no *nisab*. Finding treasure does not involve great expenditure which needs to be deducted to attenuate the burden of the payer. In this respect they are unlike minerals and grain. The later view of ash-Shafi'i is to consider the *nisab* on found treasure, because the charge is due on wealth taken from the earth, and must be treated like minerals and grains, which have a *nisab*.[1]

- It is agreed upon to abolish the condition of one year's passage. Dues are obliged immediately. In *al-Fath*, Ibn Hajar writes, "Strangely enough, Ibn al-'Arabi mentions that ash-Shafi'i retains this condition, but this is not found in any of ash-Shafi'i's writings or in the writing or his disciples."[2]

- The *hadith* does not refer to the disbursement of the fifth due on *rikaz*. Consequently, jurists have several opinions. Ash-Shafi'i and a narration from Ahmad show that it must be disbursed like *zakat*, because of a report made by Ahmad that 'Ali ibn Abi Talib ordered it to be given to the needy, and because it is wealth earned from the earth, which makes it similar to grain and fruit.

Abu Hanifa, Malik, Ahmad in another narration, and the bulk of jurists believe that this fifth should be disbursed the same way that the *fay'* is,[3] i.e. as a part of the general budget of the state. Abu 'Ubayd reports from ash-Sha'bi that a man found one thousand dinars buried on the outskirts of Madina and brought them to 'Umar, who took one-fifth (two hundred dinars) and returned the remainder to the man. Then 'Umar divided the two hundred among those Muslims who were present, until a few dinars remained. 'Umar called the finder and gave these few dinars to him. The author of *al-Mughni* comments, "If it were *zakat*, 'Umar would have restricted distribution to the deserving recipients

1. *Al-Mughni*, vol. 3, pp. 20-22. Ash-Shawkani attributes the requirement of *nisab* to Malik, Ahmad and Ishaq. This contradicts what is quoted in *al-Mughni*, especially from Ahmad.

2. *Nayl al-Awtar*, and *Fath al-Bari*, op. cit.

3. *Nayl al-Awtar*, vol. 4, p. 128.

instead of all Muslims present then and definitely would not have given the finder any part of the one-fifth." Moreover, it is argued that since the fifth is also obliged on non-Muslim finders and non-Muslims cannot be obliged to pay *zakat*, it must not be treated like *zakat*. Additionally, it is similar to war booty taken from past generations of unbelievers."[1]

Finding treasure is always rare, and more important is the following section on minerals, which usually represent a substantial sector of the economy.

Section Two: Minerals and dues obliged on them

The required dues on minerals

The importance of minerals, solid and liquid, in human life is unquestionable. If grains and fruits are liable for *zakat*, should not minerals have *zakat* paid on them too, since all come from the earth? Jurists, in total, do not dispute that there are dues obliged on minerals, although they differ on the details. Dues on minerals are obliged in accordance with the general principle established by the verse, *"O you who believe! Give away some of the good things you have earned and some of what the earth produces for you."* (2:267) No doubt, minerals are among the things produced for us by Allah from the earth.

Minerals included in this obligation

Jurists differ on whether this obligation covers all mining activities or only selected metals. It is known that ash-Shafi'i restricts it to gold and silver only, leaving all other minerals and precious stones free from *zakat*. Abu Hanifa and his disciples include metals extracted from the earth that are usually treated with heat.[2] This

1. *Al-Mughni*, vol. 3, p. 22.
2. *Al-Mirqat*, al-Qari, vol. 4, p. 149.

opinion is based on the analogy to gold and silver, whose *zakat* is confirmed by texts and *ijma'*. The Hanbali school does not make any distinction between metals treated with heat and metals that are not treated with heat. According to this school, all minerals that come from the earth are subject to *zakat*, whether solid, like iron ore, land, and copper, or fluid like petroleum and sulphur. This opinion is shared by Zayd ibn 'Ali, al-Baqir, as-Sadiq, and all Shi'ite jurists except al-Mu'ayyad, who excludes salt, petroleum and asphalt.[1]

Abu Ja'far al-Baqir was asked about salt mines. He answered, "This mineral is subject to the one-fifth due." When asked about sulphur and petroleum, he replied, "These and their likes are charged one-fifth."[2]

It seems that the Hanbali view is supported by the linguistic meaning of the word "minerals" and by reasoning, since as far as *zakat* is concerned, there is no difference between solid and liquid minerals or between those treated by heat or not so treated. All of them are kinds of wealth that must be dealt with similarly. If the great scholars from previous centuries saw the importance of petroleum, which is even called black gold, and other minerals in the economic life of the world today, they would not have hesitated about subjecting it to *zakat*. Ibn Qudama gives the following points in support of this view:

- The generality of the verse, "*and some of what the earth produces for you...*"
- The general implication of the word 'minerals' as a form of wealth extracted from the earth, which must have taken *zakat*, like gold and silver.
- Minerals are a form of wealth. If they are taken as war booty, they would be subject to a one-fifth due. The same wealth, taken from the earth, should also be subject to *zakat*.[3]

1. *Al-Bahr az-Zakhkhar*, vol. 2, p. 210.
2. *Jawahir al-Kalam*, vol. 2, pp. 1190-120.
3. *Al-Mughni*, vol. 3, p. 24.

Section Three: The rate imposed on minerals

Abu Hanifa, his disciples, Abu 'Ubayd, Zayd ibn 'Ali, al-Baqir, as-Sadiq, and all Zaydi and Imami jurists believe that the rate is one-fifth. Ahmad and Ishaq argue that the rate must be like that of gold and silver, i.e. two and one half per cent. That is also the opinion of Malik and ash-Shafi'i.[1] Malikis distinguish between minerals that take cost and effort to extract, in which case two and one half per cent is obliged, and minerals that do not require cost and effort to extract, in which case twenty per cent applies.[2]

There is yet another opinion known among Malikis, that all minerals and ores, liquid or not, are owned by the national treasury of the Islamic state, on the grounds that they in fact belong to the whole society together, and their exploitation must not be left to a few individuals. Their output must also be spent for the public interests of Islamic society.[3]

This opinion may derive support from a report by Abu 'Ubayd that Abyad ibn Harmal al-Mazini asked the Messenger of Allah (p) to grant him the salt in Ma'rib and the Messenger of Allah (p) agreed to do so. Abyad added, "When I left, the Messenger was told, 'Do you know what you have just granted him? You gave him wealth like running water.' The Prophet (p) took it back from me."[4] Abu 'Ubayd says that this granting and retrieving the grant indicates that the Prophet (p) gave Abyad the land on the assumption that he was going to use it for reclamation and agriculture. When the Prophet (p) realised that it was a huge amount of wealth in salt, he took it back from him. The Messenger's traditional practice with regard to pastureland, firewood and water is that they belong to all people together as partners. He hated to give such property to one person alone.[5] Consequently, such things as petroleum, iron ore, etc., must belong to all people together under the Islamic state.

---

1. *Al-Majmu'*, vol. 6, p. 83.
2. *Al-Muntaqa, Sharh al-Muwatta'*, p. 102.
3 *Halaqat ad-Dirasat al-Ijtima'iyya*, 3rd session, p. 250.
4. *Al-Amwal*, pp. 275-276.
5. Ibid., p. 281.

The evidence of those who believe the rate is 2.5%

In *al-Muwatta'*, Malik reports from Rabi'a ibn Abi 'Abdu'r-Rahman, from more than one narrator, that the Messenger of Allah (p) granted Hilal ibn Harith the minerals of al-Qibliya (a coastal area five days' walk from Madina) in the direction of al-Qar'a (a place between Madina and Nakhla). Those minerals are only charged *zakat* (2.5%) until today.[1] In *al-Umm*, ash-Shafi'i says after reporting this *hadith*, "This is not confirmed as authentic by critics of *hadith*. Even if it were accepted, all it indicates is that the grant was given by the Prophet (p). The application of the rate of *zakat* on minerals instead of the one-fifth rate is not narrated from the Prophet (p) in this *hadith*."[2] Abu 'Ubayd says, "This *hadith* from Rabi'a on al-Qibliya has no acceptable chain. Additionally, it does not mention that the Prophet (p) ordered the rate; all it says is that *zakat* is collected from the minerals until today. If the choice of the rate was authentically reported from the Prophet (p), it would have been irrefutable evidence."[3]

The argument of those who believe the rate is one-fifth

Abu Hanifa and his disciples present the *hadith* of the Messenger of Allah (p), "One-fifth is obliged on *rikaz*." (The Group) They add that two things can be extracted from the earth: the first is treasure buried by human beings and the second is minerals created by Allah. The word *rikaz* includes both; its literal meaning is minerals and its allegorical meaning is treasures.[4]

On the other hand, Malik, ash-Shafi'i, and most Hijazi jurists argue that minerals are not *rikaz* and that *rikaz* only means treasure buried by people in the earth. They cite the *hadith* reported by the group from Abu Hurayra that the Prophet (p) said, "Injury inflicted by animals is unclaimable, and injury sustained while (working inside) a well is unclaimable, and injury sustained while (extracting)

1. *Al-Muntaqa*, vol. 2, p. 101.
2. *Al-Umm*, pt. 2, p. 43.
3. *Al-Amwal*, p. 342.
4. *Bada'i' as-Sana'i'*, vol. 2, p. 65.

minerals is unclaimable, and one-fifth is obliged on *rikaz*." They argue that since the Prophet (p) makes a distinction between minerals and *rikaz*, using the article "and" between them, they must be two different things.

The opposing Hanafis then argue that minerals must be included in the Prophet's word *rikaz*, because when he mentioned minerals he was talking about injury sustained in their extraction. If he had then said, "And one-fifth is obliged on them," buried treasures may have remained uncharged. Because of that possibility of ambiguity, the Prophet (p) used a more general word, *rikaz*, which includes both minerals and buried treasure.[1] No language specialist could put an end to this dispute, because both Iraqi and Hijazi jurists include people who are well-versed in Arabic, such as Muhammad ibn al-Hasan and ash-Shafi'i.

It seems that the word *rikaz* has in fact two meanings. *Al-Qamus* and other Arabic dictionaries define *rikaz* as minerals Allah put in the ground and pieces of gold and silver people in the past buried. Ibn al-Athir in *an-Nihaya* says that according to the Hijazis, *rikaz* means ancient treasures buried in the ground, and according to the Iraqis, *rikaz* means minerals. Linguistically both meanings are possible because each of them is something put in the ground and made steady in it.[2]

Abu Hanifa presents another *hadith* from 'Amr ibn Shu'ayb from his father from his grandfather that, "A man asked the Messenger of Allah (p) about things found in old buildings that are being demolished. The Prophet (p) said, 'One-fifth is obliged on this and on *rikaz*.'"[3] Abu Hanifa adds that the use of the additive article "and" must mean that the two things are different, so *rikaz* cannot mean buried treasure, and consequently, must mean minerals. Some of Abu Hanifa's disciples add that even if minerals are not initially called *rikaz*, the common use of the word by people was in that meaning. Muhammad ibn al-Hasan, a renowned scholar of the Arabic language, says, "Arabs say *'rakaza al-ma'din'*, for mineral ore

1. *Sharh at-Tirmidhi,* vol. 3, p. 139.

2. *An-Nihaya*, vol. 2, p. 107.

3. Reported by Abu 'Ubayd in *al-Amwal*, al-Hakim in *al-Mustadrak* and Abu Dawud. Al-Mundhiri says it is reported by at-Tirmidhi, an-Nasa'i, and Ibn Majah. At-Tirmidhi calls it good. See *Mukhtasar Sunan Abu Dawud*, vol. 2, p. 420.

when it has a high ratio of gold and silver in it.[1] The author of *al-Bada'i'* writes "*Rikaz* is derived from the verb *rakaza, which* means to make stand still, minerals stand still in earth while buried treasures are put in it."[2]

The second argument given by Hanafis is the analogy between minerals and war booty. They say the minerals were inside the earth when it was in the hands of unbelievers and then Muslims took over when they had not dug underground to reach these minerals, leaving them untouched. Their extraction later must be subject to the same principle applied to the unbelievers, property above the ground, i.e. one-fifth must be charged.[3]

The argument is difficult to accept, because it is founded on assuming that underground wealth remains in the ownership of unbelievers until it is extracted. How could one make such an assumption about the lands of Islam and Muslims? And who is to tell us that these minerals were installed inside the land before or after Islam?

Imami jurists make an analogy between minerals and war booty on the basis of the meaning of the word *ghanima* (war booty) mentioned in the *ayat*, *"Know that when you take any booty a fifth of it belongs to Allah, and to the Messenger, and to close relatives, orphans, the very poor and travellers."* (8:41) According to the Imamis, the word *ghanima* means not only war booty, but also things extracted from land or sea.[4]

The author of *ar-Rawd an-Nadir* (in Zaydi jurisprudence) says that such a generalisation of the word *ghanima* is questionable, because first, the word mentioned in the Qur'an and *hadiths*, like "*Ghanima* has been made lawful for me," is a religious concept and not only an Arabic word. This argument is based on the principle known among the scholars of *usul* that a general word may be used for a specific meaning by additional indication in the *Shari'a*. When a word is used like this, it becomes restricted to that meaning alone.

1. *Ar-Rawd an-Nadir*, vol. 2, p. 67.
2. *Al-Bada'i'*, vol. 2, p. 67.
3. Ibid.
4. *Al-Bahr az-Zakhkhar*, vol. 2, pp. 209-214.

The judge 'Abdu'l-Wahhab al-Maliki wrote a chapter on restricting general words to specific intended meanings, in such a way that the meaning of the word in the *Shari'a* becomes only that specific one and the word may not be taken to be understood in its original linguistic meaning except by additional evidence, even though the absolute use of the word may imply that general meaning. Some disciples of ash-Shafi'i agree with that, including Abu Bakr, al-Qaffal and others. Ibn Daqiq al-'Id refers in his commentary on *al-'Umda* to the principle that the context sometimes indicates the specific meaning of a general word or gives more weight to one or more of the meanings included.[1]

To sum things up, it appears that the only strong argument for the rate of twenty per cent on minerals is that minerals are *rikaz* and *rikaz* is charged at one-fifth. This is the view selected by the great scholar Abu 'Ubayd, also reports from 'Ali ibn Abi Talib a statement in its support.[2]

A distinction made on the basis of the cost of extraction

Some jurists argue that if the cost of extraction is high, relative to the amount of mineral taken, the rate should be 2.5%. On the other hand, if the cost involved is small or negligible, relative to the cost of mineral extracted, the rate should be one-fifth. This is also a narration from Malik and ash-Shafi'i.[3] This trend is instigated by the attempt to reconcile the *hadiths* which indicate that gold and silver, which are minerals, are charged at 2.5 % and the *hadiths* which indicate that the charge on minerals is one-fifth. Another instigation for this approach is the fact that the rate of *zakat* on agriculture differs according to irrigation costs.

Ar-Rafi'i, a Shafi'i, says, "In reconciling all the texts together, minerals obtained without cost or toil must be charged at one-fifth, while those obtained by effort and cost must be charged at 2.5%, just as irrigation costs change the rate on agriculture."[4] Obviously,

1. *Ar-Rawd*, vol. 2, p. 419.
2. *Al-Amwal*, pp. 240-241.
3. *Ash-Sharh al-Kabir and al-Wajiz*, on the margins of *al-Majmu'*, vol. 6, pp. 88-89.
4. Ibid.

the difference between 20% and 2.5% is substantial. It may be reasonable to impose a rate of 10% or 5% according to the value of the extracted minerals relative to the cost involved. This is not an invention of new rates in the *Shari'a,* but an application of clear analogy, because *Shari'a* makes a similar distinction in rates according to the value of the item and the cost of its production.

Section Four: *Nisab* of minerals

Is there a *nisab* for minerals?

Abu Hanifa, his disciples, and the scholars of Ahl al-Bayt believe that dues on minerals apply to any quantity regardless of the amount, on the grounds that the *hadiths* do not refer to any *nisab* or to the passage of one year on *rikaz*. Malik, ash-Shafi'i and his disciples, Ahmad, and Ishaq argue that there must be a *nisab*, and that it is equal to the *nisab* of money, since general *hadiths* determine a *nisab* for gold and silver, as in "No *zakat* is obliged on anything less than five *uqiyyas* (of silver) and nothing is obliged on a hundred and ninety dirhams," and since *ijma'* sets the *nisab* of gold at twenty dinars.

The correct view seems to be that we must consider the *nisab*, but the passage of one year is not required since, as ar-Rafi'i states, the *nisab* is needed for the wealth to be substantial enough to relieve the recipient, while the passage of one year is given for wealth to be invested and grow. Minerals extracted from the ground are themselves the increase, like plants and fruits. So, like on grains and fruits, there must be a *nisab*, but there is no need for the passage of one year.[1]

The time span for the accumulation of the *nisab*

The *nisab* need not be produced at one time. Things extracted are added together and if they add up to the amount of the *nisab* in

1. *Ash-Sharh al-Kabir*, op. cit., p. 92.

the period of one year, then *zakat* applies, even though the output, may be sold as time passes. This period is similar to the season in the case of crops. Small interruptions in production do not affect this accumulation, but after a long interruption a new period of accumulation starts.[1]

I believe such a matter should be left to specialists, in accordance with the advice of the Qur'an: *"Ask the people of the Reminder if you do not know."* (16:43, 21:7)

Section Five: The passage of one year

The majority of jurists argue that dues on minerals are payable at the time of extraction, after initial preparation and refinement. Malik notes, "Minerals are like crops. Dues on them are collected on similar dates, i.e. the day of extraction, without any need for the passage of one year."[2] According to an-Nawawi, this is the view of the vast majority of scholars, both from the *Salaf* and later generations. It is confirmed in most Shafi'i writings,[3] and is the approved opinion in the school of Ahmad.[4]

Ishaq and Ibn al-Mundhir disagree. They require the passage of one year because of the *hadith*, "No *zakat* is obliged on wealth until one year has passed."[5] This *hadith* is, however, weak and it is unanimously agreed that it does not apply on all cases, since agriculture is excluded. Minerals should, by analogy, likewise be excluded. The author of *al-Mughni* writes, "Since minerals are wealth earned from the earth, like agriculture and buried treasure, there is no need for the condition of the passage of one year. Moreover, this condition is made in order to allow wealth to grow. Minerals are, like fruits, the result of the process of growth itself, so there is no such condition."[6]

1. *Al-Wajiz*, al-Ghazali, op. cit., pp. 83-96.
2. *Al-Muntaqa*, printed with *al-Muwatta', vol.* 2, p. 104.
3. *Al-Majmu'*, vol. 6, p. 81.
4. *Al-Mughni*, vol. 3, p. 26.
5. Ibid.
6. Ibid.

The author of *al-Muhadhdhab*, a Shafi'i, says, "Dues on minerals are payable when minerals are obtained, without any consideration of the period of one year – according to the better of the two views – because the lapse of such a period is meant to give time for the asset to grow, but minerals are the fruits and growth of land, like agricultural produce."[1]

Section Six: Disbursement of dues on minerals

Jurists differ in categorising dues on minerals. Abu Hanifa and a group of jurists classify these dues with *fay'* and argue that they must be disbursed the same way *fay'* is. Malik and Ahmad consider it *zakat*. We have two reports from the Shafi'is. Some Shafi'i jurists say it is like *zakat*, and others say it depends on the applied rate – if 20% is applied, it must be treated like *fay'*, but if 2.5% is applied, it must be treated like *zakat*.

Those who do not classify this due as *zakat* apply the charge of one-fifth to non-Muslims too, while those who classify it as *zakat* do not, because *zakat*, as a form of worship, is not applicable to non-Muslims, and there is no worship without intention.[2]

Section Seven: Extractions from the sea

Materials extracted from the sea, such as pearls and coral

According to Abu Hanifa, his disciples, al-Hasan ibn Salih, and Zaydi jurists, nothing is due on such materials. This is also the opinion of Ibn 'Abbas, as reported by Ibn Abi Shayba and others. Ibn 'Abbas said, "Amber is not *rikaz*. It is something thrown up by the sea and nothing is imposed on it."[3] Apparently, this means that no charge is obliged on it. Additionally, Jabir ibn 'Abdullah is reported to have said, "Amber is not *ghanima*. All of it goes to the one who acquires it," meaning that the one-fifth due on *ghanima* is

1. *Al-Muhadhdhab* and its commentary, *al-Majmu'*, vol. 6, p. 80.
2. *Al-Majmu'*, vol. 6, p. 76.
3. *Al-Majmu'*, vol. 6, p 76.

not obliged on amber. Abu 'Ubayd comments, "Here we find two Companions of the Prophet (p) believing that it is not charged anything."[1]

On the other hand, it is authentically reported that Ibn 'Abbas said about amber, "If anything is charged on it, it must be one-fifth." It seems that Ibn 'Abbas changed his opinion after a specific incident. 'Abdu'r-Razzaq reports via a correct chain that Ibrahim ibn Sa'd, who was governor of Aden, asked Ibn 'Abbas about amber. Ibn 'Abbas' reply was, "If anything is charged, it must be one-fifth."[2] Aden was an area where amber was produced. Thus, Ibn 'Abbas gave a different opinion in consideration of interests recognised in the *Shari'a.* It is reported via al-Hasan ibn al-'Umara from Ibn 'Abbas from 'Umar ibn al-Khattab that one-fifth must be charged on amber and every jewel extracted from the sea.[3]

Additionally, Ibn 'Abbas is reported to have said that Ya'la ibn Munya wrote to 'Umar about a piece of amber found at the coast. 'Umar asked the Companions who were present, and they suggested that one-fifth should be collected from it. 'Umar wrote, "One-fifth is obliged on it and on every jewel that comes out of the sea."[4] There is also another report from 'Umar that runs in opposition to this one, which says he wrote, "Collect one-tenth from jewels of the sea and amber." None of these reports from 'Umar reach the level of authenticity, and if they were authentic, they would simply indicate that the issue of the rate is subject to *ijtihad.*

Obliging one-fifth on amber and pearls is reported from some Followers also. Abu 'Ubayd reports it from al-Hasan al-Basri and Ibn Shihab az-Zuhri.[5] 'Abdu'r-Razzaq and Ibn Abi Shayba report it from 'Umar ibn 'Abdu'l-'Aziz.[6] This is the view of Abu Yusuf.[7] Ahmad is reported to have said that amber and pearls have *zakat* paid on them like minerals.[8]

1. *Al-Musannaf*, vol. 4, p. 21, and *al-Amwal*, p. 346.
2. *Al-Muhalla*, vol. 6, p. 117, *Musannaf Ibn Abi Shayba*, vol. 4, p. 21, also mentioned in *Nasb ar-Raya*, vol. 2, and in *at-Talkhis*, p. 184.
3. *Al-Muhalla*, op cit., al-Hasan ibn al-'Umara is disregarded.
4. *Ar-Rawd an-Nadir*, vol. 2, p. 419.
5. *Al-Amwal*, p. 346.
6. *At-Talkhis*, p. 184.
7. *Al-Kharaj*, Abu Yusuf, p. 70.
8. *Al-Mughni*, vol. 3, p. 27.

Abu 'Ubayd took the view that no charge is placed on things extracted from the sea, arguing that people at the time of the Prophet (p) and the first Khalifs used to extract minerals from the sea and no charge on that is reported in the *Sunna*. This indicates that these materials are exempt, the same way that horses and slaves are exempt. Those who oblige one-fifth on things extracted from the sea do so only by analogy to minerals extracted from the land. Those who do not do so believe that things extracted from the sea are not the same as land minerals, since the Prophet (p) distinguished between them by stating that one-fifth is obliged on *rikaz* while remaining silent on things extracted from the sea.[1] But one may argue, what is analogy but applying the ruling mentioned in the texts to something similar about which the texts are silent?

If things extracted from the sea are not a form of *ghanima*, they are then similar to minerals and agriculture from the land, and must be treated likewise. For these reasons, I choose to oblige a charge on them, whether this charge is called *zakat* or not. The rate of this charge must be determined by people of wisdom and knowledge, as indicated by 'Umar when he consulted the Companions. Different rates are applied in the *Shari'a* on agricultural products, depending on the cost and effort involved in irrigation. Here, also, the rate must be chosen in consideration of expenses involved, as well as the value of the materials extracted. Whenever cost is minimum and value is high, the rate should be the higher one. There are reports from ash-Shafi'i and Malik to this effect concerning minerals.

When I discussed the rate of minerals, I supported the view through *ijtihad* that a rate of one-tenth or one-half a tenth should be selected, according to the situation being considered. Abu 'Ubayd reports that 'Umar imposed one-tenth, and comments, "I know of no reason why one-tenth is selected, because sea extracts are not treated like *rikaz* (where 20 % applies) or like minerals (where 2.5% applies), according to the view of jurists of Madina. 'Umar imposed one-tenth, which seems to be making an analogy with agricultural produce, and I know of no one else who

1. *Al-Amwal*, p. 347.

expressed such a view."[1] This means that there is nothing to prevent expressing it now or in the future as long as it is founded on valid evidence and reasoning.

The obligation on fish

The fishing industry is important in today's economic life, producing millions of dollars worth of fish. What is its treatment in the *Shari'a* from the point of view of *zakat*?

Abu 'Ubayd reported from Yunus ibn 'Ubayd, "'Umar ibn 'Abdu'l-'Aziz wrote to the governor of 'Uman, 'Do not take anything from fish until it reaches two hundred dirhams in value similar to the *nisab* of money. Once it becomes two hundred dirhams, take *zakat* from it.'"[2] A similar view is reported from Ahmad. The Imamis believe that the rate must be one-fifth, like on *ghanima*. Here I also offer the opinion which I expressed regarding other things extracted from the sea.

1. Ibid., p. 348.
2. *Al-Mughni*, vol. 3, p.26.

Chapter Eight

Zakat on Buildings, Factories and Assets Meant for Exploitation

Section One: *Zakat* on exploited assets

Exploited assets are defined as forms of wealth that are not themselves subject to *zakat* and are not obtained for trade, but for growth, and yield their owners benefits and earning through rental or selling their products. They include assets rented for profit, such as residential buildings, means of transportation, jewellery, and other material used for rental purposes. Also in this category are livestock raised for milk, wool, or meat, and factories, plants or equipment used for producing goods. In Chapter Six, I discussed livestock products and concluded that they must be treated like honey, whereby one-tenth should be charged on the net output, but the producing animals are exempted. Therefore, it is not necessary to include a discussion of livestock in this chapter.

The difference between assets used for exploitation and those used for trading is that the former remain as permanent capital, while the latter changes hands. Exploited assets used in the industrial, transportation and service sectors, represent a large portion of contemporary economies.

Those who restrict *zakat*

Two extreme opinions exist among jurists. There are those who expand the concept of *zakat* to include all or most assets and those who limit *zakat* to only a few kinds of wealth. Those who tend to limit *zakat* argue that:

- The Messenger of Allah (p) defined assets on which *zakat* is taken and did not mention among them these exploited ones such as buildings, rented animals, and productive machinery. The principle is that people must not be obliged to pay any charge without a clear text. There is no such text.
- Jurists throughout the history of Islam and in all its various countries did not oblige *zakat* on those assets.
- We have available scholarly opinions that negate the idea of *zakat* being taken on exploited assets. Jurists have stated that residential homes, craftsmen's tools, transportation animals, home furnishings, cars, planes, and ships are not subject to *zakat*, regardless of their size, value or income.

All agree that when the earnings from such assets are received, retained for one year, and exceed the *nisab*, they are then liable for *zakat*, like money.

Restricting the kinds of assets on which *zakat* is paid is a well-established stance in jurisprudence. It is defended by Ibn Hazm and later by ash-Shawkani and Siddiq Hasan Khan, to the extent that they excluded trading assets and fruits and vegetables from *zakat*. The author of *ar-Rawda an-Nadiya* argues for this opinion: "Imposing *zakat* on assets that are agreed as being not subject to *zakat*, such as residential buildings, real estate and animals, simply because they are rented for profit without being exchanged in trade, was unheard of in the first generations of Islam, not to mention the lack of support for it from the Qur'an or *Sunna*."[1]

Those who expand the concept of *zakat*

On the other side there are jurists who expand the category of zakatable assets and impose *zakat* on exploited assets like factories and buildings. This is the position of some Malikis, Hanbalis, and, although not very famous, the followers of al-Hadi among the Zaydis. It is also the view of contemporary scholars, including Abu Zahra, 'Abdu'l-Wahhab Khallaf, and 'Abdu'r-Rahman Hasan, as

1. *Ar-Rawda an-Nadiya*, vol. , p. 94.

we shall see in this section. In my opinion, this approach is more valid, for the following reasons:

- Allah obliges a defined due on each asset, *"and on their wealth there is a known due"* and *"take sadaqat from their wealth."* The Prophet (p) also exhorts us to "Pay the *zakat* on your assets." These texts do not distinguish between the different kinds of assets. Ibn al-'Arabi disproves the opinion of the Zahiris, who negate *zakat* on trade assets for lack of a correct text. "The verse, *'Take sadaqa from their wealth'* is general," he remarks. "It includes all kinds of wealth, regardless of classification, name and purpose. Whoever wishes to impose any restriction on this generality is asked to bring proof."[1]
- The reason for which *zakat* is imposed with respect to assets is growth, as noted by jurists who look for the reasons behind the rulings of the *Shari'a* in order to use them in analogy. They include practically all jurists of the Islamic *Umma* except for a few Zahiris, Mu'tazilites and Shi'ites. Consequently, *zakat* is not obliged on houses inhabited by owners, clothes, jewellery, craftsman's tools, or horses used for fighting, by unanimous agreement. This is also why *zakat* is waived from camels and cows used as personal transportation, and from every asset that does not grow on its own or by human action. Since the reason for the *zakat* on an asset is its growth, then if growth exists, an item must have *zakat* charged on it.
- The objectives of the legislation of *zakat* imply that *zakat* must be imposed, because owners of exploited assets need to be cleansed and purified, the poor and needy need relief, and Islam and its state have many uses for the proceeds of this form of *zakat*. Al-Kasani explains the reasoning behind the obligation of the one-tenth charge on the produce of the earth, "The payment of the tenth to the poor is an expression of gratitude for blessing, a relief for the incapable and poor so they can perform their religious and social role. It is also needed for the purification of the payer's soul from miserliness and sin, and the cleansing of his or her spirit and wealth." Is it reasonable to

1. *Sharh at-Tirmidhi*, vol. 3, p. 104.

claim that farmers need this cleansing, purification, and expression of gratitude, while owners of factories, buildings, ships and planes do not, although the latter usually have higher incomes than the former?

Disproving the evidence of the restricters

The fact that the Prophet (p) does not mention a certain asset as being liable for *zakat* is not an indication of complete exclusion from *zakat*, because the Prophet (p) only mentions growing assets common in Arab society at his time, such as camels, cows, lambs, wheat, barley, dates, raisins and silver money. Muslims throughout generations obliged *zakat* on many assets by analogy to those mentioned by the Prophet (p) because of the general terms used in the texts, and in consideration of the objectives of *zakat*. Some examples are:

- Ash-Shafi'i says in *ar-Risala* about the *zakat* due on gold, "The Messenger of Allah (p) imposed *zakat* on silver. Afterwards, Muslims collected *zakat* on gold, either by virtue of a text from the Prophet (p) that did not reach us, or by analogy, since gold is used by people as a determinant of value for their exchange, before and after Islam."[1]

  The possibility that there is a saying that did not reach ash-Shafi'i is very remote. The only reason, then, is analogy, as stated by Abu Bakr ibn al-'Arabi in *Sharh at-Tirmidhi*: "The Arabs' trade at the time of the Prophet (p) made use of money of all kinds. His mentioning of silver was understood as inclusive of all kinds of money. But when people in later generations started asking for a specific text on everything, Allah closed the door of guidance and they deviated from the track of their Predecessors."[2]

- There is no clear text about the *zakat* on trade assets. In spite of this, Ibn al-Mundhir reports that they are zakatable by *ijma'*. Only the Zahiris disagree.

1. *Ar-Risala*, ed. Ahmad Shakir, pp. 193-194.
2. *Sharh at-Tirmidhi*, vol. 3, p. 104.

- 'Umar ordered *zakat* on horses because he realised that they had become a valuable form of wealth. Abu Hanifa agrees with 'Umar on this issue as long as the horses are retained for growth and pastured naturally.
- Ahmad obliges *zakat* on honey, on the basis of the report from the Companions and by analogy with grains and fruits. He further obliges *zakat* on all minerals by analogy to gold and silver, and by virtue of the general verse, "*and some of what the earth produces for you...*"
- Az-Zuhri, al-Hasan and Abu Yusuf obliged a one-fifth charge on pearls, amber, and other extracts from the sea, by analogy with *rikaz* and minerals.
- All known schools of thought utilise analogy in the rules of *zakat*. For example, the Shafi'is use analogy in applying the condition of *zakat* on food items, although the hadiths mention only a few of these items by name.

The claim that no Muslim jurists impose *zakat* on exploited assets is refuted on the basis that the concept of retaining the asset and exploiting it for production or rental is a modern innovation that did not exist at the time of the great Muslim jurists. Yet we find that their statements indicate that *zakat* would be taken on such assets.

The fact that jurists exempt residential houses and craftsmen's tools from *zakat* cannot be extended to include buildings exploited for rent and factories or plants established by industrial growth. Riding animals of the past are by no means similar to modern cars, planes and gigantic ships while personal home furnishings of the past differ substantially from today's furniture rental businesses.

Our predecessors did not err when they decided that furniture and tools are not subject to *zakat*. They applied strictly and rationally the rules for *zakat* to the circumstances of the age in which they lived. The author of *al-Hidaya* rationalises the exemptions of such times, "... because they are utilised for essential needs and also do not grow."[1] The author of *al-'Inaya* comments, "Each of these

1. *Al-Hidaya*, with *Fath al-Qadir*, vol. 1, p. 487.

two traits is alone an obstacle to *zakat*. Residential quarters are indispensable for people as is clothing. As for growth, it may either be a characteristic of the item itself, as in the case of gold and silver, or it may be merely by designation, as in the case of trade goods."[1]

Jurists agree that *zakat* is not paid on a house used as a residence by its owner. This exemption is an expression of Islamic justice, especially when compared with most contemporary real estate taxes, which do not usually give such consideration.

It is essential to point out that the rationalisation of the exemption of housing, clothing, tools, etc., from *zakat* on the basis that they are non-growing and utilised for essential needs, is itself an indication that any of these items becomes subject to *zakat* if it is used for growth for non-essential needs.

Section Two: The calculation of *zakat* on buildings, factories and similar items

*Zaka*t on growing assets discussed in previous chapters are of two kinds:

- Assets whose *zakat* is calculated on the principal and its increments together once every year, such as *zakat* on livestock and trade goods. In this case, the asset and its increment are integrated very closely, and the rate of *zakat* is two and a half per cent.
- Assets whose *zakat* is calculated only on the growth or increase once the harvest is obtained. The asset may be materially fixed, such as land, or non-fixed, such as bees. The rate of *zakat* on this kind of asset is 10% or 5%, as we have seen earlier in this book.

If buildings and factories are subject to *zakat*, on what basis must *zakat* be calculated and how are these assets to be treated with regard to *zakat*?"

1. *Al-'Inaya*, ibid.

Two Established Trends

Many people may think that past jurists did not discuss whether rented houses are subject to *zakat* because the practice was not common in the past. This justification is generally valid, but one may find a few jurists who expressed the view that such houses are amenable to *zakat*, although they have different ways of calculating it. Some suggest that rented houses be treated like trade goods, appraised every year and *zakat* paid on the appraisal value at a rate of 2/5%, while others calculate *zakat* on the income these assets bring in, to see if it reaches the *nisab* and fulfils other conditions for *zakat* to be charged.

The first trend: treatment similar to that of trade assets

This view requires an appraisal of the asset used for income such as rented buildings, aeroplanes, shops, etc., every year. *Zakat* is then charged on the basis of this appraisal plus whatever net earnings remain at the end of the year, at the rate of 2.5% this view is shared by jurists from Sunni and Shiite schools of thought.

Ibn 'Aqil, a great sharp-minded Hanbali jurist, expresses this view, as quoted approvingly by Ibn al-Qayyim in his book, *Bada'i' al-Fawa'id*: "Ibn 'Aqil, in application of Ahmad's belief in *zakat* on jewellery which is rented, says that *zakat* must also be applied to buildings designated for rent and every asset or commodity that is used for rental purposes " Ibn al-Qayyim continues, "Ibn 'Aqil points out that this view is the logical extension of our treatment of jewellery. Jewellery, according to our school, is not subject to *zakat*, but if jewellery is used as a rental item, *zakat* becomes obliged. If the designation for rent obliges *zakat* on an item that was originally not subject to *zakat*, this must apply to all non-zakatable items, i.e. the zakatibility of an item depends on its state. Gold and silver are amenable for *zakat*, but when they are made into women's ornaments designated for personal use, *zakat* is abolished on them. If again that same piece of jewellery changes its state into a rental item, *zakat* is imposed on it again. This necessarily indicates that buildings, animals used for riding, utensils, and furniture become liable for *zakat* when they are rented out."[1]

In my opinion, this view of Imam Ahmad is very strong. It is based on the important principle that *zakat* is not obliged on non-growing assets or on assets used to fulfil essential needs but is obliged on growing assets. An asset that generates rental income is undoubtedly a growing one. Lawful jewellery used for personal ornamentation does not grow and also fulfils a need for the woman who wears it, but if it is used for rental purposes it becomes a growing asset subject to *zakat*. This is also one opinion of Malik, according to Ibn Rushd.[2]

If we apply this principle to buildings, furniture, cars, ships, planes, machinery, and industrial equipment, we can find an answer to their relationship to *zakat*. If any of these is assigned for personal use, *zakat* is not obliged, but when they are used for rental or for generating income, they become subject to *zakat*. *Zakat* on them is similar to that on trade goods as far as the *nisab* and rates are concerned. This means that owners of such assets must appraise their buildings, cars, etc., add to the appraisal value other cash capital and loans to others, and pay 2.5% on the total.

The claim of exemption from *zakat* on the basis that these are fixed assets like the exempted store fixtures of merchants is disproved by the fact that the productive capital itself is these fixed rental assets. They are the ones that generate gains and profit. Exemption from *zakat* covers assets that are not themselves used for growth but help other assets to produce, such as buildings where industrial equipment is placed. The industrial equipment is the productive asset. On the other hand, land and structure in rented buildings, hotels and cinemas are themselves the productive assets.

The school of Hadawi

The author of *al-Bahr az-Zakhkar* writes that the Hadawis, who are Zaydi Shi'ites, oblige *zakat* on all items used for making profit, on the basis that the verse, *"take* sadaqat *from their wealth"* is general

1. *Bada'i' al-Fawa'id*, vol. 3, p. 143.
2. *Bidayat al-Mujtahid*, vol. 1, p. 147.

and applies to these assets These assets are intended for income generation and must be treated similarly to trade goods so that *zakat* must be paid if they reach the *nisab*.[1] The author of *Matn al-Azhar* and its commentators, also Zaydi, adopt the same opinion regarding all assets whose benefits renew without exhausting the asset itself. Thus *zakat*, according to them is not obliged on horses, mules, donkeys, houses, etc., except when they are used for trade and productive exploitation.

Al-Hadi is reported to have said that if a person purchases a horse for the purpose of selling its offspring, the horse and its off-spring are all subject to *zakat*. Al-Mu'ayyad Abu'l-'Abbas and Abu Talib say this is "... because all become like trade goods." Al-Mu'ayyad continues, "The same applies to the silkworm." Al-Huqayni says the same also applies to a person who has purchased a tree in order to sell its fruit. It is also said to be applied to cows and sheep bred for their offspring, milk and dairy products and wool.[2]

The author of *al-Bahr az-Zakhkhar* states as evidence to support this view:

- The generality of the texts regarding the obligations of *zakat*.
- The similarity between assets used for production and exploitation and trade goods; both are forms of wealth intended for profitable growth.

Objections of the opponents

Scholars who tend to restrict the obligation of *zakat*, such as ash-Shawkani and Siddiq Hasan Kahn, object to this opinion. This is not surprising because they also object to *zakat* on trade goods and vegetables. Their argument concentrates on two points:

- The text of the saying, "No *zakat* is obliged on a Muslim's slaves and horses" is general in its exemption of horses from *zakat*. This exemption includes cases in which horses are used for renting or for trade

1. *Al-Bahr az-Zakhkhar*, vol. 2, p. 147.
2. *Sharh al-Azhar*, Ibn Miftah, and its commentaries, vol. 1, pp. 450-451 and 475.

• The obligation of *zakat* on assets known to be exempted, such as houses, buildings and riding animals, simply because they are being rented, was unheard of among the Companions and the generations that followed them, not to mention its lack of support from Qur'an and *Sunna*. In spite of the fact that they used to hire and rent their houses, orchards, and animals, it never occurred to any of these people to pay, at the end of the year, a 2.5% tax on their real estate or animals. They passed away with their peace of mind unbroken by such a harsh obligation, until the end of the third century of the Hijra, when this form of *zakat* was claimed on the basis to mere analogy to trade goods, which is in itself dubious. Moreover, this analogy is itself incorrect because in renting one exchanges the benefit of the asset, while in trade one exchanges the asset itself.[1]

In brief, this view says that people are not obliged to pay anything in principle, except when there is clear evidence that requires them to do so. In the case in hand, such evidence does not exist. Nothing is reported from the *Salaf*, no *ayat* or *hadith* talks about it. As for the analogy to trade assets, it is erroneous because of the difference between them.

Weighing and discussion

One can argue that the *hadith*, "No *zakat* is obliged on a Muslim's slaves and horses" founds the exemption on the basis that these items are for personal use that satisfies the essential need for services and transportation. The great majority of scholars, as early as the third generation, oblige *zakat* on them if they are designated for trade. Ibn al-Mundhir even mentioned that there is *ijma'* on this. The wording of the *hadith* never prevented such an understanding.

The lack of reports from the Companions concerning the *zakat* on rented and productive assets may be attributed to the rarity of such incidents during their time. The use of fixed assets for productive purposes or rent was not so common as to make it important

1. *Ar-Rawda*, op. cit.

enough for people to give their opinions about it. The author of *al-Bahr az-Zakhkhar* notes that the claim that Hadawis contradict *ijma'* on this issue is baseless, because there are no reports from the *Salaf* on this issue either way.[1] The author of *Sharh al-Azhar* comments, "I believe that the view of al-Hadi does not contradict *ijma'*, because the Companions and the Followers never discussed this issue at all. No harm is done by discussing it anew and expressing an opinion on it."[2]

The analogy between productive rented assets and trade goods makes some sense because each is a growing capital that produces income, and the owners of each are businessmen who intend to invest their capital in income generating activities for the purpose of profit. The difference between exchanging the utility of the item or exchanging the item itself is not substantial enough to warrant different treatment. One may even argue that a person who exchanges only the utility and preserves the principal has more guarantee of profitability than the person who exchanges the item itself. However, if we think deeply we may find a few differences between these two forms of business.

First of all, the best definition of trade goods is anything obtained for the purpose of resale for profit, as stated in the *hadith* from Samura in which the Prophet (p) used to command them to pay *zakat* on that which they prepared for sale. It is obvious that buildings and factories are not prepared for sale by their owners, but rather for rent and productive use. Contractors and property developers buy buildings or build them for the purpose of resale.

Secondly, if we consider each owner who has an asset that is productive and profitable as a merchant, even though his or her assets are not themselves intended for sale, owners of agricultural land and orchards must be included, implying that they are required to appraise the value of their land and trees each year and pay *zakat* at the rate of 2.5%. This is not acceptable and contradicts the ample evidence that we have.

Thirdly, the productive use of these assets may be halted sometimes for a particular reason, such as a lack of raw material or a

1. *Al-Bahr az-Zakhkhar*, vol. 2, p. 148.
2. *Hashiyat Sharh al-Azhar*, vol. 1, p. 450.

market. In those cases, how can the owner pay his or her *zakat*? Can owners of trade goods sell some of them or pay *zakat* in kind? Are owners of real estate required to sell in order to be able to pay *zakat*? This is an obvious hardship which is not required in the *Shari'a*.

Fourthly, from the practical point of view, the required yearly appraisal is subject to many non-objective elements in addition to price changes and depreciation because of wear and tear. It is a cumbersome practice that requires hiring specialised experienced people and involves the payment of substantial expenses that may end up being paid from the *zakat* itself.

For these reasons, I select the view that *zakat* on buildings and factories must be taken on the basis of their income, which coincides with the other two opinions, which differ only in whether the percentage of *zakat* is 2.5%, 10% or 5%.

The second trend: *zakat* taken on an asset's income

Ahmad is reported to have said that *zakat* is obliged on the rent of rented houses whether the rent is received or not. This is quoted by Ibn Qudama.[1] In the writings of the Malikis, Zarruq states in *Sharh ar-Risala*, "There are two opinions on the zakatability of assets used for income, such as rented housing. One is that *zakat* is obliged on their value received when sold and the second is that *zakat* is due on their income and yield when it is acquired. In either case, *zakat* becomes due after the passage of one year according to the famous view among jurists or it becomes due upon receipt of yield or sale value like the case of a monopolistic trader selling his merchandise according to some jurists."[2] The second opinion is important for our purpose here and has its roots in older views from some Companions and Followers.

The view of a group of Companions

All those who say that earned funds are subject to *zakat* when acquired (without the passage of a year) can apply the same rule

1. *Al-Mughni*, vol. 3, pp. 29 and 47.
2. *Sharh ar-Risala*, vol. 1, p. 329.

with regard to *zakat* on income earned from the output of factories and rental incomes of cars, buildings, planes, equipment, furniture and the like. We shall see in the next chapter that this is the opinion of Ibn 'Abbas, Ibn Mas'ud, Mu'awiya, an-Nasir, al-Baqir, and Da'ud. It is also attributed to 'Umar ibn 'Abdu'l-'Aziz, al-Hasan al-Basri, az-Zuhri, Makhul, and al-Awza'i.

The evidence for this opinion is the generality of the statement, "One-quarter of one-tenth is obliged on minted silver." Some jurists add the same argument given by al-Hadi, the analogy of assets designated for renting or production and assets designated for sale, on the grounds that selling the benefit of the item is like selling a commodity. But the analogy implies that the *nisab* of rented assets should be calculated on the basis of earned income, as was stated by the author of *al-Hasir fi Madhhab an-Nasir*, who said if the rent and return from houses, shops, and assets for exploitation reached two hundred dirhams, then 2.5% should be paid and if it does not reach that limit, there is nothing due.[1]

Thus the difference between the earlier view and this view is that the earlier view obliges *zakat* on the asset itself, while this view obliges it on the income at the rate of 2.5%, and therefore the condition of the passage of one year does not apply here.

A modern view: the sort of *zakat* obliged is like that on crops

There is another modern view which coincides with the second view: namely, that *zakat* can be taken from the revenue generated by these assets. However, there is disagreement about the amount which is taken, and whether it is 10% or 5%, based on an analogy with agricultural land. The first analogy was based on treating these assets as trading goods, whereas this analogy is based on agricultural land and the revenue being equated with crops, since there is no difference between an owner who reaps the revenue of his cultivated land and an owner who receives the revenue of his factories and buildings. Some of the modern jurists who accept this second analogy which likens such revenue to agricultural produce, include

1. *Hawashi Sharh al-Azhar*, vol. 1 , pp. 450-451.

Abu Zahra, 'Abdu'l-Wahhab Khallaf, and 'Abdu'r-Rahman Hasan. In the conference which they held in 1952 in Damascus about *zakat*,[1] they divided property into three categories:

- Assets which satisfy personal needs, like houses in which the owners live and food stored up for the owner's needs. There is no *zakat* on these assets.
- Assets acquired in the hope of making a profit. These assets are usually stored in vaults or storage places. They are unanimously liable for *zakat*. They include the items mentioned by the Prophet (p) as zakatable. Other items are added to this category on the basis of similarity.
- Assets that are sometimes used for growth or profit and sometimes for personal needs, such as jewellery and domestic animals. Jurists differ on the *zakat* on these items.

The application of this classification to the kinds of assets we have in our time must necessarily lead us to include zakatable items that are used today for growth and profit but did not exist at the time of our great *Salaf*. The three scholars mention two kinds of these assets.

Firstly, they talked of industrial equipment, plants and machinery that represent productive capital, because they are the assets that produce income. This machinery and plant are not like the tools of a blacksmith or carpenter who works with his hands. These three scholars reached the conclusion that *zakat* should be paid on plant and equipment because they are productive and growing. Jurists in the past did not oblige *zakat* on the tools of craftsmen because these tools were very primitive, not much more than basic hand tools; production was in fact dependent upon the ability and skill of the craftsman himself.

On the other hand, today's plants and factories represent productive growing capital. Consequently, we conclude that craftsmen's tools which the owner uses personally are exempted from *zakat* because they are essential for his or her personal needs, but

1. *Halqat ad-Dirasat al-Ijtima'iyya lil-Jami'a al-'Arabiya*, third session, pp. 241-242.

plant and machinery are liable for *zakat*. No one can claim that by stating this we stand against the opinion of preceding jurists, since they never expressed an opinion on factories they never saw. If they had seen them, they would have given the same ruling, we are merely applying their standards and criteria to modern times.

Secondly, they discussed buildings designated for rental purposes and not the personal residence of the owner which are growing assets and not assets that satisfy essential personal needs of their owners. Accordingly, we divide residential houses into two categories, houses that are residences of their owners, which are *zakat*-free as stated by the jurists, and houses designated for renting. *Zakat* is due on those. In this manner we do not contradict the opinions of preceding jurists, who did not oblige *zakat* on houses, because they meant only houses occupied by owners. Rental housing was rare; it was the exception and not the rule. Today, rental housing is a well-known, profitable form of investment, which must be charged *zakat* as a growing asset, especially since *zakat* is imposed on similar assets, like agricultural land. Justice requires that these two similar kinds of assets be treated similarly.

It is fair to mention that Ahmad used to pay *zakat* on the income of a few shops he rented out, although that was his only source of income (see *Manaqib al-Imam Ahmad by Ibn Abi Ya'la*, p. 225). We have seen that the Prophet (p) imposed *zakat* on mobile assets at the rate of 5%, and we also find him imposing *zakat* on the income and not the principal of productive capital, because the principal is indivisible, so one must collect from its output. Then the rate of *zakat* on the output becomes one-tenth, or one-half of a tenth, in accordance with rates decreed by the Prophet (p) which distinguish between fixed and mobile assets. We conclude that productive assets of our time must also be subject to *zakat*, with the same distinction between fixed and mobile assets. On the mobile items, the rate of *zakat* must be 2.5%, while on the fixed, it should be 10% or 5% taken out of its income.

This means that *zakat* on rented buildings and fixed industrial assets is taken out of their income and not out of the principal at the rate of 10% or 5%. When it is possible to know the net income after deducting costs, as is the case in business corporations, *zakat* is calculated on the net income at the rate of 10%. The Prophet (p) took 10% from crops watered by rain or natural springs, as if he were taking it from the net product. When it is difficult to determine the net income, *zakat* is calculated at the rate of 5% of the profit.[1]

This is the opinion of these three great scholars, who spent their whole lives studying and teaching Islamic jurisprudence. Their opinion can only be described as the opinion of men of great experience, and I believe it is a correct *ijtihad*, based on sound analogy.

Discussion and consideration

The view of these three respected scholars is consistent with the second trend in charging *zakat* on the income of buildings and factories. The only difference is the rate applied. This opinion is most persuasive, since it is based on the sound analogy between the income of fixed assets and that of agricultural land. This is my considered view with the following remarks.

This opinion includes factories and buildings among assets on which *zakat* may be levied, without providing general criteria that can be applied to all similar productive capital. This present era witnesses other forms of profitable investment, such as cattle and poultry farms and transport rental firms. All these forms of invested capital are similar to factories and buildings, and should be treated like them, without distinction between the different forms invested capital may take. We have noted that the Prophet (p) collected *'ushr* from honey, which is the produce of bees, a mobile asset, unlike buildings.

Also, the similarity between rented houses and agricultural land is not free of dispute. The claim that there is no difference between an owner who gets income from his agricultural land and an owner who collects income from buildings is rejected on the grounds that *zakat* on agriculture is not based on ownership of the land, but on ownership of the crops themselves, which can occur even though the land is rented. The sound analogy must be between the owner of rented land who gets only its rent, and the owner of a rented

1. Ibid., pp. 249-250.

building who also obtains rent. Such an analogy must certainly be preceded by a discussion of *zakat* on rent of agricultural land, which was covered in earlier chapters, and the conclusion was that *zakat* must be paid on it.

Lastly, the analogy between buildings and agricultural land is not accepted, because agricultural land is a perpetual source of income that is not exhausted as years go by, while buildings have a certain number of years at the end of which they will be debilitated and possibly demolished. This difficulty in analogy can be overcome by accepting the exemption of capital depreciation used in today's taxation systems, whereby a certain amount is deducted every year from the income of fixed assets, with the purpose of accumulating a sufficient amount to acquire a new asset at the end of the old one's productive span.[1] With this consideration of depreciation or amortisation, the buildings and machinery that have a finite life span can become similar to agricultural land, whose life span is not finite in the same way.

Section Three: The *nisab* on buildings and similar assets

The three renowned professors do not discuss the issue of the *nisab* on the income of buildings and factories. How much should this *nisab* be? Is it like that of crops and fruits, i.e. five *wasqs*, or is it like the *nisab* of money? It seems that the *nisab* should be that of money, as long as the owners of buildings and factories receive their income or rent in monetary form.

The period in which the *nisab* condition is fulfilled

Since the flow of income is always time-related, the question of the time for the accumulation of income arises. Should we apply the *nisab* to the monthly, weekly or yearly income? It seems that the yearly interval is the most suitable period of time for the con-

1. *'Ilm al-Maliyya*, Rashid ad-Daqr, p. 238.

sideration of the *nisab*, especially since incomes of individuals and states, as well as rental procedures, are usually estimated and considered on a yearly basis. It is mentioned that some of the scholars who believe that earned income is liable for *zakat* when acquired also believe that if the yearly rent reaches *nisab*, *zakat* must be taken when rent is obtained.

Consequently, monthly earned rent and income will be treated like fruits that are collected periodically and then all the collections are added together, which is the opinion of the school of Ahmad. The author of *al-Mughni* says, "Fruits collected on several pickings are added together as long as they are of the same year's harvest, whether they all ripen together or not, and then the first harvest comes, the second growing of the same plants during the year must be added to the first, like in the case of palm trees that carry fruit twice a year. Both harvests are added together."[1]

Deduction of expenses and debts from income

My opinion is that *zakat* must be calculated on the basis of net income, after deducting expenses and costs such as wages, maintenance, taxes, debts, etc. It should be noted that expenses in agriculture and fruits are deductible, according to the opinion of 'Ata' and others. 'Ata' says, "Deduct your expenses and pay *zakat* on the remainder." This is also supported by Ibn al-'Arabi in his *Sharh at-Tirmidhi*.

Deduction of a minimum cost of living

Undoubtedly, there exist people whose only source of income is the rent from a house, the earnings from a small craft shop, or something similar. Such incomes may belong to an old retired person, a widow or orphaned children. Are these and similar owners whose only source of income is rent or output derived from fixed assets allowed a certain amount as a deduction for their cost of living? Or must *zakat* be calculated on the gross income?

---

1. *Al-Mughni*, vol. 2, p. 733.

It is obvious that an exemption of a minimum cost of living is consistent with the justice of Islam, so long as such a minimum is determined by experts who are righteous. *Zakat* must be calculated on the remainder only if it equals the *nisab*. This opinion is substantiated by two points:

- Jurists consider assets which are needed by owners to satisfy basic needs as exempt from *zakat*. They give the example of water for a thirsty person. A thirsty person can use soil to purify himself (*tayammum*), in spite of the presence of water, because as long as the water is needed to satisfy the thirst of the person, it cannot be counted.
- *Hadiths* mentioned earlier order the estimators of dates and grapes to make it easy on the owners. The Prophet (p) told them to "...discount one-third, and if you do not discount one-third, then discount one-fourth." This discount from the total quantity from which *zakat* is taken is a consideration for what they eat to fulfil their needs. It might even be easier and simpler in calculation to discount one-third or one-fourth of such income in compliance with the spirit of these *hadiths*.

Chapter Nine

Zakat on the Earnings of Labourers and Professionals

Salaries and wages are among the most important sources of income in the modern day. Earnings generally take the form of a professional's salary or a labourer's wages. This chapter deals with the *zakat* on these two forms of income, neither of which was common at the time of the great scholars who preceded us.

Section one: Jurists' opinions on the income from labour and professions

A contemporary opinion

The three later scholars we referred to previously, 'Abdu'r-Rahman Hasan, Muhammad Abu Zahra, and 'Abdu'l-Wahhab Khallaf, mentioned this matter in their lecture in Damascus in 1952, and reached the following conclusion:

> "Income from labour and the professions is subject to *zakat* if it reaches the *nisab* and one year passes. We note that Abu Hanifa, Abu Yusuf and ash-Shaybani believe that the *nisab* conditions must be satisfied at least in the beginning and the end of the year without reaching zero during the year. On the basis of this opinion, *zakat* can be imposed on income from labour on a yearly basis. Earnings from labour are amenable to *zakat* for the same reason other earnings are subject to *zakat*. The consideration of the *nisab* is also an essential factor, because *zakat* is imposed

on the rich and the *nisab* determines wealth. The Hanafi approach to the fulfilment of this condition at the two ends of the year is easy to satisfy."

Discussing the rate of *zakat* on different items, the three professors continue:

"We know of no case similar to that of *zakat* on income from labour and professions in existing jurisprudence. Perhaps the only exception is an opinion from Ahmad that rent, if it is acquired and reaches the *nisab*, is subject to *zakat* at the time of acquisition, regardless of the condition of the passage of a year. This, in fact, is similar to income from labour, and consequently the latter is liable for *zakat* if it reaches the *nisab*. This is in addition to what we remarked upon earlier, that professionals and workers are most likely to have the *nisab* at least at the beginning and end of the fiscal year."[1]

Wages and salaries are earned income

The conclusion of their analysis is that *zakat* on salaries applies only to the last month of the year, because they require the fulfilment of the condition of the *nisab* at the beginning of the year and at its end [i.e. they do not impose *zakat* on the flow of income itself during the year, but only consider its two ends.]

It is rather astonishing that they claim there is no similarity to the case of *zakat* on salaries in the writings of jurists except for rent, because the most similar case to earnings from labour is the well-known case of earned income, and I believe this similarity should be the foundation for imposing *zakat* on labour income. A group of Companions believed in the *zakat* on earned income. This included Ibn 'Abbas, Ibn Mas'ud and Mu'awiya. They are followed by a few jurists, such as as-Sadiq, al-Baqir, an-Nasir, and Da'ud. This opinion is also reported from 'Umar ibn 'Abdu'l-'Aziz, al-Hasan, az-Zuhri, and al-Awza'i. *Zakat* on earned income is dis-

1. *Halaqat ad-Dirasat al-Ijtima'iyya*, p. 348

cussed in several well-circulated books, including *al-Muhalla* (vol. 6, p. 83), *al-Mughni* (vol. 2, p. 6), *Nayl al-Awtar* (vol. 4, p. 148), *ar-Rawd an-Nadir* (vol. 2, p. 412) and *Subul as-Salam* (vol. 2, p. 129).

Analysis of the different views concerning earned income

It is extremely important to reach a strong ruling on this matter, because earned income is a major category of wealth in our time, including wages and salaries, professional fees, gains from invested capital, etc. Earned income may be merely an increase in a zakatable asset, such as profit from trade assets or increase in the number of cattle or sheep. These increments are added to the principal and become subject to *zakat* at the end of the fiscal year. On the other hand, earned income may be the acquired value of an asset, such as crops sold after *zakat* is paid on them. This earned income is not subject to *zakat* until one year elapses, in order to avoid duplication. Our discussion is restricted to earned income not covered by the two previous cases, such as wages and salaries, capital gains and dividends, gifts, etc., whether the earned income is of the same kind as its source or not.

For such forms of earned income, is the passage of one year necessary, or must earned income be added to similar already-owned assets, applying the year of that asset on newly earned increments? Or should earned income have *zakat* taken from it at the time of acquisition, provided that the necessary conditions such as *nisab*, non-existence of debts, and being in excess of essential needs, are met? In fact, each of these three propositions is taken by a few jurists, although it is commonly known among scholars that the passage of one year is a required condition on all funds liable to *zakat*, whether they are owned assets or earned income. This is based on the general terms of the *hadiths* on this matter, as understood by many jurists. Consequently, an analysis of these *hadiths* and their authenticity is indispensable when discussing this mattter.

Hadiths on the passage of one year are weak

The condition of the passage of one year is reported from four Companions: 'Ali, Ibn 'Umar, Anas and 'A'isha, but all these *hadiths* are in fact weak and cannot substantiate the point in hand.

The hadith from 'Ali is reported by Abu Dawud under the title, "*Zakat* on pastured livestock." Abu Dawud says, "Sulayman ibn Da'ud al-Mahri informed me that Ibn Wahb told him that Jarir ibn Hazim told him (and he named another) from Abu Ishaq, from 'Asim ibn Damura and al-Harith al-A'war from 'Ali that the Prophet (p) said, "And if you have two hundred dirhams and one year elapses on them, there is five dirhams obliged as *zakat*, and nothing is obliged on you in gold until you have twenty dinars. When you have twenty dinars, and a year elapses, there is half a dinar obliged as *zakat*. What is above that is proportional." The narrator adds, "I do not know whether 'Ali added 'proportional' or attributed it to the Prophet (p)." "And there is no *zakat* obliged on a fund until one year elapses." Jarir says that Ibn Wahb adds to the *hadith*, "And there is no passage of a year."

Critics of this *hadith* have the following to say:

- Ibn Hazm, followed by 'Abdu'l-Haqq in al-Ahkam, notes, "Abu Ishaq mentions 'Asim and al-Harith together in his narration, and al-Harith is a liar. It may pass unnoticed by many that al-Harith is the one who extends his narration to the Prophet (p), while 'Asim does not. Associating them together is incorrect. Shu'ba, Sufyan and Ma'mar narrate the same *hadith* from 'Asim from 'Ali, stopping there. This is also the way it is narrated by any trustworthy narrator. If it had been the narration of Jarir that extends the chain through 'Asim to the Prophet, the *hadith* would have been accepted."[1]

- In *at-Talkhis*, Ibn Hajar says that at-Tirmidhi reports this *hadith* from Abu 'Awana from Abu Ishaq from 'Asim from 'Ali, attributed to the Prophet (p).[2] I argue that the words of the *hadith* from Abu 'Awana do not include the passage of a year

1. *Al-Muhalla*, vol. 6, p. 3, and *Nasb ar-Raya*, vol. 2, pp. 328-329.
2. *At-Talkhis*, p. 182.

and so it cannot stand as evidence. At-Tirmidhi reports the following words: "On each forty dirhams, pay one dirham as *zakat*. Nothing is due on a hundred and ninety dirhams, but if it reaches two hundred dirhams, pay its due *zakat*, which is five dirhams."[1]

- 'Asim himself is not free of criticism. Al-Mundhiri, in *Mukhtasar*, says,[2] "Al-Harith and 'Asim are not accepted." Adh-Dhahabi says, "The four report his narration, Ibn Ma'in and Ibn al-Madini grade him trustworthy. Ahmad grades him higher than al-Harith, and to me he is accepted." An-Nasa'i says he is all right. On the other hand, Ibn 'Adi says he is singled in several *hadiths* from 'Ali; the problem comes from him. Ibn Hibban says, "He had a bad memory and made very bad errors. He often attributes the statement of 'Ali to the Prophet (p), and he deserves to be abandoned ... Anyhow he is better than al-Harith."[3] This supports the opinion of al-Mundhiri that he is not accepted.

- The *hadith* has a defect in its chain, referred to by Ibn Hajar in *at-Talkhis*.[4] He warns, "The *hadith* just mentioned from Abu Dawud has a defect discovered by Ibn al-Mawaq: Jarir did not hear from Abu Ishaq. Trustworthy disciples of Ibn Wahb, namely Sahnun, Harmala, Yunus and Bahr narrate it from Ibn Wahb from Jarir from al-Hasan ibn 'Umara from Abu Ishaq. It seems that Sulayman made the mistake of omitting the name of al-Hasan ibn 'Umara, who is agreed to be abandoned."[5] Ibn Hajar does not criticise the opinion of Ibn Mawaq, which indicates that he probably changed his opinion, mentioned earlier in *at-Talkhis* itself, that "...the *hadith* from 'Ali is all right as far as its chain is concerned; it is supported by other narrations, to the extent that makes it an acceptable evidence."[6]

---

1. *Sunan at-Tirmidhi*, part on *zakat*, Chapter "*Zakat* on gold and silver".
2. *Mukhtasar as-Sunan*, vol. 2, p. 191.
3. *Mizan al-I'tidal*, vol. 2, pp. 352-353, biography no. 4052.
4. *At-Talkhis*, op cit.
5. See his biography in *Mizan*, vol. 1, pp. 513-515, no. 1918.
6. *At-Talkhis*, p. 175.

In conclusion, this *hadith* is unacceptable as evidence. It is apparent that there are so many problems connected with it that I speculate that those who grade it good would have changed their opinion had they known these defects, especially the one mentioned by Ibn al-Mawaq, that is so substantiated by correct evidence as to be overwhelming in its effect on the acceptability of the *hadith*.

The *hadith* from Ibn 'Umar is, according to Ibn Hajar, reported by ad-Daraqutni and al-Bayhaqi. In its chain there is Isma'il ibn 'Ayyash, and his narration is weak when it comes from other than narrators in Syria. Ibn Numayr and Mu'tamir report it via 'Ubaydullah ibn 'Umar, from Nafi' as stopping at Ibn 'Umar. Ad-Daraqutni grades the narration that ends at Ibn 'Umar as correct.[1]

The *hadith* from Anas is reported by ad-Daraqutni. It had Hasan ibn Siyah in its chain and he is weak. He narrates alone from Thabit, as in *at-Talkhis*. Ibn Hibban says in *ad-Du'afa'*, "his narrations are very unacceptable. Whenever he is narrating alone, he cannot stand as acceptable."[2]

The *hadith* from 'A'isha is reported by Ibn Majah, ad-Daraqutni, al-Bayhaqi, and al-'Uqayli in *ad-Du'afa'*. Ibn Abi'r-Rijal, who is weak, is in its chain.[3] Ibn al-Qayyim says, "This *hadith* is reported from 'A'isha via a correct chain. Muhammad ibn 'Ubaydullah ibn al-Munada says that Abu Zayd Shuja' ibn al-Walid informed him … that 'A'isha said, 'I heard the Messenger of Allah (p) saying, "No *zakat* is obliged on any fund until one year elapses." Abu'l-Husayn ibn Bishran narrates it from 'Uthman ibn as-Samak from Ibn al-Munada."[4]

I wonder how Ibn al-Qayyim could grade this *hadith* as having a correct chain, since Shuja' ibn al-Walid is graded poor, not strong, and not accepted by Abu Hatim. Even more importantly, he narrates from Haritha, who is graded weak by ad-Daraqutni and al-'Uqayli. According to adh-Dhahabi: "Ahmad and Ibn Ma'in grade him weak, an-Nasa'i says he is abandoned, al-Bukhari says his narrations are disregarded, and no one accepts him as narrator." Ibn al-

1. Ibid.
2. *Nasb ar-Raya*, vol. 2, p. 330.
3. *At-Talkhis*, p. 175.
4. *Tahdhib Sunan Abi Dawud*, vol. 2, p. 189.

Madini says, "Our colleagues still grade him weak." And Ibn 'Adi says, "The bulk of what he narrated is disregarded."[1] This means grading him weak and abandoning his narrations are agreed upon. How then could a narration he alone gives be graded sound? Confusion caused by not mentioning the full name of his father may have caused this in the mind of Ibn al-Qayyim.

Hadith about earned income

At-Tirmidhi reports from 'Abdu'r-Rahman ibn Zayd ibn Aslam from his father from Ibn 'Umar that the Messenger of Allah (p) said, "He who earns income is not subject to *zakat* until a year elapses during which it remains in the possession of its owner." At-Tirmidhi also reports from Ayyub from Nafi' that Ibn 'Umar said, "He who earns income..." etc., without connecting it to the Prophet (p). At-Tirmidhi says that the last *hadith* is more correct than the *hadith* from 'Abdu'r-Rahman. Ayyub and 'Ubaydullah ibn 'Umar and others narrate from Nafi' from Ibn 'Umar the same *hadith* as being said by Ibn 'Umar. 'Abdu'r-Rahman is graded weak by Ahmad, Ibn al-Madini and others. He makes frequent mistakes.[2]

The narration of 'Abdu'r-Rahman is reported by ad-Daraqutni and al-Bayhaqi; al-Bayhaqi, Ibn al-Jawzi and others conclude that as a statement of Ibn 'Umar himself, the *hadith* is correct. Ad-Daraqutni mentions in the peculiarities of Malik, the same, and comments, "The saying is weak. The sound position is that its report via Malik is *mawquf* at Ibn 'Umar. Al-Bayhaqi reports statements of Abu Bakr, 'Ali, and 'A'isha similar to that of Ibn 'Umar and says that we can count on those of Abu Bakr, 'Uthman, Ibn 'Umar and others."[3]

This makes it clear that there is no authentic *hadith* going back to the Prophet (p) that supports the condition of the passage of a year especially regarding earned income, as is confirmed by al-Bayhaqi. Even if there were a sound *hadith* about the year, it would be applied to assets other than earned income, in order to reconcile

1. *Mizan*, vol. 1, pp. 445-446, biography no. 1659.
2. At-Tirmidhi, with commentary of Ibn al-'Arabi, vol. 3, pp. 125-126.
3. *As-Sunan al-Kubra*, vol. 4, p. 95, and *at-Talkhis*, p. 175.

the different texts. However, it is agreed upon that any item subject to *zakat* must not be charged with *zakat* again until one year has elapsed. In this sense, *zakat* is yearly. *Hadiths* that imply *zakat* is not imposed until one year elapses may be interpreted in this manner, as was explained in detail in Chapter One. Lastly, the fact that the Companions do not agree on this condition with regard to earned income implies that there was no sound text.

Differences among Companions and Followers regarding earned income

It is reported correctly from al-Qasim ibn Muhammad that Abu Bakr did not take *zakat* from any fund until one year had elapsed. 'Amra bint 'Abdu'r-Rahman narrates from 'A'isha, "No *zakat* is due until a year elapses," regarding earned income. 'Ali is reported to have said, "He who earns income is not obliged to pay *zakat* on it until one year has passed." A similar statement is reported from Ibn 'Umar.[1] On the other hand, Ibn Hazm quotes Ibn Abi Shayba and Malik in *al-Muwatta'* as saying, "It is correctly reported from Ibn 'Abbas that *zakat* is obliged on any income when acquired by any Muslim."[2] Ibn Mas'ud and Mu'awiya, both Companions, and 'Umar ibn 'Abdu'l-'Aziz, al-Hasan and az-Zuhri, Followers, are also reported to oblige *zakat* on earned income when acquired.[3]

It is known that when the Companions differ on an issue, the matter is rendered to other texts and to the general principles of Islam. No one may claim any *ijma'* on such a disputed matter.

Reports from Companions and Followers on this issue

Abu 'Ubayd reports from Ibn 'Abbas about a man who earns income, "He must pay its *zakat* the day he earns it."[4] Similar state-

1. Ibn Hazm reports these statements, *al-Muhalla*, vol. 5, p. 276.

2. *Al-Muhalla*, vol. 6, p. 83. Abu 'Ubayd reports the same in *al-Amwal*, pp. 413-414, and interprets it in a different, far-fetched way.

3. *Al-Muhalla*, vol. 6, p. 834-85. The narration from 'Umar and al-Hasan is slightly different.

4. *Al-Amwal*, p. 413, reported via two chains.

ments are reported by Ibn Abi Shayba.[1] The report is correct from Ibn Hazm. It obviously does not require the passage of one year for *zakat* to be obliged, as understood by most people from Ibn 'Abbas. Abu 'Ubayd disagrees, saying, "People understand that Ibn 'Abbas meant gold and silver, but I do not believe that. In my opinion, Ibn 'Abbas knows better than that, because such a view would put him in opposition to the majority of people. I assume he only meant agricultural produce, because people of Madina call lands "*mal*" (the word used in the *hadith* of Ibn 'Abbas), and there seems to be no other interpretation to his statement!"[2]

Abu 'Ubayd is undoubtedly a leading expert in financial affairs and has good insight into *zakat*, but I believe that his interpretation of Ibn 'Abbas' view is weak. It contradicts what immediately comes to mind and the understanding of most scholars. If it were simply related to agricultural produce, nothing would be new about this statement and it would not be worth being pointed out by many people as distinguishing Ibn 'Abbas. In principle, words must be taken to mean their apparent meaning, except when that becomes impossible. Is there anything in this statement that prevents us from taking the apparent meaning of *mal*? The reason cited by Abu 'Ubayd is not acceptable for the following reasons:

- Ibn 'Abbas is not alone in this opinion. Both Ibn Mas'ud and Mu'awiya agree with him, in addition to some Followers.
- A Companion who exerts efforts to find a *Shari'a* ruling is not required to wait for agreement or approval of other scholars to express his or her conviction.
- A Companion may even be alone in expressing certain opinions, and this is not unusual in the history of jurisprudence. The fact that Ibn 'Abbas was alone in expressing this opinion must not be an excuse to twist the apparent meaning of his words to make them consistent with the opinions of other Companions.
- We must note that Abu 'Ubayd is not certain about his interpretation, because he uses the words "I assume."

1. *Al-Musannaf*, vol. 3, p. 160.
2. *Al-Amwal*, p. 414.

Abu 'Ubayd also reports that Hubayra said, "'Abdullah ibn Mas'ud used to give us salaries in small bags and collect *zakat* from them."[1] Abu 'Ubayd also interprets this collection as related to *zakat* that was due on assets other than these salaries.

This interpretation seems to me to be very far-fetched. It contradicts the apparent meaning of the statement. Moreover, it is also in contradiction with sound reports from Ibn Mas'ud which provide the obvious explanation. Hubayra says, "Ibn Mas'ud used to collect *zakat* on salaries at the rate of twenty-five from each thousand," as reported by Ibn Abi Shayba[2] and at-Tabarani.[3] This explanation of the practice of Ibn Mas'ud is reported by Hubayra himself, but one may assume that Abu 'Ubayd did not hear of this second report."[4]

In *al-Muwatta'*, Malik reports from Ibn Shihab, "The first one who collected *zakat* from salaries was Mu'awiya ibn Abi Sufyan."[5] He probably means the first head of state, since Ibn Mas'ud collected it before him, or perhaps Ibn Shihab did not hear the report about Ibn Mas'ud. Mu'awiya, as head of the Islamic state, used to collect *zakat* from salaries in the state administration. Many Companions lived during the era of Mu'awiya, but none of them

1. Ibid., p. 412.

2. *Al-Musannaf*, vol. 3, p. 114.

3. The author of *Majma' az-Zawa'id*, vol. 3, p. 63, says its narrators are those of the *Sahih* books, except Hubayra, but he is trustworthy.

4. Perhaps what helped Abu 'Ubayd in his interpretation is another saying. Abu 'Ubayd says it is attributed to Sufyan from Khasif from Abu 'Ubayda that 'Abdullah said, "A person who earns income does not pay *zakat* until one year passes." But this hadith is weak for two reasons. Firstly, Abu 'Ubayd does not determine the connection between him and Sufyan; he only says it is attributed to Sufyan. And secondly, Khasif is accused of having a bad memory and many illusions, to the extent that his narrations are disturbed, and do not stand as evidence. The best that is said about him may be the statement of Ibn Hibban, "He was righteous, knowledgeable, also a good worshipper, but he makes many mistakes in what he narrates, and is singled out alone in narrations from famous men, while no one agrees with his narration. He is honest, but in fairness to him, he must only be accepted when his narrations coincide with those of the trustworthy and to be abandoned when they do not." See *Tahdhib at-Tahdhib*, vol. 3, pp. 143-144. In the case on hand, we notice that sound narrations from Ibn Mas'ud contradict that which is narrated by Khasif.

5. *Al-Muwatta'*, with *al-Muntaqa*, vol. 3, p. 95.

objected to his action, although Mu'awiya was the target of much criticism.

Around the end of the first century after Hijra, 'Umar ibn 'Abdu'l-'Aziz reconfirmed by his practice the collection of *zakat* from salaries and grants. Abu 'Ubayd reports that when 'Umar ibn 'Abdu'l-'Aziz paid anyone a salary, he collected *zakat* out of it. He also collected *zakat* on grants before they were delivered.[1] Ibn Abi Shayba also reports that 'Umar ibn 'Abdu'l-'Aziz used to collect *zakat* on salaries and prizes.[2]

Scholars among the Followers and others

The subjection of earned income to *zakat* is reported from az-Zuhri, al-Hasan and Makhul, as Ibn Hazm mentions. Some of these reports will be mentioned in the next section. The same is also reported from al-Awza'i. Even Ahmad is reported to have said similar things concerning rent on land. The author of *al-Mughni* says, "Ahmad and several others say that rent should have *zakat* taken from it when it is collected."[3]

The view of Al-Baqir, as-Sadiq, an-Nasir, the first three scholars among the descendants of the Prophet (p), and that of Da'ud, is that whoever earns the equivalent of the *nisab* must pay *zakat* immediately.[4] They argue that this is based on general texts which oblige *zakat* on money, such as the *hadith*, "There is 2.5% due on silver currency." (Agreed upon)

This removes the condition of the passage of one year, according to these scholars. The *nisab* need only be fulfilled at the end of the year, as was apparent from the practices of the Prophet (p) and his *zakat* collectors in taking *zakat* at the end of the year, without keeping records at the beginning of the year.[5]

1. *Al-Amwal*, p. 432.
2. *Al-Musannaf*, vol. 3, p. 85
3. *Al-Mughni*, vol. 2, p. 626 and vol. 3, p. 29 and 47.
4. *Ar-Rawd an-Nadir*, vol. 2, p. 241, and *Nayl al-Awtar*, vol. 4, p. 148.
5. *Ar-Rawd*, ibid.

Disagreement of the four schools about *zakat* on earned income

Ibn Hazm mentions that Abu Hanifa believes that earned income is not liable for *zakat* until a year has passed, except when the owner has assets of the same kind as the earned income, adding up to the amount of the *nisab* from the beginning of the year. In this case, the earned income is added to the assets in the calculation of *zakat*. Malik has a similar view on the requirement of the passage of a year regardless of the presence of assets of the same kind, except when it comes to livestock. If the owner of livestock has assets of the same kind of animal from the beginning of the year adding up to the amount of the *nisab* the total becomes liable for *zakat* at the end of the year. He also drops the condition of the *nisab* at the beginning of the year if earnings result from animal reproduction. Ash-Shafi'i says earned income needs the condition of the passage of a year for *zakat* to be taken in the case of calves, provided that their mothers reach the *nisab*.[1]

Ibn Hazm objects to all these opinions, describing them all as erroneous, and says, "Their differences are themselves evidence that they are not based on solid proofs. They are all empty claims not supported by the Qur'an, *Sunna*, *ijma'*, *qiyas*, or any rationality that can stand up to scrutiny." Ibn Hazm himself considers the condition of the year obligatory with regard to all items, whether assets or earned income, thus contradicting his colleague Da'ud, who does not require this condition regarding earned income.

Zakat on earned income at the time it is acquired outweighs other opinions

In view of the texts on *zakat*, its objectives, and the general interests of Islam and Muslims, I believe that *zakat* is due on earned income, whether salaries, wages, professional fees, or return on capital invested in other than trade, such as shipping, planes, and hotels, when received, without the requirement of the passage of one year. This opinion is substantiated by the following points:

1. *Al-Muhalla*, vol. 6, p. 84.

- The requirement of the passage of one year with respect to all funds, including earned income, is not based on any sound or good *hadith*, which is necessary in order to derive a ruling in *Shari'a*, or to restrict one of its general texts. All that exists are the opinions of some Companions.

- Companions and Followers did not agree on requiring the passage of one year on earned income. Some oblige *zakat* when earned income is received. When Companions and Followers differ, no one can claim that the view of some must be taken, and this issue must then be settled by other texts in accordance with the general principles of Islam. Allah says, *"If you have a dispute about something, refer it back to Allah and the Messenger."* (4:59)

- The lack of a text or *ijma'* allows for schools of jurisprudence to disagree on the issue of earned income to such a degree that Ibn Hazm accused them all of being mere claims, unfounded on correct texts from the Qur'an, *Sunna*, *ijma'*, analogy, or sound rationalisation. I myself have examined these differences as well as differences on the same issue inside each school of thought, and noted many unnecessary details and complications, so many that I do not believe it is at all likely that our easy-flowing *Shari'a*, which is addressed to all people, can accommodate such minute, complicated details, especially with regard to one of the essential pillars of Islam.

- The view that the passage of one year is not required with regard to earned income is in fact closer to the generality of the texts. Texts of the Qur'an and *Sunna* that oblige *zakat* are general and absolute, and do not mention a condition of the passage of a year, such as the *hadiths*, "Bring 2.5% of your *amwal*," and "On money, 2.5% is required." This is also supported by the general implication of the *ayat*, *"O you who believe! Give away some of the good things you have earned."* (2:267) Earning in the *ayat* is general and applies to trade, professions or employment. Jurists use this *ayat* to support the zakatibility of trade; why can we not use it to support the zakatability of earned income? When jurists require the passage of one year with regard to *zakat* on trade assets, it is only to allow for the principal to produce its earnings. The case of salaries is different. They are earned when they are received.

• Sound analogy also supports our view. Earned income is most similar to crops and fruits when harvested. If farmers, even those who have rented the land, are charged one-tenth or one-twentieth, why not charge employees and physicians one-fortieth of their earnings, especially since Allah associates earnings with the produce of land in the above-quoted *ayat* that continues *"...and of the fruits of the earth which we have produced for you."* Why should we treat differently things that Allah associates together, while both of them are of the same grace of Allah? It is true that the grace of Allah is more obvious in the produce of the earth, and consequently, gratitude for that is more stressed, but this is not sufficient grounds for exempting the other earnings from the obligation of *zakat*. The difference in applicable rates is sufficient reflection of the difference in the emphasis of thankfulness.

• The requirement of the passage of one year regarding earned income implies the exemption of many highly paid employees and professionals from the obligation of *zakat*. These may either expend all their earnings during the year, thus escaping totally any *zakat*, or save and invest part or all of their earning, [thus becoming amenable for *zakat* after one year]. This approach results in putting all the burden of *zakat* on moderate or thrifty income earners and exempting extravagant spenders. It is improbable that our wise and just *Shari'a* would make it difficult for the moderate spenders while making the burden of the extravagant spenders null.

• The requirement of the passage of one year on earned income ends up creating contradictions not acceptable to the justice of Islam. Take the example of a farmer who rents his land. He is required to pay ten per cent or five per cent if his total output reaches 653 kilos of grain, while the owner of the land is not required to pay any *zakat* on the incoming rent money. Such a contradiction cannot be reconciled except by applying *zakat* on earned income regardless of the passage of one year.

- The obligation of *zakat* on earned income is more beneficial to the poor and other deserving categories. This form of *zakat* may produce huge proceeds, especially since the cost of collection is minimal and convenient for the *zakat* payers, as *zakat* can be deducted at the source, as done by Ibn Mas'ud, Mu'awiya and 'Umar ibn 'Abdu'l-'Aziz. Ibn Abi Shayba reports from Hubayra, "Ibn Mas'ud used to deduct from salaries and periodical grants 25 out of each thousand." This is also reported by at-Tabarani. 'Awn ibn Muhammad says, "I saw the governors deducting *zakat* when they gave salaries and periodical grants."[1] 'Umar ibn 'Abdu'l-'Aziz is reported to have been deducting *zakat* from salaries and grants. Moreover, in *al-Muwatta'*, Malik reports from Ibn Shihab, "The first to take *zakat* from salaries was Mu'awiya ibn Abi Sufyan."[2]

- The obligation of *zakat* on earned income is consistent with the spirit of Islam in nourishing the values of brotherhood and caring. Allah describes believers as *"those who spend out of the provision We have given them,"* and commands, *"O you who believe, spend out of what We have provided for you."* The Prophet (p) obliged charity on Muslims out of their wealth and their earnings." Al-Bukhari reported from Abu Musa al-Ash'ari from the Prophet (p), "*Sadaqa* is obliged on every Muslim." His listeners asked, "O Prophet of Allah, what about the person who finds nothing to spend from?" He replied, "He must work with his hands, so he can benefit himself and give charity." "And if he cannot find a job?" they asked. He replied, "He must help the person who is desperate for help." They asked, "What if he cannot?" The Prophet (p) then answered, "He must do what is known as good and abstain from evil; this is a charity for him." (*Sahih* al-Bukhari)

The exemption of those renewable incomes from obligatory *zakat* for the excuse of the passage of one year allows many

1. *Musannaf Ibn Abi Shayba*, vol. 4, pp. 42-44.
2. *Al-Muntaqa*, with *al-Muwatta'*, vol. 2, p. 95.

people to earn, spend and enjoy without sharing in the needs of others and without assigning part for the sake of Allah.

- The elimination of the condition of the passage of a year with respect to earned income provides administrative convenience and procedural easiness in the calculation and collection of *zakat* for the *zakat* administration, as well as *zakat* payers. The condition of a year implies that payers and the administration must keep records of every segment of income earned in order to monitor its changes for one full year, which means that the payment of *zakat* shall be as frequent throughout the year as the frequency of the segments of income acquired. This is very cumbersome and difficult to pursue.

A contemporary view

At the end of this section, and in fairness to contemporary Muslim writers, it is imperative to mention the opinion of Shaykh Muhammad al-Ghazali, presented in his book, *al-Islam wa'l-Awda' al-Iqtisadiyya*, more than twenty years ago. After stating that *zakat* is either on the stock or capital – such as *zakat* on money and business assets – or on income – such as crops and fruits, he continues:

> "The conclusion is that whoever has an income equal to that of *zakat*-paying farmers must be subject to *zakat* on equal footing regardless of capital and related conditions. Consequently, physicians, lawyers, and other professionals and employees are subject to *zakat* on their income for the following two reasons:
>
> - Firstly, the general texts: The *ayat*, *"O you who believe! Give away some of the good things you have earned."* (2:267) There is no doubt that the income of those categories is included in good earnings referred to in the *ayat*. It is by this obligatory spending that they become integrated among believers described in the *ayat*, *'Those who believe in the Unseen and establish the prayer and give of what We have provided for them.'* (2:3)

- Secondly, it is beyond imagination to assume that Islam may impose *zakat* on a poor farmer who produces the *nisab* and exempt the owner of buildings that produce many times the income of the farmer, or a physician whose daily income may equal that of the farmer for one full year.

Accordingly, *zakat* must be obliged on all of them as long as they share the same reason for the conditions of *zakat*. This form of analogy does not accept hypocritical manipulation. A question may arise regarding the calculation of *zakat* and its rates. Its answer is found in the rules of *zakat* themselves. The rate on crops and fruits is one-tenth or one-twentieth, according to the efforts involved in irrigation. *Zakat* on income may likewise be related to efforts in earning. It is always possible to make details and refinements once that principle is agreed upon, although such an exercise must be done by a group of scholars."[1]

These are excellent words that reflect depth in understanding Islamic principles. The two substantiating arguments given by al-Ghazali are undoubtedly strong, but the approach I selected in this chapter in providing evidence from the practice of some Companions and Followers is more consistent with jurists' methodology. Even though our results may not have precedents in the four known schools of jurisprudence, we are not obliged to follow any of these schools.

Section Two: The *nisab* of earned income

Zakat is only imposed on the rich in order to realise the meaning of the excess or surplus, mentioned in the Qur'an as the subject of spending. *"They will ask you what they should give away. Say, 'Whatever is surplus to your needs.'"* (2:219) The Prophet (p) also says, "No *sadaqa* is obliged except out of wealth." All this requires

1. *al-Islam wa'l-Awda' al-Iqtisadiyya*, pp. 166-168.

the condition of the *nisab* for *zakat*. What should the *nisab* be in regard to earned income? Al-Ghazali, as quoted at the end of Section One, determined this *nisab* as the equivalent of the *nisab* of grains and fruits, but who can be sure whether or not this *nisab* was set for a special purpose related to agricultural products? Why not take the *nisab* of money, which is 200 dirhams of silver, 20 dinars of gold, or its equivalent, i.e. eighty-five grams of gold, especially since earned income is usually paid and calculated in monetary terms?

The time period for estimating *nisab*

Since we are talking about a flow of income, the question arises as to whether there is any time span through which income accumulates with regard to the amount of *nisab*, especially since earned income is paid at intervals, sometimes equal like salaries and other times unequal, like physicians' fees. There are two opinions on this matter.

The first is that each amount of earned income is considered alone when it is received. Monthly salaries, if they reach the *nisab* or more, are charged *zakat*, payments received at short intervals are not charged, except for the payment that is equal to the *nisab* or more. This opinion exempts small salaries and wages from *zakat*. It is consistent with the apparent meaning of the report about the practice of the Companions and Followers. But this means exemption of many highly paid professionals, such as physicians, who receive their income in small increments that add up to large amounts in one week and perhaps one day. Shall all these small amounts be exempted from *zakat* while a salaried employee whose monthly income is just above the *nisab* be liable for *zakat*? This explains the merits of the second opinion.

The second opinion is that increments of income and other earned funds must be added to each other as long as they are received at short intervals. We noticed earlier that when talking about minerals, jurists state that increments of an ore extracted at short intervals are added together in order to make the *nisab*. The same thing is applied by Hanbalis in the case of several crops of the harvest of the same year.[1] Consequently, the year must be considered at the time set for the calculation of *nisab* (i.e. earned income received during the same year is added together, and the *nisab* is considered on the basis of yearly income. In fact, a period of one year occurs in *zakat* studies on more than one occasion, like the condition of the passage of one year. It is useful at the end of this sub-section to mention some of the reports from the Salaf on how *zakat* is taken on earned income.

Az-Zuhri is reported to have stated, "If a person earns income and wants to spend it before the end of his fiscal year, he then must wait to pay *zakat* on the total at the end of his fiscal year."[2] Similarly, it is reported from al-Awza'i that money received from the sale of items on which *zakat* is not due, like a residential house or a slave, must have *zakat* taken from it when received, except when the payer has already established a fiscal year with respect to *zakat*, in which case the *zakat* of the acquired money can be postponed until the end of the year.[3]

Makhul is reported to have said that if a person has an established fiscal year, earned income that is spent before the end of this fiscal year is not charged *zakat*, but funds received in the months when *zakat* becomes due must be included in the calculation of *zakat*. When the person does not have an established *zakat* year, earned income must have *zakat* taken when it is received.[4]

It is clear that Makhul's opinion favours the payer who has an established fiscal year, which is awkward, because this privilege is given to the richer, who already own some wealth, while those who have no previous wealth are disadvantaged.

This is why I select the opinion of az-Zuhri and al-Awza'i with regard to earned income that reaches the *nisab*, and the opinion of Makhul for income not reaching *nisab*, received in the same month when *zakat* is due on other wealth owned by the person who received the income, observing, however, that income needed for personal and family expenses is exempt from *zakat*. And for the case when received income is less than the *nisab*, and the earner

1. *Sharh Ghayat al-Muntaha*, vol. 2, p. 59.
2. *Al-Musannaf*, Ibn Abi Shayba, vol. 2, p. 59.
3. *Al-Mughni*, vol. 2, p. 626.
4. *Al-Musannaf*, op cit.

does not have previous assets that *zakat* is due on, earned income must accumulate until it reaches the *nisab* and then *zakat* becomes due.

Zakat applies on net earned income

Zakat on earned income applies only to the net amount. Debts and a minimum standard of living for the income earner and his family are deductible, because they are among essential needs, and *zakat* is only obliged on a *nisab* that is above essential needs.[1] Business expenses, for professional and other income earners are also deductible, in accordance with the view I select with respect to farming, and palm trees that *zakat* is due on the remainder after payment of expenses. This is the opinion of 'Ata' and others.

After the above-mentioned deductions have been made if the remainder of salaries or other earned income reaches during the year an amount equal to the *nisab* of money then *zakat* is due on this amount. That exempts small earnings and wages.

It should be noted that if earned income is charged *zakat* when received, the next *zakat* is not required until one year elapses, since two amounts of *zakat* cannot be imposed in the same year. When a person has an established fiscal year with respect to his or her *zakat,* he or she may delay the payment of *zakat* on earned income until the end of that fiscal year. To give an example, a person earns income in the second month of his fiscal year and pays its *zakat* as he earns it. *Zakat* on the part saved from this earned income is not due at the end of the twelfth month of the fiscal year during which it is earned, but becomes due the next year on all assets then owned.

Section Three: *Zakat* rate on earned income

Al-Ghazali calls for collective research on the part of Muslim scholars to determine the applicable rate on earned income. My

1. See the condition of being above essential needs in Chapters One and Three.

personal opinion is to distinguish between earned income resulting from capital and labour together, and earned income resulting from labour alone.

Income that is earned as a return on capital or on capital and labour together should pay *zakat* of one-tenth of the net income, after deduction of all expenses, debts and allowance for essential needs. This is in analogy to agricultural produce grown without irrigation costs. It applies to returns from factories, buildings, printing facilities, hotels, renting cars, transportation businesses and the like. I mentioned earlier the opinion of Abu Zahra and his two colleagues that the rate of *zakat* on buildings and factories should be ten per cent of the net income, if expenses and costs are determined and deducted, or five per cent of gross income if expenses cannot be determined. This distinction is – in my opinion – acceptable. It is noted, however, that capital in this regard does not include trade goods discussed earlier in Chapter Four.

Income that results from labour alone, such as wages, salaries and professional fees has a rate of 2.5% only, in application of general texts that oblige a rate of 2.5% on money, whether it takes the form of assets or earned income. It is also in accordance with the Islamic principle of reducing the applicable rate in proportion to effort spent and with the practice of Ibn Mas'ud, Mu'awiya and 'Umar ibn 'Abdu'l-'Aziz. Analogy of salaries and professional fees with salaries paid by those leaders is much sounder than a claimed analogy with income generated by farming. On the other hand, income from farming may be closer to income from buildings and factories.

Lastly, this distinction means that income from labour is treated with consideration of effort spent, which reduces the rate as compared to income from capital. This is a principle also followed by contemporary taxation systems, in which it is considered just to charge higher rates on the return of capital than on employment income.[1]

---

1. *Mabadi' 'Ilm al-Maliyya al-'amma*, Dr. Muhammad Fu'ad Ibrahim, vol. 1, p. 284.

Chapter Ten

Zakat on Shares and Bonds

Stocks, shares and bonds are forms of financial assets that were not known in the past. Many taxation specialists call for imposing certain taxes on these assets or at least on their returns.[1]

Shares or stocks represent ownership of a certain part of the capital of a corporation. Bonds are certificates of loans borrowed by a corporation, government or municipality. A bond is usually paid back at a certain future point of time and the loan it represents carries interest. The basic difference between a share and a bond is that the first represents a contribution to the capital and carries profits or losses, while the second is only a borrowing instrument that carries predefined terms of interest and schedules of repayment. Usually, bond holders do not have any authority or control in the administration of the corporation concerned.

When issued, both shares and bonds may have a market value that is different from their face value. They are traded in exchange markets, like other commodities in their respective markets. Their prices go up and down according to different factors that affect their supply and demand, including the success of the corporation that issues them and the local and international economic and political situation.[2]

The issue, holding and circulation of shares – in their common form – is permissible in the *Shari'a*, except when the very activity of the issuing corporation is prohibited in Islam, such as breweries of alcoholic beverages or interest-based financial corporations. On the other hand, bonds are interest-bearing instruments, and interest is prohibited in Islam. But regardless of the lawfulness of holding bonds, they represent capital owned by people and their conditions

1. *Mawarid ad-Daula*, Sa'd Mahir Hamza, p. 180.
2. *Al-Mu'amalat al-Haditha wa Ahkhamuha*, pp. 68-69.

for *zakat* must be discussed. Two broad opinions are formulated among contemporary scholars on this issue.

The first opinion regarding *zakat* on shares and bonds

One view distinguishes between shares and bonds and deals with shares in accordance with the nature of the economic activity of the corporation whose capital they represent. Shaykh 'Abdu'r-Rahman 'Isa, in his book, *Al-Mu'amalat al-Haditha wa Ahkhamuha* (Modern Transactions and their *Shari'a* Rulings) presents this opinion:

> "Some people who own corporation shares may not know the *Shari'a* ruling on their zakatability, or may think that they are not zakatable. This is wrong. Others may think that *zakat* is obliged on all such shares, and this too is wrong. It is imperative to distinguish between shares by examining the the nature of economic activity of the corporation itself. The shares of purely industrial corporations that do not practise any trade activities, such as corporations dealing with refrigeration, hotels, advertising, public transport, shipping and airline industries, are not zakatable, since the capital of these corporations and the shares which represent it are invested in machinery, offices, and buildings, that *zakat* is not due on. But dividends distributed on these shares are added to the other assets of the shareholders and are subject to *zakat* at the end of the year, according to the rule of *zakat*.
>
> "Trading corporations that deal only with the purchase and sale of commodities, such as import/export dealers and retail trading, along with corporations that have a mixture of trading and industry, such as corporations that transform raw materials, extracted by the same corporation or purchased elsewhere, and sell their final products, are zakatable as far as their shares are concerned. Thus, the criteria for the zakatability of shares is whether the corporation is trading or not, no matter whether it is engaged in production

> or not. Shares are evaluated at their present value. A deduction is made for the percentage of capital used in buildings, machinery, and tools owned by these corporations. After deducting this percentage from the present value of the share, the residual is charged *zakat*. (pp. 73-73)

This opinion of Shaykh 'Isa is based on the well-known view that factories, machinery, buildings for exploitation and non-trading exploitable assets, are not subject to *zakat*, neither on capital and profit together as with trade assets, nor on profit alone, as with agricultural land. Because of that, he differentiates between industrial and trading corporations. This means that people who own different shares, even of the same value, may be charged *zakat* differently according to whether these shares happen to be of a trading or industrial corporation.

In Chapter Eight, the zakatability of buildings and factories was analysed, and it was concluded that there are three opinions in addition to the traditional one of non-*zakat*:

- Treating them like trade assets and estimating *zakat* at the rate of 2.5% on their total net value at the end of each year.
- Subjecting the return of factories and buildings to *zakat*, like money, on the basis of being earned income.
- Drawing an analogy with agricultural land and imposing *zakat* at ten or five per cent on their net return and profit.

In Chapter Three, I selected this last view as being the most appropriate. Here I must add that the distinction between trade and industry has no foundation, or evidence from Qur'an, *Sunna*, *ijma'* or sound analogy. There seems to be no sense in imposing *zakat* on the shares of trading corporations, while at the same time leaving exempt the shares of industrial corporations. Both kinds of shares are growing capital that earns annual renewable returns, which may in fact be higher in industries than trade.

If such a distinction is to be made, I suggest that we treat corporations like individuals, whereby *zakat* is imposed at the rate of ten per cent on the dividends of shares. While it is imposed at the rate of 2.5% on the market value of shares of corporations engaged mainly in industry and using most of their capital in fixed assets plus the profit of corporations most of whose capital is invested in actual trading, certainly after deducting the percentage invested in fixed assets, i.e. treating trading shares like we treat trade goods.

Zakat on bonds

Regarding bonds, Shaykh 'Isa continues, "Since bonds represent a loan made by companies or the government of definite amounts at definite interest rates, the holder of a bond is like the creditor of a deferred debt. At the due date, when it is paid, it must be charged *zakat* for only one year, if it remains in the holding of its owner for one year or more. This is the opinion of Malik and Abu Yusuf regarding such loans. Unless the bond is redeemed, or if it is not in a person's possession for at least a year, it is not subject to *zakat*.

It was shown earlier that the most acceptable opinion about debts which are expected to be repaid is that *zakat* is taken every year. This is the view of the majority, and the choice of Abu 'Ubayd and others, because such debts are like assets in hand. Accordingly, bonds being specific forms of debt that have legal assurances in addition to the interest they earn, must be liable for *zakat* every year. The fact that interest is prohibited is no reason for exempting these bonds from *zakat*, because a person who commits what is prohibited must not be given any privilege. It is known, for example, that jurists unanimously agree on subjecting prohibited jewellery to *zakat*, although they disagree on the *zakat* on lawful jewellery.

The second opinion

This opinion treats all shares and bonds alike, regardless of the economic activity of the issuing corporation. Professors Abu Zahra, 'Abdu'r-Rahman Hasan, and Khallaf believe that shares and bonds are used in exchange, like commodities, purchased and sold, usually at a market value that is different from its face value. They are thus like commodities that are purchased for resale at a profit. Like any other business goods, they have *zakat* taken.[1]

This means that *zakat* is calculated on shares and bonds on the dividends or interest, provided the total equals at least the *nisab*, or if added to other funds owned by the same holder, they make up at least the *nisab*. The rate is 2.5%, and deductions for essential needs or minimum cost of living is applied in the case where shares are the only source of income It seems to me that this opinion is more suitable to individual *zakat* payers, because it is simple and easy to know the market value and add earnings to it on all kinds of shares. This is as long as individuals are asked to make their own calculations, but if an Islamic state adopts the laws of *zakat*, it may be advisable to collect *zakat* directly from corporations, on the basis of the first opinion.

Zakat on corporations in addition to shareholders

If shares are treated like trade goods and subjected to *zakat*, is it lawful to impose *zakat* on the earnings of the corporations themselves, in addition to the *zakat* on the shareholders?

Professors Abu Zahra and his two colleagues consider that since shares are treated like commodities owned by shareholders, corporations are liable for *zakat* on their own activities, because their assets are growing assets invested in business and industry, while shares for those who trade shares and hold them are merely trade goods.[2] According to this opinion, the corporations should pay *zakat* on their earnings before distribution, and shareholders must also pay another *zakat* on their shares, including earned dividends.

1. *Halaqat ad-Dirasat al-Ijtima'iyya*, third session, p. 242. It is noted that the three professors treat stocks and bonds similarly, without the distinction made by Shaykh 'Isa. This unified treatment is, in my opinion, correct. One may object on the grounds that bonds represent debts and may change hands from one creditor to another, which makes them forbidden, according to many jurists. Their reply to this objection is to emphasise that bonds have become commodities which, if exempted from *zakat*, would encourage investors to hold more bonds. Exempting them from *zakat* is not a means to reduce undesired holdings and transactions. Moreover, it is not prohibited to spend unlawful earnings on charity when the original lawful source of that earning is not determined.

2. Ibid.

This means that *zakat* is taken from the shareholders once on the earnings of the company and once on their own assets and distributed profits. This kind of duplication in *zakat* is prevented in the *Shari'a*. I believe that only one of these two amounts of *zakat* must be applied in order to avoid such duplication.

It may be useful to give some examples from jurists' writings that can shed some light on this matter. In Chapter Two, we saw that *zakat* is obliged on pastured livestock unanimously, but that when livestock are obtained for trading purposes by livestock merchants, they are only subject to *zakat* either at the rate of livestock or at the rate of business goods. Ibn Qudama discusses the difference in treatment of this issue as follows:

> "Malik and the new opinion of ash-Shafi'i say that *zakat* on such livestock must be taken at the rate normally applied to livestock on the grounds that *zakat* on livestock is stronger, being unanimously agreed upon and mentioned by name in the *hadiths*. On the other hand, Abu Hanifa, ath-Thawri, and Ahmad say that *zakat* must be taken as from trade goods because this *zakat* gives more benefits to the *zakat* recipients in addition to being proportional. If the number of livestock held by the merchant reaches, in value, the *nisab* of trade goods but does not reach in number the *nisab* of livestock, *zakat* on trade goods applies indisputably.[1] ... but it is impossible to oblige the two kinds of *zakat* together, because this leads to duplication, which must be avoided in accordance with the *hadith* of the Prophet (p), 'No duplication in *sadaqa*.'"[2]

The author of *al-Mughni* gives another example: the case of palm trees on land purchased for resale, but whose land was farmed, or the trees harvested, before being resold. If the *zakat* year of business ends at the time of the harvest, and the value of the land and/or trees equals the *nisab*, then *zakat* on crops and fruits must be

1. *Al-Mughni*, vol. 3, pp. 34-35.
2. Reported by Abu 'Ubayd in *al-Amwal*. p. 275, and Ibn Abi Shayba, *al-Musannaf*, vol. 3, p.218.

paid at the rate of ten per cent or five per cent, and *zakat* on the land and trees must be paid at the rate of 2.5 %. This is according to Abu Hanifa and Abu Thawr. Al-Qadi and his Hanbali colleagues say that the land and crops must all have *zakat* taken at the rate of business assets because all are considered business stock. Ibn Qudama argues that the first opinion gives more proceeds and is thus better for the poor and claims that this case is different from the case of livestock as trade goods, since the rate of livestock is anyway below that on trade goods.[1]

One can reply that increasing the proceeds of *zakat* is not reason enough, since *zakat* aims at providing a just and bearable burden on payers as well. The justice of Islam is featured in applying the high rate of one-tenth when *zakat* is only on the return, while the *zakat* on the principal and return, should be paid at the rate of 2.5%, as in business assets. It is not known that two rates can be applied together on the same principal and on its return. It is imperative to select one of the two forms of *zakat* in order to avoid duplication or payment of more than one *zakat* in the same year.

The argument that in the above-mentioned examples there are two reasons for *zakat*, namely, trade and agriculture, is not valid, because only one of them was originally intended. The other came incidentally. This is taken by the author of *Sharh al-Ghaya*, a Hanbali, who says, "A person who owns the *nisab* of pastured livestock for the purpose of trading only is subject to *zakat* on trade goods alone, even if the year of the *nisab* of livestock ends before the *nisab* of business is reached, since the intention of holding trade goods removes the description as holding livestock."

By the same token, he argues that land held as inventory for trade is liable for *zakat* along with its crops or fruits at the rate of *zakat* as applied to trade goods, because crops and fruits are clearly an increase in the stock the owner had. But if the total does not reach 200 dirhams, while the fruit alone reaches their own *nisab*, or the livestock reaches its *nisab*, they must be subject to *zakat* applied on their own cases, so that *zakat* may not be waived at all.[2]

1. *Al-Mughni*, vol 3, pp. 35-36.
2. *Matalib Uli'n-Nuha*, vol. 2, pp. 100-101.

Ibn Hazm quotes al-Hasan ibn Hayy, "What is farmed for business is subject to *zakat* on business, and nothing else."[1] Al-Kasani says, "Our colleagues, the Hanafis, say *'ushri* or *kharaji* land purchased for trade is only subject to *'ushr* or *kharaj*, and *zakat* on trade may not be obliged at the same time as *kharaj* or *'ushr*." This is their well-known opinion. Muhammad is said to have obliged *'ushr* or *kharaj* along with *zakat* on trade, i.e. *zakat* of trade of the land, and *'ushr* on crops, assuming these are two different properties. The rationale behind this is that trade's *zakat* is obliged on the land while agriculture's *zakat* is obliged on the crops. This is so that two *zakats* are not charged on the same asset.[2]

I believe that only one of the two forms of *zakat* must be applied, and that it is not correct to allow duplication in *zakat* as is the common view of the Hanafis and others. As for which of the two forms of *zakat* should be selected, I think this should be left to the *zakat* administration or the *zakat* payer. Each of the two alternatives had its merits. We must recall that the bulk of Muslim jurists, perhaps all of them, do not approve of any duplication of *zakat* on the same asset, although in certain instances, we find some who disagree, such as the above-mentioned case of Muhammad ash-Shaybani.

1. *Al-Muhalla*, vol. 5, p. 249.
2. *Al-Bada'i'*, vol. 2, p. 57.

Part Four
The Distribution of *Zakat*

Prologue

Like prayer, the injunction of *zakat* as defined in the Qur'an is not elaborated upon in detail. The Qur'an does not give rates, *nisabs*, the kinds of wealth that are zakatable, or the conditions for *zakat*. The *Sunna*, or the words and actions of the Prophet, provides the details of *zakat*. As the second source of *Shari'a* after the Qur'an, knowledge of the *Sunna* is essential for any explanation of *zakat*. Allah says:

> *"And We have sent down the Reminder to you so that you can make clear to mankind what has been sent down to them so that perhaps they may reflect."* (16:44)

Abu Dawud reports that a man told the Companion, 'Imran ibn Husayn, "O Abu Nujayd, you tell *hadiths* that we do not find in the Qur'an." 'Imran was upset and told the man, "Do you find, 'On each forty dirhams, one dirham is obliged; on such-and-such an amount of sheep, one sheep is obliged, and on such-and-such an amount of camels, so much is obliged?' Do you find all this in the Qur'an?' The man replied, "No." Then 'Imran asked, "Where do you get these from? You took them from us and we got them from the Prophet (p). He mentioned this along with similar matters.[1]

Zakat distribution as defined by the Qur'an

Although the collection of *zakat* is discussed in the Qur'an as a general concept, where it can be spent is specifically mentioned in the Qur'an; it was not left to rulers or those with personal opinions to decide according to their whims. At the time of the Messenger, some greedy individuals tried to take some proceeds of *zakat*, but when the Prophet did not yield to their attempts, they criticised

1. Al-Mundhiri, *Mukhtasar Sunan Abi Dawud*, vol. 2, p. 174.

and censured the Prophet to such an extent that Allah sent verses deploring their greed and uncovering their hypocrisy. Those same verses go on to name the categories of those who deserve *zakat*:

> *"Among them there are some who find fault with you concerning the collected* sadaqa*. If they are given some of it, they are pleased but if they are not given any, they are angry. If only they had been pleased with what Allah and His Messenger gave them and had said, 'Allah is enough for us. Allah will give us of His bounty as will His Messenger. It is to Allah that we make our plea.' Collected* sadaqa *is for: the poor, the destitute, those who collect it, reconciling people's hearts, freeing slaves, those in debt, spending in the way of Allah, and travellers. An obligation imposed by Allah. Allah is All-Knowing, All-Wise."* (9:58-60)

Abu Dawud reports from Ziyad ibn al-Harith as-Suda'i, "I came to the Messenger of Allah and gave him my pledge." The narrator recounts a long story and then adds, "A man came to the Prophet and said, 'Give me some of the proceeds of the *sadaqa*.' The Messenger of Allah said, 'Allah does not leave the distribution of the *sadaqa* to a Prophet or anyone else. He Himself ordains the distribution to eight categories. If you are in any of these categories, I will give you what you deserve."[1]

The significance of *zakat* distribution details in the Qur'an

Economists and sociologists note that in taxation systems, the determination of the usage of proceeds is more important than the collection of funds, because governments usually have sufficient means to collect taxes efficiently and justly. It is in the usage of these funds that misconduct occurs most often. It is essential that the proceeds of *zakat* be distributed and not kept in the state treasury as was done before Islam by emperors and kings with the levies they imposed on their subjects. History tells us that in most

1. The chain contains 'Abdu'r-Rahman ibn Ziyad ibn An'am al-Ifriqi. More than one scholar criticises him. See al-Mundhiri, op. cit., vol. 2, p. 230.

cases, taxes were imposed on the weak and poor to be spent on luxury by kings and lords.

With the emergence of Islam, *zakat* was imposed as a relief for the poor and the weak, but it was necessary that the words of Allah Himself specify the deserving categories.

Chapter One

The Poor and the Needy

The poor and the needy are the first two categories of people deserving of *zakat* mentioned in *Surat at-Tawba*, which highlights the fact that the primary aim of *zakat* is to eliminate poverty and destitution from society. This purpose of *zakat*, being the most important, is mentioned alone in some *hadiths*, such as the *hadith* narrated by Mu'adh, when the Prophet sent him to Yemen, "Inform them that Allah has prescribed on them *sadaqa*, taken from the rich among them and rendered to the poor among them."

Definitions of the "poor" and "needy"

Abu Yusuf, the disciple of Abu Hanifa, and Ibn al-Qasim, the disciple of Malik, believe that the poor and needy are to be considered as one category.[1] The majority of scholars disagree. In fact, the poor and needy are two subsets of one category. Jurists and commentators on the Qur'an differ as to the specific meaning of "the poor" (*faqir*) and "the needy" (*miskin*), especially when the two words are mentioned together. Many scholars argue that these two words are interrelated, so that if one of them is mentioned, it includes both, but when they are mentioned together in one statement, they carry slightly different meanings. In the verse, "*Sadaqa* is only for ..." the two words appear together.

At-Tabari takes the view that the word "poor" refers to the person who is in need, but is also modest enough not to beg,[2] while the needy is the person who is in need but humbles himself in begging. He argues that the word "need" has this connotation, as in the verse regarding the Jews, *"Abasement and destitution were*

1. *Hashiyat ad-Dusuqi*, vol. 1, p. 492, and *Sharh al-Azhar*, vol. 1, p. 509.
2. *Tafsir at-Tabari*, vol. 14, pp. 308-309.

stamped upon them." (2:61) The sound *hadith*, "A needy person is not one who is satisfied with a date or two ... but the person who is modest," is not a linguistic explanation of the word "needy", but rather an assertion by the Prophet concerning modesty. This is similar in style to the *hadith*, "The strong is not the one who conquers others in wrestling, but the one who controls himself when he is angry."[1] Commenting on the *hadith* regarding the needy, al-Khattabi rightly argues that "the needy person is someone who goes around begging, since the Prophet brought the attention of his audience to the fact that beggars' needs may be satisfied by what they receive, while a person who is in need but does not beg may be forgotten, so his or her need passes unsatisfied."[2]

Jurists also differ as to whose state is worse, the poor or the needy. Shafi'is and Hanbalis believe the status of the poor is worse, while Malikis and Hanafis believe the circumstances of the needy is direr. They all provide semantic arguments to support their views. But while determining that differences in the meaning of "poor" and "needy" may remain unresolved, this is ultimately irrelevant to the analysis of *zakat*.[3]

Hanafis define the poor as a person whose property is either below the *nisab* or used for basic needs like shelter and clothing.

---

1. The *hadith* is agreed upon as narrated by Abu Hurayra. See *Bulugh al-Maram*, p. 302. See also *al-Mughni*, vol. 6, p. 457.

2. *Ma'alim as-Sunan*, vol. 2, p. 232.

3. The orientalist Joseph Schacht stoops to cheap slurs in the *Encyclopaedia of Islam* when he discusses the difference between the poor and the needy. He writes. "The difference usually stated between the poor and the needy is merely arbitrary. Anyhow, Muslim scholars are accustomed to interpret definitions in such a way that they themselves are included in one of these two categories." Scholars like as-Sarakhsi, Ibn al-'Arabi. an-Nawawi, Ibn Qudama, Ibn Hazm, and other jurists who discuss these definitions obviously had no ambition to receive payments of *zakat*. All these scholars were rich and known donors to charity, in addition to their renowned modesty of living. This is plain to all who study their biographies. As for Schacht's claim that the difference in definitions is always arbitrary, this can only be a result of his ignorance of the Arabic language, since it is known to scholars of Arabic that if two terms are linked by an additive article in the same context, there must be a difference between them, although we know that the semantic difference in definition is immaterial here because both poor and needy persons are included among the recipients of *zakat*.

The needy is a person who owns nothing. According one deserving of *zakat* in this category, whether poor of needy, may be:

- A deprived individual who owns nothing.
- A person who has shelter, furniture, clothing (regardless of value), but not in sufficient quantity to satisfy his basic needs.
- A person who has less than the *nisab* of money.
- A person who has less than the *nisab* of resources other than money, such as camels, provided the value of his or her property is less than two hundred dirhams.[1]

According to the other three major schools of jurisprudence, the poor and needy are not defined with regard to the *nisab*, but according to satisfaction of essential needs. A poor person is one whose wealth and income are far from satisfying his or her essential needs while a needy person is one whose wealth and income fall short of satisfying essential needs. According to this criteria, one who deserves *zakat* as a poor or needy person may be:

- A person who has no property or income at all.
- A person whose wealth and income only partially satisfy his/her essential needs.
- A person whose wealth and income satisfy more than half of his essential needs but still fall short of fulfilment of those needs.

As for satisfaction of needs, Malikis and Hanbalis consider a one year period for such satisfaction, while Shafi'is look to the expected life of the person. Shams ad-din ar-Ramli argues that by taking the rest of the expected life of the poor or needy person, one may not expand the category of those deserving *zakat* to include the rich, because a person who owns some property that yields a return sufficient to satisfy essential needs cannot be categorised as poor or needy.[2] If poor or needy people own an adequate residence in

1. *Majma' al-Anhur*, printed with *Durr al-Muntaqa*, pp. 220 and 223.
2. *Nihayat al-Muhtaj*, vol. 6, pp. 151-153.

which they live,[1] but their income is not sufficient to cover their essential needs, they are not required to sell this residence before being entitled to receive *zakat*.

Furthermore, someone who owns property which he rents out but whose rent is below that required for satisfying his needs, is also considered poor or needy, except when the property is high in value and it can be substituted by another, the income from which would be sufficient. In this case, the person is required to sell it. The same may be said of adequate clothing, women's jewellery, books, and tools for craftsmen. Moreover, property not under the control of the owner which the owner cannot use to reduce the level of his poverty is not counted either, such as property in another country, or that under legal obstacles that prevent the owner from using it.[2]

Contrasting the poor and needy with the rich

It may be necessary to look at the definition of wealth as given by jurists, since by doing that we may be able to determine the exact boundary of the poor and needy category. *Zakat* must not be given to the rich. The Prophet said, *"... to be taken from the rich and rendered to the poor,"* and "Sadaqa *is not lawful for the rich."* (Abu Dawud and at-Tirmidhi) Giving the rich *zakat* means that some poor person is being deprived of it, which violates the objectives of *zakat*, as stated by Ibn Qudama.[3] By knowing who the rich are, we can define the poor and needy by contrast.

Here again jurists are not unanimous in their opinion. According to Sufyan, Ibn al-Mubarak and Ishaq ibn Rahawayh,[4] the amount of wealth that excludes a person from being a *zakat* recipient is fifty dirhams, a quarter of the *nisab* of money.[5] Ibn

1. Shafi'i jurists do not agree on the case of a person who is accustomed to live in rented residences and has at the same time the value of a residence, whether this person should be treated as poor or not. Ar-Ramli, in *Nihayat al-Muhtaj*, considers such a person poor while others do not. See *Hashiyat ash-Shabramallisi* on *Nihayat al-Muhtaj*, vol. 6, p. 150.

2. Ibid., pp. 150-151.

3. *Al-Mughni*, vol. 2, p. 523.

4. *Ma'alim as-Sunan*, vol. 2, p. 226.

5. One may add a second level of wealth, that is wealth that makes begging

Mas'ud narrates, "The Messenger of Allah said, 'If a person asks when he had enough to make him wealthy, whatever he receives will appear on the Day of Judgement as cuts on his face.' The Prophet was asked, 'What is wealth?' He replied, 'Fifty dirhams or its equivalent value in gold.'" Ahmad is reported to share this definition only if the property is in monetary terms, but *hadith* scholars grade this *hadith* from Ibn Mas'ud as weak.[1]

Even if it were correct, the *hadith* does not determine what constitutes eligibility for receiving *zakat*; all it indicates is the prohibition of begging or asking for charity if someone possesses fifty dirhams.[2] Some scholars argue that fifty dirhams was sufficient for the satisfaction of essential needs at the time of the Prophet and yet others interpret the *hadith* as being addressed to specific individuals for whom fifty dirhams was sufficient. Supporting the first interpretation, al-Khattabi says, "There is nothing in the *hadith* to indicate that a person who has fifty dirhams is not eligible for *zakat*. This *hadith* shows it is hateful to beg for alms, since begging may only be allowed at times of urgency, and this does not apply to anyone who has fifty dirhams.[3]

Hanafis describe a rich person as someone who has the *nisab* of any item on which *zakat* may be taken, be it camels, money or any other commodity. Their argument is based on the premise that a person who owns the *nisab* is liable for *zakat*, and such a person is considered rich because *zakat* is only taken from the rich so that anyone who owns the *nisab* cannot be described as poor. They also present a *hadith*, "He who begs while having enough to make him rich is asking people with impunity." The Prophet was asked, "What makes him rich?" and replied, "Two hundred dirhams." This *hadith*, however, is weak. Additionally, it does not concern eligibility for *zakat*, but the prohibition against begging.[4]

---

prohibited. This level of wealth is below what makes taking *zakat* prohibited, because begging is not allowed except in dire necessity.

1. Reported by Abu Dawud, an-Nasa'i, Ibn Majah and at-Tirmidhi. The latter grades it good, while others grade it weak. See *Mukhtasar as-Sunan*, al-Mundhiri, vol. 2, pp. 221-222.

2. *Al-Insaf*, a book of Hanbali *fiqh*, vol. 2, pp. 221-222.

3. *Ma'alim as-Sunan*, vol. 2, p. 226.

4. *Radd al-Muhtar*, vol. 2, pp. 880-89, and *Majma' al-Anhur*, p. 223.

Hanafis add that a person who owns items on which *zakat* cannot be taken which are in excess of a person's needs must be described as rich if the value of the surplus is two hundred dirhams or more, on the grounds that items not subject to *zakat* that are used for the satisfaction of essential needs like food, shelter and clothing are not considered when defining wealth, even if their total value is substantial. Al-Hasan al-Basri is reported to have said, "They [the Companions] used to give *zakat* to people who owned ten thousand dirhams worth of mares, personal arms, slaves and residence. Items such as these are used to satisfy essential needs.[1] In *al-Fatawa*, a person who owns houses and shops, whose rent is not sufficient for his or her needs, is also eligible for *zakat*.

According to Muhammad ash-Shaybani, such a person is poor and eligible to receive *zakat*, while Abu Yusuf disagrees. As for a person who has two hundred dirhams worth of food, it is argued that if this quantity is sufficient for only a month, the person is eligible for *zakat*, but if it is sufficient for a year, some say that the person is not eligible, whereas others argue that they are on the basis that the Prophet (p) used to save for his wives sufficient food for a year. Winter garments, not needed in the summer, are not counted when defining wealth. According to *at-Tatar Khaniya*, from *al-Mughra*, a person who owns a residence larger than his needs, so that he only uses part of it, is also eligible for *zakat*, whereas, according to Abu Hanifa and Abu Yusuf, such an individual is not eligible. Ibn 'Abidin gives the example of a woman who owns jewellery that she uses which is more than the *nisab*, and argues that she is not liable for *zakat* if jewellery is included as an essential need. He quotes from *at-Tatar Khaniya* that such a woman is liable for *zakat* according to al-Hasan ibn 'Ali, and comments that this depends on whether jewellery is counted among essential needs or not.[2]

Lastly, Malik, Ahmad in the more acceptable narration from him, and ash-Shafi'i define wealth as enough for the satisfaction of a person's essential needs, regardless of property and income. A person whose essential needs are satisfied is rich and not eligible for

1. *Bada'i' as-Sana'i'*, al-Kashani, vol. 2, p.48.
2. *Radd al-Muhtar*, op. cit.

zakat. A person whose essential needs are not fully satisfied, whether he or she has the *nisab* or more of money or other items, is eligible. Al-Khattabi quotes Malik and ash-Shafi'i as saying that the specific, objective definition of wealth depends on the particular circumstances, needs and available means of satisfying them. Ash-Shafi'i says, "Judging by money alone is not fair, because a person may be considered rich, when, in fact, his or her wealth and earnings are below what is needed for his personal and family expenses."[1]

This last definition of wealth seems to be supported by the texts and spirit of the *Shari'a*, as well as by the linguistic use of the word 'rich':

- The Prophet is reported to have told Qabisa ibn al-Mukhariq, who asked for help in a financial responsibility that he took upon himself (for the reconciliation of the two parties), "Asking [for financial help] is not permissible, except for one of three people a person who is impoverished is allowed to ask until he or she obtains sufficient sustenance...",[2] thus determining the criteria as sufficient sustenance.

- Being in need constitutes poverty; wealth is the opposite. Thus anyone who is in need is poor and anyone who can sustain himself or herself is not poor. Allah says, *"O people, it is you who are poor and in need of Allah."* An ancient poet exclaims, "And I am poor of her good doing," meaning in need of it.

So someone who has the means to satisfy his needs, whether subject to *zakat* or not, or income and earnings, is not eligible to receive *zakat*. Family needs are included. Consequently, waged or salaried individuals are not eligible as long as their periodical earning are sufficient to satisfy their essential needs, even though they may not own any *nisab* as a stock of wealth. But on the other hand someone who owns the *nisab* of one or more zakatable items may be considered poor and eligible for *zakat* if the property they own is not sufficient to fulfil their needs. Accordingly, someone who

1. *Ma'alim as-Sunan*, vol. 2, p. 227.

2. Reported by Muslim, Abu Dawud, and an-Nasa'i. See *Mukhtasar Sunan Abi Dawud*, vol. 2, saying no. 1575.

owns trade goods worth a thousand dinars or more, but whose income is below the amount needed to satisfy their needs – because of a slump in the market or because of a big family – is eligible to receive *zakat*.

The same applies to other zakatable items on which *zakat* is due. So being a recipient of *zakat* does not necessarily preclude a person from being subject to *zakat* at the same time, since the level of wealth that makes *zakat* obligatory is defined by owning the *nisab*, along with other known conditions, while wealth that prevents receiving *zakat* is defined by the satisfaction of essential needs.[1] Ahmad says that someone who owns real estate or a farm, whose income is ten thousand dirhams or more, is eligible for *zakat* if that income does not satisfy their essential needs.[2]

The poor who are capable of earning

A person who chooses to be idle and to live at the expense of society through charity and financial help, despite being strong enough to and capable of working and earning, is not eligible for *zakat* according to Shafi'i and Hanbali scholars, who say *zakat* must not be expended under the category of poor and needy to a rich person or a person capable of working at a job whose income would be adequate for personal and family needs.[3] In my opinion, this view is supported by the texts and principles of the *Shari'a*, to the extent that some Hanafis, who permit giving *zakat* to the poor person capable of earning, say it is not good for such a person to take *zakat*, i.e. although paying him is permissible, it is not correct on his part to receive *zakat*. The majority of Hanafis maintain that receiving *zakat* is not prohibited in this case but it is undesirable.[4] Some Malikis support the Shafi'is and Hanbalis in their view.[5]

In principle, Islam obliges each capable man to work. Jobs and economic opportunities should be provided for people to work and

1. *Sharh Ghayat al-Muntaha*, vol. 2, p. 135.
2. *Al-Mughni*, vol. 2, p. 664.
3. Al-*Majmu'*, vol. 6, p. 228.
4. *Majma' al-Anhur*, p. 220.
5. The author of *Hashiyat ad-Dusuqi*, vol. 1, p. 1494, attributes it to Yahya ibn 'Umar.

earn their sufficiency. The Prophet says, "No person could eat food better than that earned by his own hand's work."[1] It is not permitted for a person who finds a job within his ability that would give him sufficient income to refuse it and live on charity or begging. In one of his *hadiths*, the Messenger of Allah states frankly, "*Sadaqa* is not lawful to a rich person or a capable and not handicapped person."[2]

At-Tabari reports from Zuhayr al-'Amiri that he met 'Abdullah ibn 'Amr ibn al-'As and asked him to whom *zakat* belongs. 'Abdullah replied, "It is for the lame, the blind, and every handicapped or disabled person." Zuhayr asked, "Is there not a right on the part of administrators of *zakat* and fighters for the sake of Allah?" 'Abdullah said, "Fighters and administrators are permitted by Allah inasmuch as their work deserves it," and continued, "*Sadaqa* is not lawful to the rich or to strong people who are not handicapped."[3] This last sentence of 'Abdullah is reported to have been attributed to the Prophet by 'Abdullah himself and several other Companions.[4]

Physical power and ability alone is not sufficient because what matters is earning sufficient income. An-Nawawi says, "If a capable person cannot find employment, *zakat* is lawful for him because he is unable to earn.[5] In another *hadith*, the Prophet adds further explanation. 'Ubaydullah ibn 'Adi ibn al-Khiyar narrates that two men told him they went to the Prophet and asked for some *zakat*. The Prophet looked at them thoroughly and found them strong and said, "If you wish, I will give you, but the rich and the strong who earn have no share in it [*zakat*]."[6] The Prophet gave them the

1. Reported by al-Bukhari and others. See ar-*Targhib wa't-Tarhib* of al-Mundhiri, vol. 2, beginning of chapter on sales contracts.

2. Reported by the five. At-Tirmidhi grades it good.

3. Commentary on at-Tabari, edited by Mahmud Shakir, vol. 14, p. 231.

4. Extended to the Prophet by Abu Hurayra, Hubshi ibn Junada, Jabir, Talha, 'Abdu'r-Rahman ibn Abi Bakr, and Ibn 'Umar. See *Nasb ar-Raya*, vol. 2, pp. 399-401, and *Musannaf* Ibn Abi Shayba, vol. 3, pp. 207-208.

5. *Al-Majmu'*, vol. 6, p. 191

6. Reported by Ahmad, Abu Dawud, and an-Nasa'i. Ahmad comments, "What a good saying it is?" An-Nawawi says, "This hadith is correct." See *al-Majmu'*, vol. 6, p. 189. Abu Dawud and al-Mundhiri make no comment. See *Mukhtasar as-Sunan*, vol. 2, p. 233.

choice because he did not know the truth of their circumstances. They appeared to be strong and capable, but they may not have been able to find jobs that would give them income for at least sufficient subsistence. This *hadith* is used by scholars to show that officers of *zakat* are required to advise the potential *zakat* recipient, whose real circumstances are not evident, that *zakat* is not lawful for the rich or the strong who can earn sufficient income.[1]

It is noted that sufficiency of earning is what matters and not only having an income, since absolute inability is not a condition for receiving *zakat*.[2] According to an-Nawawi, what matters is an occupation that suits the person who is able but insists on remaining idle, in spite of the availability of suitable jobs.

In summary, a capable person must satisfy the following conditions in order to be prevented from receiving *zakat*:

- The existence of available employment which is lawful according to *Shari'a*.
- The employment being within the person's ability.
- The employment being suitable for the person, his social status, and physical and spiritual ability.
- The employment earning him sufficient income for his personal and family needs.

This implies that every capable person is required to find employment which gives him an income sufficient to satisfy his needs. Society at large, and the state specifically, are required to help such a person find a job. A person who is incapable of earning – because of a disability such as age, sickness or handicap, or because of lack of job opportunities – and all those whose incomes are not sufficient to satisfy their needs, are eligible to receive *zakat*. This is the justice and mercy of Islam. One must compare it with unjust and unmerciful principles of materialist thinkers who say, "No food for anyone who does not earn."

1. *Nayl al-Awtar*, vol. 4, p. 170.
2. *Al-Majmu'*, vol. 6, p. 190.

Individuals totally devoted to worship are not eligible for *zakat*

One of the admirable rulings recorded by Muslim jurists is that people who are able to earn their own livelihoods but spend all their time worshipping, praying, fasting, etc., without having an income or resources of their own, are not eligible to receive *zakat*, because the reward of worship is confined to the worshipper,[1] and because they are commanded in the Qur'an to work and to travel the earth in search of sustenance. Islam does not recognise asceticism or monasticism. Working to earn sufficiency of sustenance is a high-ranking form of worship, provided it is performed with good intention and commitment to the limits imposed by Allah.

Full-time students are eligible for *zakat*

Devoting all one's time to acquiring a useful branch of knowledge does not preclude a person's eligibility to receive *zakat*. Such a person may be given *zakat* in order to help him or her achieve that purpose, including the cost of necessary books, regardless of whether the knowledge sought is secular or religious. Seeking knowledge is a social obligation that some members of society must undertake. The benefit of this knowledge extends to society as a whole and *zakat* is due to two kinds of persons - those in need of relief and those needed by Muslim society.

Some jurists add the condition that a student, if he or she is able to earn, must be outstanding in order to be eligible for *zakat*.[2] This is usually practised by governments today when they offer scholarships.

The modest poor take precedence in receiving *zakat*

It must be stressed that the people who deserve *zakat* most are not beggars, especially since many of them adopt begging as a pro-

1. *Ar-Rawda*, an-Nawawi, vol. 2, p. 309, and *al-Majma'*, vol. 6, p. 191.

2. Ibid., *Sharh Ghayat al-Muntaha*, vol. 2, p. 127, and *Hashiyat ar-Rawd al-Murbi'*, vol. 1, p. 400.

fession, but rather those whose modesty prevents them from asking for help. The Prophet (p) emphasises that "A needy person is one who is modest. Read, if you like, '*They do not ask people insistently.*'" (2:273) The *ayat* describes the poor *Muhajirun* who were serving Islam and did not have sufficient resources to satisfy their essential needs, but did not ask people or beg for help, out of modesty.[1] Such people deserve the help of *zakat* more, as the Messenger of Allah (p) indicated. In another version of the same *hadith*, the Prophet (p) says, "The needy person is not one who goes around begging from people, who can be satisfied by a bite or two or a date or two. The truly needy person is one who finds no sufficiency, but it does not come to the mind of others to give to him, nor does he stand begging people."[2] This brings our attention to many individuals and families who have financial difficulties but rarely indicate their condition to others.

Al-Hasan al-Basri was asked whether a person who owns a house and servant can take *zakat*. His answer was affirmative, if the person is in need.[3] Muhammad ash-Shaybani gave a similar response when asked about a person who owns land and buildings whose income does not fulfil all his needs, as reported by Ibn 'Abidin.[4]

The opinion of Ahmad concerning such cases was mentioned earlier,[5] while similar examples are reported from both the Shafi'is[6] and Malikis.[7] *Zakat* does not aim only to improve the state of the totally deprived and financially broken, but also of those who do not find full satisfaction of their basic needs.

How much are the poor and needy to be given?

The divergent views of jurists on this issue can be grouped into two main approaches. The first opinion is to give as much as will

1. Commentary of Ibn Kathir, vol. 1, p. 324.
2. Agreed upon.
2. *Al-Amwal*, p. 556.
3. *Radd al-Muhtar*, vol. 2, p. 88.
4. *Al-Mughni*, vol. 2, p. 525.
5. *Al-Majmu'*, vol. 6, p. 192.
6. *Sharh al-Kharashi bi Hashiyat al-'Adawi 'ala Khalil*, vol. 2, p. 215, and *Hashiyat ad-Dusuqi*, vol. 1, p. 494.

sufficiently satisfy the essential needs commonly accepted in society, without determining a specific amount, while the second is to give a specific amount on the exact determination of which jurists differ.

The first approach seems to be more consistent with the texts and objectives of *zakat*. Within this, two major opinions can be noted: one which says the amount to be given should satisfy essential needs for a lifetime, and the other which says this amount should cover those needs for one year only.

The first opinion: satisfying a lifetime's needs

This opinion aims at giving the poor what is sufficient to remove them from the poverty level forever, in such a way that they will not need *zakat* in the future. In *al-Majmu'*, an-Nawawi says:

> Our Iraqi colleagues, along with many from Khurasan [north-east of what is today Iran], believe that the poor and the needy must be given in such a way that they are permanently removed from poverty into sufficiency. This is the opinion of ash-Shafi'i. They provide as supportive evidence the *hadith* from Qabisa ibn al-Mukhariq al-Hilali that the Messenger of Allah said, "Begging [or asking] is not permissible, except for one of three cases. It is lawful for a person who carries a financial charge of [reconciling] disputing people to ask until he obtains sufficiency of sustenance; a person who is struck by a disaster that wipes out his wealth is permitted to ask until he reaches sufficiency of sustenance; and a person struck by poverty to the extent that three wise clansmen confirm that he is really hit by poverty is permitted to ask until he obtains sufficiency of sustenance. O Qabisa, any asking beyond these three cases is evil on the part of the person who asks." (Reported by Muslim in his sound collection)
>
> Our colleagues argue that asking is permitted by the Messenger of Allah until sufficiency is reached. This means the purpose of the distribution of *zakat* is to make the poor

> and needy reach their sufficiency as stated above. A craftsman would be given an amount sufficient to buy tools and equipment that allow him to work and gain his sustenance. This certainly differs according to the time, country, and ability of the individuals concerned. Some of our colleagues give examples that a person who sells vegetables might be given five or ten dirhams, while a person whose profession is selling jewels might be granted ten thousand dirhams if he cannot reach sufficiency with less than that amount. People of other professions would be given according to the requirements of their profession. Farmers would be given enough farming land to enable them to gain sufficiency of sustenance. As for those who have no craft or ability, they must be given sustenance sufficient for the rest of their lives.[1]

Shams ad-Din ar-Ramli, the commentator on *al-Minhaj* of an-Nawawi, says about this *hadith*, "The poor and needy who are not earners should be given what suffices them for the average life expectancy in their area, because the aim of *zakat* is to ensure that the poor are no longer under pressure of need. If they live longer, *zakat* should continue on a yearly basis. It is not necessary to give the poor and needy money to suffice for the rest of their lives. They may be given investments whose return would be sufficient for their maintenance, provided that ownership of the investment transfers to the poor person and can be bequeathed to their heirs." Ar-Ramli continues:

> The *zakat* officer, but not the payer when he distributes *zakat* directly, has the right to force the recipient to buy, for example, real estate, and to prevent him or her from disposing of it. If the return of such an investment becomes less than sufficient, additional distribution must be made to the same recipient. Al-Mawardi says, "A person who has, for example, ninety but needs a hundred to be able to earn sufficient return, should be given the difference, even though the ninety, if spent on living expenses, instead of

1. *Al-Majmu'*, vol. 6, pp. 193, 195.

> the investment, may be sufficient for many years, but not for a whole life. This applies only to individuals who cannot earn by work or profession. As for professionals and workers, they should be given the capital necessary for their productive work, that would provide them with sufficient income, taking into consideration social, personal and geographical circumstances. If a person knows more than one profession, the least amount of capital needed would be given, and if that profession does not produce sufficient income, an added capital investment such as real estate should be granted.[1]

This is what ash-Shafi'i mentions in *al-Umm* and what later became the view of the majority of his disciples. Ahmad ibn Hanbal is reported to have expressed a similar view, and is followed by some Hanbalis. Al-Khattabi comments on the *hadith* from Qabisa, "The upper limit of giving in *zakat* is the provision of sufficiency of sustenance. This differs from one person to another, and there is no definite amount that applies to all people in all their different circumstances."[2]

This view is also consistent with what is reported from 'Umar. 'Umar declared, "When you give, make the recipient rich."[3] In his actual practice, he indeed gave amounts that made the poor rich. A person came to him complaining of poverty. 'Umar gave that person three camels just to help him out of need, camels being the most valuable assets for Arabs at that time, and went on to advise his *zakat* officers to "repeat the distribution of *sadaqa* to people, even if you give them a hundred camels."[4] In another incident, he declared his policy when he said, "Indeed, I shall repeat the distribution of *sadaqa* to the poor, even if one of them has one hundred camels."[5] 'Ata' says, "I would have loved to see a *zakat* payer give what is due to one Muslim family in such a way that makes them really relieved."[6]

1. *Nihayat al-Muhtaj* with *Sharh al-Minhaj*, ar-Ramli, vol. 6, p. 159.
2. *Al-Insaf,* vol. 3, p. 238.
3. *Ma'alim as-Sunan*, vol. 2, p. 239.
4. *Al-Amwal*, p. 565.
5. Ibid.
6. Ibid.

It is obvious that, according to this opinion, the Muslim state can establish factories and businesses, making them all owned by the poor and needy, whose returns and income would be sufficient to maintain the recipients and prevent them from disposing of these properties, so that such properties become like some form of perpetual trust for these poor persons.

The second opinion: giving one year's sustenance

This is the view of the Malikis, most of the Hanbalis, and most other jurists. They argue that the poor and needy must be given their sufficiency for one full year, no more and no less, on the grounds that the Prophet (p) used to keep for his family the amount of food needed for one year and that *zakat* is collected on a yearly basis, so its distribution must be on a yearly basis too.[1]

Sufficiency for one year cannot be determined by any given amount, since it depends on the circumstances, needs, and size of family.[2]

Enlarging upon the concept of sufficiency

In order to fully understand the concept of sufficiency or satisfaction of basic needs as used in Islamic jurisprudence, we must mention several points. Basic needs include, in addition to food, clothes, and shelter, the fulfilment of other essential human drives, especially the sexual drive. Islam, while not allowing celibacy, does forbid wanton sexual practices. Islam ordains marriage for everyone who can afford it, as the Prophet (p) says, "He who has the means and ability must get married because this helps to lower the gaze and guard modesty." (al-Bukhari) Consequently, the *Shari'a* is expected to help those who want to be married but do not have the necessary financial means. Scholars argue that marriage expenses

1. Some Malikis agree on giving the sufficiency for more than one year if *zakat* is not distributed every year. See *Hashiyat ad-Dusuqi*, vol. 1, p. 494.

2. *Sharh al-Kharashi*, vol. 2, [. 215. It states in *Hashiyat ad-Dusuqi*, vol. 1, p. 494, that "It is lawful to give the poor once every year what is needed for their expenses, including clothing, but if there are plenty of funds, the value of a servant and the dowry of a wife may be added."

are included in the level of sufficiency for those who have no spouses and need to get married.[1] Some scholars go as far as assuming that, for a man who is not satisfied with one wife, the cost of marrying a second wife is also part of his level of sufficiency.[2]

'Umar ibn 'Abdu'l-'Aziz, who is usually called the fifth of the Rightly-guided Khalifs, ordered people to search for the needy, those under burden of debt, and those seeking marriage, in order to help them from the treasury of the Muslim state.[3] This view is originally based on the *hadith* from Abu Hurayra that a man came to the Prophet (p) and said, "I have married a woman of the Ansar." The Prophet (p) asked, "How much *mahr* did you give her?" The man answered, "Four *uqiyyas* (160 dirhams]." The Prophet (p) exclaimed, "Four *uqiyyas*? As if you are cutting silver from the side of the mountain! We do not have what we can give you to help, but we may send you on a mission where you may gain something."[4] This *hadith* indicates that the Prophet was wont to give funds from the treasury for such a purpose but did not have enough at the moment, so he tried other means for help.

By the same token, seeking knowledge is a basic need in Islam. Knowledge is the door that opens to faith and is the guide for practising righteousness. Faith by imitation is not accepted, nor is worship with ignorance. Allah says clearly, *"Are they the same – those who know and do not know?"* (39:9) and *"The blind and seeing are not the same nor are darkness and light."* (35:19-20) And the Messenger says, "Seeking knowledge is an obligation on every Muslim."[5] Knowledge which is urged to be taught is not confined to knowledge of religion. It includes every branch of knowledge that is useful to Muslims in their earthly life, such as knowledge of the human body, economics, construction, technology, and military

1. *Hashiyat ar-Rawd al-Murbi'*, vol. 1, p. 400, and the footnote on p. 147, vol. 2, of *Matalib Uli'n-Nuha.*

2. *Sharh Kitab an-Nil wa Shift' al-Ail*, in Ibadi Jurisprudence, vol. 2, p. 135.

3. *Al-Bidaya wa'n-Nihaya*, Ibn Kathir, vol. 9, p. 200.

4. *Nayl al-Awtar*, vol. 6, p. 316. One *uqiyya* equals forty dirhams, while one sheep is estimated at five to ten dirhams. Thus such an amount is rather too much for the person who asked for help here.

5. Reported by Ibn 'Abdu'l-Barr from Anas in the chapter on knowledge. As-Suyuti grades it correct.

science. All these are societal requirements that must be undertaken by some individuals according to the confirmed opinions of great scholars.

It is no surprise that jurists of Islam declare that knowledge seekers who devote all their time to study and research are deserving of *zakat*, while those who devote all their time to worshipping Allah are not included, because worshipping according to Islamic standards does not require devoting all one's time, while seeking excellence in a branch of knowledge does. A worshipper benefits himself or herself only, while a learned person benefits other people too.[1] Jurists go even further in deciding that a poor person who seeks knowledge may take *zakat* to pay for the books necessary for his or her study.[2] Furthermore, some Hanafis permit transporting the proceeds of *zakat* from one country to another for poor individuals who seek knowledge, in spite of the fact that transporting *zakat* is generally not allowed.[3]

Discussion and analysis

In comparing these two views, one must note that they are not mutually exclusive. Each of them may be the best when applied in the proper instance.

The poor and the needy may be classified into two sub-categories. First are the poor and needy who can work and earn sustenance, such as craftsmen and those who know any kind of business that needs capital or equipment for its practice. It is obliged to give them what they need in order to enable them to earn their sustenance for the rest of their lives, so that they are no longer on the list of *zakat* recipients. Secondly, there are those who are incapable of earning because of a physical handicap, like the elderly, or the socially handicapped, like widows who are bringing up children. They may be given sufficiency for one year, provided that it is repeated every year. It may even be advisable to give them monthly payments instead of yearly payments if is feared that they may be

1. *Al-Majmu'*, vol. 6, p. 190.
2. *Al-Insaf*, vol. 3, pp. 165 and 218.
3. *Radd al-Muhtar*, vol. 2, p. 94.

extravagant in spending on unnecessary matters, especially since monthly and periodical payments are common nowadays as salaries and aid.

It is noteworthy that after I made this distinction of the sub-categories of the poor and needy, I discovered that I was preceded by some Hanbali scholars. The commentator on *Ghayat al-Muntaha*, after mentioning the opinion of Ahmad on the case of a person who owns real estate which yields returns that are not sufficient for the person's living, writes, "Such a person has the right to be given his sufficiency from *zakat*, such as an amount needed to buy equipment, or needed capital, if the person is a businessman. On the other hand, other kinds of the poor and needy should be given what suffices them for one year, since *zakat* is repeated every year."[1]

The approach that suggests giving a definite amount

Abu Hanifa and his disciples argue that no more than two hundred dirhams per person can be given to any poor or needy individual. Others decide a maximum of fifty dirhams can be given. Yet others argue that food for one day is to be given. Ibn Hazm rejects these opinions because "payment of *zakat* may be very large or very small, without any limitation, since neither Qur'an and *Sunna* oblige any limit."[2]

The opinion of al-Ghazali

In the *Ihya'*, al-Ghazali selects the view of giving what is sufficient for one full year and argues that this has its origin in the fact that the Messenger used to keep food sufficient for one year for his own family (reported by al-Bukhari and Muslim). Moreover, one year is a reasonable span for estimating the needs of the person. Al-Ghazali adds:

1. *Matalib Uli'n-Nuha*, vol. 2, p. 136.
2. *Al-Muhalla*, vol. 6, p. 156.

There are different opinions as to how much should be given. Some scholars say as little as the sustenance for one day and night, arguing that this is indicated by the *hadith* reported from Sahl ibn al-Hanzaliya that the Prophet (p) prevented the rich from begging. When he was asked what wealth was, he answered, 'Lunch and supper.' (Abu Dawud and Ibn Hibban) Others argue that payment must be up to the limit of wealth, as determined by the *nisab*, since Allah only obliges *zakat* on the rich. Those scholars add that the poor may take from *zakat* an amount equal to the *nisab* for each person in the family. Yet other jurists determine wealth at fifty dirhams or its equivalent in gold, basing this on the *hadith* reported from Ibn Mas'ud that the Messenger (p) said, "He who begs while he has enough to make him rich will appear on the Day of Judgement with cuts on his face." The Prophet (p) was asked, "What is wealth?" He answered, "Fifty dirhams or its equivalent in gold."[1] It is argued, however, that the chain of transmission for this *hadith* is not strong enough. Some others also say that the limit is only forty dirhams, as quoted by 'Ata'.

At the other extreme, we find jurists going on the high side. Some say that the poor person should be given what is needed to buy a farm that would enrich him for the rest of his life, or business capital for the same, in accordance with 'Umar's statement, "When you give, you must enrich." Some people go as far as saying that a person who is impoverished must be given to the extent that brings him back to his previous standard of living, even if that takes ten thousand dirhams. When Abu Talha was so occupied with working in his orchard that he missed prayer, he decided to give the orchard away as charity, but the Prophet said, "Give it to your relatives, that is better for you..." Abu Talha then granted it to Hassan and Abu Qatada. An orchard for two men is certainly enrichment.

1. Al-'Iraqi comments, "This *hadith* is reported by the four. At-Tirmidhi grades it *hasan*, while an-Nasa'i and al-Khattabi grade it weak."

> The claim that one day's food is enough in *zakat* distribution looks unacceptable. The supportive *hadith* refers only to the matter of begging and not to *zakat* distribution. If one has to choose between this opinion and that which provides for the price of a farm, the latter is more sensible, although it is inclined towards extravagance. I believe that the most rational is to be moderate in giving one year's sufficiency of sustenance, since giving more is extravagant, while giving less is too restrictive.[1]

Interestingly, al-Ghazali makes this argument in a book devoted generally to the manners of modesty and Sufism.

Abu 'Ubayd prefers giving more

After mentioning the story of Abu Talha's giving of the orchard to Hassan and Abu Qatada, Abu 'Ubayd asks how much the value of such an orchard would be, especially if it is added that Abu Talha tried to hide his charity out of fear that somebody might think of his action as showing off on his part, because it was so large. Abu 'Ubayd adds, "Although this charity was only voluntary, what applies to it applies to the obligation of *zakat*, since if it were forbidden to take large amounts from the proceeds of zakat, it would be more forbidden to take large amounts from voluntary charity, and if it is lawful to take that much in charity, it should be as lawful to take that much in the form of obligatory *zakat*."[2]

Abu 'Ubayd goes on to mention the statements of 'Umar, 'Ata', and others, referred to earlier in this chapter, then says, "All narrations and evidence indicate that what is given to the poor and needy has no limit. Rather, it is preferred that more be given, as long as the distributors make their decisions without bias or personal preferences. A rich man who sees that a righteous family is in need of a residence and buys that residence for them, paying a big amount in order to provide that family with a decent home out of his *zakat*, would not only be performing his *zakat*, but also doing

1. Al-Ghazali, Ihya' 'Ulum ad-Din, vol. 1, p. 201.
2. *Al-Amwal*, p. 551.

the best that would please Allah. The same applies to a rich man who frees a slave who is under oppression, although he may have to pay a large lump sum.[1]

The aim is to provide an adequate level of living

The preceding discussion shows that the objective of *zakat* distribution is to realise an adequate and suitable standard of living and to help Muslims stay above the poverty level. The minimum of such standards is the provision of reasonable food, clothing, and shelter, as stated by Ibn Hazm, an-Nawawi and many others.

An-Nawawi says, "According to the view of our colleagues in the Shafi'i school, the consideration is for food, clothes, shelter and other needs, at a standard that is suitable but not extravagant for the poor person and all members of his family.[2]

Using contemporary terms, the other needs must include education, health care, and other social necessities that can only be determined by time and locale. No absolute definition can be applied to all cases.

Zakat provides regular help

It is essential to observe that the preceding discussion leads to the view of *zakat* as regular and continuous relief to the poor, whether newly impoverished or disabled and handicapped, whereby people who need to be removed from poverty are given what satisfies their needs, while people who cannot earn are given regular relief at certain intervals. Let us look at an incident from the time of 'Umar, which provides insight into the distribution of *zakat*.

'Umar was napping at midday in the shade of a tree. A bedouin woman came and looked around, then approached him. She said, "I am a needy woman and I have children. 'Umar, the *Amir al-Mu'minin*, sent Muhammad ibn Maslama to distribute *zakat* in our area, but he did not give us any. Would you please talk to him on

1. Ibid., p. 567.
2. *Al-Majmu'*, vol. 6, p. 191, and *ar-Rawda*, vol. 2, p. 311.

our behalf?" 'Umar told his servant Yarfa', "Bring me Muhammad ibn Maslama." The woman, not knowing to whom she talking, said, "It would be more helpful is you went with me to Muhammad ibn Maslama." 'Umar said, "He will come, Allah willing." Then Yarfa' came with Muhammad to 'Umar and he said, "Peace be upon you, Amir al-Mu'minin..."

The woman felt embarrassed upon discovering she had been addressing the Caliph. 'Umar said, "By Allah, I have always selected the best of you as officers. What will we answer Allah when He asks us about this woman?" Muhammad's eyes filled with tears, and 'Umar continued. "Allah sent His Prophet to us and we believed him and followed him as he was doing what Allah commanded him to do. He distributed *sadaqa* to those who deserved it among needy people until Allah took his soul. Then Allah gave us Abu Bakr as a ruler, and he followed the tradition of the Messenger (p) until he died. Then Allah made me ruler and I did my best to select the best of you as my officers. When you go next time to her area, give her the *sadaqa* for last year and the year before. I do not even know whether I want to send you any more."

Then 'Umar asked for a camel to give her along with some flour and oil, and addressed the woman, "Take these and meet us in Khaybar, for we are heading there." When the woman met him in Khaybar, he gave her two more camels, saying, "This might sustain you until Muhammad ibn Maslama reaches you. I have ordered him to give you your right from last year and the year before it."[1]

This story is rich in lessons on the purpose and manner of *zakat* distribution. It tells how deep is the feeling of responsibility a Muslim leader has toward his people. It also illustrates how well citizens were educated about their rights and how freely they could approach the state and its officers to pursue their rights. It also shows that *zakat* is the basic pillar of solidarity in Muslim society, in addition to being a regular and continuous relief for the person who is in need. Lastly, this story indicates that 'Umar's policy was to give enriching amounts and that he felt in so doing he was following the tradition of the Messenger and Abu Bakr.

1. *Al-Amwal*, p. 599.

Chapter Two

Workers in *Zakat* Administration

Workers in the collection and distribution of *zakat* are the third category of *zakat* recipients. They are made recipients in order to avoid any possible attempt on their part to impose additional duties on *zakat* payers for their own benefit. This emphasises the autonomy of the *zakat* institution. The very mention of this category in the Qur'an immediately after the poor and the needy, who are the major benefitters of *zakat*, is itself a clear indication that *zakat* collection and distribution are the function of an organised body of paid employees. It is part of the social structure of the Islamic state and not an individual practice.

The state is required to collect and distribute *zakat*

Jurists say that the Islamic state is required to appoint collectors and distributors of *zakat*. The Prophet (p) and his Successors used to assign people to fulfil these duties. For example, Abu Hurayra is reported by al-Bukhari and Muslim to say that the Messenger of Allah (p) appointed 'Umar ibn al-Khattab to administrate the *sadaqa*. It is also reported by al-Bukhari and Muslim from Sahl ibn Sa'd that the Prophet (p) appointed Ibn al-Lutabiya to administrate the *sadaqa*. There are many other *hadiths* that refer to such appointments. It is to be expected that there will always be people who have wealth but do not know how much they are required to pay, and people who know what to pay but have a tendency to be miserly. Officials are thus needed for both information and collection.[1] The state must send officials at the time of harvest to farmers and must establish *zakat* payment months so that the payersof other kinds of *zakat* know when collection officers are expected.[2]

1. *Al-Majmu'*, vol. 6, p. 167.
2. Ibid., p. 170

Duties of workers in the *zakat* organisation

Jobs involved in *zakat* administration include collecting, keeping records, gathering information and distribution. This can be classified into two major functions directly related to *zakat*: the collection function and the distribution function.

The collection function is similar to that of taxation officials. It certainly includes gathering statistics of *zakat* payers and their zakatable assets, the actual collection of *zakat*, in money or in kind, and keeping payments in suitable storage facilities. One can divide this function into several sections:

- *Rikaz* and minerals
- Grains and fruits
- Livestock
- Money and business assets

As for the distribution of *zakat*, many of its activities are similar to the activities of social insurance or welfare departments in the modern state. Workers in this section must be trained to exert their best efforts to seek out those who deserve it, discover the degree of their need, and assure that the distributed *zakat* reaches them quickly. An-Nawawi says, "The state and its *zakat* distribution officials should keep records of those who deserve, their number, and their individual needs, so that their due *zakat* can reach them quickly, especially since some collected items may be perishable."[1]

This function may be divided into several sections:

- The incapable poor and needy, which include the elderly, orphans, widows raising children, handicapped and retarded persons.
- The needy who can earn.
- Those burdened by liabilities.
- Refugees, street people and asylum-seekers.
- Funds used to help propagate the message of Islam in non-Muslim countries and to help liberate Muslim lands, etc.

1. *Ar-Rawda*, vol. 2, p. 337.

The distribution of the total proceeds of *zakat* among the different categories of recipients is subject to the discretion of the state and its *shura* council, taking the local, national, and global interests of Muslims as one people into consideration.

Additional notes on those who merit *zakat*

Officials charged with the distribution of *zakat* must do their utmost to be sure that recipients truly deserve *zakat*, and that it is fairly distributed among those who deserve it. A few notes and regulations deduced by jurists from the available *hadiths* are of help in this regard.

- The wealth of poor and needy recipients must be less than is needed for their complete sustenance. Incapacity is not a condition, since an earner may not find a job, and someone who earns less than they actually need deserves help to satisfy their needs.
- Work must be sufficient and suitable for the person concerned. For example, a scholar or professor is not obliged to work as a manual labourer. *Zakat* is lawful for such persons until they find a suitable job.
- A person who can earn but is a full-time student (i.e. if he or she were to take an earning job they would have to quit seeking education) is eligible for *zakat*. Such people can benefit other Muslims by their knowledge. But people who are not expected to master a branch of knowledge and are able to work and earn are not eligible for *zakat*, even if they reside at a school.
- People who own real estate but whose income is below their needs are counted poor. They should be given from *zakat* the amount needed to supplement their income. A student or teacher is not required to sell his or her books as long as they are needed for their work.
- If a person, known to be wealthy, claims to be in need, the claim should not be accepted without evidence.

- A person known to be poor needs no evidence of poverty.
- If a person whose general conditions would normally preclude them having income (such as an old or disabled person) claims to be in need, their claim is accepted without evidence. But if the claimant is young and strong, he may be asked to testify under oath, according to a minority of Shafi'ites. Most Shafi'is do not require such swearing, since Ahmad, Abu Dawud and an-Nasa'i report that two men asked the Prophet (p) to give them *sadaqa*. The Prophet (p), after looking them over thoroughly, found them strong and said, "If you like, I will give you, but there is no share in this *zakat* for the rich or the strong who can earn." It is the duty of the distributor to remind and teach recipients about *zakat*.
- If a poor person claims that he or she has a family, evidence is required.
- The same is true for people who claim to be overburdened by debt. Evidence can be testimony of two honest people or that the need of the person be publicly known. It is not meant to take the form of court procedures.[1]

Some *hadiths* mention "…a person so struck by poverty that three wise individuals from his clan say he is impoverished." Al-Khattabi comments, "This applies to someone who is known to have been affluent, and suddenly something happens to his wealth, especially if poverty is not visible in his lifestyle. If doubt arises, his poverty must be confirmed by people who know him well enough to give their opinions. The description of these three people of discrimination is mentioned to establish that they are not likely to be fooled. This is not a form of legal testimony. If a group of a person's neighbours know that he is in need, that is sufficient evidence to justify giving him *zakat*.[2]

1. *Al-Majmu'*, vol. 6, p. 189[illegible].
2. *Ma'alim as-Sunan*, vol. 2, p. 238.

Eligibility conditions for *zakat* workers

It is necessary for them to be Muslim since working in *zakat* is part of the direct governance (*wilaya*) of the Muslims. In all positions of direct governance, being Muslim is a requirement. Certain jobs not directly related to the collection and distribution of *zakat* are exempt from this condition, such as guards and drivers. Ahmad is reported to have permitted non-Muslims in *zakat* jobs because the term "*zakat*-workers" is general and not limited to Muslims and what is paid to them is only compensation for their work.[1] However, although this is a gracious position of Ahmad, it is still preferred in his opinion that "those who implement this critical obligation of Islam be Muslims." Ibn Qudama says, "Because these jobs require honesty and entail some control over Muslims, the condition of being Muslim must be fulfilled, especially since it is unreasonable that people who do not believe in *zakat* should be entrusted to implement it. Moreover, disbelievers are described in the Qur'an as not trustworthy and 'Umar said, 'Do not take them as confidants, since Allah labels them unreliable.' 'Umar condemned the appointment of a Christian as registrar by Abu Musa. *Zakat* as a pillar of Islam is more important than registration."[2]

Zakat workers must be sane and past the age of puberty. Trustworthiness is also a requirement, since they will be handling public funds. They must be righteous and honest so as not to oppress the rich or neglect the rights of the poor.

General and complete knowledge of *zakat* rulings and regulations is essential for officials who are in charge of the overall organisation of *zakat*. An ignorant person cannot perform well and would make many errors that would make him or her a liability to the *zakat* institution.[3] As for workers whose jobs are strictly limited, they are only required to know their own jobs.

Efficiency and performance is required. Officers of *zakat* must be efficient in their work and capable of achieving the aims of *zakat*. Allah says, *"The best person to hire is someone strong and trust-*

1. *Al-Mughni*, vol. 2, p. 654.
2. Ibid., vol. 6, p. 460.
3. *Al-Majmu'*, vol. 6, p. 167, and *Sharh Ghayat al-Muntaha*, vol. 2, p. 137.

worthy." (28:26) Recalling Yusuf's words, Allah says, *"Entrust to me the country's stores. Truly I am a knowing guardian."* (12:55)

The candidate may not be a member of the Prophet Muhammad's family, according to most scholars. His family includes all descendants of Hashim [the Prophet's grandfather] because al-Fadl ibn al-'Abbas and al-Muttalib ibn Rabi'a [cousins of the Prophet Muhammad] asked the Prophet (p) to employ them administrating *sadaqat*. One of them said, "O Messenger of Allah, we come to you seeking jobs in administrating *sadaqat*, so we can earn some of it like other people, and perform [the service] that is due on us like others." The Prophet said, "Indeed, *sadaqa* is not to be given to Muhammad or the family of Muhammad. It is the impurities left after cleansing the wealth of people." (Reported by Ahmad and Muslim)

In another version reported by the same two, the Prophet says, "*Sadaqa* is not lawful for Muhammad or for the family of Muhammad."[1] This *hadith* discourages the family of the Prophet (p) from taking *zakat*. Because *zakat* is public property, the Prophet (p) did not want his family to have any inclination to take from it. The use of the word 'impurities' is apparently figurative, as *zakat* purifies the wealth of the payers as stated in the Qur'an, "so that you might purify and cleanse them."

An-Nasir believes it is permissible for descendants of Hashim to be employed in the *zakat* organisation and receive compensation. This is also expressed by ash-Shafi'i and Ahmad. Abu Ya'la says, "It is permissible to appoint to the collection and distribution of *zakat* a person otherwise forbidden to receive *zakat*, such as the descendants of Hashim and slaves, because what they receive is not *zakat* but merely the price of their labour. Certainly, the amount given depends on the amount of labour provided."[2] Al-Khiraqi says, "*Sadaqa* must not be paid to descendants of Hashim, disbelievers, or slaves, unless they are employees of the *zakat* agency. Then they may be paid the price of their labour." This means these scholars interpret the *hadith* mentioned above as a discouragement and not a prohibition.

1. *Nayl al-Awtar*, vol. 4, p. 175.
2. *Al-Ahkam as-Sultaniyya*, Abu Ya'la, p. 99, and al-*Majmu'*, vol. 6, p. 168.

Those who understand the *hadith* as a prohibition argue that payment of *zakat* to descendants of the Prophet (p) is prohibited, but their appointment to the *zakat* agency is not prohibited, as long as they either work for free or receive compensation from other funds.[1]

Must the sex of the appointee be male? Some jurists add this condition on the grounds that these jobs entail control over public funds and in jobs of public administration, women should not be appointed. They have no evidence to support their view except the *hadith* of the Prophet (p), "A people who give control of their affairs to a woman will not succeed." (al-Bukhari) But this *hadith* applies only to positions that entail public posts whose decisions have national consequences. Jobs in *zakat* administration cannot be included in the context of this *hadith*.

Some jurists argue that it is not reported that a woman was ever appointed as a *zakat* official. This is not, in my opinion, sufficient reason, because of the circumstantial economic and social surroundings of women in those ages. Additionally, not doing something at some time is not evidence that it is prohibited. Others also argue that the literal meaning of the verse, "and those who work in it" does not include females, because the word used for workers is the masculine plural.[2] If this argument were correct, women would also not be given *zakat* if they are poor, because the word used in the Qur'an for the poor is in the masculine plural. This is totally contrary to *ijma'*, since grammatically women are included in the Arabic masculine plural, unless otherwise is implied by the context.

The truth is that there is no basis to the claim that women must not be appointed to *zakat* administration positions, as long as Islamic standards of conduct – modesty, avoidance of unnecessary competition and mixing with men – are observed. In fact, although these general rules make men more suited to jobs that require daily contact with *zakat* payers, there are certain jobs in the *zakat* organisation which women can do better than men, such as contacting widows and handicapped women and assessing their needs.

1. *Nayl al-Awtar*, vol. 4, p. 175.
2. *Sharh Ghayat al-Muntaha*, vol. 2, p. 137.

Some jurists add the condition that appointees of the *zakat* agency must be free, i.e. slaves cannot be employed by this agency. This is denied by other jurists because of a report by al-Bukhari and Ahmad that the Messenger of Allah (p) said, "Listen and obey, even if an Abyssinian slave whose head is like a raisin is appointed over you," especially since the job itself can be performed regardless of the free or slave status of the employee.[1]

Amount of worker compensation

Workers in the *zakat* agency should be paid salaries equal to the market value of their labour. Ash-Shafi'i is reported to have suggested that total compensation for workers must not exceed one-eighth of the total proceeds of *zakat*, based on his opinion that the total proceeds must be divided equally among the eight categories of recipients. The majority does not accept such limitation. One may suggest that the Shafi'i opinion has the merit of restricting the cost of collection.

Workers in the *zakat* organisation need not be poor in order to receive compensation for their labour. Abu Dawud reports that the Prophet (p) says, "*Sadaqa* is not lawful for any rich person, except these five: a fighter for the sake of Allah, a *zakat* administrator, a person under the burden of liabilities, a person who buys a *zakat* item from a recipient, and a person given a gift by a needy person who receives this gift as *zakat*."[2]

The Prophet (p) was very strict in protecting the public funds of *zakat*, and disallowed non-deserving people from taking any of them under any guise. 'Adi ibn 'Umayra reports, "I heard the Messenger of Allah saying, 'Whoever is employed in any collection job and hides from us even a needle or more, it is misappropriation, and he will bear what he misappropriated on the Day of

1. Ibid., p. 138.

2. In *al-Majmu'*, an-Nawawi says, "This *hadith* is *hasan* or *sahih*, reported by Abu Dawud via two chains. One of them is via 'Ata' from Abu Sa'id from the Prophet, and the other from 'Ata' from the Prophet as *mursal*. Its two chains are *hasan*." In *Mukhtasar as-Sunan*, al-Mundhiri says, "It is also reported from the Prophet by Ibn Majah." Abu 'Amr an-Nahwi adds, "It is linked to the Prophet (p) by a group, through Zayd ibn Aslam."

Judgement.'[1] A black man of the Ansar – I can almost see him now – stood and said, 'O Messenger of Allah, accept my resignation from the job.' The Prophet (p) asked, 'Why?' and the man replied, 'I heard you saying (such and such).' The Prophet (p) continued, 'And I say now, whoever we employ in a job must bring forward all that he collects, the little and the big. What we give him after that, he should take, and what we do not give him, he should leave alone.'" (Reported by Muslim, Abu Dawud and others.)

In another *hadith*, Abu Rafi' says he was passing by the cemetery of al-Baqi' with the Prophet (p). The Prophet (p) said, "Woe to you! Woe to you!" Abu Rafi' says, "I was stunned and retreated to the back, afraid that he meant me. The Prophet (p) said, 'What is the matter? Come on.' I asked, 'Did I do anything wrong?' and he said, 'Why do you ask that?' I answered, 'You said "Woe" to me.' The Prophet (p) said, 'No, not to you, but to the person in the grave. I sent him to collect *zakat* from the land of so-and-so, and he misappropriated a *namira* [a special garment made of wool] He is clothed in one like it from the Fire.'" (Reported by an-Nasa'i and Ibn Khuzayma in his *Sahih* collection.)

It is reported from 'Ubada ibn as-Samit that the Messenger of Allah (p) appointed him over the *sadaqa* and told him, "O Abu'l-Walid, fear Allah. You must not appear on the Day of Judgement carrying a camel that bellows or a cow that lows or a sheep that bleats (out of misappropriation)." 'Ubada said, "O Messenger of Allah, could that happen?" He replied, "Yes, in the name of Him in Whose Hand is my soul." 'Ubada said, "In the Name of Him who sent you with the Truth I do not accept appointment to any job at all by you." (Reported by at-Tabarani in *al-Muj'am al-Kabir* via a correct chain) 'Ubayda, a great and renowned Companion, responded as he did because he wanted to be on the safe side.

Gifts to *zakat* officials are unlawful

As well as being required to declare everything they collect and put it in the *zakat* fund, *zakat* collectors are forbidden to accept

1. In reference to 3:161: *"Those who misappropriate will arrive on the Day of Rising with what they have misappropriated."*

gifts from *zakat* payers. Any such gift is considered a bribe because it may influence the estimation of *zakat* due at the expenses of those entitled to it.

Abu Humayd as-Sa'idi says that the Prophet (p) appointed a man from the tribe of al-Azd named Ibn al-Lutabiyya for the *sadaqa* collection. When he came back, the collector said, "This is yours and this was given to me as a gift." The Messenger of Allah (p) stood, addressing the gathering, and praised and thanked Allah, then said, "I employed a man from you to do a job that Allah gives me control over. Then he comes and says, 'This is yours and this was given to me as a gift.' Why does he not sit in his father and mother's house and wait for his gift to be brought to him, [if he sincerely thinks that it is an innocent gift on their part?] By Allah, there is nothing which any of you takes without true right which will be not carried by you when you face Allah on the Day of Judgement. Let me not recognise any of you coming before Allah carrying a camel that is bellowing, or a cow that is lowing or a sheep that is bleating." Then he raised his hands so high that the whiteness of his underarms was seen and said, "O my Lord, did I convey to them?" (Reported by al-Bukhari, Muslim and Abu Dawud)[1]

Kindness to the rich

The Prophet (p) advised his *zakat* collectors to be kind, courteous and moderate, and he selected them from the best of his Companions. It was mentioned that the Messenger of Allah (p) advised estimators, "Be easy in estimation, since orchards may have trees assigned to the poor, needy, family, and passers-by."

It is advisable for collectors to pray for *zakat* payers, since Allah tells His Messenger, "*Take sadaqa from their wealth to purify and cleanse them and pray for them. Your prayers bring relief to them.*" (9:103) 'Abdullah ibn Abi Awfa narrates that his father came to the Messenger of Allah (p) and gave him the *zakat* due on his wealth. The Prophet (p) said, "My Lord, have mercy on the family of Abu Awfa." (Ahmad, al-Bukhari and Muslim)

1. *At-Targhib wa't-Tarhib*, al-Mundhiri, vol. 1, p. 277.

Can other public officials be paid from *zakat*?

Ibn Rushd mentions that some jurists approve of this on the grounds that the benefit of these public officials' work extends to all Muslims.[1] In *an-Nil* and its commentary in Ibadi *fiqh*, it is stated that *zakat* may be given to workers in the *zakat* organisation as well as other public officials, such as judges and governors. These people may be given as much as their labour is worth, even if they are rich, because they are occupied by public service from pursing their own interests.[2] The majority of scholars argue that such officials must be paid from other resources of the state.

1. *Bidayat al-Mujtahid*, vol. 1, p. 267.
2. *An-Nil* and its commentary, vol. 2, p. 134.

Chapter Three

Those Whose Hearts are Being Reconciled

Those whose hearts are being reconciled include persons who have recently become Muslim or who need to strengthen their commitment to this faith, and individuals whose evil can be forestalled or who can benefit and defend Muslims.

Implications drawn from the inclusion of this category

The very presence of this category as recipients of *zakat* emphasises the fact that *zakat* is not personal charity or merely an act of worship left to individual discretion. Distribution of this category is not, by nature, a job that individuals acting independently can undertake. It is a political decision made by the decision-making body of the state. Only the state can determine the need at any given time for reconciling hearts and the qualifications of those who are entitled in this category.

Subdivisions of this category

One group in this category is that of individuals who are close to becoming Muslims or whose clans may become Muslim, like Safwan ibn Umayya, who was granted safety by the Prophet the day of the Muslim conquest of Makka. The Prophet gave him so many camels loaded with goods after the Battle of Hunayn that he stated, "This is the giving of one who fears no poverty." Muslim and at-Tirmidhi report from Sa'id ibn al-Musayyab that Safwan said, "By Allah, when the Prophet gave to me, he was the person I hated most. He continued to give to me until he became the person I loved most."[1] Safwan became a committed Muslim.

1. *Commentary of Ibn Kathir*, vol. 2, p. 325.

Ahmad reports via a sound chain from Anas, "Never was the Messenger of Allah (p) asked to give anything for accepting Islam but that he gave it. A man once came and asked to be given something for accepting Islam. The Messenger (p) ordered him to be given enough sheep to fill the space between two hills from the sheep collected as *sadaqa*. The man went back to his clan saying, 'O my people, accept Islam, for Muhammad gives like someone who does not fear poverty.'"[1]

A second group includes those who may do harm to Muslims but to whom giving *zakat* will stop them from doing it. Ibn 'Abbas narrates that certain people came to the Prophet (p) who, if they were given *sadaqa*, would praise Islam and declare it a good religion, but if not, would malign Islam.[2]

A third group consists of individuals who have just embraced Islam, to whom giving will help them to be steadfast. When az-Zuhri was asked who are those whose hearts are to be reconciled, he said, "Whoever among the Jews and Christians embraces Islam." He was then asked, "Even if they are rich?" "Even if they are rich," he replied.[3] Al-Hasan answered a similar question by saying, "They are individuals who embrace Islam."[4] It is understandable that persons who embrace Islam may have to make several sacrifices and may be persecuted, ostracised, or even threatened financially by the communities in which they live. Such a person is undoubtedly in need of support and encouragement.

Also in this category are prominent Muslims whose social status is respected by disbelievers who have status in their own communities, such that giving these Muslims encourages their non-Muslim counterparts to consider embracing Islam. It is said that Abu Bakr's giving to 'Adi ibn Hatim and az-Zibriqan ibn Badr, who were obviously committed Muslims, was of this nature.[5]

Other groups coming under this category are:

1. *Nayl al-Awtar*, vol. 4, p. 166.
2. *Commentary of at-Tabarani*, vol. 14, p. 313.
3. Ibid., p. 314, and *al-Musannaf*, vol. 3, p. 223.
4. *Al-Musannaf*, ibid., and *al-Iklil*, as-Suyuti, p. 119.
5. Commentary *al-Manar*, vol. 10, pp. 574-577.

- Muslim leaders whose faith is not firm. Such individuals may have great influence on Muslims and giving to them generously is likely to strengthen their faith and commitment. An example is the Makkans who were given to generously by the Prophet (p) after the Battle of Hunayn.[1]
- Muslims living on the borders of a Muslim country who are expected to defend Muslim land against any attack from enemies.
- Muslims whose influence is needed in the process of collecting *zakat* to persuade would-be rebels to pay their *zakat*. By using such influence, the government avoids having to fight those who refuse to pay *zakat*.[2]

All these groups are covered by the general term, "those whose hearts are being reconciled", whether they are Muslims or disbelievers. Ash-Shafi'i says that those whose hearts are being reconciled includes new Muslims but that disbelievers must not be given *sadaqa*. He argues that the gift of the Prophet (p) to some unbelievers after the Battle of Hunayn was not from *zakat*, but from either *fay'* or the Prophet's personal property. Ash-Shafi'i adds, "Allah makes it mandatory that the *zakat* of Muslims be rendered to Muslims and not to disbelievers.[3] The Prophet (p) told Mu'adh *zakat* was, "...to be taken from the rich among them and rendered to the poor among them."

Ar-Razi in his commentary quotes al-Wahidi as saying, "Allah does not make Muslims in need of reconciling the hearts of unbelievers. The head of state may find it beneficial to Muslims to reconcile the hearts of some individuals. This is only permissible if those individuals are Muslims, since it is not allowed to extend *zakat* to unbelievers. Unbelievers whose hearts must be reconciled can be given from *fay'* and not *sadaqat*." Ar-Razi comments, "The statement of al-Wahidi may give the impression that the Prophet (p) gave unbelievers *zakat*, but such a thing never happened.

1. *Commentary al-Qurtubi*, vol. 8, pp. 179-181.
2. *Al-Majmu'*, vol. 6, pp. 196-198 and *Ghayat al-Muntaha* and its commentary, vol. 2, p. 141f.
3. *Al-Umm*, vol. 2, p. 61.

However, the verse of *zakat* distribution nowhere specifies that the hearts being reconciled are those of unbelievers, since the term, *'those whose hearts are being reconciled'*, may include Muslims as well as non-Muslims.[1]

By the same token, since the term used in the Qur'an can include Muslims and non-Muslims, there is no reason for restricting it to Muslims. Unbelievers may be reconciled to Islam by *zakat*. Qatada says, "Those whose hearts are being reconciled were often pagan bedouins whom the Prophet (p) used to reconcile through giving *zakat* in order to bring them to faith."[2] In the *hadith* from Anas quoted earlier about the man to whom the Prophet (p) gave sheep from *zakat* and who returned and said to his clan, "Accept Islam. This is the giving of one who fears no poverty," it appears he was not Muslim before being given that *zakat*. Granting unbelievers *zakat* in order to bring them to Islam is, according to al-Qurtubi, "a form of *jihad*." "There are three kinds of unbelievers: those who understand reason and dialogue; those who do not and must be conquered; and those who can be reconciled by generosity and benevolence. The Muslim state should deal appropriately with each group."[3]

Did giving for reconciliation end with the death of the Messenger?

Ahmad and his followers believe the ruling on heart reconciliation is permanent, which is also the opinion of az-Zuhri and Abu Ja'far al-Baqir.[4] It is also taken up by the Ja'fari and Zaydi schools[5] Yunus says, "I asked az-Zuhri about this matter, and he said he knew of no change regarding this ruling." Abu Ja'far an-Nahhas comments, "Accordingly, the ruling on heart reconciliation is firm. Whenever there is a need for reconciling a person's heart, he or she may be given *zakat*."

1. *Commentary ar-Razi*, vol. 16, p. 111.
2. *Commentary* of at-Tabari, vol. 14, p. 314.
3. *Commentary* of al-Qurtubi, vol. 8, p. 179.
4. *Commentary* of at-Tabari, vol. 14, p. 314-316, and *al-Mughni*, vol. 2, p. 666.
5. *Al-Bahr*, vol. 2, p. 179, and *Sharh al-Azhar*, vol. 1, p. 513, and *Fiqh al-Imam Ja'far,* vol. 2, p. 90.

Al-Qurtubi quotes al-Qadi 'Abdu'l-Wahhab – a Maliki – as saying, "If such persons are needed sometimes by the state, they may be given *zakat*." Likewise, al-Qadi Ibn al-'Arabi remarks, "The way I see it, if Islam becomes strong, the allocation to this group of recipients becomes redundant, but if they are needed, they may be give their share, the same way the Messenger of Allah (p) used to give to them. It is correctly reported that Islam started strange and unfamiliar and will again become strange and unfamiliar as it started."[1] It is mentioned in *an-Nil* and its commentary on Ibadi *fiqh* that "this category is dropped as long as the state is strong and in no need of reconciling people, but reconciling is permitted when need arises, to avoid harm to Muslims or bring them benefit."[2]

At-Tabari quotes al-Hasan as saying, "Today there must be no reconciliation of hearts from *zakat*."[3] Ash-Sha'bi says, "Those whose hearts are to be reconciled were a group at the time of the Prophet (p), which, when Abu Bakr took command, came to an end." An-Nawawi quotes ash-Shafi'i as saying, "If unbelievers are reconciled, they must only be paid *fay'* and not *zakat*, since the latter must not be given to non-Muslims." As for reconciling Muslims' hearts, ash-Shafi'i is reported to disallow giving to them after the state of Islam becomes strong. A second view says it is permissible to give to them the same way they were given to by the Prophet (p).[4]

As for Malikis, they also have two opinions, one allowing and one disallowing giving this group *zakat*.[5] Hanafis believe there must be no giving for reconciliation after the death of the Prophet (p). This, according to al-Kasani, is the correct and authentic view, because the Companions were unanimous on that count. Neither Abu Bakr and 'Umar gave anything from *zakat* funds for reconciling hearts and none of the Companions disapproved of this. It is reported that, upon the death of the Messenger of Allah (p), indi-

1. Al-Qurtubi, op. cit.
2. *An-Nil*, vol. 2, pp. 134, 136.
3. At-Tabari, vol. 14, p. 315.
4. *Al-Majmu'*, vol. 6, pp. 197-198.
5. Al-Qurtubi, op. cit. In *Ma'alim as-Sunan*, vol. 2, p. 231, al-Khattabi says "Their share is fixed and must be paid to them." Ibn Qudama says the same in *al-Mughni*, vol. 2, p. 666.

viduals who were given *zakat* for reconciling their hearts asked Abu Bakr to document this in writing. Abu Bakr did so, and they went and showed it to 'Umar, whereupon 'Umar grabbed the document and tore it up, saying, "Indeed, the Messenger of Allah (p) used to give to you in order to reconcile you to Islam but today Allah has strengthened this religion. If you remain steadfast in Islam, it is well and good, but if you do not, there is nothing between us but the sword." They left him and ran to Abu Bakr, complaining, "Is the khalif you or 'Umar?" Abu Bakr replied, "He is if he so wishes," and approved of 'Umar's action.

Al-Kasani adds, "This was known to the bulk of the Companions and not disapproved. This becomes a unanimous *ijma'*. Furthermore, the Prophet used to give to these people in order to reconcile them to Islam. The Muslim state was then weak and its people were few, while the disbelievers were more numerous and stronger. But thanks be to Allah, the Muslim state today is strong. Its people are more in number and in strength and it is well established on earth, while the unbelievers are humiliated. It is a rule in *Shari'a* that whenever a ruling can be rationally attributed to a specific reason, if a reason is nullified, the ruling is dropped."[1]

In brief, the opinion of al-Kasani can be summarised into two main points: the ruling is nullified by the *ijma'* of the companions; and the ruling of reconciliation is caused by a rational reason and should, therefore, be dropped if its cause no longer exists.[2]

Refuting claims of annulment

In fact, these two main points of al-Kasani are incorrect. The ruling is not annulled and the need to reconcile hearts has not ceased. The action of 'Umar does not indicate annulment of this category, since those whose hearts needed to be reconciled at one time did not need to be at another. At each time the determination of the need to reconcile hearts and the specification of the individuals to be included is decided by the executive authority according to what benefits Islam and the Muslims.

1. *Al-Bada'i'*, vol. 2, p. 45.
2. *Radd al-Muhtar*, vol. 2, p. 89, quoting from *al-Bahr*.

Scholars of *usul* affirm that the dependency of a ruling on a defined element is an indication that the element is the cause of the ruling. The spending of *zakat* in the case in hand depends on the need for reconciliation of hearts. This indicates that reconciliation is the reason for payment. Consequently, whenever the need for reconciliation exists, payment is permissible, and vice versa. At a given time, the process of reconciling certain persons may be finished, and the step taken by 'Umar would then be taken, in the same way that *zakat* workers would not be paid if at one point there were no workers of *zakat*.

That does not mean that this category is eliminated from future consideration. 'Umar did not annul payment to *'individuals whose hearts are being reconciled'* nor was there an *ijma'* on such annulment. He simply judged that there were none entitled in that category at that point in time.[1] The statement of al-Hasan and ash-Sha'bi that "today there are no individuals who are being reconciled" is understood similarly as a fact of the age in which they lived.

Abrogation of a ruling enacted by Allah can only be made by Allah through Revelation to His Messenger and can, therefore, only take place during the time of the Message. Abrogation is dictated only when two authentic texts of Qur'an or *Sunna* contradict one another and we know that one of them came after the other chronologically. In the case in hand there is only one text which determines this category as a recipient of *zakat*. There is no text contradicting the Qur'anic verse. How can abrogation be attributed to an *ayat* in the Qur'an without another text? Ash-Shatibi writes,

1. This disproves the claim of some contemporary writers that it is permissible to neutralise or contradict texts if it is to the Muslims' common benefit, which they base on 'Umar's action regarding those whose hearts were being reconciled. Such a claim is made by Subhi al-Mahmasani, among others, in *Falsafat at-Tashri'*, p. 178, where he claims, "'Umar dared to oppose the text about reconciliation because such opposition was prompted by the public interest of Muslims." Similarly, Mahmud al-Lababidi makes the claim that "the nation, as represented by its consultative authority, can freeze or oppose certain texts for the common benefit." See his article, "*As-Sulta at-Tashri'iyya fi'l-Islam* (Legislative Authority in Islam) in the review *Risalat al-Islam*, issued by Dar at-Taqrib bayn al-Madhahib, Cairo. The latter uses this action of 'Umar as an example. Scholars from al-Azhar replied to al-Lababidi in several articles, such as the article *"Bahth 'ala Bahth"* (Analysis of an Article) by the late Muhammad al-Madani.

"Rulings of the *Shari'a*, after they are confirmed, cannot be claimed to be null except through confirmed, authentic evidence, since the rulings were initially obliged by completely authentic evidence. This is why scholars unanimously agree that a sound but single-chain *hadith* cannot annul the Qur'an or a *hadith* narrated by a group, because the single chain narration, though authentic and sound, is not absolutely confirmed like narration by groups."[1]

Needless to say, the sayings and actions of a Companion cannot abrogate Qur'anic texts, especially since the action of the Companion in point does not even signify abrogation. Ibn Hazm, even before ash-Shatibi, says, "It is not permissible for any Muslim who believes in Allah and the Last Day to claim that anything in the Qur'an or *Sunna* is abrogated without affirmative evidence, because Allah says, *"We sent no Messenger except to be obeyed by Allah's permission,"* (4:64) and *"Follow what has been sent down to you from your Lord."* (7:3) Everything sent by Allah as Qur'an or established by the Messenger (p) as *Sunna* must be followed, and anyone who claims that something is annulled implies that it must not be followed and is not required, which is obviously disobedience to Allah, unless authentic and confirmed proof support it. Accepting anything to the contrary of the above rule would lead to wiping out the whole of the *Shari'a*, since what would then be the difference between a claim of annulment and a rejection of an *ayat* or *hadith*? This kind of behaviour represents total apostasy from Islam. We cannot allow an ordinance made by Allah or His Messenger to be waived, except by equally undeniable and authentic evidence."[2]

In conclusion, payment for reconciliation of hearts is part of *zakat* distribution, determined by a clear *ayat* in *Surat at-Tawba* and not abrogated by anything. Abu 'Ubayd remarks, "This *ayat* is a clear text. We know of no annulment of it in the Book or the *Sunna*. Whenever there are individuals who can be brought closer to Islam by being given to generously and it is not to the benefit of Muslims to let them be driven away or to fight them, the ruler may decide to give them *zakat* to reconcile their hearts. This action is supported by three facts: the texts of the Qur'an and *Sunna*, pro-

1. *Al-Muwafaqat*, vol. 3, p. 64.
2. *Al-Ahkam fi Usul al-Ahkam*, part 20, p. 458, vol. 1.

motion of the best interests of the Muslims, and the hope that such individuals may be guided to the path of Islam once they have the opportunity to study it."[1] In *al-Mughni*, Ibn Qudama, supporting the view of Ahmad that this category of recipients is permanent, says:

> On our side is the Book of Allah and the tradition of His Messenger (p). Allah mentions reconciliation of hearts among the categories of *zakat* spending and the Prophet (p) used to give generously for reconciliation, as stated in famous reports. He continued to do this until he died. It is unacceptable to abandon the Book of Allah and the tradition of the Messenger (p) except by authentic annulment from Allah or His Messenger, and annulment is not confirmed by mere possibility. Moreover, such annulment could only take place during the life of the Prophet (p), because the texts required for annulment ceased to be revealed upon his death. A text in the Qur'an can only be annulled by another text in the Qur'an itself; there is no such text. By what virtue is one asked to abandon Qur'an and *Sunna* and revert to mere human opinion or the statements of a Companion? Scholars do not consider a statement of a Companion strong enough to stand in opposition to analogy, so how could such an opinion stand against the Qur'an and *Sunna*? Az-Zuhri also says, "I know of nothing that annuls the category of those whose hearts are being reconciled."[2]

1. *Al-Amwal*, p. 607.

2. Hanafis differ on the determining factors that annul the ruling of heart reconciliation which is confirmed by a text in the Qur'an. Some of them claim the annulling factor is *ijma'*, attempting to make ijma' out of 'Umar's position. This is far-fetched, as explained above. Some try to find documentation on which such *ijma'* is based. Here they also diverge into two groups. Ibn Hujaym in *al-Bahr* presents the *ayat* in *Surat al-Kahf, "It is the Truth from your Lord. So let whoever wills believe and whoever wills reject,"* which was quoted by 'Umar in arguing with his opponents. Ibn 'Abidin says, "*Ijma'* cannot be the annulling factor, because annulment cannot be made after the death of the Prophet (p)." Others claim the annulling factor is the Prophet's instructions to Mu'adh when he sent Mu'adh to Yemen. (See *Radd al-Muhtar*, vol. 2, p. 83.)

Lastly, 'Umar's action does not contradict the Qur'an or *Sunna* since, when Muslims do not need those individuals who were paid in the past, they may choose to cease such payment, and if the need arises in the future to pay the same individuals or others, that can be done. In reality, this principle applies to all categories. A category may not exist at a certain time, but that does not mean it is eliminated because it may exist at some later time.[1]

The need to reconcile hearts does not cease

The claim that there is no more need for heart reconciliation after the spread of Islam and the establishment of its state is rejected for the following reasons:

- Some Malikis assert that the reason for giving *zakat* to a person whose heart is to be reconciled is not that person's benefit to the Muslims but only to bring him closer to Islam and break any barriers that may be hindering him from opening his mind to Islam. In other words, the purpose of the payment is to save the recipient from the fire of Hell.[2] Thus, this payment is a form of calling to Islam (*da'wa*) that may be effective with some people. It is the obligation of Muslims to help others seek the guidance if Allah and lead them out of the darkness of ignorance and the agony of disbelief that leads to Hellfire. People may convert to Islam for material gains but once they start

The fact is that all these attempts are fruitless. The *ayat* from *Surat al-Kahf* is Makkan. It cannot annul a Madinan *ayat*, which was revealed a long time afterwards. Additionally, there is no contradiction between the two *ayats*. The *hadith* from Mu'adh is not an annulling factor; it mentions only the poor as recipients because the poor are the most important category. If this *hadith* annuls one category, it must eliminate all the rest of them. Why should it only eliminate the category of heart reconciliation? 'Ala'd-Din ibn 'Abdu'l-'Aziz, a Hanafi, says, "The best way out is to assume that the Prophet's action was appropriate to his time, because strengthening the call of Islam could be served by payments to reconcile hearts. After his death, the same objective could be achieved without such payments." But Hanafis do not generally agree with the explanation of 'Ala'd-Din, which is clear from the efforts of Ibn al-Humam to negate the opinion of 'Ala'. (See Commentary al-Alusi, vol. 3, p. 327.

1. *Al-Mughni*, vol. 2, p. 666.
2. *Hashiyat as-Sawi* on *Bulghat as-Salik*, vol. 1, p. 232.

understanding it they may embrace it wholeheartedly. Abu Ya'la reports from Anas, "A man came to the Messenger of Allah (p), embracing Islam for some earthly gain, not accepting Islam except for that purpose, but by nightfall Islam became dearer to him than the whole earth and what is on it." In another version, "A man asked the Prophet (p) for some earthly material gain for which he would embrace Islam..."[1]

This applies when the person whose heart is being reconciled is an unbeliever but not all who are given under this title are unbelievers. Some may have embraced Islam very sincerely, but are oppressed and persecuted by their communities. Giving to them is a required relief. It encourages them on the path of truth and supports them while their faith is still tender.

- The claim that there is no longer a need for heart reconciliation is based on the erroneous assumption that it is only needed when the Muslim state is weak. This is an unnecessary restriction and an unrealistic assumption. In contemporary politics we observe that strong states like the United States provide help to poor states in order to reconcile these small and weak states to the objectives of the government of the United States. At-Tabari says in this regard, "Allah makes *zakat* fulfil two objectives, namely satisfying the needs of Muslims and strengthening the cause of Islam. The cause of Islam covers rich and poor alike, since what is given for this purpose is not aimed at erasing destitution but at strengthening commitment to Islam. Fighters for the sake of Allah are given *zakat* regardless of whether they are rich or poor. Payments to those whose hearts are being reconciled are made regardless of their wealth, because giving them is supporting the call of Islam. The Prophet (p) gave *zakat* for reconciliation of hearts after Allah had opened for him most of Arabia and after the Islamic state was well-established. There is no support in the *Sunna* for those who claim that after the strengthening of Islam and its state there is no need for reconciling hearts."[2]

1. The author of *Majma' az-Zawa'id* says it is reported by Abu Ya'la; the men of its chain are among the men of the *Sahih* collections. Vol. 3, p. 104.

2. *Commentary at-Tabari*, vol. 14, p. 316.

- Lastly, times have, in any case, changed and Muslims are no longer masters of the land. Actually, Islam has returned to being a stranger. The Muslim nation suffers under pressure and aggression from many other states. Muslims are weak and can only complain to Allah. If weakness is a reason for distribution towards reconciling hearts, it certainly exists today.[1]

Who has the right to pay for heart reconciliation?

Decisions regarding reconciling hearts are the duty of the Islamic state. The Prophet (p) and his Successors affirmed this responsibility as part of the state's executive affairs. If the state does not fulfil its responsibility in collecting and distributing *zakat*, Muslim organisations can make decisions about distributing to individuals whose hearts are being reconciled.[2] If the government does not undertake this duty and there are no organisations that distribute *zakat*, can a Muslim individual who distributes his own *zakat* use part of it for reconciling an unbeliever's heart? In my opinion, a Muslim individual must not make decisions concerning heart reconciliation, except in the very rare case where no other destination of *zakat* is available. Such a case may apply to Muslims living in non-Muslims countries, although it is preferable even under such circumstances to dispose of *zakat* for the spread of Islam or to send it to the poor and needy in Muslim countries.

1. Hanafis themselves say that if one attributes a ruling to certain reasons, and those reasons cease to exist, that is not sufficient proof to negate the ruling, since a ruling does not require the continuous presence of its reason, as in the case of slavery. Thus there is always need for proof to indicate that such a ruling is waived, even when its reason does not exist anymore. But they go on to argue that we need not specify the reason whenever *ijma'* exists. (See *Radd al-Muhtar*, vol. 2, pp. 82-83.)

2. In *Sharh al-Azhar*, vol. 1, p. 513, it is said that reconciling hearts is allowed if done by the state for the benefit of Muslims, but is not permissible to anyone else, Some Zaydis allow individual *zakat* payers to give towards heart reconciliation.

How can the share of heart reconciliation be spent today?

If we agree that reconciliation of hearts by payment from *zakat* is permissible, to whom should this share be given today? In order to answer this question, we must remember that the purpose of this share is to bring hearts closer to Islam, affirm their commitment to its cause, support the weak, and prevent harm that could be inflicted on Muslims or on their religion. These objectives could be achieved by giving aid to non-Muslim countries, persons, organisations and tribes to bring them closer to the cause of Islam.

It could also be extended to support research and utilise mass media that teaches the religion of Islam and defends its cause against attackers. Many people enter into the fold of Islam every year who do not find encouragement or support from their governments and communities, or even from the governments of Muslim countries. The share of heart reconciliation can be extended to such people, an idea consistent with the opinions of az-Zuhri and al-Hasan.

Christian missionaries spend millions every year for the spread of their religion, even though theirs does not have an institution like *zakat* devoted to this purpose. It is true that Islam spreads on its own merit because of its inner persuasive power but it is equally true that most of those who embrace Islam in non-Muslim countries do not receive even nominal support or compensation for the sacrifices they make when they embrace Islam. There are many Islamic organisations which attempt to fill this gap but remain desperate for financial support, especially in areas like Africa and many other poor countries.

Payment for heart reconciliation from sources other than *zakat*

It is always possible that the Muslim state appropriate some of its funds derived from sources other than *zakat* for the purpose of heart reconciliation, if the total proceeds of *zakat* are insufficient to satisfy the other categories of *zakat* recipients. This is consistent with the opinion of ash-Shafi'i that payments for heart reconciliation must be made from sources other than *zakat*.

Chapter Four

Emancipation of Slaves

The Qur'anic verse that lists the categories of *zakat* recipients (9:60) cites eight categories, mentioning four of them using the preposition "to" (*ila*) – to the poor, the needy, the workers, and those whose hearts are to be reconciled – and then using the preposition "in" (*fi*) with the other four categories – in freeing slaves, in aid of those in debt, in the Cause of Allah, and in aid of the traveller. The Qur'an is perfect. Not even a change of preposition is done without reason, so why is "to" used in the first instances and "in" used later?

Az-Zamakhshari says the use of the preposition "*fi*" for the last four categories indicates that they are more deserving of *zakat* than the first four, since "*fi*" indicates a place inside which things are put, meaning that the last four categories are containers in which *sadaqat* should be put.[1] In *al-Intisaf*, Ibn al-Munayyir comments on az-Zamakhshari's note, "The other, more important difference is that *zakat* is given to the first four categories in such a manner that they become its owners while *zakat* is not necessarily given to persons in the last four categories but spent for their benefit. In other words, *zakat* is given to the slave's owner to gain the slave's freedom. It is also given for the Cause of Allah, to the creditor of those in debt, or to help a traveller return home."[2] Ar-Razi notes, similarly to Ibn al-Munayyir, that "*ila*" indicates ownership, while "*fi*" connotes the purpose of spending. In summary, *zakat* is given to the first four categories, while it is given for, but not necessarily to, the last four categories.[3] This is also mentioned in al-Khazin's commentary.[4]

1. *Al-Kashhaf*, vol. 2, pp. 45-46.
2. *Al-Intisaf min al-Kashshaf*, in the margin of the above commentary.
3. *At-Tafsir al-Kabir*, ar-Razi, vol. 16, p. 112.
4. Quoted by al-Jamal in his notes on the *Commentary al-Jalalayn*, vol. 2, p. 292.

Rashid Rida[1] followed by the late Mahmud Shaltut,[2] divides the categories that deserve *zakat* into two kinds: individuals and interests. Individuals include the first four along with those in debt and travellers, while interests include freeing slaves and the Cause of Allah. The author of *al-Manar* uses the additive conjunction "and" before the words "those in debt" and "travellers", relating these two categories to the first four, since the preposition "*fi*" is used immediately before "freeing slaves" and "Cause of Allah."

However, this non-sequential addition does not show proper respect for the eloquence of the Qur'an. It is better to take the additions in sequence, grouping the last four categories together, because they are preceded by the preposition "*fi*", which is the choice of az-Zamakhshari, Ibn al-Munayyir, ar-Razi and others. Ibn Qudama supports the view of ar-Razi and his colleagues:

> Four categories receive *zakat* in such a way that it becomes their property forever and they do not need to return it. The other four categories do not receive *zakat* except to spend it for a pre-determined purpose and if they do not spend it for that purpose, it can be taken back. The last four categories receive *zakat* in order to use it toward fulfilling particular objectives, while the first four categories are themselves objectives of *zakat*. For example, the purpose of *zakat* is fulfilled by giving to the poor, thus making the poor rich. On the other hand, if a person in one of the last four categories was given an amount of *zakat* for a purpose which can be achieved by spending a lesser amount, the remainder must be returned, except in the case of the fighter in the Cause of Allah."[3] (This last exception does not apply to military equipment such as weapons and horses, which must be returned to the *zakat* fund.)

This distinction made by Ibn Qudama is undoubtedly correct. He could have supported it by quoting the change of preposition

1. *Commentary al-Manar*, vol. 10, pp. 586-590.
2. *Al Islam, 'Aqida wa Shari'a*, pp. 111-113.
3. *Al-Mughni*, vol 2, p. 760.

used in the Qur'an with the listed categories, as noted by the commentator of *Ghayat al-Muntaha.*[1]

The meaning of "freeing slaves"

Spending *zakat* to free slaves may take two forms:

- Such *zakat* can be used to help a contracted slave pay his master. A contracted slave (*mukatab*) is a slave who has an agreement with his master that upon paying the master an agreed amount, the slave will gain his freedom. Allah orders Muslims to give slaves who desire it a contract of liberation. Allah also commands Muslims to help slaves provide such contractual ransoms to their masters. Allah says, *"If any slaves you own desire to make a contract to free themselves, write it for them if you know of good in them and give them some of the wealth Allah has given you."* (24:33) In other words, Allah also orders masters to help their own slaves pay their contractual sum. In addition to this, Allah assigns a share of *zakat* for this purpose. Abu Hanifa, ash-Shafi'i, their disciples and al-Layth ibn Sa'd consider the verse of *zakat* to refer to contracted slaves. They present as evidence a report that Ibn 'Abbas interprets the verse *"... and freeing slaves"* to mean contracted slaves. This is said to be supported by the last sentence of the verse.[2]

- The second way of freeing slaves is to buy the slave outright with the proceeds of *zakat* and emancipate him or her. This can be done by the state, a *zakat* payer, or a group of *zakat* payers together. This is the opinion held by Malik, Ahmad, and Ibn Ishaq. Ibn al-'Arabi argues that this is apparent from the words of the Qur'an, because the word used translates as "necks" which, whenever used in reference to slaves in the Qur'an, means freeing them. If Allah had meant the specific sub-category of contracted slaves, He would have mentioned it by its name. According to Ibn al-'Arabi, the contracted slave

1. *Matalib Uli'n-Nuha*, vol. 2, p. 151.
2. *At-Tafsir al-Kabir*, vol. 16, p. 112. See also *al-Hidaya* and *Fath al-Qadir*, vol. 2, p. 17.

may be given zakat as a person in debt and not under the title of freeing slaves except by over-generalising the term.[1]

Actually the verse includes both meanings. It is, however, said that Ibrahim an-Nakha'i and Sa'id ibn Jubayr, both Followers, did not like purchasing slaves with *zakat* and then freeing them, since such an action benefits the emancipator as a result of the concept known in Islam as *wala'* (mutual support) between the emancipator and the freed slave. *Wala'* between them means that if the freed slave has no other heirs, his emancipator may inherit his estate upon his death. Malik argues that since *zakat* is due for Allah's sake, the emancipator must not gain any personal benefit. Thus, the person who liberates slaves from the proceeds of his own *zakat* should not be granted the *wala'* of the freed slave. This *wala'* belongs to all Muslims as represented by their state.[2]

Abu 'Ubayd reports that Ibn 'Abbas finds nothing wrong in a person freeing slaves with his own *zakat* and comments that Ibn 'Abbas is much more of an authority than an-Nakha'i and Ibn Jubayr, and his opinion is much preferred, especially as al-Hasan, a Follower, and the majority of scholars agree with Ibn 'Abbas. Abu 'Ubayd adds that even if the emancipator inherits the ex-slave's estate as a result of *wala'* between them he may also have to pay, for example, the ransom for a killing which the freed slave may commit, in application of the same principle of *wala'*.[3]

It should be realised that the difference in opinion applies only to the case where an individual *zakat* payer frees slaves out of his *zakat*, but if the Islamic state takes that action, the Muslims agree that the state can use any combination of the two forms of slave emancipation mentioned above. Some scholars even prefer that the state use the two forms together, as suggested by az-Zuhri when he wrote 'Umar ibn 'Abdu'l-'Aziz that "the share of freeing slaves is divided into two parts, half for Muslim contracted slaves and the other half for buying Muslim slaves and freeing them."[4] Of course, there is no reason for the restriction of dividing this share in half.

1. *Ahkam al-Qur'an*, vol. 2, p. 955.
2. *Al-Amwal*, pp. 608-609.
3. Ibid.
4. Ibid.

Islam preceded other cultures in eliminating slavery

It should be noted that Islam was the first system to begin the gradual abolition of slavery through a combination of means. Islam first exhausted the sources of slavery by prohibiting the kidnapping and selling of free persons, the legal slavery of debtors and criminals, and the enslaving of prisoners of war in wars waged for aggression or economic benefit. Only one source of slavery – the taking of prisoners of war in a morally lawful war aimed at preventing aggression and oppression – remained.[1] Even in such a war, the Islamic state does not have to enslave prisoners of war. This is only a option left open in order to provide for treatment comparable to that which Muslim prisoners received from the unbelievers. Qur'anic texts regarding prisoners of lawful war do not even mention slavery as an option. The Qur'an says, *"Then when you have decimated them, tie their bonds tightly and set them free or ransom them."* (47:4)

At the same time, Islam prescribes a continuous process of freeing slaves. Islam urges the freeing of slaves and views it as an expression of submission to Allah, as well as an act of restitution performed by persons seeking forgiveness for sins or errors, such as breaking the fast in Ramadan or breaking an oath. Islam requires freeing a slave as compensation for beating him without right. Masters are ordered in the Qur'an to contract their slaves for freedom against an agreed sum and Muslim society is called upon to help contracted slaves financially and to provide them with jobs so they can earn the amount needed to gain their freedom. Allah says, *"If any slaves you own desire to make a contract to free themselves, write it for them if you know of good in them and give them some of the wealth Allah has given you."* (24:33)

In addition, Allah makes the emancipation of slaves one of the eight objectives of *zakat*. The amount of *zakat* assigned for freeing slaves may be one-eighth, or more or less, of this vast continuous source of funds in Muslim society.[2] This category may sometimes

1. 'Ali 'Abdu'l-Wahid Wafi, *Huquq al-Insan fi'l-Islam*, pp. 139-161.

2. This is in addition to raising the level of spiritual, moral and material dignity of slaves to the extent of making them like brothers to their masters. They should

take most or all of the proceeds of *zakat*, if other groups of *zakat* recipients are satisfied, as happened in the time of 'Umar ibn 'Abdu'l-'Aziz. Yahya ibn Sa'id said, "'Umar ibn 'Abdu'l-'Aziz sent me as an officer for the *zakat* of Africa. I collected it and searched for poor people to give it to but found none. We searched for worthy recipients to give *zakat* to but found that 'Umar ibn 'Abdu'l-'Aziz had made all people satisfied. Then I bought slaves and freed them with *zakat*."[1]

Freeing Muslim prisoners of war with *zakat*

The share of *zakat* proceeds used to gain the freedom of Muslim slaves can include Muslim prisoners of war who have fallen into the hands of the enemies of the Islamic state, according to Ahmad, on the grounds that both cases gain the freedom of Muslims.[2] Ibn al-'Arabi, the Maliki, says that scholars differ on whether this is permissible. Asbagh says it is not allowed while Ibn Habib believes it is allowed. The latter argues that if *zakat* is otherwise going to be used to gain the freedom of a Muslim slave owned by another Muslim in a Muslim society, freeing Muslims from an oppressive unbelieving enemy, obviously takes priority.[3] There are many ongoing wars in the world today in which Muslims fall prisoner in the hands of non-Muslims. Gaining their freedom becomes one of the objectives of *zakat*.

Helping peoples under colonialism with *zakat*

In *al-Manar*, Rashid Rida says, "Emancipation has its modern equivalent in freeing people from the humiliation and oppression of colonial power, which is mass liberation as compared with freeing individual slaves."[4] Shaykh Mahmud Shaltut emphasises, "... I

eat from the same food, wear the same quality clothes and not be forced to work more than their capacity, in addition to the prohibition of injuring and beating them, or even addressing them by the word "slave".

1. Biography of 'Umar ibn Abdu'l-'Aziz , Ibn 'Abdu'l-Hakam, p. 59.
2. *Ar-Rawd al-Murbi'*, vol. 1,. p. 402.
3 *Ahkam al-Qur'an*, vol. 2, p. 956.
4. *Commentary al-Manar*, vol. 10, p. 598.

think we have today a form of slavery that is more dangerous to humanity. It is the enslavement of people's ideas, wealth and authority, depriving them of their freedom in their own land. The enslavement of an individual ends with the death of the person but today entire nations and peoples are enslaved, generation after generation, in a continuous form of overwhelming oppression under ruthless power. This form of enslavement deserves more efforts to liberate people from it, not only by using the proceeds of *zakat* and charity but also by sacrificing all our wealth and ourselves. This must open our eyes to the tremendous responsibility of rich Muslims to help the peoples of the Muslim nation."[1]

Although Rida and Shaltut correctly describe the new phenomenon of oppression inflicted on colonised nations by aggressive powers, they do not agree on expanding the meaning of freeing slaves to such an extent because words should not be so loosely applied. As for helping oppressed peoples, we have a great opportunity under the heading of *zakat* spent "for the sake of Allah," in addition to all the resources of Muslim states and people that must contribute toward the liberation of Muslims and Muslim lands.

1. *Al-Islam, 'Aqida wa Shari'a*, p. 446.

Chapter Five

People in Debt

The sixth category of those entitled is that of people in debt. According to the Hanafi school, this group includes all who do not own the *nisab* above what is needed to pay their debts.[1] On the other hand, Malik, ash-Shafi'i and Ahmad distinguish between two types of debtors: those whose debts are for personal reasons and those whose debts are caused by their social and political responsibilities. This distinction implies differences in the ruling of these two categories, and each will be discussed individually.

Those in debt for personal reasons

This sub-category is limited to individuals who are in debt for personal reasons and who do not have an income sufficient to rid them of their debts in addition to satisfying their essential needs. Debts may have been borrowed for consumer expenditure, including marriage, medical bills, building a house for personal residence, and debts resulting from accrued liability towards others. At-Tabari reports from Abu Ja'far from Qatada that the state must pay from the treasury the debts of those who borrowed without extravagance, who do not have enough funds to repay their creditors.[2]

Also in this group are those hit by natural disasters or accidents which destroy their assets and force them to borrow in order to continue to satisfy their basic needs. Mujahid is reported to have said, "Three kinds are included in this sub-category: a person whose wealth is destroyed by flood, a person whose wealth is destroyed by fire, and a person with many dependants and no means who borrows to support his family."[3] In the *hadith* from

1. *Al-Bahr ar-Ra'iq*, vol. 2, p. 260, and *Radd al-Muhtar*, vol. 2, p. 63.
2. *Commentary of at-Tabari*, vol. 14, p. 338.
3. Ibid., and *Musannaf Ibn Abi Shayba*, vol. 3, p. 207.

Qabisa ibn al-Mukhariq, reported by Ahmad and Muslim, the Prophet (p) allowed a person afflicted by a catastrophe that wiped out his wealth to ask the state for the *zakat* which is his right, until he procures sufficiency of sustenance.

Zakat is thus an insurance against the financial effects of catastrophes and accidents, an insurance which preceded all known forms of insurance by several hundred years. This insurance is of higher quality and comprehensiveness than modern forms of insurance in the West. Western insurance compensates only subscribers with contractual amounts proportionate to the premium paid, which allows the wealthy to insure for higher sums, while Islamic insurance of *zakat* compensates those affected by disaster without requiring them to contribute premiums, and the amount of compensation is determined by the need of the affected persons and not by their ability to pay premiums.

Conditions for giving *zakat* to this sub-category

Four conditions must be met before aid is given to those with personal debts:

- The debtor must be in need of financial aid. Persons who possess sufficient wealth to cover their debts may not be given from *zakat*.[1] Individuals who do not possess sufficient wealth but can pay their debts from their earnings may still be eligible for *zakat* on the grounds that repaying the loans from their income would take time. So this condition does not imply that the debtor must be totally destitute. Scholars explicitly state that shelter, clothing, furniture, utensils, servants, and transportation, if needed, are not considered wealth from which loans must be paid. If the amount of debt is more than the available wealth of the debtor, *zakat* may be given to pay the difference.
- The debt must have originated from Islamically lawful activity, such as borrowing to support the family. Loans used for pro-

1. In another opinion attributed to ash-Shafi'i, persons with debts may be given *zakat* even if they are rich. See *al-Majmu'*, vol. 6, p. 207, and *Nihayat al-Muhtaj*, vol. 6, p. 155.

hibited practices, such as consumption of alcoholic beverages, or extravagance in lawful items, cannot be paid with *zakat*. Extravagance in lawful items is prohibited by the *ayat*, *"Children of Adam! Wear fine clothing in every mosque and eat and drink but do not be profligate. He does not love the profligate."* (7:31) This condition is based on the principle that giving *zakat* to pay a debt caused by prohibited spending is like helping sinners and encouraging others to indulge in sin. If the debtor repents, he or she may be given *zakat*, since repentance obliterates what preceded it. Some jurists add the condition that a period of time sufficient to confirm the sincerity of repentance must lapse before the repentant debtor can be given *zakat* to pay debts caused by unlawful activity.

• The debt must be due immediately. If the debt is deferred, scholars differ on whether the debtor may be given *zakat*. Some disapprove of this and others approve if the debt is due within one year. On the other hand, some scholars argue that debtors of deferred loans may be given *zakat*, regardless of the due date of their loans, on the grounds that they are included in the general definition of individuals with debts.[1] I think that any choice between these three opinions can only be made after knowing the total proceeds of *zakat* and the requirements of other categories of those entitled. Then, depending on the residue, one can expand the coverage of deferred debts or restrict it.

• The debt must be due to other human beings. Obligations to Allah, such as due *zakat* and recompenses for breaking certain conditions in *Shari'a* [*kaffarat*] are excluded.[2] Malikis mention this condition, which is not held by all jurists. On the other hand, Hanafis include *zakat* itself among debts required to be paid to people which can be paid from *zakat*.

1. For this condition, see *al-Majmu'*, vol. 6, pp. 207-209, *Nihayat al-Muhtaj*, vol. 6, pp. 154-155, and *Sharh al-Khirashi on Khalil*, vol. 2, p. 218.

2. *Hashiyat as-Sawi*, vol. 1, p. 233.

How much can be given those in debt for personal reasons?

People in debt should be given an amount sufficient to rid them of their debts. Since the *zakat* payment in this case is exclusively for the payment of debts, if any or all of the debts are repaid by other means (such as volunteers) or discounted by the creditors, the portion of *zakat* not used for the satisfaction of debts must, according to the sound view, be returned to the *zakat* institution as the receiver is not in need of it.[1]

The noble position of Islam towards debtors

It is worthwhile at this point to digress briefly and look at Islam's stance on debtors and borrowing. Islam teaches Muslims moderation and economy in living and encourages them to avoid borrowing. If circumstances force Muslims to borrow, they must do so after careful planning and with full intention of paying back the loan. The Prophet (p) says, "As for someone who takes funds from others with the intention of returning them, Allah helps him repay what he owes, but as for someone who takes funds with the intention of consuming and destroying them, Allah will destroy him."[2]

If a debtor is unable to pay all or some of his debts in spite of evidence that shows his good intentions, the state saves him from the burden and humiliation of debt. It is said that "debts are a source of depression in the night and humiliation in the day." The Prophet (p) used to pray to Allah, "O Lord, I seek refuge in You from the burden of debt and from defeat by the enemy and from giving enemies the opportunity to gloat."[3]

Debts are not only a source of anxiety and insecurity for the borrower, they also affect the borrower's behaviour and morality. The Prophet (p) often asked Allah for protection from being in

1. *Al-Majmu'*, vol. 6, p. 209.

2. Reported by al-Bukhari, Ahmad and Ibn Majah from Abu Hurayra (See *Kanz al-'Ummal*, vol. 6, p. 114.

3. In *Bulugh al-Maram*, p. 313, al-Hafiz says, "reported by an-Nasa'i and graded good by al-Hakim as from 'Abdullah ibn 'Umar, extended to the Prophet (p).

debt. He was asked why he associated seeking refuge from debts with seeking protection from punishment in the grave, from the temptation of worldly life, and from the temptation of the false Messiah. He answered, "Indeed, when a man is burdened by debt, if he speaks, he lies and if he promises, he breaks his promise." (al-Bukhari) The Prophet (p) used several means to discourage his Companions from borrowing, even declining to pray at the funeral of a person who died leaving unpaid debts. Knowing how disgraced a person would be if the Prophet (p) refused to pray at his funeral, one can realise the extensive effect of such discouragement.

When the Islamic state prospered and its resources became expanded, the Prophet (p) started paying the debts of Muslims from public funds. Abu Hurayra narrates that Messenger of Allah (p) was often brought the coffin of a man who had died in debt. The Prophet (p) would ask, "Did he leave anything to pay his debts?" If the answer was "yes" the Prophet (p) would pray for the body, but if the answer was "no" he would say, "Pray for your companion." Then, when Allah opened lands and their treasures for him, he said, "I am more responsible for believers than their own selves. If anyone dies leaving debts, I take responsibility for their payment."[1]

The Prophet (p) encouraged Muslims to help people in debt, in brotherhood, in obedience to Allah and in hope of reward from Allah. Abu Sa'id al-Khudri says, "A man at the time of the Prophet (p) suffered financial loss because of some fruits he had bought. His debts grew until he went bankrupt. The Messenger of Allah said, 'Give him charity.' People gave him charity, but it was not sufficient to pay all the man's debts. The Messenger of Allah (p) said to the man's creditors, 'Take what there is and you have nothing more.'"[2]

The last and most important means of helping debtors is the share Allah prescribes for them in *zakat* funds. By this means, Islam frees debtors from the obligation and humiliation of their debts. The world has never known another system which includes in its very constitution the rights of debtors to financial aid. By paying

1. Agreed upon. See *Bulugh al-Maram*, p. 1890, and *Kanz al-'Ummal*, vol. 6, pp. 118-122.

2. *Bulugh al-Maram*, p. 117

these debts, *zakat* achieves two objectives: relieving those burdened by debts and providing a guarantee to creditors, which helps all members of the community feel secure about extending loans to one another.

In this way. Islam relieves those in debt without forcing them to liquidate essential assets needed for their living. 'Umar ibn 'Abdu'l-'Aziz wrote to his provincial governors to "pay the debts of those in debt." Some of his governors wrote back, "There are people who own shelters, servants, horses and furniture, yet are in debt." 'Umar answered, "A Muslim needs a house to live in, a servant to help with housekeeping, a horse to ride in war, and furniture in his house. Yes, pay the debts of such people."[1]

This system of justice and mercy that came from Allah fourteen centuries ago is incomparably superior to any man-made system. In the Roman canon, if a debtor was unable to pay his debts, he had to be enslaved if free and imprisoned or killed if already a slave.[2] In pre-Islamic Arabia, debtors who could not pay their debts were sold for the benefit of the creditor.[3] Allah says, "*If someone is in difficult circumstances, there should be a deferral until things are easier. But making a free gift of it would be better for you if you only knew.*" (2:280)

Those in debt for social reasons

This category includes benevolent persons of stature who undertake activities for the public interest such as overseeing the reconciliation of disputes among groups and individuals, often by paying compensation and ransom from their own assets. There is nothing in the *Shari'a* to restrict the source of such debts to those incurred by reconciling disputing people. Such debts may also result from taking on projects of public benefit, such as building orphanages, mosques, hospitals for the poor, or schools for children, which may put people in debt. Persons of this kind are helped to pay their debts with *zakat*, even if the debts results from reconciling two groups of the people of the *dhimma*.[4]

1. *Al-Amwal*, p. 556.
2. As mentioned in *Ruh ad-Din al-Islami*, p. 328.
3. *Commentary al-Qurtubi*, vol. 3, p. 271.
4. *Ar-Rawd al-Murbi'*, vol. 1, p. 402

According to some Shafi'is, such individuals should be paid enough to repay their debts, even if they are rich, since persons in debt because of such undertakings are more worthy of assistance from *zakat* than those who have borrowed for mere personal reasons.[1] Qabisa ibn al-Mukhariq al-Hilali says, "I accepted a financial responsibility [to reconcile two disputing groups] and I went to the Messenger of Allah to ask for help. He said, 'Stay here until the *zakat* comes, so we can give you something from it.' The Prophet continued, 'O Qabisa, asking is not permissible except for three persons: Someone who accepts financial responsibility for reconciling people may lawfully ask until that financial charge is repaid. Then he must not ask for more help. Someone who is struck by a disaster that wipes out his wealth may lawfully ask until he reaches a satisfactory level of sustenance. And someone hit by poverty so that that three wise clansmen confirm that he is struck by poverty may ask until he procures sufficiency of sustenance. O Qabisa, any asking beyond that is evil. It is eaten by the person who accepts it as evil.'"[2]

This *hadith* indicates that a person who accepts financial responsibility in the process of reconciling differences among other people can ask for *zakat* to help discharge that responsibility, even if that person is rich, because the condition of sufficiency of sustenance does not apply. This is implied by the sentence in the *hadith*, "may lawfully ask until that financial charge is satisfied and then he must not ask for more help" since the poor may ask until their needs are satisfied.[3]

1. Some Shafi'is believe that a person who borrows for ransoming a prisoner of war, building a structure for public benefit, or serving guests, can be given *zakat* if he is rich, in the sense of owning real estate and not money. See *ar-Rawda*, vol. 2, p. 319. Ar-Ramli comments, "Even if those whose wealth is money are also included – that would not be unreasonable – in recognition of their benevolence." See *Nihayat al-Muhtaj*, vol. 6, p. 155.

2 Reported by Ahmad, Muslim, an-Nasa'i and Abu Dawud. See *Nayl al-Awtar*, vol. 4, p. 168.

3 *Commentary al-Qurtubi*, vol. 8, p. 184.

Paying the debts of deceased people from *zakat*

An-Nawawi says there are two opposing views among Shafi'is about this. Some believe it is not permissible to pay the debts of deceased people from *zakat*. This view is consistent with the opinion of an-Nakha'i, Abu Hanifa and Ahmad. The other opinion is to allow this on the basis of the general implication of the pertinent *ayat*. This is also the view of Abu Thawr.[1] It is reported that Ahmad argues that *zakat* payment for the debts of the deceased cannot be made because such payment must be made to the debtor himself and the debtor in this case is dead.[2]

Al-Khirashi, in his commentary on the text of Khalil, says, "It makes no difference whether the debtor is dead or alive. The state must pay the debts from *zakat*. Some jurists even argue that the debts of deceased people have priority over those of the living, since the latter may be able to pay in the future."[3] Al-Qurtubi remarks,[4] "Scholars of our school, as well as other schools, think that the debts of deceased people may be paid from *zakat* since, as a debtor, he is included in the term, 'those with debts,' especially since the Prophet (p) said, 'I am more responsible for every believer than his own self. If someone leaves wealth, it is for his family, but if he leaves behind debts or dependants, they are my responsibility,'' (Agreed upon) This is also the view of the Ja'fari school.[5]

In my opinion, the texts of the *Shari'a* do not prevent the payment of a deceased person's debts from *zakat*. This is supported by the fact that Allah, in the ayat about those entitled to *zakat*, distinguishes between two kinds of categories. The first are deserving people to whom *zakat* is paid in such a way that they become owners of what they receive, while *zakat* is not necessarily paid to the second group, but on their behalf. Those with debts are of the second kind, so it must be permissible to pay the debts of deceased

1. *Al-Majmu'*, vol. 6, p. 211.
2. *Al-Mughni*, vol. 2, p. 667.
3. *Sharh al-Khirashi*, and the notes of al-'Adami on it, vol. 2, p. 218.
4. *Commentary al-Qurtubi*, vol. 8, p. 185.
5. *Fiqh al-Imam Ja'far*, vol. 2, pp. 91-92

persons from *zakat*. This is the opinion approved by Ibn Taymiyya.[1] It is supported by the above *hadith*.

Giving loans from *zakat*

I think there is a sound analogy between borrowers and those in debt. This analogy allows giving loans from *zakat*, which is consistent with the broad objectives of *zakat*. Persons who need loans can be given *zakat* under the title of those in debt. In this way, *zakat* can contribute practically to the elimination of interest. This is the view which the late Abu Zahra, Khallaf and Hasan express in their study of *zakat*.[2] They argue that if fair debts can be paid from *zakat*, why not, even by priority, give interest-free loans from *zakat*?

Muhammad Hamidullah al-Hyderabadi expresses a similar opinion in his study, *Banking Without Interest*. He supports his opinion by stating that individuals in debt are of two kinds: those who cannot pay back already used debts, and those who need loans which they can pay back in the future.[3] Thus Hamidullah considers people who need loans as people in debt. It may be argued that persons who need loans are obviously not in debt before they receive the loan. Consequently, the argument of Abu Zahra and his two colleagues is stronger.

1. *Fatawa Ibn Taymiyya*, vol. 1, p. 299.

2. *Halqat ad-Dirasat al-Ijtima'iyya*, p. 254.

3 Published by Maktabat al-Mansar, Kuwait, in its series, *"Towards a Sound Islamic Economy"*, no. 2 pp. 8-9.

Chapter Six

For the Cause of Allah

The seventh category of *zakat* distribution is expressed in the Qur'an as *fi sabili'llah* ["In the Way of Allah, for the Cause of Allah"]. To whom is this share of *zakat* to be paid? The linguistic meaning of the term is quite obvious. *Sabil* means 'way' and *sabili'llah* is the way that leads to pleasing Allah. Ibn al-Athir says, "*Sabili'llah* is general enough to cover every action or deed sincerely intended for the sake of Allah, including fulfilling religious obligations and voluntary acts of worship. When the term, *'fi sabili'llah',* is not modified, it usually means jihad, so the term often appears to be restricted to the meaning of *jihad*."[1] The analysis of the term *fi sabili'llah* by Ibn al-Athir shows two important points:

- The term originally means every action intended solely to serve the Cause of Allah, including all good deeds, both individual and collective.
- Unmodified, the term is commonly understood to mean fighting for the sake of Allah, since frequent usage almost restricts the meaning to fighting for the sake of Allah.

These two meanings of the term reveal a wide range of opinions among jurists regarding this seventh category of *zakat* distribution. Obviously all agree that fighting for the sake of Allah is included in it. Their differences centre on whether this category may also cover other good actions intended to please Allah.

The Hanafi view

According to Abu Yusuf, the category of *fi sabili'llah* includes fighters who do not have sufficient funds for mounts and expenses

1. *An-Nihaya*, Ibn al-Athir, vol. 2, p. 156.

to an extent that impedes them from fighting. *Sadaqa* is lawful to them, even if they are able to earn income, since working would deter them from fighting. Ash-Shaybani understands the term to include those who want to perform pilgrimage but cannot do so for lack of money. He presents as evidence a report that a man who devoted his camel for the Cause of Allah was ordered by the Messenger of Allah (p) to carry pilgrims on it. Additionally, pilgrimage is for the sake of Allah, as it is obedience of His ordinances.

Some Hanafis argue that this category includes full-time students. The author of *al-Fatawa az-Zahiriyya* mentions only this category in his interpretation of the term *'fi sabili'llah'*. Others reject this interpretation on the grounds that when the *ayat* was revealed, the concept of full-time students did not exist. Others reply that studying full-time can mean acquiring knowledge of the *Shari'a*, as practised full-time by those Companions who kept the company of the Prophet (p) in order to obtain knowledge from him in Madina, known as the People of *as-Suffa* [the name of the place in front of the Prophet's mosque in Madina where these people used to live in tents].

In *al-Bada'i'*, al-Kasani says all those who perform acts of obedience to Allah and promote good actions can be helped *fi sabili'llah* if they are in need, following the original linguistic meaning of the term. In *al-Bahr*, Ibn Nujaym comments, "It is obvious that the condition of poverty is necessary in all cases,[1] but Rashid Rida[2] argues that such a restriction eliminates the whole category 'in the Cause of Allah' as a separate group of recipients, since the first category, i.e. the poor and needy, covers all poor persons.[3]

1. *Al-Ikhtiyar li-ta'lil al-Mukhtar*, vol. 1, p. 119; *al-Bahr ar-Ra'iq*, vol. 2, p. 260, and *Radd al-Muhtar*, vol. 2, pp. 83-84.

2. *Tafsir al-Manar*, vol. 1, p. 580.

3. Hanafi scholars raise this objection and do not give a satisfactory answer. The author of *al-Bahr* quotes from *an-Nihaya*, "Take detached isolated fighters and pilgrims. If they have no wealth in their homes, they are poor, and if they do, they are travellers. Then they are but a special category of poor, that is, detached and isolated poor." See *al-Bahr*, vol. 2, p. 260, and *Radd al-Muhtar*, vol. 2, p. 84. Nevertheless, a special kind of poor is poor anyway. In his commentary, al-Alusi says, "The correct view is that mentioned by al-Jassas in *al-Ahkam*: 'He who is rich in his home does not deserve *zakat*, but if such a person joins the fighting in the

In conclusion, jurists of the Hanafi school agree on the necessity of poverty as a condition in all their interpretations of 'in the Cause of Allah', but it is argued that their interpretations are merely semantic exercises, in view of this condition, since it means that all persons in this category can be considered as poor except someone who is employed to collect *zakat*. The Hanafis thus add nothing, because the poor and the needy get their share of *zakat*, regardless of whether they can be qualified as being amongst those 'in the Cause of Allah' or not. The question remains, why does Allah make 'in the Cause of Allah' a separate category?

It must be noted that all Hanafis agree that *zakat* must become the owned property of its necessarily human recipients – it cannot be spent to build mosques, parks, dams, irrigation projects, roads, and highways or for pilgrimage or even *jihad*, because all these do not fulfil the condition that recipients become possessors of *zakat*.[1]

The Maliki view

In *Ahkam al-Qur'an*, Ibn al-'Arabi quotes Malik's remark, "The ways of Allah are manifold, but I know of no disagreement that what is meant by *fi sabili'llah* here is fighting, as distinct from other ways of Allah." Muhammad ibn 'Abdu'l-Hakam says, "From *sadaqa*, the value of food, arms and other equipment of warfare [for the fighters] can be paid. This includes preventing enemies from invading Muslim lands, since all these are actions related to fighting for the sake of Allah. The Prophet (p) gave one hundred camels from the *sadaqa* in reconciliation after the attack against Sahl ibn Abi Hathma. He did so in order to prevent a major violent disturbance."[2]

The author of *Sharh ad-Dardir*, the commentary on the text of Khalil, writes, "*Zakat* can be given to fighters and border guards, and to buy war equipment, such as weapons and horses. Fighters may take *zakat* even if they are rich, since they are given it because

---

Cause of Allah, he needs weapons, transportation and maintenance, things not needed when he is at home. Such a person may be given *zakat* in spite of his wealth." (vol. 3, p. 328.

1. *Radd al-Muhtar*, vol. 2, p. 85.
2. *Ahkam al-Qur'an*, vol. 2, p. 957.

they are fighting for the sake of Allah and not because of poverty. Spies can also be given *zakat*, even if they are unbelievers."[1]

The Maliki view can be summarised as follows:

- They agree that 'in the Cause of Allah' is restricted to fighting and guarding Muslim territory.
- They approve of giving *zakat* to fighters and to border guards even if they are rich. The Maliki view seems closer to the apparent meaning of the Qur'anic text which distinguishes between 'the Cause of Allah' as a category and the poor as another category. It is also closer to the *Sunna* because the Prophet (p) says, "*Sadaqa* is not lawful for any rich person except in five cases ..." and he mentions the fighter for the sake of Allah. Ibn al-'Arabi disregards the condition of poverty held by the Hanafis, saying that this is an addition to the text and, according to the Hanafis themselves, an addition to a text is a modification or an annulment of the original text which can only be done by another text from the Qur'an.[2]
- The bulk of the Malikis allow general spending for military purposes, such as buying arms and horses, and building barracks and fighting ships.

The truth is that Maliki opinion is more in harmony with Qur'anic expression, which uses the preposition *'fi'* instead of *'ila'* when introducing this category. Qur'anic expression apparently indicates that spending must be in the interest of fighting, not necessarily to the fighters.

The Shafi'i view

Along with an-Nawawi in *al-Minhaj* and Ibn Hajar al-Haythami in his commentary on it, Shafi'is believe that the category 'in the Cause of Allah' includes voluntary fighters who do not receive salaries from the government. To use Ibn Hajar's words, "Volunteer fighters fight without salaries and otherwise they work

1. *Ash-Sharh al-Kabir* with *Hashiyat ad-Dusuqi*, vol. 1, p. 497.
2. *Ahkam al-Qur'an*, op. cit.

in business and crafts." He adds, "Linguistically, *sabili'llah* means the way that leads to Him. It is often used to mean fighting for His Cause, which may mean martyrdom that leads to pleasing Allah. Then the term was applied to those who fight without compensation, since they sacrifice more than salaried soldiers and deserve to be given what helps them undertake this duty, even if they are rich."[1]

Ash-Shafi'i says in *al-Umm*, "Neighbours of the area where *zakat* is collected who fight can be given the share for the Cause of Allah, whether they are poor or rich. People other than fighters must not be given this share unless they defend or guard the fighters. *Zakat* may be given to those who prevent unbelievers from attacking them."[2] His condition that only neighbours can be given *zakat* is based on his principle that it must not be transferred from one area to another.

In *ar-Rawda*, an-Nawawi says, "Fighters can be given their expenses and clothing for the period from the time they leave to fight until the time they come back, even if they stay at border points for a long period. Two opinions exist about paying all their expenses or only those caused by travelling to war. A fighter may also be given money to buy a horse, weapons, and other tools of war. What he buys becomes his permanently. However, it is permissible to lease the mount and weapons from someone else and supply them to the fighters. This depends on the availability of funds. Fighters who do not know how to fight mounted should not be given the value of a horse." An-Nawawi adds, "In some commentaries on *al-Miftah*, it is stated that the fighter may be given his expenses as well as the expenses of his family during the entire period he is absent. Most scholars do not mention the expenses of his family but it seems reasonable. The state may give the fighter's mount and arms to him permanently, rent or lease them for him, or buy and keep them in trust [*waqf*] which after the end of the war would be returned to the state to be used by other fighters."[3]

---

1. *Tuhfat al-Muhtaj*, with *Sharh al-Minhaj*, vol. 3, p. 96, and *Nihayat al-Muhtaj*, vol. 6, pp. 155-56.

2. *Al-Umm*, vol. 2, p. 60.

3. *Ar-Rawda*, vol. 2, pp. 326-327.

Shafi'is discuss whether regular salaried soldiers can be given this *zakat* if the state's resources are insufficient to pay its enlisted army and there is a need to defend Muslims against outside aggression. According to an-Nawawi, the correct answer is negative, since financing those payments is obliged on the rich in addition to *zakat*.[1] The question remains, what if rich Muslims do not have sufficient surplus wealth to pay the regular army? Ibn Hajar feels it is permissible to pay them *zakat*.[2]

It is remarkable that Shafi'is agree with Malikis on restricting this category to fighting and fighters, giving to even rich fighters, and spending on the necessities of the fighters, such as weaponry and equipment. They differ only in that Shafi'is require that fighters be unsalaried volunteers in order to deserve such payment and restrict this share to one-eighth of the total proceeds of *zakat*. This is based on the opinion of ash-Shafi'i that the eight categories of those entitled must receive equal shares, which we shall discuss in the next chapter.

The Hanbali view

Like Shafi'is, Hanbalis restrict the term *'fi sabili'llah'* to volunteer fighters who receive no regular salaries or who receive less than is sufficient to cover their expenses, even if they are rich. Border guards are also included. It is stated in *Ghayat al-Muntaha* and its commentary that the state may buy horses with *zakat* and give them to the fighters, even if the fighters pay *zakat*. It is permissible to buy warships, as well as all other equipment, as decided by the state. On the other hand, an individual *zakat* payer has no authority to buy a horse and devote it to fighting for the sake of Allah, because individual *zakat* payers are required to pay *zakat* and this is not payment.[3]

There are two reports from Ahmad concerning pilgrimage. The first is that pilgrimage is included in this category. A poor person may be given *zakat* to perform the obligatory pilgrimage, based on

1. Ibid., p. 321.
2. *Tuhfat al-Muhtaj*, vol. 3, p. 96.
3. *Matalib Uli'n-Nuha*, vol. 2, pp. 147-148.

a report from Umm Ma'qil al-Asadiyya. Her husband had devoted a camel for the Cause of Allah and she planned to perform *'umra.* When she asked to use the camel, her husband refused. She mentioned this to the Prophet (p). The Prophet (p) ordered him to let her use the camel saying, "*Hajj* and *'umra* are for the sake of Allah."[1] This is reported from Ibn 'Abbas and Ibn 'Umar. It is also the opinion of Ishaq.

The second report from Ahmad is that pilgrimage must not be paid for with *zakat.* This is consistent with the opinion of the majority of scholars. In *al-Mughni,* Ibn Qudama states, "This is better, because the term 'in the Cause of Allah', when not qualified, applies only to *jihad.* Most use of the term *'fi sabili'llah'* in the Qur'an is intended to mean *jihad,* so the *ayat* regarding *zakat* must be understood in the same way. The fact is that *zakat* can be expended on two kinds of people: those who need *zakat,* such as the poor and needy or debtors, and those who are needed by the Muslims, such as fighters, people whose hearts are being reconciled, and people in debt as a result of their efforts in mediating between disputing groups. Pilgrimage of the poor fits into neither group. It is not in the public interests of Muslims nor do the poor need it, because poor persons are not obliged to perform the pilgrimage. Allah makes possession of sufficient financial means a condition for the obligation of pilgrimage. Preferably, such help must not be given to the poor from *zakat,* but saved, to be used for the public benefit of the Muslims."[2]

The *hadith* from Umm Ma'qil is disputed because of weakness in its chain of narrators. Even if it were correct, some Shafi'is reply that pilgrimage is for the sake of Allah, no doubt, but nevertheless the term *'fi sabili'llah'* in the *ayat* on *zakat* distribution refers only to fighting because, the Prophet's words "*Sadaqa* is not lawful for the rich, except one of the five cases...", mention the one who fights in the Cause of Allah. Moreover, the use of the *hadith* from Umm Ma'qil is irrelevant, since the camel was devoted for the sake of

1. Reported by Ahmad and the four. The *hadith* is weak because there is an unknown person and a criticised person in its chain. Additionally, the *hadith* is disrupted. Abu Dawud reports the same through another chain, which includes Muhammad ibn Ishaq, who is also criticised. See *Nayl al-Awtar,* vol. 4, p. 181.

2. *Al-Mughni,* vol. 6, pp. 470-471.

Allah, but not necessarily to fighting in the Cause of Allah. 'For the Cause of Allah' here may include carrying people to pilgrimage or giving rides to those who need rides without granting them ownership of the camel, while *zakat* requires transfer of ownership.[1]

Points of agreement of the four schools

The four schools agree on three points:

- *Jihad* is definitely included in the category *'fi sabili'llah'*.
- It is lawful to give fighters *zakat*. Spending *zakat* on equipment and arms is not agreed upon.
- It is not permissible to spend *zakat* on public works or general beneficial deeds such as the building of irrigation canals, mosques, schools, roads and highways, etc. These must be paid for from other state funds, such as *fay'* and *kharaj*. Hanafis do not allow this on the grounds that the recipients must possess what is paid to them, while the others do not allow it on the grounds that such spending is not included in the eight categories. As for al-Kasani's interpretation that 'for the Cause of Allah' includes deeds of obedience, it is restricted in its meaning by his condition that *zakat* must be possessed by the recipient and that he must be poor.

Abu Hanifa alone requires that the fighters be poor in order to be given *zakat* and Ahmad alone allows payment to pilgrims and visitors to the Sacred Mosque in Makka. Shafi'is and Hanbalis share the condition that fighters be volunteers, while all but the Hanafis agree on spending *zakat* on equipment, arms and other necessities of *jihad*.

Those who extend the meaning of 'in the Cause of Allah'

Some scholars, both early and contemporary, tend to extend the meaning of the term 'in the Cause of Allah' to include good deeds

1. *Tuhfat al-Muhtaj*, vol. 3, p. 96.

in general, in accordance with the original indication of the term. Ar-Razi in his commentary on the Qur'an remarks that the apparent meaning of the term *'fi sabili'llah'* is not restricted to fighters. He adds, "For this reason, al-Qaffal's explanation of the verse mentions that some jurists allow spending *sadaqat* on all kinds of good deeds, including supplying coffins for the deceased and building fortifications and mosques, since 'in the Cause of Allah' covers all these."[1] But ar-Razi does not name these jurists, and makes no comment on his quote from al-Qaffal.

Ibn Qudama attributes this opinion to Anas ibn Malik and al-Hasan al-Basri, who says, "*Zakat* on bridges and highways is acceptable."[2] He concludes that this statement allows spending *zakat* on building and repairing bridges and roads, but Abu 'Ubayd's elucidation of the context of this statement gives it a different meaning. He explains that Muslim merchants used to pass by the *'ushr* officers on bridges and highways to pay dues on merchandise brought into the country. Abu 'Ubayd reports that some Followers, including Ibrahim and ash-Sha'bi, say it is permissible to count what is paid to those tax officers as obligatory *zakat*. This is explicitly attributed to al-Hasan who, Abu 'Ubayd argues, agrees with Anas, Ibrahim, ash-Sha'bi and Muhammad al-Baqir.[3] A similar story is reported by Ibn Abi Shayba from Anas and al-Hasan under the title, "Counting what is paid to *'ushr* officers as *zakat*."[4] Ibn Qudama's understanding of the statement made by Anas and al-Hasan is thus incorrect since it refers to payment made **at** bridges, not **for** them.

The Ja'fari view

Al-Mukhtasar an-Nafi' explains that 'in the Cause of Allah' includes everything that benefits Muslims or brings them closer to Allah, such as pilgrimage, fighting and building irrigation systems.

1. *Tafsir ar-Razi*, vol. 16, p. 113.
2. *Al-Mughni*, vol. 2, p. 167.
3. *Al-Amwal*, pp. 573-575.
4. *Al-Musannaf*, vol. 3, p. 166. The text of this narration is: "Whatever is taken from you on bridges is *zakat* that satisfies the duty of *zakat*."

Some Ja'faris say it only relates to *jihad*.[1] The author of *Jawahir al-Kalam fi-Sharh Shara'i' al-Islam*, a Ja'fari encyclopaedia of jurisprudence, states that public works, such as irrigation, mosques, *hajj*, and all good deeds are included under 'in the Cause of Allah'. He adds, "This is the view of the bulk of later scholars, supported by the implication of the term itself, since *'sabil'* means 'way', and the Way of Allah includes everything that pleases Allah, whether fighting for His cause or other things."[2]

The Zaydi view

It is mentioned in *ar-Rawd an-Nadir*, a book of Zaydi jurisprudence, that *zakat* must not be spent on buying coffins for the deceased or building mosques. Zaydis who allow this argue that such good deeds are included in 'in the Cause of Allah', and although the term is often used for fighting, especially in the early period of Islam, this popular usage must not restrict the original meaning of the term. All that brings a person closer to Allah must be included, except when the term is restricted by qualifiers. The author of *al-Bahr* agrees that the term is clearly general, except when restricted by specific evidence.[3]

The author of *Sharh al-Azhar* partially agrees, saying it is permissible to spend the residue of this share on the public interest of Muslims, as stated by al-Hadi. Abu Talib emphasises, "This can be done only after satisfying the needs of the poor." Some commentators on *Sharh al-Azhar* propose that not only this share's residue should be spent for the general interest of Muslims but also what is left over from any of the eight categories, and the poor may also be give to from non-*zakat* funds.[4]

The opinion of Siddiq Hasan Khan

In *ar-Rawda an-Nadiyya*, Siddiq Hasan Khan, a follower of *Ahl al-Hadith* with an independent mind, says, "*Sabili'llah* means the

1. *Al-Mukhtasar an-Nafi'*, p. 59.

2. *Jawahir al-Kalam*, vol. 2, p. 79, *Shara'i' al-Islam* by al-Hilli, vol. 1, p. 87, and *Fiqh al-Imam Ja'far*, vol. 2, p. 92.

3. *Ar-Rawd an-Nadir*, vol. 2, p. 428, and *al-Bahr*, vol. 2, p. 182.

4. *Sharh al-Azhar* and its commentary, pp. 515-516.

'Way to Him'. No doubt the greatest Way to Allah is fighting for His sake, but there is no proof that this share of *zakat* is restricted to this meaning alone. It is therefore permissible to spend on any way to Allah. Since this is the linguistic meaning of the term, we must stick to it as long as we have no evidence transmitted from the Revelation to the contrary." He continues, "Among the ways to Allah is supporting scholars who achieve public and religious interests for the sake of Allah, whether they are rich or poor. This is especially important, because scholars are the heirs of the Prophets and the torchbearers of religion. Through them the *deen* of Islam is preserved."[1]

Contemporary opinions

In his commentary on the Qur'an, the late Jamal ad-Din al-Qasimi quotes without comment ar-Razi's statement that the apparent meaning of the term is not restricted to fighters, the statement attributed by al-Qaffal to some jurists, and a statement from at-Taj that every way intended for Allah which is good is in itself included under, 'in the Cause of Allah'.[2] Al-Qasimi's non-objection to these quotations may implicitly indicate his personal approval.

In *al-Manar*, Rashid Rida says, "The truth is that *'in the Cause of Allah'* includes all public interests of Muslims necessary for the establishment of religion and state, not including individual interests. Thus pilgrimage is not included because it is an individual obligation required from those who can afford it, but the general establishment of the pillar of pilgrimage is included. Spending *zakat* on building highways for pilgrimage and providing pilgrims with water and health services are included if there are no other uses in the Cause of Allah."[3]

He continues, "The Cause of Allah covers all legitimate public interests by which religion and state are maintained. No doubt fighting and buying weapons and spending on soldiers top this list.

1. *Ar-Rawda an-Nadiyya*, vol. 1, pp. 206-207.
2. *Mahasin at-Ta'wil*, vol. 7, p. 3181.
3. *Tafsir al-Manar*, vol. 10, p. 585.

The fighting that is meant here is that which is done in order to make Allah's word supreme on the earth. A similar view is reported from Muhammad ibn 'Abdu'l-Hakam, who includes in this share of *zakat* building military and charitable hospitals, roads, non-commercial railroads, military airports, fortifications and military ships. Also included are expenses of training and travelling for speakers, writers and the like who go to the lands of the unbelievers to inform them about Islam and spread the word of Allah. Allah says, *"Let there be a community among you who call to the good..."* (3:104)[1]

Mahmud Shaltut interprets *fi sabili'llah* to mean also "the public interests that are not individually owned, but owned by Allah for the benefit of His creatures. The first of these is military preparation through which Muslims can prevent aggression and preserve the integrity of their society. This includes funding research and building roads, hospitals, and military equipment, in addition to sending Muslims to unveil the beauty of Islam to unbelievers. It also includes supporting those who preserve and memorise the Qur'an, for through them Allah keeps this Glorious Book intact until the Day of Judgement."[2]

Shaltut says in response to a question about building mosques, "If the mosque to be built is the only one in the village or if the existing mosque is not sufficient for all the people of the village, it is permissible in the *Shari'a* to spend *zakat* for building and repairing mosques. Building the mosque in this case is included under the category of 'in the Cause of Allah' in the verse on *zakat* distribution. It is necessary, however, to mention that this issue is disputed among scholars, but what I feel comfortable with and give my religious opinion about is what is cited above, if the mosque cannot be done without."[3]

Shaykh Hasanain Makhluf answered affirmatively a question on the payment of *zakat* to charitable Islamic organisations, based on the interpretation of *fi sabili'llah* taken by al-Qaffal and other scholars.[4]

1. Ibid., p. 587.
2. *Al-Islam, 'Aqida wa Shari'a,* pp. 97-98.
3. Mahmud Shaltut, *al-Fatawa*, p. 219.
4. Hasanain Makhluf, *Fatawa Shari'iyya*, vol. 2.

Analysis

Those who extend the meaning of 'in the Cause of Allah' depend upon the original linguistic meaning of the term, while those who restrict the meaning to fighting for Allah's Cause (who are the majority of scholars from the four schools of jurisprudence) depend on two points: firstly, that *zakat* must become owned by the recipient,[1] and that public interest projects are not owned by any individual, and secondly, the *ayat* is exclusive because it reads, "*Sadaqat* ***is only*** *for …*" as is the *hadith* of the Prophet (p), "Indeed, Allah gives His ruling on *zakat*, and divides it into eight parts …" This is presented as an argument by Ibn Qudama in *al-Mughni*.[2]

As for the first point, the preposition used with the category of 'in the Cause of Allah' is '*fi*', which does not imply ownership. Basing their opinion on this distinction, scholars say it is permissible to buy and free slaves or pay debts of a deceased person from *zakat*, although *zakat* paid in these cases is not owned by the recipients. Moreover, the requirement of making *zakat* owned by the recipient is fulfilled when *zakat* is paid to the government's *zakat* agency. Once received by the state, it can be spent at the state's discretion.

As for the second point, the restriction of the expenditure of *zakat* proceeds to the eight categories cannot convince those to extend the meaning of 'in the Cause of Allah', because they always argue that things like building mosques are included in the share of *fi sabili'llah*. It is necessary to determine whether this category is restricted to fighting and defending Muslims or covers other public interests too. To do this, we must survey the use of the term in the Qur'an.

The term *'sabili'llah'* in the Qur'an

The term *'sabili'llah'* appears in the Qur'an more than sixty times, in either of two ways: more frequently preceded by the preposition 'in' (*fi*) as in the *ayat* on *zakat* distribution, and, in twenty-three places, preceded by one of two verbs that mean 'to

1. *Fath al-Qadir*, vol. 2, p. 20.
2. *Al-Mughni*, vol. 2, p. 167.

prevent or mislead', such as *"Those who reject and bar access to the way of Allah have gone far into misguidance,"* (4:167); *"Those who disbelieve spend their wealth to bar access to the Way of Allah,"* (8:36); and *"But there are some people who trade in distracting tales to misguide from Allah's Way without any knowledge."* (31:6) When the term *'sabili'llah'* is preceded by 'in', as in the *ayats*, *"Spend in the Way of Allah," "those who emigrate in the Way of Allah," "fight in the Way of Allah, "those who fight in the way of Allah, they kill and are killed,"* and *"Do not say about those killed in the Way of Allah, 'they are dead,'"* how should the term be interpreted?

The word *'sabil'* means 'way' and *'sabili'llah'* is the path that leads to the nearness and pleasure of Allah. Allah sent Prophets to guide His creatures to Him, and ordained the last of His Messenger to *"Call to the Way of your Lord with wisdom and fair admonition,"* (16:125) and ordered His Messenger to say: *"This is my way. I call to Allah with inner sight, I and all who follow me."* (12:108) Opposition to the Way of Allah is the way of the *taghut* or evil transgression, which is called for by Shaytan and his followers and which ends at the Fire and earns the wrath of Allah. Comparing these two ways, Allah says, *"Those who believe fight in the Way of Allah. Those who reject fight in the way of false gods."* (4:76) Those who call to the Way of Allah are few and those who prevent people from it are many: *"They spend their wealth in order to bar people from the Way of Allah", "...and there are people who buy vain talk in order to divert from the Way of Allah", "And if you obey most of those who are on the earth, they would divert you from the Way of Allah."*

The responsibilities and demands of the Way of Allah are sizeable, and people's worldly desires usually oppose it. The Qur'an warns against pursuing those desires. *"And do not follow your whims, because that will mislead you from the Way of Allah."* If the enemies of Allah expend money and effort to bar people from the Way of Allah, it is the duty of the supporters of Allah's Cause to sacrifice effort and wealth in the Way of Allah. This is why Islam devotes part of obligatory *zakat* to this cause, in addition to the general encouragement of believers to spend for the sake of Allah.

The term *'sabili'llah'* associated with spending

The term *'sabili'llah'*, when associated in the Qur'an with spending, is used in two ways:

- The general meaning, derived from the original linguistic one, covers all virtues and good deeds, as in the *ayats*: *"The likeness of those who spend their wealth in the Way of Allah is that of a grain which produces seven ears, in every ear there is a hundred grains. Allah gives such multiplied increase to whoever He wills"* (2:261), and *"Those who spend their wealth in the Way of Allah, and then do not follow what they have spent by demands for gratitude or insulting words will have their reward with their Lord. They will feel no fear and know no sorrow."* (2:262) No one can claim that *'sabili'llah'* is restricted to fighting for the Cause of Allah in these *ayats*. Condescension and insult to the recipient mentioned in the verse can only be done toward the poor and needy. *'Sabili'llah'* has a broad meaning in the *ayat*, *"And promise those who hoard up gold and silver and do not spend it in the Way of Allah a severe punishment,"* as stated by Ibn Hajar, and is not restricted to fighting. Otherwise, giving wealth to the poor, needy and traveller would be a form of hoarding.[1] Some contemporary writers claim that *'sabili'llah'*, when associated with spending, is restricted to fighting,[2] but such a claim is unsupported by evidence.

- The second meaning restricts *'sabili'llah'* to supporting the *deen* of Allah, fighting its enemies, and raising high the Word of Allah on earth. The context within which the term is used determines whether it refers to the broad or restricted meaning. When the term is used in association with the idea of fighting for Allah's sake, it must also mean spending for His Cause, as in *"Spend in the Way of Allah. Do not cast yourselves into destruction."* (2:195) "Spending" here refers to raising high the Word of Allah by fighting the enemies of Islam, because fighting in the Way of Allah is mentioned in the *ayat* before it.

1. *Fath al-Bari*, vol. 3, p. 172.
2. *An-Nizam al-Iqtisadi fi'l-Islam*, an-Nabhani, p. 208.

Other examples are in the *ayats*, *"And how is it with you that you do not give in the Way of Allah, when the inheritance of the heavens and the earth belongs to Allah? Those of you who gave and fought before the Victory are not the same as those who gave and fought afterwards. They are higher in rank. But to each of them Allah has promised the Best."* (57:10) And *"Arm yourselves against them with all the firepower and cavalry you can muster, to terrify the enemies of Allah and your enemies, and others besides them whom you do not know. Allah knows them. Anything you spend in the Way of Allah will be repaid to you in full. You will not be wronged."* (8:60)

It is obvious that "in the Way of Allah" refers to fighting the enemies of Allah, as elucidated by the sound *hadith*, "He who fights to make the word of Allah supreme is fighting for the sake of Allah." (agreed upon) This specific meaning is what is usually called *jihad*, but it must be noted that support of the Cause of Allah includes more than fighting, especially when the term used is "perform *jihad* in the Way of Allah."

Which meaning applies to the *ayat* on *zakat* distribution

In my opinion, the general meaning is not suitable to this *ayat*, since the verse lists specific categories entitled to *zakat*, as confirmed by the *hadith* of the Prophet (p), "Indeed, Allah does not accept the ruling of a Prophet (p) or anyone else on *sadaqat*, so He Himself gave His ruling, and divided it into eight parts." Moreover, the general meaning of *'sabili'llah'* includes in fact the other seven categories. Why then does Allah enumerate the other seven? The glorious words of Allah are void of useless repetition or redundancy. So there must be a distinct meaning for the category of 'in the Way of Allah".

Therefore Muslim jurists and Qur'an commentators have for centuries understood this term to mean *jihad* (fighting for His Cause) as well as supporting fighting. Scholars state, "Whenever the term *'sabili'llah'* is left unrestricted, it means fighting for Allah's sake." Ibn al-Athir says, "The term became specific to *jihad* as a result of frequent use." This understanding is supported by a report of at-Tabarani that one day, some Companions were with the Messenger of Allah and saw a strong young man. They said, "This youth and strength were used in the Way of Allah,"[1] meaning in *jihad*.

Several sound *hadiths* from the Prophet (p) and his Companions indicate that the immediate meaning of the term *'sabili'llah'* is *jihad*. Among these is the sound report that 'Umar said, "I gave a horse in the Way of Allah," meaning for *jihad*, and the *hadith* reported by al-Bukhari and Muslim that, "A departure in the morning or in the afternoon in the Way of Allah is better than the world and what is in it." A *hadith* reported by al-Bukhari states, "He who tethers a mare in the Way of Allah out of faith in Him and belief in His promise, will have the eating, drinking, excretion and urination of the mare added to the scale of his good deeds on the Day of Judgement", while a *hadith* reported by an-Nasa'i and at-Tirmidhi states, "He who spends an amount in the Way of Allah, it is recorded for him seven hundred-fold." Another *hadith* reported by al-Bukhari says, "He whose feet are dirtied in the Way of Allah will never be touched by the Fire."[2] No one understands *'sabili'llah'* in those quotations to mean anything other than *jihad*.

Above all, the interpretation of *'sabili'llah'* to mean fighting is supported by the tradition that *zakat* is not lawful for the rich except in five cases, among them being the fighter in the Way of Allah. Accordingly, I do not extend the meaning of the term *'fi sabili'llah'* to include all good deeds. On the other hand, I do not restrict it to military fighting alone. *Jihad* for the sake of Allah includes supporting His Cause by writing and speaking as much as by fighting. *Jihad* may be educational, journalistic, social, economic or political *jihad* as much as military *jihad*. We must remember that in all kinds of *jihad*, the essential condition is that the action helps make Allah's word supreme on earth.

At-Tabari says "*'Fi sabili'llah'* means spending to support the *deen* of Allah, its way of life, its law which is Allah's gift to humanity, and to fight all its enemies, the unbelievers." The first

1. In *at-Targhib*, al-Mundhiri says, "reported by at-Tabarani. The people of the chain are the same as the people of the *Sahih* collection," vol. 3, p. 4.

2. Al-Mundhiri in *at-Targhib* lists all these chapters, vol. 2, *Jihad* chapter.

part of at-Tabari's statement obviously indicates that all actions aimed at establishing this *deen* are *'fi sabili'llah'*, but fighting unbelievers mentioned in the last part is only one way of supporting Islam, since religion can sometimes be supported by cultural means instead.

The majority of scholars in the four schools of jurisprudence restrict this share to financing fighters and defenders of Islam. Today we must add fighters of opposing ideologies, since cultural colonialism is worse than military colonialism. This expanded meaning of *jihad* is supported by the fact that *jihad* is not restricted to military action When the Prophet (p) was asked which *jihad* is better, it is authentically reported that he answered, "A word of truth in the presence of an oppressive ruler."[1]

Muslim reports from Ibn Mas'ud in his *Sahih* Collection that the Messenger of Allah (p) said, "There was no Prophet sent by Allah to any nation before me but that he had from among his people close companions and friends who followed his practice and followed his orders. After them, generations come who say what they do not do, and do what they are not ordered to do. He who makes *jihad* against them with his hands is a believer; he who makes *jihad* against them with his tongue is a believer; and he who makes *jihad* against them in his heart is a believer. Not a single grain of faith exists beyond that." The Prophet (p) also says, "Make *jihad* against those who associate partners with Allah, with your wealth, your selves and your tongues."[2]

Furthermore, writing, lecturing and organising work in the Way of Allah are included in *jihad* by analogy, even if they are not mentioned specifically by the Prophet (p), since such efforts are necessary to support and defend Islam, to resist aggression against its teachings, society, and state, and to make Allah's Word supreme on earth. We noted earlier in this book that Ibn Rushd said, "Those

---

1. Reported by Ahmad, an-Nasa'i, al-Bayhaqi in *ash-Shu'ab*, and ad-Diya' al-Maqdisi from Tariq ibn Shihab. Al-Mundhiri says it is reported by an-Nasa'i and its chain is sound. See al-Munawi, *at-Taysir*, vol. 1, p. 182.

2. Reported by Ahmad, Abu Dawud, an-Nasa'i, Ibn Hibban and al-Hakim, from Anas. Al-Hakim says it is sound. This is approved by others. See *at-Taysir*, vol. 1, p. 485.

who allow payment to *zakat* workers even if they are rich also allow payment to judges and persons who work for Muslims' public interest."[1]

We also noted that some Hanafi jurists include in the category of travellers every person detached from his or her wealth and unable to make use of it, even if such a person is in his or her hometown. By the same token, all activities that fulfil the same purpose of fighting for the sake of Allah must be treated like *jihad*. Analogy can be applied in *zakat*; every school of jurisprudence applies analogy in *zakat* one way or another, and this is an appropriate analogy.

I believe the term 'in the Way of Allah' includes fighting and all activities that achieve the same goal as fighting, which is consistent with the opinion of the majority of jurists with a little expansion. It must also be noted that certain activities may be included as being 'in the Way of Allah' in certain periods in certain countries,which may not be included in other lands or times.

Establishing an Islamic school, for example, though beneficial to Muslims, is not included in *jihad*. Yet in a country whose educational institutions are dominated by secularists, communists or missionaries, one of the best means of *jihad* is establishing an Islamic school to protect Muslim children from such destructive and demoralising preaching. Likewise, an Islamic library may sometimes be only a good and beneficial project, but may at other times in other places be a *jihad*. The same thing may be stated about an Islamic hospital that protects Muslims patients from being exploited by missionary hospitals, and other cultural projects that perform similar tasks.

Activities included under 'in the Cause of Allah' today

The wars in which the Companions and Followers battled were fought solely to help people quit the worship of human creatures for the worship of Allah, the Creator, to eradicate oppression and establish the justice of Islam. Some people think this kind of war does not happen anymore and that contemporary wars in Muslim

1. *Bidayat al-Mujtahid*, vol. 1, p. 267.

countries are merely nationalistic, having nothing to do with religion, so *zakat* must not be given to Muslims who fight such wars.

Such thinking is grossly erroneous, because, first of all, Islamic *jihad* is not restricted to the wars in which the Companions fought. It is true that the wars fought by the Companions and Followers are unique in the history of humanity in regard to the goals of the Muslims fighters, their manners, and their moral behaviour during and after the wars. No doubt the wars of the Companions are the most ideal wars in Muslim history, but history has witnessed many other wars in which Muslims defended their values, sacred places and communities which are no less sacred than the wars of the Companions and Followers, such as those which defended Muslim lands against Mongol and Crusader aggressors.

If the fighting of the Companions and Followers were for the Cause of Islam, the fighting of leaders like Nur ad-Din, Salah ad-Din, and Qutuz were in defence of the homelands of Islam. *Jihad* is obligatory in order to protect Muslim land as much as it is obligatory to protect the Islamic faith. Fighting in defence of Muslim land is legitimate from an Islamic standpoint if it is not based simply on love of country. A Muslim may leave the homeland of his ancestors and go to live where Islam is fully implemented, as the Prophet and his Companions did by emigrating from Makka to Madina for the sake of Allah.

The most honourable form of *jihad* nowadays is fighting for the liberation of Muslim land from the domination of the unbelievers, regardless of their religion or ideology. The communist and the capitalist, the Westerner and the Easterner, Christian, Jew, pagan or unbeliever, all are aggressors when they attack and occupy Muslim land. Fighting in defence of the home of Islam is obligatory until the enemy is driven away and Muslims are liberated.

Today Muslim land is occupied in Palestine, Kashmir, Eritrea, Ethiopia, Chad, Western Somalia, Cyprus, Samarqand, Bukhara, Tashkent, Uzbekistan, Albania and several other occupied countries. Declaring a holy war to save these Muslim lands is an Islamic duty, and fighting for such purposes in those occupied territories is in the Way of Allah for which *zakat* must be spent.

Not all fighting by Muslims is in the Way of Allah

Some people believe that every military action taken by Muslims is in the Way of Allah, regardless of its objectives. An essential distinction must be made between fighting for the sake of Allah and nationalistic or class wars. Fighting for the sake of Allah is motivated purely by Islamic vision and directed towards making the Word of Allah supreme,or defending the homeland of Islam and Muslims. Any war devoid of this spiritual content is an earthly war, whether waged by Muslims or unbelievers. Wars disassociated from the above goals and directions cannot be financed by *zakat*.

Only fighting for the establishment of the *deen* of Allah on earth is sacred in Islam, and only this kind of war deserves the sacrifice of human lives and material wealth. Fighting for the liberation of Muslims and Muslim land from colonialism and other forms of oppression are acceptable as means to establishing Islam on earth, but fighting for the sake of liberating the soil and mud in order to establish other ideologies is not recognised as *jihad* and cannot be financed by *zakat*.

Abu Muhammad 'Abdu'l-Ghani al-Hafiz reports, via his own chain of transmission from 'Abdu'r-Rahman ibn Abi Nu'm, "I was sitting with 'Abdullah ibn 'Umar when a woman came up and said, 'O Abu 'Abdu'r-Rahman, in his last will my husband says his wealth should be spent in the Cause of Allah.' Ibn 'Umar said, 'Let it be spent as he wished, in the Cause of Allah.' I said, 'You did not answer her question.' 'Abdullah said, 'What do you want me to tell her? Should I tell her to give the money to these troops that destroy land and cut off roads?' I said, 'What would you tell her then?' 'Abdullah replied, 'I would tell her to give it to righteous people, to those making *hajj* to the sacred House of Allah. They are those who come to the All-Merciful. They are those who come to the All-Merciful. They are those who come to the All-Merciful."[1]

1. *Tafsir al-Qurtubi*, vol. 8, p. 185. It seems that this story is the source of the report that Ibn 'Umar said, "*Hajj* is 'in the Way of Allah'" as one understands from the context in al-Qurtubi. It must be noted that the words of Ibn 'Umar indicate that 'the Way of Allah', when not restricted, means *jihad*, and he gives it another interpretation only because of the corruption of the troops.

Ibn 'Umar hesitated to describe the war of his time as being in the Way of Allah, although the troops at that time had only one banner, one slogan, and one direction – that of Islam. What would Ibn 'Umar say about the armies of our time, that do not even mention the name of Allah or the word Islam, armies whose men do not pray or worship Allah and whose generals are sunk in drinking and immorality? What would he say about armies whose ideologies are based on secularism which has no place for Allah, His Messenger, or His Sacred Book?

The Messenger of Allah (p) was asked about a man who fights out of bravery, a man who fights out of patriotism, and a man who fights out of pride to be seen – which of these is for the sake of Allah. The Prophet (p) answered, 'He who fights for the Word of Allah to be supreme is for the sake of Allah.'"[1] This *hadith* provides the criteria to distinguish between *jihad* and non-Islamic war, between the Way of Allah and the way of aggression. The Way of Allah aims at making the *deen* of Allah supreme.[2]

Re-establishment of the Islamic state is *jihad*

The best way to spend the share of 'in the Way of Allah' today is, as the reformist Rashid Rida suggests, to establish an organisation of Islamic activists to collect *zakat* and spend it to re-establish the Islamic state. He suggests that *jihad* for establishing the Islamic state is even more important than *jihad* to protect it, and that one of the ways to re-establish the Islamic state is to promote the call to Islam and defend its ideology when defending it by the sword is not needed.[3]

The most important form of *jihad* today is serious, purposefully organised work to rebuild Islamic society and state and to implement the Islamic way of life in the political, cultural and economic domains. This is certainly the most deserving area of *zakat*.

Armies are normally financed by the state's regular resources. This was the case in the early Islamic state which financed the army

1. This is mentioned in *al-Muntaqa*. See *Nayl al-Awtar*, vol. 7, pp. 226-227.
2. Ibid.
3. *Tafsir al-Manar*, vol. 10, p. 598.

from *fay'* and *kharaj*. It is also the case today that the government's general budget provides for its army. Financing a regular army requires huge resources that by far exceed the proceeds of *zakat*. If modern armies were to depend on *zakat*, they would take perhaps all of its proceeds and still need more.

Therefore I believe that cultural, educational and informational *jihad* in the Way of Allah should be given priority today, as long as such *jihad* is a purely Islamic effort that aims at re-establishing the Islamic state. Examples of activities that desperately need finance from *zakat* in order to serve the cause of making the Word of Allah supreme are building centres for the call to Islam (*da'wa*), which provide correct and pure Islamic information to men and women throughout the world, and establishing Islamic centres, even in Muslim countries, to provide Islamic education and training and protect the faith of Muslim youth from deviation, agnosticism, and behavioural corruption. Such centres are crucial for they prepare Muslim youth to support Islam and resist the aggression of its enemies. Another example would be the establishment of a purely Islamic newspaper which would provide guidance to Muslim men and women in their daily lives and increase Islamic political and social awareness.

Issuance of Islamic books is yet another area where *jihad* in the Way of Allah can be practised, for it is crucial to reveal the treasures of this religion as a better way of life. Yet another example of *jihad* is to provide for full-time workers in the Way of Allah. These and similar activities deserve the share of *zakat* in the Way of Allah.

Chapter Seven

Travellers

According to the majority of scholars, a traveller (*ibn as-sabil*) is someone on the way from one location to another. Literally, the term means 'son of the road'. This form of expression, 'son of such-and-such', is common in Arabic.

At-Tabari reports from Mujahid, "Travellers have a right to *zakat* even if rich, as long as they are cut off from their wealth. Ibn Zayd says, "A traveller is anyone travelling, rich or poor, who has lost his means of expenditure or depleted them while on the road. Helping this person is obligatory."[1]

Care for the traveller in the Qur'an

The Glorious Qur'an mentions travellers eight times, in the context of encouraging kindness toward them. In Makkan *suras*, Allah says, *"Give relatives their due, and the very poor and travellers but do not squander what you have"* (17:26) and *"Give relatives their due and the poor and travellers"* (30:38). In Madinan *suras*, Allah designates for travellers a share of wealth spent in the Way of Allah. Allah says, *"They will ask you what they should give away. Say: 'Any wealth you give away should go to your parents and relatives and orphans and the very poor and travellers.'"* (2:215)

Allah ordains doing good to travellers in the verse, *"Worship Allah and do not attribute partners to Him. Be good to your parents and relatives and to orphans and the very poor, and to neighbours who are related to you and neighbours who are not related to you, and to companions and travellers and your slaves."* (4:36) Allah also gives travellers a share in the fifth taken from war booty: *"Know that when you take any booty a fifth of it belongs to Allah, and to the Messenger, and to close rela-*

1. *Tafsir at-Tabari*, vol. 14, p. 320.

tives, orphans, the very poor and travellers." (8:41) Also Allah provides a share of the *fay'* to travellers, saying, *"Whatever booty Allah gives to His Messenger from city dwellers belongs to Allah and to the Messenger and to near relatives and orphans and the very poor and travellers."* (59:7) Lastly, Allah gives a share of *zakat* to travellers in the verse we are studying. Moreover, helping travellers is one of the deeds of righteousness in the verse: *"Who, despite their love for it, give away their wealth to their relatives and to orphans and the very poor, and to travellers and beggars and to set slaves free, and who establish the prayer and pay* zakat*."* (2:177)

The reason for the attention given to travellers

The reason for the attention given travellers in the Qur'an is that Islam encourages travelling for several reasons.

- Travelling for work and opportunity. Allah says, *"Walk its broad trails and eat what it provides"* (67:15) and *"And others are travelling in the land seeking Allah's bounty, and others are fighting in the Way of Allah."* (73:20) The Prophet (p) said, "Travel so that you become rich."[1]
- Travelling to seek knowledge and meditate on the signs of Allah in the world and on His animal and human communities. Allah says, *"Travel in the earth and see how He brought creation out of nothing"* (29:20); *"Whole societies have passed away before your time, so travel the earth and see the end result of the deniers"* (3:137) and *"Have they not travelled in the land and have they not hearts to understand with or ears to hear with?"* (22:46) The Messenger (p) says, "He who takes a path seeking knowledge, Allah will make easy for him a way to the Garden,"[2] and "He who goes out in pursuit of knowledge is in the Way of Allah until he returns."[3] Early Muslim scholars provide ideal examples in their ardent travelling in pursuit of knowledge, which is recorded with admiration by contemporary scholars.

1. Mentioned by al-Mundhiri in *at-Targhib wa't-Tarhib*, vol. 2. He adds, "Reported by at-Tabarani in *al-Awsat* via a trustworthy chain."
2. In *at-Targhib*, al-Mundhiri says, "Reported by Muslim and others."
3. Ibid., reported by at-Tirmidhi, who rates it good.

• Travel for *jihad* in the Way of Allah. This includes defending Muslim land, calling to Islam, liberating the oppressed and punishing those who break pledges with the Muslims. Allah says, *"Go out to fight, whatever your circumstances or desires, and do jihad with your wealth and yourselves in the way of Allah. That is better for you if you only knew."* (9:41) Then He speaks of the hypocrites: *"If it had been a case of easy gains and a short journey, they would have followed you, but the distance was too great for them..."* (9:42) Allah promises, *"Nor will they give away any amount, whether large or small, nor will they cross any valley, without it being written down for them so that Allah can recompense them for the best of what they did."* (9:121) The Prophet (p) says, "A single departure in the morning or in the afternoon in the Way of Allah is better than this world and what it contains." (al-Bukhari)

• Travel to perform pilgrimage to the Sacred House of Allah, the fifth pillar of Islam. Allah says, *"*Hajj *to the House is a duty owed to Allah by all mankind – those who can find a way to do it."* (3:97) *"Announce the* Hajj *to mankind. They will come to you on foot and on all sorts of lean animals, coming by every distant road so that they can be present at what will profit them and mention Allah's name on particular days."* (22:27-28)

These are kinds of travelling and journeying in the land that Islam calls for or encourages in order to realise its objectives on earth and affirm its teachings among people. Admittedly, there are other reasons for travelling, yet a religion that specifically encourages the above listed kinds of travel must provide for travellers, especially those who are cut off from families and wealth. Helping travellers reaffirms the solidarity of the Muslim community, regardless of geographic location or place of origin.

Care for travellers builds social solidarity

This form of social insurance is unique to Islam. In its social programme, Islam not only guarantees the provision of somewhere to stay, but provides security from unforeseen mishaps that affect people who are on the road. To get the complete picture of this insurance, one must remember that it came at a time when there were no hotels, restaurants, or rest areas for travellers. Motivated by this idea of taking care of travellers, 'Umar ibn al-Khattab established stations on the road between Makka and Madina to help travellers and provide transportation for those who needed it between oases. He also established a food storage area for those who needed food on the road and in the city.[1]

'Umar ibn 'Abdu'l-'Aziz asked az-Zuhri to write him a detailed outline on how to spend *zakat* based on his knowledge of the practice of the Prophet and the first four Khalifs. Among other things, az-Zuhri wrote, "The share of travellers must be divided in accordance with the density of traffic on the road, so that roads with a higher number of people passing along them are assigned a bigger proportion of the *zakat* proceeds. Each traveller who has no means to continue or return must be provided with food until he achieves the purpose of his journey or reaches home. Places of shelter must be established, and trustworthy people assigned to manage them so that any passing traveller can be provided food, shelter, and fodder for his animal, until all the *zakat* funds you assign are used up."[2] Has humanity ever witnessed such a level of caring for needy men and women wherever they may be?

Is someone who wants to go on a journey considered to be a traveller?

Jurists differ on whether a traveller is only someone actually on a journey or whether the term also includes someone who is at home but desires to begin a journey. The majority believe that someone who wants to start travelling is not a traveller, for the following reasons:

- The term *'ibn as-sabil'* means someone on the road and does not include someone who is at home.
- A traveller is a person who is cut off from his financial means at home. A person who has not yet started travelling is not cut

1. Ibn Sa'd, *at-Tabaqat*, vol. 3, p. 283.
2. *Al-Amwal*, p. 580.

off from his means. Travellers must be helped until they reach their home, regardless of whether their financial help for travelling or other purposes is given as a poor person or as a traveller.[1]

Ash-Shafi'i believes that "travellers" also includes people who want to start a journey but do not have sufficient means, on the grounds that such persons need help to travel just like the person on the road.[2]

In my opinion, the view of the majority is sounder. *Zakat* funds must not be spent on those who desire to initiate a journey. However, ash-Shafi'i's view may be applicable if the intended travel is for the service of the Muslim community, for instance to call people to Islam or for a scientific mission needed for the Muslim community, provided that such a need is recognised by people of knowledge. Helping such potential travellers may also be included in the category of "in the Way of Allah." This is supported by the fact that travellers are listed after, and in addition to, the term 'in the Way of Allah' in the *ayat* we are studying.

Keeping in mind that the wording of the *ayat* – the use of in (*fi*) instead of to (*li*) – allows payment to be made to a third party on behalf of the traveller, such as a transport or airline company, since the *ayat* indicates that *zakat* should be spent on the traveller and not necessarily given to him, Hanbalis believe that a traveller who is on his way to a town other than his own must be provided with what he or she needs to reach the destination, fulfil the objective of the journey, and return home. This applies when the travelling is either in obedience to Allah, such as on *hajj* or visiting parents, or merely permissible, such as on business.

Hanbalis differ about travelling for the purpose of amusement only. Some argue that this travelling is not essential or needed, and consequently *zakat* funds should not be spent on it,[3] while others take it at face value as travelling, meaning that a traveller on a pleasure journey can also be helped from *zakat*. If a traveller who is on

1. *Ash-Sharh al-Kabir*, with *al-Mughni*, vol. 2, p. 702.
2. *Al-Majmu'*, vol. 6, and *Nihayat al-Muhtaj*, vol. 6, p. 156.
3. *Ash-Sharh al-Kabir*, vol. 2,. pp. 702-703.

a business or pleasure journey may be given help out of *zakat*, he who travels for the service of Islam and Muslims must be more entitled to such funds.

Conditions for payment

The first condition is that the traveller must be in need when on the road, since the primary purpose of *zakat* is to help travellers reach their home. If he has the means of reaching his home, no payment can be made. This is unlike fighters in the Way of Allah who, according to other than the Hanafis, are given *zakat* regardless of their need since the purpose of giving to the fighters is to uplift their spirit and support their stand against the enemy.

The second condition is that the journey must not be in disobedience to Allah. This exclusion means that those who travel for sinful purposes or traders whose commodities are forbidden must not be given *zakat*, except if the their lives are at stake. Saving life then becomes an obligation in the *Shari'a*.[1] The purpose of this condition is obviously to refrain from helping wrongdoers.

Travelling which is not disobedience to Allah is of three kinds: travelling to do good deeds or worship Allah, such as *hajj*, *jihad* and seeking knowledge; travelling for lawful earthly reasons, such as on business or in search of a job; and travelling for amusement and tourism. Only giving to travellers of the third group is disputed among jurists,[2] while giving to travellers in the first two is unanimously lawful, On the other hand, Shafi'is, who believe in giving to the person who is starting a journey, differ as to whether such a person may be given *zakat* if the trip is not necessary.

Some Malikis and Shafi'is add a third condition, that the traveller must not be able to borrow to satisfy his or her needs.[3] This applies only if the traveller is rich at home. This condition is not upheld by some other scholars of the two schools. Ibn al-'Arabi in

1. *Hashiyat ad-Dusuqi*, vol. 1, p. 498. Some Malikis believe he must not be given anything, even if his life is threatened, since he always has the means to safety by repentance. See *Hashiyat as-Sawi*, vol. 1, p. 233.

2. *Al-Majmu'*, vol. 6, pp. 214-215, and *ash-Sharh al-Kabir*, vol. 2, pp. 701-702.

3. *Sharh al-Khirashi*, on the text of Khalil, vol. 2, p. 219, and *Nihayat al-Muhtaj*, vol. 6, p. 156.

Ahkam al-Qur'an, and al-Qurtubi in his *Tafsir* reject this condition, since a traveller need not be obliged to anyone if he or she can only be obliged to Allah.[1] An-Nawawi adds that even if, by taking *zakat*, the traveller can borrow money, he or she is not required to take a loan and may take *zakat*.[2] Hanafis recommend taking loans if possible, but do not oblige it, on the grounds that taking a loan exposes the borrower to the possibility of becoming unable to pay the loan back and he or she need not take that chance.[3]

How much should travellers be given?

- Travellers should be given their sufficiency of food and clothing until they reach their home or a place where they have funds of their own. If a traveller has less than is needed, *zakat* should be given to supplement the existing funds until they are sufficient.
- For long journeys, a means of transportation must also be provided. Long journeys are those in which the prayer is shortened, i.e. approximately 80 km [50 miles]. Rides may be purchased or rented for the traveller depending on the circumstances, need and availability of *zakat* funds.
- All necessary expenses should be given and not only those expenses caused by travelling.
- Payment can be made to travellers regardless of their ability to work and earn
- As for travellers' expenses at their destination, Shafi'is say that they should be met if the stay there is less than four days, excluding days of arrival and departure, the same number of days as in the case of shortening the prayer because of travelling. This restriction does not apply to fighters in the Way of Allah whose expenses should be met for the whole period they stay at frontier posts, no matter how long it may be. Some scholars believe travellers should be given funds for the whole

1. *Ahkam al-Qur'an*, vol. 2, p. 958, and *Tafsir al-Qurtubi*, vol. 8, p. 187.
2. *Al-Majmu'*, vol. 6, p. 216.
3. *Fath al-Qadir*, vol. 2, p. 18, and *Radd al-Muhtar*, vol. 2, p. 64.

period of their stay in the place of destination, regardless of its length.[1]

- If a traveller returns home with leftover *zakat* money, this residue must be returned to the *zakat* fund, according to Shafi'is.[2] Hanafis argue that travellers are not obliged to give back any *zakat* left over from their trip.[3]

Are there travellers today?

Some contemporary scholars assert that today there are no more travellers in the original sense of the word because of the transportation, accommodation, and banking facilities that make travelling easy and wealth accessible anywhere in the world. This is argued by the late Ahmad Mustafa al-Maraghi in his explanation of the Qur'an.[4] I beg to differ with him, since there are as many travellers today as there were in the past.

- Some people may be rich, but do not do business with banks, so that when they are away from their towns they are actually detached from their wealth, or they may be crossing some desert far from urban centres and unable to contact their banks.
- There are refugees who are driven out of their homes and lands by aggressors or who flee from dictatorial governments. They may live for an undetermined period of time outside their countries, unable to reach their wealth which is often confiscated by the government. Amongst those are political refugees who seek asylum in countries other than their own.
- Some Hanafis consider individuals who, although they are rich and live in their own towns, have no access to their wealth, such as businessmen whose wealth is in the form of unremittable loans to others.[5] These jurists assert that such individuals may be treated as travellers and given *zakat*.[6]

1. *Al-Majmu'*, vol. 6, pp. 215-216, and *ash-Sharh al-Kabir*, vol. 2, pp. 701-702.
2. *Al-Majmu'*, vol. 6, p. 216.
3. *Fath al-Qadir*, vol. 2, p. 18, and *Radd al-Muhtar*, vol. 2, p. 64.
4. *Tafsir al-Maraghi*, vol. 28, explanation of 59:6.
5. *Al-Bahr ar-Ra'iq*, vol. 2, p. 260.
6. *Radd al-Muhtar*, vol. 2, p. 64.

• There are those who intend to initiate journeys for public service or for individual affairs that are beneficial to the public, such as students who want to pursue training abroad.

• Some Hanbalis include, under the definition of travellers, tramps or street beggars who have no homes[1] Such persons are literally *ibn as-sabil*, or children of the street. They may be given from the share of travellers as well as from the share of the poor.

• And lastly, foundling infants may be included in this category, according to Rashid Rida, who says the term *ibn as-sabil* perfectly describes foundlings since they are in fact children of the street. Islam takes good care of orphans, and foundlings are even more in need of care than orphans with known relatives.[2]

1. *Al-Insaf*, vol. 3, p. 237.
2. *Tafsir al-Manar*, vol. 5, p. 94.

Chapter Eight

Issues Related to the Deserving Categories

Must *zakat* be divided equally between the eight categories?

In the Qur'an Allah mentions eight categories who deserve *zakat*. Should *zakat* be distributed each year to all eight categories? Should the proceeds be equally divided between them?

Some jurists understand the verse in this sense, like ash-Shafi'i in *al-Umm*. In *al-Majmu'*, an-Nawawi says, "Ash-Shafi'i and his disciples believe that when *zakat* is distributed by the payer or the payer's representative, the share of *zakat* workers is dropped, and the amount due must be distributed to the other seven categories, if they exist. It is not permissible to abandon an existing category. If an existing category is abandoned, its share is guaranteed by the owner. This is also the view of 'Ikrima, 'Umar ibn 'Abdu'l-'Aziz, az-Zuhri and Da'ud."[1] In one of several reports, Ahmad agrees with ash-Shafi'i on the equal distribution between all categories and on the rule that at least three persons in each category except *zakat* collectors (who might be one) should be given *zakat*, because the *ayat* uses the plural form and three is the minimum number for which a plural form is used. This is the view preferred by Abu Bakr, a Hanbali.[2] The Maliki, Asbagh, also prefers the Shafi'i opinion.[3]

Ibn al-'Arabi says, "It is agreed that it is not permissible to give all the proceeds of *zakat* to *zakat* workers since this does not fulfil the objectives of *zakat* which is to satisfy the poor and the needs of Islam, as at-Tabari puts it. Shafi'is argue that the *ayat* in *zakat* distri-

1. *Al-Majmu'*, vol. 6, p. 185.
2. *Al-Kafi*, Ibn Qudama, vol. 1, p. 146.
3. As quoted from al-Khirashi by as-Sawi in his *Hashiyat*, vol. 1, p. 334.

bution uses the preposition "to" (*li*) which means that proceeds must be given so that each recipient becomes owner of what he or she is given. This implies giving to all of them.[1] Shafi'is also present as evidence the *hadith* reported by Abu Dawud from Ziyad ibn al-Harith as-Suda'i: "I came to the Messenger of Allah (p) and gave him my covenant. A man came and said, 'Give to me from the *sadaqa*.' The Messenger of Allah (p) said, 'Allah did not leave the distribution of *sadaqat* to a Prophet or anyone else. He gave the ruling and divided the proceeds into eight parts. If you are in any of these parts, I will give you your right.'"

Malik, Abu Hanifa and their disciples disagree with ash-Shafi'i. They do not require distribution to cover all categories, asserting that the preposition 'to' (*li*) in the *ayat* does not mean one must make the recipient own what is given but means 'for whom'. These scholars offer as evidence the following *ayat*: *"If you make your* sadaqa *public that is good. But if you conceal it and give it to the poor, that is better for you."* (2:271) This *ayat* only mentions the poor and makes no reference to other categories, and they also cite the *hadith*, "I am commanded to take *sadaqa* from the rich among you and render it to the poor among you." They argue that *sadaqa* in the Qur'an means *zakat* unless specified otherwise and that not mentioning the other categories in these two texts is an indication that giving to the poor alone is satisfactory.[2]

Abu 'Ubayd reports that Ibn 'Abbas said, "If you spend *zakat* on one of these categories, it is all right, since Allah says, 'Sadaqat *is only for the poor and needy...'* which means *zakat* must not be given outside these categories." The same is reported from Hudhayfa. Ibn Shihab says, "The category which deserves *zakat* most is the one that is bigger in number and whose need is greater." Sufyan and jurists from Iraq (Abu Hanifa and his followers) believe that spending *zakat* on one of the right categories is enough. An-Nakha'i suggests that when funds are plenty, it is better to distribute it to all categories, but when funds are limited, one category is sufficient. A similar opinion is attributed to 'Ata'.[3]

---

1. *Ahkam al-Qur'an*, vol. 2, p. 947.
2. Ibid.
3. *Al-Amwal*, pp. 576-578.

Abu Thawr suggests that when the owner distributes his own *zakat*, it may be given to one category only, but when *zakat* is distributed by the state, all categories must be included. Malik adds, "It is left to the state's *zakat* agency to distribute to those categories whose needs are greater. This is what I have heard expressed by scholars whom I respect." In my opinion, this last view is the soundest and most reasonable.

The opinion of Siddiq Hasan Khan

In *ar-Rawda an-Nadiya*, Siddiq Hasan Khan argues that the fact that Allah restricts *zakat* distribution to the eight categories does not necessarily mean *zakat* proceeds must be divided equally between them. Obliging Muslims to divide their *zakat* equally between the eight deserving categories entails great hardship and difficulty, and furthermore such a course differs from the course followed by the Muslims, both in early and later times. A situation might result in an insignificant amount being divided between all categories in such a way that it would be of no use to anyone.

In such a case, it is better to give it to one category. The *hadith* reported by Ziyad ibn al-Harith about dividing *zakat* into eight categories may refer to the suitable areas in which *zakat* can be spent. It does not mean that if one of the categories is absent, that amount cannot be given to another category. Such a conclusion would be contrary to the consensus of the Muslims. If that refers to *zakat* which has been collected by the ruler and not the *zakat* of the individual, then such equal distribution is not mandatory.

When the ruler has collected all the *zakat* of the area and the eight categories exist, each category should receive what Allah has allotted to it. However, the distribution does not have to be equal or include all of them. Some categories may be given more than others and some of those entitled may be given to rather than others if the ruler deems that to be in the best interests of the Muslims. For example, the *zakat* may be collected at a time when *jihad* is in progress and so defence of Islam against the unbelievers takes precedence and may exhaust all of the *zakat*."[1]

1. *Ar-Rawda an-Nadiya*, vol. 1, pp. 207-208.

The opinion of Abu 'Ubayd

This is also the opinion of Abu 'Ubayd. He mentions what az-Zuhri said to 'Umar ibn 'Abdu'l-'Aziz about the shares and distribution of *zakat* according to the *Sunna*, and how he defined the eight categories. Then he gives the details of what each category was given and how the share was divided among the sub-categories of each of the eight. Abu 'Ubayd then says, "This is the manner in which *zakat* is distributed when all eight categories exist. However, I think this is only a restriction on the ruler who has a large quantity of the Muslims' *zakat* collected, when all categories are entitled to receive something and such distribution is possible. As for the person who only has his own personal *zakat*, he can give it to some rather than others based on the position of the scholars we named."

The basis for this is the *hadith* reported from the Prophet (p) in which he said, "Take it from their rich and give it to their poor." In this instance, the Prophet (p) only mentioned one category. Later he obtained wealth and used some of it in another category: reconciling hearts in the case of al-Aqra' ibn Habis, 'Uyayna ibn Hisn, 'Alqama ibn 'Ulatha and Zayd al-Khayl. Gold was given to them from the money of the people of Yemen. Then there was more money and it was allotted to a third category: debtors. The Prophet (p) also said to someone, "Stay here until the *zakat* comes, so we can give you something from it." So we see that the Prophet (p) gave it to some categories rather than others. Therefore the ruler can choose whether he thinks he should divide it between all of them or give it to some rather than others when it is based on *ijtihad*, and not bias and abandoning the truth.[1]

The opinion of Rashid Rida

In his explanation of the Qur'an, Rashid Rida says, "The fact that our leading scholars differ on this issue is an indication that there is no agreed upon report from the Prophet determining whether or not all categories must be included in each *zakat* distribution. Therefore this issue must be determined after consideration

[1. *Al-Amwal*, pp. 576-578.

of the Muslim community's needs and interests and the size of *zakat* proceeds. The views that fit public interest best are those of Malik and an-Nakha'i, while the opinion farthest from the texts and public interests is that of Abu Hanifa,[1] except when funds are very small. Giving *zakat* to the deserving of only one category, when proceeds are huge, is not acceptable because it does not fulfil the objective of *zakat*. This matter must be settled by the state decision-makers so as to do justice to the general interests of the Muslims, especially since certain categories may sometimes be more important than others."[2]

Summary

After surveying all these views, one can briefly summarise them as follows:

- When funds are plenteous and there are deserving people in all categories, distribution must cover all of them. It is not acceptable to deprive deserving people who are in need. The duty of the state is to collect *zakat* and distribute it according to the needs of the entitled categories.
- Distribution among the eight categories need not be equal, i.e. each group need not receive exactly one-eighth of the total proceeds since the criteria is need of the recipients. I believe the view of Malik and az-Zuhri is most suitable in distributing to the categories on the basis of their respective needs and number.[3]
- The total amount of *zakat* collected may be given to certain categories when this is necessary. Preference must be based on

1. As mentioned earlier, Abu 'Ubayd reports from Ibn 'Abbas and Hudhayfa that this is permissible. Also, the opinion of Abu Hanifa that *zakat* may be give to one category does not prevent distribution according to needs and public interests of Muslims.

2. *Tafsir al-Manar*, vol. 10, p. 593.

3. In *ash-Sharh as-Saghir*, vol. 1, p. 234, ad-Dardir says, "It is encouraged to give preference to those in more need, such as giving them more or giving only to the needy.

actual needs and public interest and not on personal opinion or bias.[1]

- The poor and the needy are the most important category of all. Satisfying their needs is the main objective of *zakat*, as repeatedly mentioned in the *hadiths* of the Prophet. It is not permissible to spend *zakat* on the army while tremendous need exists for food and shelter among the poor and needy. However, there may be exceptionally urgent needs for diverting funds from the poor and needy in response to emergencies in other categories, such as defence.

- The suggestion of ash-Shafi'i regarding *zakat* workers should be applied so that their share does not exceed one-eighth of total proceeds in order to preserve the major part of *zakat* for fulfilling its objectives.

- When *zakat* proceeds are small, as when an individual payer distributes his small amount of *zakat*, all of it may be spent on one deserving person since dividing such a small amount diminishes its usefulness and would not enrich *zakat* recipients, as urged by the Shafi'i school.

1. In *Sharh al-Azhar*, vol. 1, p. 518, it is noted, "The state can make such preference, provided no injustice is done to the other categories. Injustice exists when one poor person is given more than his needs, while a another is given less than what he needs."

Chapter Nine

Categories to whom *Zakat* must Not be Paid

Since *zakat* is a special tax that aims at achieving particular objectives in the lives of individuals as well as society as a whole, it is obvious that there are certain categories of people to whom *zakat* must not be given. These categories are:

- The rich.
- Those capable of earning.
- Disbelievers and apostates who fight against Islam and, according to the majority of jurists, People of the Pledge.
- The children, parents and wives of *zakat* prayers.
- Descendants of the Prophet.

These will be studied in the following sections.

The Rich

Based on the *hadith* of the Prophet (p), "*Sadaqa* is not lawful for the rich," and his statement to Mu'adh that *zakat* is "...to be taken from their rich and rendered to their poor", Muslim jurists unanimously believe that *zakat* must not be given to the rich. Giving it to the rich violates the very purpose of *zakat* which is to enrich the poor. Yet, when it comes to defining wealth that prevents receiving *zakat*, jurists do not have a unified opinion, as was shown earlier when we discussed the definition of the poor and needy.

There is also disagreement about giving *zakat* to the rich under the category of 'in the Way of Allah' or those in debt. Hanafis do not allow this on the basis of the above *hadiths*. They make an exception for *zakat* workers and reconciliation of hearts since what is paid to workers is merely the price of their labour, and in the case of reconciliation of hearts, the Hanafis believe it must be abandoned as a category after the spread of Islam.[1]

Other leading jurists contend that the *hadith* from Mu'adh mentions only the poor because enriching this category is the major goal of *zakat*. They point out that if *zakat* could only be given to the poor and needy, there would be no meaning to the other six categories mentioned in the *ayat* on distribution of *zakat*. By the same argument through which Hanafis exempt workers, those scholars permit paying *zakat* to the rich if they are fighters in the Way of Allah or in debt for mediating disputes.

The fact is that the *ayat* on distribution of *zakat* includes two kinds of deserving recipients. The first group encompasses those who are in need: the poor, the needy, slaves needing emancipation, individuals with personal debts, and travellers. All these are given *zakat* because they need help and relief. The second group comprises those whom the Muslim community needs: workers for the *zakat* agency, individuals whose hearts are being reconciled, persons in debt due to public service, and fighters in the Way of Allah. These people are given to regardless of their poverty or wealth.

The Prophet (p) himself specified, "*Sadaqa* is not lawful for the rich, except in five cases: the fighter in the Way of Allah, the *zakat* worker, the debtor, a person who buys from a recipient of *zakat* an item given as *zakat*, and a person whose poor neighbour receives *zakat* and gives him a gift from it." An-Nawawi comments, "This is a sound or good *hadith*, reported by Abu Dawud through two chains, one *mursal* and the other linked to the Messenger (p).[2]

1. *Fath al-Qadir*, vol. 2, p. 21.

2. An-Nawawi says, "The chains of both narrations are good. Al-Bayhaqi collects all the chains of this *hadith*. Malik and Ibn 'Uyayna report it *mursal*, while Ma'mar and ath-Thawri link it to the Prophet. If a hadith is reported *mursal* and linked, it is considered linked, as long as the chain through which it is linked is accepted, according to the correct rule of hadith research." See *al-Majmu'*, vol. 6, p. 206.

Children are rich if their father is rich

Whether a child is male or female, if the father is rich, the child is also considered rich. However, if the son or daughter is adult, the wealth of the father is not considered in the determination of the wealth or poverty of the child.[1] Wives are also considered according to the prosperity of their husbands. A poor woman does not deserve *zakat* if her husband is rich.

Hanafis consider giving *zakat* to the wife of a rich husband permissible, but Abu Yusuf disagrees, arguing that a wife's needs should be satisfied by the wealth of her husband.[2] Most Hanafis argue that the nature of the husband's obligation to spend on his wife is contractual while a father is obliged to spend on his young child by virtue of parenthood.[3] Some Shafi'is go along with the Hanafis and allow payment of *zakat* to the wife of a rich man. Some even allow giving *zakat* to a rich man's child.[4] As for Malikis, they believe it is not permissible to give *zakat* to any poor person whose subsistence and expenses are the responsibility of a wealthy person, except if the wealthy person responsible for the expenses of the poor cannot be reached.[5]

In my opinion, *zakat* should not be given to any person whose living expenses are the responsibility of a wealthy person, such as the wife or young child of a rich man. This does not apply to other relatives whose expenses are not the duty of the rich person concerned.

Those capable of earning

Several *hadiths* prohibit payment of *zakat* to the rich and to men who have no physical or mental defects or handicaps. *Zakat* is not given to the strong because they are required to work and earn instead of depending on charity. If a capable person cannot find a job, he may be given *zakat*, since the issue is the availability of jobs

1. *Fath al-Qadir*, vol. 2, p. 23.
2. Ibid,
3. Ibid., p. 24.
4. *Al-Majmu'*, vol. 6, p. 191.
5. *Sharh al-Khirashi* on the text of Khalil, vol. 2, p. 214.]

in the market at which he can earn his living, as well as the ability of the person concerned.[1]

Hanafis believe that *zakat* may be given to an income earner if he owns less than the *nisab*, on the grounds that such a person is, in fact, poor. Ibn al-Humam points out that several scholars do not allow income earners to take *zakat*, in accordance with the *hadith*, "*Sadaqa* is not permissible for the rich or the strong who are free of defects," and the Prophet's answer to two strong and capable men who asked for *zakat*, "Indeed you have no right to it, but if you wish, I will give to you." The last sentence indicates that asking for *zakat* is not permissible, while receiving it without asking is allowed.[2]

One may argue that the Prophet (p) gave them the option of receiving *zakat* because he was not sure about their true situation, although they looked capable of earning. This is the essence of the comment of Abu 'Ubayd. He adds that strength and the ability to work must be associated with the availability of suitable jobs yielding sufficient income. A person who is able to work but does not find a job may be given *zakat*, as is indicated by the *ayat*, "*And the beggars and deprived received a due share of their wealth.*" (51:19) Ibn 'Abbas is reported to have described 'the deprived' as craftsmen who do not earn sufficiently.[3]

Can *zakat* be paid to non-Muslims?

Apostates and hostile unbelievers cannot be given *zakat*

Scholars unanimously agree that *zakat* cannot be paid to unbelievers who fight Muslims.[4] This *ijma'* is based on the *ayat*: *"Allah merely forbids you from taking as friends those who have fought you in the*

1. The author of *al-Bahr*, vol. 2, p. 175, mentions the condition of ash-Shafi'i that the poor must be weak, chronically ill, and not beggars, but the above-mentioned *hadith* negates this condition. Ibn al-'Arabi considers restricting giving to the chronically ill false, as mentioned earlier.

2. *Fath al-Qadir*, vol. 2, p. 28.

3. *Al-Amwal*, p. 557.

4. The author of *al-Bahr az-Zakhkhar*, vol. 2, p. 195, quotes this *ijma'*.

deen *and driven you from your homes and who supported your expulsion. Any who do take them as friends are the wrongdoers."* (60:9) Financial help to such enemies would be used against Muslims in one way or another. Unbelievers who deny the existence of Allah, the principle of prophethood, or faith in the Hereafter likewise cannot be given *zakat*, and neither can apostates who turn their backs on Islam and the Muslim community after having tasted faith.

Giving *zakat* to People of the Pledge

As for the People of the Pledge, i.e. the People of the Book, and all who like them live within Muslim society, pledging their sincerity to the state and obeying its laws, there are differences among Muslim scholars regarding giving them *zakat* and charity.

Giving voluntary charity to the People of the Pledge

There is nothing to prevent Muslims from giving voluntary charity to the People of the Pledge out of humanitarian concern, as well as in consideration of their pledged mutual commitment with Muslims. Being non-Muslims does not prevent them from being given charity by Muslims as long as they are not fighting against Islam, for *"Allah does not forbid you from being good to those who have not fought you in the* deen *or driven you from your homes, from being just towards them. Allah loves those who are just."* (60:8)

This *ayat* was sent particularly for those Muslims who hesitated to give charity to their unbelieving relatives. Ibn 'Abbas says, "They (the Companions) used to dislike giving charity to their kin and relatives who were unbelievers. They asked and were permitted to do so by this verse: *'You are not responsible for their guidance, but Allah guides whoever He wills. Whatever good you give away is to your own benefit, when you give desiring only the Face of Allah. Whatever good you give away will be repaid to you in full. You will not be wronged.'* (2:272)"[1] According to Ibn Kathir, the *ayat* means that if the giver of charity aims to please Allah, he will be rewarded by Allah regardless of whether the recipient of charity is righteous or

1. *Tafsir Ibn Kathir*, vol. 4, p. 349.

not, or deserving or not. The giver is rewarded for his intention.[1] In another *ayat*, Allah praises those who *"... give food, despite their love for it, to the poor and orphans and captives."* (76:8) Captives in Muslim society were obviously unbelievers, as reported by al-Hasan and others.[2]

Giving *zakat al-fitr* to non-Muslims

Zakat al-fitr, expiation (*kaffara*) and vows are like voluntary charity as far as giving to People of the Pledge is concerned. Abu Hanifa, Muhammad, and some other jurists permit paying these charities to People of the Pledge on the grounds that texts about these charities are general, such as the *ayats*, *"If you make your* sadaqa *public, that is good. But if you conceal it and give it to the poor, that is better for you, and We will erase some of your bad actions from you"* (2:271), and *"The expiation in that case is to feed ten poor people with the average amount you feed your family"* (5:92), and *"And anyone who is unable to do that must feed sixty poor people."* (58:4)

These *ayats* make no distinction between poor believers and unbelievers which is an expression of the generally required good treatment of the People of the Pledge. Obviously these scholars believe it is undoubtedly better to give to the Muslim poor since it helps a person who obeys Allah. Abu Hanifa established the condition that an unbeliever must not be fighting against Muslims in order to be given *zakat al-fitr*.[3] Lastly, Abu 'Ubayd and Ibn Abi Shayba report that some Followers gave monks *zakat al-fitr*.[4]

The view of the majority

The majority of scholars believe that *zakat* should not be given to any non-Muslims. Ibn al-Mundhir claims this is unanimous.[5] This view is founded on the *hadith* reported from Mu'adh, "Allah

1. Ibid., vol. 1, p 324.
2. *Musannaf Ibn Abi Shayba*, vol. 4, pp. 39-40.
3. *Al-Bada'i'*, vol. 2, p. 49.
4. *Al-Amwal*, pp. 613-614 and *Musannaf Ibn Abi Shayba*, vol. 4, p. 39.
5. *Al-Majmu'*, vol. 6, p. 228. The above-mentioned *ijma'* does not include heart reconciliation.

prescribed *zakat* on their wealth, to be taken from the rich among them and rendered to the poor among them," in which the pronoun "them" refers to Muslims.

The claimed *ijma'* is disputed. Ibn Sirin and az-Zuhri reportedly allowed paying *zakat* to unbelievers.[1] In *al-Mabsut*, as-Sarakhsi notes that Zafar, a disciple of Abu Hanifa, allowed giving *zakat* to the People of the Pledge. As-Sarakhsi adds, "This is implied by analogy since the objective of *zakat* – enriching the poor – is fulfilled by giving to any poor persons regardless of their faith." This is refuted by virtue of the above *hadith* from Mu'adh.[2]

Ibn Abi Shayba reports that when Jabir ibn Zayd was asked to whom *sadaqa* was to be distributed, he replied, "To people in your area, Muslims and the People of the Pledge," and continued, "The Messenger of Allah (p) gave the People of the Pledge from *sadaqa* and the one-fifth."[3] The question is obviously about *zakat*, but it may mean voluntary *sadaqa* as well, although only *zakat* was collected and distributed at the time of the Prophet (p). At any rate, the *hadith* is only *mursal*.

Ibn Abi Shayba also reports 'Umar's comment that the *ayat*, *"Sadaqa is only for the poor..."* (9:60) includes People of the Pledge who are chronically ill.[4] Abu Yusuf reports that 'Umar assigned a regular subsidy for an elderly Jewish man from the treasury of the Muslim state on the grounds that the old man was covered by the above verse.[5] The author of *ar-Rawd an-Nadir* comments that these stories indicate that 'Umar believed it was permissible to give *zakat* to the People of the Book.[6] A similar opinion is quoted from the Zaydis by the author of *al-Manar*. The author of *al-Bahr* quotes az-Zuhri and Ibn Sirin as saying the same, the latter adding, "This

1. Ibid.

2. *Al-Mabsut*, vol. 2, p. 202.

3. *Musannaf Ibn Abi Shayba*, vol. 4, p. 40.

4. Ibid.

5. *Al-Kharaj*, Abu Yusuf, p. 126. Similar to this is what is reported by al-Baladhuri in his history, p. 177, "'Umar ibn al-Khattab, upon his journey to al-Jabiya (a place close to Damascus), passed by some Christian lepers and ordered them to be given *sadaqa* and that food should be served to them." It is obvious that *sadaqat* means obligatory *zakat*, since this *zakat* was under the governor's authority, from which foodstuff was usually given.

6. *Ar-Rawd an-Nadir*, vol. 2, p. 426.

action is done because of the generality of the term 'the poor' in the verse."[1]

At-Tabari reports that 'Ikrima believed that the word 'needy' (*miskin*) in the verse refers to the poor among the People of the Book.[2] 'Ikrima says, "Do not call poor Muslims needy. The term "needy" refers to poor people of the People of the Book."[3] Some jurists argue that giving *zakat* to People of the Pledge is only permissible if no deserving Muslims are found, as reported by al-Jassas from 'Ubaydullah ibn al-Hasan.[4] Some Ibadis believe the same.[5]

Analysis

The argument of the majority depends mainly on the *hadith* from Mu'adh which is agreed upon as correct. However, this hadith does not clearly exclude the non-Muslim poor since it may simply mean that *zakat* should be collected and distributed in the same area. This *hadith* is often quoted to support the policy of non-transportation of *zakat* from one land to another.

On the other hand, the general argument forwarded by Hanafis with regard to the *zakat al-fitr* is very strong. It is supported by 'Umar, az-Zuhri, Ibn Sirin, 'Ikrima, Jabir ibn Zayd and Zafar. It is further supported by the *ayat*, *"Allah does not forbid you from being good to those who have not fought you in the* deen *or driven you from your homes, from being just towards them. Allah loves those who are just."* (60:8)[6] After comparing these arguments, one may conclude that *zakat* must first be given to poor Muslims since it is taken from

1. *Al-Bahr az-Zakhkhar*, vol. 2, p. 185.

2. *Tafsir at-Tabari*, vol. 14, p. 308.

3. The late Abu Zahra, 'Abdu'r-Rahman Hasan, and 'Abdu'l-Wahhab Khallaf comment that the interpretation of the word 'needy' (*miskin*) in the verse to mean needy People of the Book establishes two points: one that the poor and needy are two different categories, and two that it is permissible to give *zakat* to the poor People of the Pledge, provided they are chronically ill or completely disabled. Able People of the Pledge are charged *jizya*, and it is not rational for them to be charged *jizya* and given *zakat* at the same time. See *Halqat ad-Dirasat al-Ijtima'iyya*, p. 202.

4. *Ahkam l-Qur'an*, al-Jassas, vol. 3, p. 315.

5. *Sharh an-Nil*, vol. 2, p. 123.

6. *Al-Bada'i'*, vol. 2, p. 123.

the Muslim rich alone. But there is nothing to forbid giving *zakat* to the poor people among the People of the Pledge, as long a such action does not harm the privileges of the Muslim poor.

Obviously the above discussion refers to giving *zakat* to poor non-Muslims because of their poverty. As for giving *zakat* to People of the Pledge for reasons other than poverty, such as reconciling their hearts and bringing them closer to Islam, the Muslim community and the Islamic state, the matter is different. Earlier in the book, I argued that it is permissible to give to non-Muslims for heart reconciliation, provided that such an action is done at the discretion of the Islamic government and not of individuals.

It should be added that scholars who do not allow giving *zakat* to People of the Pledge do not mean that the poor among the People of the Pledge must not be helped. Rather they believe such subsidies must come out of sources other than *zakat*, such as war booty, *fay'* and *kharaj*. Abu 'Ubayd quotes the letter of 'Umar ibn 'Abdu'l-'Aziz to his governor in Basra, "...and look after the People of the Pledge. Find those of them who are elderly, weak, and those who do not earn, then give them regular salaries from the treasury in amounts sufficient for them."[1] This shows that the Muslim ruler has responsibility towards the People of the Pledge.

Can wrongdoers be given *zakat*?

Scholars generally permit giving *zakat* to wrongdoers, as long as they maintain the faith of Islam, on humanitarian grounds and to reconcile their hearts. *Zakat* is collected from wrongdoers so they must be covered by the general terms of the *hadith*, "...to be taken from the rich among them and rendered to the poor among them."[2] The only exception is that wrongdoers may not be given *zakat* in a form the helps them do what is condemned, such as buying alcoholic beverages. Some Malikis go as far as stating that if there is suspicion that wrongdoers may use *zakat* paid them for evil purposes, it must not be given to them.[1] According to Zaydis, it is

1. *Al-Amwal*, p. 46.
2. *Al-Bahr az-Zakhkhar*, vol. 2, p. 186.

not permissible to give *zakat* to wrongdoers, unless they are workers in the *zakat* agency, or for the purpose of reconciliation.[2]

I think that wrongdoers who do not harm Muslims or challenge the tenets and rites of Islam may be helped with *zakat*. There is no doubt at all that giving the righteous poor is much better. As for transgressors who openly challenge Islamic values, *zakat* must not be given to them, because Muslims are ordered to establish righteousness and prevent evil, and giving to such persons in no way helps evil, for Allah says, *"The men and women of the believers are friends of one another. They command the right and forbid the wrong."* (9:71) This requires that the Muslim community must withhold its help from those who oppose its values, try to vitiate its rites and openly challenge its laws. As for the families of such transgressors, *zakat* should be give to them if they are in need, in accordance with the *ayat*, *"No bearer of any burden can bear that of any other."* (6:164)

Ibn Taymiyya supports this view, saying, "One must search for the poor and needy righteous men and women who follow the *Shari'a*. How can a Muslim help those who challenge Islamic values and rites by their wrongdoing and transgression?"[3] He continues, "A person who does not fulfil the obligation of prayers must be advised to pray before being given *zakat*; if he accepts, *zakat* may be given to him, and if not, it may not be given."[4]

Giving *zakat* to deviant sects

There are two kinds of deviant sects. The first kind are those sects which deny essential principles of Islam. Those are outside the limits of this religion and are considered unbelievers. The second kind are those sects which differ from mainstream Sunnis on certain basic issues without exceeding the general boundaries of Islam. Sunnis, out of their forgiving spirit toward other sects, only exclude

1. *Ash-Sharh al-Kabir* with *Hashiyat ad-Dusuqi*, vol. 1, p. 492. This is consistent with the Ja'fari view, as stated in *Fiqh al-Imam Ja'far*, vol. 2, p. 93, and that of the Ibadis, as in *an-Nil*, vol. 2, pp. 131-132.

2. *Sharh al-Azhar*, vol. 1, p. 520-1.]

3. *Fatawa Ibn Taymiyya*, vol. 25, p, 87.

4. Ibid., p. 89.

from the benefits of *zakat* sects classified as unbelievers, and allow giving *zakat* to all Muslims regardless of any sectarian classification.[1] Obviously, the more righteous in deed and creed are preferred.

In contrast, other sects are generally strict about distributing *zakat* only inside their own sects. Ja'fari Shiites quote their Imam as saying, "Do not give *sadaqa* and *zakat* to anyone except your peers." The only exception to this rule they make is giving for reconciliation of hearts. In *Fiqh al-Imam Ja'far*, Mughniya states, "*Zakat* must only be given to individual sect members, while voluntary charity may be given to any person in need."[2] In *al-Hada'iq*, al-Bahrani says that a man asked Muhammad al-Baqir, "May the mercy of Allah be upon you. Take these five hundred dirhams from me and spend them where they belong. It is the *zakat* of my wealth." Al-Baqir answered, "You take it and give it to your needy and orphaned neighbours and your Muslim brothers."[3] This indicates that al-Baqir did not preach any discrimination and believed that brotherhood in Islam is above all other considerations.

Ibadis do not totally agree as to whether *zakat* may be given to Muslims who do not subscribe to their school of thought. Some of their jurists permit giving *zakat* to any poor person as long as he is not known to differ from their view. Some even allow giving *zakat* to people who belong to opposing schools of thought.[4]

As for the Zaydis, they forbid giving their *zakat* to certain deviant sects. The author of *ar-Rawd an-Nadir* says that some of the *Salaf* believed that *zakat* must be given on the sole criteria of need and poverty with no other questions asked. Ibn Abi Shayba reports that Fudayl asked Ibrahim about giving *zakat* to deviating people. He said, "Our ancestors asked about nothing except poverty." This is the opinion of al-Mu'ayyad, Yahya, as well as the Hanafis and Shafi'is, since the term 'poor' is general. Yahya and ash-Shafi'i are reported to have forbidden helping individuals whose wrongdoing harms the Muslims or the Islamic state, such as those who fight the Muslims.[5]

1. See, for example, *Hashiyat Ibn 'Abidin*, vol. 2, p. 75.
2. *Fiqh al-Imam Ja'far*, vol. 2, p. 93.
3. Ibid., p. 97.
4. *Sharh an-Nil*, vol. 2, p. 133.
5. *Ar-Rawd an-Nadir*, vol. 2, p. 43

Close relatives of the *zakat* payer

Relatives whose relationship to the *zakat* payer is so distant that the *zakat* payer is not legally responsible for providing their living expenses may be given *zakat* by either the *zakat* payer or the government. Scholars differ on *zakat* payers giving *zakat* to close relatives such as parents, brothers, sisters, uncles, and aunts. *Zakat* may be given to close relatives of *zakat* payers on the basis of working in the *zakat* agency or being freed from slavery or for debts or fighting in the Way of Allah because the *zakat* payer is not responsible for such activities. *Zakat* may also be given if the close relative is a traveller. Reconciliation of relatives' hearts is out of the question because such distribution can only be made by the government or public organisations and not by individuals.

As for giving on the grounds of need and poverty, one must distinguish between distribution by the government and by individual *zakat* payers. If the government distributes *zakat*, it may give to close relatives of *zakat* payers, including their children, parents, and wives,[1] since payers fulfil their obligation by delivering *zakat* to the state. When payers distribute their *zakat* directly, they cannot give it to relatives for whose provisions the *zakat* payers are responsible, such as parents, wives and children.

Ibn al-Mundhir claims an *ijma'* of scholars regarding the fact that *zakat* must not be given to a *zakat* payer's parents in cases where the *zakat* payer is obliged to provide for their living expenses, since by giving them *zakat* he is saved the obligation of providing their living expenses.[2] Moreover the Messenger of Allah (p) is quoted as saying, "You and your wealth belong to your father,"[3] and the Qur'an considers the houses of parents and their children as one and the same: *"There is no objection to eating in your own houses."*

1. *Ahkam al-Qur'an*, Ibn al-'Arabi, p. 965.

2. *Al-Mughni*, vol. 2, p. 647.

3. *Tafsir Ibn Kathir*, vol. 3, p. 305. The *hadith* is reported by Ahmad ibn Hanbal in *al-Musnad* via three chains, from 'Amr ibn Shu'ayb from his father from his grandfather. The later Ahmad Shakir grades all of them correct. See *hadiths* no. 6678, 6902, and 7001 in vol. 11 and 12. It is also reported by Ibn Majah from Jabir, via a chain whose narrators are trustworthy, and by at-Tabarani from Samura and Ibn Mas'ud via a weak chain. See *at-Taysir*, al-Munawi, vol. 1, p. 378.

(24:61) The last phrase refers to the houses of one's sons since it is obvious that there is no fault in eating in one's own house.[1] The Prophet (p) says, "The best food a man eats is that which is out of the man's own earnings. That of his son is from his own earning as well."[2]

Based on this, Hanafis argue that ownership of property is continuous between parents and their children. Thus paying *zakat* to a parent or a child is like giving it to oneself and the condition of making the poor own it is not fulfilled.[3] Children and parents are treated as one unit in *zakat* distribution. There is a *hadith* reported by al-Bukhari and Ahmad from Ma'n ibn Yazid: "My father gave a few dinars to a man in the mosque to distribute as charity. I came and took them. My father said, 'By Allah, I did not intend to give to you!' I complained to the Messenger of Allah (p) who said, 'O Yazid, you get the reward for your intention, and Ma'n, you get what you obtained.'" This *hadith*, according to ash-Shawkani, applies to voluntary charity and not to obligatory *zakat*.[4]

Only Muhammad ash-Shaybani and a report from Abu'l-'Abbas (a Shi'ite) approve of giving *zakat* to one's parents. This is supported by a group of later Zaydis. This opinion is based on the general terms of pertinent texts and lack of authentic support for parents' exclusion.[5] Additionally, Malik reportedly approves of giving *zakat* to grandchildren as well as to great grandparents.[6] It seems that Ibn al-Mundhir and the author of *al-Bahr*, who both report *ijma'*,[7] do not believe in the authenticity of the narrations from these scholars.

However, Ibn al-Mundhir limits that *ijma'* to the conditions on which parents or children can be forced to provide each others' living expenses. An-Nawawi argues that there are cases in which the *zakat* payer is not responsible for the living expenses of his parents

1 *Tafsir al-Qurtubi*, vol. 12, p. 314.

2. Reported by at-Tirmidhi, an-Nasa'i and Ibn Majah from 'A'isha. This chain is graded *hasan* by at-Tirmidhi and sound by Abu Hatim. See *at-Taysir*, vol. 1, p. 311. It is also reported by Ahmad with similar wording via a correct chain as a part of *hadith* no. 6678 and 7001.

3. *Al-Bada'i'*, vol. 2, p. 49.

4. *Nayl al-Awtar*, vol. 4, p. 189.

5. *Ar-Rawd an-Nadir*, vol. 2, p. 421

6. *Nayl al-Awtar*, op cit.

7. *Al-Bahr az-Zakhkhar*, vol. 2, p. 186.

or children.[1] Ibn Taymiyya gives as an example a poor mother whose young children are rich. Her living expenses need not be charged to the children in her care. Thus she may be given *zakat* from them.[2]

Giving *zakat* to one's wife is not permissible

Ibn al-Mundhir continues, "Scholars unanimously agree that a man must not give his wife *zakat* since he is obliged to provide all her living expenses."[3] A wife is so intimate with the husband as to be like himself. Allah says, *"Among His Signs is that He created spouses for you of your own kind."* (30:21) He refers to the husband's house as the wife's house in the *ayat*: *"Do not evict them from their homes."* (65:1)

Can a wife give *zakat* to her poor husband?

Abu Hanifa and some other jurists do not approve of this on the grounds that a wife is to her husband as a husband is to his wife. But this analogy is incorrect when applied to *zakat*, especially since we have reports to the contrary. The reasoning behind this analogy is invalid with regard to financial support, as stated by Abu 'Ubayd, since the husband is responsible for the living expenses of his wife, even if she is rich, while rich wives are not obliged to support their poor husbands.[4] Ibn Qudama notes that since wives are not responsible for the living expenses of their husbands, they can give their *zakat* to their husbands, bearing in mind that giving *zakat* to one's wife is only prohibited because the husband is responsible for his wife's living expenses.[5]

Ahmad, al-Bukhari and Muslim report from Zaynab, the wife of 'Abdullah ibn Mas'ud, "The Messenger of Allah (p) said, 'O women, give *sadaqa*, even out of your jewellery.'" She continues, "I went back to 'Abdullah and said, 'You are an empty-handed

1. *Al-Majmu'*, vol. 6, p. 229.
2. *Ikhtiyarat Ibn Taymiyya*, pp. 61-2.
3. *Al-Mughni*, vol. 2, p. 649 and *Nayl al-Awtar*, vol. 4, p. 188.
4. *Al-Amwal*, p. 588.
5. *Al-Mughni*, vol. 2, p. 650.

person, and the Messenger of Allah (p) just ordered us to give charity. Go to him and ask him if it is acceptable for me to give you charity. Otherwise I will give it to someone else.' 'Abdullah said, 'You go to the Prophet (p).'" Zaynab continues, "I went and found at the door of the Messenger of Allah a woman of the Ansar who had a question like mine. The Messenger of Allah (p) was so greatly esteemed by us that we did not like to knock on the door and disturb him. Then Bilal came out and we told him, 'Tell the Messenger of Allah (p) that there are two women at the door asking whether it is acceptable to give their *sadaqa* to their husbands or to spend it on orphans in their care. Do not mention who we are.' Bilal went in and asked the Prophet (p), who asked, 'Who are they?" Bilal answered, 'A lady from the Ansar and Zaynab.' The Prophet (p) asked, 'Which Zaynab?' Bilal replied, 'The wife of 'Abdullah.' Then the Prophet (p) said, 'Indeed they have two rewards. One for kindness to kin and one for giving *sadaqa*.'" The sentence in al-Bukhari's report reads, "Is it acceptable for me to spend it on my husband and on orphans in my care?"[1]

Ash-Shawkani says, "This *hadith* indicates that it is permissible for a wife to give her *zakat* to her husband. This is also the opinion of ath-Thawri, ash-Shafi'i, the two disciples of Abu Hanifa, a report from Malik and a report from Ahmad, also al-Hadi, an-Nasir, and al-Mu'ayyad Bi'llah." The above *hadith* can be a good argument if it makes a clear reference to obligatory *zakat*. Al-Maziri claims that it refers to *zakat* because of the words used in the *hadith* itself, "it is acceptable." Others argue that the *hadith* refers only to voluntary charity, especially since it uses the words, "out of your jewellery". Ash-Shawkani goes on, "It appears that giving a wife's *zakat* to her husband is permissible, first because there is nothing to prohibit it, and second because in the above *hadith*, the Prophet (p) makes no distinction between voluntary and obligatory *sadaqa*."[2]

1. *Nayl al-Awtar*, vol. 4, pp. 187-188.
2. Ibid.

Giving *zakat* to other relatives

Giving *zakat* to one's brothers, sisters, uncles, aunts and other relatives is disputed by Muslim scholars. Those who do not allow it do so on different grounds. Abu 'Ubayd reports from Ibrahim ibn Abi Hafsa, "I asked Sa'id ibn Jubayr whether I could give my aunt *zakat*. He said, 'Yes, as long as she does not live with you as part of your family.'"[1]

Abu 'Ubayd further reports that al-Hasan said, "It is all right for a person to give *zakat* to his relatives who are not among his dependants."[2] He reports 'Ata' as saying that relatives who are not part of the household supported by the *zakat* payer have priority in receiving his *zakat* if they are poor. Ibn 'Abbas says, "As long as you do not give to any person whom you support financially, there is no harm in giving relatives *zakat*."[3] These scholars consider whether or not the recipient is part of the *zakat* payer's household to be the criteria for permissibility of giving *zakat* to relatives. Abu 'Ubayd reports a different view from 'Abdullah ibn Da'ud, whose criterion is the legal responsibility of the *zakat* payer to support a relative, *zakat* may be given to that relative in his opinion.[4]

The third most common opinion uses the criterion of legal responsibility for financial support as set forth in the *Shari'a. Zakat* must not be given to anyone whose living expenses are the obligation of the payer. This is based on two points: firstly, that such a relative is in fact rich by the provision given or that should be given by the prayer, and secondly, that the payer, by giving *zakat* to this relative, saves himself the additional cost of supporting that relative.[5] This is the view of Malik, ash-Shafi'i, a report from Ahmad, Zayd ibn 'Ali, al-Hadi, al-Qasim, an-Nasir and al-Mu'ayyad Bi'llah, although some of these scholars do not agree on the specification of those relatives whose provisions for living is the responsibility of the payer

1. *Al-Amwal*, pp. 582-583.
2. Ibid.
3. Ibid.
4. Ibid.
5. *Al-Majmu'*, vol. 6, p. 229, and *Ahkam al-Qur'an*, Ibn al-'Arabi, part 2, p. 960.

Zayd and Ahmad believe the criterion of financial responsibility is the same as that used in the inheritance system. A person who may inherit from a certain relative is financially responsible for that relative.[1] Ash-Shafi'i restricts financial responsibility to parents, grandparents, children and grandchildren only, while Malik further restricts it to children – sons until puberty [2] and daughters until marriage – and the father and mother. In other words, Malik excludes grandchildren and grandparents. Obviously both Malik and ash-Shafi'i exclude brothers, sisters, aunts and uncles.[3]

Another group of scholars are more permissive about giving *zakat* to relatives. Some of them argue that *zakat* may be paid to relatives (other than parents and children) for whose living expenses the *zakat* payer may be responsible. These include Abu Hanifa, his disciples, and Yahya. It is the predominant report from Ahmad, according to Ibn Qudama. Abu 'Ubayd argues that this is the most acceptable opinion because the Prophet (p) said, "*Sadaqa* to the needy is merely a *sadaqa*, but it is both a *sadaqa* and a kindness to kin when it is given to relatives."[4] This *hadith* makes no distinction between obligatory and voluntary *sadaqa*, or between relatives for whose living expenses the payer is responsible and other relatives.[5]

Ibn Abi Shayba and Abu 'Ubayd say that this is also the opinion of a handful of Companions and Followers. They quote Ibn 'Abbas as saying, "A person should give *zakat* to his relatives if they are in need," and Ibrahim as reporting, "Ibn Mas'ud's wife asking him about giving the *zakat* of her jewellery to her orphaned nephews who were in her custody. Ibn Mas'ud answered, 'Yes.'" Al-Hasan was asked if it was permissible to give *zakat* to one's brother and replied, "Yes indeed." Ibrahim was asked whether a woman could give *zakat* to her sister and replied in the affirmative. Ad-Dahhak remarks, "If you have poor relatives, they have priority over your

1. *Ar-Rawd an-Nadir*, op. cit. and *al-Mughni*, vol. 2, p. 607.

2. The late Shaykh 'Ulaysh, a Maliki, was asked whether the father of a student who is strong and capable of working can give him *zakat*. The answer was affirmative since the father is not required to support an adult son who can earn, and a full-time student is entitled to *zakat* anyway. (See *Fath al-'Ali al-Malik*, vol. 1, p. 129.)

3. *Al-Mudawwana al-Kubra*, vol. 1, p. 256.

4. Reported by the five, except Abu Dawud.

5. *Al-Mughni*, vol. 2, p. 648.

zakat compared to other people." Mujahid adds, "One's *zakat* is not accepted if it is given to others while one has needy relatives."[1]

Comparison and analysis

After surveying all these opinions, I feel that allowing *zakat* to be given to all relatives except parents and children is the most appropriate. This is also the opinion of Abu 'Ubayd and the majority of scholars since the era of the Companions and Followers. This opinion is supported by:

- The generality of texts about the poor which make no distinction between poor relatives and non-relatives like, "*Sadaqat* are only for the poor and the needy ..." and the *hadith*, "... to be taken from the rich among them and rendered to their poor." These texts include relatives and any attempt to remove relatives from the categories of those entitled to *zakat* requires an appropriate text. This is not the case with the wife, parents and children who are all unanimously excluded from *zakat*.
- Texts that encourage helping one's relatives such as, "*Sadaqa* to the needy is merely a *sadaqa*, but that given to one's relatives has two merits: both a *sadaqa* and a kindness to kin when it is given to relatives."[2] "Indeed, the best *sadaqa* is that which is given to a relative, even one who conceals hatred,"[3] and the report from Ibn Mas'ud'a wife mentioned earlier.

The argument that in giving *zakat* to these relatives, the payer benefits himself is not absolute. It indeed applies to the *zakat* payer's wife, children and parents, but not to other relatives, since

1. These statements are mentioned in *Musannaf Ibn Abi Shayba*, vol. 4, pp. 47-8, and *al-Amwal*, pp. 581-2.

2. Reported by Ahmad, an-Nasa'i, at-Tirmidhi, Ibn Hibban, al-Hakim and ad-Daraqutni. At-Tirmidhi grades it *hasan*. See *Nayl al-Awtar*, vol. 4, p. 189.

3. Reported by Ahmad and at-Tabarani from Abu Ayyub. They also report a similar *hadith* from Hakim ibn Hizam. The author of *Majma' az-Zawa'id* comments that its chain is *hasan*. In *al-Muj'am al-Kabir* at-Tabarani reports the same from Umm Kulthum bint 'Uqba; its chain of narrators are those of the *Sahih* collections. See *ar-Rawd an-Nadir*, vol. 2, p. 422.

supporting relatives other than the wife, children and parents is the responsibility of the Islamic state from *zakat*, *fay'* and other sources. Relatives are responsible only when the state does not fulfil its obligation. A *zakat* payer may support relatives other than his wife, parents and children out of his own *zakat*.

We should notice that Hanafi scholars make no connection between permissibility of giving *zakat* to relatives and financial responsibility for supporting them as determined in the *Shari'a*. They hold that charging the payer with the responsibility of supporting his relatives does not prevent allowing him to give them *zakat*, as long as what is given to them is made their own property, since there is no continuity of property between relatives other than parent and children.[1] The Zaydi author of *ar-Rawd an-Nadir* argues that giving *zakat* to relatives does not imply saving an otherwise obligatory financial support, since the obligation of support is only temporary.[2]

Ash-Shawkani adds that, in principle, giving one's *zakat* to relatives is permissible, since no text prevents it and the burden of proof is on anyone who claims otherwise.[3]

The descendants of the Prophet Muhammad (p)

Hadiths prohibiting *sadaqa* to Muhammad's family

Ahmad and Muslim report that al-Muttalib ibn Rabi'a (the first cousin of the Prophet) "... went with al-Fadl ibn al-'Abbas to the Prophet (p). One of them said, 'O Messenger of Allah, we come to ask you to appoint us to collect *sadaqat* so we can earn from it like other people and bring you what we collect like other people do.' The Prophet (p) said, 'Indeed, *sadaqa* must not be taken by Muhammad or the family of Muhammad. It is merely the impurities cleansed from people's wealth.'" In a version mentioned in *al-*

1. *Al-Bada'i'*, vol. 2, pp. 49-50.
2. *Ar-Rawd an-Nadir*, vol. 2, p. 423.
3. *Nayl al-Awtar*, vol. 4, p. 183.

Muntaqa, the Prophet says that it "… is not lawful to Muhammad nor to the family of Muhammad."[1]

Abu Dawud and at-Tirmidhi report that Abu Rafi' said, "The Messenger of Allah (p) appointed a man from the clan of Banu Makhzum to collect the *sadaqa*. The man said to me, 'Come with me (to help me) and you will get some of it.' I said, 'Not until I ask the Messenger of Allah (p).' When I asked him, he told me, 'The ex-slave of a clan is one of them, and we are a family to whom *sadaqa* is not lawful.'"[2] Abu Rafi' was an ex-slave of the Prophet.

Al-Bukhari reports from Abu Hurayra, "Al-Hasan ibn 'Ali took one date from the dates of the *sadaqa* and put it in his mouth (he was a child at the time). The Prophet (p) said, 'Yech! Yech!' to get him to take it out of his mouth, and continued, 'Don't you know we do not eat from the *sadaqa*?'" Muslim's version (as stated by Ibn Hajar) reads, "We are those to whom *sadaqa* is not lawful," and in a version from Ma'mar, "Indeed *sadaqa* is not lawful to the family of Muhammad." Ahmad and at-Tahawi report from al-Hasan ibn 'Ali, "I was with the Prophet (p). We passed by a crate of dates collected as *sadaqa*. I took one and put it in my mouth. The Prophet (p) grabbed it with the saliva on it and said, 'For us, the family of Muhammad, *sadaqa* is not lawful.'" Its chain is strong.[3]

These *hadiths* indicate that *zakat* is not permissible to the Prophet and his family and descendants. It is important to determine who numbers among the family of the Prophet (p), and whether either *zakat* or voluntary charity is permissible for them.

Whom does the family of Muhammad include?

Ibn Hajar in *al-Fath* and ash-Shawkani in *an-Nayl* state that there are differences among Muslim scholars in specifying the Prophet's family.[4] Ash-Shafi'i and a group of scholars believe that the family of the Prophet includes the descendants of Hashim and of al-Muttalib. Hashim is the great-grandfather of the Prophet (p)

1. Ibid., p. 175.
2. *Al-Majmu'*, vol. 6, p. 228.
3. *Fath al-Bari*, vol. 3, p. 228.
4. Ibid., p. 227 and *Nayl al-Awtar*, vol. 4, pp. 182-4.

and al-Muttalib is Hashim's brother. Ash-Shafi'i argues that the Prophet (p) included the children of al-Muttalib as well as the children of Hashim in the share assigned to the kin of the Prophet (p), and did not include any other clan. Ash-Shafi'i continued that this share is given in compensation for preventing them from taking *sadaqa*. Al-Bukhari reports from Jubayr ibn Mu'tim, "I went to the Prophet (p) with 'Uthman ibn 'Affan and said, 'O Messenger of Allah, you have given to the children of al-Muttalib out of the one-fifth from Khaybar and did not give to us. We and they are at the same level.' The Messenger of Allah (p) said, 'The children of al-Muttalib and the children of Hashim are one thing.'"

This argument is challenged on the grounds that the children of al-Muttalib were given from the share of the kindred only because of their alliance with, and support of, the family of the Prophet, (p) and not as recompense for preventing them from taking *sadaqa*. Consequently Abu Hanifa, Malik and the Hadawis believe the family of the Prophet (p) includes the descendants of Hashim alone. There are two reports regarding the view of Ahmad. One goes along with Abu Hanifa while the other agrees with ash-Shafi'i.

The descendants of Hashim include the families of 'Ali, 'Aqil, Ja'far, al-'Abbas and al-Harith. Notice that the family of Abu Lahab is not included, because it is said that none of them embraced Islam during the life of the Prophet (although the author of *Jami' al-Usul* reports that his two sons, 'Utba and Mu'attib, became Muslims in the year the Muslims conquered Makka and that the Prophet was pleased by their conversion and prayed for them). Ibn Qudama says, "We know of no dispute that *zakat* is not permissible for the children of Hashim." Ibn Rislan and Abu Talib claim there is *ijma'* on this.

According to at-Tahawi, at-Tabari quotes that Abu Hanifa allowed paying *zakat* to the family of the Prophet (p) if they are denied the share of the kindred. A similar opinion is attributed to al-Abhari, a Maliki, and to some Shafi'is, as stated by the author of *al-Fath*. Abu Yusuf is claimed to have permitted members of the Prophet's family to receive *zakat* paid by other members of the same family. We find a similar opinion is attributed in *al-Bahr* to Zayd ibn 'Ali, al-Murtada, Abu'l-'Abbas and the Imamis. The same is mentioned in *ash-Shifa'* as attributed to the two children of al-Hadi as well as to al-Qasim.

Al-Hafiz said, "There are four views on this among the Malikis: permission, prohibition, permission with regard to *zakat* but not voluntary *sadaqa* and its reverse. Ash-Shawkani contends that the *hadith* which indicates this prohibition seems to cover all cases. Some scholars even claim that these *hadiths* may reach the grade of *mutawatir* with regards to their meaning. This is supported by a few *ayats*: *"Say: 'I do not ask you for any wage for this – except for you to love your near of kin.'"* (42:23) *"Say: 'I do not ask you for any wage for it, nor am I a man of false pretentions.'"* (38:86) and *"Take* sadaqa *from their wealth to purify and cleanse them."* (9:103) and the *hadith*, "*Sadaqa* is only the impurities of people's wealth," reported by Muslim.[1]

As for permitting members of the Prophet's family to take *zakat* from other members of the same family, it is founded on a report narrated by al-Hakim via a chain all from Banu Hashim that al-'Abbas said, "I told the Messenger of Allah (p), 'You have prohibited us from taking *sadaqa* from people. Is the *sadaqa* of some of us lawful for others among us?' He replied, 'Yes.'" The authenticity of this *hadith* is controversial.

It may be useful here to quote the different schools' positions on this issue. In *Majma' al-Anhur*, Abu Hanifa is reported to have permitted the giving of *zakat* to the descendants of Hashim. Ash-Shaybani, in *al-Athar*, is quoted as saying, "There are two narrations from Abu Hanifa. We hold to the one that allows giving them *zakat*, since the prohibition is restricted to the era of the Prophet (p)." In *Durr al-Muntaqa*, Abu Hanifa is reported to have allowed paying *zakat* from one member to another of the descendants of Hashim. He is also reported to have approved of giving them *zakat* in general. At-Tahawi adds, "This is what we support. This is approved by al-Quhustani and others." [2] Ibn Taymiyya also

1. Al-Hafiz says, "This indicates that it is permissible to give voluntary donations but not obligatory *zakat*. This is the opinion of most Hanafis and the accepted view among Shafi'is and Hanbalis. As for the opposite (allowing *zakat* but not voluntary donations), it is argued that there is no humiliation in taking obligatory *zakat*, contrary to taking what is volunteered." See *al-Fath*, vol. 3, p. 227.

2. *Majma' al-Anhur*, printed with *Durr al-Muntaqa*, p. 224.

permits giving *zakat* from one member to another of the descendants of Hashim.[1] Ja'farites hold the same opinion too.[2]

The most restrictive opinion is that of the Zaydis who consider the prohibition of paying *zakat* to a member of the Prophet's family absolute and final to the extent that they consider eating the flesh of dead animal not as bad as a member of the Prophet's family taking *zakat*.[3]

Can what is not war booty or *fay'* be given the Prophet's family?

Can the Prophet's family be given *zakat* if their share of war booty and *fay'* is not given to them? This question is answered in the affirmative by a few scholars. These include some Malikis who point out that members of the Prophet's family are prevented from taking *zakat* partly because a share of war booty and *fay'* is assigned to them. Therefore, if they are not given that share and are struck by poverty, they can be given *zakat*.[4] Hanafis have a similar argument, as quoted in the preceding sub-section. Among the Shafi'is, Abu Sa'id al-Istakhri believes the family of the Prophet (p) must be given *zakat* if they are not paid their share of booty and *fay'*. An-Nawawi quotes ar-Rafi'i saying that Muhammad ibn Yahya (a disciple of al-Ghazali) believed the same.[5] Ibn Taymiyya and Qadi Ya'qub, Hanbalis, presented similar arguments.[6] This is also the view of the Ja'fari school.[7]

The majority of scholars believe that since the family and descendants of the Prophet (p) are not given *zakat* in order to honour them, their deprivation from booty is not sufficient grounds to give them *zakat*.[8]

1. *Matalib Uli'n-Nuha*, vol. 2, p. 157.

2. *Fiqh al-Imam Ja'far*, vol. 9, pp. 94-95. It is stated, "*Zakat* that is not obliged by texts, such as *zakat* on trade, can be given to them, but certainly not *zakat* on wheat, barely, dates, and raisins."

3. *Sharh al-Azhar* and its commentaries, vol. 1, pp. 520-523.

4. Ibid.

5. *Al-Majmu'*, vol. 6, pp. 227-228.

6. *Matalib Uli'n-Nuha*, op. cit.

7. *Fiqh al-Imam Ja'far*, op cit.

8. *Al-Majmu'*, op cit.

Comparison

In our times, payment of *zakat* to descendants of the Prophet (p) must be permissible since they are not given a share of booty and *fay'*, either because these do not exist at all or because of arbitrary decisions by rulers. The share of the Prophet's kin is referred to in the Qur'an several times: *"Know that when you take any booty a fifth of it belongs to Allah and to the Messenger, and to close relatives, orphans, the very poor and travellers"* (8:41), and *"Whatever booty Allah gives to His Messenger from city dwellers belongs to Allah and to the Messenger and to near relatives and orphans and the very poor and travellers, so that it does not become something which merely goes by turn to the rich among you."* (59:7)

Claiming that the family of the Prophet (p) is prevented from receiving *zakat* to honour them is not a strong argument. It might be better to explain it by their support to the Prophet (p) in Makka. It seems more reasonable that they are so prohibited because of the share they are granted in those two verses. Thus, if the compensation assigned to them does not exist, they must be able to receive *zakat*, especially since many scholars believe that the share of the family, after the death of the Prophet (p), must be diverted to supporting fighters in the Way of Allah,[1] thus leaving the family and descendants of the Prophet (p) with nothing to support them in case of need.

The opinion that permits the family of the Prophet (p) and their descendants to receive *zakat* is further supported by the fact that all

1 Abu 'Ubayd, Abu Yusuf in al-Kharaj, and at-Tabari in his commentary on *Surat al-Anfal* (8) reported from al-Hasan ibn Muhammad ibn al-Hanafiyya that he was asked about the shares of the Messenger and his family and answered, "People differed, after the Prophet's death, on these two shares. Some say that the share of the family belongs to the relatives of the Prophet. (p) Others hold it belongs to relatives of the khalif, whoever he might be. Still others say that the share of the Prophet (p) belongs after his death to the khalif. So they came to a unanimous agreement that they must spend these two shares on horses and equipment for the sake of Allah." He continues, "This practice continued through the periods of Abu Bakr and 'Umar." See *al-Amwal*, p. 332, and *Bidayat al-Mujtahid*, vol. 1, pp. 390-391. In fact, when 'Ali became khalif he continued the same practice as Abu Bakr and 'Umar. See *al-Amwal*, ibid.

the *hadiths* presented in support of the prevention do not clearly name the reason for the prevention, as shown below.

- The refusal of the Prophet (p) to appoint his cousins to collect *zakat* was based on his desire to have the members of his family set a good example in honesty and sacrifice by not taking anything from the income of the state.[1] The narration of al-Bukhari implies this by the wording, "Indeed, *sadaqa* is not suitable for the family of Muhammad." This is so in order to prevent accusations and rumours of any abuse of state funds, which is perhaps why even ex-slaves of the family are prevented from taking *zakat*, as indicated by the report from Abu Rafi'. This shows that they are not prevented from *zakat* because they are too honourable.
- The Prophet's statement to al-Hasan ibn 'Ali, "*Sadaqa* is not lawful for us," is most likely a reference to the Prophet (p) in his capacity as head of state. 'Umar understood that, as head of state, he must not take anything out of *zakat*. Once he drank some milk, but when he realised it was part of the *sadaqa*, he made himself vomit it up. (*al-Muwatta'*) The author of *al-Bahr* argues that *sadaqa* is not lawful to the ruler and his family since the Prophet (p) prohibited it to his family.[2]
- We must reconsider the texts concerning this issue. The term that appears in the *hadiths* is "*Ali Muhammad*" which literally means the family or the people of Muhammad. By what authority can anyone claim that this word must include the descendants of Muhammad (p) and his relatives through the centuries?

The word *'al'* is used in several other *ayats*, such as, *"Allah chose Adam and Nuh and the family (*al*) of Ibrahim and the family (*al*) of 'Imran over all other beings,"* (3:33) and *"then the family (al) of Pharaoh picked him up,"* (28:8) and *"drowned the people (*al*) of Pharaoh."* (2:50) This word has nothing to do with their descendants. All it means in these usages is the close family: wives, children, and all those close-

1. *The Biography of the Prophet* by Ibn Hisham, vol. 4, p. 32.
2. *Al-Bahr az-Zakhkhar*, vol. 2, p. 184.

ly associated by the bond of family relation. There is nothing that allows us to include their descendants in all centuries to come. Hence arises the opinion of Abu Hanifa and his follower, ash-Shaybani, that this bar only applies to the Prophet's family during his lifetime and that it ceased after his death. This is also a view attributed to Malik, according to the author of *al-Bahr.*[1]

Two points must be kept in mind. Firstly, Islamic laws do not discriminate between the members of the Prophet's family and others. The Prophet (p) himself says, "By Allah, if Fatima, the daughter of Muhammad, stole, I would cut off her hand," (Agreed upon) and "He whose deeds make him slow in his path towards Allah, his family ties do not make him progress faster." (Agreed upon) Secondly *zakat* is a basic obligation and a determined right collected by the state and distributed to defined deserving people. Why then should some people be excluded from being deserving?

Finally, we must remember that there is no *ijma'* on preventing the descendants of the Prophet (p) from receiving *zakat*, since Abu Hanifa, some Malikis and some Shafi'is disagree. Thus one can rightly claim that all that is indicated by the *hadiths* is that the Prophet (p) and members of his family are prevented from *zakat* in order to purify them from suspicion of abuse of *zakat* proceeds at a time when the legislation of the *Shari'a* was still being formed. Shah Waliyu'llah ad-Dihlawi adds that this was a very good move on his part, one which nipped in the bud any attempt to accuse him of financial abuse.[2] Additionally, it must be added that there are the same reports in support of the permissibility of giving to the relatives of the Prophet (p) from the *zakat*. For instance, it is mentioned in *al-Bahr* that the Prophet gave *sadaqa* to widows of the Banu'l-Muttalib[3] and Abu Dawud reports from Ibn 'Abbas, "My father sent me to the Prophet (p) for camels which were given to him from the *sadaqa*."[4]

1. *Al-Bahr*, op. cit.
2. *Hujjat Allah al-Baligha*, vol. 2, p. 512.
3. *Al-Bahr*, vol. 2, p. 184.
4. Reported by Abu Dawud in chapter on *sadaqa*. He and al-Mundhiri did not make any comment on it, also reported by an-Nasa'i.

Errors in judgement in *zakat* distribution

Giving *zakat* to non-deserving people by error of judgement

If a *zakat* payer gives his *zakat* to a person whom he thought was entitled and then finds that he was incorrect, does that payment fulfil the payer's obligation of *zakat*? There are three major opinions on this matter. The first is that such distribution fulfils the obligation of *zakat*. This is the opinion of Abu Hanifa, Muhammad ash-Shaybani, al-Hasan and Abu 'Ubayd. This view implies that no other payment is required from the *zakat* payer and is founded on a few *hadiths* of the Prophet (p).

Al-Bukhari and Ahmad report from Ma'n ibn Yazid, "My father gave a few dinars as *sadaqa* to a man in the mosque in order for him to give them away. Not knowing, I came by and took them. My father said, 'By Allah, I did not intend to give to you.' I complained to the Prophet (p) who said, 'O Yazid, you get the reward of your intention and, O Ma'n, you get what you have taken.'" This *hadith* does not make any distinction between voluntary and obligatory *sadaqa*.

Abu Hurayra narrates that the Prophet (p) said, "A man [of the Israelites] once said, 'Surely I am going to give charity tonight.' He went out with his *sadaqa* and put it unknowingly in the hands of a thief. The next morning it was rumoured that a thief had been given *sadaqa* the night before. The man said, 'My Lord, praise be to You alone, indeed I shall give another *sadaqa*.' He went out with the *sadaqa* and put it in the hands of a prostitute. The next morning it was circulated that a prostitute had been given *sadaqa*. The man said to himself, 'My Lord, praise be to You alone, surely I shall give *sadaqa*.' He went out with the new *sadaqa* and put it in the hands of a rich man. The next morning, the people were saying that a rich man had been given *sadaqa* the night before. The man said, 'My Lord, praise be to You! Should I be giving to a prostitute, a thief and a rich man!' While he was asleep, he was told, 'As for your *sadaqa* to the thief, it may help him to be satisfied and cease stealing. As for the prostitute, she may take the *sadaqa* and give up prostitution. And as for the rich man, he may take the lesson and start spending out of what Allah has given him.'" (Ahmad, al-Bukhari and Muslim)

There is also the *hadith* in which the Prophet (p) told a man who asked him for *zakat*, "If you are among those categories of those entitled, I would give you your right," and the answer of the Prophet (p) to the two strong and capable men who asked him for *sadaqa*, "If you wish, I would give to you out of it, but the rich and those capable of earning have no share in it." If the condition was truly wealth, he would have investigated their case and not merely accepted their claim.[1]

The second opinion inclines towards the other extreme and considers that if an error of judgement results in giving *zakat* to a person who is not entitled, the *zakat* obligation is not fulfilled and another amount must be given. Ash-Shafi'i subscribes generally to this view, [2] while we have two reports about the view of Ahmad on mistakenly giving *zakat* to a rich man, one similar to that of ash-Shafi'i.[3] As for giving *zakat* to an unbeliever, a member of the Prophet's family, or a relative of the payer who is not allowed to receive the payer's *zakat*, Ahmad firmly believes such payment does not fulfil the requirement of *zakat*.

The third opinion covers the area between these two extremes. There are varying views in this area according to the conditions of distribution. According to Hanafis, if the payer makes a reasonable effort to find those entitled and then discovers that he has paid *zakat* to those who are not entitled, such a payment is acceptable and the payer is not required to repeat his payment. However, when *zakat* is distributed without proper investigation, such payment is not acceptable if it is found that it was given to those not entitled. When payment is given to unbelievers, Abu Yusuf believes that the *zakat* payer is required to make a second payment, even if *zakat* was distributed after proper investigation. As for Abu Hanifa, there are two reports from him: one is like Abu Yusuf and the other is the opposite.[4]

1. *Al-Mughni*, vol. 2, p. 667.
2. *Ar-Rawda*, vol. 2, p. 328.
3. *Al-Mughni*, vol. 2, p. 668.
4. *Radd al-Muhtar*, vol. 2, pp. 73-74.

According to Malikis, payment to those who are not entitled as a result of error in judgement does not relieve the *zakat* payer of his responsibility, and a second payment must be made unless that which was given to those not entitled can be retrieved and redistributed to those entitled.[1]

Zaydis believe giving *zakat* to persons considered unanimously to be undeserving, by mistake, does not fulfil the obligation of *zakat*. Individuals who are unanimously treated as undeserving are unbelievers, parents and offspring of payers, and the wealthy. If a person gives his *zakat* to individuals to whom he believes *zakat* can be given, another payment is not required.[2]

Finally, in my opinion, if a *zakat* payer makes sufficient efforts to find those entitled but makes a mistake and gives his *zakat* to those who are not entitled by an error of judgement, he is not responsible for that mistake, nor is he required to repeat the payment. Allah says, *"Allah does not charge any self beyond what it can bear."* (2:286) Allah would not suffer the reward of such a person to be lost, exactly like the person mentioned in the *hadith* who gave his *sadaqa* to a thief, a prostitute and a rich person. However, if the *zakat* payer does not make an adequate search, he must be charged for the result of his mistake in judgement.

In all cases, whoever takes *zakat* knowing that he is not entitled to it must return it, or at least give it to someone who is entitled to it. Otherwise what he takes is unlawful. If the *zakat* agency makes a mistake in giving *zakat* to those not entitled, the *zakat* agency is not required to repeat the payment. Rather the law enforcement body must be used to recover what was unjustly given, as recommended by Malikis.

1. *Ash-Sharh al-Kabir* with *Hashiyat ad-Dusuqi*, vol. 1, pp. 501-502.
2. *Sharh al-Azhar*, vol. 1, pp. 526-527, and *al-Bahr*, vol. 2, p. 187.

Part Five
Methods of *Zakat* Distribution

Chapter One

The Role of the State

State responsibility with regard to *zakat*

As a confirmed obligation from Allah, *zakat* is not merely charity left to individuals to implement nor is its fulfilment dependent on the benevolence of the wealthy. *Zakat* is rather a social welfare institution supervised by the state and an organised tax administered by a specific governmental body.

The state's role in the collection and distribution of *zakat* is best supported by the *ayat* that mentions, *"those who collect* zakat*"* (9:60) as one of the categories to whom *zakat* is distributed. This *ayat* is explicit evidence that there should be a specialised body with workers who derive their incomes from the work they do. Moreover, Allah says, *"Take* sadaqa *from their wealth to purify and cleanse them."* (9:103) "Take" is addressed to the Prophet as head of the Islamic state, to the extent, that when Abu Bakr succeeded the Prophet (p) as head of state, he continued using state authority to collect and distribute *zakat*. Scholars recognise that the verb 'take' in the above *ayat* is addressed to the Prophet (p) and to whoever runs the affairs of Muslims after him.

As for the *Sunna*, there are *hadiths* that confirm that administering *zakat* is one of the responsibilities of the Islamic state. Al-Bukhari, Muslim and others report from Ibn 'Abbas that the Prophet told Mu'adh when he sent him to Yemen, "Inform them that Allah obliges *sadaqa* on their wealth, to be taken from the rich among them and rendered to the poor among them. If they obey you in that, carefully avoid their dear wealth..." This *hadith* indicates that *zakat* is taken from the rich and rendered to the poor by the state. Ibn Hajar says, "This *hadith* is evidence that the state is the authority which takes *zakat* and distributes it. Those who refuse to pay are forced to do so.[1] Ash-Shawkani quotes the same from Ibn Hajar in *Nayl al-Awtar*.[2] Additionally, there are several *hadiths* which instruct *zakat* workers, who were called *as-su'at* or *al-musaddiqin*. Most of these *hadiths* are mentioned in chapter two of part four of this book. There are also many *hadiths* that advise *zakat* payers on their conduct towards collectors.

In addition to the Qur'an and *Sunna*, the assertion that the Islamic state is responsible for the collection and distribution of *zakat* is supported by the actual practice of the Prophet (p) and the Rashidun Khalifs after him. In *at-Talkhis*, Ibn Hajar notes that the fact that the Messenger of Allah (p) and the Khalifs sent out *zakat* collectors is well-known. Al-Bukhari and Muslim report from Abu Hurayra that the Prophet (p) sent 'Umar as a collector of *zakat*. They report from Abu Humayd, "The Prophet (p) employed a man from the tribe of al-Azd named Ibn al-Lutabiya as a *zakat* collector." They also report that 'Umar employed Ibn as-Sa'di for that job. Abu Dawud reports that the Prophet (p) employed Ibn Mas'ud as a *zakat* collector. Ahmad reports that the Prophet sent Abu Jahm ibn Hudhayfa and 'Uqba ibn 'Amir as *zakat* collectors and from Qurra ibn Da'mus that the Prophet sent ad-Dahhak ibn Qays as *zakat* collector. Al-Hakim reports in *al-Mustadrak* that the Prophet sent Qays ibn Sa'd and 'Ubada ibn as-Samit as *zakat* collectors, and al-Walid ibn 'Uqba as a *zakat* collector to the Banu'l-Mustaliq.

Al-Bayhaqi reports from ash-Shafi'i that Abu Bakr and 'Umar used to send *zakat* collectors. In a version reported by ash-Shafi'i from Ibrahim ibn Sa'd from az-Zuhri, it is added that they did not delay its collection in any year. Ash-Shafi'i, in his former opinion, narrates that in the year of the famine, 'Umar postponed *zakat* and then sent collectors to take twice as much in the following year. Ibn Sa'd reports in *at-Tabaqat* that the Prophet (p) sent collectors to Arab tribes at the beginning of al-Muharram 9 AH. This *hadith* is also cited by al-Waqidi in *al-Maghazi*.[3]

1. *Fath al-Bari*, vol. 3, p. 23.
2. *Nayl al-Awtar*, vol. 4, p. 124.
3. *At-Talkhis*, vol. 2, pp. 159-160.

Ibn Sa'd names *zakat* collectors and the tribes to which they were sent. The Prophet, he reports, sent 'Uyayna ibn Hisn to the Banu Tamim to collect and distribute *zakat*, Burayda ibn al-Hasib to Aslam and Ghifar, 'Abbad ibn Bishr al-Ashhali to Sulaym and Muzayna, Rafi' ibn Makith to Juhayna, 'Amr ibn al-'As to Fazara, ad-Dahhak ibn Sufyan al-Kilabi to Banu Kilab, Busr ibn Sufyan al-Ka'bi to Banu Ka'b, Ibn al-Lutabiya to Banu Dhubyan, and a man from Sa'd Hudhaym to his tribe. Ibn Sa'd adds, "The Messenger of Allah (p) told his collectors to take only from the surplus and to avoid the choicest assets of the payers."[1]

Ibn Ishaq names yet other collectors the Prophet (p) sent to various tribes and provinces of the Arabian peninsula. For example, he sent al-Muhajir ibn Abi Umayya to San'a, Zayd ibn Labid to Hadramawt, 'Adi ibn Hatim to Tay' and Banu Asad, Malik ibn Nuwayra to Banu Hanzala, az-Zibriqan ibn Badr to a part of the Banu Sa'd, Qays ibn 'Asim to the other part of Banu Sa'd, al-'Ala' ibn al-Hadrami to Bahrayn, and 'Ali to Najran.[2]

In *at-Taratib al-Idariyya*, al-Kattani quotes Ibn Hazm as saying in *Jawami' as-Siyar,* "Az-Zubayr was the *zakat* clerk appointed by the Messenger of Allah. When az-Zubayr was absent, Jahm ibn as-Salt and Hudhayfa ibn al-Yaman used to substitute for him."[3] Al-Kattani also quotes Ibn Hajar in *al-Isaba* as naming Companions employed for this job by the Prophet. These include al-Arqam ibn Abi al-Arqam, Hudhayfa ibn al-Yaman, Kafiya ibn Sab' al-Asadi, Kahl ibn Malik al-Hudhali, Khalif ibn al-Bara', Khuzayma ibn 'Asim al-'Ukli, etc."[4] Thus it is obvious that the Prophet (p) covered practically all Arabia with *zakat* collectors. He provided them with advice and instructions on how to treat those who paid *zakat* and collect the right amount. He also instructed them to avoid the choicest wealth of payers, and when they came back, he sometimes used to ask them for a full account of what they had done.[5]

Scholars agree that the state must appoint *zakat* collectors, because the Prophet and the Khulafa' ar-Rashidun after him sent

1. *Tabaqat Ibn Sa'*d, vol. 2, p. 160.
2. *Zad al-Ma'ad*, vol. 2, p. 472.
3. *At-Taratib al-Idariyya*, p. 398.
4. Ibid., pp. 396-8.
5. *Zad al-Ma'ad*, vol. 2, p. 472.

collectors, and because there are always people who own assets but do not know how to pay their due *zakat*, and people who dislike paying because of greed.[1]

Owners of zakatable assets are advised to help collectors and not hide any part of their wealth. Jarir ibn 'Abdullah says, "A group of nomadic Arabs came to the Messenger of Allah (p) and said, 'Some *zakat* collectors did us an injustice.' The Messenger of Allah (p) said, 'You must please your collectors,'" (Muslim), and Jabir ibn 'Atik narrates that the Prophet (p) said, "People that you may not like [collectors] shall come to you. When they come, you should welcome them and let them do what they want. If they do justice, the result will be on their own souls, but if they do injustice, the punishment will also be on their own souls. It is necessary for completing your *zakat* that you please them so they will pray for you.'"[2]

Anas narrates, "A man asked the Messenger of Allah (p), 'If I give *zakat* to the person you send, would I be fulfilling it as far as Allah and His Messenger are concerned?' The Prophet (p) answered, 'Yes, if you give it to my messenger, you are freed of that obligation as far as Allah and His Messenger are concerned. You deserve its reward, and if it is tampered with later, the sin is on whoever alters it."[3]

Companions' opinions on the role of the state

Sahl ibn Abi Salih narrates that his father said, "I accumulated a zakatable amount of wealth. I asked Sa'd ibn Abi Waqqas, Ibn

1. *Al-Majmu'*, vol. 6, p. 167 and *ar-Rawda*, vol. 2, p. 155.

2. Reported by Abu Dawud, according to *Nayl al-Awtar*, vol. 4, p. 155. Al-Munawi says in al-Fayd, "There is no doubt the Prophet never appointed an unjust officer. All his officers and *zakat* collectors were scrupulous in their sense of justice. They include persons like 'Umar, 'Ali and Mu'adh. So the *hadith* must mean that you are going to have collectors whom you may think are unjust." Al-Mazhari adds, "This may be a reference to the future when collectors may in fact be unjust. Yet rejection of payment to them may lead to general unrest and disturb the public order of the whole state." See *Fayd al-Qadir*, vol. 1, p. 475.

3. According to *Nayl al-Awtar*, ibid., the author of *al-Muntaqa* attributes quoting this hadith to Ahmad.

'Umar, Abu Hurayra and Abu Sa'id al-Khudri whether I should distribute *zakat* myself or give it to the government. They all ordered me to pay it to the government and none of them disagreed." Another version reads, "I said, 'Don't you see what this government does?' It was the time of the Umayyads. 'Should I still give it my *zakat*?' They all answered, 'Yes, you must.'" This is reported by Sa'id ibn Mansur in his *Musnad*.[1]

Ibn 'Umar says, "Pay your *sadaqa* to whoever runs your affairs. If he does it right, it is his soul that will be rewarded, and if he does evil, it is on himself." Qaz'a reports from Ibn 'Umar, "Give them your *zakat* even if they drink wine." An-Nawawi says, "These two statements are reported by al-Bayhaqi via correct or good chains."[2] Al-Mughira ibn Shu'ba once asked a slave of his who was managing his assets in at-Ta'if, "What do you do with the *zakat* on my wealth?" The manager said, "I distribute part of it and pay part of it to the government." Ibn Shu'ba said, "Why do you do that?" He answered, "They buy land and marry women with what we give them." Al-Mughira said, "Give it to the government, for the Messenger of Allah (p) orders us to give it to them." (Reported by al-Bayhaqi in *as-Sunan al-Kabir*)

Rationalisation of this evidence

The above-mentioned *ayats*, *hadiths* and opinions of the Companions indicate that in principle, *zakat* must be administered by the Islamic government. It is an important responsibility of the Islamic state and the public *zakat* organisation.

It might be asked that if the purpose of religions is to awaken the human conscience, enlighten people with truth, and induce them to behave ideally by the motivation of love of Allah or fear of His punishment, why should Islam interfere with the organisation of society instead of leaving this to the political authorities? Our answer is that this may be relevant to religions other than Islam, but Islam is both creed and system, moral values and laws, a guiding Book and an organised state.

1. As stated by an-Nawawi in *al-Majmu'*.
2. Ibid.

From the point of view of this religion, human beings' lives cannot be divided up with one part for religion and the other for worldly life. Life cannot be partitioned into one allegiance to Caesar and another separate allegiance to Allah. Life is one complete thing, as is the human being, as is the entire universe, all submitting to Allah, One and Almighty. Islam brings forth comprehensive and universal guidance which gives liberty and dignity to the individual and, at the same time, betterment and happiness to society. Within this unified framework, the system of *zakat* is enacted, its collection and distribution being the business of the state. Islam implants the desire to pay *zakat* in the hearts of the believers while entrusting the state with *zakat* collection and distribution for the following important reasons.

- Some individuals may not have awakened consciences that force them to fulfil this obligation. In such cases, the right of the poor would be lost if *zakat* payment were left to individuals.
- When poor persons receive their right from the government and not directly from the rich, their dignity is preserved and there is no possibility of their humiliation in front of the payer.
- If the distribution of *zakat* is left to individuals, it is bound to come out uneven, since each individual always has his or her personal bias which means that one poor person may be given to by several rich people while another poor person may be forgotten or neglected.
- Deserving categories include public interests such as softening hearts, fighting for Allah's sake or calling to Islam that can only be determined by authorities who have an overall vision of the entire society and its major needs.
- Islam is both a religion and a state, and the state needs funds to play its role. *Zakat* is one of the financial resources of the Islamic state.[1]

1. Al-Qaradawi, *Mushkiliyat al-Faqr wa kayfa 'Alajaha'l-Islam*, pp. 94-5.

The treasury of *zakat*

If *zakat* is handled by the state, it must be run independently since Allah determines its distribution in the Qur'an. Thus *zakat* should have a separate treasury and administrative body supervised by the Islamic state. The verse on *zakat* distribution refers implicitly to this autonomy by assigning a share to its collectors. The historical practice of the Muslims was to establish several sub-treasuries in the state. Four sub-treasuries are clearly identified and described by the Hanafis:

- *Zakat*
- *Jizya* and *kharaj*
- War booty and *rikaz* (according to those who do not include it in *zakat*).
- Lost and found assets and similar things such as the estates of those who die without heirs, etc.[1]

Apparent and non-apparent assets

Jurists usually divide zakatable assets into two groups. Apparent assets are those that are visible and can easily be counted by people other than the owner. They include agricultural crops and livestock. Non-apparent assets are those that can easily be hidden away by the owner. They include money and business assets.

As for apparent assets, jurists agree almost unanimously that the collection and distribution of their *zakat* must be undertaken by the state. Their *zakat* should not be left to individuals, especially since we have many reports that the Prophet (p) sent his collectors to take *zakat* on these assets. It is obvious that the state is responsible for enforcing this collection and must fight, if necessary, those who refuse to pay this *zakat*, as Abu Bakr did after the death of the Prophet.[2] As for non-apparent assets, it is agreed that the state has the right to collect and distribute the *zakat* on them. However, jurists have several opinions about enforcing its payment to the government.

1. *Al-Mabsut*, vol. 3, p. 18, *al-Bada'i'*, vol. 2, pp. 68-69, and *Radd al-Muhtar*, vol. 2, pp. 59-60.

2. *Al-Amwal*, p. 531.

Hanafis argue that *zakat* on non-apparent assets should be left to the owners to distribute. They add that although, in principle, the state has the right to administer this kind of *zakat*, unlike the apparent assets for which the authority of collection is vested in the state,[1] since the time of 'Uthman this task has been assigned to the owners of wealth. This assignment does not eliminate the state's authority to supervise payment of *zakat* on non-apparent assets. If the state is informed that owners of wealth in certain areas do not pay *zakat* on their non-apparent assets, its payment can be enforced by the public law enforcement authority.[2] *Zakat* on trade assets may be collected by the state if they are being transported from one place to another, but if trade assets are not transported, they are treated like other non-apparent assets.[3]

Malikis argue that *zakat* must be given to a just government without differentiation between apparent and non-apparent assets.[4] If the state is just only in the matter of *zakat* collection and distribution and is unjust in other affairs, some Malikis argue that all *zakat* must still be paid to the state. These include ad-Dardir, as stated in *ash-Sharh al-Kabir*. Ad-Dusuqi does not agree in his commentary. Al-Qurtubi says, "If the government is just with regard to *zakat* collection and distribution, owners are not justified in distributing *zakat* on money or other items independently, although some say the distribution of *zakat* on money is the responsibility of the owners. Ibn al-Majishun adds, "Distribution to the poor and needy by *zakat* payers may be acceptable, but individuals should not be allowed to distribute to the other categories of those entitled. Such distribution must only be made by the state."[5]

Shafi'is believe that owners are allowed to distribute due *zakat* on their non-apparent assets independently. As for the apparent assets, the prominent view in the Shafi'i school is that their *zakat* may also be distributed by the payer. The other opinion is that it must be given to the government if it is just. Some Shafi'is argue that *zakat* on apparent assets must be given even to an unjust gov-

1. *Al-Mughni*, vol. 2, p. 643.
2. *Radd al-Muhtar*, vol. 2, p. 5.
3. Ibid., pp. 41-42.
4. *Hashiyat ad-Dusuqi*, vol. 1, pp. 503-4.
5. *Tafsir al-Qurtubi*, vol. 8, p. 177.

ernment. It is, however, agreed upon by all Shafi'is that, when the government carries out the task of collecting *zakat* on apparent assets, this *zakat* must be paid to the government. If the government does not carry out this responsibility, owners have the right to distribute *zakat* on their apparent assets themselves. Al-Mawardi argues that the distribution of *zakat* on non-apparent assets must, in principle, be left to payers who, however, have the right to surrender this authority to the government. An-Nawawi adds that the government also has the right to see that owners are actually fulfilling this obligation and to demand payment to the state in case owners of non-apparent assets do not distribute their due *zakat*.[1]

Hanbalis believe that giving *zakat* to the government is not obligatory, although the government has the right to undertake this task. They do not differentiate between apparent and non-apparent assets or between just and unjust states. On the other hand, Hanbalis agree that payers are allowed to distribute their *zakat* by themselves. Ibn Qudama argues in *al-Mughni* that it is preferred for the *zakat* payer to distribute his or her *zakat* by himself, so as to be sure it is given to the true deserving categories, no matter whether it is on apparent or non-apparent assets. Ahmad says, "I would like the payer to distribute his due *zakat* although it is permissible to give it to the government.

Makhul, al-Hasan, Sa'id ibn Jubayr and Maymun believe the owner should distribute his *zakat* himself if the state does not use it properly. Ath-Thawri even allows the owner to cheat the government so as not to give it the *zakat* due, while 'Ata' says it is all right to surrender *zakat* to the government "if you know it is going to be distributed justly." Ash-Sha'bi and Abu Ja'far also say that it should not be given to a government if it is not just. Ibn Qudama adds, "Distribution of *zakat* by the owner guarantees that it will be given to the true deserving categories, in addition to saving the amount paid to *zakat* workers. As well as that, collectors and distributors of *zakat* are not necessarily above betraying the trust placed in them, and in any case, *zakat* may not reach the neighbours and kin of the payer, who deserve the payer's grace more

1. *Ar-Rawda*, vol. 2, pp. 205-6.

than anyone else."[1] On the other hand, Ahmad is reported to have said that it is desired that *'ushr* be paid to the state because it is similar to *kharaj* while other forms of *zakat* may be distributed to deserving persons by their owner.

Zaydis believe the responsibility for collecting and distributing *zakat* belongs to the government alone, regardless of whether assets are apparent or not. If there exists a just government, the owner has no right to distribute *zakat* on his own. Their view is based on their understanding of the *ayat* that addresses the Prophet (p), *"**Take** sadaqa from their wealth ..."* and the *hadith* that *zakat* is "...**taken** from the rich..." and by the fact that the Prophet (p) and his Successors sent *zakat* collectors. They add that if the government collects *zakat* and a person decides to distribute his *zakat* by himself, he is required to make another payment of *zakat* to the government, even if the person was not aware that the government collects *zakat*.[2] If there is no Islamic government, or the *zakat* payer is not under its authority, the payer must distribute *zakat* independently.[3]

Ibadis argue that the responsibility for collecting *zakat* is the government's. They agree with the Zaydis that if a person distributes his own *zakat* while the government takes responsibility for collection, this person is required to make another payment of the *zakat* due to the government.[4]

Ash-Sha'bi, al-Baqir, Abu Razin, and al-Awza'i believe the government has the exclusive right to collect *zakat*, because it has better means of knowing those who deserve it. They add that Ibn 'Umar used to give his *zakat* to collectors sent by the rulers of the time– Ibn az-Zubayr sometimes and Naja al-Haruri at other times – and that Suhayl reported that Abu Salih asked Sa'd ibn Abi Waqqas, "I have wealth and I want to give its due *zakat*, and you see these rulers, the way they are. What should I do?" Sa'd replied, "Give it to them." Abu Salih adds, "I went to Ibn 'Umar, Abu

1. *Al-Mughni*, vol. 2, pp. 641-4.
2. *Sharh al-Azhar*, vol. 1, pp. 527-9.
3. Ibid., pp. 534-5.
4. *Sharh an-Nil*, vol. 2, pp. 137-8.

Hurayra and Abu Sa'id, and they gave me the same answer." A similar opinion is reported from 'A'isha.[1]

Comparison

Before I select one of these opinions, I should mention that almost all jurists agree on two points. Firstly, the Islamic state has the right to collect and distribute *zakat* on any and all assets, apparent and non-apparent. This right is emphasised if there exists suspicion that people are not eager to pay their *zakat* by themselves. Some jurists even state that all differences with regard to the role of the state arise about the case in which the government does not administer *zakat*, but when it does, those jurists claim there is *ijma'* on the obligation of giving *zakat* to the state.[2] Even those who disagree accept the principle that once *zakat* collection is carried out by the state, *zakat* must be given to the state, because it is a disputed issue and any disputed issue can be settled by a political decision like legal disputes that are decided by court judgements.[3]

The second point of agreement is that if the state neglects *zakat* collection, owners of assets must distribute their own *zakat*. This is based on the fact that *zakat* is a form of worship and a religious obligation that must be fulfilled by each individual, to the extent that if a government dares to exempt people from paying *zakat*, Muslims must distribute their own *zakat* independently.

Once these two points of unanimous agreement are understood, we can look at differences about whether the government has the authority to collect *zakat* on non-apparent wealth. It seems to me from examining texts on *zakat* collection and the authority of the Islamic state that texts make no distinction between apparent and non-apparent wealth. It is stated that the Islamic state is required to administer both *zakat* collection and distribution, without any exceptions. This understanding is supported by the following points:

1. *Al-Mughni*, vol. 2, pp. 642-3.
2. *Sharh al-Azhar*, vol. 1, p. 529.
3. *Al-Bahr*, vol. 2, p. 190.

- Ar-Razi in explaining the *ayat*, "*Collected* sadaqa *is only for the poor…*" says, "This *ayat* indicates that the government and its representatives are the authority responsible for collecting and distributing *zakat*, especially since Allah assigns a share to *zakat* workers. This means workers are needed to fulfil this obligation. Workers are appointed by the Islamic government. Thus the government is the authority that collects *zakat*. This is emphasised by the *ayat* which reads, *'**Take*** sadaqa *from their wealth …'* Jurists who permit the owner to distribute his *zakat* on non-apparent wealth find supportive evidence elsewhere, such as in the *ayat*, *'And the beggars and deprived received a due share of their wealth,'* on the grounds that, since this right belongs to the beggars and the deprived, it may be given to them directly by the owner of the wealth."[1] In my opinion, this last sentence of ar-Razi is not acceptable, since the share mentioned above also applies to apparent items, and there is overwhelming evidence and agreement that the state collects and distributes *zakat* on apparent items.

- Ibn al-Humam, a Hanafi, says, "It is evident that the *ayat 'Take* sadaqa *from their wealth'* requires that the right of collecting all *zakat* belongs to the Islamic government. This was the fact at the time of the Messenger of Allah (p) and his first two successors. When 'Uthman was elected, he did not like to search for people's non-apparent wealth, so he left the payment of *zakat* on such wealth to the owners themselves. The other Companions did not quarrel with him about this. This certainly does not eliminate the state's right to collect *zakat*, since if it becomes known that certain people do not pay their *zakat* on non-apparent items, the state reserves the right to enforce payment of *zakat* to the state treasury."[2]

- Abu 'Ubayd, at-Tirmidhi and ad-Daraqutni report, "The Prophet (p) once appointed 'Umar as a *zakat* collector. 'Umar asked al-Abbas for the amount of *zakat* due on his wealth. Al-'Abbas answered, 'I have pre-paid the *sadaqa* for two years to the Messenger of Allah (p).' 'Umar told this to the Prophet (p)

1. *Tafsir ar-Razi*, vol. 16, p. 114.
2. *Fath al-Qadir*, Ibn al-Humam, vol. 1, p. 487.

who said, 'My uncle tells the truth. We have taken from him the *sadaqa* of two years in advance.'"[1] This is evidence for collecting wealth on non-apparent wealth, since al-'Abbas was a merchant and did not own agriculture or livestock.

• A similar report reads, "The Prophet sent his collector to take *zakat*. Some malicious individuals spread a rumour that Ibn Jamil, Khalid ibn al-Walid and al-'Abbas ibn 'Abdu'l-Muttalib refused to pay *zakat*. The Messenger of Allah (p) gave a speech in which he refuted the accusation on behalf of al-'Abbas and Khalid, and confirmed it about Ibn Jamil. The Prophet said, 'They do an injustice to Khalid. Khalid devotes his shields and weapons for the sake of Allah.' (Apparently Khalid's wealth consisted of them.) He continued, 'As for al-'Abbas, the uncle of the Messenger of Allah (p), we took his *zakat* for two years.'"[2]

• Abu Dawud also reports that the Prophet (p) said, "Bring me one-fourth of the tenth, one dirham out of each forty dirhams...",[3] which indicates that he collected *zakat* on money.

• Moreover, there are several reports to the effect that Abu Bakr, 'Umar, 'Uthman, Ibn Mas'ud, Mu'awiya, 'Umar ibn 'Abdu'l-'Aziz and others used to collect *zakat* out of salaries and grants given by the state. Abu Bakr used to ask the recipients whether they owned any wealth. If the answer was affirmative, he took out of the salary the due amount of *zakat* on the wealth. Ibn Mas'ud collected *zakat* on the salaries themselves at a rate of twenty-five per thousand. (It is known that he did not require the passage of one year on earned income, as shown earlier in this book.) 'Umar, when giving salaries counted the wealth of merchants, both current and future, and took *zakat* out of both.[4] Qudama narrates, "'Uthman ibn

1. *Al-Amwal*, p. 589. The *hadith* is reported via several chains that are not safe from weakness, but they strengthen each other. See *Fath al-Bari*, vol. 2, p. 214. Jurists use this *hadith* as evidence to indicate the lawfulness of prepayment of *zakat*.

2. *Al-Amwal*, pp. 592-3. The *hadith* is reported by al-Bukhari, Muslim and Ahmad. See *Nayl al-Awtar*, vol. 4, p. 149.

3. *Ma'alim as-Sunan*, vol. 2, pp. 18809. See also the notes on this *hadith* by Ibn al-Qayyim in *Tahdhib Sunan Abi Dawud*.

4. *Musannaf Ibn Abi Shayba*, vol. 4, p. 44.

'Affan used to ask me when I went to receive my salary, 'Do you have any wealth on which *zakat* is due?' If I said yes, he would collect the *zakat* out of my salary, and if I said no, he would give me my salary."[1]

- Lastly, the religious opinions reported from Ibn 'Umar and some other Companions indicate that *zakat* must be paid to the government, even if it is oppressive, without any distinction between apparent and non-apparent items of wealth.

The view of Abu 'Ubayd

A few scholars distinguish between apparent and non-apparent wealth on the grounds of the actual practice of the Prophet. They argue that no overwhelming or widespread evidence reaches us which shows that the Messenger (p) sent people to collect and distribute *zakat* on money and business assets, as he did with respect to apparent wealth. Consequently, some leading scholars argue it is permissible either to give the *zakat* due on non-apparent wealth to the government or distribute it without discrimination between recipients. Abu 'Ubayd says:

> "This is, I believe, the view of *Sunni* scholars in both the Hijaz and Iraq. As far as gold, silver and trade goods are concerned, Muslims are trusted to fulfil this obligation, while *zakat* on livestock, grain, and fruits must only be administered by the Islamic government. Owners must not hide due *zakat* away from the Islamic government. If owners distribute the latter on their own, that does not satisfy the requirement and *zakat* must again be given to the state. The texts we gave from *Sunna* and the Companions warrant this distinction. We see that Abu Bakr fought the apostates in order to collect the *zakat* due on livestock. He did not do that for *zakat* due on gold and silver."[2]

1. *Al-Umm*, ash-Shafi'i, vol. 2, p. 14.
2. *Al-Amwal*, p. 573.

Abu 'Ubayd goes on to give a few reports in support of this position, but upon close examination of his quoted statements, we find them all speaking about exceptional circumstances, such as corruption in government and its *zakat* agency and not normal situations. This is obvious from the fact that such opinions come about only after political unrest and conspiracies that led to the murder of 'Uthman. Abu 'Ubayd reports, via his own chain, that Ibn Sirin says, "*Sadaqa* was paid to the Prophet (p) or his commissioners, then to Abu Bakr or his commissioners, then to 'Umar or his commissioners, then to 'Uthman or his commissioners. When 'Uthman was killed, people differed. Some, like Ibn 'Umar, continued to give *zakat* to the state and some started distributing it directly."[1] This is well-known about Ibn 'Umar who said, "As long as they [the rulers] establish the prayer, you must give *zakat* to them." It is even reported that he dropped this condition, saying, "Give it to them even if they use it to buy dog meat for their own dishes." In answer to another person, he said, "Pay it to them even if they use it to buy clothes and perfume for themselves."

But we have certain narrations to the effect that Ibn 'Umar withdrew this last opinion, saying, "Put it [*zakat*] where it must properly be put."[2] A friend of his asked him, "What do you say about *zakat* since these rulers do not put it where it belongs?" Ibn 'Umar said, "Pay it to them." The man said, "If they delayed the prayer, would you still pray with them?" He answered, "No." The man said, "Is not *zakat* like prayer?" Ibn 'Umar said, "They confuse us, may Allah confuse them!"[3] This is seen as acceptance of the man's point of view.

It is also reported that Ibrahim an-Nakha'i and al-Hasan al-Basri said, "Distribute it properly among yourselves and hide it from the rulers."[4] Maymun ibn Mihran is reported to have said, "Put it in small bags and distribute it among the deserving categories that you know. Be keen to do away with all of it by the end of the month."[5] Abu Yahya al-Kindi said, "I asked Sa'id ibn Jubayr about

1. *Al-Amwal*, p. 567.
2. Ibid.
3. Ibid.
4. Ibid.
5. Ibid.

zakat. He said, 'Give it to the rulers.' When Sa'id left, I followed him and asked, 'Should I give it to the rulers although they do with it so-and-so?' Sa'id answered, 'Put it where Allah ordered you. You asked me in the presence of a public audience, and I could not give you my personal opinion there.'"[1]

All these narrations and opinions mentioned by Abu 'Ubayd were given after the beginning of political unrest, the rise of anger against some Umayyad commissioners and the deviation of many of them from standards established during the period of the *Khulafa' ar-Rashidun*. Lastly, it must be noted that any authentic report that the Prophet (p) made a distinction between apparent and non-apparent items of wealth and that he did not send commissioners to collect *zakat* on non-apparent items is caused by either of the two following reasons:

- People used to bring that *zakat* to the Messenger of Allah (p) out of their faith and awakened consciences.
- Reckoning of this kind of wealth was practically impossible, except by the owner, so owners were charged with that obligation.

This continued during the era of the first Khalif, Abu Bakr. During the caliphate of 'Umar, the state expanded and salaries were assigned to all people, including the new born. Even the People of the Pledge were covered by this social insurance. This program required huge resources, so it became indispensable to appoint commissioners to collect *zakat* on all wealth, both apparent and non-apparent. Consequently, 'Umar established an administration for *zakat* collection called the system of *"al-'Ashirin"*, i.e. "collectors of the tenth", since one-tenth was collected from foreign merchants (in application of the same treatment Muslim merchants were given in foreign countries), half a tenth was collected from merchants of the People of the Pledge (according to the treaties 'Umar had with them) and one-fourth of a tenth from Muslim merchants as *zakat*.[2]

1. *Al-Amwal*, ibid.
2. Ibid., p. 531.

Scholars consider the system of collection established by 'Umar as a great facilitation for the entire society for, otherwise, zakatable people would have had to cover great distances to bring their due *zakat* to Madina. Thus the same principle was applied by the Prophet, Abu Bakr and 'Umar, except that 'Umar improved the method of collection. When 'Uthman came, huge amounts of proceeds from *fay'*, *ghanima*, *kharaj*, *jizya*, and *sadaqat* started pouring into the state treasury, so 'Uthman decided to collect the *zakat* of apparent wealth only and to leave *zakat* on non-apparent wealth to owners to distribute themselves under the supervision of the state. 'Uthman, at his own discretion, depended on the awakened consciences of Muslims at his time to stimulate scrupulous payment. Some jurists interpret this action of 'Uthman as the appointment of owners as representatives of the state regarding distributing *zakat* on non-apparent wealth. In *al-Bada'i'*, al-Kasani says:

> The Prophet (p), Abu Bakr, and 'Umar collected it [*zakat*] on non-apparent items. But when funds became abundant at the time of 'Uthman, he found it was to the public benefit to assign distribution to owners. This was done with the approval of the Companions. Owners of such items became agents of the state, especially since 'Uthman said, "Whoever owes any debt must first pay it back, then distribute *zakat* on the residue." This authorises owners to distribute their *zakat*. Thus the right of the state is not waived. Consequently, our colleagues hold that if it becomes known to the state that people in certain areas do not fulfil this requirement, the state reserves the right to collect it through its own commissioners.[1]

Finally, we reach the conclusion that, in principle, it is the state's duty to collect *zakat* on all wealth, both apparent and non-apparent. Exceptionally, when the treasury's resources are great (as with 'Uthman), owners of wealth may be authorised to distribute *zakat* on non-apparent assets on the condition that, if they fail, the state can take charge of this collection and distribute again.

1. *Al-Bada'i'*, vol. 2, p. 7.

Who is responsible for administering *zakat* today?

This matter is discussed by professors Khalaf, al-Hasan and Abu Zahra in their lecture on *zakat* in Damascus, 1952. They say:

> It is imperative that the government take responsibility for collecting *zakat* on all wealth, apparent and non-apparent, for two reasons. Firstly, many people have now abandoned this obligation on all their wealth. They do not fulfil the terms of agency given by 'Uthman and scholars after him, and jurists state that if people do not fulfil the obligation of distributing *zakat* due on their non-apparent wealth, the state may take charge of this obligation again, and that if people do not in general pay their *zakat*, the state must force them to do so.
>
> Secondly, most formerly non-apparent items of wealth have become apparent today, especially trade goods and monetary assets, since merchants usually keep accounting records for their businesses. The same rules that apply to calculating taxes on income and profit must be used with regard to *zakat* obliged by Allah for the poor and deprived. Money and monetary assets are mostly deposited in banks and knowing their balances at the end of the year is an easy matter.
>
> We know that jurists agree that if non-apparent items of wealth become apparent, responsibility for the collection of their *zakat* reverts to the state. The fact that the institution of *al-'Ashirin* remained during and after 'Uthman's period supports this point, since *al-'Ashirin* used to collect *zakat* on money and merchandise being transported from one place to another. Thus the ability to reach and count non-apparent items obviously means they should be treated like apparent items.[1]

It must be noted that each Islamic state is called upon to establish an organisation for collecting and distributing *zakat*, although I

1. *Halqat ad-Dirasat al-Ijtima'iyya*, third session on *zakat*.

prefer that a fraction of the *zakat* due (one-fourth or one-third) be left for individuals to distribute to deserving people whom they personally know, especially their kindred and neighbours. This is by analogy to the Prophet's practice of leaving part of the harvest uncounted during pre-estimation of *zakat* due on it.

Undoubtedly, assigning the responsibility of *zakat* collection and distribution to the state applies to a government that takes Islam as its basis, Islamic laws as the foundation for its constitution, and Islamic social, economic, cultural and political standards as a basis for its social structure, even if such a government may deviate slightly in the minute details. Governments which reject Islam as the basis of the state are prohibited from collecting *zakat* because they cannot be entrusted with its proper fulfilment.

Refusal to pay and cheating

Authorising the state to penalise those who do not fulfil the obligation of *zakat* and to take the due amount by force is itself an assertion of the state's vital role in *zakat* collection.

Hanafis believe that *zakat* officers may only accept payers' disclosures if ascertained under oath. A payer may claim that payment has been made to another officer, that he is in debt, or any other factor that reduces or eliminates *zakat* payment. Hanafis add that if it is discovered, even years later, that a statement made under oath about the payment of *zakat* is invalid or false, then the *zakat* due must be collected. *Zakat* officers must not accept any claim that *zakat* on apparent wealth was paid directly by the individual.[1] However, the officer may accept a statement made under oath that *zakat* on non-apparent items was already distributed to deserving categories by the payer himself.[2]

Malikis assert that, in case of a refusal to pay, *zakat* must be collected by force, as long as it is known that the payer is wealthy,

1. It is noticed that many Hanafis do not consider *'ushr* to be *zakat*, on the grounds that it is a fee on land. But Ibn al-Humam, a leading Hanafi, rejects this view and asserts that *'ushr* is undoubtedly *zakat*. See this book, chapter on *zakat* on agriculture.

2. *Radd al-Muhtar*, vol. 2, pp. 42-43 and 54.

whether he or she owns apparent items or non-apparent items. Imprisonment may be the penalty for certain cases of denial of *zakat* payment. It is said that the Islamic government may go as far as to declare those who refuse to pay *zakat* rebels and fight them until the due *zakat* is collected.[1]

Shafi'is argue that anyone who refuses to pay *zakat* may be forced to do so and a penalty must be imposed. However, if such a refusal is caused by denial of the obligation itself, it is considered apostasy and the penalty is death. Ash-Shafi'i, in his older opinion, asserts that the penalty for refusing to pay *zakat* is a fine of half the person's wealth in addition to the due amount of *zakat*. This is in accordance with the *hadith* narrated by Bahz ibn Hakim from his father from his grandfather from the Messenger of Allah (p): "And he who refuses to pay, we shall surely take it, along with half his wealth. It is one of the obligations of our Lord, and none of it belongs to the family of Muhammad."[2] But imposing penalty only is the correct view. The author of *al-Muhadhdhab* adds, "The government may fight those who refuse to pay *zakat* as Abu Bakr, the Truthful, fought them."[3]

Unanimity about penalising those who refuse to pay *zakat*

It is agreed that those who deny the obligation of *zakat* itself are treated as apostates, provided they have no excuse, such as being very new to Islam and therefore not having grasped all its requirements. There is no disagreement that *zakat* must be collected by force if the payers refuse to give it without the use of force.[4]

1. *Hashiyat ad-Dusuqi*, vol. 1, p. 503.

2. This *hadith* is reported by Ahmad, Abu Dawud and an-Nasa'i. See part one of this book. The *hadith* is also reported by al-Hakim in *al-Mustadrak*, who, followed by adh-Dhahabi rates it sound. Yahya ibn Ma'in says, "Its chain would be sound if those below Bahz are trustworthy." Ahmad says, "I do not know what to grade it. Its chain is all right." See *Nayl al-Awtar*, vol. 4, p. 122 and *Tahdhib at-Tahdhib*, vol. 1, pp. 498-9, autobiography no. 924 and *Mizan al-I'tidal*, autobiography no. 1324.

3. *Al-Majmu'*, vol. 5, pp. 331-332.

4. *Al-Bahr az-Zakhkhar*, vol. 2, p. 190.

However, scholars do not agree about imposing a fine on those who refuse to pay *zakat*. Some, including Ishaq, a report from Ahmad, al-Awza'i, and the older opinion of ash-Shafi'i, believe that a fine of half the payer's wealth must be collected along with the due amount, in accordance with the *hadith* mentioned above. As for the majority, including the later opinion of ash-Shafi'i, only the due amount of *zakat* must be collected. This is based on three points:

- The *hadith*, "Nothing is obliged on wealth except *zakat*."
- *Zakat* is an act of worship, and not fulfilling an act of worship is not something that incurs fines.
- Many people refused to pay *zakat* during Abu Bakr's time. Although Abu Bakr fought those who refused to pay, no report is available from him or any of the Companions that a fine was imposed on those who were forced to pay *zakat*.[1]

As for the *hadith* from Bahz, al-Bayhaqi quotes ash-Shafi'i as saying, "It is not considered authentic by scholars of *hadith*. If it were authentic, I would have bowed to its implication."[2] Al-Bayhaqi adds that neither al-Bukhari or Muslim use Bahz in their chains of narrators. [3] But one may reply that this is not a sufficient reason for grading a *hadith* weak, since there are many sound *hadiths* outside the collections of al-Bukhari and Muslim. Some scholars claim the *hadith* of Bahz is abrogated by a *hadith* from al-Bara' ibn 'Azib that might virtually mean eliminating all financial penalties. This cannot be supported since it requires knowledge of the chronological order of the two *hadiths* and such knowledge is not available.[4] Al-Mawardi considers Bahz's *hadith* in contradiction to the *hadith*, "Nothing is obliged on wealth except *zakat*," and concludes that the *hadith* from Bahz is not meant for actual punishment but only to create fear of violating the obligation of *zakat*.[5]

1. *As-Sunan al-Kubra*, vol. 4, p. 105.
2. Ibid.
3. Ibid.
4. Ibid., and *al-Majmu'*, vol. 5, p. 334.
5. Al-Ahkam as-Sultaniyya, p. 121.

An-Nawawi adds that the *hadith* of Bahz is graded weak by ash-Shafi'i and other *hadith* scholars.[1]

All the objections to the *hadith* from Bahz can easily be shown as invalid, but as stated earlier in this book, the fine was imposed by the Prophet in his capacity as a head of state. Thus imposing such a fine or not is up to the Islamic state, as argued by al-Qarafi, ad-Dihlawi and others.

The contrast between the *hadith* from Bahz and the *hadith*, "Nothing is obliged on wealth except *zakat*..." is invalid. Firstly, because there are several financial obligations on wealth besides *zakat* confirmed by glorious *ayats* of the Qur'an and explicit, sound *hadiths*, and secondly, the authenticity of the latter saying is disputed.[2]

The objection that Islam does not impose financial penalties is refuted. In *at-Turuq al-Hukmiya*, Ibn al-Qayyim shows that we have at least fifteen cases reported from the Messenger of Allah (p) and the Khulafa' ar-Rashidun in which a financial penalty was imposed.[3]

Lastly, grading the *hadith* from Bahz as weak is irrational, since it is not so graded because of weakness in the chain, but rather because an imagined weakness in the text itself, on the grounds of the previous two objections. Since these two objections have been shown to be incorrect, grading the *hadith* weak on those grounds is also incorrect. It is noted that Bahz himself was graded weak because of this *hadith* and not because of any weakness in his own trustworthiness. Ibn Hibban says, "If it were not for this *hadith*, I would grade Bahz trustworthy." After narrating the opinion of several leading scholars about the trustworthiness of Bahz and the grading of his narrations as correct by Ahmad, Ishaq and Ibn al-Madini in *Tahdhib Sunan Abi Dawud*, Ibn al-Qayyim adds:

> He who rejects this *hadith* has no acceptable evidence since the claim that it is abrogated is unfounded and has no truth. We have several *hadiths* about the existence of

1. Ar-Rawda, vol. 2, p. 209.
2. *Al-Bahr az-Zakhkhar*, vol. 2, p. 190, *al-Mughni*, vol. 2, p. 573, and *al-Ahkam as-Sultaniyya*, al-Mawardi, p. 121.
3. *At-Turuq al-Hukmiya*, p. 687.

> financial penalties. As for the contradiction between this hadith and that from al-Bara', it is absurd because the story in the *hadith* from al-Bara' does not contain an action that deserves any penalty but merely injury caused by an animal without any intention on the part its owner. Interpreting the *hadith* as intending merely to create fear of violation is even more absurd. The words of the Prophet cannot be taken to mean other than what the words say. As for Ibn Hibban's statement, 'If it were not for this *hadith*, I would consider Bahz among the trustworthy', it is illogical to consider Bahz weak because of this *hadith* while this *hadith* is rejected because Bahz is weak. Narrating this *hadith* is by no means a reason for weakness anyway since he does not differ from any trustworthy narrator on it."[1]

Strangely enough, many authors such as ash-Shirazi, al-Mawardi and Ibn Qudama object to this correct *hadith* from Bahz on the grounds that it contradicts the *hadith*, "Nothing is obliged ..." which has no value at all from the point of view of authenticity.

The Hanbali opinion is similar to that of the Shafi'is. Ibn Qudama says, "He who refuses to pay *zakat* while still believing in its obligation must be forced to pay it by the government. However, nothing in excess of the due amount may be taken." On the other hand, Ishaq and Abu Bakr 'Abdu'l-'Aziz believe a fine of one-half the wealth of the payer must be collected in accordance with the *hadith* reported from Bahz ibn Hakim.

Those who refuse to pay *zakat* may be fought by the Islamic state until *zakat* is collected without any additional fine. Al-Maymuni reports that Ahmad says, "Those who refuse to pay *zakat*, to the extent that they fight against the Islamic government in order to defend their position of refusal, should not be treated like Muslims in matters of inheritance and funerals." 'Abdullah ibn Mas'ud says, "He who abandons *zakat* is not Muslim." This is based on Abu Bakr's stance toward those who refused to pay *zakat*.

1. *Tahdhib as-Sunan* with the summary of al-Mundhiri and *al-Ma'alim*, vol. 2, p. 194.

When they were pressured at the battle front, they told Abu Bakr they would pay the due *zakat* if he discontinued the fight, but his answer was, "No, I do not accept your due *zakat* until you testify that our martyrs are in heaven and those who were killed on your side are in the Fire." None of the Companions is reported to have disagreed with Abu Bakr's statement, a statement that implies the rebels were unbelievers.

The other opinion which does not mark as unbelievers those who refuse to pay *zakat* is supported by the fact that *zakat* is one of the Islamic obligations whose abandonment does not negate basic faith, as long as its obligation is not entirely denied.[1]

Lastly, according to Zaydis, a claim by a person that he does not owe any *zakat* may be accepted according to the discretion of the *zakat* commissioner and the trustworthiness of the person,[2] while a claim that the due amount was distributed directly by the payer must be supported by evidence. Otherwise the collectors should charge the *zakat* payer the due amount, disregarding any claim of direct distribution.[3]

Payment of *zakat* to oppressive governments

Muslim scholars differ on paying *zakat* to oppressive governments. Some believe it is unconditionally permissible and others declare it prohibited in all cases, with a whole spectrum of views between these two extremes.

As for those who say it is unconditionally allowed to pay *zakat* to oppressive governments, their main argument is derived from a few *hadiths* mentioned by the author of *al-Muntaqa* as follows[4]:

- It is reported from Anas that a man said, "O Messenger of Allah, if I give my *zakat* to your commissioner would I be fulfilling it as far as Allah and His Messenger are concerned?" The Prophet said, "Yes, if you give it to my commissioner, you

1. Al-*Mughni*, vol. 2, , pp. 573-5.
2. *Sharh al-Azhar* and its commentaries, vol. 1, p. 530, and *al-Bahr*, vol. 2, pp. 190-1.
3. Ibid.
4. *Nayl al-Awtar*, vol. 4, pp. 164-5.

have completed it from the point of view of Allah and His Messenger; you get its reward, and the evil of tampering with it is on whoever tampers with it.'"[1]

- It is reported from Ibn Mas'ud that the Messenger of Allah (p) said, "There shall be selfishness and matters you disapprove of after I am gone." People said, "Messenger of Allah, what would you order us to do then?" He replied, "Fulfil the obligation that is on you and ask Allah for what is yours." (Agreed upon)
- It is reported from Wa'il ibn Hajar, "When the Messenger of Allah (p) was asked by a man, 'What would you say if we happened to have rulers who prevented us from getting our rights and yet ask us for their right?' I heard him reply, 'Listen and obey. They have the burden of what they do and you have that of your deeds.'" (Muslim and at-Tirmidhi)

These *hadiths* have an important implication. The Islamic state always needs funding for its social insurance programs and for public services and if people withhold making payments to the state because of the injustice of some rulers, many essential public services would be disrupted. Thus it is important that *zakat* keep flowing into the state treasury. However, making such payments to the state by no means implies abstaining from resisting oppression by all lawful means.

Muslims are required to pay financial dues obliged on them while continuing to admonish and advise the rulers in application of the general principle of commanding what is good and forbidding what is evil. Additionally, Islamic society has the right – in fact, it is obliged – to remove rulers who make public their explicit disbelief. Moreover, a Muslim is obliged by Allah to disobey any order that conflicts with obedience to Allah or that requires him or her to do anything Allah forbids. This is in accordance with the sound *hadith*, "Listening and obeying is a true obligation on any Muslim, both in matters he likes and in matters he does not like,

1. Reported by Ahmad. See *Nayl al-Awtar*, vol. 4, pp. 154-5.

unless ordered to disobey Allah. If he is ordered to disobey Allah, then there is no listening nor obeying."[1]

As for the jurists who do not allow giving *zakat* to oppressors, their argument is based on the *ayat*, *"My contract does not include the wrongdoers."* (2:124) They say paying *zakat* to oppressors does not fulfil the 'religious worship' aspect of *zakat*. Ash-Shafi'i, in one report, subscribes to this opinion. So do the *Ahl al-Bayt*, as stated by al-Mahdi in *al-Bahr*. Ash-Shawkani objects to this opinion, arguing that the general meaning of the above-mentioned *ayat* is at least restricted by the *hadith* mentioned at the beginning of this sub-section.[2]

Between these two extreme opinions several views exist. Malikis assert that a ruler who is known to abuse *zakat* funds must not be given *zakat*. All effort must be made to avoid paying *zakat* to such a ruler, according to ad-Dardir in *ash-Sharh al-Kabir*, who continues, "But if a ruler is just in the collection and distribution of *zakat*, despite being oppressive in other issues, *zakat* must be given to him."[3] In his commentary, ad-Dusuqi disagrees and says, "It is rather undesirable to give zakat to such a ruler."[4] In *Sharh ar-Risala*, Zarruq says:

> *Zakat* may not be paid to an unjust government unless it enforces payment and the payer cannot escape it. If the *zakat* payer can distribute the *zakat* directly, payment to the oppressive government does not fulfil the religious obligation. Ashhab notes that if *zakat* is taken by force, the religious obligation is fulfilled although it is preferable that an equal, additional amount be directly distributed to deserving people. Ibn Rushd quotes differences among Malikis on whether, if an oppressive government collects *zakat* by force and does not distribute it justly, such collection fulfils the religious requirements of payers. He adds that the prominent view among Malikis is that *zakat* collected by force satisfies the religious requirement, provided

1. Reported by the group from Ibn 'Umar; see *al-Jami' as-Saghir*.
2. *Nayl al-Awtar*, vol. 4, p. 165.
3. *Ash-Sharh al-Kabir*, vol. 1, p. 502.
4. *Hashiyat ad-Dusuqi*, vol. 1, p. 504.

it is collected as *zakat* and at the proper rates and conditions.[1]

Hanafis believe that the collection of *zakat* by oppressive governments fulfils the religious requirement of the payers, provided that funds collected are distributed justly. If they are not distributed justly, *zakat* payers are religiously required to make another payment directly to the deserving categories. This applies to *zakat* on apparent assets. As for non-apparent wealth, some Hanafis argue that the enforced collection of this *zakat* by oppressive governments does not fulfil the religious requirement of *zakat*.[2]

Hanbalis, according to Ibn Qudama in *al-Mughni*, believe that *zakat* collected by oppressors satisfies the religious obligation of the payer regardless of the manner in which funds are distributed or of the use of force in collection. Abu Salih says, "I asked Sa'd ibn Abi Waqqas, Ibn 'Umar, Jabir, Abu Sa'id, and Abu Hurayra, 'Should I pay my *zakat* to this government when you see what it does?' They all answered, 'Yes.'" Ibn Qudama adds, "The statement of these Companions is not disputed according to what reaches us about their positions."[3] The author of *Matalib Uli'n-Nuha* says, "There is no disagreement in our school that it is permissible to pay *zakat* to the government, be it just or not, regardless of whether it is *zakat* on apparent or non-apparent wealth." He adds, "This is based on what is reported from the Companions. Ahmad says, 'They (the Companions) used to pay *zakat* to the government although they knew how it was spent. Why should I say something different?'"[4]

In my opinion, Muslims are not required to repeat payment if they are forced to pay *zakat* to oppressive governments, as long as what is paid takes the name of *zakat*. Moreover, *zakat* should be paid to unjust governments as long as they collect and distribute justly to the categories named in the *Shari'a*, even if such governments are otherwise oppressive. Governments which do not distribute *zakat* properly yet enforce its collection may be given due *zakat* as long as Muslims cannot avoid doing so.

1. *Sharh ar-Risala*, vol. 1, pp. 340-1.
2. *Radd al-Muhtar*, vol. 2, pp. 26-7.
3. *Al-Mughni*, vol. 2, pp. 644-5.
4. *Matalib Uli'n-Nuha*, vol. 2, p. 120.

Lastly, it must be noted that rulers to whom the above-named Companions permitted payment of *zakat* were still, at least, raising the banner of Islam and fighting its enemies although they deviated in certain areas from the Islamic system. This does not apply to many contemporary Muslim governments which have actually detached all bonds to this religion and abandoned the Qur'an to the extent that some of them suppress any Islamic voice and crush those who call for Islam. Such governments must not be given *zakat* since commitment to Islam is the indispensable condition for allowing *zakat* to be given to any government.

Muslim jurists do not allow *zakat* to be given to a traveller who is travelling in disobedience to Allah. How then could *zakat* be given to governments which stand in opposition to the Way of Allah and against His religion on earth? The later reformer Rashid Rida brilliantly says in his explanation of the Qur'an:

> The Islamic state in the Muslim land is the authority to which *zakat* must be paid. It is in charge of collection and distribution. However, most Muslims nowadays do not have governments that establish the religion of Islam, protect Muslims, and fight only for the sake of Allah, or governments that collect the obligatory *zakat* the way it should be collected and distribute it justly and rightfully. Most Muslims live either under the authority of occupying foreign troops or apostate governments that oppose Islam,[1] although these states may be headed by nominal Muslims. *Zakat* may be given to the remaining governments whose leaders believe in Islam and whose finances are not under the control of foreigners, even with the presence of certain aspects of oppression. As stated in *Sharh al-Muhadhdhab* and other works, some deeply rooted scholars suggest that "If the government is unjust and does distribute *zakat* according to the *Shari'a,* it is preferred that payers distribute *zakat* independently."[2]

1. This describes the majority of governments in Muslim countries today.
2. *Tafsir al-Manar,* vol. 10, pp. 595-6.

Chapter Two

The Place of Intention in *Zakat*

Zakat as a form of worship and at the same time a financial tax has a dual character. It is a tax-worship or a worship-tax. This two-sided characteristic of *zakat* lies at the heart of the issue of intention.

Intention is indispensable in *zakat*

The overwhelming majority of jurists believe intention is a prerequisite for performing *zakat*, since it is a rite of worship and all rites of worship demand intention. Allah says, *"They were only ordered to worship Allah, making their* deen *sincerely His as people of pure natural belief, and to establish the prayer and pay* zakat *– that is the correct* deen.*"* (98:5) The Messenger of Allah (p) says, "Actions are according to their intentions." Lack of intention makes the payment of *zakat* purposeless and spiritless. Intention for the payment of *zakat* must exist on the part of the payer, whether he pays his own *zakat* or that of persons under his guardianship.[1]

Al-Awza'i disagrees with the majority and does not consider intention to be a prerequisite for paying *zakat*. He says, "Intention is not a necessary requirement because *zakat* is a form of debt and there is no such condition when debts are paid. Because *zakat* does not require intention, it is charged on the wealth of minor orphans and taken by force from those who refuse to pay it."[2] Al-Awza'i replied that *zakat* as an act of worship requires intention, according to the *hadith*, "Actions are according to their intentions." Its analogy to debts is not complete, since a debt can be waived by the creditor, while the *zakat* due cannot be waived. Intention is further

---

1. *Hashiyat as-Sawi* on *ash-Sharh as-Saghir*, vol. 1, p. 235, and *ar-Rawda*, an-Nawawi, vol. 2, p. 208.

2. *Al-Mughni*, vol. 2, p. 638.

needed to distinguish *zakat* from general voluntary charity. Al-Awza'i's view is shared by some Malikis, but the accredited opinion in the Maliki school is that intention is required. As for taking *zakat* by force, the payer is rewarded by Allah.[1]

Intention need not be put in words. It is only a will in the payer's heart that accompanies the payment of *zakat*.[2] Some Malikis even consider acceptable intention inferred by the purposeful calculation of the due amount and its distribution to those entitled to *zakat*.[3]

Intention when *zakat* is collected by the government

If the government collects *zakat*, the *zakat* payer is required to make an intention. The intention of the collector alone does not suffice if the payer gives *zakat* willingly, according to the majority of jurists; ash-Shafi'i in one report is not included.[4] An-Nawawi remarks, "As for the person who refuses to pay *zakat*, from whom the government extracts *zakat* by force, if such a person makes intention when *zakat* is taken, the condition is satisfied, even without the collector's intention. If the payer does not make the necessary intention, that of the collector suffices as far as the application of the law is concerned and the payer need not be asked to make another payment."[5]

Ibn Qudama says, "If *zakat* is collected by the government with the use of force, the obligation of paying *zakat* is fulfilled." However, Abu'l-Khattab and Ibn 'Aqil, both Hanbalis, believe that, from the religious point of view, the worship of *zakat* is not performed in such a case because of the payer's lack of intention. Ibn 'Aqil adds, "When jurists consider *zakat* requirements satisfied in such cases, they mean that the legal, but not the religious, obli-

1. *Sharh ar-Risala*, Ibn Naji, vol. 1, pp. 317-8.
2. *Al-Mughni*, vol. 2, p. 638, and *Matalib Uli'n-Nuha*, vol. 2, p. 121.
3. As-Sawi, op cit. and *Hashiyat ad-Dusuqi*, vol. 1, p. 500.
4. An-Nawawi says, "This second view is the one approved by Qadi Abu't-Tayyib, the authors of *al-Muhadhdhab* and *at-Tahdhib*, and most of the later generations' jurists. *Ar-Rawda*, vol. 2, p. 208.
5. Ibid., pp. 208-209.

gation is satisfied."[1] Ibn al-'Arabi, a Maliki, explains that when *zakat* is collected by force, no reward is gained by the person from whom it is taken.[2] As for the Hanafis, they believe that *zakat* of non-apparent wealth cannot be fulfilled by forced payment extracted from the payer by the state since the state is not, in principle, in charge of collecting this *zakat*.[3]

Time of intention

Hanafis require that intention accompany the actual payment of *zakat* to the deserving categories, or to the government, the same as with other acts of worship.[4] According to the Malikis, intention should exist at the time of actual payment or when the payer is preparing the amount to be paid as *zakat*. If the intention of paying *zakat* does not exist at either of these two times, any following intention does not suffice.[5] Shafi'is accept an intention followed by payment. According to an-Nawawi, it is difficult to have intention simultaneously with payment.[6] Hanbalis agree with the Shafi'is that intention may precede actual payment by a short time.[7]

I believe the timing of the intention is a matter that should be founded on easiness and simplicity. Having, in general, the will to pay *zakat* satisfies the intention requirement without any need for going into minute details.

1. *Al-Mughni*, vol. 2, pp. 640-641.
2. *Sharh ar-Risala*, vol. 1, p. 318, and *ash-Sharh al-Kabir*, vol. 1, p. 503..
3. *Radd al-Muhtar*, vol. 2, p. 14.
4. Ibid., pp. 14-15.
5. *Ad-Dusuqi*, op. cit.
6. *Ar-Rawda*, vol. 2, p. 209.
7. *Al-Mughni*, vol. 2, p. 533, and *ar-Rawda*, vol. 2, p. 210.

Chapter Three

Payment in Value

Jurists' opinions on payment in value

Since *zakat* is calculated in the same commodities on which *zakat* is due (camels are taken out of camels, fruits from fruits, and money from money), the question arises whether it is permissible to give the value of what is due as *zakat* instead of payment in kind. On one side, we find jurists who allow payment in value without any reservations. These are led by the Hanafis. Scholars led by the Shafi'is and Zahiris do not accept payment in value. In between, the Malikis and Hanbalis accept payment in value in certain cases and do not approve of it in other cases.

It is maintained in *Mukhtasar Khalil* that payment in value does not suffice. Ibn al-Hajib and Ibn Bashir go along with this view. The author of *at-Tawdih* states that this is not consistent with *al-Mudawwana* in which it is stated that payment in value is undesired only.[1] In *Sharh ar-Risala*, Ibn Naji quotes Ashhab and Ibn al-Qasim as saying that payment in value is permissible and the opposite is also said.[2] The author of *al-Mudawwana* notes, "I would think payment in value would be accepted by Allah if the payer is obliged to do so by the government, since in disputed matters the government's selected practice becomes binding on all."[3]

As for Hanbalis, the author of *al-Mughni* says that it appears that Ahmad believes that payment in value unsatisfactory because it is a

1. In *al-Mudawwana*, Malik says, "One must not give food or goods if it is *zakat* of money that one is paying and it is disliked for a person to buy back what he gives as *sadaqa*." It seems that the most approved view among the Malikis is that payment in value is only disliked and not forbidden as stated by Ibn Rushd. See *Hashiyat ad-Dusuqi*, vol. 1, p. 502.

2. *Sharh ar-Risala*, Ibn Naji, vol. 1, p. 340.

3. *Sharh ar-Risala*, Zarruq, vol. 1, p. 340.

violation of the *Sunna*. However, there is a report that Ahmad approves of it except with *zakat al-fitr*.[1]

All these differences can be attributed to the different angles from which jurists perceive *zakat* as either an act of worship or a tax on wealth. Those who require payment in kind argue that, since *zakat* is an act of worship, it can only be done the very same way detailed in the *hadiths*, therefore payment must be made in the same zakatable item. On the other hand, Abu Hanifa, his disciples and others allow payment in value on the grounds that it makes no difference as far as relieving the poor is concerned.[2]

The evidence of the two parties

Those who do not approve of payment in value bring forth the following arguments:

- Al-Juwayni, a Shafi'i, argues that, since *zakat* is an act of worship, it must be done exactly the way we are ordered, because only Allah knows best the way He wants to be worshipped. *Zakat* is the sister of prayer. No one can make any change in the format or sequence of prayers and, by the same token, no one may pay money when *hadiths* state that a female camel or sheep should be paid.[3]

- This is further emphasised by Qadi Abu Bakr ibn al-'Arabi, a Maliki, who says, "The test of paying *zakat* is not realised in mere reduction (by giving away some) of total wealth – as Abu Hanifa thinks – but requires reducing the quantity of each and every item of zakatable wealth in order to break the payer's sentimental attachment to each and every item he or she owns. Payment in kind is obliged on its own merit."[4]

- Since *zakat* is meant to relieve the diverse needs of the poor, diversity of assets paid is an important convenience for the poor. It is also a sign of thankfulness and gratitude to Allah to

1. *Al-Mughni*, vol. 3, p. 65
2. *Al-Bahr*, vol. 2, pp. 140, 170-1, and *Fiqh al-Imam Ja'far*, vol. 2, pp. 70-71.
3. *Al-Majmu'*, vol. 5, p. 430.
4. *Ahkam al-Qur'an*, 2nd part, p. 945.

give to others from the very same assets He bestowed on the payer.[1]

- On top of all this is the *hadith* reported by Abu Dawud and Ibn Majah that the Prophet (p) told Mu'adh when he sent him to Yemen, "Take grain out of grain, sheep out of sheep, camels out of camels, and cows out of cows."[2] This is a text that must not be violated by payment made in value.

Hanafis and other scholars who say payment can be made in value present the following arguments:

- Allah says, *"Take* sadaqa *out of their wealth."* This is a general text which is satisfied by payment in value. The Prophet's explanation that one sheep is due for every forty sheep is made only for facilitating collection from owners of livestock and does not restrict the general ordinance of Allah. In the desert and countryside where livestock owners often live, it is difficult to find money in large quantities.[3]

- Al-Bayhaqi reports, as does al-Bukhari, that Tawus says that when Mu'adh was in Yemen he said, "Give me garments or cloth as payment of *sadaqa*. This is easier for you and better for the migrants in Madina." In another version, "Bring me cloth materials to take from you in place of corn and barley..."[4] It was known that Yemen had a flourishing textile industry at that time and it was easier for Yemenis to pay in cloth. Also Yemen had excess *zakat* that used to be sent to Madina. Mu'adh's declaration tells us that he himself did not understand the Prophet (p) to mean literally that grain must be collected out of grain and sheep out of sheep. Rather, the Prophet (p) meant to make things easier for payers, so this is an order to the collector to accept what he is given at the convenience of the payer. This is supported by the report that in paying recom-

1. *Al-Mughni*, vol. 3, p. 66.

2. Mentioned in *al-Muntaqa*. ash-Shawkani says, "Al-Hakim grades it sound according to the criteria of al-Bukhari and Muslim. In its chain 'Ata' reports from Mu'adh, but 'Ata' did not listen to Mu'adh." *Nayl al-Awtar*, vol. 4, p. 152.

3. *Al-Mabsut*, vol. 2, p. 17.

4. *As-Sunan al-Kubra*, al-Bayhaqi, vol. 4, p. 113.

pense for a killing by mistake, the Prophet (p) allowed cloth producers to make payment in cloth.[1]

- Ahmad and al-Bayhaqi report that the Prophet (p) saw an adult female camel among the camels taken as *sadaqa*. He was angered because it was too good and said, "May Allah assail whoever took this camel!" The collector said, "O Messenger of Allah, I exchanged it for two lesser-quality camels." The Prophet (p) said, "Then it is all right." This *hadith* is acceptable as far as its chain and its evidence are concerned.[2] Thus paying *zakat* in value is permissible.
- *Zakat* is meant to enrich the poor, satisfy their needs and finance public services important for the Muslim community, as well as Islam itself. This is done as well by payment in value as by payment in kind. It may even be more convenient to give the value than to collect goods and merchandise.
- It is unanimously permissible to pay an item of the same kind of zakatable asset which is not of the zakatable items themselves, such as paying with purchased wheat instead of the produced wheat itself. Why not permit, by the same logic, paying *zakat* in the form of another product? This is in answer to the argument of Ibn al-'Arabi, mentioned in the second argument above.
- Sa'id ibn Mansur reports in his *Sunan* that 'Ata' said that 'Umar ibn al-Khattab used to take money as *sadaqa* on business goods.[3]

After reflecting on the arguments of the two groups, it seems that the Hanafis succeed in their view. They are supported both by texts and the practices of the Companions, as well as by rationality. In fact, the analogy between *zakat* and the prayer, though valid in that both are pillars of Islam, is absolutely inadequate when it comes to mode of payment. This is supported by the opponents of

1. *Al-Jawhar an-Naqi*, Ibn at-Turkumani, printed with *as-Sunan al-Kubra*, vol. 4, p. 113.

2. Ibid.

3. *Al-Mughni*, vol. 3, p. 65.

the Hanafis themselves because they oblige *zakat* on the wealth of minors and insane persons, although such individuals are not required to pray.

The Hanafi opinion is also more suitable to contemporary economic life. It is easier in calculation, collection and distribution. If we imagine a governmental body collecting and distributing *zakat*, payment in value would save many storage and transportation expenses. This opinion is also attributed to 'Umar ibn 'Abdu'l-'Aziz, al-Hasan, Sufyan, and a report from Ahmad.[1] An-Nawawi says, "This is apparently the view of al-Bukhari, as shown in his *Sahih* collection."[2] Ibn Rushd comments, "Al-Bukhari, though he very often disagreed with the Hanafis, takes their view on this issue. He was indeed led by the strength of evidence."[3] In his *Sahih* collection, al-Bukhari entitles a section "Payment in value is permissible," under which he mentions the report about Mu'adh from Tawus,[4] as well as sections of Abu Bakr's letter in which twenty dirhams or two sheep substitute for one year's difference in age of camels.

Ibn Hazm undergrades the report of Tawus on the grounds that Tawus did not meet Mu'adh and says that even if it were said by Mu'adh it is not binding on us because it does not come from the Prophet (p) and because it may be in reference to *jizya* and not *zakat*.[5] These objections are invalid since, although Tawus did not meet Mu'adh, he was the leading scholar of Yemen in the era of the Followers, and the practices of Mu'adh in Yemen were very well known to him. Also, Ahmad Shakir comments that the version of Mu'adh's statement which is reported by Yahya ibn Adam explicitly mentions the word *sadaqa*, so this report is not about *jizya*. Moreover, the action of Mu'adh indicates that he believed in its consistency with the *Sunna*.

---

1. *Al-Mughni*, vol. 3, p. 65.
2. *Al-Majmu'*, vol. 5, p. 429.
3. *Fath al-Bari*, vol 3, p. 200.
4. Al-Bukhari mentions the narration of Tawus affirmatively but suspended, which indicates it is correct up to al-Bukhari. Tawus was the leading scholar in the epoch of the Followers. He was well versed in the biography of Mu'adh. Al-Bukhari's use of Tawus' narrations means it is strong evidence. See Ibid.
5. *Al-Muhalla*, vol. 6, p. 312.

Ibn Taymiyya takes a middle stand on this matter, very similar to that which I take. He says that payment in value without need or convenience is not permissible. The Prophet stipulates payment in value in case of need, for example, to make up for the difference in ages of camels. But paying in value out of necessity, convenience, justice or for the benefit of the poor is allowed; Ahmad himself permits it. It is for these reasons that Mu'adh asked for payment in value in the above report.[1]

1. *Fatawa Ibn Taymiyya*, vol. 25, pp. 82-3.

Chapter Four

Transporting *Zakat*

Fourteen hundred years ago Islam introduced its unique principle that *zakat* must be distributed in the region in which it is collected, instead of being given to some ruler to spend on palaces, servants and army, as was the practice of the time. Muslim scholars agree that *zakat* should be distributed to deserving people in the same geographical area from which it was collected.[1] This applies to *zakat* collected on livestock, grain and fruits. Whether *zakat* on money should be distributed in the area of the asset or where the owner lives is disputed, the most common view being that it should be distributed in the region where the owner resides, if the owner lives away from the area in which the *zakat* was taken from the wealth.[2]

This principle is based on the tradition of the Prophet (p) and the *Khulafa' ar-Rashidun*. When the Prophet (p) sent *zakat* officers to any area or region, he instructed them to distribute to the poor in the same region. The instructions he gave Mu'adh (and its authenticity is agreed upon) says, "*Zakat* is to be distributed to the poor among them..." Mu'adh implemented the instructions of the Prophet (p) to the letter. He divided Yemen into regions in such a way that *zakat* was collected and distributed within each region autonomously. He wrote letters to the effect that *zakat* be distributed within the same clan from which it was collected even if the owner moved away.[3]

Abu Juhayfa says, "The *zakat* officer of the Messenger of Allah (p) came and collected *zakat* from the rich among us and distributed it to our poor. I was then a minor orphan, so he gave me a she-

1. *Mushkilat al-Faqr wa kayfa 'Alajaha'l-Islam*, al-Qaradawi, p. 114.
2. *Hashiyat ad-Dusuqi*, vol. 1, p. 500.
3. *Nayl al-Awtar*, vol. 2, p. 161.
4. Reported by at-Tirmidhi, who adds, "It is *hasan*." Ibid.

camel."[4] It is correctly reported that a bedouin Arab asked the Messenger of Allah (p) several questions. Among them was, "By Allah who sent you, is it Allah who commanded you to take *sadaqa* from our rich and distribute it to our poor?" The Prophet (p) answered, "Yes."

Abu 'Ubayd reports that 'Umar wrote in his will, "I ask my successor ... to take from the peripheries of their wealth and distribute it among their poor."[1] This was the practice during the time of 'Umar himself. Sa'id ibn al-Musayyab says, "'Umar sent Mu'adh as *zakat* officer to the Banu Kilab or Banu Sa'd. Mu'adh went there, collected *zakat* and distributed all of it, leaving nothing. He came back in the same clothes that he went in." [2] 'Umar was once asked what to do with the *zakat* collected from bedouin Arabs. He answered, "By Allah, I shall render *sadaqa* to them until each of them becomes the owner of a hundred camels, male or female."[3]

Transporting *zakat* from the region where it is collected while that region still contains poor people violates the reason for which it was collected. The author of *al-Mughni* says, "Since *zakat* is meant to enrich the poor, permitting its transportation leaves the poor of that region in need."[4] Scholars and governors after the Prophet followed the same guidance. 'Imran ibn Husayn, a Companion, was appointed *zakat* officer at the time of the Umayyads. When he returned from his mission, he was asked, "Where is the money?" 'Imran said, "Did you send me to bring you money? I collected it the same way we used to at the time of the Messenger of Allah (p) and distributed it in the same way we used to."[5]

Tawus was appointed *zakat* officer in one of the regions in Yemen. He was asked for his account by the governor and his answer was, "I took from the rich and gave it to the destitute."[6] Farqad as-Sabkhi says, "I took *zakat* due on my wealth to distribute it in Makka. There I met Sa'id ibn Jubayr who said, 'Take it back

1. *Al-Amwal*, p. 595.
2. Ibid., p. 596.
3. *Al-Musannaf*, vol. 3, p. 205.
4. *Al-Mughni*, vol. 2, p. 672.
5. Reported by Abu Dawud and Ibn Majah. See *Nayl al-Awtar*, vol. 2, p. 161.
6. *Al-Amwal*, p. 595.

and distribute it in your home town.'"[1] Sufyan narrates, "*Zakat* was taken from ar-Rayy to al-Kufa, but 'Umar ibn 'Abdu'l-'Aziz ordered it taken back to ar-Rayy."[2]

Abu 'Ubayd says, "Scholars all agree that these reports mean people of every region have priority regarding their *zakat*, as long as they still have anyone in need, or until all the *zakat* is distributed." He goes on, "If the officer transports collected *zakat* while there is still need in the region from which it was collected, the government must return it to its region, as was done by 'Umar ibn 'Abdu'l-'Aziz, and as stated by Sa'id ibn Jubayr."[3]

An-Nakha'i and al-Basri allow a person to transport *zakat* in order to give it to his own kin who live away from him. Abu 'Ubayd says, "This is permitted in individual cases only, not on the massive level of *zakat* administered by the government." Abu 'Ubayd comments on the story that Abu'l-'Aliya, a Companion, used to take his due to Madina, "I believe he was taking it to his kindred and relatives."[4]

Cases in which transporting *zakat* is permissible

Scholars agree that all excess *zakat* funds may be transported to neighbouring areas or to the central government. Abu 'Ubayd reports that Mu'adh stayed in Yemen until the Prophet (p) died and during the era of Abu Bakr, then went to 'Umar who confirmed his position. One year Mu'adh sent 'Umar one third of the *zakat* collected in the year. 'Umar was annoyed and told him, "I did not send you as a collector or as a taker of *jizya*. I assigned you to take from the rich and render to the poor." Mu'adh answered, "I have not sent you anything that I can find someone to take from me here." The following year, Mu'adh sent 'Umar one half of the collected *zakat*. They exchanged statements similar to the previous year. In the third year, Mu'adh sent 'Umar all the collected *zakat*. 'Umar questioned him the same way he did the previous years,

1. *Al-Amwal*, p. 595.
2. Ibid.
3. Ibid.
4. Ibid.

whereupon Mu'adh said, "I could not find anyone who would take any of it."[1]

'Umar's objection indicates that *zakat* must be distributed in the land where it is collected but his acceptance after Mu'adh's explanation shows it is permissible to transport *zakat* when no deserving people exist in its region. Besides this agreed upon case, there are cases in which, though some need remains in the land of collection, it may be more beneficial to the total welfare of the Muslims to transport some portion of the collected *zakat*.

Shafi'is do not approve of transportation in such cases, nor do Hanbalis. It is sinful to transport *zakat* under these circumstances, although the obligation of *zakat* would be fulfilled as long as it is given to deserving persons. Some jurists say that in this case the obligation is not fulfilled.[2] On the other hand, Hanafis consider such transportation disliked but not prohibited. They add that if transporting *zakat* is done to relieve poor relatives of the payer or people or troops who are in desperate need in another land, it is not disliked. The same thing applies when *zakat* is transported for the benefit of the Muslim community by Muslims in non-Muslim land to Muslim countries, or in order to help poor scholars or students or for a *zakat* paid before its due date.[3]

Malikis oblige the distribution of *zakat* in the area of collection, but allow transportation when the need is more pressing in other areas than in the area of collection.[4] Zaydis dislike transportation except to satisfy more pressing needs, needy relatives, or students.[5] Ibadis approve of transportation if done by the government in order to strengthen the Islamic state.[6]

1. *Al-Amwal,* p. 595, and *Mushkilat al-Faqr.*

2. *Al-Ahkam as-Sultaniyya*, al-Mawardi, pp. 119-120. *Sharh al-Ghayat*, vol. 2, p. 228. At-Tibi is quoted by al-Qari as saying, "It is agreed that if *zakat* is transported and distributed the obligation is fulfilled. Only 'Umar ibn 'Abdu'l-'Aziz disagrees. He returned *zakat* transported from Khurasan to Syria to the place it was transported from." Al-Qari adds, "His action does not really indicate that he disagrees with the *ijma'*, but merely that it is better not to transport *zakat*." See *al-Mirqat*, vol. 4, pp. 118-119.

3. *Radd al-Muhtar*, vol. 2,p. 93-94.

4. *Hashiyat ad-Dusuqi*, vol. 1, p. 501.

5. *Sharh al-Azhar*, vol. 1, pp. 547-548.

6. *Sharh an-Nil*, vol. 2, p. 138.

Discussion and analysis

After this survey of the different opinions and texts on the transportation of collected *zakat*, it appears that the general principle is that *zakat* must be distributed in the area where it is collected. The poor and needy in that land have priority over all others since *zakat* is collected from their neighbours, kin and friends.

However, I find no reason why this general principle should not have exceptions, especially if the exception is made by a just government in consultation with the representative council in view of the public interests of Muslims and Islam. As Malik wonderfully puts it, "Transporting *zakat* is not permissible, except when done through the government's *ijtihad* in view of pressing need."[1] Ibn al-Qasim, Malik's disciple, adds, "If this is done out of necessity, it is all right."[2] Sahnun is reported to have said, "If the government knows that a certain land has dire need, it can lawfully transport some of the collected *zakat* there. When catastrophe befalls, relieving its victims has priority over other uses of *zakat* since a Muslim is a brother to a fellow Muslim. He does not let him down nor oppress him."[3]

In *al-Mudawwana*, Malik mentions that in the year when famine struck Madina, 'Umar wrote to 'Amr ibn al-'As who was in Egypt, "Help, help, to the Arabs. Send us a caravan whose beginning should reach me while its end is still at your place, loaded with flour wrapped in garments." When the relief arrived, 'Umar divided food and clothes among the hungry people and appointed assignees to help slaughter the camels, saying, "Arabs love camels. I am afraid they may prefer to keep them alive. Have people slaughter the camels and eat their meat and fat, and give them the garments that are used as bags for flour to wear."[4]

This opinion is supported by the three following points:

1. *Tafsir al-Qurtubi*, vol. 8, p. 175.
2. Ibid.
3. Ibid.
4. *Al-Mudawwana al-Kubra*, vol. 1, p. 246. The report is mentioned also by al-Hakim in *al-Mustadrak*. Al-Hakim adds, "Correct by the criteria of Muslim." This is approved by adh-Dhahabi, vol. 1, pp. 405-406.

- The different geographical areas in the Islamic state form one body whose members must come to the help of any member that is in pain. This unity and solidarity is required by Islam and cannot be neglected.

- There are deserving categories that can only be assessed and determined by the central government, such as reconciling hearts and spending in the Way of Allah. The central government must acquire a certain portion of *zakat* for the shares of these deserving people. In this regard, al-Qurtubi quotes some scholars as suggesting that the total collection of *zakat* should be divided into segments, "...whereby the share of the poor and needy is divided locally, while other shares may be transported at the discretion of the government."[1] This matter is undoubtedly one that must be determined by the *ijtihad* of the Islamic government. It is reported that 'Umar ibn 'Abdu'l-'Aziz once wrote to his commissioners, "Distribute half of the collected *zakat* and send me the other half." The he wrote in the following year, "Distribute it all."[2] This is apparently in accordance with needs.

- We have evidence that the Prophet (p) used to invite bedouin Arabs to send their *sadaqa* to Madina in order to spend on the poor Muhajirun and Ansar. An-Nasa'i reports from 'Abdullah ibn Hilal ath-Thaqafi, "A man came to the Messenger of Allah (p) and said, 'I was about to be killed for what amounts to a lamb or a sheep of *sadaqa*.' The Prophet (p) said, 'If it were not to be given to the poor Muhajirun, I would not have taken it.'" Similarly, the Prophet (p) told Qabisa ibn al-Mukhariq, who asked for help in paying the financial burden he incurred in reconciling two groups, "Stay until the *sadaqa* comes, and we will either help you or carry the whole burden." The Prophet (p) was prepared to give him the *sadaqa* of Hijaz, although he was from Najd.[3] 'Adi ibn Hatim is known to have carried the *zakat* collected from his tribe to Abu Bakr after the

1. *Al-Qurtubi*, vol. 8, p. 176.
2. *Al-Amwal*, p. 594.
3. Ibid., p. 600.

> death of the Prophet (p).[1] Also, 'Umar told Ibn Abi Dhubab when he sent him as a collector right after the great famine to "...collect the *zakat* due for two years. Distribute half among them and send me the other half."[2]

Mu'adh told the people of Yemen, "Bring me garments or cloth. I accept them from you in fulfilment of *zakat*. It is easier for you and more beneficial to the Muhajirun in Madina." Abu 'Ubayd comments, "All these certainly apply to *zakat* in excess of their needs."[3] But Abu 'Ubayd's explanation is not necessarily true. Needs are subjective and have different levels and the government has the right to determine where needs are more pressing and urgent. Lastly, it must be emphasised that the government must not transport all the collected *zakat* unless there is no local need at all for *zakat* funds.

It must be noted, however, that Shafi'is, who are most restrictive in the matter of transportation, do not disapprove of the transporting of *zakat* by the government or its *zakat* agency. They centre their objection only on the case when the payer distributes due *zakat* himself. An-Nawawi says, "It must be realised that the government or its *zakat* agency is permitted to transport *zakat*. The discussion on transportation is centred on the case when it is done by the payer." Ar-Rafi'i supports this position.[4] One may add that when there is no Islamic state or when the state does not collect *zakat*, individual payers can assume the same role and decide whether to transport due *zakat* to needy relatives, to people who are in dire need, for essential public interests of Muslims, or to a pivotal Islamic project in another country.

1. *Al-Amwal*, p. 594.
2. Ibid.
3. Ibid.
4. *Al-Majmu'*, vol. 6, p. 175.

Chapter Five

Pre-payment and Delayed Payment of *Zakat*

The obligation of *zakat* is immediate

The Hanafis' well-known view is that the obligation of *zakat* has an extended due time for payment unless the state determines otherwise since texts ordering its payment are not restricted time-wise. This is the opinion of Abu Bakr al-Jassas too. On the other hand, al-Karkhi, a leading Hanafi, believes that payment must be immediate from his understanding of the same ordaining text. Ibn al-Humam adds that the fact that *zakat* is relief to the poor implies that it should be immediate, for otherwise it does not fulfil its role.[1]

This seems to be the right position. It is taken from the majority of scholars, including Malik, ash-Shafi'i and Ahmad. Ibn Qudama notes:

> Ordinance of a ruling usually implies immediate execution and delay may be a reason for punishment. For example, Allah expelled Iblis and disgraced him because he disobeyed the order to prostrate. If a person orders his servant to give him water, postponement of implementation is naturally a good reason for punishment. Some delay is logically permitted in the order's implementation. Even if one believes that ordinances, in general, leave some room for delay, one would make an exception for the ordinance of *zakat*, since postponement of payment may be indefinite, and assets as well as payers are subject to destruction or death which would harm the poor and needy deserving people. Added to this is the fact that *zakat* is a repeated

1. *Fath al-Qadir*, vol. 1, pp. 482-482, and *Radd al-Muhtar*, vol. 2, pp. 13-14.

worship whose delay to the time of the following payment must be unlawful like the delay of prayer or fasting of Ramadan.

Certainly, if immediate payment may harm the payer, financially or otherwise, delay is permitted, since the Messenger of Allah (p) says, "There should be no harm or injury."[1] Postponement of payment of debts due to other people is allowed in such a case, and *zakat* need not have priority over other debts.[2]

However, all rites of worship and good deeds must, as far as possible, be carried out immediately. Allah says, *"And race to do good deeds"* (2:148, 5:48) and *"Hurry to forgiveness from your Lord and to a Garden."* (3:122) If immediacy is good in all righteous actions, it is more so in *zakat* because of the need to quickly relieve the poor and needy. Muslim scholars always emphasise that good deeds should be done without delay before obstacles and hindrances arise.[3] The Prophet (p) also says, "One's due *sadaqa* is not mixed with one's other wealth without bringing destruction to it." This is reported by ash-Shafi'i, al-Bukhari in his *History*, and al-Humaydi who explains, "This refers to due *sadaqa* that is not given away but left mixed with one's wealth."[4]

Pre-payment of *zakat*

For assets on which *zakat* is taken that require the passage of one year, such as livestock, money and trade goods, the majority of jurists believe that pre-payment of *zakat* is permitted, provided the

1. Reported by Ahmad and Ibn Majah from Ibn 'Abbas by al-Hakim, and ad-Daraqutni from Abu Sa'id, and by Ibn Majah again from 'Ubada ibn as-Samit. An-Nawawi in *al-Arba'in* grades it good, adding, "Also reported *mursal* by Malik, via several chains that strengthen each other." Al-Haythami says its chain is trustworthy. Ahmad Shakir comments on it under number 2867 of *al-Musnad*, "Its sound chain is mentioned by Ibn Majah from 'Ubayda."

2. *Al-Mughni*, vol. 2, pp. 684–685.

3. *Nayl al-Awtar*, vol. 4, p. 148.

4. Ibid.

payer owns the necessary *nisab*. This opinion is shared by al-Hasan, Sa'id ibn Jubayr, az-Zuhri, al-Awza'i, Abu Hanifa, ash-Shafi'i, Ahmad, Ishaq and Abu 'Ubayd.[1] On the other hand, Rabi'a, Malik, and Da'ud do not allow pre-payment,[2] though some Malikis approve of the pre-payment within periods of no more than one month with certain assets such as money and merchants' stock. However, such approval, they say, is accompanied by classifying the pre-payment as disliked. Pre-payment is approved by Malikis without being disliked in two cases: when *zakat* needs to be transported to more desperately needy in another area so that they arrive there at the end of the year (pre-payment is even required by some scholars in this case) and when *zakat* is collected by the *zakat* collectors a short period before the end of a full year. Pre-payment of *zakat* on fruits and grains, however, is never approved.[3]

Those who do not allow pre-payment argue that the passage of a full year is a condition for the obligation of *zakat* and that *zakat*, like the prayer, cannot be performed before the due time.[4]

Those who permit pre-payment provide as evidence the *hadith* reported by Abu Dawud and others, from 'Ali that al-'Abbas asked the Messenger of Allah (p) to allow him to pre-pay his *sadaqa* and the Prophet (p) permitted him to do so.[5] Although the chain of the *hadith* is not free of criticism, it is supported by al-Bayhaqi's report from 'Ali, "The Prophet (p) appointed 'Umar to collect *sadaqa*. It was rumoured that Ibn Jamil, Khalid ibn al-Walid, and al-'Abbas, the uncle of the Prophet (p), refused to pay *zakat*. The Prophet (p) defended Khalid and al-'Abbas, saying, "We needed some funds and took the *sadaqa* from al-'Abbas for two years in advance."[6]

1. *Al-Mughni*, vol. 2, p. 630.

2. Ibid., and *Bidayat a-Mujtahid*, vol. 1, p. 266.

3. *Hashiyat ad-Dusuqi*, vol. 1, p. 502.

4. *Al-Mughni*, op. cit.

5. Reported by the five excluding an-Nasa'i, but also reported by al-Hakim, ad-Daraqutni and al-Bayhaqi. Ad-Daraqutni and Abu Dawud give more confidence to the *mursal* version. The *hadith* is supported by other *hadiths*. See *Nayl al-Awtar*, vol. 4, pp. 159-160 and *al-Majmu'*, vol. 6, pp. 145-46.

6. *As-Sunan al-Kubra*, vol. 4, p. 111. Abu Dawud at-Tayalisi reports from Abu Rafi', "The Prophet (p) said to 'Umar, 'We pre-collected the *sadaqa* on al-'Abbas's wealth last year.'" See *Nayl al-Awtar*, ibid.

This story is reported in the *Sahih* collection of Muslim from Abu Hurayra, where the Prophet (p) reportedly adds, "As for al-'Abbas, his *zakat* is upon me and another equal amount too. Then the Prophet[1] continued, "O 'Umar, didn't you know that the uncle of a man is like his father?" Abu 'Ubayd comments, "The Prophet (p) said, 'It is upon me' because it is said he borrowed from al-'Abbas the *sadaqa* due for two years in advance."[1]

Moreover, pre-payment can be argued as acceptable by reasoning and analogy. It is like pre-payment of a debt due to another person.[2] Some object claiming that the condition of the completion of a year is a necessary condition just like having the *nisab*, but this is incorrect since owning the *nisab* is a indispensable reason for the obligation to exist, thus payment before having the *nisab* is payment of something that is not obliged, not like payment before completion of the year which is in fulfilment of a required obligation.[3] Additionally, whenever timing is added to facilitate matters, the obliged person, al-Khattabi argues, is permitted not to use this privilege, and timing in *zakat* is like timing in all debts of that kind.[4] Prayer and fasting are purely acts of worship in which timing cannot be explained, while *zakat* is both an act of worship and a financial obligation at the same time. If pre-payment is made of the *zakat* due on an asset and its increments or return together, it is invalid as for the increments and return, according to ash-Shafi'i and Ahmad, on the grounds of not being owed yet, while it is valid according to Abu Hanifa as the increase is dependent and related to the owned principal.

Lastly, Hanafis and some others allow pre-payment with no time limitation, even for several years, as long as the *nisab* is owned.[5] It must be noted that payment on time is always preferable in order to avoid the grey area of dispute.

1. *Nayl al-Awtar*, ibid.
2. *Al-Mughni*, op cit.
3. Ibid.
4. *Ma'alim as-Sunan*, vol. 2, p. 224.
5. *Radd al-Muhtar*, vol. 2, pp. 29-30, and *al-Bahr az-Zakhkhar*, vol. 2, p. 188.

Delay of *zakat* payment

Delaying the payment of *zakat* without a valid reason is not permitted, but *zakat* may be delayed in certain cases without blame, such as when there is lack of liquid funds or, according to Shams ad-Din ar-Ramli, in order to wait and give it to needy relatives or to someone in more desperate need, or to have time investigate the needs of the available deserving people. When payment is delayed, the payer must guarantee the due amount in case of destruction or loss.[1]

Ibn Qudama allows such delay only for a short time. He quotes Ahmad as saying, "It is not permitted to pay *zakat* in monthly instalments that begin on or after the due time, nor is it permitted to delay some *zakat* due on certain assets in order to combine it with *zakat* due later on some other asset."[2] Some Malikis insist that keeping the due amount of *zakat* in order to distribute it in fragments throughout the year is not permitted.[3]

The government or *zakat* commissioner may decide to postpone collection for valid reasons, such as drought, famine or depression. Ahmad quotes 'Umar's action that "One year people were in need, so 'Umar did not collect *zakat* but took that *zakat* due the following year."[4] Abu 'Ubayd reports from Ibn Abi Dhubab: "'Umar deferred the *sadaqa* the year of famine. When people were relieved the following year, he sent for me and said, 'Collect twice the amount of *zakat*. Divide among them one half and bring me the other.'"[5] We have seen in the *hadith* from Abu Hurayra that the Prophet (p) took the *zakat* due on al-'Abbas for two years. Abu 'Ubayd notes, "I think the Prophet (p) delayed collection from al-'Abbas because of an incident of need that happened to al-'Abbas."[6]

Delay in *zakat* payment without valid reason is sinful and not permitted. The author *of al-Muhadhdhab*, a Shafi'i, says, "It is not

1. *Nihayat al-Muhtaj*, vol. 2, p. 134.
2. *Al-Mughni*, vol. 2, p. 685.
3. *Hashiyat ad-Dusuqi*, vol. 1, p. 500.
4. *Matalib Uli'n-Nuha*, vol. 2, p. 116.
5. *Al-Amwal*, p. 374.
6. *Nayl al-Awtar*, vol. 4, p. 159.

permitted to delay payment of *zakat* after it becomes due, since it is a right owed to other people."[1] Hanafis also believe delaying *zakat* payment unnecessarily is sinful. At-Tahawi quotes Abu Hanifa as saying that such delay is emphatically disliked. Hanafis say it is sinful to delay payment, even for a day or two. The author of *al-Bada'i'* quotes from *al-Muntaqa*, "If *zakat* is not paid for two years, it is grossly sinful."[2] I believe that delaying *zakat* payment without reason beyond a short period is not permissible at all.

Loss of *zakat*

Ibn Rushd summarises jurists' views in the case of loss of an item or amount designated as *zakat* payment:

> If the due amount gets lost on the way to being distributed, some jurists believe the requirement is fulfilled and no new payment is needed. Other jurists argue that the payer is a guarantor until the *zakat* is actually distributed to its recipients. Yet others distinguish between the case of neglect or mishandling on the part of the prayer – some count delaying the payment as neglect – in which the payer is not considered responsible for the loss. This is the view of Abu Thawr and ash-Shafi'i. Lastly, some jurists treat the lost amount and the total assets of the payer as community property of the poor (who own a share in the proportion of lost *zakat* to the total) and the owner (who owns the rest). Accordingly, they divide the loss in proportion to their respective shares.[3]

Ibn Rushd mentioned a case, usually discussed by jurists, in which a part of the zakatable asset is lost, after the due time of *zakat* but before actual payment. Ibn Rushd adds, "In this case, some jurists say *zakat* must be calculated on what is left after the loss, while others apply the principle of community property, as in

1. *Al-Majmu'*, vol. 5, p. 331.
2. *Radd al-Muhtar*, vol. 2, p. 14.
3. *Bidayat al-Mujtahid*, vol. 1, p. 240.

partnerships." These differences exist because some jurists treat the amount of due *zakat* like interpersonal debts while others view it as a due right on the assets themselves.[1]

Can the requirement be relaxed after years pass?

If *zakat* payment is delayed, with or without a valid reason, is it waived after the passage of a certain number of years, like taxes? The answer is negative, since *zakat* is a right of the poor and needy prescribed by Allah. An-Nawawi says, "If a certain number of years pass without payment of any *zakat* that is due, the owner must pay the whole accumulated due *zakat*, regardless of the reason for the delay and the place of residence of the owner." Ibn al-Mundhir gives as an example a case in which a city falls into the hands of rebels or enemies for a few years, during which the residents of that city do not pay due *zakat*. The Islamic state, when it liberates the town, must collect the due amount of *zakat* for all those years, according to Malik, ash-Shafi'i, and Abu Thawr.

Jurists who prefer opinion (i.e. Hanafis) contend that *zakat* should not be charged for those years. The latter add that if someone embraces Islam in a non-Muslim country, then migrates to a Muslim land, he or she should not be charged *zakat* for past years.[2] Ibn Hazm notes,[3] "If two *zakat* charges or more become simultaneously due, the accumulated amount must be paid instantly, without delay and without deduction of the *zakat* calculated on the amount due for each previous year regardless of the reason of failure of post due payments."[4] *Zakat* is not similar to taxes in regard to the passage of years on unpaid amounts.

When a person dies leaving debts, any due *zakat* must be paid out of the deceased person's estate without any need for instruc-

1. *Bidayat al-Mujtahid*, vol. 1, p. 240, *al-Muhalla*, vol. 6, p. 363, and *Radd al-Muhtar*, vol. 2, pp. 79-80.

2. *Al-Majmu'*, vol. 5, p. 337.

3. *Al-Muhalla*, vol. 6, p. 87.

4. This is rightly based on the fact that *zakat* is due on the wealthy as a personal liability, not designated for any specific item of the person's assets. See *al-Mughni*, vol. 2, pp. 679-680.

tions in the will to that effect. This opinion is adopted by 'Ata', al-Hasan, az-Zuhri, Qatada, Malik,[1] ash-Shafi'i,[2] Ahmad, Ishaq, Abu Thawr, Ibn al-Mundhir,[3] and the Zaydi school.[4] Al-Awza'i and al-Layth restrict such payment to one-third or less of the estate. Ibn Sirin, ash-Sha'bi, an-Nakha'i, Hammad, ath-Thawri and others believe it can be paid only if the person's will specifies this payment. Abu Hanifa and his disciples add that without instructions in the will, *zakat* payment out of the deceased's estate does not satisfy the religious aspect of *zakat* and the heirs must not be required to make such payment, because *zakat* is an act of worship that requires intention.[5] This means the deceased is sinful for lack of payment.

Along with Ibn Qudama, I believe that, in addition to being an act of worship, *zakat* is a financial obligation and, like other debts, its payment cannot be waived as a result of death.[6] Moreover, the Prophet is authentically reported to have said, "If a person dies while still owing some fasting, his close kin may fast in compensation." *Zakat* is even more worthy of such compensation than fasting which is solely an act of worship. This allowance is a mercy from Allah for it removes the sinful consequence of neglect on the part of the deceased.

The position of *zakat* compared to other debts

The author of *al-Muhadhdhab* compares *zakat* with other debts left unpaid by a deceased person, "If *zakat* and debts to other individuals are due and the total estate is not sufficient to pay all of these obligations, jurists diverge into three opinions:

---

1. *Hashiyat ad-Dusuqi*, vol. 1, p. 502, and Bidayat *al-Mujtahid*, vol. 1, p. 241.

2. An-Nawawi says, "If *zakat* becomes due and the owner is able to pay it but dies before payment, it must be paid out of the estate." See *al-Majmu'*, vol. 5, p. 335.

3. *Al-Mughni*, vol. 2, pp. 683-84.

4. *Sharh al-Azhar*, vol. 1, p. 453, and *al-Bahr*, vol. 2, p. 144.

5. This opinion of Abu Hanifa applies to *zakat* on money. There are two contradicting reports from him about *zakat* on agriculture and livestock. See *al-Muhalla*, vol. 6, pp. 88-89, and *al-Majmu'*, vol. 5, pp. 335-336.

6. *Al-Majmu'*, ibid., and *al-Mughni*, vol. 2, pp. 683-84.

- Other people's debts must be given priority.
- *Zakat* has priority, since the Prophet (p) says in regard to pilgrimage, 'The debt owed to Allah has preference in payment.'[1]
- The estate must be divided between *zakat* and other debts, since both are equally in need of payment."[2]

Zahiris give priority to *zakat*. Ibn Hazm argues, "Neither creditors nor heirs have any right to an estate except after due *zakat* has been paid." Ibn Hazm was very critical of the Hanafi view. In *al-Muhalla*, he writes, "It is really surprising that they believe prayer must still be performed by a person who willingly delayed it until its time ran out, while they say *zakat* is waived from a person who delayed it until death … especially since *zakat* is a debt due to Allah and the right of the poor and needy." Ibn Hazm quotes the *hadith* reported by Muslim from Ibn 'Abbas, "A man came to the Prophet (p) and said, 'My mother died. She still has the fasting of one month unfulfilled. Should I fast for her?' The Prophet (p) said, 'If your mother owed some debts, would you not pay them on her behalf?' 'Yes,' said the man. The Prophet (p) went on, 'Then the debt to Allah has preference in payment.'" Ibn Hazm comments, "How can anyone claim that the debt of Allah can go without payment?'"[3]

In conclusion, the due amount of *zakat* must be paid out of the estate. It has priority above interpersonal debts. Only recently some governments have enacted laws giving priority to unpaid taxes on deceased persons' estates.[4]

---

1. The *hadith* is reported by al-Bukhari and Muslim from Ibn 'Abbas in regard to fasting. See ibid.

2. *Al-Majmu'*, vol. 6, p. 231.

3. *Al-Muhalla*, vol. 6, pp. 89-91.

4. *Mabadi' an-Nazariyya al-'Amma lid-Dariba*, 'Abdu'l-Hakim, ar-Rifa'i, and Hussain Khallaf, p. 143.

Chapter Six

Questions about *Zakat* Fulfilment

Cheating and fraud in *zakat*

Fraud and use of tricks in order to avoid *zakat* or to get it back after payment are obviously not permissible. Malikis note that it is so from the point of view of religion, as well as from the legal point of view. They add, "Any action intended to escape *zakat* payment before it becomes due, like changing the nature of zakatable assets, distributing ownership among different persons so that each of them owns less than *nisab*, or slaughtering some of a herd to reduce its number to below *nisab* – all such actions do not have any effect in waiving *zakat*, as long as it can be proved that such actions were taken in order to avoid it In cases like those, *zakat* accrues and must be collected."[1] Hanbalis agree with the Maliki view on actions meant to escape *zakat*. Ibn Qudama says:

> Exchanging an asset with a different one interrupts the year period and a new year must start for the new asset. But if this is done in order to escape *zakat*, *zakat* is levied just as if nothing had happened. By the same token, if the owner gives away or destroys some assets in order to make the remainder below the *nisab*, *zakat* is not waived and is still due at the end of the year.
>
> This opinion is also shared by Malik, al-Awza'i, Ibn al-Majishun, Ishaq and Abu 'Ubayd... This is founded on the *ayats* of Allah, *'We have tried them as We tried the owners of the garden when they swore that they would harvest in the morning but did not say the redeeming words, "If Allah wills". So a visitation from your Lord visited it while they slept and in the*

1. *Bulghat as-Salik*, vol. 1, p. 210.

> *morning it was like burnt land stripped bare.'* (68:17-20) The penalty from Allah is given because such persons embark on an action intended to escape the payment of *sadaqa.* It is known that any action meant to forsake or evade the right of another person cannot be allowed to succeed in the *Shari'a.* For example a man who divorces his wife during his death-sickness (in order to evade her sharing in his estate cannot be successful in withholding her right to a wife's share).[1]

On the other hand, Ibn Taymiyya, in *al-Qawa'id an-Nuraniya*, says that Abu Hanifa permits tricks aimed at escaping *zakat*, and that Abu Hanifa's disciples differ on whether such tricks are disliked or not. He says that ash-Shaybani dislikes them, while Abu Yusuf does not.[2] However, upon looking into Abu Yusuf's *al-Kharaj*, I find that Abu Yusuf says, "It is not lawful for anyone who believes in Allah and the Last Day to elude *zakat*, to distribute the ownership of a *nisab* that he owns to several people in order to avoid the *sadaqa* or to escape proper payment of *sadaqa* by any way or any means whatsoever."[3]

It is likely that Ibn Taymiyya is referring to what is commonly found in Hanafi writings, that use of loopholes is legally valid in waiving *zakat*, although *zakat* remains unfulfilled religiously, and that use of legal loopholes is sometimes disliked and sometimes not. Hanafis state, for example, that it is disliked to give *zakat* to a poor person on the condition that the latter give it as a gift to the payer's needy parents. By the same token, any condition made on the poor person when *zakat* is given him is invalid, even though the recipient may be willing to fulfil it.[4] It must be noted that tricks like these, whether disliked or not, apply only to the distribution of *zakat*. Hanafi books that I have seen do not discuss cheating to escape *zakat* in the first place. Additionally, Ibn Taymiyya says that ash-Shafi'i only dislikes use of loopholes in order to escape the accrual of *zakat*.

1. *Al-Mughni*, vol. 2, pp. 534-535.
2. *Al-Qawa'id an-Nuraniya*, p. 89.
3. *Al-Kharaj*, Abu Yusuf, p. 80.
4. *Radd al-Muhtar*, vol. 2, p. 69.

Lastly, Zaydis do not approve of the use of tricks, whether they are used to avoid *zakat*, to escape actual payment to deserving people, or to get it back after payment.[1] The author of *Hawashi Sharh al-Azhar* quotes ash-Shawkani, "There is no doubt that any fraud that ends up making lawful what is forbidden or vice versa must be completely prohibited. Permitting such tricks is not consistent with the *Shari'a* by any means."[2]

Exchange of prayers between collector, payer and recipient

The spiritual aspect of *zakat* is expressed – among other manifestations – in the prayers exchanged between the collector and the payer. The collector of *zakat* is asked to pray on behalf of the payer. Allah says, *"Take* sadaqa *from their wealth so that you may purify and cleanse them, and pray for them. Indeed your prayers are a source of security and comfort to them."* 'Abdullah ibn Abi Awfa narrates, "When any person brought *zakat* to the Messenger of Allah, he used to say, 'O Lord, give them mercy!' When my father, Abu Awfa' brought him his *sadaqa*, the Prophet said, 'O Lord, give mercy to the family of Abu Awfa'."[3] This prayer is not restricted to any specific form. Ash-Shafi'i says, "I like the collector to say, 'May Allah reward you for that which you give, make it a cause of purification for you, and give you blessings on what you have left for yourself.'"[4] An-Nasa'i reports that the Prophet (p) prayed on behalf of a man who sent a good she-camel, "O Lord, bless him and his camels."[5]

Zahiris and some Shafi'is consider such prayers obligatory on the part of the collector, deriving the judgement from a literal interpretation of the above *ayat*. However, the majority believes

1. *Sharh al-Azhar*, vol. 1, pp. 539-540.

2. Ibid.

3. Ash-Shawkani quotes from *al-Muntaqa*, "It is agreed upon." *Nayl al-Awtar*, vol. 4, p. 153.

4. *Ar-Rawda*, an-Nawawi, vol. 2, p. 211.

5. *Sunan an-Nasa'i*, vol. 5, p. 30.

these prayers are recommended and not obligatory, because the Prophet (p) did not include them in any of his instructions to collectors,[1] nor are government collectors required to make such prayers when they receive other dues from the payers.[2] However, these arguments do not seem to outweigh the indication of the *ayat*.

In another *hadith*, the Messenger (p) recommends payers to supplicate Allah upon payment of *zakat*. Abu Hurayra narrates that the Messenger of Allah (p) says, "When you give *zakat* away, do not forget its reward. Say, 'Our Lord, make it rewarding and not a loss.'"[3] 'Ali narrates that the Prophet (p) says, "There are fifteen things which if my nation does, it will be affected by catastrophes..." Among them he mentions "when it considers trust a means for gain and when it considers *zakat* a loss."[4] *Zakat* recipients are also recommended to pray on behalf of the payer on the basis of the *hadith* from Abu Hurayra since one of its versions reads "when you are given..."[5]

Paying *zakat* by proxy

A *zakat* payer may choose to make the payment himself or through agents, attorneys, or representatives, as long as the latter are trustworthy and dependable. Some jurists require that such agents be Muslims since *zakat* is a form of worship, while some others allow appointing a Person of the Pledge as agent to pay *zakat* as long as the proper intention is made by the owner.[6]

1. *Nayl al-Awtar*, op cit.
2. Ibid.
3. Reported by Ibn Majah, vol. 1, no. 1797, and 'Abdu'r-Razzaq in his *Jami'*, as stated by as-Suyuti in *al-Jami' al-Kabir*. As-Suyuti marks it weak, al-Munawi in *al-Fayd*, vol. 1, p. 290, says the *hadith* is not very weak. See *Nayl al-Awtar*, vol. 4, pp. 152-153.
4. Its chain is weak, as stated in *Nayl al-Awtar*.
5. In *al-Fayd*, vol. 1, p. 290, al-Munawi says, "It indicates that prayers of this kind are recommended although not usually specifically mentioned by jurists. At least they fall under the general recommendation of prayers to Allah in all circumstances."
6. *Hashiyat ad-Dusuqi*, vol. 1, p. 498.

Additionally, some Malikis consider payment via representatives less open to pride and hypocrisy than direct payment by the owner.[1] It may be necessary if the payer knows his ignorance of *zakat* payment regulations and its deserving people.

Payment in public

An-Nawawi says it is better for *zakat* to be paid in public where it is seen by others so that it serves as a reminder to other payers in the same way that obligatory prayer is recommended collectively in public.[2] This is on the grounds that *zakat* is one of the major acts of worship in Islam and should be very visible in Muslim society. Since it is required from every person liable for *zakat*, it is not an object of pride or condescension, in contrast to voluntary charity which is better done in private. Keenness to demonstrate the rites of Islam and make them dominant is a sign of faith and an indication of righteousness. Allah says, *"That is it. As for those who honour Allah's sacred rites, that comes from the fear of Allah within their hearts."* (22:32) This may be what the Prophet meant when he said, "And the showing off which is beloved by Allah is that done by a man in battle, or when giving *sadaqa*." (an-Nasa'i) This, in fact, is based on the *ayat*, "*If you make public acts of charity, it is well...*" (2:271)

Should recipients be told it is *zakat*?

When *zakat* is distributed by individuals, it is preferred that recipients should not be told that it is *zakat*, especially since many deserving people may hesitate to take *zakat* at the slightest doubt that they may not be truly deserving. The author of *al-Mughni* says, "When *zakat* is paid to those whom the payer thinks are poor, there is no need to inform recipients that it is *zakat*." Al-Hasan says, "Do you want to humiliate him? Do not tell him." And

1. *Hashiyat ad-Dusuqi*, vol. 1, p. 498.
2. *Al-Majmu'*, vol. 6, and *Fiqh al-Imam Ja'far*, vol. 2, p. 96.

Ahmad ibn al-Hasan says, "I asked Ahmad if a person who pays his *zakat* to another should tell him it is *zakat* or remain silent. Ahmad answered, 'Why should he humiliate the recipient by saying that? He should pay him and remain silent. Does he need to beat him over the head with that payment?'"[1] Some Malikis dislike mentioning that it is *zakat* since this disheartens the poor.[2]

Ja'faris also believe there is no need to tell the recipient that what is paid is *zakat*. Abu Basir says, "I asked al-Baqir about a person who may shy away from taking *zakat*. Should I give to him without calling it *zakat*? Al-Baqir answered, 'Give to him without naming it. Do not humiliate believers.'"[3]

Waiving debts as payment of *zakat*

An-Nawawi says, "Waiving the debt of a person who is unable to pay the debt back as payment of the creditor's *zakat* is not acceptable fulfilment of *zakat*, according to the most predominant opinion among Shafi'is. This opinion is shared by Abu Hanifa and Ahmad because *zakat* payment requires actually giving to the deserving categories. Another view among Shafi'is is to accept such waiving as fulfilment of *zakat* payment, a view shared by al-Hasan and 'Ata', on the grounds that if the creditor gives the debtor *zakat* in cash, the debtor would pay it back to the creditor as payment of the debt. It is not approved that the creditor give his *zakat* to the debtor under the condition that the latter pay it back in fulfilment of the debt."[4]

Abu 'Ubayd mentions that al-Hasan does not have any objection to waiving the debt which resulted from a loan, but not a sale, of one who is unable to pay it back in fulfilment of *zakat*. On the other hand, Abu 'Ubayd himself strongly opposes such an action on the grounds that payment of *zakat* in this manner may hide an

1. *Al-Mughni*, vol. 2, p. 647.
2. *Hashiyat as-Sawi* on *Bulghat as-Salik*, vol. 1, p. 335.
3. *Fiqh al-Imam Ja'far*, vol. 2, p. 88.
4. *Al-Majmu'*, vol. 6, pp. 210-211.

intention of collecting bad debts. Abu 'Ubayd adds, "It is inconsistent with the *Sunna* anyway."[1]

Ibn Hazm approves of such waiving as *zakat* payment. He quotes a *hadith* reported by Muslim from Abu Sa'id, "A man was financially straitened at the time of the Messenger of Allah (p) as a result of fruits he purchased to sell. He became overburdened by debts. The Messenger of Allah (p) said, 'Give him *sadaqa*.'" This is also the opinion of 'Ata'.[2] Ja'faris also subscribe to this view. A man asked Ja'far about loans he had given to some people who were not able to pay them back. Debtors automatically deserve *zakat*, so his question was whether he might waive the debts in fulfilment of his own *zakat* payment. Ja'far answered, "Yes."[3]

In my opinion, the view that accepts waiving debts of *zakat* deserving people in fulfilment of payment has more substance than the other. In the Qur'an, Allah calls waiving debts of persons who are in financial difficulties *sadaqa*. The *ayat* reads, *"If someone is in difficult circumstances, there should be a deferral until things are easier. But making a* sadaqa *of it would be better for you if you only knew."* (2:280)

Making things available to the poor as *zakat*

Some jurists discuss whether inviting poor persons to eat in the house of the *zakat* payer can be accepted in fulfilment of *zakat*. Hanafis and others argue that since making the poor obtain ownership of the amount given is an indispensable condition for fulfilment of *zakat*, providing them with food to eat in the payer's house can be considered to be *zakat* payment, while giving them food, even cooked, fulfils the requirement of *zakat*.[4] Some Zaydis approve of making food available to the poor as *zakat* payment under the following conditions:

1. *Al-Amwal*, pp. 595-596.
2. *Al-Muhalla*, vol. 5, pp. 105-106.
3. *Fiqh al-Imam Ja'far*, vol. 2, p. 91.
4. *Radd al-Muhtar*, vol. 2, p. 3.

- Having the intention of *zakat* payment.
- The food must not be quickly perishable. It should be something like dates or raisins.
- The amount given should be substantial, i.e. beyond what is usually eaten by people.
- The food should be at the disposal of the poor.
- The poor persons concerned must know that this is in payment of *zakat*.[1]

1. *Sharh al-Azhar*, vol. 1, p. 542.

Part Six
Objectives of *Zakat* and Its Effects on the Individual and Society

Introduction

For a long time, many taxation specialists tried to widen the gap between taxes and social or humanistic issues, in order to prevent any adverse effect such issues may have on the proceeds of taxes, claiming that taxes must have only one objective – bringing income to the treasury – and must otherwise be 'neutral'. It took deep social changes, several bloody revolutions, and great progression of ideas until financial experts came to realise that taxes can effect valuable socio-economic changes, can be used to reduce the economic balance in society.

There has been no such upheaval in the history of *zakat* for, from the beginning, *zakat*, as one of the pillars of Islam, was an essential and sacred act of worship. Muslims pay it with devotion and sincerity in accordance with the *hadith* of the Prophet (p), "Actions are according to intentions and every person will have what he intends," (al-Bukhari and Muslim) and the *ayat*, *"They were only ordered to worship Allah, making their deen sincerely His as people of pure natural belief, and to establish the prayer and pay* zakat *– that is the correct* deen*."* (98:5)

Zakat is first of all a practice in obedience to Allah and a self-purification meant to prepare the human being for eternal happiness in the Hereafter. Once a person's heart is purified and his soul is cleansed by the complete commitment to Allah's orders and obligations, such a person becomes worthy of the joy of the Afterlife as one of *"Those the angels take in a virtuous state. They say, 'Peace be upon you! Enter the Garden for what you did.'"* (16:32) It is this aspect of *zakat* that ties it to the prayer in twenty-eight places of the Qur'an and in dozens of *hadiths*, in an unbreakable bond of association that makes it known as the sister of the prayer. It is also this aspect of *zakat* that Abu Bakr had in mind when he declared war against those who refused to pay it, stating, "By Allah, I shall indeed fight those who separate prayer from *zakat*." Following this tradition, the books of *fiqh* place chapters on *zakat* immediately after chapters on prayer in the parts devoted to worship.

The obvious and essential objective of *zakat* as a transfer of ownership is supplemented by moral, humanistic, social and economic objectives which *zakat* is set to achieve by many *ayats* and *hadiths*. These objectives were fulfilled to various degrees when *zakat* was practised in early Muslim society, as will be studied in the following two chapters.

Chapter One

Objectives of *Zakat* and Its Effects on the Individual

Section One: Effects of *zakat* on payers

The foremost objective of *zakat* is to elevate the spirit of human beings above the love of material acquisition. Consequently, Islam does not view the *zakat* payer as a mere source of funds, but as a person who always needs purification and cleansing, both spiritually and materially. The Prophet (p) summarises this purpose in the *ayat*, *"Take* sadaqa *from their wealth by which you might purify and cleanse them."*

Zakat purifies the soul from miserliness

Zakat, when paid out of submission to the command of Allah, is a means of purifying the soul of a Muslim from greed and miserliness. The vices of selfishness and greed must be tamed in order for human beings to elevate their spirits, to succeed in their social relations in this life, and to gain admittance to Paradise. Allah Almighty says, *"Truly man is niggardly!"* (17:100) and *"But people are prone to selfish greed."* (4:128) Miserliness and greed are drives that incite humans to hypocrisy, cheating and betrayal, The Prophet (p) says, "Three things are devastating: obeyed niggardliness, pursued desires and self-admiration,"[1] and "Firstly avoid greed, since people before you were indeed destroyed because of greed. Greed swayed them to be misers, cut off their family and friends and to be vicious."[2]

1. Reported by at-Tabarani in *Mu'jam al-Awsat* from Ibn 'Umar via a weak chain, according to *at-Taysir*, vol. 1, p. 570.

2. Reported by Abu Dawud and an-Nasa'i. See *Mukhtasar al-Mundhiri*, vol. 2, p. 263.

Moreover, Allah makes purification from these evils a condition for success and prosperity, *"It is the people who are safe-guarded from the avarice of their own selves who are the successful."* (59:9)

Zakat is a purifier that trains Muslims to give and spend selflessly. It liberates their souls from the love of wealth and slavery to material gains and acquisitions. Life and human existence become miserable if people are overwhelmed and enslaved by the drive for material acquisition. The Prophet (p) remarks, "Miserable is he who is enslaved to the dinar, miserable is he who is enslaved to the dirham, miserable is he who is enslaved to garments. He is miserable and regressive; may he not recover from any hurt inflicted on him."[1]

Zakat trains one to give

Zakat is a means of training Muslims on the virtues of generosity as much as it is a means of purification from greed. Being paid in a repetitive pattern year after year, regular *zakat* as well as *zakat al-fitr* train Muslims to give and spend for charitable purposes. The Qur'an describes believers as the righteous who have the virtue of spending for good causes. The very second *sura* of the Qur'an begins, *"Alif. Lam. Mim. That is the Book with no doubt. In it is guidance for the godfearing: those who believe in the Unseen and establish the prayer and give of what We have provided for them."* (2:1-3) This exhortation is reiterated many times in the Qur'an, such as *"Those who give away their wealth by night and by day, secretly and openly,"* (2:274); *"Those who give in times of both ease and hardship"* (3:134), and *"The steadfast, the truthful, the obedient, the givers, and those who seek forgiveness before dawn."* (3:17)

Even Makkan *ayats* begin this training in its general form: *"Those who respond to their Lord and establish the prayer and manage their affairs with mutual consultation and give of what We have provided for them."* (42:36-38) In his commentary, al-Qurtubi considers this a general reference to both *zakat* and voluntary charity since the *ayat* describes the character of the believers,[2] although it is reported

1. Reported by al-Bukhari in the chapter on *jihad*, and by Ibn Majah in his chapter on piety.

2. *Tafsir al-Qurtubi*, vol. 1, p. 179.

from Ibn 'Abbas that the *ayat* refers to *zakat*, since it associates prayer with spending (and the only spending associated in the Qur'an with prayer is *zakat*).

One must remember, however, that other Makkan *ayats* refer more explicitly to charitable spending as one of the characteristics of believers: *"The godfearing will be among Gardens and Fountains, receiving what their Lord has given them. Certainly before that they were good-doers. The part of the night they spent asleep was small and they would seek forgiveness before dawn. And the beggars and deprived received a due share of their wealth"* (51:15-19), and *"Truly man was created headstrong. When something bad happens to him, desperate. When something good happens to him, begrudging. Except for those who pray and who are constant in their prayer. Those in whose wealth there is a known share for beggars and the deprived."* (70:19-25)

Moreover, once a person is trained to spend on public interests and to give to his brethren out of his own wealth, he is most likely to be freed from any urge to transgress on other people's wealth and possessions. Among the early verses revealed to the Prophet in Makka are those words about the characters of those who spend and those who do not spend: *"As for him who gives out and is godfearing and confirms the Good, We will pave his way to Ease. But as for him who is stingy and self-satisfied, and denies the Good, We will pave his way to Difficulty. His wealth will not help him when he plummets to the depths. Assuredly guidance is in Our hands. And both the Last and First belong to Us. I have warned you of a Fire which rages, in which only the most wretched will roast – those who denied and turned away. The most godfearing will be far removed from it: those who give their wealth to purify themselves – not to repay someone else for a favour done – desiring only the Face of their Lord Most High. They will certainly be satisfied."* (92:5-21)

The Qur'an associates the characteristics of giving and testifying to the Truth with the result of having a smooth way to bliss, and the characteristics of withholding and greediness with having a smooth path to misery.

Zakat trains people to acquire divine characteristics

If man is purified of miserliness and greed and becomes accustomed to the habit of giving and spending, his soul is elevated above the low human trait of covetousness, *"Truly man is niggardly!"* (17:100) and aspires to the height of Divine perfection, since one of the characteristics of Allah is absolute and unlimited mercy. In his *Great Commentary*,[1] ar-Razi writes, "The human soul has two powers, theoretical and practical. Its theoretical power is the soul's endeavour to perfect its submission to the Greatness of Allah and its practical power is its endeavour to perfect its mercy to the creatures of Allah. Allah obliges *zakat* in order to perfect the human soul in graciousness to other people, as the Prophet says,[2] "Train yourselves to the attributes of Allah.'"[3]

This encouragement to spend through *zakat* and voluntary charity resulted, with time, in the emergence of charitable trusts all over the Muslim world, trusts devoted not only to helping the poor and needy, but to all good causes for human beings as well as animals.[3]

Zakat as an expression of thankfulness to Allah

Gratitude and thankfulness are among the best characteristics of human beings. *Zakat* is an expression of thankfulness to Allah for the bounties He bestows on us. Allah, says al-Ghazali, has bestowed on humans spiritual and material bounties. Prayers and other acts of physical worship express gratitude for the blessing of creation, while *zakat* and other acts of donatory worship express gratitude for the material blessings of Allah. For disgraceful is he who sees

1. *At-Tafsir al-Kabir*, vol. 16, p. 101.

2. I searched for this *hadith* but never found it, nor have I found anyone who refers to it."

3. The same meaning can be expressed in different words as ar-Razi himself said and that being rich by doing without things shows more strength of soul than being rich by owning things, since wealth by possession means one is dependent on what one has while wealth by not needing things means no dependence on anything. Accordingly, wealth by not being dependent on anything is a characteristic of Allah, the creator, while wealth by acquisition is a characteristic of creatures. Allah gives His servants wealth in abundance, making them rich in the sense of having possessions, and ordains them to give *zakat* in order to teach them to do without wealth, which is a higher level than acquisition.

3. See the different examples of this kind of trust in my book, *al-Iman wa'l-Hayat* (Faith and Life), chapter on mercy, pp. 291-293.

the obvious needs of the poor and does not graciously give a tenth or one-fourth of a tenth of his wealth, or thank Allah who gave him enough bounty to remove him from the misery and pressure of poverty.[1] The concept that *zakat* is thanks to Allah for His bounties is so widespread and deeply rooted in the consciousness of Muslims that it is common to say that one must give *zakat* in thanks for the grace of sight, hearing, health, knowledge, etc. It is further reported that the Prophet (p) said, "Everything has its *sadaqa*."[2]

Zakat is a cure for the love of worldly things

As a financial obligation, *zakat* aims at attenuating the lust for material acquisition. Overwhelming love for acquisition, according to ar-Razi, takes the soul away from love for Allah and preparation for the Hereafter.[3] Ar-Razi adds, "Accumulation of wealth increases the power and control of the owner, which increases his ability of taking enjoyment from this world, and material enjoyment induces more desires and wants which demand more wealth to fulfil them, thus man enters into a vicious circle of seeking satisfaction and more wealth. *Zakat* breaks this circle because it is spending which incurs no physical joy or satisfaction. It is liberation from materialistic enslavement, and re-orientates man towards exclusive submission to Allah alone."[4]

Zakat stimulates personality growth in those who pay it

By helping others overcome their financial difficulties, *zakat* payers are enriched by feelings of self-worth and fulfilment. *Zakat* also helps offer the payer's self to others and grow through helping them and gives the payer a noble sense of victory over his base desires and material drives – over his own *shaytan*.

1. *Ihya' 'Ulum ad-Din*, vol. 1, p. 193.
2. Reported from Ibn Majah from Abu Hurayra and by at-Tabarani from Sahl ibn Sa'd. As-Suyuti marks it weak, and al-Mundhiri refers to its weakness in *at-Targhib*.
3. *At-Tafsir al-Kabir*, op. cit., p. 101.
4. Ibid.

Zakat improves ties of mutual love

Zakat links the rich and poor together with ties of brotherhood and love. The poor realise the true concern of the rich and see one manifestation of it in the stream of *zakat* revenue. Naturally, people love those who do good to them. It is said, "Hearts are kneaded by the love of those who do them good and the hatred of those who do them harm."[1] The more the rich give out of love, the more the poor love and pray for them and for the protection and preservation of their wealth. Ar-Razi says this is what is meant by the *ayat*, "*But as for that which is of use to people, it remains behind in the ground,*" (13:17) and the *hadith* of the Prophet (p), "Fortify your wealth by paying *zakat*."[2]

Zakat purifies wealth

Zakat purifies wealth. Because *zakat* is a right to the poor, not paying it means keeping something that belongs to others intermingled with one's wealth and this brings Allah's wrath on the whole wealth. The Prophet (p) says, "If you pay *zakat* on your wealth, you have taken away its evil."[3] Moreover, the fortification of wealth of *zakat* mentioned in the *hadith* at the end of the previous sub-section is especially needed today when so many destructive forces and social unrest are rampant.

Some jurists add that due *zakat* is an immediate obligation on wealth itself and not merely a personal debt on the wealthy. The Prophet says, "Due *sadaqa* is never left mixed with wealth without destroying it," and in a different version, "When *sadaqa* is due on

---

1. Reported by Ibn 'Abidin in *al-Kamil*, Abu Nu'aym in *al-Hilya*, and al-Bayhaqi in the chapter on the branches of faith, from Ibn Mas'ud, attributed to the Prophet via a weak chain. It is also described as falsified. However, al-Bayhaqi grades as *sahih* the chain that ends at Ibn Mas'ud, making the statement his instead of the Prophet's. As-Sakhawi says, "It is false in both the version attributed to the Prophet, as well as the one stopped at Ibn Mas'ud." See *at-Taysir*, vol. 1, p. 485.

2. Reported by Abu Dawud as *mursal* and by at-Tabarani, al-Bayhaqi and others from a group of Companions as linked up to the Prophet. Al-Mundhiri says the *mursal* version is better.

3. Reported by Ibn Khuzayma in his *Sahih* collection and al-Hakim from Jabir. The *hadith* is, however, criticised, as will be seen in Part Eight.

your wealth and you do not pay it, the whole wealth, lawful and unlawful (i.e. yours and the unpaid *zakat*) will be wiped out." Furthermore, when *zakat* is not performed on a large scale in a society, the nation's wealth is exposed to natural catastrophes and disasters for, "No people refuse to pay *zakat* without their rainfall being diminished, and if it were not for the animals, they would not be given any rain at all." Thus, the security of individual and national wealth from the factors of destruction and demolition can only be achieved by paying the due right of the poor obliged by Allah.

***Zakat* does not purify unlawful wealth**

Wealth earned through forbidden means cannot be purified by *sadaqa*. The Prophet (p) says, "Allah is good, and He only accepts what is good."[1] "He who acquires wealth by forbidden means, then gives it away as *sadaqa* gets no reward; the sin remains on him,"[2] and "Allah does not accept *sadaqa* out of unlawfully earned wealth, nor does he accept prayer without ablution."[3]

The Prophet (p) adds, "By Him in Whose Hand my soul is, no servant earns wealth unlawfully and gives it as *sadaqa* but that it is not accepted from him, or spends it but that it is not blessed, or leaves it behind his back [after he dies] but that it is his means to the Fire. Allah does not erase evil with evil. He rather removes evil with good. A corrupt deed does not clear another corrupt dead."[4] Al-Qurtubi comments, "Allah does not accept *sadaqa* out of unlawfully acquired wealth because such wealth is not truly owned by the payer. The payer's disposal of such wealth is thus illegal and accepting *sadaqa* from such a person is contradictory."[5] Some

1. Reported by Muslim and at-Tirmidhi. See *at-Targhib wa't-Tarhib*, vol. 3, p. 11. A similar *hadith* is reported in Sahih al-Bukhari, chapter on *zakat*, section on *sadaqa* from good earning.

2. Reported by Ibn Khuzayma, Ibn Hibban and al-Hakim. The latter says its chain is correct. See *at-Targhib* vol. 1, p. 266.

3. Reported by Abu Dawud via a correct chain, and by Muslim. See *Fath al-Bari*, vol. 3, p. 178.

4. Reported by Ahmad and others via a chain that is graded *hasan* by some critics. See *at-Targhib*, vol. 3, p. 14.

5. *Fath al-Bari*, vol. 3, p. 180.

Hanafis go as far as considering the act of knowingly giving out of unlawful wealth equal to denying Islam and becoming an unbeliever because such an act implies rejecting the Islamic criteria of lawfulness.[1]

Zakat brings growth to wealth

Although *zakat* seems reduce the capital of the wealthy, it is in fact a cause of blessing and growth to that wealth, a blessing from Allah that brings prosperity. For instance, the increase in demand for consumer goods caused by the distribution of *zakat* brings vitality to business. This may in fact be the economic explanation of the verses: *"Say: 'My Lord expands the provision of any of His slaves He wills and restricts it. Anything you expend will be replaced by Him. He is the best of Providers.'"* (34:39) *"Shaytan promises you poverty and commands you to avarice. Allah promises you forgiveness from Him and abundance. Allah is All-Encompassing, All-Knowing."* (2:268) *"What you give with usurious intent, aiming to get back a greater amount from people's wealth, does not become greater with Allah. But anything you give as* zakat, *seeking the Face of Allah – all who do that will get back twice as much."* (30:39) and *"Allah obliterates usury but makes* sadaqa *grow in value! Allah does not love any persistently ungrateful wrongdoer."* (2:276)

The effect of Providence is manifold in recompense and growth since Allah gives His grace and sustenance to those who please Him. To this, one must add the economic effect of *zakat* payment in increasing the payer's investment efforts in order to compensate for what is paid as *zakat.*

Section Two: Effects of *zakat* on recipients

Zakat frees its receiver from the humiliation of need and helps satisfy the basic requirements of a decent living since, except for workers who are paid for collecting and distributing *zakat*, fighters for the Cause of Allah who are paid for military service and those

1. *Radd al-Muhtar*, vol. 2, p. 27.

whose hearts are being reconciled, the recipients are the poor, the needy, slaves seeking freedom, persons in debt and travellers.

Zakat liberates its recipients from material needs

Living a good and prosperous life is one of Islam's objectives for all human beings. Thus men and women are urged to benefit from the grace of Allah manifest in food to eat, goods to consume, houses in which to find refuge, and happiness to savour. The satisfaction of the material needs of life is undoubtedly an essential ingredient of human happiness. The Prophet (p) says, "Three things make for happiness: a wife who pleases you when you look at her and gives you confidence about herself and your household when you are absent, a comfortable riding animal that carries you at a pace with your company, and a spacious residence with manifold utilities,"[1] and on another occasion, "Four things make for happiness: a virtuous wife, a spacious house, a good neighbour and a comfortable ride; and four make for misery: a wicked neighbour, a wicked wife, a bad ride and a cramped house." (Ibn Hibban)

Obviously, Islam likes people to be prosperous and hates poverty, especially when poverty is the result of an unjust distribution of wealth or class oppression. The essential differences between Islam and materialist systems is that, while those systems consider the betterment of material living a goal in itself, Islam sees it as a means of spiritual uplifting and as the liberation of human energy from devotion to seeking bread to worshipping and glorifying Allah.

This position of Islam is expressed in the idea that making one rich is a grace from Allah. Allah tells the Messenger, *"Did He not find you impoverished and enrich you?"* (93:8) He tells the Muslims in Madina, *"He gave you refuge and supported you with His help and provided you with good things so that perhaps you would be thankful."* (8:26) The Prophet used to pray, "My Lord, I ask You for guidance, righteousness, contentment and wealth."[2] Moreover, He prefers a grateful rich person to a patient poor person.[3]

1. Reported by al-Hakim. See *at-Targhib*, vol. 3, p. 68.

2. Reported by Muslim, at-Tirmidhi, and Ibn Majah from Ibn Mas'ud.

3. As it appears from the *hadith* which is in the two *Sahih* collections, "The wealthy took all the reward..."

Prosperity is considered part of the reward which Allah gives to righteous believers while poverty and misery are part of the punishment for disbelief and misconduct. Allah says, "*Anyone who acts rightly, male or female, being a believer, We will give them a good life.*" (16: 97) "*If only the people of the cities had believed and been godfearing, We would have opened up to them blessings from heaven and earth.*" (7:96) "*Whoever shows fear of Allah – He will give him a way out and provide for him from where he does not expect.*" (65:2-3) "*Allah makes a likeness of a city which was safe and at peace, its provision coming to it plentifully from every side. Then it showed ingratitude for Allah's blessings so Allah made it wear the robe of hunger and fear for what it did.*" (16:112)

When Adam and Eve were sent down to earth, Allah gave them the laws of life. "*He said, 'Descend from it, every one of you, as enemies to one another! But when guidance comes to you from Me, all those who follow My guidance will not go astray and they will not be miserable. But if anyone turns away from My Reminder, his life will be a dark and narrow one and on the Day of Rising we will gather him blind.'*" (20:123-124)

All the ideas which glorify and welcome poverty and condemn wealth are alien to Islam. These ideas are infiltrations from Asian religions and ancient Christianity.[1] Allah commands *zakat* in order to use the surplus wealth of society to satisfy the essential needs of those who are not lucky enough to have wealth of their own so they can enjoy the bounties of Allah and contribute to the progress of society. In case there is no Islamic state or one which does not fulfil its duty of establishing an organisation for collecting and distributing *zakat* and individuals have to distribute their *zakat* personally, Allah strongly warns them not to humiliate the poor. Allah says, "*O you who believe! Do not nullify your* sadaqa *by demands for gratitude or insulting words, like him who spends his wealth, showing off to people and not believing in Allah and the Last Day. His likeness is that of a smooth rock coated with soil, which, when heavy rain falls on it, is left stripped bare.*" (2:264)

Letting the poor know that they are not lost or forgotten and that society cares deeply about their needs is in itself an upgrading

1. See al-Qardawi, *Mushkilat al-Faqr*, chapter on how Islam views poverty.

of their sentiments and sense of brotherhood. Human dignity and the honour given human beings by Allah require that not a single person be neglected or left on the periphery of society. The martyr Sayyid Qutb explains:

> Islam hates poverty and hates seeing people pressed by needs. Islam aims to have people devote their time and energy to matters that suit the great role assigned to human beings by Allah. To do so, they need to be freed from the pressure of material needs. Allah says, *"We have honoured the sons of Adam and conveyed them on land and sea and provided them with good things and favoured them greatly over many We have created."* (17:70)
>
> Allah indeed honours humans by giving them reason, sentiments and spiritual aspirations toward what is above and beyond bodily necessities. If they are deprived of the basic needs of life, they will not have time to exert their reason, to amplify and upgrade their sentiments, aspirations and ideas. If such a thing happens, humans are indeed deprived of that honour and reduced to the level of animals seeking material needs. He is not a human being honoured by Allah who is always occupied with the pursuit of food and drink without seeking the glories involved in the honour granted by Allah.
>
> The human being is indeed the vicegerent of Allah on earth, assigned by Allah the role of upgrading life in all its aspects on this planet, filling it with glories and joys so human beings can enjoy its beauty and perfection and thank Allah for all these bounties. Human beings shall not reach such heights unless their basic material needs are satisfied – unless they are freed from running after a piece of bread.[1]

Zakat cleanses jealousy and hatred

For the recipient, *zakat* is also a means of purifying the soul from envy and hatred. A man, beaten down by poverty and pressed

1. *Al-'Adala al-Ijtima'iyya fi'l-Islam*, pp. 132-133.

by the material necessities of life, who sees others around him enjoying a high standard of living and luxuries without helping him or extending any relief to him, will doubtlessly be ravaged by the pressure of unsatisfied material needs and become full of hatred and enmity towards the entire society. Islam wants relations between people to be based on strong bonds of fraternity and solidarity. The source of this solidarity is that all are sons and daughters of Adam. As the Prophet (p) puts it, 'And be, O servants of Allah, one brotherhood," (Muslim) and "A Muslim is the brother of a fellow Muslim."[1] Such fraternity cannot be established and stabilised if one brother has a full stomach while others are left to hunger, for this nourishes hatred and envy.

Envy is dangerous to everyone. It is a deviation in the behaviour of human beings that crushes brotherhood. Allah says, *"Or do they in fact envy other people for the bounty Allah has granted them?"* (4:54) Envy and hatred are some of the most devastating social diseases that destroy people and societies. The Prophet (p) warns, "Here comes to you the illness of nations before you: enmity, envy and hatred. Hatred is the razor. I do not mean it shaves off hair, but it shaves off religion."[2] Love and brotherhood among people, poor and rich, are nourished by *zakat* which strengthens the bonds of society and cleanses the hearts and souls of people. The Prophet (p) says, "None of you is a true believer until he loves for his brother what he loves for himself."[3]

1. Agreed upon, from Ibn 'Umar. Muslim also reports it from 'Utba ibn 'Amir. Abu Dawud reports it from 'Amr ibn al-Ahwas and Qayla. See *Kashf al-Khafa*, vol. 2, p. 210.

2. Reported by al-Bazzar with a good chain and by al-Bayhaqi and others. See *at-Targhib wa't-Tarhib*, vol. 4, p. 11.

3. Reported by al-Bukhari, Muslim, Ahmad, at-Tirmidhi, an-Nasa'i and Ibn Majah, from Anas, as stated in *al-Jami' as-Saghir*.

Chapter Two

Objectives of *Zakat* in Society

A glance at the categories of people to whom *zakat* is distributed immediately reveals the social aspect of *zakat*: *"Collected sadaqa is for: the poor, the destitute, those who collect it, reconciling people's hearts, freeing slaves, those in debt, spending in the Way of Allah, and travellers. An obligation imposed by Allah."* Clearly, giving *zakat* to these categories serves important social objectives. Some of them relate to the state and public order, such as heart reconciliation and in the Way of Allah. These two categories imply that the government must collect and distribute *zakat* with the intention of spreading Islam and defending the Muslim community. This chapter will discuss the relationship between *zakat* and the moral and spiritual integrity of Islamic society.

Islam and social insurance

Zakat is the cornerstone of Islam's social insurance system. The mutual insurance that Islam ordains goes beyond the mere material aspect to include the spiritual, psychological, moral, cultural and civic aspects of a person's life, and to foster solidarity and mutual co-operation among members of Islamic society. In short, mutual social care in Islamic society extends to all branches of human life.[1] *Zakat* covers only the areas called social insurance and social security. Social insurance systems usually require the users to pay premiums and contributions in order to participate in the benefits, while social security systems may be guaranteed by the state from its own budget.

1. For details on this mutual care and solidarity, see *Ishtirakiyat al-Islam*, Dr. Mustafa as-Siba'i.

Zakat does not make it a condition for any recipient to participate or to have participated in the contributions; *zakat* simply provides relief to those in need and collects funds from whomever has excess.[1] *Zakat* is, in fact, the first system of social security ever enacted in the history of humanity, a system that does not depend on individual voluntary charity but on a governmental institution that collects regular contributions and distributes organised relief to all those who are in need.

This system of *zakat* provides regular relief as well as emergency aid. We read, for example, in the instructions prepared by az-Zuhri for 'Umar ibn 'Abdu'l-'Aziz, "There is a share in it for the ill, the handicapped, and each needy person who cannot provide for himself, a share for the destitute until they can be removed from destitution, a share for those in prison, for those who beg and those who do not, a share to whoever is burdened by debts provided such debts did not arise from disobedience to Allah, a share for every traveller in difficulty. Such travellers should be given food and shelter as well as feed for their transporting animal until they reach home."[2] This system does not cover only needy Muslims, but extends to needy Jews and Christians who live in the Islamic state, as 'Umar indicated by including the elderly Jewish man[3] and the ill Christians in this social insurance.[4]

Social security that provides help without requiring contributions is relatively new to Western society. It appeared for the first time in the Atlantic Treaty between England and the United States in 1941 as a result of the war and the internal turmoil caused by poverty and destitution.[5] It is shameful that researchers and students of social security claim that the idea of social security is a Western invention of the seventeenth century, as claimed by Daniel S. Girk, director of the study circle of the Arab League held in Damascus, 1952.[6] The Islamic system of *zakat* came fourteen centuries ago with complete provision for the poor and needy, organised and

1. *Fi Zilal al-Qur'an*, Sayyid Qutb, vol. 10, p. 81.
2. *Al-Amwal*, pp. 578-580.
3. Ibid., p. 46.
4. *Tarikh al-Baladhuri*, p. 177.
5. *Ad-Daman al-Ijtima'i*, Dr. Sadiq Mahdi, p. 126.
6. *Halqat ad-Dirasat al-Ijtima'iyya,* third session, p. 217.

implemented by the state and financed by a tax imposed on the rich only. It is part of this religion of Islam and its third pillar without which the very faith of a Muslim is incomplete.

Zakat stimulates owners to invest their wealth in order to make up for what is paid out as due *zakat*. This is very apparent in the case of money for the Qur'an warns against hoarding gold and silver. An imposition of a 2.5% charge on wealth is indeed a strong stimulus for owners to invest so that their wealth indeed does not vanish as a result of the repetitive deduction of *zakat* year after year. The Prophet (p) adds, "Invest the wealth of orphans so that it is not diminished by *zakat*.."

Zakat and the spiritual integrity of the nation

Over and above all of that, *zakat* aims at realising the ideals of Muslim society and nourishing the spiritual pillars on which society is founded and by which it is distinctively characterised. As rightly stated by al-Bahi al-Khawli:

> Nations are founded on spiritual and psychological elements in addition to material factors. Indeed, the spiritual factors count for much more in creating unity and vitality in any community. Islam pays great attention to these factors and makes spending out of the income of the community – to nourish and support these factors – one of its major obligations ...
>
> One can distinguish three major factors to which Islam gives special attention. The first is freedom or liberty. One of the objectives of *zakat* is to liberate individuals from the bondage of slavery. For the first time in the history of humanity, the liberation of slaves was made, by Islam, a social obligation for which a certain portion of the community's wealth is to be spent. Secondly, encouraging individuals to carry out projects of public interest and to spend toward smoothing out differences between segments of the community and reconciling individuals and groups in order

> to avoid social unrest... Such actions are encouraged by assigning a share of *zakat* to support those who have to bear financial responsibility for these purposes. Thirdly, spending in the Way of Allah and spreading the sound religion that comes from Him is urged. Fighting in the Way of Allah includes defending the ideals and doctrines for which Allah sent His Messengers and upholding the oneness of Allah and righteousness on earth.[1]

These three areas are essential pillars of the social life of the Muslim community. *Zakat* as an instituted tax is not detached from the principles and worship of the Islamic community, nor is it isolated from its values, morals, politics and defence. In the following sections, we shall look at six major social problems and find how *zakat* contributes to solving them and eliminating their causes. However, in my book on the problem of poverty and its Islamic solution, one may find a detailed analysis of the treatment of each problem individually.

Section One: The problem of the socio-economic gap

The presence of a great concentration of wealth alongside extreme poverty is a major social calamity that Islam does not tolerate in its society. The Qur'an emphasises, *"It is He who created everything on the earth for you."* (2:29) The Arabic word *'jami'a'* used for 'everything' may mean all things created are for you, and/or things created are for all of you.

One of the objectives Islam aims for is the reduction of socio-economic differences by providing support and financial help to the have-nots to bring them closer to the haves. Islam tackles this problem with much of its legislation, social institutions and economic directives in order to achieve justice both in the distribution of wealth and the distribution of income. Allah says, *"Whatever booty*

1. *Al-Ishtirakiyya fi l-Mujtama' al-Islami*, al-Bahi al-Khawli, pp. 141-144.

Allah gives to His Messenger from city dwellers belongs to Allah and to the Messenger and to near relatives and orphans and the very poor and travellers, so that it does not become something which merely circulates among the rich among you." (59:7)

In this section, we are discussing only the role of the institution of *zakat* in reducing economic differences. We must keep in mind that in a society which behaves according to, and is ruled by, Islam, there must necessarily be more people working and a much smaller number of idle persons because of the other means by which Islam discourages idleness and provides employment. *Zakat*, as we have seen earlier, does not only provide relief to the poor but aims also at making the poor own the means of production by giving them the tools and machinery necessary for productive work, so that persons given *zakat* are removed forever from the category of the poor and needy. This is in addition to the necessary shelter and immediate relief that *zakat* provides. We also discussed in the previous part that what is given as *zakat* must become owned by the recipient so that the recipients of *zakat* no longer remain have-nots.

Section Two: The problem of beggars and begging

Islam fights begging through education

Islam implants abhorrence of begging within each Muslim through training and education to the point that asking for any kind of assistance is disliked except in dire need. Abu Muslim al-Khawlani says that he was told by 'Awf ibn Malik, "Seven, eight, or nine of us were with the Messenger of Allah (p) when he said, 'Will you not give your pledge to the Messenger of Allah?' We had given our pledges not a long time previously, so we said, 'We have already given you our pledges!' He repeated that request three times. Then we extended our hands and gave our pledge. One of us asked, 'O Messenger of Allah, we give you our pledge, but on what basis?' The Prophet (p) said, 'That you worship Allah and do not associate any partners with Him whatsoever, that you pray the five prayers, that you listen and obey ..." and he whispered a word and continued, 'and that you do not ask people for anything.'" The narrator of the *hadith* adds, "So it might happen that the whip of one of these people would fall from his hand while riding and he would not ask anyone to hand it to him."[1]

Thawban narrates that the Messenger of Allah (p) asked, "Who will pledge to me that he will not ask people for anything so that I can guarantee him the Garden?" Thawban said, "O Messenger of Allah, I do." The Prophet (p) said, "Do not ask people for anything." Thawban never asked anyone for anything.[2]

Additionally, the Prophet (p) calls the receiving hand the lower hand and the hand of the giver the upper hand. He taught his Companions to be self-sufficient and not to look for anything from the hands of other people. Abu Sa'id says, "Some people from the Ansar asked the Messenger of Allah (p) and he gave to them. They asked him for more and he gave to them until what he had was exhausted. Then the Prophet (p) said, "Whatever I may have of good shall not be withheld from you. But he who restrains himself shall be given self-sustenance from Allah. He who enriches himself, Allah will make rich, and he who trains himself to be patient, Allah will make patient. Nothing one can be given is better than patience.'"[3]

Teachings of the Prophet on self-support

The Messenger of Allah (p) taught his Companions two essential principles. Firstly, work is the source of gaining income and means of sustenance. Muslims are urged to travel through the earth in search of the bounties of Allah through work. Work, manual or otherwise, is better than living on humiliating grants. The Prophet

1. Reported by Muslim, Abu Dawud, an-Nasa'i and Ibn Majah. See *at-Targhib*, vol. 2, Warning against Begging.

2. Reported by Abu Dawud (see ibid.) and by al-Bayhaqi in *Sunan al-Kubra*, vol. 4, p. 197.

3. Reported by the five, Ibn Majah excluded. See *at-Targhib*, ibid. Also reported by al-Bayhaqi, vol. 4, p. 195.

(p) says, "For any of you, taking some rope on your back and bringing a bunch of wood and selling it in order for Allah to preserve, with its value, the dignity of one's face is better than asking people, whether one is given to or denied."[1]

The second principle is that asking people unnecessarily is prohibited because it is undignifying. Muslims are prohibited from resorting to begging for relief except for those who are in desperate need. Anyone who asks while having what satisfies his essential needs will arrive on the Day of Rising with his begging as a scar on his face. This is reiterated in several *hadiths*. Al-Bukhari, Muslim and an-Nasa'i report from Ibn 'Umar that the Prophet (p) said, "None shall persist in begging but will come to Allah with his face stripped of flesh." The authors of the four books on *Sunan* report that the Prophet (p) says, "He who begs while he has sufficient, his begging will appear on the Day of Rising as a scar on his face."

The Prophet (p) was asked what the limit of sufficiency is. He answered, "Fifty dirhams or their equivalent in gold." (The Four) The face is the most honoured part of the human body and that is where the humiliating mark of begging will appear. In another *hadith*, we find, "He who asks while he has one *uqiyya* [equal to 40 dirhams] is overdoing it," (Abu Dawud and an-Nasa'i) and "He who asks yet has sufficient is getting more and more of the Fire or of the fuel of Hell." They said, "O Messenger of Allah, what is sufficient?" He replied, "An amount that gives him lunch and supper." (Abu Dawud) Apparently, this means a person who earns food for a day.

Shah Waliyu'llah ad-Dihlawi comments, "There is no real discrepancy in these *hadiths'* descriptions of the quantity that make up a sufficiency because people have different needs and means of earning: a craftsman is excusable until he finds tools and machines that are needed so he can earn his daily food; a farmer needs different tools at different costs; a merchant needs stock; and for him who earns his living from the *ghanima* by fighting in the Way of Allah, like most of the Companions of the Prophet (p), one *uqiyya* or fifty dirhams are sufficient. On the other hand, a person who

1. Reported by az-Zubayr by al-Bukhari.

earns through carrying loads or selling wood brought in from the mountain, his sufficiency is the requirement of his daily food."[1]

Undoubtedly, there are two limits of sufficiency, one that prohibits begging, and one that makes taking *zakat* forbidden. The former limit is indeed stricter than the latter, because the *Shari'a* is stricter on disallowing begging except in case of extreme necessity.

Practical cure for the problem of begging

The cure for the problem of begging is twofold. The first step is providing suitable jobs for all those who can work. This is one of the responsibilities of the Islamic state towards its citizens. The state must not remain paralysed when faced with the problem of unemployment. Nor must the state keep providing relief from *sadaqa* without rectifying the root of the problem. Throughout the discussion of *zakat* distribution earlier in this book, I repeatedly emphasised the Prophet's (p) saying that "*sadaqa* is not lawful to any rich person, nor to a strong and capable one." Indeed, any relief given to a person who is capable of earning is in a way encouragement of idleness.

The most proper response to such a problem is what the Messenger of Allah (p) did when a person asked him for relief. Anas ibn Malik narrates that a man of the Ansar came asking the Prophet (p) for financial help. The Prophet (p) answered, "Isn't there anything in your house?" The man said, "Yes, a piece of cloth. We use some of it to wear and spread another part to sit on, and a cup from which we drink water." The Prophet said, "Bring them to me." He brought them. The Messenger of Allah (p) took them and announced, "Who will buy these?" A man said, "I will take them for one dirham." The Prophet (p) said, "Who gives more than one dirham?" two or three times. Another man said, "I will take them for two dirhams." The Prophet (p) gave them to him and took the

1. *Hujjat Allah al-Baligha*, vol 2, p. 46. However, at-Tahawi, a Hanafi, argues in his *Mushkil al-Athar* that the Prophet (p) first made his warning strong with regard to the amount that makes asking prohibited, then made it less strong as time went by, until he reached the amount for prohibition that equals five *uqiyyas*, which is the *nisab* of *zakat* on silver. But this view is not supported by any text. Therefore ad-Dihlawi's interpretation seems to be sounder.

two dirhams and gave them to the owner, saying, "Buy food with one of them to send to your family and with the other buy an axe-head and bring it to me."

Then the Messenger of Allah (p) connected with his own hands a piece of wood to the axe as a handle and told the man, "Go and get wood and sell it ... I do not want to see you for fifteen days." The man got wood and sold it. He later came to the Prophet (p) with ten dirhams he had earned. He bought cloth with some and food with some. The Messenger of Allah (p) said, "This is better for you than the begging that comes as a scar on your face on the Day of Rising. Begging is not permissible except to one of three. A destitute poor person, or a person with overwhelming debts, or a person who has to pay ransom for an accidental homicide."[1]

We observe in this story the practical teaching of the Prophet (p) when he did not want that person to take *zakat* because he was able to earn, and such taking is not permissible except as a last resort. The government is responsible for helping to find suitable jobs for all its citizens. This *hadith* outlines the practical steps taken by Islam a long time before any other system known to humanity to wipe out poverty and unemployment. The cure is not only to extend immediate relief, but to provide means of self-support and productive work.

The Prophet (p) taught that one must use all one's abilities, no matter how few they might be, and to exhaust all means of productive work before resorting to begging or asking. He taught that any job that provides lawful sustenance is honourable and dignified, even if it is just fetching firewood on one's back and selling it, so that one is not humiliated by begging. Moreover, the Prophet (p) helped provide the means and tools of work. He did not leave the person alone to find the necessary tools and means. Beyond that, he gave the person a trial period so he would have enough time to examine his ability and the suitability of the job. This is a practical solution, an ideal example set forth by the Messenger of Allah (p),

1. Reported by Abu Dawud, at-Tirmidhi, an-Nasa'i and Ibn Majah. At-Tirmidhi comments, "This is a good *hadith* which I do not know except through al-Akhdar ibn 'Ajlan about whom Yahya ibn Ma'in says, 'He is good,' and Abu Hatim says, 'He writes his narrations.'" See *Mukhtasar Sunan Abi Dawud* by al-Mundhiri, vol. 2, pp. 239-240.

an example that we have to follow step by step to solve the problem of unemployment and begging.[1]

The role which *zakat* can play in this regard is obvious. It can provide the unemployed with the necessary tools, machinery and capital for productive work, as was explained in the part on *zakat* distribution. *Zakat* can also fund job training or job rehabilitation programmes. Above all, it can establish collective projects and industries run by poor and formerly employed workers.

The second part of Islam's cure for begging is social insurance for those who have no income. Such persons are guaranteed a minimum standard of living suitable to a given Islamic society. Unemployment may be caused by either of two reasons: physical incapability caused by age, sickness or handicap, or the inability to find a job. People in the former group are supported by *zakat* funds as long as they are incapable of earning. People who are unable to find work that produces a lawful income, in spite of their will and search, because of general economic depression or other economic and non-economic factors must also be supported by *zakat*.

Ahmad and others report the story of the two men who asked the Prophet (p) for help from *zakat*. The Messenger looked them up and down and found them strong and capable. He said, "I will give to you if you like, but there is no share in it for the rich or the strong who can earn." It is the earner who has no share in *zakat* and not the capable person who does not find means of earning.

Section Three: Brotherhood is an essential objective of Islam

Spreading brotherhood among the children of Adam in general and members of Muslim society in particular is one of the basic objectives of Islam. Social solidarity, social security and mutual co-operation strengthen brotherhood. No doubt there is a continuous need for reconciling people who involve themselves in disputes and feuds.

1. Al-Qardawi, *Mushkilat al-Faqr wa kayfa 'Alajaha'l-Islam.*

In the first Islamic society established by the Prophet in Madina, we are given an ideal picture of brotherhood, mutual love and care, in spite of the tribal and economic rivalry that existed before Islam and in spite of the ethnic and cultural differences between the *Muhajirun*, who were from the ‘Adnani branch of Arabs, and the *Ansar*, who lived in Madina before the emigration and were from the Qahtani branch of Arabs. The *Ansar* themselves were composed of two major tribes that had been fighting each other in the city for decades, in addition to a few individuals from backgrounds totally alien to both *Muhajirun* and *Ansar*, such as the Abyssinian Bilal, the Persian Salman, and the Byzantine Suhayb. On top of that, Madinan society included rough bedouins like Abu Dharr side by side with urbanites raised in luxury like Mus‘ab ibn ‘Umayr.

This society was woven into a brotherhood in a unique manner whereby each loved for his brother exactly what he loved for himself. The Qur'an describes this situation: *"It is for the poor of the Muhajirun, who were driven from their homes and wealth, desiring the favour and the pleasure of Allah and supporting Allah and His Messenger. Such people are the truly sincere. Those who were already settled in the abode, and in belief, before they came, love those who have emigrated to them and do not find in their breasts any need for what they have been given and prefer them to themselves even if they themselves are in want. It is the people who are safe-guarded from the avarice of their own selves who are the successful."* (59:8-9)

Islam legislates for real life

Although this ideal brotherhood was realised in the actual life of the first Islamic society, Islam as a way of life legislates for human life without disregarding the fact that human beings sin, make mistakes, have feuds and disputes, which may go as far as destruction of property, bloodshed and taking other people's resources.

Feuds that reach the stage of fighting are as old as humanity itself. The Qur'an tells us that the angels asked Allah when He created Adam, *"Why put on it one who will cause corruption on it and shed blood when we glorify Your praise and proclaim Your purity?"* (2:30) The story of the two sons of Adam is told in the Qur'an:

> *"Recite to them the true account of Adam's two sons: when they offered a sacrifice and it was accepted from one of them but not accepted from the other. The one said, 'I shall kill you.' The other said, 'Allah only accepts from the godfearing. Even if you do raise your hand against me to kill me, I am not going to raise my hand against you to kill you. Truly I fear Allah, the Lord of all the worlds. I want you to take on my wrongdoing and your wrongdoing and so become one of the Companions of the Fire. That is the repayment of the wrongdoers.' So his lower self persuaded him to kill his brother, and he killed him and became one of the lost. Then Allah sent a crow which scratched at the earth to show him how to conceal his brother's corpse. He said, 'O woe is me! Am I not even able to be like this crow and conceal my brother's corpse?" And he became one of the bitterly remorseful."* (5:30-34)

Since feuds, disputes and even fighting are facts of human life, the realism of Islam requires that these problems be addressed. Reconciling differences among people and removing factors that cause feuds and may lead to fighting is the collective responsibility of the community and the entire society. The Messenger (p) says, "Mischief in relations among people is indeed the razor." (Abu Dawud and at-Tirmidhi) In another version he continues, "I do not say it shaves off hair, but it shaves off religion."[1]

The action of reconciling differences among individuals, including husband and wife, so that they do not grow into big feuds is in fact a deed of the righteous. Allah says about breaches between husband and wife, *"If you fear a breach between a couple, send an arbiter from his people and an arbiter from her people. If the couple desire to put things right, Allah will bring about a reconciliation between them. Allah is All-Knowing, All-Aware."* (4:35)

1. This increment in the *hadith* is mentioned by at-Tirmidhi without a chain of narrators.

On the social level, when differences exist, Allah says, *"If two parties of the believers fight, make peace between them. But if one of them unjustly attacks the other, fight the attackers until they revert to Allah's command. If they revert, make peace between them with justice, and be even-handed. Allah loves those who are even-handed. All believers are brothers, so make peace between your brothers and show fear of Allah so that perhaps you may gain mercy."* (49:9-10)

Allah encourages reconciliation and making peace among people in more than one place in the Qur'an: *"So show fear of Allah and put things right between you. Obey Allah and His Messenger if you are believers"* (8:1), and *"There is no good in much of their secret talk – except in the case of those who enjoin* sadaqa, *or what is right, or putting things right between people. If anyone does that, seeking the pleasure of Allah, We will give him an immense reward."* (4:114) The Messenger (p) emphasises this and encourages bringing peace and reconciliation between quarrelling people. He says, "Shall I not guide you to what is higher in degree than prayer, fasting and charity? It is reconciling people [who have quarrelled], since feud among people is the razor."[1]

However, such reconciliation may require financial sacrifices, since many differences arise due to financial matters, and many others can be settled by paying ransoms. *Zakat* indeed offers a source for such payment under the title of the share of those in debt. Arbiters and mediators may accept such financial responsibility on their own shoulders knowing that the *zakat* fund will pay back such money.

The *hadith* of Qabisa ibn al-Mukhariq al-Hilali shows that he accepted certain financial charges in reconciling some disputing groups and came to the Prophet (p) seeking help. The Prophet told him to stay until the *sadaqa* came, "...so we can give you some money." Then the Prophet (p) told him that any person who carries such a financial burden in reconciling others is allowed to ask until he recovers the amount that he accepted responsibility for. Then he must stop asking. (Reported by Ahmad and Muslim) That is the case to the extent that mediators and arbiters who reconcile

1. Reported in Abu Dawud's chapter on manners, at-Tirmidhi's chapter on the description of the Resurrection. The latter comments, "It is sound."

differences between People of the Pledge, whether Christians or Jews, can also be compensated from *zakat* funds.[1]

A question arises as to whether the compensation may be paid directly to the feuding parties, or whether the reconcilers must first pay out of their own wealth and then ask for compensation? It seems from the words of jurists' texts that reconcilers must first pay out of their own wealth so as to be counted under the category of those under financial burdens and be paid back from *zakat* funds.[2] However, I believe that the spirit of the Qur'anic *ayat* and the purpose aimed at by the *Shari'a* in legislating a share for this purpose do not prevent paying the mediators or mediating committees first, then allowing those people to pay the parties that are being reconciled.

Section Four: The problem of accidents and natural calamities

Security and economic sufficiency

Islam attempts to guarantee each person in Islamic society sufficiency of sustenance and security from fear, so that each human being can devote a good part of his or her energy to worshipping Allah. In showing the tribe of Quraysh how great His bounty was to them, Allah says, *"In acknowledgement of the established tradition of Quraysh, their tradition of the winter and summer caravans: let them worship the Lord of this House who has preserved them from hunger and secured them from fear."* (106:1-4) The worst that may happen to a person or a group of people is the loss of either of these two bounties. Allah says, *"Allah makes a likeness of a city which was safe and at peace, its provision coming to it plentifully from every side. Then it showed ingratitude for Allah's blessings so Allah made it wear the robe of hunger and fear for what it did."* (16:112)

1. *Matalib Uli'n-Nuha*, vol. 2, p. 143.

2. In *Ghayat al-Muntaha* and its commentary, it is stated that the sixth category is a person who borrows for reconciling others, even if he is rich, before he pays from his own wealth. See ibid., p. 144.

Islamic law guarantees every person in the Islamic state, Muslim or not, a suitable standard of living, whereby food, clothing and shelter are available in addition to health care and education. It was shown earlier that the system of *zakat* aims at satisfying the poor and the needy and their families for life. But natural disaster may unexpectedly befall any person, wealthy or not, whether farmer, merchant, industrialist or landlord. Natural disasters may be common to a whole area, like drought, flood, insecticide contamination, explosions, or they may be individual, such as car accidents, fires or loss of assets or sources of income.

Such incidents have brought about in the West the rise of insurance and insurance companies in the last few centuries. But Islamic society had, through the public treasury of the state, its own insurance system against such accidents and happenings. This Islamic system of insurance is not based on charity and voluntary contributions or on people's charity, in spite of the fact that such charity is encouraged very much by Islamic teachings. The Prophet taught his Companions when a disaster struck a man, "Give him charity," so people gave to him.[1]

"People in debt" includes those afflicted by disaster

Individuals struck by natural disasters or accidents are not left to voluntary charity alone. They are given a share in the proceeds of *zakat*. The Prophet told Qabisa, "Asking is not permissible, except in three cases." The Prophet mentioned among them a man struck by a disaster that wipes out his wealth. Early commentators on the Qur'an include in the category of persons in debt (*al-gharimin*) "he whose house caught fire or whose wealth was wiped out by flood or who has debts that burden his family."

How much are such persons given?

In the *hadith* mentioned above, the Prophet (p) says such a person may ask, "until he secures sufficiency of sustenance." This

1. Reported by Ahmad, vol. 3, p. 36, by Muslim in the book on crop sharing, by Abu Dawud and an-Nasa'i in the chapter on sales, by at-Tirmidhi in his chapter on *zakat*, and by Ibn Majah in his chapter on rulings.

undoubtedly differs from one person to another, depending on factors such as the general standards of living, size of family, and social status. For a merchant whose stock is burned, for example, securing sustenance of living may require purchasing a minimum amount of stock sufficient for his type of business. Some jurists even argue that such people must be given amounts sufficient to put them back on their feet at the level they had before the accident took place.[1]

I believe that what determines how much persons afflicted by disasters should be given depends on the availability of funds in the *zakat* agency and on several other factors, namely other needs that draw on these funds. Lastly, it must be emphasised that the rural areas of today's Muslim countries desperately need such Islamic insurance against the financial aftermath of natural disasters and drought, because of predominant poverty and insufficiency of voluntary charity to take total responsibility for such insurance.

Section Five: The problem of involuntary celibacy

There is no monasticism in Islam

Islam, inasmuch as it does not allow an unlimited, haphazard response to, and practice of, the sexual drive, does not allow the other extreme either and does not entertain any tendency to voluntary celibacy. Suppression of the sexual drive or its elimination is not accepted by Islam which encourages marriage and forbids taking vows of celibacy and castration. A Muslim who is able to marry is not permitted to live in celibacy claiming that he is devoted to the adoration and worship of Allah.

The Prophet (p) once noted an inclination toward celibacy among some of his Companions. He immediately declared that this is an unacceptable deviation from Islam and his *Sunna*. He said, "I am indeed the most knowledgeable among you about Allah's

1. Mentioned by al-Ghazali in *al-Ihya'*, part four, chapter one.]

teachings and the one who fears Him most, but I stand in prayer in the night and I sleep. I fast and I eat, and I marry women. He who desires other than my way does not belong with me." (al-Bukhari) Sa'd ibn Abi Waqqas narrates, "The Messenger of Allah (p) rejected the vow of celibacy which 'Uthman ibn Maz'un made. If he had allowed him, we would have castrated ourselves." (al-Bukhari) Furthermore, the Prophet (p) called on youths, "O young people, whoever can afford marriage among you must marry, since marriage is better for lowering the gaze and protecting chastity." (al-Bukhari) Some scholars deduce that marriage is obligatory on each Muslim and refraining from marrying is not permissible for anyone who has the means to marry.

Muslims must not avoid marriage because of constraint in their means or because of the burden of its responsibilities. Allah promises enrichment to those who look to marriage as a means of human satisfaction and protection against the unlawful fulfilment of the sexual drive. Allah says, *"Marry off those among you who are unmarried and those of your slaves and slave girls who are righteous. If they are poor Allah will enrich them from His bounty. Allah is All-Encompassing, All-Knowing."* (24:32) The Prophet (p) says, "Three have the right to help from Allah: a man who seeks marriage in order to satisfy himself and protect his chastity, a slave who has a contract for freeing himself for a certain amount of money who intends to fulfil his duty, and a fighter in the Way of Allah."[1]

The institution of *zakat* is one of the favours Allah has given Islamic society. *Zakat* must be used to help provide marriage expenses for those who are in need, since marriage is encouraged as a human institution that helps lower the gaze and protect the chastity, and above all, helps establish the Muslim family. Allah says, *"Among His Signs is that He created spouses for you of your own kind so that you might find tranquillity in them. And He has placed affection and compassion between you. There are certainly Signs in that for people who reflect."* (30:21)

The role of the *zakat* institution in aiding marriage is not an innovation of mine but was decided by past leading scholars. They

1. Reported by Ahmad, an-Nasa'i, at-Tirmidhi, Ibn Majah and al-Hakim from Abu Hurayra via a sound chain, as stated in *at-Taysir*, vol. 1, p. 474.

declare that getting married is included in provision of sufficiency of sustenance and argue that providing unmarried poor persons with financial help for getting married is an integral part of providing essential needs.

Section Six: The problem of the homeless

It was shown earlier that help for travellers is one of the eight goals of *zakat* disbursement. In several places in the Qur'an, Allah encourages taking care of travellers. Islam prefers every person to have a home and belong to a family, and does not like anyone to be homeless. Consequently, adequate shelter for a person and his or her family is included under the essential needs, for the satisfaction of which *zakat* is imposed by Allah. An-Nawawi explains that essential needs include food, clothing, residence and everything that is indispensable for life, at a level that suits the receiver and his or her social status without extravagance or miserliness. Ibn Hazm adds, "It is an obligation for the rich people of every region to provide for all the needs of the poor in that region. If they do not fulfil this, the government must force them to do so. If the proceeds of *zakat* and *fay* are not sufficient, satisfaction of the needs for food, clothing for the summer and winter, and shelter that protects from the sun, the rain and the eyes of passers-by must nevertheless still be provided from the wealth of the rich."[1]

In the chapter on travellers in Part Four of this book, we noted that foundlings are also covered in the benefits of *zakat*, since they are indeed 'children of the street'.

1. *Al-Muhalla*, vol. 6, p. 156.

Part Seven
Zakat al-Fitr

Chapter One

Meaning, Rulings and Justification of *Zakat al-Fitr*

The meaning of *zakat al-fitr*

This *zakat* is caused by breaking the fasting at the end of Ramadan. It is sometimes called *sadaqat al-fitr*. It was shown earlier that the term *'sadaqa'* is used to mean *zakat* in the Qur'an, *Sunna*, and *Shari'a*. It is also called *zakat al-fitra* (human nature) on the basis that it is derived from the nature of the human creature. The amount paid is sometimes called *'fitra'* which is a derived term used only by one jurist.[1]

Zakat al-fitr was obliged in the second year of *Hijra*, the same year that fasting Ramadan was made obligatory,[2] in order to purify and sanctify those who fasted and to bring happiness to the poor on the day of the *'Id*.

Distinct from other forms of *zakat*, *zakat al-fitr* is levied on persons and not on wealth or income. This means there are drastic differences in the conditions of accountability for *zakat*, as will be seen in Chapter Two.

---

1. In his commentary, Ibn 'Abidin says, "The use of the word *'fitra'* to mean *zakat al-fitr* is not eloquent. It is used only colloquially and is considered a mistake by some scholars. In *al-Qamus*, *al-fitra* is listed as *zakat al-fitr* but is considered to be one of the errors in *al-Qamus* which is caused by confusing the religious and linguistic meanings. An-Nawawi says it is a derived noun, probably from *fitra*, which means 'nature' or 'creation'. Al-Abhari says *fitra* is the *zakat* of natural creation. In brief, the word *fitra* is an Arabic word that means created nature; it is used for *zakat al-fitr* because this is a *zakat* on creatures or persons themselves. It is used in the *Shari'a* to mean *zakat al-fitr* or the amount paid as *zakat al-fitr*. See *Radd al-Muhtar*, vol. 2, p, 78.

2. *Al-Mirqat*, vol. 4, p. 159.

The obligation of *zakat al-fitr*

The Group reports from Ibn 'Umar, "The Messenger of Allah (p) imposed the *zakat* of breaking the fast of Ramadan, making it one *sa'* of dates or one *sa'* of barley, on every Muslim, free or slave, male or female."[1] The majority of scholars, ancient and modern, understand the word 'imposed' to indicate obligation. Thus *zakat al-fitr* is an obligation in the *Shari'a* included in the general obligation of the *ayat*, "...and give *zakat*." (2:110, 4:77) The Prophet (p) called it *zakat* and imposed it on every Muslim. Some other sound versions of the *hadith* mention, "The Messenger of Allah (p) commanded..." which clearly shows the obligatory nature of this *zakat*.[2] Abu'l-'Aliya, 'Ata', and Ibn Sirin, as mentioned in al-Bukhari, state that this *zakat* is obligatory.[3] This is also the view of Malik, ash-Shafi'i and Ahmad.

Hanafis, who distinguish between the obligation (*fard*, which is imposed by a clear-cut text such as the Qur'an) and the requirement (*wajib*, which is imposed by texts which are not clear-cut, such as single chain *hadiths*), consider *zakat al-fitr* only *wajib*. According to Hanafis, denying a *fard* constitutes disbelief, whereas denying a *wajib* does not, since *wajib* for them is a practical obligation only, while *fard* is an ideological obligation. The other three schools do not make such a distinction, so the matter is simply a difference in definitions.[4]

There is a Maliki report from Ashhab that *zakat al-fitr* is a 'confirmed *sunna*'.[5] This is also the opinion of some Zahiris and Ibn al-

1. Mentioned in *al-Muntaqa*. See *Nayl al-Awtar*, vol. 4, p. 179.

2. *Sharh an-Nawawi*, vol. 7, p. 58, and *al-Muhalla*, vol. 6, p. 119.

3. He mentions it as suspended. In *al-Fath*, Ibn Hajar says that 'Abdu'r-Razzaq connects it from Ibn Jurayj from 'Ata', and Ibn Abi Shayba from 'Asim al-Ahwal from the other two. Al-Bukhari only mentions these names because they clearly state it is obligatory. Otherwise Ibn al-Mundhir quotes *ijma'* on it.

4. Ibn al-Humam says, "In the ultimate analysis, there is no difference between them since, according to the other schools, the nature of this obligation does not imply that he who denies it becomes a unbeliever, and this is the meaning of 'requirement' in our school. Hanafis believe it is only *wajib* because of dispute on the degree of confirmation of its texts and their indication." See *al-Mirqat*, vol. 4, p. 160

5. In *al-Muhalla*, vol. 6, p. 118, Ibn Hazm writes that Malik says that it is not obligatory, but the late Shaykh Shakir notes, "This is an error on the part of Ibn

Labban, who is a Shafi'i, on the grounds that the word "*farada*" (imposed) originally means "to estimate" linguistically, but this is disproved by what is stated at the beginning of this section. Moreover, Ibn Daqiq al-'Id says, "Linguistically, '*farada*' originally meant 'to estimate', but it is used in the *Shari'a* to mean 'to obligate', so it is better to choose this meaning." Ibn al-Humam says, "It is a must to take the meaning of the words of the Legislator that is used in the *Shari'a*, except when there is evidence to the contrary, especially in this case, in light of the other version reported by al-Bukhari and Muslim in which the word '*amara*' (commanded) is used."

The obligatory nature of *zakat al-fitr* is further supported by the fact that it is called *zakat*. This is so to the extent that, after mentioning the view of Ibn al-Labban, an-Nawawi writes, "This is a rejected and deviant opinion; it is clearly erroneous." Ibn Rahawayh says the obligation of *zakat al-fitr* is like *ijma'*, and al-Mundhiri quotes, "It is *ijma'*." But the statement of Ibn Rahawayh is apparently more precise, especially since Ibrahim ibn 'Aliya and Abu Bakr al-Asamm believe that this *zakat* was annulled when regular *zakat* was obligated. They support this view with a *hadith* reported by Ahmad and an-Nasa'i that when Qays ibn Sa'd ibn 'Ubada was asked about *zakat al-fitr*, he said, "The Messenger of Allah (p) ordained *zakat al-fitr* before *zakat* was commanded. When the *zakat* ordinance was revealed, he neither ordered us nor prevented us from continuing to pay *zakat al-fitr*, but we still do it." The chain of this *hadith* is disputed since it has an unknown narrator, according to Ibn Hajar.[1] Even if we assume it is correct, the *hadith* does not indicate any annulment of a *zakat* at breaking the fast, since revealing an obligation does not imply abolishing a previ-

Hazm, since Malik clearly says in *al-Muwatta'* that *zakat al-fitr* is obligatory on bedouins as well as on urban dwellers, because the Messenger 'imposed *zakat al-fitr* after Ramadan.'" This is also stated by Ibn Rushd in *Bidayat al-Mujtahid*, vol. 1, p. 269.

1. Followed by as-Suyuti in *Sharh an-Nasa'i* and ash-Shawkani in *Nayl al-Awtar*, vol. 4, p. 180, but Shaykh Shakir is surprised by the statement of Ibn Hajar and those who follow him, and, after mentioning the *hadith* via two chains, says, "Both chains are sound; they have no unknown person." Notes on *al-Muhalla*, vol. 6, p. 119.

ous one.[1] The original order mentioned in the *hadith* itself is still valid. An annulment requires a text.

Accordingly, it is established among Muslims that *zakat al-fitr* is obligatory, since the deviant view to the contrary is opposed by *ijma'* before and after it,[2] and Schacht's claim is nonsense.[3]

Justification for *zakat al-fitr*

Ibn 'Abbas says, "The Messenger of Allah (p) imposed *zakat al-fitr* as a purification of the faster from any vain talk and bad action indulged in during the fast and as a food provision for the needy."[3] The worshipper may be liable during Ramadan for vain, ill-advised words, or indecent feelings that require purification since perfect fasting is not merely abstention from food and drink, but abstention from wrong-doing and offensive speech to others. Pure fasting must not be polluted by any such impurities which is an impossible feat for a human being. Thus *zakat al-fitr* is obliged to make up for any impurities and imperfections in fasting, just like voluntary and

1. *Fath al-Bari*, vol. 4, pp. 110-111, *al-Mirqat*, vol. 4, pp. 159-160, *al-Muhalla*, vol. 6, pp. 118-119, *ar-Rawda* by an-Nawawi, vol. 2, p. 291, *Sharh Muslim*, vol. 7, p. 58, *Nayl al-Awtar*, vol. 4, p. 180, and *al-Fath ar-Rabbani*, vol. 9, pp. 134-137.

2. *Al-Bahr az-Zakhkhar*, vol. 2, p. 195.

3. In the *Encyclopaedia of Islam*, Schacht writes, "Jurists differ on whether *zakat al-fitr* is considered obligatory. It is only *Sunna* according to Malikis." This is grossly erroneous. Jurists are almost in total agreement that it is obligatory. Ibn al-Mundhir quotes *ijma'* on this obligation, though he knew of the presence of a disregarded deviant view expressed by one or two persons. The accepted view among Malikis is the obligatory nature of this *zakat*. See, for example, *Bulghat as-Salik*, vol. 1, p. 237, and *ash-Sharh al-Kabir* with the notes of ad-Dusuqi, vol. 1, p. 504. The view of Ashhab is rejected in the Maliki school itself. Schacht is misled by the sentence of Ibn Abi Zayd in *ar-Risala* that "*Zakat al-fitr* is an obligatory *sunna* imposed by the Prophet (p)." The commentators explain that the author means an obligation that came in the *Sunna* (as opposed to the Qur'an). See *Sharh ar-Risala*, Zarruq, vol. 1, p. 341. Malik clearly states in *al-Muwatta'* that *zakat al-fitr* is obligatory.

3. Reported by Abu Dawud in the chapter on *zakat al-fitr*; he and al-Mundhiri make no comment. Al-Hakim reports the same *hadith* and notes, correct as per the conditions of al-Bukhari. This is approved by adh-Dhahabi, vol. 1, p. 409. It is also reported by Ibn Majah, al-Bayhaqi, p. 163, and ad-Daraqutni, p. 219. The latter says, "No flaws exist in its chain of narrators." See *al-Mirqat*, vol. 4, p. 173, and *Nasb ar-Raya*, vol. 2, p. 411.

sunna prayers make up for imperfections in obligatory prayers.[1]

In addition, the *'id* is a day of joy, happiness and feasting, and the poor need help to bring the same happiness to their children and households. *Zakat al-fitr* is obliged to provide food for the poor on the day of *'id*. In another *hadith*, the Prophet is reported to have said, "Make them [the poor] satisfied on this day."[2]

1. *Nihayat al-Muhtaj*, vol. 2, p. 108.

2. The author of *Nayl al-Awtar* says it is reported by al-Bayhaqi and ad-Daraqutni from Ibn 'Umar. Al-Bayhaqi's version is "Make them satisfied this day, so they do not go around begging." Ibn Sa'd in *at-Tabaqat* also reports it from 'A'isha and Abu Sa'id, vol. 4, p. 186. See *Nasb ar-Raya*, vol. 2, p. 432, and the notes on al-*Muhalla*, vol. 6, p. 120.

Chapter Two

On Whom is *Zakat al-Fitr* Obliged?

The *hadith* reported by the group from Ibn 'Umar reads, "The Messenger of Allah p) imposed *zakat al-fitr* on every Muslim, free or slave, male or female," and in a version given by al-Bukhari, Ibn 'Umar says, "The Messenger of Allah (p) imposed ... on every Muslim, slave or free, male or female, young or old." Abu Hurayra says *zakat al-fitr* is due "on every Muslim, free or slave, male or female, young or old, poor or rich..."[1] Although these are Abu Hurayra's words, such a view is not a matter of personal opinion, so it must be taken from the Prophet (p).

These *hadiths* indicate that *zakat al-fitr* is a general obligation on all Muslim individuals, regardless of freedom, sex, age, wealth, or urban or bedouin status. Az-Zuhri, Rabi'a and al-Layth believe it is obligatory only on the urban population, i.e. nomads are exempt, but the wording of the *hadiths* disproves their view.[2] Ibn Hazm reports a similar view from 'Ata' and adds that the Messenger of Allah (p) did not make any exception.[3]

Women

The phrase in the *hadith* "male or female" implies that *zakat al-fitr* is obligatory for all women, married or not. This is the view of Abu Hanifa and the Zahiris. They continue that women must pay it from their own wealth.[4] The other three leading imams as well as al-Layth and Ishaq believe that husbands are required to pay it on behalf of their wives because *zakat al-fitr* is related to provision of

1. Reported by al-Bukhari, Muslim, Ahmad and an-Nasa'i. See *al-Fath ar-Rabbani*, vol. 9, p. 139, *hadith* no. 186.

2. *Nayl al-Awtar*, vol. 4, p. 181.

3. *Al-Muhalla*, vol. 6, p. 131.

4. *Al-Fath ar-Rabbani*, vol. 9, p. 140, *hadith* no. 187.

sustenance. Ibn Hajar argues that this view is disputed since its proponents contradict themselves in the case of a slave wife when the husband is financially unable, claiming that the wife's *zakat al-fitr* must be paid by her master while he is not obliged to spend on her sustenance. Also when the wife is not a Muslim, the husband is unanimously required to spend for her sustenance but not for *zakat al-fitr* on her behalf.

Ash-Shafi'i presents a *mursal hadith* via Muhammad ibn 'Ali al-Baqir, "Pay *sadaqa al-fitr* on behalf of those you provide for."[1] However, this *hadith* is very weak and does not stand up in argument.[2] The Imami school agrees with the Shafi'is.[3] Al-Layth adds that it must also be paid on behalf of a labourer whose wage is not defined,[4] while the Zaydis say the payer is only required to give *zakat al-fitr* on behalf on those whose sustenance he provides if they are related by kin, marriage or ownership.[5]

Children

The phrase "young or old" in the *hadith* indicates that *zakat al-fitr* is obligated on children out of their own funds if they have any. A guardian is required to pay it out of the wealth of children in his charge. If the child has no funds, the guardian must pay it like maintenance. This is the opinion of the majority. Ash-Shaybani says only a father is obliged to pay it and if a child has no father no

1. Also reported by al-Bayhaqi, vol. 4, p. 161, via the same chain and he adds 'Ali. It is interrupted. Ibn Hazm says this is very surprising since ash-Shafi'i, who does not accept *mursal hadiths*, presents the worst *mursal* which is via Ibn Abi Yahya. See *al-Muhalla*, vol. 6, p. 137. Al-Bayhaqi also reports the same from Ibn 'Umar via a not strong chain, vol. 4, p. 161. Ad-Daraqutni also reports it from him. See *Nayl al-Awtar*, vol. 4, p. 181. Al-Bayhaqi reports from 'Ali, "You must give *zakat al-fitr* on behalf of all males or females whom you are obliged to maintain." In this chain we find 'Abdu'l-A'la, who is not strong according to al-Bayhaqi, but this *hadith* is supported by the previous one. See *al-Bahr*, vol. 2, p. 199, and *Nasb ar-Raya*, vol. 2, p 413.

2. *Al-Jawhar an-Naqi* with *as-Sunan al-Kubra*, vol. 4, p. 160.

3. *Fiqh al-Imam Ja'far*, vol. 2, pp. 103-104.

4. *Al-Muhalla*, vol 6, p. 127.

5. *Al-Bahr*, vol. 2, p. 199.

zakat al-fitr is due.[1] Sa'id ibn al-Musayyab and al-Hasan al-Basri say that it is not obliged on people who do not fast because it is obliged as a purification and a child does not need that. Ibn 'Abbas says, "The Messenger of Allah (p) imposed *zakat al-fitr* as a purification for whoever fasts from vain talk and impurities." This opinion is disputed on the ground that most of those obligated usually fast,[2] and that *zakat al-fitr* is also obligated to feed the poor, a purpose better achieved if it is obligated on young and old.

Unborn babies

No *zakat* is obliged on a foetus, according to the majority of jurists. Ibn Hazm disagrees, saying that if the foetus completes one hundred and twenty days before the dawn of the last day of Ramadan, *zakat al-fitr* must be paid on its behalf. The hundred and twenty days is taken from the *hadith* which indicates that it is at this age that the soul is blown into the foetus. Ibn Hazm argues that a foetus is included by the word of the Prophet "young" and reports that 'Uthman ibn 'Affan used to pay *zakat al-fitr* on behalf of the young, old and unborn babies. Abu Qilaba says, "They used to like paying *zakat al-fitr* on behalf of the young, the old and the foetus in the womb." Ibn Hazm clarifies that Abu Qilaba met many Companions and narrates from them. Sulayman ibn Yasar answered "Yes," to a question about *zakat al-fitr* on behalf of the foetus and adds, "No Companion is known to have differed with 'Uthman on this issue."[3]

The truth is that there is no evidence on the obligation of paying *zakat al-fitr* on unborn babies in what Ibn Hazm quotes, and it is a gross extension to include the foetus in the meaning of the word "young". 'Uthman's action is not indicative of the obligation although it may mean encouragement of this action. Ash-Shawkani quotes Ibn al-Mundhir as reporting *ijma'* that it is not obligatory on

1. Ibid., p. 135, *Nayl al-Awtar*, vol. 4, pp. 180-181, and *al-Muhalla*, vol. 6, p. 137.

2. Ibid.

3. *Al-Muhalla*, vol. 6, p. 132.

unborn babies, and Ahmad considers this payment desirable but not obligatory.[1]

Conditions of *zakat*

The phrase "a free man or slave" in the *hadith* is inclusive of the poor; Abu Hurayra explicitly mentions the poor in his statement. According, the three leading jurists, along with the majority, believe that there are only two conditions of *zakat*, namely Islam and owning the amount of *zakat al-fitr* above what is needed as provision for the day of the *'id* for the person and his family. Ash-Shawkani notes that this is correct because the texts are general and inclusive of the rich and poor. The terms of *zakat* are not subject to human opinion in this case, since the purpose of this *zakat* is cleansing of vain talk, etc., and this includes the poor and the rich. On the other hand, the condition of owning food for the day of the *'id* is indispensable because, without this condition, the person deserves to receive *zakat al-fitr* and to be satisfied on the day.[2]

Abu Hanifa and his disciples disagree. They require the condition of the *nisab* for ordinary *zakat* on the basis of the generality of the *hadith* in al-Bukhari and an-Nasa'i, "No *sadaqa* is obliged except out of wealth,"[3] and wealth is defined by owning the *nisab* so, by analogy, they connect *zakat al-fitr* with other forms of *zakat* that all require the *nisab*. This is challenged on the grounds that this *hadith* does not make this condition an obligation, especially the version reported by Abu Dawud: "The best *sadaqa* is that given from wealth."[4] Moreover, another *hadith* reported by Abu Dawud and al-Hakim from Abu Hurayra stands in opposition since it reads, "The best *sadaqa* is the effort of a person who has little." The latter is supported by yet another *hadith* reported by at-Tabarani from

1. *Nayl al-Awtar*, vol. 4, p. 181.

2. Ibid., p. 186.

3. He reports it as suspended in the other chapter on the last will in his *Sahih* collection. His confirmed suspended reports are considered sound according to the majority of jurists, except Ibn Hazm.

4. Ash-Shawkani only mentions Abu Dawud, but the *hadith* is reported by al-Bukhari, chapter on expenses, an-Nasa'i, chapter on *zakat*, Ahmad in *al-Musnad*, vol. 2, p. 345, and Muslim in his chapter on *zakat*.

Abu Umama, "The best *sadaqa* is that which is given secretly to a poor person or by someone who has little."

Additionally, there is the *hadith* reported by an-Nasa'i, Ibn Khuzayma, al-Hakim (who grades it sound according to Muslim's conditions) and by Ibn Hibban, in his sound collection, from Abu Hurayra that the Prophet (p) said, "One dirham is better than a hundred thousand dirhams!" A man said, "O Messenger of Allah, how could it be?" He answered, "A man who has plenty of wealth, gives as charity a hundred thousand dirhams out of its surpluses, but a man who has only two dirhams gives as charity one dirham, which is one-half of his wealth."

Basing the argument on an analogy with the *zakat* due on wealth is not valid, as ash-Shawkani states, because it is forming an analogy between two dissimilar things since *zakat al-fitr* is connected to individuals whereas *zakat* proper is connected to wealth.[1] As for their statement that a wealthy man owns the *nisab* whereas a poor man has no wealth and therefore it is not obliged on him, they are refuted by the general texts of the sound *hadiths* related that oblige *zakat al-fitr* on every Muslim, rich or poor.

That is explicitly stated by Abu Hurayra in his *hadith*, "rich or poor" as well as what Ahmad and Abu Dawud relate from Tha'laba ibn Abi Saghir from his father that the Messenger of Allah (p) said, "Pay *sadaqat al-fitr* – one *sa'* of wheat or barley – on every person, young or old, free or slave, rich or poor, male or female. As for those of you who are wealthy, Allah will purify their wealth, and as for the poor, Allah will return to him more than he gave." Furthermore, Ibn Qudama adds that since this *sadaqa al-fitr* is a financial obligation which is not proportional to wealth, the *nisab* need not be considered. The *hadith* about no *sadaqa* being due except out of wealth should be applicable to *zakat* on *mal* wealth only.[2]

In my personal opinion, *zakat al-fitr* is obligatory for the poor as well as the rich because, in addition to the preceding arguments, there is the objective of training everyone to give and spend in obedience to Allah even just a little bit once every year. Allah

1. *Nayl al-Awtar*, vol. 4, pp. 185-186.
2. *Al-Mughni*, vol. 3, p. 74.

describes the believers who fear Allah as *"those who give in times of both ease and hardship."* (3:124) For the same reason, I also prefer the view of Abu Hanifa obligating *zakat al-fitr* on women out of their own wealth.

Lastly, it should be noted that the necessary condition of capability to pay *zakat al-fitr* must not be overlooked. Capability is defined as owning the amount of *zakat* in excess of the food of the day of the *'Id* and other necessities, such as shelter, clothing, furniture and utensils. Anything in excess of essential needs which can be liquidated for payment of *zakat al-fitr* is considered a fulfilment of this condition. Books needed for work, study or research, usual and customary amounts of jewellery, means of transportation, etc. are all included among essential needs.[1]

Deferred debt does not obstruct obligations of *zakat al-fitr*

Debts that are not due by the day of the *'Id* are disregarded in determining *zakat al-fitr*, but a person who has excess above his food for the day of the *'Id* but this excess is required to pay a debt that is due by that day is exempt from *zakat*. Deferred debts do not obstruct *zakat* because *zakat al-fitr* is emphasised and ascertained on every Muslim, including the poor, unlike *zakat* on wealth which is obliged on the rich only.[2]

1. *Al-Mughni*, vol. 3, p. 76 and *ar-Rawda*, vol. 2, pp. 299-300.
2. Ibid.

Chapter Three
Amount and Kind of *Zakat al-Fitr*

Is one *sa'* obliged?

In the *hadith* from Ibn 'Umar, "The Messenger of Allah (p) imposed … one *sa'* of dates or one *sa'* of barley …" Abu Sa'id al-Khudri said, "We used to pay *zakat al-fitr* at the end of Ramadan when the Messenger of Allah (p) was among us with one *sa'* of food, one *sa'* of dates, one *sa'* of barley, one *sa'* of raisins or one *sa'* of dried yoghurt. We continued to do this until Mu'awiya came to us in Madina and said, 'I think two *mudds* of Syrian wheat is equivalent to one *sa'* of dates.' People accepted that." Reported by the Group and the five reporters (i.e. all except al-Bukhari) add, "Abu Sa'id said, 'But I continued paying it the same way I used to.'" Thus the indication of these two texts is that one *sa'* is obligatory for each person.

Shah Waliyu'llah ad-Dihlawi says that *zakat al-fitr* is determined at one *sa'* because "this is sufficient for an average-size household. Thus it provides satisfaction for the poor without burdening the payer."[1] There is *ijma'* that from foodstuffs like dates and barley, one *sa'* is obligatory. If wheat or raisins are given, one *sa'* is obligatory, according to three of the juristic schools, including Abu Sa'id, Abu'l-'Aliya, Abu'sh-Sha'tha', al-Hasan al-Basri, Jabir ibn Zayd, Ishaq, al-Hadi, al-Qasim, an-Nasir, and al-Mu'ayyad Billah.[2]

Their argument is derived from the above-mentioned *hadith* from Abu Sa'id. Al-Mawardi says, "This *hadith* makes two important points. Firstly, the word 'food' is used in the Hijaz to mean wheat, especially when the word is used in relation to other foodstuffs, and secondly, it mentions several items whose values are dif-

1. *Hujjat Allah al-Baligha*, vol. 2, p. 509.
2. *Nayl al-Awtar*, vol. 4, p. 183, and *al-Mughni*, vol. 3, p. 57.

ferent, which means that the quantity of one *sa'* is intended regardless of the value."[1] Those who say it is one half of a *sa'* have no evidence except the story of Mu'awiya and a few other obviously weak *hadiths*.[2]

As for the story of Mu'awiya, the majority of scholars believe that it is at best the opinion of a Companion which is opposed by other Companions who knew the Prophet (p) better than Mu'awiya. However, the rule is that, when the Companions disagree among themselves, additional evidence is needed since the view of one of them does not have more weight than that of any other. The majority argue that the *hadith* itself as well as the analogy are in support of one *sa'* of all food items mentioned, including wheat, and Mu'awiya did say it was a personal view and not that he had heard it from the Prophet (p).[3] Although *ijtihad* is always permissible, it is not acceptable when there is a text.[4]

Those who say the amount is one half a *sa'* of wheat

Abu Hanifa and his disciples believe a half *sa'* of wheat is sufficient.[5] This is also the view of Zayd ibn 'Ali and Yahya.[6] Ibn Hazm says, "It is correctly attributed to 'Umar ibn 'Abdu'l-'Aziz, Tawus, Mujahid, Sa'id ibn al-Musayyab, 'Urwa ibn az-Zubayr, Abu Salama ibn 'Abdu'r-Rahman, Sa'id ibn Jubayr, al-Awza'i, al-Layth, and Sufyan." Ibn Hazm also mentions reports from several Companions to the same effect, including Abu Bakr, 'Umar, 'Uthman, 'Ali, 'A'isha, Asma' bint Abi Bakr, Abu Hurayra, Jabir, Ibn Mas'ud, Ibn 'Abbas, Ibn az-Zubayr, and Abu Sa'id. Ibn Hazm adds that reports from all of them are sound except those about Abu Bakr, Ibn 'Abbas and Ibn Mas'ud.[7]

1. *Sharh an-Nawawi* on *Sahih Muslim*, vol. 7, p. 60.

2. Ibid.

3. Ibid., pp. 61-62.

4. *Fath al-Bari*, vol. 3, p. 374.

5. His two disciples treat raisins like dates. The author of *ad-Durr al-Mukhtar* says this is the view upheld in this school. See *ad-Durr al-Mukhtar*, vol. 2, p. 83.

6. *Nayl al-Awtar*, vol. 3, p. 374.

7. *Al-Muhalla*, vol. 6, pp. 128-131, and *Nasb ar-Raya*, vol. 2, pp. 446-447.

Abu Hanifa and his group provide the following to support their view:

- Abu Dawud reports from 'Abdullah ibn Tha'laba that the Messenger of Allah (p) said, "*Sadaqa al-fitr* is one *sa'* of wheat for each two persons."[1] Al-Hakim reports from Ibn 'Abbas, attributed to the Prophet (p), "*Sadaqa al-fitr* is two *mudds* of wheat." Two *mudds* is half a *sa'*. At-Tirmidhi has a similar report from 'Amr ibn Shu'ayb from his father from his grandfather. Abu Dawud and an-Nasa'i report a *mursal hadith* from al-Hasan which goes: "The Messenger of Allah (p) imposed this *sadaqa* as one *sa'* of dates or barley, or half a *sa'* of wheat."[2] And there are a few other *hadiths* that together stand to restrict the general implications of the *hadith* about the *sa'* by excluding wheat.[3]

- It is correctly reported that several Companions believed that one half a *sa'* of wheat is obliged. Sufyan reports from 'Ali, "One half a *sa'* of wheat." It is also reported from the first four Khalifs and others.[4] Depending on such reports, Ibn al-Mundhir says, "We know of no sound report from the Prophet on wheat,"[5] which was not common in Madina. When it became abundant during the era of the Companions, they made half a *sa'* of it equal to one *sa'* of barley. They are the leaders whose view must not be ignored." Ibn al-Mundhir goes on to report via sound chains, as described by Ibn Hajar, the same from 'Uthman, 'Ali, Abu Hurayra, Jabir, Ibn 'Abbas, Ibn az-Zubayr and his mother Asma'.

1. See the versions of this *hadith* in Abu Dawud, chapter on *zakat*; ad-Daraqutni, pp. 223-224, *al-Muhalla*, vol. 6, p. 121; *as-Sunan al-Kubra*, vol. 4, pp. 167-168, and *Nasb ar-Raya*, vol. 2, pp. 406-410.

2. *Nayl al-Awtar*, vol. 4, p. 183, *al-Muhalla*, vol. 6, pp. 122-123, and *Nasb ar-Raya*, vol. 4, pp. 418-423.

3. *Nayl al-Awtar*, vol. 4, p. 183.

4. Ibid.

5. This is opposed by the *hadiths* reported by Ibn Hajar, vol. 1, pp. 410-411, about wheat; adh-Dhahabi confirms the soundness of two of them – one from Ibn 'Umar and one through Ibn Ishaq from Abu Sa'id. Both of them mention wheat. But al-Bayhaqi and Ibn Khuzayma argue that wheat is not actually mentioned in these *hadiths* and is merely an error on the part of some narrators.

At-Tahawi claims *ijma'* on this,[1] but the disagreement of Abu Sa'id mentioned in the *hadith* above disproves this claim. Moreover, Hanafis argue that Abu Sa'id's comment, "I continue to pay it the same way I used to at the time of the Prophet (p)" implies that one *sa'* of wheat is not obligatory, and no one says one cannot pay more than one half; in fact, the excess is voluntary charity.[2]

As for the interpretation of 'food' in the *hadith* from Abu Sa'id as meaning wheat, it is not agreed upon. Ibn al-Mundhir says, "Some people think that food here means wheat but this is wrong. Abu Sa'id first gives the inclusive term 'food' then its details. Al-Bukhari reports through Hafs ibn Maysara that Abu Sa'id said, 'We used to pay at the time of the Prophet (p) one *sa'* of food on the Day of *Fitr.* Our food was barley, raisins, dried yoghurt and dates.'" This is also reported by at-Tahawi via another chain with the addition of "We used not to pay anything else."[3]

Ibn Khuzayma reports from Ibn 'Umar, "The *sadaqa* at the time of the Messenger of Allah (p) was nothing but dates, raisins and barley, but not wheat." And Muslim reports from Abu Sa'id, "We used to pay one of three things: one *sa'* of dates, one *sa'* of dried yoghurt, or one *sa'* of barley." Ibn Hajar says, "All these narrations indicate that the word 'food' in the *hadith* from Abu Sa'id does not mean wheat. Food may also mean millet since it was known in the Hijaz too." Al-Jawzaqi reports via 'Iyad from Abu Sa'id "one *sa'* of dates, one *sa'* of millet..."[4]

Analysis and discussion

From all these arguments and evidence, it seems that wheat was not a common food in the Hijaz at the time of the Prophet, (p) so he did not impose one *sa'* of it. The *hadith* reported by al-Bukhari and Muslim from Ibn 'Umar supports this, since it reads "... one *sa'* of dates or one *sa'* of barley. People considered this equivalent to two *mudds* of wheat," and in another version, "People consid-

1. *Fath al-Bari*, vol. 3, p. 374, and *al-Muhalla*, vol. 6, pp. 128-131.
2. *Bada'i' as-Sana'i'*, vol. 2, p. 72, and *Nasb ar-Raya*, vol. 2, p. 418.
3. *Nayl al-Awtar*, vol. 4, pp. 192-192, and *Fath al-Bari*, op cit.
4. *Fath al-Bari*, vol. 3, p. 373.

ered it equivalent to half a *sa'*."[1] Ibn al-Qayyim quotes Abu Dawud, "It is known that 'Umar made one half of a *sa'* of wheat equal to one *sa'* of these other things."[2] It is, however, mentioned in the two *Sahih* collections that Mu'awiya was the one who did this. There are several *mursal hadiths* that strengthen one another.[3]

Ibn al-Qayyim then refers to the *hadith* from Ibn Abi Su'ayr and adds that al-Hasan al-Basri says, "At the end of Ramadan, Ibn 'Abbas gave a speech from the minbar in Basra saying, 'Pay the *sadaqa* of your fasting.' People seemed not to have understood. Then he added, 'Who here is from Madina? Stand up and teach your brothers since they do not know. The Messenger of Allah (p) imposed this *sadaqa*, one *sa'* of dates or barley, or half a *sa'* of wheat on each free person or slave, male or female, young or old...' Then when 'Ali came and noticed the low prices, he said, 'Allah has given you prosperity, would you not make it a *sa'* of anything?'" Reported by Abu Dawud and an-Nasa'i.[4] Ibn al-Qayyim adds, "Our teacher, Ibn Taymiyya, inclines toward this view, saying it is consistent with Ahmad's view about *kaffarat* in which he equates half a *sa'* of wheat to one *sa'* of other things."[5]

It seems that when the *hadiths* in support of the one half *sa'* of wheat are thoroughly scrutinised, they are not weak to the extent of being rejected, nor are they well-known among the Companions. If these *hadiths* were strong enough, they would have been known to Ibn 'Umar, Abu Sa'id, Mu'awiya, and those who heard them. It is also obvious from the text that Mu'awiya equated half a *sa'* of wheat to one *sa'* of other things on the basis of value.

1. *Sharh an-Nawawi* on *Sahih Muslim*, vol. 7, p. 60, and *Fath al-Bari*, vol. 3, pp. 271-272.

2. Ibn Hajar says, "In using the word 'people', Ibn 'Umar means Mu'awiya and his followers." This appears explicitly in the version from Ayyub from Nafi' which is reported by al-Humaydi in his *Musnad*. It is also reported by Ibn Khuzayma. See *Fath al-Bari*, vol. 3, p. 372.

3. *Zad al-Ma'ad*, vol. 1, pp. 313-314.

4. An-Nasa'i, Ahmad, Ibn al-Madini, and others say that al-Hasan did not hear Ibn 'Abbas, since the former was in Basra when the latter was in Madina. But Ahmad Shakir argues that their having met each other cannot be ruled out, since they both lived in the era of 'Uthman and 'Ali. See *as-Sunan al-Kubra, al-Jawhar an-Naqi*, vol. 4, pp. 167-169, and *Nasb ar-Raya*, vol. 2, pp. 418-419.

5. *Zad al-Ma'ad*, op. cit.

Abu Sa'id says, "That is the valuation of Mu'awiya, which I do not accept or follow."[1]

Peace of mind is achieved by remembering that the *sa'* of other foodstuffs is clearly ordained in the *hadiths* while nothing perfect is reported about wheat. The equation of Mu'awiya is based on prices which may differ from time to time and, if the principle of value is applied, it may give inconsistent results today since, for example, the price of one *sa'* of dates today is equal to the price of several *sa's* of wheat.[2]

With the above in mind, it seems the only way out of this dispute is to consider the obligation as one *sa'* of the most common items of foodstuff, and if wheat is more expensive than other items, half a *sa'* may be applied to wheat. In all cases, payment of one sa' is always better.

Is it permissible to pay more than one *sa'*?

Strangely enough, some Maliki writings express dislike of giving more than one *sa'*, since a *sa'* is the *Shari'a* prescription and it should be binding just as it is disliked to increase worship.[3] This argument is not very convincing since, although it is an act of worship, *zakat* is also a socio-financial obligation so paying more than is due does not sidetrack it from its objectives. In fact, it is better. The Qur'an says, *"And if someone does good of his own accord, it is better for him,"* in regard to compensation payment for breaking the fast of a day of Ramadan (which is the food of a person in need).

Ahmad and Abu Dawud report from Ubayy ibn Ka'b that the required amount of *zakat* due from a certain man was one one-year-old she-camel but he wanted to give a better she-camel to the collector, saying that the required one was too young to be used for riding or to give milk, but Ubayy refused to accept it and they went to the Prophet (p) for judgement. The Prophet (p) said, "This is what is obliged on you, but if you want to volunteer more, Allah

1. Reported by Ibn Khuzayma and al-Hakim in their *Sahih* collection. See *al-Fath*, vol. 3, p. 373, *al-Mustadrak*, vol. 1, p. 411, *al-Muhalla*, vol. 6, p. 130, and *Nasb ar-Raya*, vol. 2, pp. 417-418.

2. *Al-Fath*, vol. 3, p. 374.

3. *Sharh al-Kabir*, ad-Dardir, vol. 1, p. 508.

shall reward you for it and we agree to take it." Then he ordered the larger camel to be accepted and prayed to Allah to bless the man's wealth.[1]

The above clear text indicates that giving more than is due is acceptable and rewardable. 'Ali says, "If Allah gives you prosperity, you should also give more."

The amount of a *sa'*

It was shown earlier in this book that one *sa'* equals 2176 grams if measured in wheat. Since the *sa'* is a volume measure, if an item heavier than wheat is used (e.g. rice), more than 2176 grams should be given in order to make up the volume of one *sa'*. An-Nawawi argues that the *sa'*, being a measure of volume, need not be estimated in weight since food items have different weights; thus a quantity equal to the volume measure of one *sa'* must be given, regardless of its weight.[2] Ibn Hazm adds that according to the residents of Madina, a mudd is no more than one and a half ratls and no less than one and a quarter ratl. This is not a difference in the measure but the result of differences in the density of measured items, such as wheat, dates, and barley.[3]

The *hadiths* on *zakat al-fitr* mention a few food items, namely dates, barley, raisins and dried yoghurt. Some of their versions add wheat and millet. Are these the only foods that can be paid? Malikis and Shafi'is argue that these kinds are mentioned only as examples and that the requirement can be paid in the form of the most common food items in the payer's area or the most common food the payer usually eats, according to some. Many Malikis believe that the month of Ramadan is the time during which the most common food item is determined,[4] while some Shafi'is determine the most common food item on the day of *'Id al-Fitr*, as long as it is eaten by most people.[5] If several kinds are equally common,

1. Reported by Ahmad, Abu Dawud, and al-Hakim. The latter grades it *sahih* and is followed by adh-Dhahabi.

2. *Ar-Rawda*, vol. 2, pp. 301-302.

3. *Al-Muhalla*, vol. 5, p. 245.

4. *Hashiyat ad-Dusuqi*, vol. 1, p. 505.

5. *Ar-Rawda*, vol. 2, pp. 305.

any of these kinds is suitable. Certainly, it is preferred to give the best among them.[1]

On the other hand, Hanbalis believe *fitra* can only be paid in the form of one of the five items mentioned above, as long as it is available and affordable.[2] Abu Hanifa and Ahmad are quoted as permitting payment in the form of flour.[3] It seems that the Prophet (p) mentions these items merely as examples since they were the foodstuffs known to the Arabs at this time. Consequently, if rice or millet are more used in certain lands today, payment of *zakat al-fitr* must be in their form.

Ibn Hazm argues that only dates or barley is acceptable as payment on the grounds of a report from Abu Miljaz, "I asked Ibn 'Umar, 'Allah gave us prosperity. Is not wheat better than dates in payment of *fitra*?' He said, 'My colleagues went their way and I like to follow it.'"[4] Ahmad Shakir comments that taking all the *hadiths* on the matter together makes it clear that Ibn Hazm's argument is groundless. Mu'awiya, for example, suggested wheat and no Companion objected to it. (Although Abu Sa'id objected to the reduced quantity, he did not disapprove the kind.)

The report from Ibn 'Umar given by Ibn Hazm is not evidence since, in his personal action, Ibn 'Umar is known to have been very particular in following literally in the footsteps of the Prophet (p) without criticising other Companions as long as what they did was permissible. *Zakat al-fitr* is legislated in order to make the poor happy on the day of the feast and giving an item like dates or barley in a country where people are not accustomed to eating them does not solve the poor person's problem.[5]

Payment in value

The three leading scholars do not approve of payment in value. When Ahmad was asked about payment of *zakat al-fitr* in money, he answered, "I am afraid it is not satisfactory since it is in opposi-

1. Ibid.
2. *Al-Mughni*, vol. 3, p. 62.
3. Ibid.
4. *Al-Muhalla*, vol. 6, pp. 118–126.
5. Ibid., pp. 131-132.

tion to the tradition of the Messenger of Allah (p)." When he was told that it was said that 'Umar ibn 'Abdu'l-'Aziz used to accept money as payment of this *zakat*, Ahmad said, "Would they abandon the *hadith* of the Messenger of Allah (p) for the saying of someone else? Ibn 'Umar said, "The Messenger of Allah (p) imposed *zakat al-fitr* and Allah says, *'Obey Allah and obey the Messenger.'* (4:59)" This is also the view of Malik and ash-Shafi'i.[1] Ibn Hazm shares the same view on the grounds that money is only a substitute payment, and a substitute is not valid except by mutual agreement. Since *zakat* is due to Allah, one cannot negotiate a substitute.[2]

On the other hand, ath-Thawri, Abu Hanifa and his disciples believe it is permissible to pay *zakat al-fitr* in value. This is also reported from 'Umar ibn 'Abdu'l-'Aziz and al-Hasan al-Basri.[3] Ibn Abi Shayba reports from 'Awn, "I heard the letter of 'Umar ibn 'Abdu'l-'Aziz read to 'Adi in Basra (where he was governor). It said that one-half a dirham per person must be taken from all salary earners."[4] Al-Hasan is reported as saying, "It is permissible to pay *zakat al-fitr* in dirhams."[5] Abu Ishaq says, "I attended their (the predecessors) paying of the *zakat* of Ramadan in dirhams,"[6] and 'Ata' is reported to have given *zakat al-fitr* in silver currency.[7]

This view is supported by the following:

- The *hadith* of the Prophet (p), "Make them (the poor) rich on this day." Enriching them can be done by giving money as much as by giving food, more so since the poor and destitute need clothing and other materials in addition to food.

- The Companions allowed giving one half a *sa'* of wheat in place of the foodstuffs mentioned in the *hadith*. This is obviously based on the value, as explained by Mu'awiya, "I think half a *sa'* of wheat from Syria equals one *sa'* of dates."

1. *Al-Mughni*, vol. 3, p. 65.
2. *Al-Muhalla*, vol. 6, p. 137.
3. *Al-Mughni*, vol. 3, p. 65, and *al-Muhalla*, vol. 6, p. 130. It is correctly reported from 'Umar ibn 'Abdu'l-'Aziz.
4. *Musannaf Ibn Abi Shayba*, vol. 4, p. 37.
5. Ibid., p. 38.
6. Ibid.
7. Ibid.

- It is easier, especially nowadays, to give money than foodstuffs, and more useful to the poor in most countries.
- It seems to me that the Prophet (p) mentions certain food items simply because paying them was easier during his time since currency was scarce and its value not constant.

At the end of this chapter, three points need to be explained. Firstly, Abu Hanifa and Abu Yusuf argue that when money is paid its amount must equal the value of the required amount of wheat, barley or dates, while ash-Shaybani believes only the value of wheat is considered. In my opinion, the value of the most common food item is the determinant of the required amount of money.[1] Secondly, when *zakat al-fitr* is paid in kind in the form of any of the items mentioned in the *hadith*, the amount required is one *sa'* (or one-half of a *sa'* for wheat) regardless of the relative value of the item selected as payment.[2] Thirdly, Hanafis do not agree on which is better, payment in money or payment in kind. Their argument is based on which method is more beneficial for the poor.[3] Consequently, in cases where money is more useful to the poor, payment must be done in cash, and vice versa.

1. *Radd al-Muhtar*, vol. 2, p. 80.
2. Ibid., p. 83, as quoted from *al-Bada'i'*.
3. Ibid.

Chapter Four

Time of Payment

Muslims unanimously agree that *zakat al-fitr* is obliged at the end of Ramadan in accordance with the previously mentioned report from Ibn 'Umar that "the Messenger of Allah (p) imposed *zakat al-fitr* after Ramadan." However, they differ regarding the exact time this obligation becomes due. Ash-Shafi'i, Ahmad, Ishaq, ath-Thawri and Malik (in one narration) believe *zakat al-fitr* is due at sunset on the last day of Ramadan, i.e. when the last day ends. Abu Hanifa and his disciples, al-Layth, Abu Thawr and Malik (in another narration) say it is due at dawn on the day of the feast since it aims at bringing happiness to the poor on that day.[1] The difference has only one practical implication: whether new-born babies and persons who die during that night should be counted in calculating the amount of *zakat*.[2]

The last time for payment

Al-Bukhari and Muslim report from Ibn 'Umar, "The Messenger of Allah (p) ordered *zakat al-fitr* to be paid prior to the *'Id* prayer." 'Ikrima says, "One should pay *zakat* before doing the prayer. Allah says, *'He who has purified himself* [by zakat] *will have success. He who invokes the Name of his Lord and prays.'* (87:14-15)" Ibn Khuzayma reports from Kathir from his father from his grandfather that the Messenger of Allah (p) was asked about this *ayat* and answered, "It was revealed with regard to *zakat al-fitr*."[3] But this *hadith* is weak because Kathir is very unreliable.[4] Moreover, the

1. *Al-Mughni*, vol. 3, pp. 67-68.

2. *Bidayat al-Mujtahid*, vol. 1, p. 273.

3. *Nayl al-Awtar*, vol. 4, p. 195.

4. Ash-Shafi'i and Abu Dawud describe him as a "cornerstone of falsehood". See *al-Mizan*, vol. 3, pp. 406-407, *Tahdhib at-Tahdhib*, vol. 8, pp. 421-423, *at-*

ayat is Makkan, while *zakat al-fitr* was imposed after the fasting of Ramadan was prescribed in Madina. On the other hand, al-Bukhari and Muslim report from Abu Sa'id, "We used to pay, during the lifetime of the Messenger of Allah (p), on the day of breaking the fast..." implying that all the day is time for payment..

Ash-Shafi'i suggests that this *zakat* can be paid during the whole day of the *'Id*, although the best time for payment is in the early morning before the *'Id* prayer. Agreeing with ash-Shafi'i, the majority of scholars believe that delaying payment until the time for the *'Id* prayer is undesirable, since *zakat al-fitr* is meant to enrich the poor on that day, so they must be given time to use it during the day itself.

Ibn Hazm says it is prohibited to delay payment until after the time of the prayer, but that if *zakat* is not paid before prayer, it must be nevertheless be paid later because the due right to the poor must be fulfilled despite the violation of Allah's right to payment before the prayer.[1] Ash-Shawkani argues that making the payment before the prayer is obligatory on the basis of the *hadith* from Ibn 'Abbas, "He who pays it before the prayer, for him it is acceptable as *zakat*, and for him who pays it after the prayer, it is a charity like other charities." Delaying *zakat al-fitr* until after the day of *'Id* ends is unanimously considered sinful, in spite of the fact that it must be paid anyway.[2]

The question of whether *zakat al-fitr* can be paid before the day of the *'Id* also arises. Ibn Hazm's answer is an absolute no.[3] Ahmad argues that it is permissible to pay it one or two days before the *'Id*, on the grounds of the *hadith* reported by al-Bukhari from Ibn 'Umar that, "The Companions used to give it away one or two days before the *'Id*." This is also the Maliki view.[4] Some Hanbalis say it can be paid as early as the middle of the month of Ramadan. Ash-Shafi'i allows it to be paid as early as the beginning of

Ta'rikh of al-Bukhari, vol. 4, p. 217, *al-Jarh wa't-Ta'dil*, vol. 2, p. 154, and *al-Mustadrak*, vol. 1, p. 123.

1. *Al-Muhalla*, vol. 6, p. 143.
2. *Nayl al-Awtar*, vol. 4, p. 195.
3. *Al-Muhalla*, vol. 6, p. 143 The view of Ibn Hazm coincides with that of the Imami school. See *Fiqh al-Imam Ja'far*, vol. 2, p. 106.
4. *Ash-Sharh al-Kabir* with *Hashiyat ad-Dusuqi*, vol. 1, p. 508.

Ramadan since, according to him, the reason for its obligation is either fasting or breaking the fast, and once either of these exists, *zakat al-fitr* can be paid.[1] Abu Hanifa argues that, like *zakat* on wealth, *zakat al-fitr* can be paid as early as the beginning of the year. Lastly, Zaydis allow payment two years in advance.[2]

It is noticeable that the view of Ahmad and Malik seems closer to fulfilling the objective of *zakat al-fitr*, although one must confess that starting the collection and distribution process in the middle of the month is easier and more convenient, especially if the state or a social organisation takes this responsibility.

1. *Al-Mughni*, vol. 3, pp. 58-69.
2. *Al-Bahr*, vol. 2, p. 196.

Chapter Five

Recipients of *Zakat al-Fitr*

Poor and needy Muslims

According to Ibn Rushd, it is unanimously agreed that *zakat al-fitr* must be given to poor and needy Muslims since the Prophet (p) referred to them when he said, "Make them satisfied on the Day of *Fitr.*" The majority of scholars do not accept giving this religious due to poor People of the Pledge. Abu Hanifa believes this is permissible and some others allow giving only to monks of the People of the Pledge.[1] Ibn Abi Shayba reports that Abu Maysara used to give *zakat al-fitr* to monks.[2] Similar reports came from 'Amr ibn Maymun, 'Amr ibn Shurahbil and Murra al-Hamadani.[3] This is undoubtedly a humanitarian gesture from Muslim jurists in trying to make everybody happy on the day of the feast.

Can it be given to the eight categories who receive *zakat*?

The Shafi'i school argues that, like any other *zakat*, *zakat al-fitr* must be distributed equally among the eight categories except when distributed by the payer – in which case categories of '*zakat* workers' and "those whose hearts are being reconciled" are excluded.[4] This is also the view of Ibn Hazm.[5] Ibn al-Qayyim rejects this view and argues that the practice of the Prophet (p) and his Companions was to give it only to the poor and needy. This is so, he continues, to the extent that some Hanbalis believe it is not per-

1. *Bidayat al-Mujtahid*, vol. 1, p. 73.
2. *Al-Musannaf*, vol. 4, p. 39.
3. *Al-Mughni*, vol. 3, p. 144.
4. *Al-Majmu'*, vol. 6, p. 144.
5. *Al-Muhalla*, vol. 6, pp. 143-145.

missible to distribute it otherwise. Ibn al-Qayyim adds that this opinion carries more weight.[1] Malikis assert that this *zakat* must be paid exclusively to the poor and needy, even if it must be shipped to another country at the expense of the payer because of the lack of poor people in the land where it is due.[2] Al-Hadi, al-Qasim and Abu Talib share the view of the Malikis.[3]

Three opinions can be distinguished:

- *Zakat al-fitr* must be distributed among the eight categories, equally which is the view of ash-Shafi'i.
- It is exclusively for the poor and needy.
- It can be distributed to all eight groups, to some of them, or the poor alone, since it is included under the general text, "Sadaqa *is for the poor and needy...*" This is the view of the majority of jurists.

It is important to notice that the argument for the exclusivity of payment to the poor based on the *hadith*, "Make them satisfied on this day" is not specific in preventing giving to other categories. It is like the *hadith* that *zakat* is "...taken from the rich to be rendered to the poor," yet *zakat* is paid to the other categories. Thus *zakat al-fitr* must be covered by the general text of the *ayat* mentioned above, although it is conceivable that one must give priority to the poor and needy.

Categories excluded from *zakat*

As in the case of *zakat* on wealth, *zakat al-fitr* must not be given to unbelievers, apostates or the rich. It must also not be paid to people for whose expenses the payer is responsible, such as the payer's father, son or wife. The same details studied with regard to *zakat* on wealth apply here.

Lastly, the *zakat* payer may give his or her *zakat* to one or more persons, and by the same token, *zakat* collected from several payers

1. *Zad al-Ma'ad*, vol. 1, p. 315.
2. *Ash-Sharh al-Kabir* and *Hashiyat ad-Dusuqi*, vol. 1, pp. 508-509.
3. *Nayl al-Awtar*, vol. 2, p. 197.

may be given to one or more recipients since there is no evidence to prevent any of these cases,[1] although some jurists dislike dividing one's *zakat* among several recipients and giving the *zakat* of several payers to one recipient on the grounds that this may not fulfil the objective of enriching all the poor on the day of the *'Id*.[2]

As for transporting *zakat al-fitr* from one land to another, the same principle applied on other forms of *zakat* is applicable here; i.e. first the poor and needy in the area where *zakat* is due must be satisfied and the leftover may be transported, except in case of emergencies or higher priority.[3]

1. *Al-Bahr*, vol. 2, p. 197.
2. *Ad-Durr al-Mukhtar*, vol. 2, p. 85, and *ash-Sharh*, op cit.
3. *Al-Bahr*, vol. 2, p. 203.

Part Eight
Dues and Taxes Other than *Zakat*

Chapter One

The Opinion that there are No Other Financial Dues besides *Zakat*

Many jurists argue that the only financial levy approved in Islam is *zakat*.[1] Whoever fulfils the requirement of *zakat* will have his or her wealth purified and need not pay anything else except voluntarily. This is the predominant view among the later generations of jurists.

Hadiths uses in support of this view

- Al-Bukhari, Muslim and others report from Talha, "A man from Najd came to the Messenger of Allah (p). His hair was uncombed, his loud voice was heard from a distance and what he was saying could not be not understood until he came close to the Messenger of Allah (p) who said, 'Five prayers in the day and night.' The man said, 'Do I have to do more?' The Prophet (p) said, 'No, unless you volunteer.' The Messenger of Allah (p) continued, 'And the fasting of Ramadan.' The man said, 'Do I have to fast other than this?' The Prophet (p) answered, 'No, unless you volunteer...' and then the Prophet (p) mentioned *zakat*. The man said, 'Do I have to pay anything else besides it?' The Prophet (p) said, 'No, unless you volunteer.' The man turned around and left saying, 'I shall not do anything more nor less than these.' The Messenger of Allah (p) commented, 'He will be successful if he honours this promise,' or 'He will enter the Garden if he honours this promise.'"[2]

---

1. The author of *al-Bahr* attributes this to the majority, vol. 2, p. 138.
2. Reported by the five, at-Tirmidhi is excluded. See *Majma' az-Zawa'id*, vol. 1, p. 11.

- Al-Bukhari reports from Abu Hurayra, "A bedouin Arab came to the Prophet (p) and said, 'Guide me to something for which, if I do it, I shall enter the Garden.' The Prophet (p) said, 'Worship Allah and do not associate any partners whatsoever with Him, pray the obligatory prayer, fulfil the obligatory *zakat*, and fast Ramadan.' The man said, 'By the name of Him in Whose Hand is my soul, I shall not add anything to those.' When the man left, the Messenger of Allah (p) said, 'He who wants to see a man who is one of the dwellers of the Garden may look at this man.'"[1]

In the first *hadith*, the Prophet (p) says that there is nothing obligatory except *zakat*. This *hadith* is a clear text to this effect. In both *hadiths*, the two men declare that the Prophet (p) accepts that declaration and states that this is sufficient for entering the Garden. If there were other financial obligations besides *zakat*, these men would not deserve to enter the Garden unless those other obligations were fulfilled.

- At-Tirmidhi reports from Abu Hurayra, "The Prophet (p) said, 'If you pay the *zakat* due on your wealth you will have fulfilled all that is obliged on you.'"[2]
- Al-Hakim reports from Jabir that the Prophet (p) said, "If you pay the *zakat* on your wealth, you will have turned away its evil from you."[3]
- Al-Hakim reports from Umm Salama that she used to wear some pieces of gold as ornaments. She asked the Prophet, "Is this hoarding?" He answered, "If you pay its due *zakat*, it is not

1. Reported by at-Tirmidhi, vol. 3, pp. 97-99. He comments, "good and strange." Also reported by al-Hakim who comments "sound". This is approved by adh-Dhahabi, vol. 1, p. 390. But in *at-Talkhis*, p. 177, Ibn Hajar says its chain is weak.

2. Reported by Ibn Khuzayma in his *Sahih* collection, and al-Hakim, vol. 1, p. 390, who comments, "*sahih* according to the criteria of Muslim." This is approved by adh-Dhahabi. In *al-Fath*, vol. 3, p. 175. Ibn Hajar says, "Abu Zur'a, al-Bayhaqi, and others give more weight to it as a statement of Jabir himself, as is reported by al-Bazzar.

3. Reported by al-Hakim, vol. 1, p. 390.

like hoarding."[1] In some versions of this *hadith*, the Prophet says, "Anything that reaches the *nisab* for *zakat* and its due *zakat* is paid is not hoarding." (Abu Dawud) This *hadith* indicates that the Qur'an's warning against hoarding does not apply to people who pay *zakat* on their treasures, which directly means such individuals are not obliged to pay anything else. Some supporters of this view add another *hadith* in which the Prophet is reported to have said, "On wealth there are no dues except *zakat*."[2]

It is obvious that the first two *hadiths* are sound. The third *hadith* has a weak chain, and the fourth one is considered *mawquf* [a statement of a Companion not attributed to the Prophet] according to the most acceptable scrutiny. As for the fifth *hadith*, there is criticism of its chain. The *hadith*, "On wealth there are not dues except *zakat*," is very weak, and, without the slightest hesitation, unacceptable. In fact, it is wrong and may be a copying error.

Supporters of this opinion argue that all texts which indicate the existence of financial obligations besides *zakat* can be interpreted as

1. Reported by al-Hakim, vol. 1, p. 390, who comments, "sound according to the criteria of al-Bukhari." This is approved by adh-Dhahabi. However, its chain is criticised.

2. Some attribute this *hadith* to the collection of *Sunan Ibn Majah*. But in *al-Majmu'*, an-Nawawi says, "It is very weak and not known," vol. 5, p. 332. Al-Bayhaqi says, "Our colleague scholars mention this *hadith* in their suspended reports. I do not know of a chain for it." See *as-Sunan al-Kubra*, vol. 4, p. 84. Al-Hafiz al-'Iraqi objects, arguing that it is reported in some copies of Ibn Majah as "There is a right on wealth besides *zakat*," the same way it is reported by at-Tirmidhi. See *Tarh at-Tathrib*, vol. 4, p. 18. This means the word "no" (*laysa*) was included by a copying error. This is explained by the late Ahmad Shakir in his comment on quote no. 2530 in at-Tabari's explanation. He gives the following as evidence: firstly, at-Tabari (vol. 3, pp. 343-344) reports the same *hadith* under no 2527, via the same chain of Yahya ibn Adam from which Ibn Majah reports, and the text is "Indeed, there is a right on wealth besides *zakat*." Secondly, Ibn Kathir in his explanation attributes the *hadith* to both Ibn Majah and at-Tirmidhi together without any distinction between their two texts: the same is done by an-Nabulisi in the *Dhakha'ir al-Mawarith*, under no. 11699. Thirdly, al-Bayhaqi says he does not know of any chain for the *hadith*, and if Ibn Majah actually reported it with the "no", al-Bayhaqi must have known it, and so must an-Nawawi, who says that the *hadith* as stated is not known. It seems that the explanation of the late Ahmad Shakir with those reasons is very valid and convincing.

references to mere desirability and not to obligation. They also claim that before *zakat* was mandated, different financial obligations were obligatory, but when *zakat* was revealed to the Prophet as a financial obligation, all previous levies were annulled. Additionally, they reject a report by at-Tirmidhi from Fatima bint Qays that the Prophet (p) said, "There are other dues on wealth besides *zakat*,"[1] on the grounds that at-Tirmidhi himself grades it weak and it is considered inauthentic by *hadith* critics.[2]

1. At-Tirmidhi comments on this *hadith*, "Its chain is not that good. In it, Abu Maymun al-A'war is weak." At-Tabari also mentions it, vol. 3, pp. 176-177, under no 2527 and 2530, so does ad-Darimi, vol. 1, p. 385. Ibn Majah reports this *hadith* via Yahya ibn Adam, no 1786 and al-Bayhaqi in his *as-Sunan al-Kubra*, vol. 4, p. 84.

2. Ibn Hajar gives the biography of Abu Hamza, Maymun al-A'war al-Qassab in *at-Tahdhib*, so does al-Bukhari in *at-Tarikh al-Kabir*, no. 4-1-343 and Ibn Abi Hatim in *al-Jarh wa't-Ta'dil*, no. 4-1-235 and 236.

Chapter Two

The View that Other Dues besides *Zakat* may be Imposed

Other scholars, as early as the era of the Companions and Followers, believe there are other financial dues besides *zakat*. These include 'Umar, 'Ali, Abu Dharr, 'A'isha, Abu Hurayra, al-Hasan ibn 'Ali and Fatima bint Qays (all Companions), as well as the Followers ash-Sha'bi, Mujahid, Tawus, 'Ata' and several others.

The evidence

These people argue that the *ayat*, *"It is not devoutness to turn your faces to the East or to the West. Rather, those with true devotion are those who believe in Allah and the Last Day, the Angels, the Book and the Prophets, and who, despite their love for it, give away their wealth to their relatives and to orphans and the very poor, and to travellers and beggars and to set slaves free, and who establish the prayer and pay* zakat*; those who honour their contracts when they make them, and are steadfast in poverty and in illness and in battle. Those are the people who are true. They are the godfearing"* (2:177), indicates that there are dues besides *zakat*. At-Tirmidhi and others report from Fatima bint Qays that she (or someone else) asked the Prophet (p) about *zakat*. He answered, "Indeed there are dues besides *zakat* on wealth." The Prophet (p) recited this *ayat* from *Surat al-Baqara*, *"It is not devoutness ..."*

Despite its weakness, at-Tirmidhi says this *hadith* is supported and strengthened by the *ayat*. In fact, the *ayat* alone is sufficient evidence since it makes giving money one of the conditions of devoutness in addition to prayers and *zakat*. Al-Qurtubi comments, "Even despite the criticism addressed to the *hadith*, its meaning remains correct because it is implied by the *ayat* itself, which reads '*... establish the prayer and pay zakat.*' It mentions *zakat* along with prayers, which means the words at the beginning of the *ayat*, 'give away their wealth' refer to other payments not included in the word '*zakat*.' Otherwise this *ayat* would have unnecessary repetition."[1]

No one can argue that the spending mentioned in the *ayat* refers merely to voluntary contributions since the *ayat* was revealed as a reply to the Jewish inclination for formality and ritualism to show the elements of true devoutness. Thus the *ayat* lists only basic elements; as is obvious from the other elements mentioned in the *ayat*: believing in Allah and the Last Day, and practising prayer and *zakat*, fulfilling pledges and contracts, etc.

Abu 'Ubayd reports ad-Dahhak's claim that this *ayat* is abrogated because *zakat* abrogates every other *sadaqa* mentioned in the Qur'an.[2] Such a daring claim has no substance or supporting evidence. The words of Allah cannot be abrogated by other people's claims. If ad-Dahhak's claim were correct, a phrase in the *ayat*, "...and those who pay *zakat*..." must have abrogated another phrase in the very same *ayat*, "...give away their wealth." Such a thing is not possible! Moreover, the *ayat* gives information about the character of the devout, and *ayats* which give information relating to creed or basic beliefs are not subject to abrogation. Abu 'Ubayd reports from Ibn 'Abbas, "This *ayat* was revealed in Madina at the time when obligations, penalties and other behavioural requirements were being revealed."[3]

---

1. At-Tabari says, "If it is asked whether there are other dues obligatory on wealth besides *zakat*, the answer depends on the different interpretations of scholars. Some scholars believe there are obligatory dues in addition to *zakat*, based on this *ayat*, since Allah adds spending on kin and others to prayers and practising *zakat* in an additive form of expression. Thus, this spending must be different from *zakat*. Otherwise it would be senseless repetition and Allah does not say senseless words. Each of these two additives must have a different meaning." At-Tabari adds, "Other scholars believe the spending mentioned at the beginning of the *ayat* is the same *zakat* mentioned at its end." It seems that at-Tabari is inclined toward the first opinion. See *Tafsir at-Tabari*, vol. 3, p. 348, and *Tafsir al-Qurtubi*, vol. 3, p. 42.

2. *Al-Amwal*, pp. 357-358.

3. Ibid.

The second proof: dues on agriculture

After describing the bounty Allah produces for mankind, including gardens with trellises, dates, grains, pomegranates, olives, etc., Allah says, *"Eat of their fruits when they bear fruit and pay their due on the day of their harvest, and do not be profligate. He does not love the profligate."* (6:141) It is argued that this "due" is different from *zakat* on the following grounds:

- The *ayat* is Makkan and it was revealed long before *'ushr* was obligated during the Madinan period.
- The *ayat* orders giving the due on fruits on the day of harvest. This is not the time of *zakat* payment since *'ushr* or half-*'ushr* is paid after the cleaning and drying of the produce.
- The concluding sentence in the *ayat*, *"...do not be profligate,"* is inapplicable to *zakat* which is an amount defined by the *Shari'a* and not susceptible to extravagance or excess.[1]

Any claim that the proper dues mentioned in this *ayat* were later abrogated by *zakat* cannot be substantiated, because abrogation cannot be supported by mere probability and claims. Ibn Hazm adds, "Any person's claim of abrogation can only be substantiated by a text linked to the Messenger of Allah (p). Otherwise, anyone could claim the abrogation of any *ayat* or that obedience to this text of Allah is not required. This can be done by the Legislator alone."[2] He continues, "What then is the proper due ordained by the above-mentioned *ayat*? It is an undoubtedly a different due to *zakat*. It requires that owners give some of their produce on the day of harvesting. The *ayat*, however, does not require any definite amount or percentage. This is the opinion of some of the *Salaf*."[3]

In explaining this due, Ibn 'Umar says, "They used to give something besides *zakat*." 'Ata' says, "Whoever is present at the harvest must be given some of the produce. This is not *zakat*." Mujahid says, "Those poor persons present must be given some of

1. *Al-Muhalla*, vol 5, pp. 215-217.
2. Ibid.
3. Ibid.

it." He adds, "At the time of planting they should be given something like a handful, and at the time of harvesting they should also be given something."[1] Similar statements are attributed to Abu'l-'Aliya, Sa'id ibn Jubayr, 'Ali ibn al-Husayn and ar-Rabi' ibn Anas.[2] Ibn Kathir says, "Allah censures those who harvest and do not give charity, as in the story of the owners of the garden in *Surat al-Qalam*."[3]

We already discussed the issue of whether this due is *zakat* or not. What is important here is to assert that some great Companions, like Ibn 'Umar, and Followers, like 'Ata', Mujahid and an-Nakha'i, believe this *ayat* refers to a due on wealth other than *zakat*.

The third proof: dues on livestock

There are several authentic *hadiths* that describe the prescription of dues on camels and horses. Al-Bukhari reports from Abu Hurayra that the Prophet (p) said, "Camels whose proper dues are not given on the Day of Rising will come against their owner the strongest they have ever been, trampling him with their hooves, and sheep whose proper dues are not given will come against their owner the strongest they have ever been, trampling him with their hooves and butting him with their horns." The Prophet (p) adds, "One of their dues is to milk them when they come to water [and to give away that milk]."[4] Apparently, the last sentence of the *hadith* covers both camels and sheep, especially since, in a version of the *hadith* reported by Muslim and Abu Dawud, the same sentence comes just after the talk about camels.[5] It is obvious that this sentence is part of the *hadith* and is not added by the narrator. Al-Bukhari reports the last sentence alone in reference to sharecropping in another chapter.[6]

1. *Al-Muhalla*, vol. 5, pp. 216-217.
2. Ibid.
3. Tafsir Ibn Kathir, vol. 2, pp. 181-182.
4 The *Sahih* collection of al-Bukhari with the commentary, *Fath al-Bari*, vol. 3, pp. 172-173.
5. *Mukhtasar Sunan Abi Dawud*, al-Mundhiri, vol. 2, p. 248.
6. The *Sahih* collection of al-Bukhari with commentary by as-Sindi, vol. 2, p. 34.

An-Nasa'i reports from Jabir, "The Messenger of Allah (p) said, 'He who owns camels, cows and sheep who does not give their dues will be made to stand before them on the Day of Rising on a flat ground, and then the animals with hard hooves will trample him and those with horns will butt him with their horns. On that Day, none of them will have its horns broken or cut off.' We asked, 'O Messenger of Allah, what are their dues?' He replied, 'To lend the male for breeding, to lend a bucket for drawing water, and to let them be ridden in the Way of Allah…"[1] A similar *hadith* is reported by Muslim from Jabir.[2] In another *hadith* from Jabir, the Messenger of Allah (p) was asked, "What is the due on camels?" He said, "To slaughter the fat among them [for charity], to lend the male for breeding and to milk them [for the poor] on the day of watering."[3]

Ash-Sharid says, "A man came to the Prophet (p) asking him about camels. The Messenger of Allah (p) said, 'Slaughter the fat among them and give rides on the strong and fast among them and milk them [for the poor] on the day of watering.'"[4]

These *hadiths* all indicate that the dues mentioned are obligatory. They are all different from *zakat*. Ibn Hazm says, "It is obligatory on each owner of camels, cows, and sheep to milk them on the day they are watered and to give what pleases him out of that milk for charity."[5] He continues, "Whoever claims there are no rights in addition to *zakat* is wrong and has no basis for his claim from either a text or *ijma'*." Everything that is prescribed by the Prophet (p) on wealth must be taken as obligatory. As for lending the bucket and the male for breeding, they are covered by the *ayat*, *"and deny help to others."* (107:7)

There are also sound reports about dues on horses, such as that of al-Bukhari from Abu Hurayra that the Messenger of Allah (p)

1. *Sunan an-Nasa'i*, with Sharh as-Suyuti and *Hashiyat as-Sindi*, vol. 5, p. 27.

2. *Tarh at-Tathrib*, vol. 4, pp. 11-12.

3. The author of *Majma' az-Zawa'id*, vol. 3, p. 107, says, "Reported by at-Tabarani in *al-Awsat*; the people of its chain are those of the *Sahih* collections, except him from whom at-Tabarani narrates. But Ibn Abi Hatim reports from the same and no one graces him weak."

4. Ibid. Reported by at-Tabarani in *al-Kabir*. Its chain is good.

5. *Al-Muhalla*, vol. 6, p. 50.

said, "Horses for one man are source of reward, for another a means of sustenance, and for a third man a reason for sin. He for whom they are a source of reward is the man who devotes them to fighting in the Way of Allah. They are a source of satisfaction for him who keeps them for personal use and as property without forgetting the right of Allah on them and their back-riding. For he who keeps them as a matter of pride, hypocrisy or for fighting Muslims they are a reason for sin."[1]

The fourth proof: the guest's right

There are sound *hadiths* that mandate a guest's right on his host from Khuwaylid ibn 'Amr. The Messenger of Allah (p) said, "He who believes in Allah and the Last Day must honour his guest. The guest's right is to be hosted as a prize for one day and one night, and kindness to the guest is to host him for three days. What is more than that is charity."[2] This indicates that honouring one's guest is obligatory since it is related to the essence of faith, especially since what is above three days is considered to be charity.

In another *hadith* from 'Abdullah ibn 'Amr, "Your body has a certain right on you, your eye has a right on you, your guests have a right on you, and your wife has a right on you."[3] The right of guests is further emphasised in another *hadith* from Abu Hurayra, "Any guest who appears among any people and remains deprived until morning has the right to take as much as his food would be, without any blame."[4] Al-Miqdad ibn Ma'dikarib narrates that the Messenger of Allah (p) said, "If a man hosts a guest and the guest gets up in the morning still deprived, the guest's aid and support is the duty of every Muslim until the guest takes from the host's grain and wealth the equivalent of his food for the night,"[5] and, "The

1. Reported by al-Bukhari. See al-Bukhari with *Hashiyat as-Sindi*, vol. 2, p. 33.

2. Reported by al-Bukhari, Muslim, Malik, Abu Dawud and Ibn Majah. See *at-Targhib*, vol. 3, p. 241.

3. Ibid. Reported by al-Bukhari, Muslim and others.

4. Reported by Ahmad. The narrators of its chain are trustworthy, and al-Hakim comments, "the chain is sound." See *at-Targhib*, ibid.

5. Reported by Abu Dawud and al-Hakim, ibid.

food for the night for the guest is obligatory on each Muslim host. If someone has guests in his house and does not offer them food, it remains a debt on him."[1]

Ibn Hazm says that Muslim reports from 'Uqba ibn 'Amir, "We asked, 'O Messenger of Allah, you send us on certain missions and we stay overnight as guests of certain people but they do not offer us food. What do you think?' The Messenger of Allah (p) replied, 'If you bed down at the houses of some people and they offer you whatever is suitable for guests, you should accept, but if they do not, then take from them the right of the guest that is obligatory upon them.'" Ibn Hazm adds that al-Bukhari reports from 'Abdu'r-Rahman ibn Abi Bakr, "The Companions of as-Suffa were poor people. The Prophet (p) said, 'He who has food for two people must take a third with him. He who has food for four people must have a fifth. He who has food for five must take with him a sixth,' or whatever the Prophet (p) said. Accordingly Abu Bakr brought home three men with him and the Messenger of Allah (p) brought ten."

These *hadiths* indicate beyond any doubt that there is an emphasised right on the wealth of a Muslim host to the extent that if this right is not given the whole Muslim community is called upon to help the guest obtain his right. Clearly enough, this right is not *zakat*. The guest may come at any time while *zakat* is obliged at definite times. Ibn Hazm says, "Offering food to a guest is an obligation on all Muslims, urban or bedouin, knowledgeable or ignorant – one night out of righteousness and three days out of kindness. What is beyond that is not obligatory, although it is encouraged. If a host withholds this due from his guest, the guest has the right to take it by force or through the court."[2]

Ash-Shawkani adds, "Scholars have several opinions on whether the right of the guest is obligatory or only encouraged. While al-Layth says it is obligatory on the host for one night only, the majority argues that the *hadith*, 'He who believes in Allah and the Last Day…' encourages only and does not make it obligatory as the

1. Reported by Abu Dawud and Ibn Majah, *at-Targhib*, vol. 3, pp. 241-242.
2. *Al-Muhalla*, vol 9, p. 174.

word used in the *hadith* indicates encouragement rather than obligation.[1]

As for the majority's answer to the *hadiths* about the right of the guest, ash-Shawkani notes:

> Al-Khattabi says, 'The right of the guest was obligatory at the time of the Prophet (p) when there was no state treasury that took care of guests, but guests do not now have any right on individual Muslims' wealth as their support is a duty of the state. Some others argue that this was only at the beginning of Islam but not after it was well established…'[2] The truth is that honouring and offering food to guests must be obligatory for the following reasons: firstly, whoever does not offer the guest food is made punishable by these *hadiths* and a penalty can only be inflicted for neglecting an obligation; secondly, we must note the extreme emphasis in the *hadith* on taking care of guests and the consideration that this action is related to faith; thirdly, the sentence in the *hadith*, 'What is beyond that is charity' explicitly means that what is less than three days is not charity but obligation; fourthly, the sentence, 'The night of the guest is an obligatory due,' is also an explicit prescription; fifthly, the *hadiths* oblige other Muslims to aid and help the guest in order to secure his or her right – this gives the guest's right even more certainty… Once these points are granted, one realises that the view of the majority is not substantiated. Thus the *hadiths* that oblige caring for guests must be understood as restrictions of the general *hadiths* that prohibit taking anything from Muslims without their consent. It is an arbitrary extrapolation to say that the *hadiths* about guests mandate mere sustenance of guests. By the same token, restricting the applicability of these *hadiths* to bedouins in the desert is also baseless.[3]

1. *Nayl al-Awtar*, vol. 2, pp. 162–3.
2. Ibid., p. 162.
3. Ibid., p. 163.

The fifth proof

The Qur'an severely admonishes those who do not extend help to others. Allah says, *"So woe to those who pray, and are forgetful of their prayer. Those who show off and deny help to others."* (107:4-7) Abu Dawud reports from Ibn Mas'ud, "We understood 'help' at the time of the Messenger of Allah (p) to mean lending the bucket and cooking pot."[1]

Extending these small services is obligatory because the Qur'an says, "Woe" to those who refuse to do it, equating it with neglecting prayers or wanting to show off to people. Such a severe admonishment would not be given if this action were not obligatory. No doubt extending such help is not included in *zakat*, so it must be an added obligation. Ibn Hazm reports from Ibn Mas'ud, "'Offering help' is giving what people used to borrow from each other, like an axe, cooking pots and similar things."[2] He reports that Ibn 'Abbas explains 'help' as 'lending household things' and in another version, 'lending things'.[3] Ibn Hazm also reports from 'Ali[4] and Umm 'Atiyya, "It is the help in household matters that is usually exchanged by people."[5] He also reports that Ibn 'Umar explained refusing to extend neighbourly help as "refusal to give the right due on wealth." Ibn Hazm adds, "This is consistent with what was mentioned earlier and with the views of 'Ikrima, Ibrahim and others. It is not known that any of the Companions disagreed on this matter."[6]

One must mention that Ibn Mas'ud's statement mentioned above has the same weight as a *hadith*, because he gives the interpretation of the verse prevalent at the time of the Prophet (p), and if that interpretation happened to be incorrect, it would have been corrected by the Prophet (p) or the Revelation itself as a mistake in understanding the Qur'an.

1 Abu Dawud makes no comments on the *hadith*. He is followed by al-Mundhiri. See *Mukhtasar as-Sunan*, vol. 2, p. 247. The *hadith* is also reported by al-Bayhaqi, vol. 4, p. 183.

2. Mentioned by Ibn Hazm via Ibn Abi Shayba, *al-Muhalla*, vol. 9, p. 168.

3. Ibid., and al-Bayhaqi, vol. 4, pp. 183-184.

4. *Al-Muhalla*, ibid.

5. Ibid.

6. Ibid.

The sixth proof

There are several texts which overwhelmingly dictate that Muslims must co-operate in doing good, solidarity and mutual help and support and be merciful to one another. There are texts that oblige feeding the indigent as a duty implied by brotherhood, faith and religion. Allah says, *"Help each other to goodness and fear of Allah. Do not help each other to wrongdoing and enmity."* (5:2) He describes the believers as *"merciful to one another,"* (48:29) and describes the path that one must follow to deserve reward from Allah, *"But he has not braved the steep ascent. What will convey to you what the steep ascent is? Freeing a slave or feeding, on a day of hunger, an orphaned relative or a poor man in the dust. Then to be one of those who believe and bid each other to steadfastness and bid each other to compassion. Those are the Companions of the Right," (90:11-18) "Give relatives their due, and the very poor and travellers,"* (17:26) and *"Be good to your parents and relatives and to orphans and the very poor, and to neighbours who are related to you and neighbours who are not related to you, and to companions and travellers and your slaves."* (4:36)

Many *ayats* exhort people to feed the destitute, considering such an act of benevolence a sign of faith and its neglect an implication of disbelief and denial of the Hereafter, such as *"Have you seen him who denies the* deen*? He is the one who harshly rebuffs the orphan and does not urge the feeding of the poor"* (107:1-3); *"They will say, 'We were not of those who prayed and we did not feed the poor'"* (74:43-44); and *"He used not to believe in Allah the Most Great, nor did he urge the feeding of the poor."* (69:33-34)

The Messenger describes the mutual solidarity, caring, and security of the Islamic society in several *hadiths*: "A believer to a fellow believer is like the structure whose blocks are cemented together," (Agreed upon) "The example of Muslims in their mutual love, compassion, and mercy is like a single body. If one of its members aches, the other members respond with fever and insomnia," (Agreed upon) "He is not a believer who goes to sleep satiated while his neighbour is hungry."[1] 'Ali narrates that the Prophet (p) said, "Indeed, Allah prescribes for wealthy Muslims contributions

1. Reported by at-Tabarani and al-Bayhaqi. Its chain is good.

from their wealth sufficient to satisfy the poor. The poor only suffer from hunger and nakedness through deprival by the rich. Verily Allah shall make the account difficult for them and punish them with a severe punishment."[1]

Ibn Hazm defends this opinion

In *al-Muhalla*, Ibn Hazm strongly supports the view that there are financial dues besides *zakat*. He provides several arguments and quotes from the Qur'an, *Sunna*, Companions and Followers, and concludes, "Allah commands the rich of each city to take complete care of the poor in that city. If *zakat* proceeds are not sufficient and there is no available *fay'* to be used, the government must force the wealthy to spend on the poor. There must be contributions for food and clothes for the winter and summer and shelter that protects them from rain, heat, sunshine and the eyes of passers-by." His argument goes as follows:

From the Qur'an:

Allah says, "*Give relatives their due, and the very poor and travellers*" (17:26), and "*Be good to your parents and relatives and to orphans and the very poor, and to neighbours who are related to you and neighbours who are not related to you, and to companions and travellers and your slaves.*" (4:36) Thus Allah imposes a due to the poor and traveller along with the right of relatives, and prescribes good doing to parents, relatives, the very poor, neighbours and slaves. Good action requires taking care of their physical needs. Refusing to take such care is undoubtedly wrong and sinful. In another *ayat*, Allah explains the reason for dwelling in Hell: "*'What caused you to enter Saqar?' They will say, 'We were not of those who prayed and we did not*

1. In *at-Targhib*, al-Mundhiri says, "Reported by at-Tabarani in *al-Awsat* and as-Saghir." At-Tabarani adds, "Thabit ibn Muhammad az-Zahid is singled out in the chain." Al-Mundhiri continues, "but Thabit is trustworthy and truthful and someone from whom al-Bukhari and others report. Other narrators in the chain are all right. It is also reported as a statement of 'Ali. The latter seems to be more authentic." See *at-Targhib*, vol. 1, chapter on *zakat*. Ibn Hazm mentions the same in *al-Muhalla*, vol. 6, p 159, as a statement of 'Ali, via Sa'id ibn Mansur.

feed the poor." (74:42-44) Allah here associates feeding the poor with obligatory prayers.

From the *hadiths*:

The Messenger of Allah (p) is reported, through several chains, all excellent in soundness, to have said, "He who has no mercy toward people will not receive any mercy from Allah."[1] Whoever has excess wealth and sees his Muslim brother hungry, naked or lost, and does not extend help is undoubtedly devoid of mercy. 'Abdu'r-Rahman ibn Abi Bakr says, "The Companions of as-Suffa were poor people, and the Messenger of Allah (p) said, 'He who has food for two must take a third with him, and he who has food for four must take a fifth with him or a sixth." [2] Ibn 'Umar narrates that the Messenger of Allah (p) said, "A Muslim is a brother of his fellow Muslim, he does not do him injustice or let him down."[3] Leaving a Muslim to hunger or cold while one has the ability to feed and clothe him is certainly letting him down.

Abu Sa'id narrates from the Prophet (p), "He who has an extra mount must give it to him who has no mount, and he who has excess food must give it to him who has no food." Abu Sa'id continues, "And the Prophet (p) mentioned the kinds of wealth that he liked to mention, so many kinds that we saw that none of us had a right to any excess."[4] I believe that there is unanimity among the Companions, as stated by Abu Sa'id, about all that comes in this *hadith*. Abu Musa narrates from the Prophet (p), "Feed the hungry and ransom the captive." (al-Bukhari)

---

1. Reported by al-Bukhari, Muslim, Ahmad, and at-Tirmidhi from Jarir ibn 'Abdullah; also by Ahmad and at-Tirmidhi from Abu Sa'id. The meaning comes in several *hadiths* via several chains, all sound. See *at-Taysir* by al-Munawi, vol. 2, p. 447.

2. Reported by Ahmad, vol. 2, pp, 197-199, and al-Bukhari.

3. Reported by Ahmad, vol. 2, p. 91, and vol. 4, p. 104 by al-Bukhari in his chapter on oppression or compulsion; by Muslim in his chapter on piety; Abu Dawud in his chapter of manners; and at-Tirmidhi in his chapter on the description of the Resurrection, from Ibn 'Umar.

4. Reported in Muslim's chapter on marriage and on foundlings, Abu Dawud's chapter on *zakat*, and Ahmad, vol. 3, p 34.

From Companions and Followers:

'Umar says, "If I still had ahead of me as much time as what is gone, I would take the excess wealth of the rich and distribute it among the poor *Muhajirun*."[1] 'Ali says, "Allah prescribes on the wealth of the rich as much as is sufficient to satisfy the poor among them. If the latter suffer from hunger, nakedness, or exhaustion, it is because of deprivation by the rich. It is just that Allah will take them to account on the Day of Rising and punish them for it." Ibn 'Umar says, "On wealth, there is a right besides *zakat*."

'A'isha, al-Hasan ibn 'Ali and Ibn 'Umar are known to have asked people who asked them for money, "If you ask for money to pay the ransom of an aching heart or an overwhelming liability or to relieve depriving poverty, you have a right that is due." Abu 'Ubayda and three hundred Companions on a journey were near the end of their provision of food, Abu 'Ubayda ordered each individual's food be collected in two containers, and distributed equal rations to everyone. This represents an agreed-upon position of all these Companions since none are known to have disagreed. We also have correct reports to the effect that ash-Sha'bi, Mujahid, Tawus and others all said, "There is a right on wealth besides *zakat*."

We know of no one who opposes this except for ad-Dahhak's comment, "*Zakat* annuls every other right on wealth." The narration of ad-Dahhak is not even approved of, let alone his own opinion![2] The fact is that all those who accept the view of ad-Dahhak are the first ones to differ from it in actual life, since they all believe there are rights on wealth other than *zakat*, which include providing for needy parents, for one's wife, and for slaves, feeding domestic animals and paying debts and other liabilities. Furthermore, such people say he who is in such need of water that he is on the verge

1. Ibn Hazm says the chain of this quote is excellent in correctness and greatness.

2. Only Yahya ibn Sa'id grades ad-Dahhak weak. Ahmad, Ibn Ma'in, Abu Zur'a, al-'Ijli, ad-Daraqutni, and Ibn Hibban all grade him trustworthy. In *at-Taqrib*, Ibn Hajar says, "He is truthful; has many *mursal hadiths*." See *Mizan al-I'tidal*, vol. 2, pp. 325-326. *Tahdhib at-Tahdhib*, vol. 4, pp. 453-454. However, weakness in narration does not imply weakness in opinion, as claimed by Ibn Hazm. Ibn Abi Layla is graded weak by *hadith* critics but is a leading *fiqh* scholar.

of death for want of it is obligated to take water wherever it is found and even to fight anyone who denies him that right. What is the difference between fighting to avoid death from thirst and fighting to prevent death from hunger and nakedness? Indeed, the opponents' view is in opposition to *ijma'*, Qur'an, *Sunna* and analogy.

It is not permissible for any Muslim in need of food to eat the flesh of dead animals or the meat of the pig while there exists lawful food that is in excess of the needs of its owner, whether this owner is Muslim or of the People of the Pledge. It is obligatory for the owner of excess food to feed the hungry so that those in need do not have to eat pork or carrion. In such cases, the poor person is permitted to fight until his right is secured. If he is killed, whoever killed him is sinful and must pay the ransom and be subjected to the due penalty (death), but if his denier is killed, he goes to the wrath of Allah because he is an aggressor, and Allah says, *"But if one of them unjustly attacks the other, fight the attackers until they revert to Allah's command."* (49:9) For reasons similar to these, Abu Bakr fought those who refused to pay *zakat*.[1]

1. *Al-Muhalla*, vol. 6, pp. 156-159. Texts are given without their chains in order to avoid lengthiness. Ahmad Shakir comments on Ibn Hazm's view, "This and similar views in the Islamic *Shari'a* show that Islamic law is unsurpassed in its wisdom and justice. I wish our friends who are overtaken by imported man-made laws would look into these views, understand them, and realise that this religion brings forth the best law for mankind ever. If Muslims would only understand the teachings of their *deen* and go back to its clear spring and beautiful source – the Qur'an and *Sunna* – and apply what is ordained by our Lord in their private as well as their public lives, they would have been ahead of all other nations. Is it not true that all destructive uprisings and revolutions were incited by the oppression inflicted by the rich on the poor and by the former's selfishness to secure all the goods in the world for themselves, leaving their brothers dying from hunger and cold? If only the rich understood, they would realise that doing good to the poor is the first requirement necessary for the preservation of their own wealth."

Chapter Three

Discussion and Analysis

Points of agreements and differences of the two views

After surveying the pros and cons of permitting financial dues in addition to *zakat*, we find that their differences are not as great as one may think. They all agree on certain points:

- The obligation to provide for needy parents.
- The obligation to spend on the maintenance of other needy relatives, although there are differences as to the degree of relationship included in this obligation.
- The obligation is to provide for the deprived who are in desperate need of food, clothing or shelter. In *Ahkam al-Qur'an*, al-Jassas says, "The obligation is generally *zakat*, except when certain things happen that require other payments such as necessity of food for the hungry, clothes for the naked, or funerals for the deceased."[1] Similar to this is lending stools, cooking pots or axes to those in dire need, since prevention of harm is a collective obligation on all Muslims according to *ijma'*.
- The obligation to pay for public necessities such as defending Muslim land, freeing Muslim captives taken by unbelievers and curing diseases and relieving famines. This is agreed upon unanimously by Muslim scholars. In *Sharh al-Munhaj*, ar-Ramli says, "Among the collective obligations (*furud al-kifaya*) are the requirement to prevent harm to Muslims including providing clothing to the unclothed and food to the hungry if *zakat* funds and public treasury funds are not sufficient. This requirement is

1. Al-Jassas, *Ahkam al-Qur'an*, vol. 2, p. 131.

> obliged on those who have excess beyond their yearly needs. Moreover, the amount of help must equal, according to the most accepted view, the provision of sufficiency and not merely subsistence. Similar to food and clothing are necessities such as medical care and other necessary services."[1]

It is mentioned in Part Four that an-Nawawi, a Shafi'i, believes that providing for the regular army is the duty of the country's rich as well as *zakat* payment. Ibn al-'Arabi in *Ahkam al-Qur'an* adds, "If *zakat* is practised and some further need arises, the rich are obliged to provide for this need by unanimous agreement. Malik says, 'Muslims are all obliged to provide for freeing their prisoners of war, even if this were to take all their wealth.' Moreover, if a governor, by an act of oppression, does not distribute the already-collected *zakat*, the rich must still provide for the needs of the poor, according to the view I think correct."[2] In his *tafsir* of the Qur'an, al-Qurtubi emphasises the same: "Scholars are in agreement that if a need arises after the distribution of *zakat*, funds must be collected and used for that need."[3] He also attributes a similar position to Malik regarding freeing Muslim prisoners of war. In *al-I'tisam*, ash-Shatibi concludes, "If the public treasury is empty and the needs of the army for funds are still not satisfied, a just government can impose on the rich taxes sufficient to provide for these needs until the treasury has funds again."[4]

All these are clear statements that there are agreed upon cases in which financial imposts may exist in addition to *zakat*. Amazingly enough, these quotations are from scholars known to believe that there are no other financial duties besides *zakat*, which reveals that what they mean by this position is the prevention of oppressive and unneeded taxes, usually imposed by rulers and used for their own pleasures and those of their supporters. However, this does not mean there are no real differences between the two parties. The areas of real difference can be summarised as follows:

1. *Nihayat al-Muhtaj*, vol. 7, p. 194.
2. Ibn al-'Arabi, *Ahkam al-Qur'an*, part one, pp. 59-60.
3. *Tafsir al-Qurtubi*, vol. 2, p. 223.
4. *Al-I'tisam*, vol. 1, p. 103.

- The due right on agriculture at the time of harvesting
- Dues on livestock
- The right of the guest
- The duty to supply neighbourly help

All these are considered obligations by the proponents of other financial duties besides *zakat* while they are viewed as desirable areas of benevolence by their opponents except in the case of necessity, as stated by al-Jassas when he says, "Lending these tools (like the stool, cooking pit, and axe) may be obligatory in case of necessity, when refusal to lend is a cause for blame and punishment. But refusal to lend in cases where there is no dire necessity is only a sign of bad manners and low morality that is not supposed to be a trait of Muslims, since the Prophet (p) says, 'I was sent in order to complete good character.'[1]"[2]

The most important point of difference is the right of the poor to be taken care of out of the wealth of the rich which is called for by scholars who believe that there exist duties besides *zakat*.

Weighing and discussion

These areas of dispute require study in order to discover the correct position.

- The right of the poor to agricultural produce at the time of harvest was studied in Part Three, and it was concluded that this right, though mentioned in a Makkan *ayat*, is in fact the *'ushr* which is *zakat* itself. The earthly ordinance in the Makkan *ayat* proclaims the general obligation whose details come later in Madina.
- As for the right of the guest, it is apparent from the texts that this means the stranger guest travelling in an area where he knows nobody. This is almost the same as a traveller, so that Ibn 'Abbas and several Followers even explain that the traveller

1. Reported by al-Bukhari in *al-Adab al-Mufrad*, Ibn Sa'd in *at-Tabaqat*, al-Hakim in *al-Mustadrak*, al-Bayhaqi via a sound chain. See *at-Taysir*, vol. 1, p. 362.
2. Al-Jassas, op cit., p. 584.

is the guest.[1] The *hadiths* explicitly state that the guest's right is to be offered food and shelter. This is indeed different from *zakat*.

- Extending neighbourly help is undoubtedly obligated and its refusal is a cause for woe and severe censure. This due is also different from *zakat*.

- As for the right of the poor to be taken care of from the wealth of the rich, it is a matter so well-known in the *Shari'a* that the *ayats* or *hadiths* about it need not be quoted. However, scholars usually give special attention to the *ayat*, *"It is not devoutness..."* and to the *hadith*, "There are rights on wealth besides *zakat*..." because these two texts are extremely explicit and to the point in laying down this principle. It is directly derived from the basic foundations of Islam and from the very nature of its system. Mutual solidarity, co-operation, care and mercy are basic features of the Islamic system. They all imply that the strong must help the weak and the rich must care for the poor. Neglecting this obligation is tantamount to basic deviation from this *deen* and its teachings.

A man from the tribe of Tamim once came to the Prophet (p) and said, "O Messenger of Allah, I am a man with plenty of wealth, a large family and I am well-established. Tell me, how should I spend, and what should I do?" The Prophet (p) said, "Pay your *zakat*, for it is a purifier that cleanses you. Extend aid to your kindred, and know and fulfil the right of him who asks, your neighbour, and the poor."[2] The Messenger (p) established a right for relatives, he who asks, the neighbour, and the poor, over and above *zakat*, which is consistent with the *ayat*, *"Give relatives their due, and the very poor and travellers,"* (17:26) and the *hadith*, "He who asks has a right, even if he happens to come riding on a mare."[3]

---

1. *Tafsir Ibn Kathir*, vol. 1, p. 208.

2. Reported by Ahmad from Anas. Its narrators are those of the correct books. See *at-Targhib*, vol. 1, p. 263. Also reported by Abu 'Ubayd and Ibn al-Mundhir. See *ad-Durr al-Manthur*, vol. 1, p. 49.

3. Reported by Ahmad and by Abu Dawud, chapter on *zakat*. Al-Hafiz al-

The Messenger of Allah (p) said, "He who shows no mercy to others, Allah will show him no mercy,"[1] and "You will not become believers until you show mercy to one another." They said, "O Messenger of Allah, we all show mercy." He replied, "It is not the mercy of one toward his companion, but mercy to all people."[2]

The least that should be done to realise this mutual co-operation, solidarity, benevolence, and mercy is to see to it that no person in society is left out in the cold without provision for an adequate standard of living including food, clothing, shelter, medical care and necessary education. If the proceeds of *zakat* and other government resources are sufficient to cover all these needs it is well and good, but if they are not, it is an ascertained obligation on the rich – collectively – to take care of the poor. If this is not done, all rich individuals in the society are considered sinful unless at least some of them fulfil this requirement on behalf of the others. The Islamic government must interfere and collect necessary dues from the rich in order to support all the poor. This was established by the religion of Islam fourteen centuries ago, long before Western Europe opened its eyes to such "progressive" ideas.

Discussing the evidence of the opponents

From all texts of Qur'an and *Sunna* presented in argument by the opponents of financial dues besides *zakat*, it is clear that *zakat* is distinct from all other financial dues on wealth. *Zakat* is the only permanent, regular and well-defined financial obligation due from the rich. It must always be paid, regardless of the existence or non-existence of the poor and needy in society. It is performed as an act of worship to Allah and an act of thankfulness for the blessings He bestows on the rich. It is a purification and cleansing of the zakatable assets as well as the souls of those who possess them.

'Iraqi comments, "Its chain is good, and its narrators are trustworthy" as stated by as-Suyuti in *al-La'ali*, vol. 2, p. 140. (The late Ahmad Shakir grades it correct in his notes on the *Musnad* of Ahmad, vol. 3, p. 173.

1. Reported by al-Bukhari, Muslim and at-Tirmidhi from Jarir ibn 'Abdullah.

2. Reported by at-Tabarani from Abu Musa; its narrators are those of the sound books, as stated by al-Mundhiri. See *at-Targhib*, vol. 3.

As for other financial obligations such as dues collected to support the poor in case of the inadequacy of *zakat* proceeds, these obligations are temporary and measured only by the amount of need. Consequently, they differ according to circumstances. These obligations are not necessarily individual but collective, in the sense that if the needs are provided for by some of the richest payers, others may be exempted. One must not forget cases in which such a collective obligation becomes individual and specific like when there exists only one rich person available to extend help.

Ibn Taymiyya comments on the statement, "There are no other dues imposed on wealth besides *zakat*":

> It means that no dues except *zakat* are imposed only for the reason that wealth or assets are owned. Indeed, other dues are imposed on the rich, but not simply because of owning assets, such as provision for the living expenses of wives, slaves, owned livestock, needy parents and other relatives, paying due debts, feeding the hungry and clothing the naked. The latter is a collective and not individual obligation. These financial obligations are imposed for other reasons, such as family relations or the presence of dire necessity; but owning wealth is a necessary condition for their levy. Thus, owning wealth for these obligations is like being able to procure means of travel to pilgrimage: pilgrimage is obliged only on each Muslim who is able to perform it. As for *zakat*, it is obliged by reason of owning wealth and must be performed regardless of the need for its disbursement. It is a right due to Allah."[1]

1. *Fatawa Ibn Taymiyya*, vol. 7, p. 316.

Part Nine
Zakat and Taxes

Prologue

This section is a comparison between *zakat* as prescribed in this *deen* of Islam and taxes as decreed by man-made taxation systems. This comparison is, however, restricted and does not study the old and undeveloped forms of taxation systems applied in the ancient Roman and Persian empires and in Medieval Europe. The following chapters of this book take up points of similarity and difference between *zakat* and contemporary taxes from the point of view of their natures, foundations, philosophies, characteristics, ratios, proceeds, etc.

Chapter One

The Essence of *Zakat* and Taxes

A tax, as defined by taxation experts, is an obligatory due imposed on the payers and submitted to the state. Taxes are usually imposed according to the ability of the payers and regardless of the benefits the payers derive from the services performed by the public authority to whom the tax is paid. Tax proceeds are used for public expenditure to achieve economic, social, political and other objectives of the state.[1] *Zakat*, as defined by Muslim jurists, is a determined right imposed by Allah on the wealth of Muslims to the benefit of the categories mentioned in Allah's Book, such as the poor, the needy, etc. It is an expression of gratitude for Allah's blessings and is performed to seek His pleasure and to purify both soul and wealth.

Similarities between *zakat* and taxes

The above definitions reveal the following similarities:

- The elements of obligation and compulsion exist in both *zakat* and taxes.
- Both taxes and *zakat* are paid to certain public bodies, be it the local or national authority,[2] an autonomous institution enforced by law or the public treasury.
- In taxes, there is no reciprocity between the amount collected and services received by the payer. The payer is required to pay taxes as a member of society. *Zakat* is also paid, without any direct *quid pro quo*, by every Muslim to the Islamic state, regardless of the benefit that the *zakat* payer may receive from the state.

1. *Mabadi' 'Ilm al-Maliyya*, Muhammad Fu'ad Ibrahim, vol. 1, p. 261.
2. In Medieval Europe, there were taxes paid by vassals to their landlords.

- *Zakat* and, in their modern understanding, taxes have social, economic and political objectives besides their obvious financial objective.

Differences between *zakat* and taxes

Despite the above points of similarity, the differences between *zakat* and modern taxes are numerous:

- The first striking difference is the name, which has important implications. *Zakat* as a word means purity, growth and blessing. The word is selected for this pillar of Islam in order to incorporate these meanings. "Tax", on the other hand, implies imposition, estimation and charge. The Arabic word for tax, *dariba*, has the same indication of charge and imposition. Allah says, *"Abasement and destitution were stamped (*duribat*) upon them."* (2:61)

  Consequently, a tax is looked upon as a charge and liability while *zakat* inspires purity, sanctity, and growth. It is implied that hoarding wealth without cleansing it by giving the right Allah imposes to the poor makes it a source of sin and evil and that giving *zakat* – although it physically reduces the wealth – in fact brings reasons for growth. Allah says, *"Allah obliterates usury but makes* sadaqa *grow in value!"* (2:276) *"Anything you expend will be replaced by Him."* (34:39) The Messenger says, "Wealth never decreases as a result of *sadaqa*." (at-Tirmidhi)

  Moreover *zakat* is purification not only for assets on which *zakat* has been paid but for the payer himself as well as the recipient for it purifies from vanity, hatred and selfishness and provides a benevolent hand to the poor. Allah says, *"Take* sadaqa *from their wealth to purify and cleanse them."* (9:103)

- *Zakat* is an act of worship in gratitude and thankfulness to Allah whereas taxes are a mere civil obligation. Intention is one of the conditions of *zakat* since all acts of worship require intention. Allah says, *"They were only ordered to worship Allah, making their* deen *sincerely His."* (98:5) *Zakat* is always cited in the sections on worship in books of Islamic jurisprudence and is mentioned with prayer in more than twenty places in the

Qur'an and in many places in the *Sunna. Zakat* is not obliged on non-Muslim citizens of the Islamic state since Islam does not consider it fair to oblige non-Muslims to perform an Islamic rite of worship.

- *Zakat*, as an obligation from Allah, is irrevocably defined and its main features given by the Legislator. The *Shari'a* determines the ratios applied on all assets, decreeing cases to which 20%, 10%, 5% or 2.5% rates apply. These ratios and their applicability cannot be altered by anyone or any law, regardless of changing circumstances. The same applies to the *nisabs* of the wealth to which *zakat* is applied. On the other hand, a tax is enacted by people and is always subject to change and redetermination.

- *Zakat* is a fixed and permanent obligation which cannot be discontinued by any government. Even if the government does not collect it, *zakat* remains an obligation on individual Muslims. Taxes can be changed, altered or eliminated, depending on the circumstances and the decisions of legislative authorities. A tax is not permanent, continuous or fixed.

- *Zakat* defines its own disbursement. Description of its recipients is given by Allah in the Qur'an and explained by the tradition of His Messenger (p). No one may add a new category of recipients or eliminate a recipient who deserves *zakat*, to the extent that individual Muslims can, in case of need, distribute *zakat* by themselves. The disbursement of *zakat* has a humanitarian aim, among others, and is surrounded by spiritual acts, such as the exchange of prayers between payer and recipient. Furthermore, the budget of *zakat* must remain independent from the public treasury since it is "an obligation from Allah." (cf. 9:60) Taxes, on the other hand, are levied for multiple objectives, changeable with time and circumstances. The state or proper authority determines usage of tax proceeds.

- Taxes and *zakat* each have a different relationship to the state. Payment of a tax represents a relation between the payer and the local or national authorities of the state. If the tax collection is delayed by these authorities, the payer has no reason to pay the tax and cannot be blamed for lack of payment. *Zakat* represents a relationship between the payer and his Lord. It is Allah who gave him wealth, and the payer, out of obedience to Allah, pays *zakat*, seeking Allah's acceptance and pleasure. If the Islamic state does not exist or does not collect *zakat*, individual Muslims are still required to fulfil this duty, just as the prayer remains obligatory even if one does not find a mosque because "*zakat* is the sister of prayer." Muslims are supposed to pay *zakat* with their souls pleased, hoping that Allah will accept their worship. This is not the case with taxes.

- *Zakat* has spiritual and ethical objectives in addition to its socio-economic aims, while taxes have no such aspirations. The objectives of *zakat* were discussed in some detail in Part Six of this book. It is sufficient here to mention the *ayat*, *"Take* sadaqa *from their wealth to purify and cleanse them and pray for them. Your prayers bring relief to them."* The Prophet (p) used to pray for blessings for *zakat* payers and ordered his commissioners to do so to the extent that some jurists consider it obligatory. Taxes are detached from such spiritual and ethical objectives. It was even maintained by taxation specialists for a long time that taxes must have but one target: furnishing the treasury with financial resources. Only recently have scholars begun to argue for the socio-economic objectives of taxes, so that the idea of tax neutrality has become a relic of the past. But scholars who study taxation have not yet thought of spiritual or moral objectives for their taxation systems, while *zakat* established such aims fourteen hundred years ago.

- The most important difference between *zakat* and taxes is the different theoretical grounds for which each is imposed. Because of its importance, this topic will be discussed in a chapter of its own.

It is notable that Muslim scholars throughout the centuries refer to the dual meaning of *zakat* as a tax and an act of worship.[1] Thus its humanitarian, moral, social, economic and spiritual elements

1. *Bidayat al-Mujtahid*, vol. 1, p. 237.

intermingle to form one institution. The author of *ar-Rawd an-Nadir* quotes some scholars as saying:

> Allah imposes *zakat* on the wealth of the rich as a gesture of care towards their brethren, the poor, in fulfilment of the glorious right of brotherhood and in practice of love and compassion. *Zakat* includes elements of help, support and mutual co-operation, in spite of the fact that it is a test of obedience for the wealthy, similar to other forms of worship Allah prescribes be performed physically and, consequently, it requires intention. But since it is giving, it can be performed through appointed representatives or agents. Inasmuch as it is a financial obligation, the Islamic government can force owners of wealth to pay their due *zakat*, and it can be taken from the estate of the deceased. *Zakat* can be taken from the wealth of children or the insane who are otherwise not obliged to perform other forms of worship. Because *zakat* is a cherishing of the poor and needy, their needs are given priority. Because it is help to brothers and sisters, Allah imposes it only on the able – the rich who own the *nisab*. The *Shari'a* determines the *nisab* and rates for each zakatable asset. Rates differ in accordance with cost and efforts involved in the process of production. Thus, the rate is ten percent on what is watered by the sky, and five percent on what is watered by animals carrying water supplies.[1]

1. *Ar-Rawd an-Nadir*, vol. 2, p. 389.

Chapter Two
The Theoretical Foundation for Levying Taxes and *Zakat*

Legal foundation for tax levying

There are several theories explaining the legal foundation of taxes. One is the contractual theory. This was adopted by many philosophers of the eighteenth century who argued that tax levying is based on a contractual relationship between the state and the individual whereby taxes are paid in exchange for services provided by the state, such as security and other public services. This is founded on Jean Jacques Rousseau's theory of social contract. According to Mirabeau, tax is a price paid in advance by the individual for the community's protection, like in a sales contract. According to Adam Smith, the contract is a rental one whereby the state provides individuals with services and they pay rent for them, while Montesquieu and Hobbes argue that it is an insurance contract whereby the tax is a premium paid by the individual to insure protection of the rest of his wealth.

Critics of this theory believe it is ill-founded since there is no way of realising justice in any exchange between taxes and the benefits received by the taxpayer, as it is impossible to estimate the exact benefit each citizen receives from the public expenditure on security, law enforcement, judiciary system, education and national defence. Even if it were possible to measure the benefits received by each individual, this theory leads to the unjust conclusion that the poor, who usually need more of the state's services, also carry proportionally the largest burden of state finance. The "insurance" relationship is further criticised because it restricts the role of the state to security and protection only and is an incomplete insurance since an insurer normally compensates the insured for losses incurred, while the state does not give compensation for loss of property.

Another theory is that of state sovereignty. This theory explains taxes by the authority of the state as the sovereign body which has the right to distribute the burden of taxes according to the principle of solidarity of all members of society, regardless of any benefits they receive from the state's services.[1]

The theoretical basis of *zakat* levying

There are several theories that attempt to explain the theoretical basis for *zakat*. Four theories are discussed in this chapter: the theory of obligation, the theory of vicegerency, the theory of mutual solidarity, and the theory of brotherhood.

The theory of obligation

Supporters of this theory explain *zakat* the same way other obligations are explained, i.e. that Allah, who is the Creator and Provider, has the right to charge his servants with an obligation in thankfulness to Him and to test them so that wrongdoers can be distinguished from good doers. Human beings are not created to no purpose nor are they left to be lost in nothingness. Allah says, *"Did you suppose that We created you for amusement and that you would not return to Us?"* (23:115) *"Does man reckon he will be left to go on unchecked?"* (75:36)

Human beings have not been left without a role and guidance. Allah sends Messengers and Prophets to guide, to warn and to inform human beings of the commandments of Allah and the obligations He commands, *"...so that He can repay those who do evil for what they did and repay those who do good with the Very Best."* (53:31)

Thus Allah commands the performance of prayers five times every day and night, fasting one month every year and pilgrimage once in a lifetime so that man can glorify his Creator and honour His rites. In the same way Allah obliges the payment of *zakat* as a

1. For this I have depended on *Mizaniyyat ad-Dawla* by Dr. Muhammad Hilmy Murad, Nahda Misr, 1955, pp. 73-75.

financial act of worship whereby humans spend out of their assets in expression of thankfulness to Allah and in search of His pleasure. Allah says, *"It is the people who are safe-guarded from the avarice of their own selves, who are the successful."* (59:9)

The theory of vicegerency

The basic element in this theory is that all goods, in fact, belong to Allah. Human beings are only viceregents. Allah is the true owner of everything.

> *"Everything in the heavens and everything in the earth belongs to Allah."* (53:31) *"Everything in the heavens and everything on the earth and everything in between them and everything under the ground belongs to Him."* (20:6) No one, whatsoever has any share in this. *"Say: 'Call on those you make claims for besides Allah. They have no power over even the smallest particle, either in the heavens or in the earth. They have no share in them. They give Him no support.'"* (34: 22) *"Allah is the Creator of everything and He is Guardian over everything."* (39:62) *"He created everything and determined it most exactly."* (25:2)

Allah is the Bestower and Giver of all things. What humans make and produce is, in fact, owned by Allah, along with man himself. Production, according to economists, merely utilises already existing materials, changes the mixture of materials and their proportions.[1] Allah says:

> *"Our Lord is He who gives each thing its created form and then guides it."* (20:50) *"Allah is He who created the heavens and the earth and sends down water from the sky and by it brings forth fruits as provision for you. He has made the ships subservient to you to run upon the sea by His command, and He has made the rivers subservient to you, and He has made the sun and the moon subservient to you holding steady to their courses, and He has*

1. *Al-Iqtisad as-Siyasi*, Dr. Rif'at Mahjub, vol. 1, pp. 191-192, and *al-Iqtisad as-Siyasi*, Dr. 'Ali 'Abd al-Wahid Wafi, pp. 74-76.

made the night and the day subservient to you. He has given you everything you have asked Him for. If you tried to number Allah's blessings, you could never count them." (14:32-34)

Even in production, it is Allah who created the laws of mixing materials together and changing their characteristics. Allah has made these laws for humans and provides human beings with the ability to understand and use them for their own benefit. He says:

"Have you thought about what you cultivate? Is it you who make it germinate or are We the Germinator? If We willed We could have made it broken stubble. You would then be left devoid of fruit, distraught: 'We are ruined, in fact we are destitute!' Have you thought about the water that you drink? Is it you who sent it down from the clouds or are We the Sender? If We willed We could have made it bitter. So why do you not give thanks? Have you thought about the fire that you light? Is it you who make the trees that fuel it grow or are We the Grower?" (56:63-72) *"Man has only to look at his food. We pour down plentiful water. Then split the earth into furrows. Then We make grain grow in it and grapes and herbs."* (80:21-28)

Allah creates the raw materials and laws of nature governing trade and manufacturing. Allah says:

"And We sent down iron in which there lies great force and many uses for mankind." (57:25) *"We taught him the art of making garments for you to protect you against each others' violence, but do you show any thanks?"* (21:80)

In conclusion all goods belong to Allah and He makes them subject to His servants. *"Any blessing you have is from Allah."* (16:53) Therefore it is no surprise that human beings – the viceregents – should be expected to spend out of these bestowed goods for the purposes that Allah wants and to make Allah's Word uppermost. This is the least expression of gratitude and thankfulness. Allah says:

"Give away some of what We have provided for you." (2:252) *"And give them some of the wealth Allah has given you,"*

(24:33) and *"Give from that to which He has made you the successors."* (57:7)

Humans are not, in fact, the owners of goods and assets, but only viceregents.[1] Az-Zamakhshari says in explanation of the *ayat*, *"Give from that to which He has made you the successors"* to mean "The goods and funds that are in your hands belong, in the true sense, to Allah who created them. He gives them to us and authorises us to enjoy using them. Thus they are not our goods, we are only viceregents and representatives. We must spend out of these goods for the payment of rights due to Allah. Spending should not be difficult for us in that we are not doing it out of our own wealth."[2]

Moreover, the fact of all goods and creatures being owned by Allah implies one more thing: that we, as representatives, must spend in accordance with the will of the Owner. Muslim scholars express this idea very eloquently. Ar-Razi says, "The poor are dependent on Allah and the rich are Allah's treasurers because the wealth in their hands belongs to Allah. It is expected that the Owner would order His treasurers to spend some of the wealth in the treasury for the needy who are the Owner's dependants."[3] Ibn al-'Arabi says, "Allah, glorified be His absolute wisdom and praised be His commandments, gives wealth to some people out of grace and mercy to them. He makes the sign of gratitude for this blessing to spend a portion on those who have no wealth, thus representing Allah who guarantees the poor their living when He says, *"There is no creature on the earth which is not dependent upon Allah for its provision."* (11:6) If the rich do not fulfil the will of the Owner out of miserliness and selfishness, they deserve the Owner's wrath and anger."[4]

1. Ibn al-Qayyim asks, "Is it correct to say that anyone is a viceregent of Allah?" His answer is negative, since "A viceregent (*khalifa*) is a person who does things in the capacity of deputyship for the one who appoints him. Allah has no deputy, or substitute or anyone who acts on his behalf. The Messenger (p) says in his prayers, 'My Lord, You are my Companion in travel and my Viceregent in my family.' But there is nothing that prevents the use of the term for human beings in the sense that they are commanded to preserve what is under their authority and to nourish it." See *Madarij as-Salikin*, vol. 2, pp. 126-127.

2. *Al-Kashshaf*, vol. 3, p. 200.

3. *At-Tafsir al-Kabir*, vol. 16, p. 103.

4. *Ahkam al-Qur'an*, p. 945.

Many laymen in Muslim countries attribute to Allah the saying, "Wealth is Mine, the poor are My dependants and the rich are My agents. If My agents treat My dependants with miserliness, I surely will make them taste My wrath without hesitation."[1] Although there is no authenticity to these words, the idea they express is undoubtedly correct and its popularity among the Muslim masses indicates that this concept of vicegerency lies deep in the consciousness of Muslims. Amazingly, beggars throughout Muslim lands, when asking people for donations, repeat, "Out of the wealth of Allah." Lastly, there is a *hadith* that reads, "Woe to the rich from the poor on the Day of Resurrection. The latter will say 'Our Lord, they oppressed us, depriving us of our right that You ordained on them for us.' Allah will say, 'By My Might and Highness, I shall indeed make you close to me and make them far away from me.'"[2]

The theory of solidarity

Human beings are social creatures. This is known to sociologists as well as it is known to Muslim scholars. Even in the procuring of wealth and income by an individual, society plays an important role. Consequently, private wealth must have a facet that is, at the same time, part of the wealth of society as a whole. Allah addresses the Muslim community, *"Do not hand over to the simple-minded any property in your hands for which Allah has made you responsible."* (4:5) This *ayat* indicates that property and wealth belong to society as much as to individuals, to the extent that Muslim jurists deduce that abusers of their private wealth must be prevented from practising control over their assets since wealth belongs to the whole society as well. Notably the *ayat* attributes the property to "you" and not "them". Moreover, in another *ayat*, this meaning is expressed more explicitly. Allah says, *"O you who believe! Do not consume one another's property by false means, but only by means of mutually agreed trade. And do not kill yourselves. Allah is Most Merciful to you."* (4:29)

1. After research, I did not find any trace or origin of this narration.

2. Reported by at-Tabarani in *al-Muj'am al-Awsat* and as-Saghir from Anas, via a weak chain. *Jam' al-Fawa'id*, vol. 1, p. 142.

It must be noted that the *ayat* forbids eating one another's property by false means, although it expresses it as "your property".

Muslim society and community is based on mutual solidarity and mutual support. This applies to wealth as well as to persons. Consuming somebody's property by false means is like consuming society's wealth, and transgressing against someone's right is like transgressing against the whole of society on the same principle as is expressed in the *ayat*, *"If someone kills another person – unless it is in retaliation for someone else or for causing corruption in the earth – it is as if he had murdered all mankind. And if anyone gives life to another person, it is as if he had given life to all mankind."* (5:35) Commenting on the *ayat*, *"Do not consume one another's property by false means"*, Rashid Rida says, "This expression establishes an essential principle of the Islamic system: the principle that the whole society shares in the property of individuals – in the right sense. Socialists today aim at a just principle of sharing but they cannot realise it and never will as long as they continue their search outside Islam. Islam considers the entire society to have a share in the private property of each individual Muslim while still respecting the rights of private ownership. Each individual is obliged to contribute to the public interest whether the person is rich or not. Above all these decreed rights on private assets for the benefit of the whole society, Islam urges the wealthy to continuously contribute through righteous and benevolent deeds to the welfare of fellow Muslims and the welfare of the community as a whole."[1]

In conclusion, the Muslim community has a certain right on private property. This right does not deprive the individual of ownership but takes a share of individual wealth for fulfilling the interests of the whole community. The society, as represented by its state, has a share in the assets of each rich person, a share which must be paid in order to preserve the social structure, promote the message of Islam and defend fellow Muslims. Even if there are no poor and needy in a Muslim community, the rich must still contribute their *zakat* to finance such public services as promotion of faith and "the Cause of Allah" which is a continuous and permanent object of public expenditures.

1. *Tafsir al-Manar*, vol. 5, p. 39.

The theory of brotherhood among Muslims

Brotherhood, the fourth explanation for the obligation of *zakat*, is rooted deeper in the heart than solidarity and is more influential since solidarity is a mutual exchange while brotherhood implies selfless giving and sacrifice. Brotherhood is a spiritual feeling directly derived from the common humanity of men and women. It requires extending any help within one's power to one's brother and loving for one's brother what one loves for oneself.

There are two degrees of brotherhood, one based on the common human bond and the other on common faith. All human beings – regardless of colour, ethnicity, language, social status, and religion – spring from one source, one single origin, as children of Adam and Eve. Allah in the Qur'an calls humans, "O children of Adam,"[1] or "O mankind."[2] Human relations like mercy and brotherhood exist among all people.

This is emphasised in the Qur'an in more than one place: *"O Mankind! Show fear of your Lord who created you from a single self and created its mate from it and then disseminated many men and women from the two of them. Show fear of Allah in whose name you make demands on one another and also show fear of Him in respect of your families. Allah watches over you continually."* (4:1) The word "families" (literally "wombs") is a reminder that all mankind came from a single soul and are all related in this human brotherhood. The Prophet (p) emphasises this when he says, "And be, O servants of Allah, brothers." (Agreed upon)

Human brotherhood is one of the principles in the creed of this faith. Islam calls upon men and women to believe in this human brotherhood and practise it in their lives. The Messenger (p) used to say after regular prayers, "My Lord, Our Lord and the Lord and Owner of everything, I am a witness that you are the Deity alone. You have no partner, my Lord, our God and the God and Owner of everything, I am a witness that Muhammad is Your servant and

1. This appears five times in the Qur'an: four times in *Surat al-A'raf* (7) and once in *Sura Yasin* (36).

2. The beginning of *Surat an-Nisa'* (4) and *Surat al-Hajj* (22). This is also more frequent in the Qur'an.

Your Messenger. My Lord, our Lord, and the Lord and Owner of everything, I am a witness that all servants of Allah are brothers." (Ahmad and Abu Dawud) This brotherhood of all human beings has many implications. Among them is that no human being must be submerged in selfish enjoyment of the goods Allah has created while others suffer. It implies that each must share with fellow humans the blessing Allah has bestowed on all humanity.

Above this degree of brotherhood is another deeper and stronger degree – brotherhood in faith. Those who share together belief in this religion, in Allah as the only Lord of the worlds, have indissoluble spiritual and social bonds. Brotherhood in Islam is much stronger than any blood relationship. Allah says, *"Believers are a single brotherhood."* (49:10) The spiritual brotherhood of all persons who share faith together also has important implications regarding support, aid and sharing the material goods Allah has created. Brotherhood among the faithful is further strengthened when they live in one society and one land. It is known in the *Shari'a* that the lands of all Muslims are one single country for all of them and that all Muslims are members of one united society.

The Messenger of Allah (p) explained the rights implicated by this brotherhood in several of his *hadiths*, "A believer to a fellow believer is like one single structure whose parts are bonded together." (Agreed upon) "The parable of the faithful in their mutual love and mercy is like a single body: if one of its members aches, the other members respond with fever and insomnia," (Agreed upon) and "The Muslim is a brother to the fellow Muslim. He does not do injustice to him nor does he let him down."[1] He who leaves his brother hungry or naked while he is able to clothe or feed him is undoubtedly letting his brother down. The Prophet (p) says, "He does not believe in me who goes to sleep with a full stomach while he knows that his neighbour next door is hungry."[2]

1. Reported by al-Bukhari, Muslim and Abu Dawud. See *at-Targhib*, vol. 3, p. 389.

2. Reported by at-Tabarani and al-Bazzar from Anas via a good chain. Also reported by at-Tabarani and Abu Ya'la from Ibn 'Abbas and by al-Hakim from 'A'isha. See *at-Targhib*, vol. 3, p. 358.

Chapter Three

Assets Subject to *Zakat* and to Taxes

Taxable wealth, whether income or assets, is not necessarily the same as zakatable wealth. Taxation specialists count four kinds of taxes from the point of view of taxable items: taxes on capital, on income, on persons and on consumption. *Zakat* does not cover consumption; it is taken from the rich on what is left after consumption. *Zakat* is sometimes levied on assets, such as gold, silver and livestock, sometimes on income, such as agricultural produce, and on persons in the form of *zakat al-fitr*. This chapter compares *zakat* due on capital, income and persons with their tax counterparts.

Section One: *Zakat* on capital

The advantages of capital tax without its disadvantages

Zakat on capital was enacted long before European socialists called for levying taxes on capital.[1] Proponents of taxes on capital usually present the following advantages:

- Capital provides its owners with several social and economic benefits including security and opportunities to earn more wealth.
- Taxes on capital reach all private wealth including wealth that does not yield any income, as compared to income tax which is imposed only on earners.
- By taxing idle wealth, capital taxes encourage investment.

1. *'Ilm al-Maliyya*, Dr. Rashid ad-Daqr, p, 352.

- Capital tax encourages owners of capital to increase their production to make up for the loss resulting from tax payment.
- By imposing capital tax in addition to income tax, the need for raising income tax rates to provide additional resources to the state is eliminated.
- Capital tax does not burden the poor and the have-nots and is therefore considered a social reform.[1]

Opponents of capital tax list the following disadvantages:

- Levying a tax on capital very often has a negative effective on the propensity to save and the ability to invest which has a negative effect on the economy as a whole.
- It is generally difficult to determine taxable capital since there are several definitions of capital and economists and taxationists cannot agree on a common definition. Leaving determination of taxable capital to individual tax payers or to collectors raises many discrepancies, especially since some forms of capital can easily be hidden away, such as cash money.
- Repetitive collection of tax on capital year after year may exhaust the capital itself, which is a major source of income. If the state continues levying taxes on capital, it may end up transferring private capital into the public treasury, which by itself reduces future proceeds of such a tax and shrinks the economic ability of the private sector.[2]

Recommended rules for levying taxes on capital

For reasons like the ones mentioned above, some tax specialists suggest that the government observe the following rules when imposing taxes on capital:

- It is advisable that the amount of tax collected not be great. It must not take a big chunk of capital. The rate must be moder-

1. Ibid., p. 347, and *Mawarid ad-Dawla*, Dr. Sa'd Mahir Hamza, p, 166.
2. *Mawarid*, ibid., p. 168.

ate so that capital tax can be paid out of the capital income without touching the principal itself.

- Capital tax must not be the only tax in the system but must rather be supplementary to other taxes, especially income tax.[1]
- A certain minimum amount of capital must be exempt from taxes.
- Liabilities on wealth must be excluded or deducted from the taxable amount.[2]

Islam observed these rules before other systems

Looking at *zakat* as a tax, we find that it fulfils all the requirements for a healthy tax on capital by observing the necessary rules that eliminate the disadvantages of taxes on capital, while preserving the advantages.

Islam does not impose *zakat* on every kind of capital. It is only levied on growing capital. Growing capital is that wealth which usually has a yield, regardless of whether the owner renders the capital idle or profitable. This is in order to collect *zakat* from the proceeds of capital and not from the principal. The word '*zakat*' itself means, among other meanings, 'growth' in Arabic. Some jurists explain the use of the word '*zakat*' for this kind of levy in the Qur'an on the basis that *zakat* is levied only on growing assets.[3]

Accordingly, I prefer the opinion that jewellery which is not used as a growing asset is not taxable, whereas hoarded jewellery is subject to *zakat* since hoarding implies making idle what is otherwise growing. Jurists agree that houses used as the residence of the owners are not subject to *zakat*. Neither are clothes, furniture, riding animals, personal weapons, craftsmen's tools and books used for study and research because all these do not grow and are assigned for personal use to satisfy basic needs of the owners.[4] We must, however, note that, in man-made taxation systems, residential

1. *'Ilm al-Maliyya*, op. cit. p. 355.
2. *Mawarid*, p. 176.
3. *Fath al-Bari*, vol. 3, p. 168.
4. *Fath al-Qadir*, with *Sharh al-'Inaya 'ala'l-Hidaya*, vol. 1, pp. 487-488.

houses are usually taxable; even mobile forms of wealth are taxable in many countries.[1]

The *Shari'a* does not impose *zakat* on fixed capital itself, such as factories and real estate, but only on circulating capital on the grounds that fixed capital is subject to *zakat* by virtue of its yield and growth. This principle is observed in order that *zakat* does not negatively affect the desire to save and does not induce savers to spend their income to avoid taxes levied on fixed capital.

The *Shari'a* does not impose *zakat* on all amounts of capital. The *nisab* is considered a minimum level of richness below which *zakat* is not obliged and is estimated at the equivalent of eight-five grams of gold. *Zakat* is imposed on that amount of capital once every year, provided it is in excess of what is needed to satisfy the basic needs of the owner, basic needs which differ from time to time.

Islam also determines the rate of *zakat* on capital at a moderate level. Only 2.5% is demanded for money and trade assets and approximately the same with regards to livestock. At this rate, *zakat* is intended to be collected from the yield of capital and not from the principal itself. It is remarkable that some jurists explicitly mention this point, such as Ibn Qudama in *al-Mughni*, who discusses the distinction between assets for which the passage of one year is required and those for which it is not: "Kinds for which the passage of one year is requires are those designated for growth, such as livestock, trade assets and money, so that *zakat* is actually paid out of the income, thus making it easier and simpler, so that its repetition year after year does not deplete the capital itself."[2]

The author of *al-Hidaya*, a Hanafi, asserts that: "The passage of a year is necessary because there ought to be a certain period of time for growth to be realised. This period is estimated at one year, which includes the four seasons in which prices may fluctuate." Ibn al-Humam comments in *Fath al-Qadir* that the rationale for the condition of one year is that "*zakat*, in addition to being an act of worship and a test from Allah, is meant to be a relief to the poor without depriving the payer himself or making him poor, i.e. by

1. *'Ilm al-Maliyya*, op. cit., p. 355.
2. *Al-Mughni*, vol. 2, p. 625.

having the rich give out of the excess of their wealth, a little out of plenty. Obviously, obligating *zakat* on assets that do not grow would lead to depletion of such assets by *zakat* payments year after year, knowing that the *zakat* payer has other expenses too. Thus, the condition of the passage of a year for growing assets is meant to allow these assets to have sufficient time to grow and yield profits."[1]

Zakat on growing assets is meant to be collected out of the yield of the capital and not out of the capital itself. But why does the *Shari'a* make potential for growth the condition for *zakat* and not the actual realisation of profit? Ibn Qudama[2] answers this question, "Actual growth alone is not considered the criteria because it is difficult to measure and to define accurately, especially since potentiality is considered a sufficient reason for a ruling in the *Shari'a* in many instances."[3]

Section Two: *Zakat* on income and profit

Income is the most important source of taxes in modern times. Years ago, income from real estate used to be predominant, but nowadays we have income from labour, capital, or both. With the advancement of industrialisation and the increase in domestic and international trade, income from labour and capital increased vastly. Income includes profit from commercial and industrial activities, dividends of stocks and bonds, fees of professionals and wages and salaries of employees of the government, as well as of private and public establishments.

1. *Fath al-Qadir*, vol. 1, p. 482
2. *Al-Mughni*, vol. 2, p. 625.
3. This is a reference to the fact that the rulings of the *Shari'a* are only founded on explicit and definable characteristics, called by jurists "the reasons" (*al-'ilal* or *al-asbab*), and not on the existence of the ruling's objective, which is, in the ultimate analysis, the reason for having the ruling. For example, Islam allows a traveller to break the fast in Ramadan and to reduce the four *rak'at* prayers to two *rak'ats*. Clearly the objective is to reduce the difficulty of the traveller. But since difficulty cannot be accurately defined, the ruling does not depend on difficulty, but rather on a state in which difficulty is expected to exist, i.e. the state of travelling.

Financial needs of modern states are better satisfied by direct taxes on income than by the largely indirect taxes that prevailed in the past. Moreover income taxes are more acceptable to taxation scholars because they are closest to fulfilling justice in contemporary economic systems by spreading the tax burden among all income earners.[1]

What is income?

Income is the flow of new wealth from a constant and permanent source. This source may or may not be physical. Physical sources include real estate, machinery and equipment, and money, while the non-physical source is labour, whether manual or non-manual. In most cases, income results from the combination of more than one source.[2]

This definition also implies that sources of income are generally permanent and continuous. Permanency does not mean absolute permanency but relative longevity. With application of the principle of allowances for capital amortisation, capital becomes more permanent than labour.[3] Differences in the life-span of the source of income are usually bases for differences in its taxability; i.e. the tax burden is distributed in such a way that the tax rate is higher on income that flows out of financial resources and lower on income that flows out of labour alone

Zakat on income in Islam

The most obvious example of *zakat* on income is agricultural *zakat*. Its rate differs from five to ten percent – the higher rate applies when farming costs are minimum (i.e. the land is watered by rain) and the lower rate applies when water must be brought to the land. *Rikaz* (*zakat* on buried treasures and minerals extracted from the earth) has a rate of 20%. The rate on trade goods is 2.5%.

1. *Mawarid ad-Dawla*, Dr. Sa'd Mahir Hamza, p. 117.
2. *Mabadi' al-Maliyya al-'Amma*, Dr. Muhammad Fu'ad Ibrahim, vol. 1, p. 322.
3. Ibid.

Thus, Islam applies different rates of *zakat* on income, rates that vary in accordance with efforts expended. At high costs of producing the zakatable income, a low rate of *zakat* applies, and vice versa.

Other forms of *zakat* on income include *zakat* on the offspring of livestock, *zakat* on honey and other animal products, *zakat* on earnings of real estate and other fixed capital (as discussed in Part Three of this book).

Section Three: *Zakat* on persons

Taxes on people, sometimes called poll taxes, were common in many western countries and still exist in many states today, although their use is declining. The most important merit of a tax on heads is easiness in estimation and collection but the main disadvantage is that it is not based on the ability of the taxable person to pay. Many governments discontinued this form of taxation for that reason, although it is still used in some states of the United States and in France.[1]

Zakat al-fitr is on persons

Zakat al-fitr at the end of the month of Ramadan is levied on persons. It has the same advantages of simplicity of calculation and collection as the tax on persons. Above this, however, *zakat al-fitr* serves important spiritual, moral and social objectives in addition to being a transfer of funds like other forms of *zakat*. But unlike the tax on persons, individuals who cannot afford payment are exempt from *zakat al-fitr*. This is unanimously agreed upon by Muslim scholars.

By imposing this *zakat* once a year on each Muslim, Islam aims at training all Muslims to spend and sacrifice for the welfare of fellow Muslims, especially on the occasion of the religious feast days. Accordingly, exemptions from this *zakat* are much more strictly

1. *Mabadi' al-Maliyya al-'Amma*, ibid., pp. 305-307.

applied than exemptions from other forms of *zakat*. The Messenger of Allah (p) says regarding payment of *zakat al-fitr*, "As for the rich among you (who pay it), the Prophet (p) will cleanse them, and as for the poor among you (who pay it), Allah will render to them more than they give." Fortunately this *zakat* is today the most remembered and practised throughout the Muslim lands of all forms of *zakat*.

Chapter Four

Principles of Levying Taxes and *Zakat*

Taxes, as obligatory levies enforced by the state, must be based on certain principles of common sense, otherwise they cause unrest and disturbance. Scholars and taxation experts throughout the past few centuries have argued over these principles. In the eighteenth century, Adam Smith summed up these principles as: principles of justice, certainty, convenience and economy. This chapter consequently has four sections in which these principles are discussed in relation to both taxes and *zakat*.

Section One: The principle of justice

The principle of justice, according to Adam Smith,[1] means that all citizens of the state must share in financing government expenditure, each according to his ability, i.e. in proportion to his income, which is protected by the state.[2] This principle is consistent with the *Shari'a* in general and with *zakat* itself, as will be explained in this section.

Justice is a general principle in Islam. It is one of the qualities of Allah, one of His glorious Names on which the heavens and earth are based and for the establishment of which Allah sent Messengers and Books. The Qur'an declares in explicit words, *"We sent Our Messengers with the Clear Signs and sent down the Book and the Balance with them so that mankind might establish justice."* (57:25) This principle of justice is apparent in *zakat* several ways.

1. He was a British economist and philosopher of the eighteenth century. His book, *The Wealth of Nations*, is considered the "Bible" of the free economic system.

2. "Islam lays down the Foundation of Taxation," an article by Dr. Ahmad Thabit 'Awaida.

Equality in obligation

Zakat is obliged on every Muslim who owns the *nisab*, regardless of race, colour, social status or sex. Weak and strong, noble and commoner, governor and subject, learned and ignorant, all are equal in the obligation of *zakat*. This is not the case with taxes, especially in past Western applications when the nobles and clergy were exempt from taxes.[1]

Ibn Hazm says, "*Zakat* is obligatory on men and women, old and young, sane and insane, for Allah says, *'Take* sadaqa *out of their wealth so that you may purify and cleanse them.'* This covers everyone, for all are in need of the purification and cleansing of Allah. The Messenger of Allah (p) told Mu'adh, 'Inform them that Allah imposes a *sadaqa* on them, to be taken from the rich among them and rendered to the poor among them.' This text includes every rich Muslim."[2]

Exemption of wealth below the *nisab*

The principle of justice in Islam requires that those who own small amounts of wealth be exempted from *zakat*. *Zakat* is only imposed on the rich, i.e. those who own at least the full *nisab*. This makes the burden of *zakat* easier on people. Allah says, *"Take the surplus,*[3] *and command what is right,"* (7:199) and *"They will ask you what they should give away. Say, 'Whatever is surplus to your needs.'"* (2:219) Ibn 'Abbas explains "surplus" in these *ayats* as the surplus wealth of the rich.

Elimination of duplication in *zakat* levying

In application of justice in *zakat*, the Messenger (p) says, "There must be no duplication in *sadaqa*."[4] Abu 'Ubayd explains, "This

1. Ahmad Thabit 'Awaida. op. cit.

2. *Al-Muhalla*, vol. 5, pp. 199-200.

3. Surplus is interpreted by some scholars as *zakat*, since *zakat* is a little taken out of plenty.

4. Reported by Abu 'Ubayd, *al-Amwal*, p. 375, and by Ibn Abi Shayba.

means that *sadaqa* must not be collected twice in the same year."[1] Ibn Qudama and others argue that the *hadith* prevents collecting *zakat* more than once a year on the same thing.[2] Using the terms of public finance, this means that the doubling of taxes must be avoided.

The above mentioned *hadith* implies several points:

- Abu Hanifa makes the point that "if an owner sells some livestock, he need not add the price received for animals on which *zakat* has already been paid to the cash he has in hand in calculating its *zakat*, since such addition would duplicate *zakat* on livestock in the same year, which is prevented by the *hadith*."[3]

- A person who pays *zakat* on cash he has in hand, and then purchases livestock with it to add to his herd, need not add the newly bought livestock on whose value *zakat* was paid in money to the cattle he owns in the calculation of *zakat* during that same year because such addition would be a partial duplication of *zakat*.[4]

- A person who buys livestock to the amount of the *nisab* as trade stock must pay on this livestock the *zakat* of business goods, according to Abu Hanifa, ath-Thawri, and Ahmad, while Malik and ash-Shafi'i believe that the *zakat* on livestock should be paid.[5] No scholar argues that both *zakat* on livestock and *zakat* on trade should be collected on such cattle, since this would be a duplication of *zakat*.

- The argument given for exempting farm animals used in cultivation is based on the prevention of duplication of *zakat*. Since such animals work in the production of a zakatable asset (agricultural produce), imposing *zakat* on such animals would be duplication.[6] Abu 'Ubayd emphasises, "If (the animals) work in watering and ploughing, the grain that is liable for *zakat*

1. *Al-Amwal*, ibid
2. *Al-Mughni*, vol. 3, pp. 34-35.
3. *Al-Bahr ar-Ra'iq*, vol. 2, pp. 239-240.
4. Ibid., and *Radd al-Muhtar*, vol. 2, p. 21.
5. *Al-Mughni*, op cit.
6. *Al-Amwal*, p. 381.

includes the value of these animals' work. If one imposes *zakat* on the animals while the grain also has *zakat* taken, this makes duplication in the levy."[1]

- Hanafis base their argument of exempting *kharaj* land from *'ushr* on the principle of "no duplication in *zakat*". They say *kharaj* land is taxed on a yearly basis, thus *'ushr* and *kharaj* must not be combined on the same land.[2]
- Jurists, in preventing duplication in *zakat*, argue that the *nisab* must not be exhausted or burdened by debts, since assets that are due to others as debts must be deducted in the calculation of *zakat* and treated as non-existent from the point of view of *zakat*. Jurists argue that the deduction of loans from zakatable assets is based on the principle of avoiding duplication, since the creditor is required to pay *zakat* on such loans.[3]

Rates of *zakat* differ depending on effort expended

Lower rates apply when the production process requires more human effort. Accordingly, the rate of *zakat* is ten percent on grains and fruits watered by rain or rivers, and five percent when water must be carried mechanically, 20% on found treasures which require little human effort, while the rate on earned wealth is only 2.5%. The system of *zakat* is almost unique in these variations of rates according to effort spent in production.

Consideration of personal circumstances

Another important application of the principle of justice is giving attention to the personal circumstances of the *zakat* payer. *Zakat* does not deal solely with zakatable items detached from the person himself. Taxation specialists distinguish between what they call "personal taxes" and "physical taxes". Personal taxes take into consideration the following points:

1. *Al-Amwal*, ibid.
2. *Al-Bada'i'*, vol. 2, p. 57.
3. *Al-Majmu'*, vol. 5, p. 436.

- Exemption of a minimum standard of living from taxes.
- Consideration of the source of income in the levy of taxes.
- Deduction of costs and expenditures related to income
- Consideration of family responsibilities
- Consideration of debts and loans

Islam preceded all known taxation systems in providing for personal elements in the obligation, exemption, rates and deductions in the *zakat* system. Long before public finance studies recognised any distinction between physical and personal taxes, Islam established the following:

- The exemption of what is below the *nisab* from *zakat*. This is founded on the principle that *zakat* is imposed on the rich for the benefit of the poor since the *nisab* is the minimum level of wealth. Only recently have other taxation systems started exempting income beneath a certain minimum from the burden of taxes.

- The cost of a minimum standard of living is also exempt from *zakat*. The cost of living is considered among the basic needs of the *zakat* payer. Jurists define the *nisab* as that amount which is in excess of what is needed to satisfy the essential basic needs of the owner. This was discussed in Chapter One of Part Three of this book, where it was emphasised that *zakat* is only taken out of this excess. Muslim scholars define excess as what is above the provision needed for satisfying essential needs,[1] for the Prophet (p) said, "*Sadaqa* must only be given out of wealth," and "Start by providing for those whom you are responsible for."

- Debts are deducted from zakatable assets according to the majority of scholars. This is supported by the texts and spirit of the *Shari'a*.[2] Hanafis say, "Whoever owes debts that are more than his assets, whether these debts belong to other people or to Allah (such as past due *zakat*), is not liable for *zakat*. Such a person needs to pay liabilities due to other people as well as to

1. *Al-Majmu'*, ibid.
2. Ibid.

Allah, in order to avoid people's demands and the punishment of the Hereafter. Not paying due debts hinders him from entering Paradise. What need is there more than this? Thus ridding himself of these responsibilities is to him like water for the thirsty person or clothing for the naked. Such a person must be indeed exempt from *zakat*."[1]

- Production costs are deducted from zakatable income. 'Ata' says regarding *zakat* on agriculture, "Deduct your expenses, then pay *zakat* on the remainder." This is also the view of Ibn 'Umar and Ibn 'Abbas. A similar opinion is reported from Ahmad. In trade, expenses are also deducted before *zakat* is calculated.[2]

Justice in collection

In addition to justice in the levy of *zakat* itself, collection procedures are also based on justice. The system emphasises that *zakat* officers must be selected out of the best and most knowledgeable persons, who must be clearly instructed to be fair in their estimation and calculation of *zakat*. Abu Yusuf wrote to the khalif, Harun ar-Rashid, "O Amir al-Mu'minin, order your ministers to select a person who is honest, trustworthy and wise, whom you can trust and whom people can also trust. Then appoint him to collect the *sadaqat*. Instruct him to appoint only officers who can be trusted, after inspecting their opinions, behaviour and honesty, for the collection of *sadaqat* in different areas. I have come to know that some of the *kharaj* commissioners send men to collect *zakat* who do injustice and arbitrarily oppress people. They take what is not lawful to them. For *zakat*, you must only appoint righteous and trustworthy people."[3]

The Prophet ordered his *zakat* commissioners to be just and moderate and to observe, to the letter, the rules and instructions of

---

1. *Sharh al-'Inaya 'ala'l-Hidaya* and *Fath al-Qadir*, vol. 1, p, 486.

2. See section seven of the chapter on *zakat* on agriculture. Lately I came to know that the Ja'fari opinion is like that of 'Ata', as stated in *Fiqh al-Imam Ja'far*, vol. 2, pp. 80-81.

3. *Al-Kharaj*, Abu Yusuf, p. 80.

this obligation. He says, "A just worker in *sadaqa* is like a fighter in the Way of Allah.[1] He advised one of his *zakat* collectors, "O Abu'l-Walid, fear Allah, and do not appear on the Day of Rising carrying a camel that bellows or a cow that lows or a sheep that bleats (because of embezzlement)."[2]

Section Two: The principle of certainty

Certainty in taxation means the tax must be well defined in an exclusive sense without the ambiguity that leaves room for arbitrary application. Certainty refers to time and procedure of payment in addition to the calculation and definition of the amount to be paid. Adam Smith believes the principle of certainty is very important, since the taxpayer must know with certainty all his obligations. Certainty, according to Smith, may even be more important than justice itself.

There is no doubt that certainty has much to do with the stability of any tax system. If the taxpayers become accustomed to the taxes, their rates and payment procedures, tax payments become easier for them and for the government as well. Because of this, some taxation specialists, like Canard, believe that every old tax is good and every new tax is dubious. Stability of the taxation system, like stability of business law, helps build confidence in the system and its future, and thus in the prosperity of economic activities.[3]

Undoubtedly, the system of *zakat* provides a high degree of certainty. *Zakat* is imposed by Allah in His eternal Book; no one can add or delete anything in it. Allah determines the rates which have been reported to us by Allah's Messenger, and we have an enormous heritage of jurisprudence that provides explanations and details. All the basic rulings of *zakat* are fixed and unchangeable by

1. Reported by Ahmad, Abu Dawud, at-Tirmidhi, Ibn Majah and Ibn Khuzayma. At-Tirmidhi grades it *hasan*. See *at-Targhib wa't-Tarhib*, vol. 1, p. 559. Also reported by al-Hakim, vol. 1, p. 406, who grades it *sahih* according to Muslim's criteria. This is confirmed by adh-Dhahabi.

2. Reported by at-Tabarani in *al-Muj'am al-Kabir*. Its chain is *sahih*, p. 563.

3. *Mabadi' 'Ilm*, op. cit., p. 267.

any human effort. Knowing these basic rulings is obligatory for every Muslim as part of the religion of Islam. *Zakat* is the most stable financial institution humanity has ever known.

Section Three: The principle of convenience

Convenience, the third principle of taxation given by Adam Smith, means that the tax and its collection procedures must be made most convenient to taxpayers, so they give the tax with pleasure and satisfaction, or at least without doubt or inconvenience. A quick glance at Islamic laws and instructions about *zakat* reveals how much this principle is observed. This is apparent in many instances:

- Ahmad reports from 'Abdullah ibn 'Umar that the Messenger (p) said, "The *sadaqa* of the Muslims' livestock must be collected at their watering place." In another version reported by Ahmad and Abu Dawud, the Prophet (p) said, "There should be no bringing or taking away of zakatable assets. Their due *sadaqa* must not be collected except in their own locales."[1] According to al-Khattabi, "no bringing and no taking away" means *zakat* payers must not be asked to bring their assets to the collector, nor should the payers take their assets away from the collector with the intention of making it difficult for him to pursue the items subject to *zakat*. Items subject to *zakat* must be counted and *zakat* estimated in the localities of these assets."[2] Ash-Shawkani adds, "This *hadith* means the collector is

1. Ash-Shawkani says, "Abu Dawud, al-Mundhiri, and Ibn Hajar in *at-Talkhis* do not comment about this *hadith*. Muhammad ibn Ishaq is in its chain, and he says "from" (instead of explicitly stating that he "heard from" the next link in the chain). But on the same subject, Ahmad, Abu Dawud, an-Nasa'i, at-Tirmidhi, Ibn Hibban and 'Abdu'r-Razzaq have a report via 'Imran ibn Husayn. This *hadith* is also reported a little differently by an-Nasa'i. See *Nayl al-Awtar*, vol. 4, p. 156. There is also a report by at-Tabarani in *al-Muj'am al-Awsat* from 'A'isha: "The *sadaqa* of the people of the desert must be collected at their water sources and canals." Its chain is *hasan*, as stated in *Majma' az-Zawa'id*, vol. 3, p. 79.

2. *Ma'alim as-Sunan*, vol. 2, p. 205.

the one who travels for *zakat* collection, since this is easier for payers."[1]

- The Prophet's instructions command taking *zakat* out of the average quality of zakatable assets and not the best of them. In his instructions to Mu'adh, the Prophet (p) says, "Avoid the best of their wealth," since payers usually do not like to give away the best things they own. On another occasion, the Messenger (p) was displeased because a collector had taken a high quality she-camel, until the collector explained that he took that she-camel in exchange for two camels of lower quality. The Prophet (p) says, "But it (payment) must be the average of your wealth. Allah does not ask you for the best, nor does He accept the worst."

- The Prophet (p) instructs estimators of *zakat* on agriculture to be moderate and to estimate on the lower side. He even orders them to make allowances for errors and for fruits used for family and charity. Abu Dawud, at-Tirmidhi, and an-Nasa'i report that the Prophet (p) says, "When you estimate, do not count one-third. If not, then do not count one-fourth," and "Take it easy in estimation, since orchards may have trees assigned for eating (by family and passers-by) or charity." Al-Khattabi comments that one-third or one-fourth of the estimated amount of zakatable agricultural produce is deducted to make things easier for the *zakat* payer, especially since a certain proportion is always consumed or lost before the time of the harvest. 'Umar ibn al-Khattab used to instruct his estimators to make such deductions.

- *Zakat* payment may be deferred if necessary, whether for individual or general reasons, like 'Umar's delay of *zakat* in the year of the general famine.

1. *Nayl al-Awtar*, vol. 4, pp. 156-157.

Section Four: The principle of economy

The principle of economy means collection costs must be kept at a minimum. These costs include what the state pays, such as collectors' salaries and administrative and transportation costs, in addition to what the payers extend to prepare reports and accounts or to process their complaints or objections to the estimated amounts. Obviously, the purpose of a tax is to bring net income to the state to finance public expenditure. When the principle of economy is not observed, a large portion of the proceeds is used to sustain the collection process itself.[1]

Islam prohibits extravagance and commands moderation and sometimes thrift. This applies as much to public funds as to individual spending. Rather Islamic law is much keener to economise when using public funds. It was mentioned earlier how strict the Messenger (p) was with *zakat* officers and collectors. He was angered by the one who accepted gifts from payers and made clear that he had no right to do that, telling him to give these gifts to the public treasury.

Zakat, in principle, must be spent in the same locale in which it is collected, which economises on transportation costs. We saw earlier how *zakat* officers went for collection and came back with no residual funds, since they had distributed all proceeds in the same area they collected it from. Moreover, ash-Shafi'i requires that no more than one-eighth of *zakat* proceeds be spent on workers in the *zakat* administration, in order to restrict administrative costs.

1. *Mabadi' 'Ilm al-Maliyya*, op. cit. , p. 266.

Chapter Five

Proportionality and Progressiveness of Taxes and *Zakat*

Proportional and progressive taxes

Proportional taxes are those whose rates are constant, regardless of the quantity of taxable items. If, for example, the tax rate is ten percent, and this rate applies on all income regardless of its size, then the tax is proportional Progressive taxes are those whose rates increase with an increase in the amount of the taxable item. Progressive taxes are usually applied on the basis of income strata. For example, the rate may be ten percent for the first one thousand units of income, twelve percent for the second one thousand, and fifteen percent for third one thousand.[1] Progressive taxes are supported by many people nowadays who argue that this kind of taxation is more just because it distributes the burden of government expenditure according to the ability of the taxpayers. The following arguments are usually forwarded in support of progressive taxes:

- Wealthy people benefit from the economic law of increasing returns, so that the more they accumulate, the higher returns and more accumulation they can obtain. This ability to accumulate and to earn increases more than proportionally, so the tax applied on such persons must also be more than proportional.

- Progressive taxes are the most accessible means of eliminating great differences in income and wealth in a society. Whenever we are confronted with the situation of badly distributed

1. *Mabadi' an-nazariya al-'Amma lid-Dariba*, Husayn Khallaf and 'Abdu'l-Karim ar-Rifa'i, p. 151.

wealth, progressive taxes rectify the situation and shrink the economic gap between rich and poor.

Zakat is proportional

It is clear that *zakat* is proportional, i.e. it does not take the principle of increasing the rate with increases in the quantity of the zakatable item. The applicable rate on an item is constant. This applies to all zakatable assets: agricultural produce, livestock, trade goods, or cash. Some contemporary researchers even think that *zakat* on livestock has a regressive rate, i.e. the rate declines as the amount of livestock increases. They consider such regression as an attempt to encourage cattle raising in the harsh desert environment of the Arabian peninsula.

This interpretation may have an aspect of truth, but a closer look shows its flaws. In fact, the rate of *zakat* on cattle is generally 2.5%, with slight differences that relate only to segmental increases in the number of animals subject to *zakat*. The rate of 2.5% (generally speaking) is seen in the case of cows and camels, while in the case of sheep there is a misunderstanding that arises from the inclusion of lambs. In estimating the *nisab* of forty sheep, young lambs are not counted, and the rate is one sheep for forty sheep (2.5%). As the number of sheep increases above forty, baby animals are included in the total count of zakatable heads, but these babies are not acceptable in *zakat* payment. The rate is thus reduced to one sheep for each additional hundred sheep to make up for this inclusion of lambs. There is an opinion reported from Ibrahim and Abu Hanifa that *zakat* on horses has a rate of 2.5%, based on evaluation of their price. This supports the general understanding that the rate on livestock is 2.5%

Why is *zakat* not progressive

Zakat as an eternal religious obligation does not change because of changing circumstances. It is an act of worship required from every Muslim in all ages and environments, while progressive taxes are imposed to achieve a rectification of the transitory problem of unequal distribution of wealth and income. They are malleable tools whose rates may be altered to achieve their target.

Islam does not prevent the imposition of additional taxes in exceptional circumstances. These taxes may have progressive rates if this is needed to achieve justice and to fulfil the rights of the poor, provided such taxes are enacted by legitimate authority which rules righteously in the light of the Holy Book sent by Allah.

Zakat itself redistributes income and wealth from the rich to the poor. Consequently it fulfils the objective of progressive taxes by specifically raising the tandard of living of the poor and levying the whole burden on the rich while taxes, even progressive ones, are usually expended, in the form of public services, to all members of society, including the rich.

Islam resolves the problem of concentration of wealth and income through several means. *Zakat* is but one of them. These means include the inheritance system, confiscation of wealth and income that arises from unlawful sources, prohibition of interest, usury and monopoly. Thus the objectives of progressive taxes are fulfilled through all these means together.

The principle of progressiveness in taxation is, in any case, criticised by many thinkers, economists and experts on public finance, who point to the following weaknesses:

- The determination of income strata for progressiveness is very arbitrary. It has no agreed upon or rationally accepted formulation. This leads sometimes to arbitrariness in the determination of the tax itself. Equality in sacrifice, which is the dominant foundation for progressiveness, has no steady and stable rules for its application. What rate applies such equality at each additional stratum of income? Is it an increment of one percent or two percent? How wide should each band of income be? And should taxpayers be divided into classes according to their incomes? All these pose real obstacles in the practical application of any progressive tax.[1]

1. *'Ilm al-Maliyya*, Rashid ad-Daqr, p. 379.

- Continuous progressiveness is mathematically impossible, since an increase of one percent at each additional one thousand units of income makes the rate 129 % on an income of two million units. This means the tax is at this level more than the taxed item, which is physically impossible to carry out.[1]
- Progressiveness in taxes may crush the rich and liquidate all accumulated capital, especially in socialist countries that are dominated by the class struggle.[2]
- Progressive taxes usually take away the amount assigned for saving and investment and do not reduce the consumption of taxpayers. They usually discourage the wealthy from investment and reduce their motivation to produce more income, and thus have negative effects on production.[3]

1. *'Ilm al-Maliyya*, ibid.
2. Ibid.
3. *Mabadi' 'Ilm al-Maliyya*, Muhammad Fu'ad Ibrahim, vol. 1, p. 279.

Chapter Six

Enforcement of Taxes and of *Zakat*

Attempts to escape taxation

Taxes are always susceptible to evasion, even by individuals who are just and honest in their transactions with other people. Several reasons account for tax evasion: selfishness and love of wealth, the belief that a certain tax is not just, or that tax proceeds are unjustly utilised, etc. The heavier the tax, the more people will attempt to escape paying it. Escaping tax payment takes several forms. The most common is to take utmost advantage of loopholes in the taxation system itself. This form of evasion is undoubtedly within the law. Another way of escaping takes is to present incorrect information which leads to total or partial elimination of the tax or by failure to submit an accurate tax return. Certainly cheating on taxes is harmful from several aspects:

- It reduces the proceeds of the tax.
- It disturbs the just distribution of the tax aimed for originally by its enactment.
- It may lead sometimes to an increase in tax rates in order to make up for funds lost because of tax cheating.
- It may reduce some useful government activities because of limited resources.
- It spreads dishonesty in society because people tend to imitate methods of tax evasion.

Consequently all tax legislation attempts to provide legal and administrative procedures to prevent tax evasion in the following ways:

- Authorising tax officers to inspect the documents and books of taxpayers.
- Requiring the payer to submit a tax return given under oath or at the risk of legal penalties for giving incorrect information.
- Rewarding anyone who informs the government of cases of tax evasion.
- Deducting certain taxes at the source, such as deducting income tax from salaries before they are paid to income earners.
- Imposing heavy financial fines and other penalties for tax evasion.
- Giving the tax department a legal lien on all the assets of tax payers with priority over other creditors.[1]

Despite all these preventive measures, treasury officers always declare their inability to wipe out tax evasion, especially when information can easily be hidden. This is because any solution to this problem must be sought in the consciences of payers before legal measuress.

Endorsement of *zakat* in the *Shari'a*

Zakat differs from taxes in several ways. Its enforcement is supported by religious, moral, legal and administrative sanctions.

The religious and moral endorsement of *zakat*

Muslims treat *zakat* as a link between them and Allah before any other thing. This is the meaning of worship. Muslim jurists emphasise this aspect of *zakat* very often. Ibn al-'Arabi says, "*Zakat* is, in fact, a right owed to Allah, but He transfers His right to those for whom he guarantees sustenance when He says, *'There is no creature*

1. *Mabadi' an-Nazriyya al-'Amma lid-Dariba*, 'Abdu'l-Karim ar-Rifa'i and Husayn Khallaf.

on the earth which is not dependent upon Allah for its provision.' (11:6) Al-Kasani, a Hanafi, says, "The core of *zakat* is giving part of the owned *nisab* to Allah. This is done by making it the property of the poor through actual delivery to them… Allah says, *'Do they not know that Allah accepts repentance from His slaves and acknowledges their gifts of* sadaqa*?'* (9:104) and the Messenger (p) said, 'The *sadaqa* reaches the hands of the All-Merciful before it reaches the hands of the poor.'[1] Moreover, *zakat* is worship, and worship is the devotion of an action completely to Allah."[2]

When paying *zakat*, the payer has not the slightest resentment or feeling of injustice, since *zakat* is legislated by Allah who oppresses none. Allah is the most just Legislator and Nourisher and Sustainer of His servants. Why would a believer try to escape *zakat*, knowing that Allah, for whom it is given, knows what is secret and even what is more hidden than a secret, and that Allah is going to inspect everyone's account on the Day of Judgement?

Consequently, Islamic values and ethics inculcated by faith, education and upbringing are the strongest guarantee that payers pay their dues properly. Muslims are educated and trained to look toward the Hereafter and to be moderate in their love of worldly benefits. They seek reward from Allah, and they spend for Allah's sake. They prefer what pleases Allah and His Messenger above all other things.

A believer will not hesitate between what pleases Allah and His Messenger, on the one hand, and all earthly benefits and enjoyments on the other. In the Qur'an Allah makes the matter clear. *"Say: 'If your fathers or your sons or your brothers or your wives or your tribe, or any wealth you have acquired, or any business you fear may slump, or any dwelling-places which please you, are dearer to you than Allah and His Messenger and fighting hard in* jihad *in His Way, then*

1. In his *Tafsir*, at-Tabari attributes this statement to Ibn Mas'ud. See texts 17163-17166, vol. 12, pp. 459-461. A report from 'A'isha, linked up to the Prophet (p) says: "A person should give *sadaqa* out of good earnings, for Allah only accepts the good. The All-Merciful receives it with His hand and He cares for it as any of you would care for a foal or colt or infant servant." Reported by al-Bazzar via a chain of trustworthy narrators. See *Majma' az-Zawa'id*, vol. 3, p. 112.

2. *Al-Bada'i'*, vol. 2, p. 39.

wait until Allah brings about His command. Allah does not guide degenerate people.'" (9:24)

This kind of faith is not consistent with escaping *zakat* payment. Rather believers are eager to pay, as is evident in many occasions in the Qur'an and *Sunna*. Twice in the Qur'an it is reported that believers asked the Messenger of Allah (p) about spending and Allah answers them once regarding what to spend and once regarding to whom one should give: *"They will ask you what they should give away. Say: 'Whatever is surplus to your needs'"* (2:219), and *"They will ask you what they should give away. Say: 'Any wealth you give away should go to your parents and relatives and orphans and the very poor and travellers.' Whatever good you do, Allah knows it."* (2:215)

The willingness of Muslims to volunteer their wealth is a recurring theme in the tradition of the Prophet (p). Anas says, "A man from the Banu Tamim came to the Messenger of Allah (p) and said, 'O Messenger of Allah, I have plenty of wealth. I have a family and a residence. Tell me what to do and how to spend.' The Messenger of Allah (p) said, 'Give the *zakat* on your wealth for it purifies you. And do good to your kindred, and recognise the right of the poor, the neighbour and the beggar.' The man said, 'O Messenger of Allah, reduce it for me.' The Prophet (p) said, 'Give kindred their right, and the poor, and the traveller, and do not be extravagant.' He said, 'O Messenger of Allah, if I give the *zakat* I owe to your collector, is that sufficient to fulfil my duty to Allah and His Messenger?' The Messenger of Allah (p) said, 'Yes, if you give *zakat* to my collector, you have fulfilled it. You deserve its reward, and (if it is altered later) the sin for altering it is upon whoever changed it.'"[1]

Abu Hurayra narrates that a man said, "O Messenger of Allah, I have one dinar." The Prophet (p) said, "Give it as *sadaqa* to your own self." The man said, "I have another." The Prophet replied, "Make it *sadaqa* to your children." The man continued, "I have a third." The Prophet (p) said, "Make it *sadaqa* to your wife." The man said, "I have a fourth." The Prophet said, "Make it *sadaqa* to

1. In *Majma' az-Zawa'id*, vol. 3, p. 63, al-Haythami says, "It is reported by Ahmad and at-Tabarani in *al-Muj'am al-Awsat*. Its narrators are those of the *Sahih* collection.

your servant." "I still have another," the man went on. The Prophet said, "You know better (or you can divide it yourself)."[1]

Some faithful believers sometimes brought the Prophet (p) all their wealth to be spent as charity in spite of their need for it. The Prophet (p) disapproved of this, and usually informed such people not to give away all they had. Jabir narrates, "We were with the Messenger of Allah (p) when a man brought a gold nugget the size of an egg and said, 'O Messenger of Allah, I gained this from a mine. Take it. It is charity from me. I own nothing beside it.' The Prophet (p) turned his face away from him. The man came from the Prophet's right side and repeated what he had first said. The Prophet (p) turned away again. Then the man came from the left side and the Prophet (p) turned away from him again. At last the man came from behind. The Messenger of Allah (p) took the piece of gold and threw it to the man such that if it had hit him it would have hurt and said, 'One of you would bring all he owns and say, "This is *sadaqa*." Then he would go begging from people! The best *sadaqa* is that which comes out of wealth.'"[2]

The keenness of Muslims to pay *zakat* was great, as it was part of their religious requirements. Once a group of people from Syria asked 'Umar ibn al-Khattab to take *zakat* from them for their mares and slaves, saying, "We gained some wealth in the form of mares and slaves, and we would like to pay *zakat* on them in order to be purified."[3] Another man asked 'Umar to take *zakat* on honey, saying, "A property from which *zakat* is not taken is no good."[4] After paying the tenth or half-tenth on his agricultural produce, Ibn

1. Reported by Abu Dawud, an-Nasa'i and al-Hakim. The latter grades it sound by the criteria of Muslim, and this is confirmed by adh-Dhahabi. See *al-Mustadrak*, vol. 1, p. 415.

2. Reported by Abu Dawud and al-Hakim. The latter grades it sound by the criteria of Muslim, and this is confirmed by adh-Dhahabi, *al-Mustadrak*, vol. 1, p. 413.

3. Reported by Ahmad and at-Tabarani in *al-Muj'am al-Kabir*. Its narrators are trustworthy, as stated in *Majma' az-Zawa'id*, vol. 3, p. 69. Also reported by al-Hakim in *al-Mustadrak*, vol. 1, pp. 400-401. He grades it sound, and this is confirmed by adh-Dhahabi.

4. Reported by al-Bazzar and at-Tabarani in *al-Muj'am al-Kabir*. Its chain contains Munir ibn 'Abdullah, who is weak, as stated in *Majma' az-Zawa'id*, vol. 2, p. 77.

Mas'ud used to divide the remainder into three equal parts, one for his family, one to buy seeds for the following year, and one for charity.[1]

Muslims believe that paying *zakat* is purification and cleansing for themselves and their wealth, and a source of protection and a blessing for the rest of their wealth. Abu Dawud reports from Suwayd ibn Ghafala, "I went along with the Prophet's *zakat* officer or someone who went along told me … A man wanted to give the officer a large she-camel with a huge hump. The officer refused to accept it, so the man gave another smaller she-camel which he accepted, saying, 'I shall take this, but I am afraid the Messenger of Allah (p) may be displeased by my action. He may tell me, 'You went to a man and selected the best of his camels.'"[2]

Ubayy ibn Ka'b says, "The Messenger of Allah (p) sent me out as a *zakat* collector. I went to a man who collected his herd for me and I found that he only owed one two-year-old she-camel. I told him, 'Pay the two year old she-camel. This is the *sadaqa* due on you.' The man said, 'This camel does not give milk nor is it good for riding. Here is a better she-camel, stronger (but still young) with a huge hump. Please take it.' I said, 'I would be taking more than I am ordered to. The Messenger of Allah (p) is nearby. If you like, go to him and make him the offer you are making me. If he accepts, I will accept it, and vice versa.' The man said, 'I shall do that.' So he went with me, taking with him the she-camel, which he had offered to me, to the Messenger of Allah (p). The man said, 'O Prophet of Allah, your collector came to take the *sadaqa* of my camels. By Allah, no one came to me before, not the Messenger of Allah (p) nor his collector. So I gathered my herd for him to inspect and he said that I owe one two year old she-camel. Such an animal does not give milk and is not good as a ride, so I offered him a bigger she-camel that is strong and still young, but he refused

1. Reported by at-Tabarani in *al-Muj'am al-Kabir*, from Masruq. Its narrators are those of the *Sahih* collection, as in *Majma' az-Zawa'id*, vol. 3, p. 68.

2. Al-Mundhiri says, "Reported by an-Nasa'i and Ibn Majah. In its chain is Hilal ibn Habbab, who is considered trustworthy by more than one critic, although he is criticised by others. See *Mukhtasar as-Sunan*, vol. 2, p. 196. Also reported by ad-Daraqutni and al-Bayhaqi. See *Nayl al-Awtar*, vol. 4, p. 133.

and gave it back to me. This is it. I have brought it to you, O Messenger of Allah. Take it.'

"The Messenger of Allah (p) answered. 'That was what is due on you, but if you volunteer more, Allah will reward you more for it and we accept it from you.' The man said, 'Here it is. I brought it to volunteer it. Take it.' The Messenger of Allah (p) ordered that it be accepted and prayed for blessings on the wealth of the man." In the version of this *hadith* reported by Ahmad, it says, "The man said, 'I would not give Allah an animal that does not give milk and was not good for riding.'"[1] Clearly the man felt that paying *zakat* is a transaction between him and Allah, and therefore shied away from giving Allah anything less than the best.

These beliefs and sentiments are the best guarantee for the proper fulfilment of *zakat.* Tax cheating is the rule and not the exception in Western countries. In France, 1936, Vincent Orion remarked, "If it were not for cheating, the rates of taxes would have been reduced." President Roosevelt said about tax evasion in the United States, "Many tax cheaters use loopholes in taxation acts; many others commit violations of the law. Either way, the spirit of the law is not observed and we must fight all forms of tax evasion." The British Times newspaper notes that a good part of Britain's budget deficit could be reduced if only the Finance Minister could discover practical means to prevent tax evasion. [2]

---

1. Reported by Ahmad, Abu Dawud, and al-Hakim. The latter grades it sound according to Muslim's criteria, which is confirmed by adh-Dhahabi. See *al-Mustadrak*, vol. 1, pp. 399-400. In its chain is Muhammad ibn Ishaq, about whom leading critics do not agree, when he mentions in his narration the word "from" instead of explicitly, saying that he "heard from". But in this *hadith* he explicitly mentions his hearing. See *Mukhtasar as-Sunan*, vol. 2, pp. 198-199, and *Nayl al-Awtar*, vol. 4, p. 115. In *al-Majmu'*, vol. 5, p. 427, an-Nawawi says, "It is reported by Ahmad and Abu Dawud via a sound or good chain." Ibn Ahmad adds in the *Musnad* of his father, "The reporter from Ubayy ibn Ka'b, who is 'Umara ibn 'Amr ibn Hazm, says, 'I was commissioned on *sadaqat* at the time of Mu'awiya. I took from the same man thirty she-camels, four to five years old, due on 1500 camels." This means that the Messenger's prayer for blessing was accepted by Allah.

2. From the lecture, "Islam Laid Down the Foundations of Modern Taxes" by Muhammad Thabit 'Awayda.

Legal and organisational endorsement of *zakat*

The *Shari'a* provides legal and organisational endorsement of *zakat*, in addition to the religious and moral ones. These legal and organisational guarantees includes the following directions.

Payers ordered to co-operate with collectors

Several *hadiths* explicitly indicate that payers are required to help *zakat* collectors. The Messenger of Allah (p) said, "You shall receive a group of collectors whom you may dislike. When they come, welcome them. All owe them to do what they want. If they do justice, that benefits their own selves on the Day of Judgement, and if they do injustice, it is their own souls they harm. It is part of completing *zakat* that you please them. They also should pray on your behalf."[1]

Jarir ibn 'Abdullah says, "Some bedouin Arabs came to the Messenger of Allah (p) and said, 'Some of the *zakat* collectors do injustice to us.' The Prophet (p) said, 'You must please your collectors.' They said, 'Even if they are oppressive towards us?' The Prophet (p) repeated, 'You must please your collectors.'" Jarir adds, "Since I heard this from the Messenger of Allah (p), no *zakat* collector left me without being pleased."[2] Bashir ibn al-Khasasiya says, "We asked the Messenger of Allah (p), 'Some *zakat* collectors transgress against us. Should we hide some of our wealth in amounts equal to the amount of their transgressions?' The Prophet said, 'No.'"[3]

These *hadiths* indicate that *zakat* payers must help *zakat* collectors and are not allowed to hide any information needed for the

1. Reported by Abu Dawud, chapter on pleasing *zakat* collectors. Its chain contains Thabit ibn Qays al-Madani al-Ghifari, who is disputed from the point of view of his memory. Ahmad grades him trustworthy. See *Mukhtasar as-Sunan*, vol. 2, p. 202.

2. Reported by Abu Dawud (the version mentioned is his), Muslim and an-Nasa'i. Ibid.

3. Reported by Abu Dawud, with no comment, and without comment also from al-Mundhiri. Also reported by 'Abu'r-Razzaq. In its chain is Daysam as-Sadusi. Ibn Hibban mentioned his name among the trustworthy. The author of *at-Taqrib* says he is "accepted". See *Nayl al-Awtar*, vol. 4, p.156.

estimation of *zakat*, even in the case when collectors do not behave rightly and do injustice to the payers. Of course, as any such action on the part of payers disturbs the state's finances. In cases of clear-cut oppression on the part of the collector, *zakat* payers have the right to refuse to pay the unjust part and complain to the proper authorities. In the *hadith* reported from Anas, it is stated, "He, among the Muslims, who is asked for *zakat* at the proper rate and amount must pay it, but he who is asked for more must not give more." That is since the Prophet determined all *zakat* rates, and these are known to all Muslims, both payers and collectors.

Cheating and tricks to waive *zakat* are forbidden

Islam prohibits cheating in all its forms, especially when it is used to avoid *zakat* payment. The laws of *zakat* do not have loop-holes, but some cheating, though forbidden, may take a legal form such as interrupting the passage of the year by a nominal change of ownership (e.g. giving one's wealth to one's wife and then taking it back after a few days.) Prohibition of this kind of practice is clear in the general *hadith* of the Messenger (p), "Actions are only by intention, and each person has only what he intends." Al-Bukhari argues that the *hadith* reported from Anas on *zakat* which states, "What is combined must not be separated and what is separated must not be combined in order to avoid *sadaqa*,"[1] stands firmly against cheating and tricks.

Malik explains this *hadith* with the example that "Three people, each one owning forty sheep, each being obliged to give one sheep, cannot combine their herds together and pay only one sheep for the hundred and twenty sheep. Or, two partners, each owning 101 sheep, are obliged to give as a partnership three sheep, and must not divide their sheep so that each pays only one sheep."[2] Abu Yusuf says, "It is not lawful for anyone who believes in Allah and the Last Day to withhold *sadaqa* or to change property only to

1. Mentioned by Ibn al-Qayyim in *Ighathat al-Lahfan*, vol. 1, p. 376. In *I'lam al-Muwaqqi'in*, Ibn al-Qayyim studies this subject in some detail. See vol. 3.

2. *Al-Muwatta'*, chapter on *sadaqa* of partners, vol. 1, p. 264.

avoid the payment of *sadaqa*. It is not lawful to cheat or use any trick to avoid *sadaqa*, by any means and for any reason."[1]

Both Hanbalis and Malikis prohibit all tricks, legal or not, that aim at escaping the payment of *zakat*. One finds in Hanbali writing such statements as, "He who purchases real estate in order to escape *zakat* must be charged the amount of *zakat* on the value of the real estate, such a person must be treated exactly the opposite of his intention, like someone who escapes *zakat* by selling or by other actions."[2] In Maliki writings one finds similar things, as studied in Chapter Six of Part Five of this book. Purchasing exempted women's jewellery in an attempt to evade *zakat* does not avert the *zakat* for the amount used for the purchase.

Imposing fines and penalties for *zakat* evasion

The *hadith* reported by Ahmad, Abu Dawud and an-Nasa'i mentions fines for rejecting payment of due *zakat*. It reads, "... and he who holds off payment, we shall take it, along with half his wealth, an imposition decreed by our Lord, none of which is lawful to the family of Muhammad." The author of *Muntaqa al-Akhbar* comments, "This is evidence for collecting *zakat* from those who reject paying it, and spending it where it belongs."[3]

Fines were discussed earlier in this book and it was concluded that a fine of half the zakatable asset is maximum. Imposition of such fines is to be decided by the executive authority in Muslim society, although there are scholars who do not allow imposing any fines, on the grounds that in another *hadith* the Prophet (p) announced, "Indeed Allah has made unlawful to each one of you each other's blood and wealth," (Muslim) and that the Companions fought those who refused to pay *zakat*, but charged them no fines above the due amount of *zakat*.[4]

---

1. *Al-Kharaj*, Abu Yusuf, p. 80.
2. *Sharh Ghayat al-Muntaha*, vol. 1, p. 101, and *al-Qawa'id an-Nuraniyya*, p. 89.
3. *Nayl al-Awtar*, vol. 4, p. 122.
4. In *at-Turuq al-Hukmiyya*, Ibn al-Qayyim mentions fifteen cases in which a fine was imposed by the Prophet (p) and the first Khalifs. See p. 287. Refer also to chapter one of part five of this book.

Those who withhold payment of *zakat* are subject to other penalties as well. When objection to payment of *zakat* takes on a collective form, as at the time of Abu Bakr, it represents a rebellion against Islamic law. Such rebels must be fought by the Islamic state, as Abu Bakr and the Companions fought them upon the death of the Messenger of Allah (p). Ibn Hazm says:

> The ruling regarding anyone who does not pay *zakat* is to collect it by force, whether he likes it or not. If he continues defending himself against law enforcement, then he is treated as a rebel. Moreover, negating the obligation is a form of apostasy. But he who evades payment through methods of cheating, without denying or deferring payment, is doing an evil act and must be subjected to legal penalties until he pays up what he owes. If he dies during the period of the penalty, he goes to Allah's wrath. This is according to the *hadith*, "He who sees an evil act must change it with his hand if he can." Withholding payment of *zakat* is undoubtedly an evil act which he must change with his hand if he can. Withholding payment of *zakat* is undoubtedly an evil act that must be changed.[1]

In Part Five I discussed in detail that the due amount of *zakat* is not waived, even by the passage of years, and it must be collected by the law enforcement body of the Islamic state, for such a right belongs to Allah and is assigned to the poor and needy. No one has any authority to waive it.

1. *Al-Muhalla*, vol. 11, p. 313.

Chapter Seven

Is it Permissible to Levy Taxes Besides *Zakat*?

Zakat is levied for particular purposes decreed by Allah on the wealth of Muslims and is collected and distributed by the Islamic state. Is the Islamic state permitted to impose other taxes in addition to *zakat* or is *zakat* the only levy permitted on the wealth of Muslims? We will study in the following three sections the evidence concerning imposing taxes in addition to *zakat*, the necessary conditions for levying such taxes, and the objections raised by opponents.

Section One: Evidence permitting levying taxes beside *zakat*

The fundamental of social solidarity

There is no need to say any more concerning social solidarity between members of Muslim society, which we have discussed in previous chapters. However, the solidarity and brotherhood of the Muslims, that is the foundation for *zakat* itself, are also grounds for the imposing of taxes when the necessity arises.

Distribution of *zakat* is predetermined while the state's needs are many and variable

Since *zakat* can only be dispensed to the eight categories described in Part Four of this book, Muslim scholars argue that *zakat* must have an autonomous budget. Abu Yusuf, for example, says that the proceeds of *kharaj* must not be added to the proceeds of *sadaqat* since *kharaj* is to serve all Muslims while *zakat* must only serve the categories named by Allah.[1] Scholars usually agree that *zakat* must not be spent on building bridges, highways, canals, mosques, schools, etc.[2]

No one can argue with the fact that services for which *zakat* cannot be used include certain public necessities, like schools and mosques, and these require financial resources. If the proceeds of *kharaj*, *ghanima* and *fay'* are sufficient, there is no need for imposing taxes, but if some sources do not exist or do not yield a sufficient amount, other taxes need to be levied since the principle of *usul* states, "Something without which an obligation cannot be fulfilled is also obligatory."

We have seen earlier in this book that Shafi'is do not allow payment of *zakat* to the regular army and restrict payment to voluntary fighters. When an-Nawawi was faced with the problem of insufficiency of other resources to finance the regular army, he suggested, as do many other Shafi'is, that rich Muslims should be obliged to finance the regular army.[3]

General rules in the *Shari'a*

The permissibility of imposing taxes besides *zakat* does not only depend on the above-mentioned rule. The general rules and principles of the *Shari'a* allow the levying of taxes when need arises. Principles which imply such possibility include the state's responsibility to care of the public interests of the Muslims, the rules that "avoiding evil has priority over bringing benefit," "small benefit can be sacrificed for greater benefit," and "individual harm may be tolerated in order to prevent common harm."[4]

Undoubtedly, application of these general rules leaves room for imposing taxes. In fact, it may be deduced from these rules that

1. *Al-Kharaj*, Abu Yusuf, p. 59.
2. *Al-Mughni*, vol. 2, p. 667.
3. *Ar-Rawda*, vol. 2, p. 321, and *Tuhfat al-Muhtaj*, vol. 3, p. 96.
4. For these and similar principles and rules of *ahkam*, see *al-Ashbah wa'n-Naza'ir* by Ibn Nujaym, section on general rules. See also *Usul at-Tashri'*, al-Khudari.

taxes, on certain occasions, **must** be imposed to secure important interests of society and state, and to prevent harm and danger. For such reasons derived from the *Shari'a* principles, Muslim scholars think that financing the treasury with taxes imposed by the Islamic government is needed in exceptional circumstances to prevent a danger or fulfil an important benefit.

Al-Ghazali, a Shafi'i known for his restrictive views regarding unspecified public interest, says, "When there are no funds and the state income is not sufficient to pay for army needs and there is danger that an enemy may transgress against Muslim land or that evil rebels may arise, the Islamic government is allowed to impose on the rich sufficient taxes to pay for the soldiers, since we know the rule that when one must choose between two evils or two harms, the more dangerous of them must be avoided. Every sacrifice made by the rich, including the sacrifice of lives and wealth, is a lesser harm than the lack of means to defend Islamic society against aggression or sinful rebellion."[1] Ash-Shatibi, a Maliki, says:

> If we happen to have an Islamic government that needs to increase the number of its soldiers in order to defend Muslim borders and lands and the treasury is empty, the leader, provided he is just, has the right to impose on the rich what is sufficient to fulfil defence needs until the treasury has funds again. The government has the right to make these impositions on agriculture or other products. The reason no such opinion is reported from the scholars of the early generations is the abundance of treasury funds during their times. If the Islamic government does not impose such taxes, its strength would vanish and our country would be exposed to unbelievers' aggression. The backbone of the government and defence is the army. Those who evade the payment of levied taxes would realise that if the army were abolished, they will be hurt personally and all their wealth, not only a part of it, would be confiscated by the aggressors. If such enormous harm is

1. *Al-Mustasfa*, vol. 1, p.104.

contrasted with the harm of tax payment, no one can argue that the latter is much lesser.[1]

Jihad and its financial requirements

Islam prescribes *jihad* on both persons and their wealth. Allah says,

> *"Go out to fight, whatever your circumstances or desires, and do jihad with your wealth and yourselves in the way of Allah."* (9:41) *"The believers are only those who have believed in Allah and His Messenger and then had no doubt and done* jihad *with their wealth and themselves in the Way of Allah. It is those who are the truthful."* (49:15) *"That you believe in Allah and His Messenger and do* jihad *in the Way of Allah with your wealth and yourselves."* (61:11) *"Spend in the way of Allah. Do not cast yourselves into destruction."* (2:195)

All these *ayats* command spending out of wealth and property in the Way of Allah. *Jihad* in respect of wealth is an obligation in itself, like the obligation of *zakat*. Armaments and army expenditures today are huge, in addition to the fact that the might of a nation is not only measured by the size of its army. National strength requires superiority in several areas, including scientific research, industry and the general economy. All these require abundant financial resources which cannot be secured except by imposing taxes. These taxes are a form of *jihad* with wealth whereby all individuals contribute to the strength and defence of their state. Such contributions pay back, in the form of protection for the individual himself, his religion and his assets.

Sharing the burdens as the gains are shared

Resources collected in the form of taxes are spent on public services which benefit all members of society, such as defence and security, judicial institutions, education, health services, transporta-

1. *Al-I'tisam*, vol. 2, p.104.

tion, irrigation, etc. Each individual benefits from the presence and power of the state as well as from the services it provides. Thus each must share the financial burden that allows these services to be performed. Just as each individual benefits from the state's services and its presence, he or she is required to pay the necessary taxes in application of the principle that gains must be comparable to sacrifices.

Section Two: Conditions for imposing taxes

There are four conditions for imposing taxes: real need, just distribution, lawful use of funds and due consultation.

Real need for funds and shortage of other sources

There should be a real need for the services to be financed by additional financial resources as well as inadequacy of treasury funds and other state resources to meet it. In principle, private wealth is protected and free from any financial obligation and no charge should be made on it beyond *zakat*. It is unlawful to violate this rule except in extreme need. If such necessity does not exist or if the government has other financial resources, it is not lawful to impose taxes.

Leading scholars have emphasised this condition for centuries. Some go as far as requiring the treasury to be completely empty in order to deter rulers from imposing taxes without need. Islamic history reveals several instances in which Muslim scholars stood fast, confronting rulers who wanted to impose taxes while they still had other resources.

When Sultan Qutuz of Egypt was preparing his troops to fight the Mongols, who by then had occupied most of Syria, he gathered all scholars, jurists and judges to consult with them on whether he could impose taxes for *jihad*. Among them were 'Izz ad-Din ibn 'Abdu's-Salam and Badr ad-Din as-Sinjari. After discussion, the leaders of opinion agreed that 'Izz ad-Din speak for them. He said:

> If the enemy transgresses on the lands of Islam, all Muslims are obliged to fight. It is then permissible for you to collect taxes from people in the amount that helps you to fight this *jihad*, provided there is nothing in the public treasury and that you sell all gold ornamented clothes and all fancy tools and utensils that you and your courtiers and soldiers own, so that each person in the army has only a mount and a weapon and all become equal to the common people. As for collecting funds from the public while your men and soldiers still have assets and luxurious things - no, it is not permissible.[1]

A similar stand was taken later by an-Nawawi before Sultan az-Zahir Baybars. When the Sultan wanted to fight the Tatars in Syria, he had insufficient funds in his treasury, so he asked scholars in Syria whether he could impose taxes to help the government and army fight the enemies of Islam. All the scholars present approved and wrote their approval to the king. An-Nawawi was not there and the Sultan asked if there were any scholars who did not respond to his appeal. They said, "Yes, there is an-Nawawi." When he came, the Sultan asked him to add his approval to those of the others, but an-Nawawi refused. When asked for a reason, he replied, "I know that you were a slave of the previous ruler, Bandaqdar. Then you owned nothing and Allah gave generously to you and made you a king. I hear that you own one thousand slaves, each of whom has a gold ornamented garment, and that you also own 200 female slaves, each of whom has a basket of jewellery. If you spend all that, your slaves wear woollen garments only, and your slave women keep their clothes but dispense with their jewellery, after that I approve of your collecting taxes from people."

The Sultan was furious and ordered an-Nawawi out of the city. An-Nawawi obeyed and went to his village, Nawa [about fifty miles south of Damascus]. When some other scholars negotiated for his return and the Sultan permitted it, an-Nawawi refused and announced, "I will not go to Damascus as long as az-Zahir Baybars

1. *An-Nujum az-Zahira*, vol. 7, pp. 72-73, *as-Suluk lil-Ma'rifat Duwal al-Muluk*, vol. 1, pp. 416-417, and *Tabaqat ash-Shafi'iyya*, Ibn as-Subki for the biography of 'Izz ad-Din ibn 'Abdu's-Salam.

is there," but the king died after a month.[1] An-Nawawi wrote a letter to az-Zahir explaining, "It is not lawful to collect anything from people as long as the treasury has wealth in any form, money, property, land or anything that can be sold. All scholars agree to this. And the treasury now, praise be to Allah, has much property and goods, may Allah always increase it."[2]

Just distribution of the tax burden

The burden of taxes must be distributed justly among people so that no one is over-burdened when others are exempted without reasonable cause. Justice does not require equality among taxpayers, since treating equally what is different is as unjust as treating differently what is equal. There must be objective criteria for distributing the tax burden among the rich members of society.

Abu 'Ubayd reports from Ibn 'Umar that 'Umar used to collect from the Nabatites [foreign merchants who used to bring goods into the country] half a tenth on oil and wheat to encourage them to bring more of these goods to Madina, and one-tenth on beans."[3] It is known that the general principle of this tax laid by 'Umar was to collect one-tenth from foreign merchants from the People of War, one-half from merchants who were People of the Pledge, and one-fourth of a tenth from Muslim merchants,[4] as reported by Anas and by as-Sa'ib ibn Yazid, who says, "I was a commissioner to the Madinan market during 'Umar's time and we used to collect one-tenth from the Nabatites."[5]

1. *Al-Islam al-Muftara 'Alayh*, Muhammad al-Ghazali, pp. 222-223.

2. Biography of an-Nawawi, by as-Sakhawi.

3. *Al-Amwal*, p. 533.

4. On roads used for transporting goods from one town to another, *'ushr* collectors used to stand to collect the required tax. 10% was collected from foreigners, on the basis of equal treatment, since Muslim merchants abroad were also charged 10%, according to what Abu Musa wrote to 'Umar. (See *al-Kharaj* by Yahya ibn Adam, p. 172.) 5% was collected from merchants who were People of the Pledge, in accordance with the treaties signed with them. (See *al-Amwal*, p. 532.) This, however, did not apply to the Christians of Banu Taghlib who were treated differently by special agreement. See Chapter One of Part Two of this book.

5. *Al-Amwal*, p. 532.

But with regard to oil and wheat, 'Umar apparently reduced the tax to 5% for an important economic reason, i.e. encouraging food imports that were required in the fast growing town of Madina, the Islamic capital. This action of 'Umar indicates that the rate of this specific levy was changed to meet the particular economic target it aimed at achieving.

Proceeds must benefit society

Tax collection is aimed only at serving the nation. Thus tax proceeds must not be used for the whims and desires of the rulers and their inner circles or to fulfil dictatorial purposes or individual ambitions. Allah establishes this principle when He details *zakat* distribution, not leaving it to be determined by any ruler. The *Khulafa' ar-Rashidun*, along with the great Companions, were extremely strict regarding the disbursement of public funds. In the *Tabaqat*, Ibn Sa'd reports from Salman that 'Umar ibn al-Khattab once asked, "Am I a king or a khalif?" Salman replied, "If you collect one single dirham from the Muslim land, or less or more, and spend it on anything other than its right and proper disbursement, then you are a king and not a *khalifa*." 'Umar, hearing this, wept.[1]

Sufyan ibn Abi'l-'Awja' said, "'Umar ibn al-Khattab once said, 'By Allah, I am not sure whether I am a *khalifa* or a king. If I am a king, this is indeed an awful thing.' A man answered 'O Amir al-Mu'minin, there is indeed a great difference between them.' 'Umar asked, 'What?' The man said, 'The *khalifa* does not take anything except what is right and does not spend it except on what is right. You, praise be to Allah, are of that kind. Kings oppress arbitrarily. They take from this and give to that.' 'Umar remained silent."[2]

At-Tabari reports, "A man who was a relative of 'Umar asked 'Umar for a grant. 'Umar turned him down and asked him to leave. Then someone spoke to 'Umar about him, 'O Amir al-Mu'minin, so-and-so asked you, but you turned him down and ordered him out.' 'Umar answered, 'He indeed asked me to give to him from the property of Allah [meaning the property of society

1. *Tabaqat Ibn Sa'd*, vol. 3, pp. 306-307.
2. Ibid.

and the state]. If I did so, what would be my excuse? Then I would meet Allah as a betraying king!'"[1]

Due consultation

Since private property is protected by Islamic law, any levy on individuals must be approved after due consultation with the relevant authorities. It is not sufficient that the ruler alone or his administrative commissioners make such a decision. *Shura* consultation is required by the Qur'an and *Sunna*. Allah commends, *"...those who respond to their Lord and establish the prayer, and manage their affairs with mutual consultation and give of what We have provided for them."* (42:38) *Shura*, or consultation, is associated with accepting the Message of Allah, establishing prayer and spending for His sake. This *ayat* establishes the essential principles of the Islamic system as early as the Makkan period.

Later in Madina, Allah sent down the *ayat*, *"And consult with them in the affair. Then when you have reached a firm decision, put your trust in Allah."* (3:59) Revealed in Madina, in the era when details of Islamic law and life were laid down, this *ayat* gives a general outline for the governmental structure of this society. This *ayat* was revealed just after the Battle of Uhud before which the Prophet had consulted his Companions on whether to stay in Madina and let the enemy come there or to go out and fight the invaders outside the city limits.

The majority of Companions wanted to go out, while the Prophet's opinion was to stay in Madina and fortify it, but in tune with the majority, he went out and the result was a defeat and about seventy great Companions were killed. Even despite that, the *ayat* reaffirmed that consultation is an essential part of the Islamic system, as if to say, "You should continue to consult them and make your decisions by consultation, even after what happened as a result of following the majority's opinion."

The Prophet used to consult his Companions on all matters of substance whenever he was not given clear revelation from Allah about the matter. At the time of Badr, the first battle in Islam, the

1. *Tarikh at-Tabari*, vol. 5, p. 19.

Prophet asked the opinion of both the *Muhajirun* and *Ansar* on whether they should seek out the Qurayshi caravan and where to camp in that battle. In the Battle of Uhud, he also based his decisions on consultation. At the Battle of al-Ahzab, the Prophet (p) consulted his Companions when he wanted to accept the peace treaty offered by the unbelievers, which required that he give them one-third of the produce of Madina that year, but the leading Companions advised him not to accept, so he refused that offer.

On the Day of al-Hudaybiyya, he based his decision to hold back from fighting on consultation, for he was told by Abu Bakr, "We did not come here to fight. We came only to visit the House of Allah." When his wife 'A'isha was accused, he also consulted the Muslims, saying, "O Muslims, give me your opinion. What should I do with those who accuse my wife?" He also consulted 'Ali and Usama on how to deal with 'A'isha.[1] Ibn Kathir comments, "The Prophet (p) used to consult the Companions on battles and for other decisions. Jurists dispute whether this was obligatory for him or only recommended (by Allah) in order to keep them happy."[2]

If this can be disputed when it comes to the Messenger (p) who is guided by Allah and His Revelation, it should certainly be respected by other leaders who are simply elected men. The *ayat* explicitly commands consultation, and commands mean obligation. Add to that the keenness of the Prophet (p) to implement this *ayat* in all important matters. All this makes consultation obligatory for leaders, especially in view of the historical experience of the Muslim nation of suffering from tyrants and dictators.

Is a ruler bound by consultation?

The answer is certainly affirmative, on the grounds that the Prophet used to generally accept the opinion of the majority of his Companions after consultation. Ibn Kathir mentions that Ibn Mardawayh reports that 'Ali said, "The Messenger of Allah (p) was asked about the meaning of the *ayat*, *'When you have reached a firm decision…'* and he answered that it meant 'consult people of knowl-

1. *Tafsir Ibn Kathir*, vol. 1, p 420.
2. Ibid.

edge and then follow them.'"[1] If a decision based on consultation (*shura*) is not binding on the government, *shura* loses its meaning. This makes a mockery of consultation, whereby rulers consult people and then do what they want, regardless of the majority opinion.

Moreover, the Muslims in a community can make *shura* binding by making it a condition on the leader when he is appointed. The Prophet (p) says, "Muslims are bound by their contractual conditions."[2] Honest fulfilment of such conditions are binding on a ruler, without doubt, regardless of juridical opinions on whether *shura*, when unassociated with such conditions, is only informative or is binding.

The *ayats* do not specify on what affairs *shura* is required. No doubt the words "matters" or "affairs" in the verse are general and include all affairs, yet the mot important are those affairs that affect Muslim society and its future. Certainly taxes are of such importance.

Section Three: Arguments against taxes

Some scholars believe it is unlawful to impose any taxes besides *zakat*. They use three main arguments to support their views: firstly, the rule that nothing is obliged on wealth except *zakat* is commonly known among jurists; secondly, private property is protected

1. Ibid.

2. Reported by Abu Dawud in his chapter on judgements, Ibn Majah's chapter on rulings, al-Hakim from Abu Hurayra. Al-Hakim grades it sound according to the criteria of al-Bukhari and Muslim. It is also graded sound by Ibn Hibban and at-Tirmidhi, through Kathir ibn 'Abdullah ibn 'Amr ibn 'Awf al-Muzani from his father from his grandfather. At-Tirmidhi comments, "Good sound". The version of at-Tirmidhi reads, "Muslims are bound by their conditions, except a condition that makes unlawful what is lawful or makes unlawful what is prohibited." It is objected that Kathir is very weak, but Ibn Hajar comments, "This *hadith* is considered by numerous chains." Al-Hakim reports it from Anas and 'A'isha via a weak chain, and at-Tabarani from Rafi' ibn Khadij via a good chain, as stated by al-Munawi in *at-Taysir*, vol. 2, p. 457. Ash-Shawkani comments, "It is not secret that these different *hadiths* and chains support each other. Thus the least that can be said about the text of these narrations is that it is good." See *Nayl al-Awtar*, vol. 5, p. 254, *Kashf al-Khafa'*, vol. 2, p. 209, and *Fayd al-Qadir*, vol. 6, p. 272.

and any charge on it must be supported by a text. The Prophet (p) said, "He who is killed while defending his wealth is a martyr." (The Group) It is, therefore, unlawful to take any part of Muslims' private property without their consent. Thirdly, several *hadiths* discredit levies on people and prohibit even the collection of the tenth (*'ushr*), such as the following:

- Abu'l-Khayr says, "Maslama ibn Mukhallad, who was governor of Egypt, offered Ruwayfi' ibn Thabit the position of *'ushr* collector. Ruwayfi' refused, saying, "I heard the Messenger of Allah (p) say, 'Tax collectors are in the Fire.'"[1]
- 'Uqba ibn 'Amir says he heard the Messenger of Allah (p) say, "Tax collectors do not enter Paradise."[2]

Although these two *hadiths* are criticised by *hadith* critics, they are supported by a *hadith* reported by Muslim at the end of a story about a married woman who committed adultery and was stoned. The Prophet (p) said, "She made such sincere repentance that, if similar repentance was made by a tax collector, he certainly would be forgiven." This shows that the sin of tax collectors is in fact more severe than that of the woman who committed adultery. This is further supported by the several *hadiths* that censure *'ushr* collectors.

Although none of these *hadiths* reach the level of good or sound, they support each other. In *al-Muj'am al-Kabir*, at-Tabarani reports from 'Uthman ibn Abi'l-'As that the Prophet (p) says, "Allah descends close to his creatures and forgives anyone who asks forgiveness, except a prostitute [who earns] by her body and an *'ushr* collector."[3] In *an-Nihaya*, Ibn al-Athir explains than an *'ushr*

1. Reported by Ahmad via Ibn Lahi'a and by at-Tabarani who adds, "It means *'ushr* collector." See *at-Targhib*, vol. 1, p. 568.

2. Reported by Abu Dawud, Ibn Khuzayma, and al-Hakim via Muhammad ibn Ishaq. Al-Hakim calls it "sound according to the criteria of Muslim." Al-Mundhiri adds, "But Muslim only reports from Muhammad ibn Ishaq supporting narrations." See *at-Targhib*, vol. 1, pp. 566-567.

3. In *Majma' az-Zawa'id,* vol. 3, p. 88, al-Haythami mentions the *hadith* in different versions, as quoted from *al-Muj'am al-Kabir* and *al-Muj'am al-Awsat*, both of at-Tabarani, and from Ahmad. He adds, "The people of the chain of Ahmad are

collector is a tax collector.[1] Al-Baghawi adds, "A tax collector is the officer who collects from merchants who pass by him a tax called *'ushr*."[2] Al-Mundhiri adds, "Nowadays they collect a tax named *'ushr*, in addition to other nameless taxes that they take unlawfully. It is as if they are eating fire in their stomachs. They shall have no excuse when they meet their Lord, may the wrath of Allah be upon them, and indeed they will be severely punished."[3] Al-Munawi says, "The tax collector is the *'ushr* collector: he is an officer who collects taxes from people."

Al-Munawi quotes at-Tibi says saying, "The *hadiths* indicate that collecting such a levy is among the most dangerous sins." Adh-Dhahabi considers it a great sin.[4] Al-Munawi continues, "A tax collector is like a highway robber, who is worse than normal thieves, since oppressing people and imposing undue taxes on them is heavier than stealing. The tax collector, his clerk, policemen who aid him, and even those who receive salaries and grants out of such taxes, are all partners in taking unlawful property."[5]

Additionally, there are *hadiths* which call for the lifting of *'ushr* from the shoulders of the Muslim people. Sa'id ibn Zayd said, "I heard the Messenger of Allah (p) say, "O Arabs, thank Allah that He removed the *'ushr* [10%] from you.'"[6] A man narrates from the Prophet (p) that "The *'ushur* are only on Jews and Christians; there should be no *'ushr* on Muslims." Another version reads, "And there is no *'ushr* on the people of Islam."[7] In *at-Taysir*, al-Munawi com-

those of the *Sahih* Collections except 'Ali ibn Zayd who is criticised but who is nevertheless considered trustworthy by some."

1. *An-Nihaya*, Ibn al-Athir, vol. 4, p. 110.

2. *At-Targhib*, vol. 1, p. 567.

3. Ibid.

4. *Al-Kaba'ir*, adh-Dhahabi, p. 119. Adh-Dhahabi does not define the word *maks* exactly; he only says, "The *maks* collector is a real helper of oppressors. He is, in fact, one of the oppressors, since he takes what is not due and gives it to those who do not deserve it." Ibn Hajar al-Haytami in *az-Zawajir* has a similar view.

5. *Fayd al-Qadir*, vol. 6, p. 449.

6. Al-Haythami in *Majma az-Zawa'id*, vol. 3, p. 87, says, "Reported by Ahmad, Abu Ya'la, and al-Bazzar. In its chain is a narrator whose name is not given but the rest of the narrators are trustworthy."

7. Reported by Ahmad, vol. 3, p. 474, via 'Ata' ibn as-Sa'ib, from a man of the tribe of Bakr ibn Wa'il from the man's uncle, who said, "O Messenger of Allah, should I collect *'ushr* from my clan?" The Prophet said, "The *'ushr* are only

ments on this *hadith*, "It explicitly says the 10% levy is on Jews and Christians, if they made their treaty of surrender on that condition, or if they enter our country to trade. There is no such levy on Muslims, except what is required as the *'ushr* of *zakat* on agriculture. This text explicitly prohibits imposing any levies on Muslims."[1]

In the remainder of this section, we shall discuss the second and third objections, since the first objection was discussed at length in Part Eight of this book.

Discussion of the second objection against taxes

The protection of private ownership in Islam is not contradictory to charging certain dues on this ownership. The poor, weak and needy have a right on the wealth of the rich based on their brotherhood in humanity and in religion, as was shown when we studied the theoretical foundations of *zakat*. Society also has rights on private property since individuals earn their wealth only in the framework of society and, one way or another, society contributes to the earning of individual property, and because without social services, life would be very inconvenient for urban people. Before

on..." The same is reported via 'Ata' from Harb ibn 'Ubaydullah ath-Thaqafi from Abu Umayya, who is from the tribe of Taghlib and who heard the Prophet (p) say, "There are no *'ushur* on Muslims..." Also reported by Abu Dawud from Harb ibn 'Ubaydullah ibn 'Umayr from his maternal grandfather from the latter's father linked up to the Prophet. See Mukhtasar as-Sunan, hadiths no. 2924, 2926, and 2927, vol. 4, pp. 253-254, and the comments of al-Mundhiri. 'Abdu'l-Haqq says, "This is a *hadith* whose chain is disputed and I know it is not via an acceptable chain." Ibn al-Qaffal says, "Ibn Ma'in was asked about Harb and answered, "He is known but this is not sufficient to consider him trustworthy. Many known persons are not accepted as narrators of *hadiths*. As for Harb's grandfather, no one knows him, it is worse when it comes to the latter's father." Al-Munawi says, "Al-Bukhari reports it in *at-Ta'rikh al-Kabir*, mentioning the disturbance in its chain, and comments, 'There is no support for this narration.'" At-Tirmidhi, in the chapter on *zakat* under the title, "No *jizya* in Islam," mentions this *hadith* without any chain. Ahmad mentions it in his *Musnad*. Al-Haythami says, "'Ata' is in its chain, who was mentally disturbed, but the rest of the chain is trustworthy." See *al-Fayd*, vol. 2, p. 561. Strangely enough, al-Munawi mentions in *at-Taysir*, vol. 1, p. 358, that its chain is good or sound.

1. *At-Taysir*, Ibid.

all this, Allah has rights on private wealth. He is the Creator and true Owner of wealth. Goods are in fact Allah's property before anything else, and people are merely viceregents.

If, in Islamic society, there exist needy persons whose needs are not satisfied by all the proceeds of *zakat*, if there are public needs, military, economic and otherwise that require resources, and if the spread and establishment of Islam requires funds, Islam approves, in exceptional circumstances, of imposing taxes on the rich to achieve these targets in application of the rule, "Something without which an obligation cannot be fulfilled is also obligatory."

Discussion of the third objection

The *hadiths* that discredit levies are not always reliable, as we have seen earlier. Even those which reach the level of acceptance do not explicitly prohibit every tax, since the word used in them for tax is the Arabic *maks*, which has several meanings. In *Lisan al-'Arab*, the most respected Arabic dictionary, *maks* is defined as money collected from vendors in pre-Islamic markets. It is also defined as what is collected by the *'ushr* officer. Ibn al-'Arabi says that *maks* is an added dirham collected by the *zakat* officer above the due *zakat*, the collection of which the Prophet (p) prohibited. He mentions the *hadith*, "A *maks* collector does not enter Paradise." *Maks* is also defined as the tax collected by the *maks* officer. Originally the word *maks* means collection. *Maks* also means reduction, making it a discount in the cost of a sale." Al-Bayhaqi says, "*Maks* is deduction. If the officer skims from the proceeds of *zakat*, he is called a *maks* collector."[1]

Accordingly, the demeaning of *maks* collectors can be understood as a warning to *zakat* officers, for a *maks* collector is the dishonest and unjust *zakat* officer who takes from payers more than is due or keeps part of the proceeds that belong to the poor for himself. This understanding is supported by some narrators' explanation of the *'ushr* collectors mentioned in the *hadith* as being officers who take *sadaqa* improperly.[2] Moreover, Abu Dawud mentioned such

1. *Fayd al-Qadir* vol. 6, p. 449.
2. *Majma' az-Zawa'id*, vol. 3, pp. 87-88.

hadiths in the chapter on the collection of *sadaqa*. This understanding is also supported by *hadiths* that threaten collectors who are not just in their calculation and collection of *sadaqa*. (Some of these *hadiths* are mentioned earlier in Chapter Two of Part Four.) Such *hadiths* inadvertently convinced some Companions to refuse positions as *zakat* collectors because of the great responsibility involved.

However, there is another understanding of *hadiths* on *maks* which may be more convincing. *Maks* in these *hadiths* is explained as unjust taxes that were predominant all over the world at the time of Islam's spread. Taxes were collected without due right and spent for the benefit of rich people, taxes that were mainly imposed on the poor, from which the rich lords were exempted. The author of *at-Tabyin*, a Hanafi, says texts that degrade *'ushr* collectors are references to those who "take funds from people unjustly, as done by tyrants today."[2] In *ad-Durr al-Mukhtar* and other books, one finds similar statements.[3] These taxes are the best interpretation of the word *maks*. Also the *'ushr* collectors threatened in the *hadiths* are collectors used by tyrants and oppressors to collect unjust taxes.

This understanding in consistent with adh-Dhahabi's opinion, expressed in *al-Kaba'ir*: "The *maks* collector is the right hand of the oppressor. Such collectors are in fact themselves oppressors, since they take what is not due and give it to those who do not deserve it."[4]

Taxes levied under the conditions listed in Section Two of this chapter to provide for needed services in the public interest, to improve the standard of living, to educate the ignorant, to provide jobs for the jobless, to feed the hungry, to protect the frightened and to cure the ill are not unjust. They can be lawful, and the Islamic government has the right to impose them in exceptional circumstances.

The *hadith* that *'ushr* is eliminated for Muslims is not explicit in indicating that all taxes are prohibited. In fact there are several other interpretations of this *hadith* that make it consistent with just taxation.

---

1. *Al-Bahr ar-Ra'iq*, vol. 2, p. 249.
2. *Radd al-Muhtar*, vol. 2, p. 42.
3. *Al-Kaba'ir*, adh-Dhahabi, p. 119.

Abu 'Ubayd comments on this and similar *hadiths*:

> *Hadiths* in which *'ushr* and *maks* collectors are denounced clearly refer to the predominant *Jahiliyya* (pre-Islamic) practice of both Arab and non-Arab kings, i.e. imposing taxes (10%) on merchants who passed through their land. This is obvious from the messages the Prophet (p) wrote to the different regions of Arabia in which he said, 'People should not be forced to gather in processions nor charged *'ushr.*' From this we know that it was a *Jahiliyya* practice which Allah abolished with Islam and which was substituted by the purifying obligation of *zakat* at the rate of one-fourth of a tenth, i.e. five dirhams out of each two hundred dirhams.
>
> Commissioners who collect *zakat* correctly are not *'ushr* collectors. They do not take *'ushr.* They only take one-fourth of *'ushr.* This is explained in the *hadith* that reads, 'No *'ushur* are imposed on Muslims. *'Ushur* are only for Jews and Christians," and in the *hadith* linked up to the Prophet that the *'ushr* collector is he who collects *sadaqa* without due right. Also, this is the reason Ibn 'Umar answered the question, 'Do you have any information that 'Umar collected *'ushr* from Muslims?' by replying, 'No, I do not.' The *hadith* of Ziyad ibn Hudayr that, 'We used not to charge *'ushr* (10%) on Muslims or People of the Pledge' means that he collected from Muslims one fourth of one-tenth and from People of the Pledge one-half of one-tenth.[1]

Thus, abolishing *'ushr* is the abolition of an oppressive pre-Islamic tax imposed at the rate of 10% by Arabs and non-Arab kings, and substituting it by *zakat* at the rate of 2.5% on trade goods. And what is meant by Jews and Christians in this *hadith* is not People of the Pledge, but foreign Jews and Christians who bring merchandise from outside the Islamic state. They were

1. *Al-Amwal*, pp. 707-708.

charged 10%, as reported by Abu 'Ubayd from 'Abdu'r-Rahman ibn Ma'qil, who says, "I asked Ziyad ibn Hudayr whom he used to charge 10%.' He replied. 'Traders from non-Muslim countries since they used to charge our merchants 10% when they went there.'"[1]

This is on the basis of equal treatment, a very common practice among nations even today. As for People of the Pledge – Jews and Christians within Muslim lands – they were not charged 10%, nor were they charged 2.5% like Muslims. They were charged 5%, as stated by Abu 'Ubayd, who adds, "At first I did not know the reason. Then I studied a report from 'Umar and found that he made the treaty with them on that basis."[2] It seems that duplicating the rate for them as compared to the rate applied on Muslims was compensation for their exemption from any tax on livestock and money, while Muslims still had to pay *zakat* on these properties.[3]

At-Tirmidhi gives another interpretation of the *hadith* abolishing *'ushr*. He argues that by the *hadith* indicating that the Muslims are not charged *'ushr*, the Prophet meant the *jizya* on persons, as the *hadith* itself indicates when the Prophet continues, "*'Ushr* [i.e. *jizya*] is only on Jews and Christians and not on Muslims." In some versions of the *hadith* reported by Abu Dawud, the words are, "There is no *kharaj* on Muslims." The word *kharaj* was used to mean *jizya* which used to be called "*kharaj* on heads."

Strangely, in *at-Taysir*, al-Munawi attempts to conclude that the above-mentioned *hadiths* prohibit all taxes:

> It seems that this *hadith* did not reach 'Umar since he imposed *maks*. Al-Maqrizi and others say 'Umar was informed that when Muslim merchants went to India they were charged 10%. He then wrote to Abu Musa al-Ash'ari, then governor of Basra, "Collect from each Muslim merchant that passes by you at the rate of five dirhams from each 200 dirhams, and from the *dhimmi* merchants at the

1. *Al-Amwal*, ibid.
2. Ibid., pp. 709-710)
3. *Ahkam adh-Dhimmiyyin wa'l-Musta'inin fi Dar al-Islam*, 'Abdu'l-Karim Zaydan, chapter on business taxes

rate of one dirham out of each 20 dirhams." Later 'Umar ibn 'Abdu'l-'Aziz abolished this *maks*."[1]

This is a reference to what 'Umar ibn 'Abdu'l-'Aziz wrote to one of his governors, "Abolish the *maks,*" and to another, "Ride to the house in the city of Rafah that is called the House of *Maks* and demolish it."[2]

In fact, this opinion of al-Munawi lacks accuracy and correctness for the following reasons:

- He grades the *hadith* about *'ushr* good or sound. The *hadith* is neither sound nor good, as he himself mentions in his comments on *Fayd al-Qadir.*
- He presumes 'Umar took an action contrary to a sound *hadith*, and not one Companion brought that to 'Umar's attention, despite their large number and their keenness to fulfil the commands of the Prophet (p), especially in a matter that relates to masses of people.
- He suggests that 'Umar, with full approval of all the Companions, committed a denounced action that is one of the great sins. A *maks* collector does not enter Paradise. This is an obvious contradiction to the command of the Prophet (p) that we must follow the tradition of the *Khulafa' ar-Rashidun* of whom 'Umar is one.
- His last statement implies that 'Umar ibn 'Abdu'l-'Aziz abolished this oppressive ruling of 'Umar ibn al-Khattab. It is a historical fact that the later 'Umar was keen to follow in the footsteps of 'Umar ibn al-Khattab and for that reason he is considered similar to Ibn al-Khattab by many historians. 'Umar ibn 'Abdu'l-'Aziz abolished oppressive levies and practices of the Umayyads, his own clan, because his obedience to Allah and His Messenger would not allow him to follow his family. It is obvious that 'Umar ibn 'Abdu'l-'Aziz abolished unjust dues that exceeded what was right and proper, and ordered *zakat* collectors to be fair and just in their estimation and collection.

1. *At-Taysir, Sharh al-Jami' as-Saghir,* vol. 1, p. 368.
2. *Al-Amwal,* op cit., p. 704.

> For reasons like this he is called the fifth of the *Khulafa' ar-Rashidun* by many Muslim scholars. The position of 'Umar ibn 'Abdu'l-'Aziz is clarified by Ibn Hazm who reports from Zurayq ibn Hayyan ad-Dimishqi, a commissioner in Egypt, that 'Umar ibn 'Abdu'l-'Aziz wrote him, "Look after whoever passes by you of the Muslims and take from what is apparent of their wealth (the trade goods they have) at the rate of one dinar out of each forty dinars. What is less than that is charged proportionately."[1]

What concerns this study is that the *hadith*, "There are no *'ushur* on Muslims," cannot be used to prohibit imposing taxes on Muslim people when the Islamic state needs them in exceptional circumstances. This *hadith* is not accepted from the point of view of its authenticity as well as its indication.

Jurists from the four schools allow just taxes

Very seldom do jurists use the Arabic word *dariba* which means tax. But in their writing they refer to regular levies using other names. Sometimes they call them "government charges", "duties", "*kharaj*" or "allotments".

Hanafis of both early and later generations mention taxes and distinguish between unjust and proper taxes and oppressive ones. Ibn 'Abidin says, "Some allotments are justified, such as fees for making water pools on rivers, for distribution of water, for irrigation, to pay night watchmen, to finance the army or to free captives when such things are needed and the public treasury does not have funds. But some allotments are not right, such as many which are collected in out times.'

In *al-Qunya*, Abu Ja'far al-Balkhi is quoted as saying, "What is imposed by the Islamic government on people to pay for public interests is a religiously obliged financial due similar to *kharaj*. Our teachers say, 'What is collected by the government to provide for public interests becomes obligatory, such as salaries for guards who protect roads and buildings and entrances to highways. This should

1. *Al-Muhalla*, vol. 6, p. 66.

be known among scholars but not made public in order to avoid its abuse by rulers. Similarly to these just taxes is what is collected in Khwarizm [a Muslim area in Russian-occupied Central Asia] to repair the banks of the Oxus and to pay the frontier guard. Such duties are obligatory, since they are not oppressive. Every taxable person must pay them. The government must not be denounced for such levies but nor must it be encouraged to exceed what is necessary."[1] Ibn 'Abidin, after quoting al-Balkhi's statement in his *Radd al-Muhtar*, comments, "This only applies when there are no funds sufficient for these purposes in the public treasury."[2]

Al-Maliqi, a Maliki, says, "Imposing *kharaj* on Muslims is subject to given public interests. There is no doubt in our school that it is permissible. It is obvious that we have such needs in Andalusia today, especially since we pay war booty to the enemies of Muslims, in addition to what is needed for public services and in regard to the weakness of the treasury. All this provides sufficient grounds for the lawfulness of such taxes in Andalusia today. What is important, though, is to determine the amount needed and not to impose taxes beyond that. This is left to the discretion of the Islamic government."[3]

In Section One of this chapter, the views of al-Ghazali and ash-Shatibi that it is permissible to impose taxes if real need arises and there are no funds in the public treasury were cited. Ibn Taymiyya has a similar view, and approves of taxes that are just and consistent with needs, while he disapproves of some others, as mentioned by the author of *Ghiyath al-Umam*.[4] This means we have opinions from each of the four major schools that when real needs exist, and the public treasury does not have sufficient funds, taxes – under certain strictly defined conditions – may be levied on people.

1. *Radd al-Muhtar*, vol. 2, p. 58.

2. Ibid., p. 59.

3. *Tahdhib al-Furuq wa'l-Qawa'id as-Saniyya*, Muhammad 'Ali ibn Husayn, printed on the margins of *al-Furuq* by al-Qarafi, vol. 1, p. 141.

4. *Ghiyath al-Umam*, as mentioned in *Kashf az-Zunun*, vol. 2, p. 1213, chapter on the state, by al-Juwayni, a Shafi'i, who died in 478 AH.

Comments on unjust taxes

Several legal rulings and opinions deal with unjust taxes, such as the following:

- Transactions, such as a guarantee agreement of unjust taxes, are legal, in the sense that if a guarantor had to pay the amount of unjust taxes to the government, he has the right to collect what he paid from a guaranteed person. This does not, however, mean the government has the right to collect unjust taxes from guarantors.[1]
- Whoever takes responsibility for the just distribution of the burden of such unjust levies is rewarded by Allah, since leaving distribution of the burden up to the oppressive authority leads to very unjust distribution of the burden of these levies.[2]
- It is lawful to cheat the government with regard to these levies, unless it is known that such an endeavour ends up putting more burden on other tax payers. If so, it is preferred that one not cheat in payment.[3] Ibn Taymiyya says "When communities are charged levies by oppressive authorities whether on heads or on their animals, trees or wealth, or are overcharged in *zakat* or *kharaj* or other levies that are not justified in the *Shari'a* (such as sales taxes), such charges must be justly distributed among the oppressed. No one of the people unjustly charged with such taxes has any right to throw his share of the collective burden on others... They are required to distribute the burden of those unjust taxes in a fair way, as if they were lawful, since from the point of view of collection and payment, people are forced to pay unjust taxes the same way they are forced to pay just taxes. The evil of unjust taxes is carried by those who impose and collect them and not by the payers. Payers in such cases are required to pay their share of the burden fairly and justly. No one has the right to escape payment if such and escape throws the burden on others..."[4]

1. *Radd al-Muhtar*, vol. 2, pp. 58-59.
2. Ibid, p. 59.
3. Ibid, p 58.
4. *Matalib Uli'n-Nuha*, vol. 3, pp. 569-570.

Chapter Eight

Can Taxes Substitute for *Zakat*?

Wealthy individuals in most contemporary societies pay several taxes, progressive and otherwise, at rates very often several times the rates of *zakat* decreed in the *Shari'a*. These taxes provide resources for the government's budget and finance state expenditure. No doubt several objectives of the expenditure of contemporary states are similar to those of *zakat*, such as funds for welfare programmes that help the poor, the disabled and street beggars, or programmes which provide jobs and training for the jobless. Most contemporary governments have one or more departments for such social and welfare matters. Therefore, the question arises, do these taxes make up for the *zakat* required by the *Shari'a*? Or must Muslim taxpayers pay *zakat* in addition to the taxes paid to the government?

In order to answer this question, we must remember that there are three essential features of *zakat* without which *zakat* does not exist. These are:

- The rates as determined in the *Shari'a* (2.5%, 5 % or 10 %).
- The specific intention of fulfilling a worship in obedience to Allah.
- Distribution to the eight categories mentioned in the Qur'an.

Do taxes have these three characteristics? Tax rates do not follow the rates determined in the *Shari'a* which are described in this study. Tax rates are more than *zakat* rates on certain assets and less on others. Some zakatable assets are not taxable at all, while some taxable assets and incomes are not liable for *zakat* in the *Shari'a*.

As for intention, can it be fulfilled simply if Muslim tax-payers have the intention of paying *zakat* when they pay their taxes? An objection may arise since the intention of worship is not pure in this case. This may be answered on the ground that what matters is giving *zakat* in fulfilment of the obligation.

As for the third characteristic of *zakat,* when the state collects *zakat* it must distribute its proceeds according to the Qur'an. Moreover, if the government collects *zakat*, this collection must take the name of *zakat*, since *zakat* loses its essence without its name, form and purpose (i.e. proper distribution). For such reasons, Malikis specifically argue that if an oppressive government collects *zakat* in the name and form of *zakat*, payment to such a government fulfils the *Shari'a* requirement for individual payers. This is also implicitly understood from other jurists' positions. But levies and taxes collected under other names, such as *maks* and *dariba*, do not replace *zakat* and cannot be counted as *zakat* as long as they do not carry the name and the form of *zakat*, especially since they may be distributed to categories which are not approved in the *Shari'a.*

Lastly, we must realise that sincere Muslims are in most countries today charged more financial dues than non-Muslims, since Muslims are required to pay taxes like everybody else and, in addition, they are required to pay *zakat*, either by direct distribution or through Islamic organisations. This heavy burden on sincere Muslims is the cause for such a question [and a solution should be explored on the basis of justice].

Contradictions in Muslim societies

This question would not have arisen if there were not gross contradictions in Muslim societies today. On one hand there are still Muslims who hold to the basics of Islam and Islam is the official religion in most Muslim countries. Yet Islamic law has been stripped from the legislative system of most Muslim lands. Take *zakat* as an example. Although it is one of the pillars of Islam and although many Muslims implement it individually and would like it to be part of their social system, most countries do not have a system for collecting and distributing *zakat*. In all eras there have been stingy persons whose love of accumulation prevents them from paying *zakat*. Such people used to be forced to pay it by the government, but now the lack of law enforcement and the lack of *zakat* legislation in most Muslim countries leave these miserly wealthy people free not to pay *zakat*.

In most cases, the transfer from Islamic law to imported Western laws was a result of the Western colonialism which dominated Muslim lands in the nineteenth and the first half of the twentieth century. The cultural and legislative impact of colonialism was far deeper and more dangerous to Muslim society than military occupation. After the aggressive troops withdrew from most Muslim lands, we found ourselves with penal codes that are not Islamic, whereby prostitution, pornography, night clubs, adultery and drinking are legalised; with civil codes that are not Islamic, whereby interest and other unlawful transactions are made permissible in such a way that social and economic activities become dominated by foreigners and minorities.

As a result of the heavy impact of the military, economic and legislative domination of the West on Muslim lands, we found ourselves with social standards and financial codes whereby *zakat* is wiped out and taxes have been imposed which are alien to Islam. As a result of cultural colonialism, we find "geographic", or nominal, Muslims, many of whom even oppose the idea of re-establishing *zakat* and other Islamic reforms, like some so-called Muslim members of the Egyptian parliament who objected to the proposed re-instatement of a *zakat* law, on the grounds that they want their country secular and detached from religion like Western states in Europe.

What is required from Muslim governments regarding *zakat*?

Muslim governments today are called upon to adopt the Islamic system in all aspects of societal organisation, and especially to give sufficient attention to *zakat* and establish an autonomous department to collect and distribute *zakat*, the third pillar of Islam. It is necessary to enact an accurate and detailed law of *zakat*. Muslim individuals are also called upon to pay *zakat* to the state, if the state collects it, and if not, to any other organisation, or, failing that, individually, because this is a basic rite of Islam.

Scholars who seem to approve of taxes replacing *zakat*

We have some religious opinions given at different times by renowned scholars implying that Muslim tax payers may hold the intention that taxes they pay may wholly or partially fulfil the requirements of *zakat*. Among them is an-Nawawi who says, "Shafi'is agree that levies collected unjustly do not stand in place of *'ushr*. But if the government takes such levies in place of *'ushr* (*zakat* on agriculture), scholars have two opinions on whether the obligation of *'ushr* is thus fulfilled or not. If the correct amount collected by the state is less than the required *'ushr*, the difference must be paid by the payers."[1] Although levies referred to in this statement are not far-removed from contemporary taxes, it is important to observe that an-Nawawi says, "If such levies are collected in place of *zakat*," while governments today do not have in mind to collect such taxes in place of *zakat*, nor do they expend their proceeds on the correct *zakat* categories.

Similarly, a Hanbali writer says, "Ahmad was asked about a land in which the government takes half of one's produce. He answered, 'That is unjust. The government does not have such a right.' Then he was asked whether the payer must distribute *zakat* on the other half. He answered, 'What is paid to the government fulfils the obligatory *zakat* if the owner makes that his intention.'"[2] Ibn Taymiyya is quoted as having said, "Levies taken by the government in the name of *maks* (taxes) can be given with the intention of paying *zakat*, and obligatory *zakat* is thus fulfilled, even such payments do not take the form of *zakat*."[3] This quote from Ibn Taymiyya seems to contradict his statement in *al-Fatawi*, "What is collected by rulers in names other than that of *zakat* cannot be

1. *Al-Majmu'*, vol. 5, pp. 541-543.
2. *Sharh Ghayat al-Muntaha*, vol. 2, p. 133.
3. This is quoted by Muhammad al-Manqur in *al-Fawakih al-'Adida fi'l-masa'il al-mufida*, vol. 1, p. 154.

counted as *zakat* payment."[1] I wonder which of these two quotes is the correct one, or what was the final opinion of Ibn Taymiyya?

Whatever the motivation behind such opinions, they were given with the desire to avoid over-burdening sincere Muslims who were already charged several oppressive taxes. The case in contemporary society is slightly different since it is presumed that existing taxes are necessitated to provide people with basic services, including defence, i.e. it is presumed that existing taxes have acceptable justifications. Therefore, these taxes cannot make up for *zakat*, even with the intention of the payer to pay *zakat*.

Scholars who do not allow considering taxes *zakat*

The majority of scholars do not approve of intending *zakat* payment when taxes are paid and come down hard against opinions that allow it. Ibn Hajar al-Haytami, a Shafi'i, says in *az-Zawajir*:

> Some corrupt merchants think that the *maks* they pay can be counted as *zakat* if they make the intention of paying *zakat*. This is an unfounded notion. It is false and incorrect according to the Shafi'i school. The government – when it collects taxes – does not intend to consider these taxes *zakat*, nor do they collect *zakat* according to the *Shari'a*, regarding both rates and zakatable assets. The government levies these taxes with the claim that their proceeds need to be spent on the army and the public interests of the Muslims, which I do not want to argue at this point, but even given that the taxes are legitimate and their proper conditions are fulfilled, these taxes are different from *zakat* and must not be considered *zakat*, for they do not even carry its name.
>
> Some merchants tell me that they make intention of paying *zakat* when they give this *maks* to collectors, and if these collectors give it to non-*zakat* receivers, it is their problem. This idea is also false. *Maks* recipients do not usually deserve *zakat*. They are mostly rich or powerful and can earn. By what virtue can *zakat* be given to this kind of

1. *Majmu' al-Fatawi*, vol. 25, p. 93.

people? The selfishness of the merchants makes them blind so they do not see right from wrong. All they want is to save themselves the properly due *zakat* since they are forced anyway to pay these taxes. They must realise that the *zakat* obligated by Allah is not fulfilled by these tax payments, even if accompanied by their wicked intentions. As for the oppressive taxes themselves, payers of those taxes are rewarded by Allah inasmuch as they are oppressed.

Muslim scholars consider *maks* collectors thieves or armed robbers. They may, in fact, be much worse. Evidently, money collected by armed robbers cannot be considered *zakat* by the robbed. Muslim scholars warn Muslim payers repeatedly that making the intention of paying *zakat* when they pay taxes to *maks* collectors is improper and meaningless. Scholars consider those who do that merely ignorant.[1]

Ibn 'Abidin, a Hanafi, after quoting some opinions of Ibn Hajar, goes on to say:

Nowadays *maks* collectors contract the government for a certain amount which they pay the government, above which they collect for themselves, very oppressively and aggressively. Payments to *maks* collectors are taken by force repeatedly, more than once a year, even when an asset is not liable for *zakat* at all. Such payment cannot be counted as *zakat* in the Hanafi school. The *maks* collector is not like the *zakat* collector appointed by the Islamic government to collect *zakat* from merchants passing on the roads. In *al-Bazzaziyya* it is stated, 'If the payer makes the intention of paying *zakat* when handing over obligated *maks*, the correct opinion is that this cannot be considered *zakat*, as confirmed by as-Sarakhsi.'[2]

Shaykh 'Ulaysh, a Maliki, was asked whether a person who owns the *nisab* of livestock and is forced to pay a certain amount every year to the government can count his payment as *zakat*.

1. *Az-Zawajir*, Ibn Hajar al-Haytami, vol. 1, p. 149.
2. *Radd al-Muhtar*, vol. 2, p. 42.

'Ulaysh answered, "No, not even with the intention of *zakat* payment, as is also the opinion of an-Nasir al-Laqani and al-Hattab."[1]

Rashid Rida was also asked whether taxes collected by British Christians from Indian Muslims, which sometimes reach one-fourth or one half of the land rent, could be considered *zakat*. His answer was:

> The *'ushr* and half-*'ushr* obliged as *zakat* on land produce must be expended on the right categories given in the Qur'an. If the Islamic government or its representatives collect this *zakat*, the *zakat* payer fulfils his duty by paying it to the government or its representatives who are obliged in the *Shari'a* to distribute the proceeds properly. But if the Islamic government does not collect *zakat*, owners must distribute their due *zakat* according to the commandment of Allah. What is collected by Christians and others from Muslims in lands they have conquered are kinds of taxes whose payment does not fulfil the obligation of *zakat*. Muslims are required to pay *zakat* on the remainder after these impositions.[2]

What is pertinent of his opinion is his statement, "What is collected by Christians and others," since it means taxes cannot stand for *zakat*, whether collected by Christians or non-Christians, including national governments in Muslim countries.

Mahmud Shaltut, the former Shaykh al-Azhar, was asked whether taxes could be counted as *zakat*. His astute answer ascertained that since *zakat* is "a financial act of worship", it is far from being similar to taxes. Although there are certain similarities between tax and *zakat*, the differences are much greater. Taxes and *zakat* differ in their respective legislative sources, in their theoretical foundation, their objectives, rates, exemptions and in the expenditure of their proceeds. He adds:

1. *Fath al-'Ali al-Malik*, vol. 1, pp. 229-280.
2. *Tafsir al-Manar*, vol. 7, p. 576, and *Fatawa al-Imam Muhammad Rashid Rida*, vol. 1, pp. 229-230.

> *Zakat* is decreed by Allah as an obligation based on faith that must be performed whether there are poor and needy or not, and is a permanent flow of resources for the poor and needy that exists at all times among all people, while taxes are ordained by governments when there is need. With all the differences between them, one cannot substitute for the other. Accordingly, *zakat* remains due according to the conditions known in the *Shari'a*, regardless of the payment of taxes.
>
> Taxes are obligated by law and *zakat* is obligated by the religion of Allah. If this sometimes makes the burden heavy for rich persons, the poor must not be made to pay for this by being deprived of their right. Instead, governments must be asked to economise in their expenditure and reduce taxes. Governments must be questioned on the efficient use of the tax money they collect. This is one of the basic principles of the Islamic political system.[1]

Lastly, in *Tanzim al-Islam li'l-Mujtama'*, Muhammad Abu Zahra answers the question as follows: "No substantial portion of tax proceeds is devoted to social welfare, which is the essential objective of *zakat*. *Zakat* is obligatory first of all. It may substitute for certain taxes, since they do not fulfil the needs of the poor."[2]

Abu Zahra's answer gives only one aspect of the importance of *zakat* and may oversimplify the issue. Obviously, even if a sufficient proportion of taxes is devoted to the same objectives as *zakat*, *zakat* must still be collected because it is commanded by Allah and no one has any authority to freeze or abolish it. It must be collected under the same name of "*zakat*" and at the same rates and conditions prescribed by Allah. It must also be spent on the proper deserving categories mentioned in the Qur'an. Even if in certain countries the poor and needy happen to be satisfied, *zakat* must still be collected from the rich in that society and spent in the Way of Allah or to make His Word supreme.

1. *Fatawa ash-Shaykh Shaltut*, pp. 116-118.
2. *Tanzim al-Islam li'l-Mujtama'*, p. 165

I must add that the opinion of Shaltut and other scholars that taxes do not make up for *zakat* is the one with which I feel comfortable, since it is based on legitimate considerations and is safer from the point of view of practical application, since *zakat*, as a pillar of Islam, must not be forgotten in actual practice. True, this means that sincere Muslims have to pay *zakat* in addition to taxes which they are obliged to pay by law, but this is one way of striving for the re-establishment of this religion on earth, especially in a time like ours.

Muslims are called upon to struggle to correct the abnormal situations prevailing in their countries and to erase the contradictions spawned by colonialist authority over Muslim lands. The legal and economic situation in Muslim countries must be brought back to compliance with the Islamic system. Without enormous efforts to reform Muslim societies under the guidance of the Islamic system, Muslims will remain burdened financially, psychologically and socially, since they live in a society whose laws and regulations are against the nature of Islam.

If Muslims find that in certain parts of the world governments take care of the poor and needy, this does not mean *zakat* is no longer needed, since *zakat* has several other objectives, including the call to Islam, reconciling hearts to it, preparing, training and supporting Muslim callers and Islamic centres, in addition to actual *jihad* for making the Word of Allah supreme. If some Muslims do not find deserving categories of *zakat* in their areas, they can always send their *zakat* to the nearest country where there is need for *zakat* proceeds.

As for the opinions attributed to Ibn Taymiyya, an-Nawawi, and Ahmad, they deal with circumstances that are essentially different from ours in a time when governments were generally Islamic and collected *zakat* regularly. If it were to be permitted to count as *zakat* taxes paid to governments today, this would be a final abolition of this religious obligation and even the remnants that exist now would be done away with, just as it was erased from the laws and legislation of governments. This is something no one can approve of, justify, or accept in any time or place.

Epilogue

Zakat: a new and unique system

The reader should realise by now that *zakat* is a unique system with no precedent in any Divine or man-made laws. It is a blend of financial, economic, social, political, moral and religious requirements. It is a well-defined financial tax imposed at times on individuals, like *zakat al-fitr*, and at other times on capital and produce. Thus it represents a permanent and continuous flow of resources to the public treasury of the Islamic state, devoted to liberating men and women from the bondage of need and fulfilling their economic necessities. It fights accumulation of wealth and discourages hoarding it away from circulation and investment.

It is a social system because *zakat* secures individuals against disability, accidents and catastrophes. It realises humanistic aspirations of social solidarity and co-operation in which the haves help the have-nots, the strong carry the weak, and the rich give to the poor and travellers. The distance shrinks between the rich and the poor, and elements of jealousy, vanity and hatred are diminished. Moreover, the *zakat* system financially aids reformers and mediators of disputes to carry on such tasks in order to fulfil the noble social and moral objectives of *zakat*.

It is political as well, because the institution of *zakat* is part of the state. The Islamic government takes full responsibility for collecting and distributing *zakat* according to the principles of justice, and for appointing personnel necessary to accomplish that. Additionally, some categories of distribution can only be decided by the state, such as reconciliation and, in general, the share spent 'in the Way of Allah."

It has a moral purpose because the very objective of *zakat* is to cleanse and purify the souls of the rich from selfishness and desire for accumulation. It aims to train the rich to sacrifice and contribute to the welfare of other people. *Zakat* is a sword against jealousy and vanity. It aims at making brotherhood and love prevail among all people in society.

Above all, it is an act of worship; for performing *zakat* establishes an essential pillar of Islam. It is one of the basic forms of worship through which men and women obey Allah and please Him. Additionally, some of its expenditure deals directly with the progress of religion: making Islam known to all people and reconciling hearts to Islam whether they are hearts of new or prospective converts. The spending of *zakat* "in the Way of Allah" aims at making the word of Allah supreme – what a glorious religious objective!

Lastly, *zakat* is incisive evidence that this religion is from Allah, for Muhammad (p), an unlettered man from an illiterate and backward society, could never have devised such a unique and just system on his own, not with all the information and resources he could muster, were it not for the Revelation sent down to him by Allah verse after verse as a guidance for all human beings and had it not been taught to him by the All-Knowing Creator of the universe. Indeed, the bounties of Allah on Muhammad (p) and on all humanity are magnificent.

Non-Muslim writers give testimony

This unique system of *zakat*, which is misunderstood and often badly applied by many Muslims, finds ample appreciation among non-Muslim writers who have studied it and given their opinions about it. In his book, *The Preaching of Islam*, Thomas Arnold describes some of the rites of Islam, especially pilgrimage, and then goes on to speak about *zakat*, "Besides the institution of pilgrimage, we find the performance of *zakat,* another basic obligation, which reminds every Muslim of the *ayat* of Allah, 'Believers are but one brotherhood,' which is a religious ideal realised magnificently in Islamic society in a way that surprises all of us. It is seen in all acts of tenderness toward fellow Muslims, regardless of race, sex, colour or ancestry. A Muslim becomes a member of the bond of believers and immediately takes his place equal to other Muslims."

Lloyd Rouch says "I find in Islam the solution of the two major social problems that occupy the minds of the world. The first is the statement of the Qur'an, 'Believers are but one single brotherhood.' This is the most beautiful principle of socialism. The second is the obligation of *zakat* on every wealthy person and allowing the poor to take it by force if the rich refuse to pay it voluntarily, and this is a recipe for anarchy."

Muhammad Kurd 'Ali quotes another foreign writer as saying about *zakat*, "This tax, in addition to being a religious obligation required from all, is a social system and a source of income for the Muhammadan state which is used to supply and enrich the poor in a systematic, straightforward way, without any arbitration or enslavement. It is not a casual event in the life of Muslim society. This marvellous system was established by Islam for the first time in the history of mankind. This tax, *zakat*, which is obliged on landlords, merchants, and the wealthy in order to be spent on the poor, needy and disabled, brought down the barriers that divide the nation into classes, and unifies the Islamic nation into one social group based on justice. By that the Islamic system proves it is not based on hatred or selfishness."

Muhammad 'Ali also quotes a renowned French orientalist, Massignon, as saying, "This religion of Islam has the ability to be strict in realising the principle of equality by imposing *zakat* on every individual, paid to the public treasury and by working against interest loans and indirect taxes that are usually imposed on necessities. At the same time, this religion stands in support of private ownership and commercial capital. Thus Islam stands once more in the middle, balanced between the theories of bourgeois capitalism and Bolshevik communism."

The Italian writer Vaglieri says in her book, *In Defence of Islam*, "All religions recognise to a certain degree the great moral and social importance of giving charity and encourage it as a material expression of mercy. But Islam alone achieves the glory of making such charity obligatory, thus transforming the teachings of Christ into ordinances and then reality in the world. Each Muslim is obliged by law to devote a certain fraction of his wealth to the poor and needy, travellers and strangers, etc. By performing this religious obligation, believers exercise such deeper humanistic feelings that they purify their souls from selfishness and niggardliness and hope for divine reward." (p. 69)

Quotations from Muslim reformists

After quotations from these orientalists, we give a few quotations from Muslim writers about *zakat*. Muhammad Rashid Rida, in his explanation of the Qur'an, notes:

> In imposing *zakat*, Islam is distinct from all religions and legislations, as confessed by most writers of many origins. If Muslims would only establish this pillar of their religion, no poor or needy person or anyone under pressure of debts would ever exist in their societies. Unfortunately, many Muslims neglect this obligation and consequently cause harm to their religion and their nation. So they have become the worst of all nations in political and financial matters to the extent that they even lost control of their own countries and became dependent on other nations, even for the education of their children. Muslim children today are educated in Christian missionary schools, whereby they lose all their ties to their nations and become enslaved to foreigners.
>
> If they are asked, 'Why don't you establish high-performing schools yourselves instead of sending your children to missionary schools?' They answer, 'We do not have the financial resources to do so.' In reality, they do not possess the zeal, the mind and the will to implement their religion. And they see with their own eyes other people spending to finance schools and charitable and political organisations. Thus I say to these Muslims that they have lost their religion and have indeed also lost their worldly living. Allah says, *'...those who forgot Allah so He made them forget themselves. Such people are the degenerate.'* (59:19)
>
> Those who call for the reform of Muslim societies are required to start by saving the remnants of their religion

> and dignity by establishing *zakat* and distributing it according to the *Shari'a*. They must realise that the share of freeing slaves must be used to liberate people who suffer from colonialism if there is no one in the bondage of actual slavery, and that the share of 'in the Way of Allah' must be used to re-establish the Islamic system through the glorious form of *jihad* which preserves Islam before the aggression of unbelievers. They must spend to call to Islam and to defend its values by writing and speaking, if such defence is not viable by weapons.
>
> We must realise that if all, or the majority of Muslims, paid *zakat* correctly and spent it according to its proper designation, that would be sufficient to re-establish the glory of Islam, to regain what was stolen from Muslim land by foreigners, and to salvage Muslims from enslavement to unbelievers. This can be done only by spending one-tenth or one-quarter of a tenth from the wealth owned by the rich. We observe with our own eyes that many people who dominate Muslim lands spend more than that for their own national interests and ideologies, without even being obligated by their Lord.[1]

In his comment on the *hadith* from Mu'adh that the Prophet (p) told him, "Inform them that Allah imposes on them a *sadaqa* on their wealth, to be taken from the rich among them and rendered to the poor among them." Shaykh Mahmud Shaltut, the former Shaykh al-Azhar, says:

> These instructions from the Prophet indicate that *zakat* in Islam is simply a transfer of the excess wealth of the nation within itself, since it is taken from the rich and given to the poor. In other words, *zakat* only changes control of a proportion of wealth from one hand – the hand that invests and protects – to the other hand – the hand that works and struggles (when the yield of that work

1. *Tafsir al-Manar*, vol. 2.

is not sufficient of for all their needs), or to the hand that cannot work, which is the hand of the poor.[1]

In his book, *Economic Foundations in Islam Compared to Other Contemporary Systems*, Abu'l-A'la al-Mawdudi talks about the role and place of *zakat*:

> What Islam, in fact, wants is that wealth must not be concentrated in a few hands in society; that those who acquire wealth because of good fortune or good abilities must not hoard it and must spend at least part of it to help the unfortunate who cannot obtain sufficiency of sustenance. In order to achieve this objective, Islam works through two channels.
>
> Firstly, Islam encourages generosity, co-operation, and helping others, by all means of moral encouragement and religious stimulus, so that people, who naturally like to accumulate, are taught to like giving some of their wealth voluntarily. Secondly, Islam enacts a law that requires the rich to give away a certain well-defined fraction of their wealth. This payment is *zakat*. One must not forget that *zakat* is a very important element in the Islamic economic system. It is next to prayer as a pillar of Islam. The Qur'an even explicitly states that hoarding wealth is not permitted without payment of *zakat*. *"Take* sadaqa *from their wealth to purify and cleanse them."* (9:103)
>
> The word *zakat* itself indicates that wealth accumulated by men and women is dirty and sinful if it is not purified and sanctified by paying 2.5% of it for the sake of Allah every year. Undoubtedly Allah is rich, nothing of this payment is given to Him nor does He need it. Therefore the 'sake of Allah' means that one seeks to improve the lot of the poor, as well as to initiate activities that benefit the nation as a whole. Allah says, *'Collected* sadaqa *is for: the poor, the destitute, those who collect it, reconciling people's hearts, freeing slaves, those in debt, spending in the way of Allah, and travellers.'* (9:60)

1. *Al-Islam, 'Aqida wa Shari'a*, Mahmud Shaltut.

Zakat is thus an organisation of mutual co-operation on the social level, among all Muslims. It is their insurance company and their reserve fund. This is the wealth that guarantees the jobless, the disabled, the sick, the orphans and widows among them and, above all, it is the institution that helps Muslims not to worry about their material future.

The simple principle established by Islam is; if you are rich today, help others for you will receive help if you become poor, or your wife and children will receive help if they become poor after you die, or if you lose the means to earn if an accident befalls you, or if you get lost on a journey without any financial means. *Zakat* is always there to enrich you, to save you, to relieve your worry about such accidents or mishaps. All you need is to pay 2.5% of all your wealth to this insurance institution established by Allah, and you feel secure about yourself and your family for all the future. You do not need this excess wealth today, so why not give it to those who need it for sustenance, and when you need help, it will be extended to you.

Thus the contrast becomes clearer between the Islamic way and the capitalist way. Capitalists urge people to accumulate wealth and to collect interest on it so that they acquire more of other people's wealth. This is not consistent with the nature of this religion. Islam commands that if wealth happens to accumulate in your hands, it must flow through the channels of distribution provided by Islam so that life flourishes around you.

Wealth circulation is restricted in capitalism, while it is free in the Islamic system. In capitalism, you must have some wealth to acquire anything from the common pool of wealth, while in Islam, if you have excess wealth, you must give a fraction to society and those who need it will come and take it from the common pool. The two systems

> are different in both nature and approach and cannot co-exist in one place.[1]

Abu'l-Hasan an-Nadwi, in *The Four Pillars*, explains that the principle feature of *zakat* is that it is based on faith and is performed for the sake of pleasing Allah. This does not exist in any other tax. He goes on to the second essential characteristic of *zakat*:

> The second distinguishing characteristic of *zakat*, in contrast with other taxes and financial charges imposed by kings, dictators, or even republics and people's government's today, which makes *zakat* different from them from beginning to end in method, objectives and effects, is the legislative position given it by the Prophet (p) in his statement, "…to be taken from the rich among them and rendered to the poor among them."
>
> Thus *zakat* is collected from the rich, as defined in the *Shari'a*, and distributed to the categories determined by Allah in the Qur'an, which are not left to any man or group of people to decide. Moreover, it is always preferred that *zakat* be spent on the poor and needy in the same land it is collected from. This was the general practice of *zakat*, even by governments that did not strictly follow the teachings of Islam in minute detail and did not realise the Islamic ideals in politics and government. Even under these governments, the poor and needy were not deprived of their rights, and Islamic law was not abolished.[2]
>
> This is very different from taxes and fees imposed by governments today. In most cases, taxes are collected from the poor and middle class and rendered to the chiefs, the rich and the powerful. They are taken from the sweat of farmers, labourers, small craftsmen and small businesmen, who work hard day and night on their jobs, and spent for

1. *Usus al-Iqtisad fi'l-Islam*, Abu'l-A'la al-Mawdudi, pp. 128-131.

2. See *al-Kharaj*, Abu Yusuf. The introduction especially is clear evidence of the concern of the head of the Abbasid state regarding the principles of *kharaj*, *zakat*, and *sadaqat*. The introduction states that the book was written at the request of the Amir al-Mu'minin, Harun ar-Rashid.

> visiting chieftains, ceremonies and food and drink for celebrations as lavish as those described in *One Thousand and One Arabian Nights*.
>
> They are also spent freely by embassies of the country in other countries, and on propaganda for the government that exhausts the blood and resources of people. Proceeds are paid also to foreign journalists to write articles praising the government, something done by all kinds of governments, whether democratic, Communist, capitalist or socialist. The most truthful description of these taxes is "collected from the poor among them and given to the rich."
>
> *Zakat*, which is imposed by Allah on the rich to help the poor, is a form of kindness and mercy to the whole nation, a bounty from Allah, incomparable to all other taxes. It is a tax, if one must use the term, that is the least burdensome and the most beneficial.[1]

It is now my turn to present this study to thinking men and women, to experts of financial legislation and taxation, so they can know by how much Islam preceded modern financial and tax systems in legislating this *zakat*, based on principles of justice, that aims at the noblest objectives, and that is supported by the strongest bonds, in the hope that these thinkers and people of law may realise that they must observe the beliefs of this Muslim nation when they enact laws and establish *zakat* by law in all Muslim countries.

I present this study to specialists in social insurance so they may recognise that *zakat* is the first organised system of welfare in the history of mankind, that the history of governmental action in social welfare started in the seventh century with the Revelation of the Qur'an, and not in Western Europe in the seventeenth century. They must realise that social welfare and insurance are not contemporary inventions borrowed from the West, but part of the original Islamic system, provided by this religion to Muslims and non-Muslims alike.

1. *Al-Arkan al-Arba'a*, Abu'l-Hasan an-Nadwi, pp. 120-122.

I present this study to the contemporary intelligentsia in Muslim countries who have Muslim and Arab names and faces, but European, American, Russian or Chinese hearts and minds, so they realise that Islam is not a religion of asceticism that lives in the mosque alone, but a religion and a state, a system and a faith, encompassing knowledge and action, meditation and active life, freedom and justice, rights and obligations. All these are most justly manifested in the system of *zakat.*

I present this study to all Muslim people and their contemporary governments so they can revise their position vis-à-vis the Islamic law and system, especially *zakat*, in order to remove the contradictions imposed on our lives by the imperialistic powers, and rid their societies of the effects of cultural and legislative colonialism, now that they have rid their lands of military colonialism, and return to Islam as a source of law and legislation.

Lastly, I present this study to all who are concerned with Islamic jurisprudence and Islamic culture, those who call for implementing the Islamic system in the light of the Qur'an and *Sunna* which strengthens their faith so that this religion can endure the onslaught of so-called 'modernism' and can respond to the needs of contemporary life. Islam can again lead societies and direct their affairs toward truth, goodness and justice under its ever rich and fertile *Shari'a,* that is suitable to all ages and lands. And the close of our call will always be "Praise be to Allah, the Cherisher and Sustainer of the universe."

Biographical Notes

Since a great many names are mentioned in this book, this index is restricted to names which appear in the text itself and not the footnotes. This list is also restricted to names of persons who have opinions about *zakat*. I do not mention the names of narrators in this index, nor do I list the names of the leaders of the four schools of *fiqh* because of their renown. Persons are listed according to their most well-know name, whether it is the first name, last name, or title. The following are not considered in the listing of names: al-, ibn, umm, ibn Abi, etc. Each name is followed by a very brief description of the person.

Translator's Note

In the sequence of English letters, the letter with no punctuation marks of transliteration is listed before the letter with such marks. For example, the letter "s" when it represents the Arabic letter *sin* is before the letter "s" when it represents the letter *sad*.

*****

Al-Abhari, Muhammad ibn 'Abdullah ibn Salih, Abu Bakr, the leading supporter of Malik's view in Iraq, renowned among scholars of his age. (d. 375 AH).

Ahmad Thabit 'Awayda, contemporary legislation expert in Egypt, who has a good lecture on *Islam and Taxation*.

Ahmad Shakir: *see* Shakir, Ahmad.

Abu'l-A'la al-Maududi, founder of the Jama'ati Islami party in Pakistan and a great modern Islamic thinker, d. 1979 CE.

Al-Amidi, Abu'l-Hasan 'Ali, a jurist and scholar of *usul*, author of *al-Ahkam*, d. 631. AH.

Anas ibn Malik ibn an-Nadr al-Ansari, who served the Prophet (p). He is one of a small number of Companions who narrate more *hadiths* than anyone else, d. 92 or 93 AH.

Asbagh ibn al-Faraj, Egyptian jurist. He is Abu 'Abdullah, trustworthy and truthful, a disciple of Ibn Wahb, the most knowledgeable of his age about Malik's companions, d. 225 AH.

Ashhab ibn 'Abdu'l-'Aziz al-Qaysi, a jurists from Egypt, a Maliki and great defender of the Maliki school. Abu Dawud and an-Nasa'i use him in their chains. d. 204 AH.

Asma' bint Abu Bakr as-Siddiq, one of the early Muslims. The wife of az-Zubayr ibn al-'Awwam and mother of 'Abdullah and 'Urwa. She is known as "she of the two waist-bands", d. 72 AH.

Ibn al-Athir, 'Ali ibn Muhammad, author of the history, *al-Kamil*, d. 630 AH.

Ibn al-Athir, Majdu'd-din al-Mubarak ibn Muhammad, author of *an-Nihaya*, d. 606 AH.

Author of *Ghiyath al-Umam*. *See* al-Juwayni.

Author of *al-Hidaya*. *See* al-Marghinani.

Author of *al-Hawi*. *See* al-Mawardi.

Author of *al-'Inaya*, a Hanafi.

Author of *ar-Rawd an-Nadir*. *See* al-Husayn ibn Ahmad.

Al-Awza'i, 'Abdu'r-Rahman ibn 'Amr, a well-known leading jurist, *hadith* critic and one of the 'pillars of knowledge', d. 157 AH.

Ayyub as-Sakhtiyani, Ibn Abi Taymiyya al-Hasri, one of the trustworthy persons. Shu'ba used to call him 'master of jurists'. Malik describes him as one of "scholars who practise their knowledge and who fear Allah," d. 131 AH.

Al-A'zami, Muhammad Mustafa, an Indian scholar who studied at al-Azhar, author of a good study in English in which he refutes the claims of Schacht.

Ibn 'Abbas. *see* 'Abdullah.

Abu'l-'Abbas, Ahmad ibn Ibrahim al-Hashimi al-Hasani, a jurist from *Ahl al-Bayt*. He was Ja'fari, then became a Zaydi. Some people say he remained Ja'fari, d. 353 AH.

'Abdullah ibn 'Abbas ibn 'Abdu'l-Muttalib, cousin of the Prophet (p). He was the most renowned commentator on the Qur'an and a leading knowledgeable scholar, d. 67 AH.

'Abdullah ibn 'Amr ibn al-'As, a leading scholar among the Companions and a great man of worship, d. between 63 and 77 AH.

'Abdullah ibn Da'ud ibn 'Amr al-Hamadhani ash-Sha'bi, known as al-Khuraybi, a trustworthy man of worship, d. 213 AH.

'Abdullah ibn Mas'ud al-Hudhayli, one of the great early Companions, known as a reciter and a great jurist, likened to a mountain of knowledge, d. 32 or 33 AH.

'Abdullah ibn al-Mubarak ibn Wadih al-Hanzali. He was from Marw (now in Russian-occupied south Central Asia), known as a great scholar and one of the persons most agreed to be trustworthy, a leading man in knowledge, righteousness and morality, d. 181 AH.

'Abdullah ibn Shaddad ibn al-Had al-Laythi, Abu'l-Walid al-Madani, one of the great Followers and trustworthy persons. He revolted against the Umayyads with Ibn al-Ash'ath and was killed in the year 81 or 82 AH.

'Abdullah ibn 'Umar ibn al-Khattab, a leading Companion in knowledge and piety, great scholar and jurist, taught for about sixty years and freed 1000 or more slaves, d. 73 or 74 AH.

'Abdu'l-'Ali al-Laknawi, known as the "Ocean of Knowledge", the author of *Rasa'il al-Arkan al-Arba'a*.

Ibn 'Abdu'l-Barr, Abu 'Umar, Yusuf ibn 'Abdullah al-Namari al-Qurtubi, the scholar of the West (Andalusia) and their jurist, author of *at-Tamhid*, *al-Istidhkar*, *al-Isti'ab*, and other works, d. 463 AH.

Ibn 'Abdu'l-Hakam, Muhammad ibn 'Abdullah, Egyptian jurist, trustworthy, and a leading Maliki, d. 268.

'Abdu'r-Rahman Fahmy, secretary of the Islamic Art Museum in Cairo.

'Abdu'r-Rahman Hasan, former deputy chairman of al-Azhar Mosque.

'Abdu'r-Rahman 'Isa, a graduate of al-Azhar, director of Islamic teachings in al-Azhar.

Ibn 'Abdu's-Salam, Muhammad ibn 'Abdu's-Salam ibn Yusuf. He was a judge in Tunisia and one of the leading Malikis, d. 749 AH.

'Abdu'l-Wahhab ibn 'Ali, a Maliki jurist and judge, d. 422 AH.

Ibn 'Abidin, Muhammad Amin, renowned Hanafi scholar, author of *Radd al-Muhtar* and other books, d. 1252 AH.

'A'isha bint Abu Bakr, the truthful daughter of the Truthful, Mother of the Believers, and the most knowledgeable woman of this Muslim nation, d. 58 AH.

'Ali ibn Abi Talib, Amir al-Mu'minin, son-in-law of the Prophet (p) and his cousin, and father of the Prophet's two grandchildren, an ocean of knowledge and the Companion most famous for his judgements, d. 40 AH.

'Ali ibn al-Husayn ibn 'Ali ibn Abi Talib, a great Follower, one of the most trustworthy and pious persons, known as *"Zayn al-'Abidin"* (the Best of the Worshippers), and the leading person of *Ahl al-Bayt* during his time. Ibn al-Musayyab says about him, "I have not seen a more pious person than him." d. 93 AH.

'Ali Mubarak Pasha ibn Mubarak ibn Sulayman, Egyptian historian and minister in the Egyptian government, founder of the Egyptian National Library, d. 1311/1893.

Abu'l-'Aliya, Rufay' ibn Mihran ar-Riyakhi al-Basri, lived in the *Jahiliyya* and accepted Islam two years after the death of the Prophet (p). He met Abu Bakr and prayed behind 'Umar, and is unanimously known as trustworthy, d. 90 AH.

'Amr ibn al-'As ibn Wa'il as-Sahmi, well-known Companion who conquered Egypt, d. 43 AH.

'Amr ibn Dinar al-Makki, Abu Muhammad al-Athram al-Jumahi, a Follower, scholar, and opinion leader in Makka, d. 125 or 126 AH.

'Amr ibn Maymun al-Awdi al-Kufi. He accepted Islam while the Prophet (p) was alive, but did not meet him. One of the most trustworthy Followers, d. 74 AH.

'Amr ibn Shurahbil al-Hamdani, Abu Maysara, a trustworthy and pious man of worship, one of the best disciples of Ibn Mas'ud, a Follower and a colleague of Masruq, d. 63 AH.

'Amra bint 'Abdu'r-Rahman ibn Sa'd ibn Zurara. She was one of the Ansar who lived in Madina and was raised by 'A'isha, from whom she narrates. She was among the most knowledgeable persons in Madina, d. 98 or 103 or 106 AH.

Ibn 'Aqil, Abu'l-Wafa, 'Ali ibn Muhammad ibn 'Aqil al-Baghdadi, a jurist and scholar of *usul*, a leading Hanbali of distinguished view which sometimes differ with the Hanbali school, though he was a great admirer of Ahmad and his disciples, d. 513 AH.

Ibn al-'Arabi, Muhammad ibn 'Abdullah ibn Muhammad al-Ma'afiri, Qadi Abu Bakr, a Maliki *mujtahid*, and leading scholar, d. 543.

Ibn 'Arafa, Muhammad ibn Muhammad ibn 'Arafa al-Warghami, Abu 'Abdullah, a Maliki, Tunisian jurist, artistic in *usul* and jurisprudence, d. 803 AH.

'Ata' al-Khurasani ibn 'Abdullah, lived in Damascus; Muslim and the four authors of the *Sunan* report his narrations, d. 135 AH.

'Ata' ibn Abi Rabah, a great Follower and jurist, d. 114 AH.

'Atiyya al-'Awfi ibn Sa'd ibn Junada al-Qaysi al-Kufi, Abu'l-Hasan, Abu Dawud, at-Tirmidhi and Ibn Majah report his narrations, so does al-Bukhari in works other than his *Sahih* Collection. The majority grades him weak, d. 111 AH.

Umm 'Atiyya, Nusayba bint Ka'b (or al-Harith), from the Ansar, a great Companion who went to battles with the Prophet to take care of the wounded and to fight when needed, d. 13 AH.

Al-Bahi al-Khawli, contemporary writer and early caller for the Islamic movement in Egypt, author of *Tadhkirat ad-Du'at*, *al-Islam wa'l-Mar'a al-Mu'asira*, and other books.

Al-Bayhaqi, Ahmad ibn al-Husayn, a *hadith* scholar and collector and a leading scholar, author of *as-Sunan al-Kubra* and other books, d. 458 AH.

Al-Baji, Abu'l-Walid, Sulayman ibn Khalaf ibn Sa'd, a Maliki judge, a commentator on *al-Muwatta'*, d. 474 AH.

Abu Bakr 'Abdu'l-'Aziz ibn Ja'far, known as "*Ghulam al-Khallal*", leading Hanbali jurist and pious man of worship, d. 353 AH.

Abu Bakr al-'Asamm 'Abdu'r-Rahman ibn al-'Asamm al-'Abdi. Ibn Mufti says about him, "He is trustworthy. He was one of the Qadaris." Abu Hatim says, "He tells the truth and his narrations are all right; Muslim reports one *hadith* from him, and an-Nasa'i also reports one."

Abu Bakr ar-Razi. *see* al-Jassas.

Abu Bakr ibn Abi Shayba, 'Abdu'r-Rahman ibn 'Abdu'l-Malik al-Madani. His trustworthiness is disputed; some grade him weak. Al-Bukhari reports only two *hadiths* from him and an-Nasa'i reports from him, d. 335 AH.

Abu Bakr as-Siddiq, 'Abdullah ibn Abi Quhafa, the successor of the Messenger of Allah as head of state, his right-hand minister and Companion, mentioned even in the Qur'an as the Prophet's Companion, d. 13 AH.

Al-Baghawi, 'Abdullah ibn Muhammad al-Baghdadi, Abu'l-Qasim, the great trustworthy author and *hadith* critic, d. 317 AH.

Al-Baladhuri, Ahmad ibn Yahya, well-known historian, author of *Futuh al-Buldan*, d. 279 AH.

Al-Balkhi, Abu Ja'far, a Hanafi jurist.

Al-Baqir, Abu Ja'far, Muhammad ibn 'Ali, the best of worshippers, a leading jurist of *Ahl al-Bayt* as well as a great Muslim scholar, d. 118 AH.

Ibn Bashir, a Maliki jurist.

Bilal ibn Rabah, the *mu'adhdhin* of the Prophet (p). One of the very early Muslims who were harshly tortured by the disbelievers. He was present at all the battle of the Prophet (p), d. 17, 18 or 25 AH.

Ibn Daqiq al-'Id, Muhammad ibn 'Ali ibn Wahb, Abu'l-Fath, Taqi'd-din, leading scholar, most trustworthy, and the renovator of the seventh century, d. 702 AH.

Abu'd-Darda', 'Uwaymir ibn Zayd, a Companion from the Ansar, known as a great worshipper, d. 32 or 33 AH.

Ad-Dardir, Ahmad ibn Muhammad al-'Adawi, a Maliki professor at al-Azhar in Egypt, a great scholar and worshipper, d. 1201 AH.

Da'ud az-Zahiri ibn 'Ali ibn Khalaf, leading jurist and scholar, founder and head of the Zahiri school, d. 270 AH.

Ad-Dihlawi, Ahmad ibn 'Abdu'r-Rahim, known as Shah Waliyu'llah, the renovator of Islam in India, d. 1176 AH.

Draz, Dr. Muhammad 'Abdullah, one of the great professors of al-Azhar in modern times and a great writer, author of *an-Naba' al-'Azim*, *ad-Din*, and other important studies.

Ad-Dusuqi, Muhammad ibn 'Arafa, Egyptian Maliki professor at al-Azhar, a great scholar, d. 1230 AH.

Ad-Dahhak ibn Muzaham al-Hilali, known as a commentator on the Qur'an, died after 100 AH.

Adh-Dhahabi, a Shafi'i scholar who, among his numerous works, composed a small treatise on determination of the dirham and the *mithqal.*

Abu Dharr al-Ghifari, Jundub ibn Junada, pious Companion known as "the Truth-teller", one of the early Muslims, d. 32 AH.

Al-Fakhr ar-Razi, Muhammad ibn 'Umar ibn al-Husayn, Fakhru'd-din, leading scholar and Qur'an commentator, a Shafi'i, d. 606 AH.

Fatima bint Qays ibn Khalid al-Qurashiyya al-Fihriyya, a female Companion who was one of the early Muhajriun, d. 50 AH.

Al-Ghazali, Muhammad ibn Muhammad, Abu Hamid, the famous scholar of Islam, d. 505 AH.

Al-Ghazali, Muhammad, contemporary Muslim scholar from al-Azhar, one of the early workers and writers of the contemporary Islamic movement, d. 1421 AH.

Al-Hadi, Abu Muhammad Yahya ibn al-Husayn ibn al-Qasim, leading *Ahl al-Bayt* scholar, founder of the Hadawi school, d. 298 AH.

Ibn al-Humam, Kamal ad-Din, Muhammad ibn 'Abdu'l-Wahid as-Siwasi, then as-Sakandari, the great Hanafi scholar who reached the level of *ijtihad*, author of *al-Musayara*, *al-Fath* and other books, d. 861 AH.

Abu Hurayra ad-Dawsi. His original name is disputed; he became famous as Abu Hurayra, the Companion with the sharpest memory, d. 67 or 69 AH.

Ibn Habib, 'Abdu'l-Malik, Marwan, a leading Maliki jurist, d. 238 AH.

Ibn Hajar, Ahmad ibn Muhammad al-Haytami, author of *al-Minhaj* and *az-Zawajir*, d. 947 AH.

Ibn Hajar, Ahmad ibn 'Ali al-'Asqalani, the Shaykh al-Islam, famous as al-Hafiz, great *hadith* critic, author of *al-Fath*, *at-Tahdhib* and other works, d. 852 AH.

Ibn al-Hajib, 'Uthman ibn 'Umar, a Maliki scholar of *usul* and grammar, d. 646 AH, in Alexandria.

Ibn Hamid, al-Hasan ibn Hamid ibn 'Ali, Abu 'Abdullah al-Baghdadi, Hanbali leader of his time, d. 403 AH.

Hammad ibn Abi Sulayman, Abu Isma'il al-Kufi, great jurist, teacher of Abu Hanifa, and the most knowledgeable disciple of Ibrahim an-Nakha'i. Al-Bukhari reports from him in *al-Adab al-Mufrad*. Muslim and the other four also report from him, d. 119 or 120 AH.

Al-Harbi, Ibrahim ibn Ishaq, the *hadith* critic and trustworthy narrator, d. 285 AH.

Al-Hasan al-Basri, Ibn Abi'l-Hasan, Abu Sa'id, a leading scholar of Islam and one of the most famous Followers, d. 110 AH.

Al-Hasan ibn 'Ali ibn Abi Talib, grandson of the Messenger of Allah (p), one of the two "Masters of Young Men" in heaven, as stated by the Prophet (p), d. 49 or 50 AH.

Al-Hasan ibn 'Ali, a Hanafi. In *al-Jawahir al-Mudi'a*. There are several persons with this name. I could not tell which one was indicated.

Al-Hasan ibn Salih ibn Hayy, sometimes called al-Hasan ibn Hayy, al-Hamdani, a jurist and pious man of worship who refused leadership, was honest in telling *hadiths* and had an accurate memory. Graded sound in his narrations, Muslim and the other four report from him. Al-Bukhari reports from him in *al-Adab al-Mufrad*. Some grade him weak because he was a Shi'i and did not use to go to Friday congregational prayers as he did not permit prayer behind deviant persons, d. 166 AH.

Abu Hathma, 'Abdullah or 'Amir al-Ansari, well-known Companion, the guide of the Prophet (p) in the Battle of Uhud. The Prophet (p) also sent him as an estimator of fruits. He died early in the era of Mu'awiya.

Ibn Hazm, 'Ali ibn Ahmad, Abu Muhammad az-Zahiri, He was a leading scholar, a *mujtahid*, and the author of *al-Muhalla*, *al-Ihkam*, *al-Fasl*, and several other books, d. 456 AH.

Al-Hazimi, Abu Bakr Muhammad ibn Muhammad ibn Musa, a *hadith* critic, author of *al-I'tibar* and other books, d. 584 AH.

Al-Huqayni, 'Ali ibn Ja'far ibn al-Hasan al-Husayni al-Hashimi, known as al-Huqayni as-Saghir, from a small village close to Madina, a Zaydi jurist, d. 490 AH.

Al-Husayn ibn 'Abdi ibn Muhammad ibn Ziyad al-'Abdi an-Naysaburi, a great pillar of *hadith* criticism and an author, known as al-Qabbani, d. 289 AH.

Al-Husayn ibn Ahmad as-Siyaghi az-Zaydi, Sharaf ad-Din, a moderate Zaydi scholar, author of *ar-Rawd an-Nadir.*

Ibrahim. *See* an-Nakha'i.

Ishaq ibn Ibrahim ibn Mukhlid al-Hanzali, known as Ibn Rahawayh al-Marwazi. He lived in Nisapur and was a leading scholar in knowledge, jurisprudence and *hadith*, and a teacher of al-Bukhari and Muslim, d. 237 or 238 AH.

Abu Ishaq, 'Amr ibn 'Abdullah as-Sabi'i al-Kufi, a trustworthy Follower, d. 156 or 159 AH.

Al-Istakhri, Abu Sa'id, al-Hasan ibn Ahmad, renowned Shafi'i jurist who authored several books, d. 328 AH.

'Ikrima ibn 'Abdullah al-Barbari, ex-slave of Ibn 'Abbas and his student, one of the great jurists of Makka, and a Follower, d. 107 AH.

'Imran ibn Husayn al-Khuza'i, a famous Companion, d. 52 AH.

'Isa 'Abduh, modern Egyptian professor of economics and accounting.

Iyad ibn Musa al-Yahsubi, Abu'l-Fadl, the judge, a great scholar from the Islamic West, and a Maliki jurist, d. 544 AH.

'Izz ad-Din ibn 'Abdu's-Salam, 'Abdu'l-'Aziz as-Sulami, Shafi'i jurist from Damascus, known as the "King of Scholars", and the "Seller of Princes", one of the most brilliant leaders of knowledge in Syria and Egypt, d. 660 AH.

Jabir ibn 'Abdullah ibn Haram al-Ansari as-Sulami, one of the Companion scholars, d. 70 AH.

Jabir ibn Zayd al-Azdi, Abu'sh-Sha'tha', al-Basri, a trustworthy Follower and jurist, d. 93 AH.

Jabir as-Sadiq ibn Muhammad al-Hashimi al-Husayni, a great scholar and leading figure from *Ahl al-Bayt*, d. 148 AH.

Al-Jassas, Ahmad ibn 'Ali, Abu Bakr ar-Razi, renowned Hanafi scholar and author, d. 370 AH.

Ibn al-Jawzi, 'Abdu'r-Rahman ibn 'Ali, Abu'l-Faraj, jurist, *hadith* critic and historian, a great Hanbali, d. 597 AH.

Al-Juwayni, 'Abdu'l-Malik ibn 'Abdullah, Abu'l- Ma'ali, who is usually known as Imam al-Haramayn, author of *Ghiyath al-Umam*, *al-Irshad*, *an-Nizamiyya*, and several other books; a leading Shafi'i, d. 478 AH.

Al-Karkhi, Abu'l-Hasan 'Ubaydullah ibn Dallal, Hanafi jurist, a great scholar and worshipper, the leader of the Hanafis of his time in Baghdad, p. 587 AH.

Al-Kasani, 'Ala ad-Din Abu Bakr ibn Mas'ud, called 'the King of Scholars', a leading Hanafi, d. 587 AH.

Ibn Kathir, Abu'l-Fida' Isma'il al-Qurashi, known as a commentator on the Qur'an, *hadith* scholar and critic, historian and jurist, d. 774 AH.

Abu Khaythama, Zuhayr ibn Harb, a trustworthy and accurate *hadith* scholar. Muslim reports 1281 *hadiths* from him in his *Sahih* Collection, d. 234 AH,

Ibn Khaldun, 'Abdu'r-Rahman ibn Muhammad, the philosopher and historian, great renovator and scholar, founder of sociology, d. 808 AH.

Khalil ibn Ishaq al-Jundi, Egyptian-raised Maliki scholar, author of *al-Mukhtasar*, a famous compendium of Maliki jurisprudence, d. 776 AH.

Khallaf, 'Abdu'l-Wahhab, professor of *Shari'a* at al-Azhar and a great modern scholar.

Al-Kharashi, Abu 'Abdullah Muhammad, a Maliki, the commentator on the *Mukhtasar* of Khalil, d. 1101 AH.

Abu'l-Khattab, Mahfuz ibn Ahmad al-Kalwadhani al-Baghdadi, a leading Hanbali jurist of independent opinions, d. 510 AH.

Al-Khattabi, Muhammad ibn Muhammad ibn Ibrahim, Abu Sulayman, well-known leading jurist, *hadith* scholar and scholar of the Arabic language, d. 388 AH.

Al-Khiraqi, Abu'l-Qasim, 'Umar ibn Husayn ibn 'Abdullah, a Hanbali jurist, d. 334 AH.

Ibn al-Labban, Muhammad ibn 'Abdullah ibn al-Hasan, Abu'l-Husayn, a trustworthy Shafi'i scholar, especially knowledgeable in inheritance law, d. 402 AH.

Ibn Abi Layla, Muhammad ibn 'Abdu'r-Rahman al-Ansari al-Kufi, jurist and famous judge in Kufa, lived at the same time as Abu Hanifa, honest, but had a bad memory, d. 148 AH.

Al-Layth ibn Sa'd ibn 'Abdu'r-Rahman, leading Egyptian scholar, trustworthy and a most generous person. Ash-Shafi'i says, "Al-Layth had more knowledge than Malik, but his knowledge was lost by his disciples." d. 175 AH.

Al-Lakhmi, 'Ali ibn Muhammad, a renowned, Maliki scholar, d. 748 AH.

Massignon, Louis, French orientalist who lived at the turn of the century.

Maghniya, Muhammad Jawad, contemporary Lebanese Shi'ite scholar, author of several books.

Al-Mahdi, Ahmad ibn Yahya ibn al-Murtada al-Hasani al-Hadawi, author of *al-Bahr az-Zakhkhar,* and a leading Zaydi scholar, d. 840 AH.

Mahmud Abu Sa'ud, contemporary economist with special interest in Islamic economics, d. 1415 AH.

Ibn al-Majishun, 'Abdu'l-Malik ibn 'Abdu'l-'Aziz, a jurist son of a jurist and opinion leader in Madina at his time. Ibn Habib grades him as more knowledgeable than most disciples of Malik, d. 212 213, or 214 AH.

Makhluf, Hasanayn Muhammad Hasanayn al-'Adawi, leading Egyptian scholar and one of the great scholars of al-Azhar.

Makhluf, Muhammad Hasanayn al-'Adawi, an Egyptian, leading Maliki scholar, famous as a Qur'an commentator and as a scholar of Arabic literature. He was deputy chairman of al-Azhar, d. 1355/1936.

Makhul, great Follower, one of the most trustworthy and knowledgeable of scholars. He lived in Damascus, d. 112 or 113 AH.

Al-Maliqi, Muhammad ibn al-Hasan, a Maliki jurist who has a commentary on the *Mukhtasar* of Ibn al-Hajib in jurisprudence, d. 771 AH.

Al-Maqrizi, Ahmad ibn 'Ali, historian of Egypt with several volumes of writings, known as *Khitat al-Maqrizi*, d. 845 AH.

Al-Maraghi, Ahmad Mustafa, modern Egyptian, author of a commentary on the Qur'an.

Marwan ibn al-Hakam ibn Abi'l-'As, an Umayyad, born in Madina two years after the emigration of the Prophet (p). We have no sound report that he listened to the Messenger of Allah (p). He was a clerk under 'Uthman and governor of Madina in Mu'awiya's time. He became khalif after Mu'awiya II, son of Yazid, and remained so for nine months. Criticism is known to be addressed to him, d. 65 AH.

Masruq ibn Ajda' al-Hamdani, a Follower, great jurist and worshipper, a disciple of Ibn Mas'ud, d. 62 AH.

Ibn Mas'ud. *See* 'Abdullah.

Al-Mawardi, Abu'l-Hasan, 'Ali ibn Muhammad ibn Habib al-Basri al-Baghdadi, renowned Shafi'i scholar, known as the best judge, author of *al-Hawi*, *al-Ahkam as-Sultaniyya*, and other books, d. 450 AH.

Maymun ibn Mihran al-Jazri ar-Raqqi, one of the great trustworthy scholars, a jurist, pious worshipper, and leading Follower, who was appointed by 'Umar ibn 'Abdu'l-'Aziz as *kharaj* collector and judge in the area of Jazira (northeast Syria and northwest Iraq), d. 116 or 117 AH.

Abu Maysara. *See* 'Amr ibn Dhurahbil.

Al-Maziri, Muhammad ibn 'Ali ibn 'Umar at-Tamimi, a known Maliki jurist and *hadith* critic, who wrote a commentary on Muslim's *Sahih* Collection, d. 536 AH.

Mu'adh ibn Jabal ibn 'Amr al-Ansari, one of the leading Companions, d. 18 AH.

Mu'awiya ibn Abi Sufyan, founder of the Umayyad caliphate, a Companion and one of the scribes who wrote the Qur'an for the Prophet (p), d. 60 AH.

Al-Mu'ayyad Bi'llah, Ahmad ibn al-Husayn ibn Harun, leading scholar of *Ahl al-Bayt*, a Zaydi jurist, d. 411 AH.

Ibn al-Mubarak. *See* 'Abdullah.

Ibn Muflih, Muhammad Abu 'Abdullah, Shamsu'd-din, a Hanbali, d. 763 AH.

Al-Mughira ibn Shu'ba ath-Thaqafi, famous Companion, one of the shrewdest Arabs, d. 50 AH.

Muhammad 'Abdullah al-'Arabi, modern professor of finance and economics in Egyptian universities, has a good study on Islamic economics.

Muhammad 'Abduh, famous as one of the reformers in religious matters in Egypt in his time, d. 1905 CE.

Muhammad Baqir as-Sadr, modern Shi'ite scholar from Najaf, Iraq, author of *Iqtisaduna* and *Falsafatuna*.

Muhammad Hamidullah, from Hyderabad, a contemporary Indian Muslim scholar, professor at the University of Paris and University of Istanbul.

Muhammad ibn al-Hanafiyya (ibn 'Ali ibn Abi Talib), Abu'l-Qasim, trustworthy Follower, d. 73 or 93 AH.

Muhammad ibn al-Hasan ash-Shaybani, disciple of Abu Hanifa, a great scholar, writer of the original books in the Hanafi school, d. 189 AH.

Muhammad ibn Ka'b al-Qurazi, knowledgeable scholar on the Qur'an and a trustworthy Follower, d. 108 or 120 AH.

Muhammad ibn Maslama, a Hanafi scholar.

Muhammad Uzayr, contemporary Pakistani economist who wrote on Islamic economics.

Muhammad ibn Yahya, disciple of al-Ghazali, head of the Shafi'is in Nisapur, d. 548 AH.

Mujahid ibn Jabr al-Makki, a renowned Follower, d. 135 AH.

Al-Munawi, Muhammad 'Abdu'r-Ra'uf, a great scholar in jurisprudence and *hadith*, Shafi'i Egyptian, author of *Fayd al-Qadir* and *at-Taysir* as a commentary *on al-Jami' as-Saghir*, d. 1031 AH.

Ibn al-Munayyir, Ahmad ibn Muhammad ibn Mansur, Nasiru'd-din 'Abdu's-Salam says, "The land of Egypt is proud of having two persons, Ibn Daqiq al-'Id and Ibn al-Munayyir." d. 683 AH.

Ibn al-Mundhir, Muhammad ibn Ibrahim an-Naysaburi, Abu Bakr, a great jurist. He was a *mujtahid* and leader in knowledge. He wrote many books, d. 319 AH.

Al-Mundhiri, Zaki'd-din 'Abdu'l-'Adhim, known leader and *hadith* critic, author of *at-Targhib wa't-Tarhib* and *Mukhtasar Sunan Abu Dawud*, d. 656 AH.

Murra al-Hamdani ibn Shurahil as-Saksaki, Abu Isma'il al-Kufi, trustworthy Follower, known as a great worshipper, used to be called "Murra at-Tayyib" or "Murra al-Khayr", d. 76 AH.

Al-Murtada, Muhammad ibn Yahya al-Hadi ibn al-Husayn al-Hashimi al-Hasani, a leading Zaydi jurist who inherited knowledge from his father al-Hadi, d. 310 AH.

Musa ibn Talha ibn 'Abdullah al-Qurashi at-Taymi, trustworthy Follower, a leading Muslim figure of his time, d. 103, 104 or 106 AH.

Abu Musa al-Ash'ari, 'Abdullah ibn Qays, famous Companion. The Prophet (p) appointed him to Yemen and 'Umar appointed him as a judge, d. 44 AH.

Al-Muzani, Isma'il ibn Yahya, a *mujtahid*, an Egyptian disciple of ash-Shafi'i, and a man of great worship, d. 264 AH.

An-Nadwi, as-Sayyid Abu'l-Hasan 'Ali al-Hasani, secretary of Nadwat al-'Ulama' in Lucknow, India, one of the greatest figures in the contemporary Islamic movement and a famous Islamic writer.

Ibn Nafi', 'Abdullah as-Sa'igh, Abu Muhammad al-Madani, a disciple of Malik, the best versed in Malik's opinions. Ash-Shafi'i praises him, but others criticise the accuracy of his memory, d. 206 or 107 AH.

An-Nahhas, Abu Ja'far, Ahmad ibn Muhammad, an Egyptian scholar, d. 338 AH.

Ibn Naji, Qasim ibn 'Isa, Maliki jurist, author of *Sharh ar-Risala*, a commentary on *ar-Risala*, which is by Ibn Abi Zayd, d. 837 AH.

An-Nakha'i, Ibrahim ibn Yazid ibn Qays al-Kufi, a great jurist, a Follower, and one of the pillars of knowledge in Kufa, d. 96 AH.

An-Nasir, al-Hasan ibn 'Ali al-Husayni al-Hashimi, d. 304 AH.

An-Nawawi, Abu Zakariyya, Muhyi'd-din Yahya ibn Sharafu'd-din, great jurist by the unanimous opinion of scholars, a Shafi'i scholar and critic in *hadiths* and jurisprudence, d. 676 AH.

Ibn Nujaym az-Zayn, a great Hanafi scholar, called the second Abu Hanifa, author of *al-Ashbah an-Naza'ir, al-Bahr ar-Ra'iq* and several other books, d. 970 AH.

Al-Qadi 'Abdu'l-Wahhab. *See* 'Abdu'l-Wahhab ibn 'Ali.

Al-Qadi Ya'qub. *See* Ya'qub.

Al-Qaffal. He is most likely 'Abdullah ibn Ahmad al-Qaffal as-Saghir, d. 417 AH.

Al-Qarafi, Shihabu'd-din Abu'l-'Abbas Ahmad ibn Idris ibn 'Abdu'r-Rahman, jurist and scholar of *usul*, a great Maliki, d. 684 AH.

Ibn al-Qasim, 'Abdu'r-Rahman al-'Utaqi, Abu 'Abdullah, Egyptian jurist, disciple of Malik, and a great defender of Malik's school, d. 191 AH.

Al-Qasim ibn Ibrahim ibn Isma'il ibn al-Hasan ibn 'Ali, a leading scholar of the Ahl al-Bayt, d. 242 or 244 AH.

Al-Qasim ibn Muhammad ibn Abi Bakr the Truthful, one of the pillars of knowledge in the era of the Followers, and a great Follower, d. 108 AH.

Al-Qasimi, Jamalu'd-din ibn Muhammad, the famous scholar of Syria, who wrote a commentary on the Qur'an called *Mahasin at-Ta'wil*. He was a *hadith* scholar and critic, d. 1332 AH.

Qatada ibn Di'ama as-Sadusi, Abu'l-Khattab al-Basri, one of the most knowledgeable Followers, d. 117 AH.

Ibn al-Qayyim, Abu 'Abdullah, Shamsu'd-din Muhammad ibn Abi Bakr, an important Hanbali scholar, author of many beneficial books, d. 751 AH.

Ibn Qilaba, 'Abdullah ibn Zayd al-Jurami al-Azdi al-Basri, great Follower and trustworthy jurist, d. 104 AH.

Ibn Qudama, Abu Muhammad 'Abdullah ibn Ahmad, great Hanbali scholar and jurist, author of *al-Mughni*, d. 620 AH.

Al-Quhustani, Ahmad ibn Muhammad ibn 'Abdullah, Abu'l-Qasim, a Hanafi jurist.

Al-Qushayri, 'Abdu'r-Rahman ibn 'Abdu'l-Karim ibn Hawazin, great Shafi'i jurist, d. 514 AH.

Al-Qurtubi, Abu 'Abdullah Muhammad ibn Ahmad al-Ansar, author of a commentary on the Qur'an and a great Maliki jurist, d. 774 AH.

Al-Qurtubi, Ahmad ibn 'Umar, commentator on the *Sahih* collection of Muslim, d. 656 AH.

Ar-Rabi' ibn Anas al-Bakri al-Hanafi al-Basri, then al-Khurasani. Al-'Ijli and Abu Hatim say, "He is honest." An-Nasa'i says, "He is all right," d. 139 or 140 AH.

Rabi'a ibn Abi 'Abdu'r-Rahman at-Taymi, known as Rabi'a ar-Ra'i, teacher of Malik, a trustworthy Follower and renowned jurist, d. 136 AH.

Ar-Rafi'i, Abu'l-Qasim 'Abdu'l-Karim ibn Muhammad ibn 'Abdu'l-Karim, a leading Shafi'i figure, d. 623 AH.

Ar-Rafi'i, Mustafa Sadiq, modern writer in Islamic studies and Arabic literature, author of *Wahi al-Qalam*, d. 1356/1937.

Ar-Ramli, Shamsu'd-din, author of the commentary on an-Nawawi's *al-Minhaj*.

Rashid Rida, author of the commentary on the Qur'an, *Tafsir al-Manar*, and publisher of the journal, *al-Manar*, d. 1354 AH.

Ar-Rayyis, Dr. Muhammad Diya', professor of Islamic history at Egyptian universities, modern author of several useful books, including *al-Kharaj fi'd-Dawla al-Islamiyya*.

Abu Razin, Mas'ud ibn Malik al-Asadi, a trustworthy Follower who lived in Kufa in 85 AH.

Ibn Rushayd, Muhammad ibn 'Amr ibn Muhammad, Abu 'Abdullah Majdu'd-din al-Fihri as-Sabti, a Maliki jurist as well as a Qur'an and *hadith* scholar, d. 721 AH.

Ibn Rushd, Muhammad ibn Ahmad, the grandfather, one of the greatest scholars in the Maliki school, d. 520 AH.

Ibn Rushd, Muhammad ibn Ahmad al-Qurtubi al-Andalusi, the judge and famous philosopher, known as Ibn Rushd the grandson, d. 595 AH.

Sa'd ibn Abi Waqqas az-Zuhri, one of the early Muslims, one of the ten persons promised heaven, and one of the six persons selected by 'Umar to choose the next khalifa, d. 55 AH.

Sahl ibn Abi Hathma al-Ansari al-Khazraji, the Companion son of a Companion. His year of death is not known.

Sahnun, 'Abdu's-Salam ibn Sa'id at-Tanukhi, a famous Maliki jurist, head of scholars in the Islamic West, author of *al-Mudawwana*, d. 240 AH.

Sa'id ibn 'Abdu'l-'Aziz at-Tanukhi ad-Dimishqi, a contemporary of al-Awza'i, about whom al-Hakim says, "He is for Syria like Malik for Madina in knowledge and leadership," d. 167 or 168 AH.

Sa'id ibn Jubayr al-Kufi, a great Follower and scholar of his time, d. 95 AH.

Abu Sa'id al-Khudri, Sa'd ibn Malik ibn Sinan al-Khazraji al-Ansari, one of the great Companions, one of the seven persons who narrate more than one thousand *hadiths* from the Prophet (p), d. 74 AH.

Sa'id ibn al-Musayyab al-Qurashi al-Makhzumi, known as 'the Master of the Followers', d. 95 AH.

Salama ibn al-Akwa' al-Aslami, famous Companion who attended the pledge or covenant known as *'Bay'at ar-Ridwan'*, d. 74 AH.

Abu Salama ibn 'Abdu'r-Rahman ibn 'Awf az-Zuhri al-Madani, great Follower and jurist, d. 94 or 104 AH.

Salim ibn 'Abdullah ibn 'Umar ibn al-Khattab al-Madani, the great jurist, one of the seven jurists of Madina and a leading Follower, d. 107 AH.

Salman al-Farisi, Abu 'Abdullah, known as 'the son of Islam,' a great Companion, d. 33, 36 or 37 AH.

As-Sarakhsi, Muhammad ibn Ahmad, Abu Bakr, 'the sun of scholars', a great Hanafi jurist who dictated his great book, *al-Mabsut*, while in prison, d. 483 AH.

Sayyid Qutb, Islamic thinker and writer, author of *Fi Zilal al-Qur'an*, *al-'Adala al-Ijtima'iyya*, *Khasa'is at-Tasawwur al-Islami*, and several other books, who was martyred in Egypt in 1386/1966.

Schacht, Joseph, contemporary orientalist, author of the section on *zakat* in the *Encyclopaedia of Islam*, known for his antagonistic views toward Islam and the *Sunna*.

Ash-Sha'bi, 'Amir ibn Sharahil al-Kufi, a leading Follower and scholar, d. 105 AH.

Shahr ibn Hawshab al-Ash'ari, a Follower. His trustworthiness is disputed. Muslim, the four and al-Bukhari in *al-Adab al-Mufrad* report from him. At-Tabari says he was a jurist and a knowledgeable scholar, d. 100, 111, or 112 AH.

Shakir, Ahmad ibn Muhammad, the modern Egyptian judge and scholar of *hadith* and Arabic language, known for his editing of many important books, such as *al-Muhalla*, *ar-Risala*, *Musnad Ahmad*, *Tafsir at-Tabari*, and several others.

Shaltut, Mahmud, the former chairman of al-Azhar, a modern Egyptian known for his famous religious opinions and explanations of the Qur'an. He has several useful books.

Sharik ibn 'Abdullah an-Nakha'i al-Kufi, a jurist and judge, trustworthy and honest. Muslim and the four report from him, but he used to make many mistakes, d. 177 or 187 AH.

Abu'sh-Sha'tha', Salim ibn Aswad ibn Hanzala al-Muharibi al-Kufi, a trustworthy Follower, d. 85 AH.

Ash-Shatibi, Abu Ishaq, Ibrahim ibn Musa al-Lakhmi al-Gharnati al-Maliki, a great scholar from Andalusia, author of the two distinguished books, *al-Muwafaqat* and *al-I'tisam*, d. 790 AH.

Ash-Shawkani, Muhammad ibn 'Ali al-Yamani az-Zaydi, an independent *mujtahid*, d. 1255 AH.

Ash-Shaybani. *See* Muhammad ibn al-Hasan.

Ibn Shibruma, 'Abdullah ibn at-Tufayl al-Basri al-Kufi, the judge, one of the trustworthy jurists, d. 144 AH.

Ibn Shihab. *See* az-Zuhri.

Shurayh ibn al-Harith ibn Qays al-Kindi, the great judge and one of the greatest Followers, d. 87 AH.

Ash-Shirazi, Abu Ishaq, Ibrahim ibn 'Ali ibn Yusuf, a leading Shafi'i, author of *al-Muhadhdhab* and other books, d. 476 AH.

Ibn Sirin, Muhammad Abu Bakr al-Basri, a great Follower and jurist, d. 110 AH.

Smith, Adam, founder of modern Western economics, famous for his book, *The Wealth of Nations*, d. 1776 CE.

As-Suddi, Isma'il ibn 'Abdu'r-Rahman al-Kufi, known as as-Suddi al-Kabir, famous for his explanations of the Qur'an. Some people grade him trustworthy and others do not. Muslim and the four report from him, d. 127 AH.

Sufyan ath-Thawri. *See* ath-Thawri.

Sufyan ibn 'Uyayna al-Hilali, a great trustworthy scholar and *hadith* critic, about whom ash-Shafi'i says, "If it were not for Malik and Sufyan, knowledge in the Hijaz would have been wiped out," d. 198 AH.

Sulayman ibn Harb, Abu Ayyub al-Basri, lived in Makka and was a judge there; a trustworthy *hadith* scholar, d. 224 AH.

Sulayman ibn Musa ad-Dimishqi, a jurist of Syria at his time, the most knowledgeable disciple of Makhul, d. 115 AH.

Sulayman ibn Yasar al-Hilali al-Madani, a former slave of Maymuna (the Mother of the Believers and wife of the Messenger (p)), a great Follower and one of the seven renowned jurists, d. 110 AH.

As-Sadiq. *See* Ja'far as-Sadiq.

Sadr ash-Shari'a Mas'ud ibn Ahmad ibn Burhan, Hanafi jurist and scholar.

As-Saymari, 'Abdu'l-Wahid ibn al-Husayn, the judge and leading Shafi'i scholar, d. after 386 AH.

As-San'ani, Muhammad ibn Isma'il al-Yamani az-Zaydi, author of *Subul as-Salam* and other books, d. 1182 AH.

As-Sawi, a Maliki jurist.

Siddiq Hasan Khan, rajah of Bhopal, India, great independent-minded scholar, similar to ash-Shawkani, d. 1307 AH.

Ibn Taymiyya, Ahmad ibn 'Abdu'l-Halim, leading scholar and *mujtahid*, 'Shaykh al-Islam' and the political and scholarly leader of his time, d. 728 AH.

Abu Thawr, Ibrahim ibn Khalid al-Kalbi, jurist and *mujtahid*, disciple of ash-Shafi'i, d. 240 AH.

Ath-Thawri, Sufyan ibn Sa'id, Abu 'Abdullah al-Kufi, the Amir al-Mu'minin in *hadith* and knowledge, one of the most famous Muslim jurists and worshippers, d. 161 AH.

At-Tabari, Muhammad ibn Jarir, Abu Ja'far, master of Qur'an commentators, and unrivalled leader of historians, a *mujtahid* and independent person, d. 310 AH.

At-Tahawi, Ahmad ibn Muhammad ibn Salama, a jurist and leading Hanafi of his time, d. 321 AH.

Talha ibn 'Abdullah ibn 'Awf az-Zuhri al-Madani, well-known judge, trustworthy Follower and jurist, nephew of 'Abdu'r-Rahman ibn 'Awf, d. 97 AH.

Abu Talib, Yahya ibn al-Husayn ibn Muhammad, brother of al-Mu'ayyad Bi'llah, leading scholar of *Ahl al-Bayt*, d. 424 AH.

Tawus, Dhakwan ibn Kisan al-Yamani, Abu 'Abdullah, a great renowned trustworthy Follower, d. 106 AH.

'Ubada ibn as-Samit al-Ansari al-Khazraji, Abu'l-Walid, one of the chairmen selected by the Prophet (p) on the night of the Pledge of al-'Aqaba, one of the Companions who collected the Qur'an during the life of the Prophet 9P), d. 34 AH.

'Ubaydullah ibn al-Hasan ibn Husayn al-'Anbari, trustworthy Egyptian jurist and judge, d. 168 AH.

Abu 'Ubayd, al-Qasim ibn Sallam, leading scholar and *mujtahid*, author of *al-Amwal*, d. 225 AH.

Abu 'Ubayda ibn al-Jarrah, 'Amir ibn 'Abdullah, one of the early Muslims, a great Companion, one of the ten persons promised Paradise, the most trustworthy person of this Umma, d. 18 AH.

Al-Ujhuri, 'Ali ibn Muhammad, a Maliki, d. 1066.

'Ulaysh, Muhammad ibn Ahmad, Egyptian, leading Maliki, d. 1229 AH.

Ibn 'Ulayya, Isma'il ibn Ibrahim al-Basri, named in relation to his mother or grandmother, one of the most trustworthy scholars and a leader in *hadith* studies and criticism, known as 'the Rose of the Jurists', d. 193 or 194 AH.

'Umar ibn 'Abdu'l-'Aziz ibn Marwan, Amir al-Mu'minin, the fifth of the *Khulafa' ar-Rashidun*, renovator of the first century of Islam, d. 101 AH.

Ibn 'Umar. *See* 'Abdullah.

'Umar al-Hafiz ibn Ahmad ibn Muhammad ibn Musa an-Naysaburi, Hanafi scholar, disciple of Abu 'Abdu'r-Rahman as-Sulami, d. 467 AH.

'Umar ibn al-Khattab, Amir al-Mu'minin, one of the ten promised Paradise, the great leader of the Islamic state, second Khalif of the Prophet (p) about whom the Prophet (p) said, "Allah made truth come on his tongue and in his heart," d. 23 AH.

'Urwa ibn az-Zubayr ibn al-'Awwam al-Asadi al-Madani, one of the seven pillars of jurisprudence in Madina, a great Follower and scholar, d. 91 or 101 AH.

'Uthman ibn 'Affan, Amir al-Mu'minin, "the Man with the Two Lights", one of the ten promised Paradise, d. 35 AH.

Vagleri, Italian orientalist.

Ibn Wahb, 'Abdullah ibn Wahb ibn Muslim, master of knowledge in Egypt and its great jurist, trustworthy disciple of Malik who combined jurisprudence, *hadith* and piety, d. 197 AH.

Al-Wahidi, Abu'l-Hasan 'Ali ibn Ahmad, the leading scholar of his time in explanation of the Qur'an and in Arabic grammar, d. 468 AH.

Waki' ibn al-Jarrah, Abu Sufyan al-Kufi, one of the most famous scholars and trustworthy persons of his time, known for his knowledge of *hadith* and for his piety, d. 196 or 197 AH.

Yahya ibn Adam, Abu Zakariyya al-Kufi, one of the most trustworthy persons, scholar and *hadith* critic, author of *al-Kharaj*, d. 203 AH.

Yahya ibn Hamza ibn 'Ali al-Hashimi al-Husayni, knowledgeable Zaydi scholar and leader, d. 749 AH.

Abu Ya'la, Muhammad ibn al-Husayn al-Farra', the judge, a great Hanbali scholar, d. 458 AH.

Ya'qub ibn Ibrahim ibn Satura al-Barzabimi, Abu 'Ali, the judge and great Hanbali jurist, d. 486 AH.

Abu Yusuf, Ya'qub ibn Ibrahim, the disciple of Abu Hanifa, the great judge at the time of the Abbasids, a *mujtahid*, d. 132 AH.

Abu Zahra, Muhammad, professor of Shari'a at various Arab universities in Egypt and elsewhere, a great modern scholar and writer.

Az-Zamakhshari, Mahmud ibn 'Umar, a Mu'tazili, good writer, author of the explanation of the Qur'an called *al-Kashshaf*, also the author of *al-Asas*, *al-Fa'iq* and other books, d. 538 AH.

Az-Zarkashi, Badru'd-din 'Abdullah ibn Muhammad, a great Shafi'i scholar, d. 794 AH.

Zarruq, Ahmad ibn Muhammad ibn 'Isa al-Burnusi al-Maliki, a great Maliki jurist in the Islamic West, d. 899 AH.

Ibn Zayd. *See Jabir ibn Zayd*.

Ibn Abi Zayd, 'Abdullah ibn 'Abdu'r-Rahman, Abu Muhammad al-Qayrawani, Maliki jurist and well-known scholar who wrote *ar-Risala* on Maliki jurisprudence, d. 386 AH.

Zayd ibn 'Ali ibn al-Husayn ibn 'Ali ibn Abi Talib, leader and founder of the Zaydi school. Abu Ishaq as-Sabi'i says, "I have not seen anyone like Zayd in knowledge or grace among all of the *Ahl al-Bayt*," d. 120 or 121 AH.

Zayd ibn Thabit al-Ansari, scribe of the Qur'an, the one who collected the Qur'an at the time of Abu Bakr and 'Uthman, a great knowledgeable Companion, d. 45 AH.

Zembaur, modern orientalist, one of the writers of the *Encyclopaedia of Islam.*

Ibn az-Zubayr, 'Abdullah ibn az-Zubayr ibn al-'Awwam al-Asadi al-Qurashi, a Companion, great scholar and courageous person, who was elected *khalifa* after the death of Mu'awiya and remained so for a few years until he was killed by al-Hajjaj in 78 AH.

Az-Zuhri, Muhammad ibn Muslim ibn ibn Shihab, leading scholar of his time, with one of the best memories in the history of *hadith* and jurisprudence, d. 124 AH.

Zufar ibn Hudhayl ibn Ways al-'Anbari, one of the great jurists, disciple of Abu Hanifa, about whom his master said, "He is the most knowledgeable in analogy among my disciples," d. 158 AH.

Glossary

agreed upon: in reference to a *hadith*, it means it is reported by both al-Bukhari and Muslim.

ahkam: plural of *hukm,* rulings of the *Shari'a* and its injunctions.

Ahl al-Bayt: the family of the Prophet (p), i.e. descendants of his great grandfather, Hashim and the latter's brother, al-Muttalib.

Ahl al-Hadith: specialists in the studies of the Prophet's sayings. It refers sometimes to a quasi-school of *fiqh* characterised by emphasizing *hadiths* at the expense of analogy.

Ahl ar-Ra'y: or people of opinion, those scholars who believe in rationale based on logical anaylysis, especially analogy as one of the sources of deriving *Shari'a* rulings and *ahkam.* They usually include, among others, the Hanafis and Malikis.

amwal: the plural of *mal,* generally all kinds of assets and income.

Ansar: the singular is *Ansari.* Helpers, the people of Madina who accepted the *deen* of Islam and became Companions of the Prophet (p) after he emigrated to Yathrib.

ardab: a volume measure used specially for grain.

ayat: a verse of the Qur'an.

dinar: a golden coin used as currency, equal to one *mithqal* of weight.

dirham: a silver coin used as currency. One dinar equals ten dirhams.

fiqh: the science of knowing details of the *ahkam* of the *Shari'a.*

Followers: the *Tabi'un*, the generation of Muslims who met the Companions or any of them, but not the Prophet (p).

furq: a volume measure.

ghanima: property of the enemy acquired in war, booty.

good: *hasan*, for a *hadith*, a degree of acceptability of a *hadith* putting it below the correct one, but still in the range of acceptability.

hadith: saying attributed to the Prophet (p). Categorically includes what he said, did or approved.

hadiy: sacrificial animal (camel, cow, sheep or goat) taken to be slaughtered when performing the *Hajj*.

Hajj: the pilgrimage to Makka.

Hijaz: the central western part of the Arabian peninsula, that includes Makka and Madina.

Hijra: the emigration of the Prophet (p) from Makka to Madina.

hukm: see *ahkam*.

ihram: a special state required for entering Makka on *Hajj* or *'umra*. It entails intention, unsewed garment (for men) and observation of certain conduct.

ijma': unanimity, agreement among all scholars on a certain ruling.

ijtihad: exertion of effort in finding a ruling or something not mentioned clearly, following a certain known methodology.

Imam: a leader in his field.

Imami: a follower of the Shi'ite school of *fiqh*.

jihad: use of military force to defend Islam, its people and land, or the religious freedom of any people.

jizya: a tax imposed on non-Muslims who are defeated in *jihad* and stay under the authority of the Islamic state in exchange for protection and security.

kaffara: giving to the poor and needy in recompense for a missed act of worship, e.g. feeding three poor people for an unfulfilled vow.

Khaybar: a small town northwest in the Arabian peninsula, about 400 km north of Madina.

khalifa: pl. *khulafa'*, khalif, the head of the Islamic state in the Islamic poltiical system.

al-Khulafa' ar-Rashidun: the four successors of the Prophet (p) in leading the Islamic state in Madina: Abu Bakr, 'Umar, 'Uthman and 'Ali. They ruled from 11 to 40 AH, and are all 'the Rightly-guided Khalifs."

khilafa: name of the position of the head of state in the Islamic political system.

mahr: an amount granted to the bridge as part of the marriage contract.

mal: see *amwal*.

milk: ownership

minbar: a pulpit in the mosque for the speech given on Fridays.

mithqal: a weight measure which is equal to a gold dinar, sometimes used to mean a gold dinar.

mudd: a volume measure.

Muhajirun: Emigrants, people from Makka who accepted Islam at the time of the Prophet (p) and migrated to Madina to escape persecution.

mursal: in *hadiths*, when a Follower omits the name of the Companion through whom the *hadith* was received.

musnad: when the chain of the *hadith* is complete all the way to the Prophet (p).

nash (or **nashsh**): a weight measure, equal to half an *uqiyya*.

nawa: a weight measure.

nisab: a minimum amount which determies if a person's wealth is subject to *zakat*.

People of the Pledge: *Ahl al-'Ahd* or *Ahl adh-Dhimma*, non-Muslims permitted in the Muslim state temporarily or permanently.

qafiz: a volume measure.

qirba: a volume measure.

ratl: a weight measure.

riba: any increase in repayment of a loan, generally interest.

rikaz: buried treasure, or sometimes natural ores which are found underground.

sa': a volume measure.

sadaqa: plural *sadaqat*, charitable donation.

sahih: see sound.

Salaf: the Predecessors, referring to the early generations of Isam.

Shari'a: the total legal system of Islam

shuf'a: right of preference given to neighbour or parter in buying real estate.

sound: with respect to hadith, a *hadith* whose chain of narrators is (1) linked without interruption, and (2) consists of trustworthy persons both in morality and faith and in memory provided that its text is not off (*shadhdh*) or there is a good reason to reject it (*ma'lul*).

Sunna: path or method of the Prophet, sometimes used as synonymous with *hadith*.

sura: a chapter of the Qur'an.

tafsir: with respect to Qur'an, commentary or explanation.

tawhid: the Oneness of Allah.

tayammum: using clean earth as a substitute for ablution with water.

uqiyya: a weight measure.

'urud at-tijara: trade inventory, merchandise acquired for the purpose of re-sale.

'ushr: plural, *'ushur*, one tenth; it also refers to the one-tenth (pr one twentieth) given as *zakat* in agriculture.

usul al-fiqh: the science of *fiqh* methodology and axiomatic system.

wasq: a measure of volume used in agriculture.

wudu': use of water to wash certain parts of the body in preparation for prayer, ablution.

Zahiri: a follower of the school of *fiqh* that puts its main emphasis on the literal meaning of the text.

Zaydi: a follower of the school of *fiqh* initiated by Zayd ibn 'Ali ibn al-Husayn.

Bibliography

Note: References are classified according to subject. In each subject, the order of authors is according to the year of their death. Books whose place of printing is not mentioned were printed in Cairo. Sometimes I refer to other printings not mentioned in this reference.

I. The Qur'an and Qur'an Studies

The Glorious Qur'an.

Tafsir gharib al-Qur'an, Abu Muhammad 'Abdullah ibn Muslim ibn Qutayba, d. 276 AH, ed. Ahmad Saqr, 'Isa al-Babi, al-Halabi print.

Jami' al-bayan 'an ta'wil al-Qur'an, known as *Tafsir at-Tabari*, Imam at-Tabari, d. 310, Dar al-Ma'arif print, ed. Mahmud Muhammad Shakir, al-Halabi print.

Ahkam al-Qur'an, Imam al-Jassas, d. 370 AH, al-Matba'a al-Bahiyya print, Egypt.

Asbab an-nuzul, Abu Hasan 'Ali ibn Ahmad al-Qahidi an-Nisaburi, d. 468 AH.

Mufradat al-Qur'an, al-Husayn ibn Muhammad ibn al-Mufaddal, known as ar-Raghib al-Isfahani, d. 502 AH, printed in the margins of *an-Nihaya*, Ibn al-Athir, al-Halabi print.

Al-Kashshaf 'an haqa'iq at-tanzil wa daqa'iq at-ta'wil, Mahmud ibn 'Umar az-Zamakkshari, d. 538 AH.

Ahkam al-Qur'an, al-Qadi Abu Bakr ibn al-'Arabi, d. 543 AH, al-Halabi print, ed. 'Ali al-Bijawi.

Majma' al-Bayan fi tafsir al-Qur'an, Abu 'Ali al-Fadl ibn al-Hasan at-Tabarsi ash-Shi'i, d. 548 AH.

At-Tafsir al-Kabir, called *Mafatih al-Ghayb*, al-Imam Fakhru'd-din ar-Razi, d. 606, al-Misriyya print, 1938.

Al-Jami' li-ahkam al-Qur'an, Imam al-Qurtubi, d. 774 AH, Dar al-Kutub print.

Tafsir al-Qur'an al-A'dhim, al-Hafiz Abu'l-Fida' Isma'il ibn Kathir al-Qurashi, d. 774, al-Halabi print.
Al-Intisaf min al-Kashshaf.
Al-Burhan fi 'ulum al-Qur'an, al-Imam Badur'd-din 'Abdullah ibn Muhammad az-Zarkashi, d. 794 AH, al-Halabi, ed. Abu'l-Fadl Ibrahim.
Ad-Durr al-manthur fi't-tafsir bi'l-ma'thur, as-Suyuti, d. 911 AH, al-Maymaniyya print.
Al-Iklil fi istinbat at-ta'wil, as-Suyuti.
Al-Itwan fi 'ulum al-Qur'an, as-Suyuti.
Ruh al-Ma'ani, Shihabu'd-din Mahmud al-'Alusi al-Baghdadi, d. 1270 AH.
Al-Futuhat al-Ilahiyya, known as Hashiyat al-Jamal.
Mahasin at-ta'wil, Jamalu'd-din al-Qasimi, d. 1332/1914, al-Halabi print, ed. Muhammad Fu'ad 'Abdu'l-Baqi.
Tafsir al-Qur'an al-Hakim, known as *Tafsir al-Manar*, Muhammad Rashid Rida, d. 1354 AH.
Tafsir al-Qur'an al-Karim: The First Ten Parts, Shaykh Mahmud Shaltut, Dar al-Qalam print.
Fi Zilal al-Qur'an, Sayyid Qutb, al-Halabi print.
At-Tafsir al-hadith, Muhammad 'Izzat Darwaza.
Al-Muj'am al-mufahras li alfaz al-Qur'an al-Karim, Muhammad Fu'ad 'Abdu'l-Baqi, Jaridat ash-Sha'b print.

II. Studies of *Hadith* and Narrators

Al-Muwatta', Malik ibn Anas, d. 179 AH, printed on the margins of its commentary, *al-Muntaqa,* al-Baji, second volume, as-Sa'ada print or al-Halabi print.
Al-Musannaf, al-Imam Abu Bakr ibn Abi Shayba, d. 355, Multan print, Pakistan, or Hyderabad print, India.
Al-Musnad, al-Imam Ahmad ibn Hanbal, d. 241 AH, Dar al-Ma'arif print, ed. Ahmad Muhammad Shakir, al-Maymaniyya print.
At-Ta'rikh al-Kabir, al-Bukhari, Hyderabad print.
Sahih Muslim, al-Imam Muslim ibn al-Hajjaj al-Qushari an-Naysaburi, d. 261 AH, with commentary by an-Nawawi, al-Misriyya print, and al-Azhar print, first ed., 1348 AH.
Sunan Abu Dawud, al-Imam Abu Dawud Sulayman ibn al-Ash'ath as-Sijistani, d. 275 AH, as-Sa'ada print.

Sunan Ibn Majah, al-Hafiz Abu 'Abdullah Muhammad ibn Yazid al-Qazwini, known as Ibn Majah, d. 275 AH, al-Halabi print.

Jami' at-Tirmidhi, al-Imam Abu 'Isa Muhammad ibn 'Isa at-Tirmidhi, d. 279 AH, with its commentary by Ibn al-'Arabi, known as *'Aridat al-Ahwadhi*, or with commentary by al-Mubarakpuri known as *Tuhfat al-Ahwadhi*, or printed alone as ed. by Ahmad Shakir.

Sunan an-Nasa'i, al-Imam Abu 'Abdu'r-Rahman, Ahmad ibn Shu'ayb an-Nasa'i, printed with the explanation by as-Suyuti and notes by as-Sindi.

Mushkil al-Athar, al-Imam Abu Ja'far at-Tahaqi, d. 321, Hyderabad print, 1333 AH.

Al-Jarh wa't-Ta'dil, Ibn Abi Hatim ar-Razi, Hyderabad print.

Ma'alim as-Sunan, al-Imam Abu Sulayman al-Khattabi, d. 388, Ansar as-Sunna print. Printed along with *Mukhtasar Sunan Abu Dawud*, by al-Qayyim, ed. Ahmad Shakir and Muhammad Hamid al-Faqi.

Al-Mustadrak 'ala's-Sahihayn, Abu 'Abdullah Muhammad ibn 'Abdullah, known as al-Hakim an-Naysaburi, d. 405 AH, Hyderabad print.

As-Sunan al-Kubra, al-Hafiz Abu Bakr Ahmad ibn al-Husayn al-Bayhaqi, d. 348 AH, Hyderabad print.

Al-Jawhar an-Naqi, 'Ala' ad-Din 'Ali ibn 'Uthman al-Maridini, known as Ibn at-Turkumani, d. 745 AH, Hyderabad print.

Al-I'tibar fi'n-nasikh wa'l-mansukh li'l-athar, al-Hazimi, d. 584, Hyderabad print.

'Umdat al-Ahkam, al-Hafiz 'Abdu'l-Ghani ibn 'Abdu'l-Wahid al-Maqdisi, d. 600 AH, printed with its explanation, called *al-Ihkam*, Ibn Daqiq al-'Id, as-Sunna al-Muhammadiyya print, ed. Ahmad Shakir.

Muntaqa al-akhbar li ahadith Sayyid al-Akhyar, known as *al-Muntaqa*, Abu'l-Barakat ibn Taymiyya, the grandfather, d. 652 AH.

At-Targhib wa't-tarhib, al-Mundhiri, d. 656 AH, al-Halabi print.

Mukhtasar Sunan Abu Dawud, al-Mundhiri, printed with *Ma'alim as-Sunan.*

Sharh an-Nawawi on Sahih Muslim, an-Nawawi, d. 676 AH.

Al-Ahkam, sharh 'umdat al-Ahkam, al-Imam Abu'l-Fath Muhammad ibn 'ALi ibn Wahb Taqiyyi'd-din, known as Ibn Daqiq al-'Id, d. 702 AH, printed with *'Umdat al-Ahkam.*

Mishkat al-Masabih, al-Hafiz Waliyyu'd-din Muhammad ibn 'Abdullah al-Khatib al-'Umari at-Tabrizi, d. 737 AH, ed. Nasiru'd-din al-Albani, al-Maktab al-Islami print, Damascus.

Talkhis al-Mustadrak, al-Imam al-Hafiz adh-Dhahabi, d. 748 AH, Hyderabad print.*Mizan al-I'tidal*

Mizan al-I'tidal, adh-Dhahabi, al-Halabi print.

Tahdhib Sunan Abu Dawud, al-Imam Abu 'Abdullah Shamsu'd-din Muhammad ibn Abi Bakr, known as Ibn al-Qayyim or Ibn Qayyim al-Jawziyya, d. 751 AH, printed with *Ma'alim as-Sunan.*

Nasb ar-Raya li ahadith al-Hidaya, al-Hafiz Jamalu'd-din Abu Muhammad 'Abdullah ibn Yusuf az-Zayla'i al-Hanafi, d. 762 AH, Dar al-Ma'mun print, printed with the commentary, *Bulghat al-alma'i fi takhrij az-Zayla'i.*

Takhrij ahadith al-Ihya', al-Hafiz Zaynu'd-din Abu'l-Fadl 'Abdu'r-Rahim ibn Husayn al-'Iraqi, d. 806 AH, pritned with *al-Ihya'.*

Tarh at-Tathrib sharh at-taqrib, al-'Iraqi, completed by his son Abu Zar'a, d. 827 AH.

Majma' az-Zaw'id wa manba' al-fawa'id, al-Hafiz Nuru'd-din 'Ali ibn Abu Bakr al-Haythami, d. 807 AH, Maktaba al-Qudsi print.

Fath al-Bari, commentary on the *Sahih al-Bukhari*, Shaykh al-Islam al-Hafiz Ahmad ibn Hajar al-'Asqalani, d. 852 AH, al-Khayriyya print, 1319 AH, also al-Halabi print.

Bulugh al-Maram min adillat al-ahkam, Ibn Hajar.

Talkhis al-Habir fi takhrij ahadith ar-Rafi'i al-kabir, Ibn Hajar, printed in India.

Tahdhib at-Tahdhib, Ibn Hajar, Hyderabad print.

Taqrib at-Tahdhib, Ibn Hajar, ed. 'Abdu'l-Wahhab 'Abdu'l-Latif, Dar al-Kitab al-'Arabi print.

Takhrij ahadith al-Kashshaf, Ibn Hajar.

'Umda al-Qari, commentary on *Sahih al-Bukhari*, Badru'd-din Abu Muhammad Mahmud ibn Ahmad al-'Ayni, d. 855 AH, printed by Idarat at-Tiba'a al-Muniriyya.

Al-Jami' as-saghir min hadith al-bashir an-nadir, known *as al-Jami' as-Saghir*, as-Suyuti, d. 911, al-Halabi print.

Al-La'ali al-masnu'a bi'l-ahadith al-mawdu'a, as-Suyuti, second volume, al-Maktaba al-Idariyya print.

Zahr ar-Ruba 'ala'l-Mujtaba, as-Suyuti.

Tadrib ar-rawi 'ala taqrib an-Nawawi, as-Suyuti, ed. 'Abdu'l-Wahhab 'Abdu'l-Latif.

Khulasat tadhhib al-kamal fi asma' ar-rijal, Safiyu'd-din al-Khazraji, d. 923 AH.

Kanz al-'Ummal fi sunan al-aqwal wa'l-af'al, 'Ali al-Muttaqi 'Ala'u'd-din al-Hindi, d. 975, Hyderabad print.

Mirqat al-Mafatih, commentary on *Mishkat al-Masabih*, 'Ali al-Farisi, d. 1014 AH, Multan print.

Al-Mubin al-Mu'ain li fahm al-Arba'in, al-Farisi.

Fayd al-Qadir, commentary on *al-Jami' as-Saghir*, al-Munawi, d. 1031 AH.

At-Taysir, commentary on *al-Jami' as-Saghir*, al-Munawi, al-Maktab al-Islami print, Beirut.

Kashf al-Khafa' wa muzil al-ilbas, Isma'il al-'Ajluni, d. 1162 AH.

Subul as-Salam, commentary on *Bulugh al-Maram*, as-San'ani, d. 1182 AH, Sabih print.

Nayl al-Awtar, commentary on *Muntaqa al-Akhbar*, ash-Shawkani, d. 1250 AH, al-Halabi print.

Al-Fawa'id al-majmu'a fi'l-ahadith al-mawdu'a, ash-Shawkani.

Ar-Raf' wa't-takmil fi'l-jarh wa't-ta'dil, Shaykh Muhammad 'Abdu'l-Hayy al-Laknawi al-Hindi, d. 1304 AH, ed. 'Abdu'l-Fattah Abu Ghidda, Dar Lubnan print.

Al-Ajwiba al-Fadila, al-Laknawi, with comments by Abu Ghidda, al-Matba'a as-Suriyya print, Aleppo.

Tuhfat al-Ahwadhi, commentary on at-Tirmidhi, Muhammad 'Abdu'r-Rahman ibn 'Abdu'r-Rahim al-Mubarakpuri, d. 1353 AH, Dar al-Ittihad al-'Arabi li't-Tiba'a print, Cairo.

Al-Fath ar-Rabbani, a study of *Musnad Ahmad* and its commentary. *Bulugh al-Amani*, Ahmad 'Abdu'r-Rahman al-Banna, Matba'a al-Fath ar-Rabbani print, 1357 AH.

Miftah kunuz as-Sunna, A.I. Wensinck, translated by Muhammad Fu'ad 'Abdu'l-Baqi.

Silsilat al-ahadith as-sahiha, Muhammad Nasiru'd-din al-Albani, al-Maktab al-Islami print.

Silsilat al-ahadith ad-da'ifa wa'l-mawdu'a, al-Albani.

Al-Muj'am al-mufahras li alfaz al-hadith, a group of orientalists with the help of Muhammad Fu'ad 'Abdu'l-Baqi, Brill print, Leiden, Holland.

Mir'at al-Mafatih, commentary on *Mishkat al-Masabih*, Abu'l-Hasan 'Ubaydullah ibn Muhammad 'Abdu's-Salam al-Mubarakpuri, vol. 3, Indian print, 1282/1962.

III. Books on jurisprudence

A. Hanafi *fiqh*

Al-Kharaj, Abu Yusuf, d. 182 AH, as-Salsafiyya print, 1352 AH.

Al-Mabsut, voluminous book of Hanafi *fiqh*, as-Sarakhsi, d. 483 AH, as-Sa'ada print, 1324. It is a commentary of *al-Kafi* by al-Hakim ash-Shahid, which is a collection of the books known as *Kutub Zahir ar-Riwaya*, al-Imam Muhammad ibn al-Hasan ash-Shaybani, the disciple of Abu Hanifa, d. 189 AH.

Sharh Siyar al-Kabir, commentary on *as-Siyar al-Kabir* by al-Imam Muhammad, as-Sarakhsi, Hyderabad print, 1335 AH.

Bada'i' as-Sana'i', a voluminous book of *fiqh*, al-Kasani, d. 587 AH, printed by Sharika al-Matbu'a al-'Ilmiyya, 1327 AH.

Al-Hidaya, voluminous book of *fiqh*, Shaykh al-Islam Burhanu'd-din 'Ali ibn Abu Bakr al-Marghinani, d. 593 AH, Mustafa Muhammad print.

Sharh al-'Inaya 'ala'l-Hidaya, commentary on *al-Hidaya*, Akmalu'd-din Muhammad ibn Mahmud al-Barbari, d, 776 AH, printed on the margins of al-Hidaya.

Fath al-Qadir, Ibn al-Humam, d. 861 AH. It too is a commentary on *al-Hidaya.*

Majma' al-Anhur, commentary on *Multaqa al-Abhur*, Shaykh Zadah, d. 951 AH, printed in Istanbul.

Al-Bahr ar-Ra'iq, a commentary on *Kanz ad-Daqa'iq*, az-Zayn ibn Nujaym, d. 870 AH.

Ad-Durr al-Mukhtar, commentary on *Tanwir al-Absar*, al-Haskafi, d. 1077 AH.

Durr al-Muntaqa, commentary on *al-Multaqa*, printed on the margins of *Majma' al-Anhur*, al-Haskafi.

Radd al-Muhtar, commentary on *ad-Durr al-Mukhtar*, Muhammad Amin ibn 'Abidin, d. 1252 AH, al-Maymaniyya print and Istanbul print. *Ad-Durr al-Mukhtar* is printed on its margins. This book is known as *Hashiyat Ibn 'Abidin.*

B. Maliki *fiqh*

Al-Mudawwana al-Kubra, al-Imam Malik ibn Anas, as reported from him by Sahnun ibn Sa'id at-Tanukhi from 'Abdu'r-Rahman ibn al-Qasim, al-Khayriyya print, 1423 AH.

Ar-Risala, Ibn Abi Zayd al-Qayrawani, d. 386 AH. This is printed with its two commentaries by Zarruq and Ibn Naji.

Al-Muntaqa, commentary on *al-Muwatta'* of Malik, Qadi Abu'l-Walid Sulayman al-Baji, d. 494 AH, vol. 2, as-Sa'ada print. *Al-Muwatta'* is in its margins.

Bidayat al-Mujtahid, Qadi Ibn Rushd, d. 595 AH, al-Istiqama print, 1371 AH, vol. 1. It is, in fact, a comparatve study of fiqh.

Mukhtasar Khalil, Abu'd-Diya' Khalil ibn Ishaq, d. 776 AH, printed with its commentary by ad-Dardir and commentary by ad-Dusuqi.

Sharh ar-Risala, Ibn Naji, d. 837 AH, al-Jamaliyya print.

Sharh ar-Risala, Zarruq, b. 899 AH. This and the previous work are printed together with ar-Risala.

Sharh al-Kharashi, Abu 'Abdullah Muhammad al-Kharashi, d. 1101 AH. It is a commentary on *Mukhtasar Khalil.*

Sharh az-Zurqani, commentary on *al-Muwatta'*.

Tahdhib al-Furuq wa'l-qawa'id as-saniyya, commentary and notes on *al-Furuq*, Shaykh Muhammad 'Ali ibn Shaykh Husayn, a Maliki.

Ash-Sharh al-Kabir Ahmad ibn al-'Adawi al-Khalwati, known as ad-Dardir, d. 1201 AH. It is a commentary on *Mukhtasar Khalil.*

Ash-Sharh as-Saghir, comments on *Aqrab al-Masalik*, both by al-'Adawi, al-Halabi print.

Hashiyat ad-Dusuqi, Muhammad ibn 'Arafa ad-Dusuqi, d. 1230 AH.

Bulghat as-Salik li Aqrab al-Masalik, Ahmad ibn Muhammad as-Sawi, d. 1241 AH.

Fath al-'Ali al-Malik, Muhammad 'Ulaysh, d. 1299 AH, Mustafa Muhammad print.

C. Shafi'i *fiqh*

Al-Umm, al-Imam Muhammad ibn Idris ash-Shafi'i, d. 204 AH, al-Amiriyya print in Bulaq, Egypt.

Al-Ahkam as-Sultaniyya, al-Qadi Abu'l-Hasan al-Mawardi, d. 450 AH, al-Halabi print.

Al-Muhadhdhab, Abu Ishaq ash-Shirazi, d. 476 AH, al-Muniriyya print.

Al-Wajiz, al-Imam Abu Hamid Muhammad al-Ghazali, d. 505 AH.

Fath al-'Aziz, commentary on *al-Wajiz*, ar-Rafi'i, d. 623 AH.

Al-Majmu', commentary on *al-Muhadhdhab*, an-Nawawi, d. 676 AH. The previous four books are printed by al-Muniriyya along with *Talkhis al-Qadir* by Ibn Hajar.

Rawdat at-Talibin, al-Imam an-Nawawi, second volume, printed by al-Maktab al-Islami.

Al-Minhaj, an-Nawawi, printed with the following two commentaries:

Tuhfat al-Minhaj, Ibn Hajar al-Haytami, d. 974 AH.

Nihayat al-Muhtaj, ar-Ramli, d. 1004 AH, al-Halabi print, along with its two commentaries, one by ash-Shabramallisi, d. 1087 AH, and the other by ar-Rashidi, d. 1096 AH.

D. Hanbali *fiqh*

Mukhtasar al-Khiraqi, Abu'l-Qasim 'Umar ibn Husayn ibn 'Abdullah al-Khiraqi, d. 334 AH, printed with *al-Mughni*.

Al-Ahkam as-Sultaniyya, Qadi Abu Ya'la al-Hanbali, d. 458 AH.

Al-Mughni, Shaykh al-Islam Ibn Qudama al-Maqdisi, d. 630 AH, al-Manar print. It is a commentary on *Mukhtasar al-Khiraqi*.

Al-Kafi, Ibn Qudama, printed by al-Maktab al-Islami, Damascus.

Ash-Sharh al-Kabir, Ibn Qudama, the grandson, d. 681 AH. It is a commentary of *al-Muqni'* by the grandfather.

Fatawa Ibn Taymiyya, Kurdistan print in Cairo, 1326 AH.

Al-Ikhtiyarat, Ibn Taymiyya, printed with the fourth volume of his *Fatawa*.

Al-Furu', Ibn Muflih, d. 763 AH, printed with its commentary, *Tashih al-Furu'*.

Tashih al-Furu', commentary on *al-Furu'*, Abu'l-Hasan al-Mardawi, al-Hanbal, d. 875 AH, printed by Dar 'Umar li't-Tiba'a, second edition, 1381 AH.

Al-Insaf, al-Mardawi, printed by Matba'a as-Sunna al-Muhammadiyya.

Ar-Rawd al-Murbi', commentary of *Zad al-Mustaqni*, Mansur ibn Yunus al-Buhuti, d. 1051 AH, printed with its commentary by 'Abdu'l-'Aziz al-'Anqari, as edited by 'Abdu'l-Latif as-Subki, Matba'a as-Sunna al-Muhammadiyya, 1374 AH.

Ghayat al-Muntaha, Shaykh Mar'i ibn Yusuf al-Karami, d. 1033 AH, printed with the following commentary.

Matalib Uli'n-Nuha, commentary on *Ghayat al-Muntaha*, Mustafa as-Suyuti ar-Rahbani, d. 1243 AH, printed by al-Maktab al-Islami, Damascus, first printing 1380 AH.

Manar as-Sabil (*Sharh ad-Dalil*), Ibrahim ibn Muhammad ibn Salim ibn Dayyan, d. 1353 AH, printed by al-Maktab al-Islami.

E. Zahiri *fiqh*

Al-Muhalla, al-Imam Abu Muhammad 'Ali ibn Ahmad ibn Sa'id ibn Hazm al-Andalusi, d. 546 AH, al-Muniriyya print, ed. Shaykh Ahmad Shakir

F. Zaydi *fiqh*

Majmu' Fiqh al-Kabir, al-Imam Zayd ibn 'Ali, d. 132 AH, printed with his commentary, *ar-Rawd an-Nadir.*

Al-Bahr az-Zakhkhar, al-Imam al-Mahdi Yahya ibn al-Murtada, d. 840 AH, as-Sa'ada print. It is, in fact, a study of comparative *fiqh.*

Matn al-Azhar, printed with its commentary.

Ar-Rawd an-Nadir, commentary on *Majmu' Fiqh al-Kabir*, Sharafu'd-din al-Husayn ibn Ahmad ibn al-Husayn as-Siyaghi as-San'ani, d. 1221 AH, as-Sa'ada print. It is also a book in comparative fiqh.

Sharh al-Azhar, Abu'l-Hasan 'Abdullah ibn Muftah, d. 877 AH, printed by Sharikat at-Tamaddun, 1332 AH.

G. Imami Ja'fari *fiqh*

Shara'i' al-Islam fi fiqh al-Imamiyya, Ja'far ibn al-Hasan al-Hilli, d. 771 AH.

Al-Mukhtasar an-nafi' fi fiqh al-Imamiyya, a summary of *Shara'i' al-Islam*), al-Hilli, printed by Dar al-Kitab al-'Arabi.

Jawahir al-Kalam, commentary on *Shara'i' al-Islam*, Muhammad Hasan an-Najafi, printed in Iran, 1278 AH, second volume.

Fiqh al-Imam Ja'far as-Sadiq, Muhammad Jawad Mughniyya, printed by Dar al-'Ilm li'l-Malayin, Beirut.

IV. Financial and Administrative Islamic Law

Al-Kharaj, Abu Yusuf, mentioned earlier. It was written at the request of the khalifa, Harun ar-Rashid.

Al-Kharaj, Yahya ibn Adam, d. 203 AH, Salafiyya print, 1352 AH, ed. Ahmad Shakir.

Al-Amwal, al-Imam Abu 'Ubayd al-Qasim ibn Sallam, d. 234 AH, ed. Muhammad Hamid al-Faqi.

Al-Ahkam as-Sultaniyya, al-Mawardi, mentioned earlier.

Al-Ahkam as-Sultaniyya, Abu Ya'la, mentioned earlier.

As-Siyasa ash-Shar'iyya, Shaykh al-Islam Ibn Taymiyya, d. 728 AH, printed by Dar al-Kitab al-'Arabi.

V. General References in Jurisprudence

Al-Qawa'id an-Nuraniyya al-fiqiyya, Ibn Taymiyya.

Majmu' fatawa Shaykh al-Islam Ibn Taymiyya, collected by 'Abdu'r-Rahman ibn Muhammad ibn Qasim al-'Asimi an-Najdi al-Hanbali, printed by Matabi' ar-Riyad.

Zad al-Ma'ad fi hady khayri'l-'ibad, Ibn al-Qayyim, printed by Matba'a as-Sunna al-Muhammadiyya, ed. Muhammad Hamid al-Faqi.

At-Turuq al-Hukmiyya, Ibn al-Qayyim, al-Madani print.

Ar-Rawda an-Nadiyya, Siddiq Hasan Khan, printed by Idarat at-Tiba'a al-Muniriyya.

Ad-Durar al-Bahiyya, al-Imam ash-Shawkani, printed with *ar-Rawda an-Nadiyya.*

Ad-Din al-Khalis, Mahmud Khattab as-Subki, d. 1352 AH, eighth volume, al-Istiqama print, 1370 AH.

Fatawa al-Imam Muhammad Rashid Rida, printed by Dar al-Kitab al-Jadid, Beirut.

Halqat ad-dirasat al-ijtima'iyya li jami'at ad-duwal al-'arabiyya, 3rd session, lectures of professors 'Abdu'r-Rahman Hasan, Muhammad Abu Zahra, and 'Abdu'l-Wahhab Khallaf, on *zakat* and expenditures on relatives, 330 pages.

At-Tibyan fi zakat al-athman, Muhammad Hasanayn Makhluf al-'Adawi.

Bahjat al-Mushtaq fi hukm zakat al-awraq, Ahmad al-Husayni.

Al-Fiqh 'ala'l-madhahib al-arba'a, by a committe supervised by the Ministry of Awqaf in Egypt, fifth printing.

Muqarana al-Madhahib fi'l-fiqh, Mahmud Shaltut and Muhammad 'Ali as-Sayes, Sabih print, 1372 AH.

Al-Islam, 'Aqida wa Shari'a, Mahmud Shaltut, al-Azhar print.

Al-Fatawa, Mahmud Shaltut, Dar al-Qalam print or al-Azhar print.

Fatawa Islamiyya, Husayn Muhammad Makhluf, al-Halabi print.

Ahkam al-Mu'amalat ash-shar'iyya, 'Ali al-Khafif.

Al-Mu'amalat al-haditha wa ahkamuha, 'Abdu'r-Rahman 'Isa, Mukhaimir print.

Ahkam adh-dhimmiyyin wa'l-musta'minin fi Dar al-Islam, 'Abdu'l-Karim Zaydan.

Fiqh as-Sunna, Sayyid Sabiq, third volume, printed by Dar al-Kitab al-'Arabi.
Al-Halal wa'l-haram fi'l-Islam, al-Qardawi, printed by al-Maktab al-Islami.

VI. References on *Usul* and General Rules of *Fiqh*

Ar-Risala, al-Imam ash-Shafi'i, ed. Ahmad Shakir, al-Halabi print.
Al-Ihkam fi usul al-ahkam, Ibn Hazm, al-Muniriyya print or al-Imam print.
Al-Mustasfa min 'ilm al-usul, al-Imam al-Ghazali, Mustafa Muhammad print.
Usul as-Sarakhsi, as-Sarakhsi, Hyderabad print.
Rawdat an-Nazir wa jannat al-manazir, Ibn Qudama, author of *al-Mughni*.
Al-Ihkam fi usul al-ahkam, Abu'l-Hasan 'Ali ibn Abi 'Ali al-Amidi, d. 631 AH, Sabih print.
Takhrij al-furu' 'ala'l-usul, al-Imam az-Zanjani, d. 656 AH, ed. Muhammad Adib Salih, University of Damascus print.
Al-Furuq, al-Imam al-Qarafi, d. 684 AH, al-Halabi print.
Al-Ihkam fi tamyiz al-fatawa min al-ahkam, al-Qarafi, ed. 'Abdu'l-Fatth Abu Ghidda, printed in Aleppo.
Al-Qiyas, Shaykh al-Islam Ibn Taymiyya, as-Salafiyya print.
I'lam al-Muwaqqi'in, Ibn al-Qayyim, d. 751 AH, as-Sa'ada print, ed. Muhammad Muhyi'd-din 'Abdu'l-Hamid.
Al-Muwafaqat, al-Imam ash-Shatibi, d. 790 AH, ed. 'Abdullah Draz, printed by Matba'a ash-Sharq al-Adna fi'l-Muski, Cairo.
Al-I'tisam, ash-Shatibi, al-Manar print.
Al-Ashbah wa'n-Naza'ir, Ibn Nujaym, d. 970 AH.

VII. General Islamic Studies

Ihya' 'Ulum ad-Din, Al-Imam al-Ghazali, al-Halabi print.
Talbis Iblis, al-Imam Abu'l-Faraj 'Abdu'r-Rahman ibn al-Jawzi, d. 597 AH, al-Muniriyya print.
Al-Kaba'ir, adh-Dhahabi, al-Bayan print, Beirut.
Ighathat al-Lahfan, Ibn al-Qayyim, al-Halabi print.
Madarij as-Salikin, Ibn al-Qayyim, as-Sunna al-Muhammadiyya print.
Az-Zawajir, Ibn Hajar al-Haytami al-Makki.

Hujjatu'llah al-Balighha, by the great scholar of India, Ahmad ibn 'Abdu'r-Rahim ad-Dihlawi, known as Shah Waliyyu'llah, d. 1176.

At-Taratib al-Idariyya, 'Abdu'l-Hayy al-Kattani al-Fasi, al-Ahliyya print, Rabat, 1346 AH.

Al-Wahi al-Muhammadi, Muhammad Rashid Rida, al-Manar print.

Al-Islam, din 'amm khalid, Muhammad Farid Wajdi.

Al-Arkan al-Arba'a, Abu'l-Hasan an-Nadwi, Ma'tuq Ikhwan print, Beirut.

Usus al-Iqtisad fi'l-Islam, Abu'l-A'la al-Maududi, al-Hashimiyya print, Damascus.

Al-Islam wa'l-awda' al-iqtisadiyya, Muhammad al-Ghazali, fifth print.

Al-Islam al-muftara 'alayh bayna ash-shuyu'yyin wa'r-ra's-maliyyin, Muhammad al-Ghazali.

Al-Ishtirakiyya fi'l-mujtama' al-Islami, al-Bahi al-Khawli, printed Matba'a al-Istiqlal al-Kubra.

Ishtirakiyyat al-Islam, Mustafa as-Siba'i, printed by ad-Dar al-Qawmiyya, Cairo.

Al-Iqtisad wa's-siyasa fi daw' al-Islam, authored under the supervision of the Islamic Studies Society in the College of Commerce, University of Cairo, 1951.

Tanzim al-Islam li'l-Mujtama', Muhammad Abu Zahra.

Haqa'iq al-Islam wa abatil khusumih, 'Abbas Mahmud al-'Aqqad.

Khutut ra'isiyya fi'l-iqtisad al-Islami, Mahmud Abu's-Sa'ud.

Da'irat al-ma'arif al-Islamiyya al-Awrubbiyya, (*Islamic European Encyclopaedia*) published in Arabic by Ahmad ash-Shantatawi, 'Abdu'l-Hamid Yunus and Ibrahim Khurshid.

Ad-Da'wa ila'l-Islam (*The Preaching of Islam*), Thomas Arnold, translated by Dr. Hasan Ibrahim Hasan and a colleague of his, printed by Lajnat al-Bayan al-'Arabi.

Sirat ar-Rasul, Muhammad 'Izzat Darwaza.

Al-'Ibada fi'l-Islam, Yusuf al-Qardawi, first printing, an-Nasr print.

Al-'Adala al-ijtima'iyya fi'l-Islam, Sayyid Qutb, fifth printing, al-Halabi print.

Falsafat az-zakat 'inda'l-Muslimin, 'Abdu'l-'Aziz Sayyid al-Ahl, printed in Beirut.

Majmu'a'l-watha'iq as-Siyasiyya fi 'ahd ar-Rasul wa'l-Khulafa' ar-Rashidin, Muhammad Hamidullah al-Hayderabadi, second printing, Dar al-Irshad print, Beirut.

VIII. Taxation and Public Finance

Mabadi' 'ilm al-maliyya al-'Amma, Muhammad Fu'ad Ibrahim, first volume.

'Ilm al-Maliyya, Rashid ad-Daqr, Damascus print.

Mawarid ad-Dawla, Sa'd Mahir Hamza, printed by al-Matba'a al-Maliyya.

Mabadi' an-nasariyya al-amma li'd-dariba, Husayn Khallaf and 'Abdu'l-Karim ar-Rifa'i.

Nizaniyat ad-Dawla, Muhammad Hilmi Murad.

Tashri' ad-Dara'ib, Muhammad Hilmi Murad, first volume, Nahdat Misr print, 1955 CE.

an-Nuzum an-naqdiyya wa'l-masrafiyya, 'Abdu'l-'Aziz Mar'i.

Al-Iqtisad as-Siyasi, 'Ali 'Abdu'l-Wahid Wafi, al-Halabi print, fifth edition.

Al-Iqtisad as-Siyasi, Rif'at al-Mahjub.

IX. Social Studies

Ad-Daman al-Ijtima'i, Sadiq Mahdi as-Sa'id.

Halqat ad-dirasat al-ijtima'iyya, mentioned earlier.

'Ilm al-Ijtima', Ahmad al-Khashab.

X. Biography of the Prophet, History, and Other Biographies

Sirat Ibn Hisham, by Ibn Hisham, ed. Muhammad Muhyi'd-din 'Abdu'l-Hamid.

Sirat 'Umar ibn 'Abdu'l-'Aziz, Ibn 'Abdu'l-Hakam, Dar al-Fikr print, Damascus.

Ta'rikh al-Umam wa'l-Muluk, Abu Ja'far at-Tabari, al-Husayniyya print.

Wafayat al-A'yan, Ibn Khallikan, d. 681 AH.

Al-Bidaya wa'n-Nihaya, Abu'l-Fida' Isma'il ibn Kathir, as-Sa'ada print.

Al-Jawahir al-Mudiyya fi Tabaqat al-Hanafiyya, Muhyi'd-din al-Qurashi, d. 775 AH, Hyderabad print.

Tabaqat al-Hanabila, Ibn Abi Ya'la, d. 527.

Tabaqat ash-Shafi'iyya, Taju'd-din as-Subki, d. 771 AH.

Ad-Dibaj al-Mudhdhab fi ma'rifat a'yan al-madhhab, Ibn Farhun, d. 799 AH.

Al-Fawa'id al-Bahiyya fi Tabaqat al-Hanafiyya, Abu'l-Hasanat 'Abdu'l-Hayy al-Laknawi, d. 1304 AH.
Nuzhat al-Khawatir, 'Abdu'l-Hayy ibn Fakru'd-din al-Hasani al-Lakhnawi, d. 1341, director of Nadwat al-'Ulama, Lucknow, India, d. 1341 AH, the father of Abu'l-Hasan an-Nadwi.
Al-A'lam, Kayr ad-din az-Zirikli.
Al-Kharaj fi'd-Dawla al-Islamiyya, Muhammad Diya'd-din ar-Rayyis, Nahdat Misr print.
An-Nuqud al-'Arabiyya wa 'ilm an-numiyyat, Father Anstas al-Karmali.
An-Nuqud al-'Arabiyya, madiha wa hadiruha, 'Abdu'r-Rahman Fahmy.
Sanj as-Sikka fi fajr al-Islam, 'Abdu'r-Rahman Fahmy.

XI. Language and Dictionaries

Gharib al-Hadith, Abu 'Ubayd al-Qasim ibn Sallam, d. 225, Hyderabad print.
An-Nihaya fi gharib al-hadith wa'l-athar, Abu's-Sa'adat Maju'd-din al-Mubarak ibn Muhammad, known as Ibn al-Athir, d. 606 AH, al-Khayriyya print.
Lisan al-'Arab, Jamalu'd-din Abu'l-Fadl Muhammad ibn Mukarrm ibn Mansur al-Ansari al-Ifriqi al-Misri, d. 711, Beirut printing, 1956 CE.
Al-Misbah al-Munir, Ahmad ibn Muhammad ibn 'Ali al-Muqri al-Fayumi, d. 770 AH, al-'Amiriyya print, Egypt, 1912 CE.
Al-Qamus al-Muhit, Majdu'd-din al-Fayruzabadi, d. 817 AH.
Taj al-'Arus fi sharh al-Qamus, Muhammad Murtada az-Zabidi, d. 1205 AH.
Al-Muj'am al-Wasit, collected by the Arabic Language Congress in Cairo.

XII. Miscellaneous References

The Bible, Old and New Testaments
Al-Muhadarat al-'Amma li Idarat ath-Thaqafa al-Islamiyya bi'l-Azhar (Public Lectures of the Directorate of Islamic Culture in al-Azhar), first, second and third sessions, al-Azhar print.
*Al-Mu'tamar al-Awwal li Majma' al-Buhuth al-Islamiyya (*The First Conference of the Congress of Islamic Research) in Cairo, by a group of researchers, al-Azhar print.

Majallat al-Azhar (al-Azhar Review).
Majallat Hadarat al-Islam (Islamic Culture Review), Damascus.
Majallat al-Muslimun (The Muslims Review), Cairo.